# BARRON'S

# TOEFL iBT®

## Internet-Based Test

## SIXTEENTH EDITION

Pamela J. Sharpe, Ph.D.

# BARRON'S

**To my students at home and abroad with best wishes
for success on the TOEFL and after the TOEFL**

## About the Author

Dr. Pamela Sharpe is an internationally recognized educator in the field of English as a second language (ESL). She has been a member of the faculty at many prestigious colleges and universities in the United States including the University of Florida, University of Texas at Austin, Miami Dade Community College, and the Ohio State University. In addition, she was the founding director of the American Language Institute at the University of Toledo, a curriculum specialist for federal bilingual education programs, and chair of Modern Languages at Arizona Western College. As a member of the statewide television faculty of Northern Arizona University, she taught graduate courses for teachers via the interactive television network throughout the state of Arizona. She has received numerous awards for teaching. An educational consultant for schools across the globe, Dr. Sharpe has been actively involved in teacher training and development both in the United States and as a Fulbright Scholar in Latin America.

Dr. Sharpe is a preeminent authority in test preparation for the TOEFL and the TOEIC. Her text, *Barron's TOEFL iBT*®, is in the sixteenth edition, and has been a consistent best seller worldwide. She has published twelve books, including four for TOEFL preparation, that have been used successfully by millions of students.

Dr. Sharpe earned her bachelor's degree Phi Beta Kappa with honors from the Ohio State University, her master's degree in Linguistics from the University of Florida, and her Ph.D. in TESL, the Teaching of English as a Second Language, from the Ohio State University.

© Copyright 2019, 2016, 2013, 2010, 2006 by Kaplan, Inc., d/b/a Barron's Educational Series

Previous edition under the title *How to Prepare for the TOEFL Test: Test of English as a Foreign Language* © copyright 2004, 2001, 1999, 1996, 1994, 1989, 1986, 1983, 1979, 1977 by Barron's Educational Series, Inc.

Published by Kaplan, Inc., d/b/a Barron's Educational Series
750 Third Avenue
New York, NY 10017
**www.barronseduc.com**

ISBN: 978-1-4380-1187-5

10 9 8 7 6 5 4 3 2 1

Kaplan, Inc., d/b/a Barron's Educational Series print books are available at special quantity discounts to use for sales promotions, employee premiums, or educational purposes. For more information or to purchase books, please call the Simon & Schuster special sales department at 866-506-1949.

# TABLE OF CONTENTS

About the Author   ii

## 1 STUDY PLAN   1

✔ *Develop a personal study plan*

Study Habits   2
A Checklist for Success   4
Timetable for the TOEFL iBT®   6

## 2 ORIENTATION   7

✔ *Inform yourself about the TOEFL iBT®*

Overview of the TOEFL   7
Frequently-Asked Questions   8

## 3 PRETEST FOR THE TOEFL iBT®   17

✔ *Evaluate your strengths and weaknesses*

Model Test 1: Pretest   17
Answer Keys   63

## 4 REVIEW OF TOEFL iBT® SECTIONS   65

✔ *Study the most frequent question types*

Reading   65
Listening   96
Speaking   126
Writing   149

# 5 ACADEMIC SKILLS 165

✔ **Master the most important academic skills**

Campus Vocabulary **165**
Taking Notes **181**
Paraphrasing **202**
Summarizing **229**
Synthesizing **251**
Answers and Audio Scripts **278**

# 6 USAGE AND STYLE FOR THE TOEFL iBT® 323

✔ **Learn the grammar that adds points**

Usage Problems **324**
Style Problems **368**

# 7 ONE-HOUR TOEFL iBT® PRACTICE TESTS 395

✔ **Practice taking short tests**

Practice Test 1 **396**
Practice Test 2 **405**
Practice Test 3 **414**
Practice Test 4 **423**
Practice Test 5 **433**
Practice Test 6 **442**
Practice Test 7 **451**
Practice Test 8 **460**

# 8 PROGRESS TESTS FOR THE TOEFL iBT® 469

✔ **Practice taking full-length model tests**

Model Test 2: Progress Test **471**
Model Test 3: Progress Test **518**
Model Test 4: Progress Test **565**
Model Test 5: Progress Test **609**
Model Test 6: Progress Test **654**
Model Test 7: Progress Test **702**
Model Test 8: Progress Test **749**

# 9  SCORE ESTIMATES  797

✔ *Estimate your score*

Procedures for Scoring   **797**
Reference Charts   **799**

# 10  RESOURCES  803

✔ *Use resources to support your preparation*

Websites for TOEFL   **803**
Tutors and Onlline Teachers   **804**
Dr. Sharpe's Website   **805**
TOEFL iBT® Resource Centers   **805**
Teaching Tips   **806**

# PERSPECTIVES FOR TEACHERS  809

# ACKNOWLEDGMENTS  810

# LANDING PAGE

Welcome to Barron's online TOEFL site. This is your resource page for the online material referenced in *Barron's TOEFL iBT® 16th Edition*. When you see this icon in the book, visit the resource page, at http://bit.ly/Barrons-TOEFL and click on the arrow that corresponds to the material you are studying.

➤ **PowerPoint Presentations**
   ➤ **Study Skills Presentation**
   ➤ **Review Presentations**
      ➤ Reading Section
      ➤ Listening Section
      ➤ Speaking Section
      ➤ Writing Section

➤ **Audio Only**
   ➤ **Review Scripts**
      ➤ Listening Review
         ➤ Conversation
         ➤ Lecture
      ➤ Speaking Review
         ➤ Question 3: Talk
         ➤ Question 4: Lecture
         ➤ Question 5: Conversation
         ➤ Question 6: Lecture
      ➤ Writing Review
         ➤ Integrated Essay: Lecture
   ➤ **Quick Quizzes**
      ➤ Listening Quiz
         ➤ Written Script
      ➤ Speaking Quiz
         ➤ Written Script
      ➤ Writing Quiz
         ➤ Written Script
         ➤ Example Answers
   ➤ **Academic Activities**
      ➤ Campus Vocabulary
      ➤ Taking Notes
      ➤ Paraphrasing
      ➤ Summarizing
      ➤ Synthesizing
   ➤ **One-Hour Practice Tests**
      ➤ Practice Test 1
         ➤ Listening
         ➤ Speaking
         ➤ Writing
      ➤ Practice Test 2
         ➤ Listening

         ➤ Speaking
      ➤ Practice Test 3
         ➤ Listening
         ➤ Speaking
      ➤ Practice Test 4
         ➤ Listening
         ➤ Speaking
         ➤ Writing
      ➤ Practice Test 5
         ➤ Listening
         ➤ Speaking
      ➤ Practice Test 6
         ➤ Listening
         ➤ Speaking
      ➤ Practice Test 7
         ➤ Listening
         ➤ Speaking
         ➤ Writing
      ➤ Practice Test 8
         ➤ Listening
         ➤ Speaking
         ➤ Writing

➤ **Video**
   ➤ **Academic Skills**
      ➤ Mini-Lesson for Note Taking
      ➤ Mini-Lesson for Paraphrasing
      ➤ Mini-Lesson for Summarizing
      ➤ Mini-Lesson for Synthesizing

➤ **Onscreen**
   ➤ **Full-Length Model Tests**
      ➤ Model Test 1
      ➤ Model Test 2
      ➤ Model Test 3
      ➤ Model Test 4
      ➤ Model Test 5
      ➤ Model Test 6
      ➤ Model Test 7
      ➤ Model Test 8

➤ **Flashcards**
   ➤ Campus Vocabulary

# 1

# STUDY PLAN

## ✔ *Develop a personal study plan*

Many students do not prepare for the TOEFL iBT® before they take the test. They do not even read the *TOEFL iBT® Information and Registration Bulletin* when they register. You have an advantage. By using this book and the online materials that supplement it, you have a plan for success.

---

**User-friendly icons will help you navigate from the book to the online material in each chapter.**

 When you see the Internet icon in the book, go to the Barron's TOEFL site online at *http://bit.ly/Barrons-TOEFL* to continue.

 When you see the speaker icon online, click to hear the audio for the presentation.

 When you see the book icon online, return to the book from your online preparation.

 When you see the headphone icon in the book, go to Barron's TOEFL site online at *http://bit.ly/Barrons-TOEFL* and listen to the MP3 file referenced in the audio.

---

# STUDY HABITS

 To see and hear this presentation online, go to the Barron's TOEFL site at *http://bit.ly/Barrons-TOEFL* and click on the icon for **Presentations**, then select **Study Habits**.

## Study Habits

A habit is a pattern of behavior that is acquired through repetition.

Research indicates that it takes about 21 days to form a habit.

The study habits here are characteristic of successful students.

Be successful!

Form these habits now.

They will help you on the TOEFL and after the TOEFL.

## Accept responsibility

- Don't rely on luck
- Work diligently

Successful students understand that the score on the TOEFL is their responsibility. It doesn't happen because of luck. It's the result of their own efforts.

Take responsibility for *your* TOEFL score. Don't leave it to chance.

## Get organized

- Find a study area
- Keep your materials in one place

You'll need a place to study where you can concentrate. Try to find a place where you can organize your study materials and leave them until the next study session. If that isn't practical, then find a bag that you can use to store all your TOEFL materials so that you have everything you need when you go to the library or another place to study. This will save time, and you'll be less likely to lose important notes for your TOEFL prep.

### Set realistic goals

- Evaluate your English
- Set a goal that you can achieve

Be honest about your preparation. Students who are just beginning to learn English are not prepared to take the TOEFL. Give yourself the time you need to prepare. By setting an unrealistic goal, for example, to finish preparing with this book in one week, you will probably be very disappointed. Even advanced students need time to learn academic skills and review language skills as well as to take model tests.

### Manage time

- Schedule study time
- Use unscheduled time well

Successful students have a schedule that helps them manage their time. Preparing for the TOEFL is planned for on a regular basis just like a standing appointment. If it is written down on a schedule, it is more probable that you will give TOEFL preparation the time necessary to achieve your goal.

Learn to use time while you are waiting for an appointment or commuting on public transportation to study. Even a 5-minute review will help you.

### Learn from mistakes

- Study the explanatory and example answers online
- Review your errors

If you knew everything, you wouldn't need this book. Expect to make mistakes on the practice tests and model tests.

Read the explanatory and example answers online and learn from your mistakes. If you do this, you will be less likely to make those mistakes again on the official TOEFL iBT®.

### Control stress

- Use stress for motivation
- Avoid panic and worry

Some stress is normal and good. Use it constructively. It will motivate you to study. But don't panic or worry. Panic will cause loss of concentration and poor performance. Avoid people who panic and worry. Don't listen to them. They will encourage negative thinking.

### Choose to be positive

I know more today than I did yesterday.
I am preparing.
I will succeed.

Your attitude will influence your success on the TOEFL iBT®. To be successful, you must develop patterns of positive thinking. To help you develop a positive attitude, memorize the sentences on the left side of the screen, and bring them to mind after every study session. Say them aloud when you begin to have negative thoughts.

# A CHECKLIST FOR SUCCESS

This book is easy to use. Each chapter corresponds to one of the goals on the checklist. More than 2 million Barron's students have succeeded on the TOEFL. You can be successful, too, by checking off each of these goals as you finish another chapter.

✔ *Develop a personal study plan*
✔ *Inform yourself about the TOEFL iBT®*
✔ *Evaluate your strengths and weaknesses*
✔ *Study the most frequent question types*
✔ *Master the most important academic skills*
✔ *Learn the grammar that adds points*
✔ *Practice taking short tests*
✔ *Practice taking full-length model tests*
✔ *Estimate your score*
✔ *Use resources to support your preparation*

A *syllabus* is a study plan for a course. This syllabus can be used either for self-study or for a classroom. If you would like to download a copy of this syllabus, go to the Barron's TOEFL site online at *http://bit.ly/Barrons-TOEFL*. If you need help preparing a different syllabus for a shorter class, contact Dr. Sharpe *sharpe@teflprep.com*.

## Barron's TOEFL iBT® 16th Edition

| WEEK | GOALS | BOOK | ONLINE | HOMEWORK |
|------|-------|------|--------|----------|
| 1 | *Develop a personal study plan* *Inform yourself about the* *TOEFL iBT®* *Evaluate your strengths and* *weaknesses* | Chapter 1 Chapter 2 Chapter 3 | Presentation: Study Habits Download: Syllabus Pretest: Model Test 1 Explanatory and Example Answers | Organization Self-Evaluation |
| 2 | *Study the most frequent* *question types* | Chapter 4 | Presentation: Reading Presentation: Listening Presentation: Speaking Presentation: Writing | |
| 3 | *Master the most important* *academic skills* Taking Notes Paraphrasing | Chapter 5 | Campus Vocabulary | Activities 1–10 Activities 11–20 Activities 21–30 |
| 4 | Summarizing Synthesizing | Chapter 5 | Campus Vocabulary | Activities 31–40 Activities 41–50 |
| 5 | *Learn the grammar that adds* *points* | Chapter 6 | | Usage Problems Style Problems |
| 6 | *Practice taking short tests* One-Hour Test 1 One-Hour Test 2 One-Hour Test 3 One-Hour Test 4 | Chapter 7 | | |
| 7 | One-Hour Test 5 One-Hour Test 6 One-Hour Test 7 One-Hour Test 8 | Chapter 7 | | |
| 8 | *Practice taking full-length* *model tests* | Chapter 8 | Progress Test: Model Test 2 Explanatory and Example Answers Progress Test: Model Test 3 Explanatory and Example Answers | Review Model Test 2 Review Model Test 3 |
| 9 | | Chapter 8 | Progress Test: Model Test 4 Explanatory and Example Answers Progress Test: Model Test 5 Explanatory and Example Answers | Review Model Test 4 Review Model Test 5 |
| 10 | | Chapter 8 | Progress Test: Model Test 6 Explanatory and Example Answers Progress Test: Model Test 7 Explanatory and Example Answers | Review Model Test 6 Review Model Test 7 |
| 11 | | Chapter 8 | Progress Test: Model Test 8 Explanatory and Example Answers | Review Model Test 8 |
| 12 | *Estimate your score* | Chapter 9 | | Individualized Review |

## Individualized Study

*Barron's TOEFL iBT®, 16th Edition,* is designed to support self-study or classroom preparation. After analyzing the Pretest, the teacher can assign individualized review by selecting the chapters and pages that focus on the most challenging sections of the test for each student. It is often helpful to divide the class into groups of students who have similar patterns of error on the Pretest. Model tests provide a process for monitoring individual progress and redirecting student effort. Students who are not in a class can determine which sections of the test require the most time for self-study. *Barron's Practice Exercises for the TOEFL, 8th Edition*, and *Barron's TOEFL Strategies and Tips: Outsmart the TOEFL, 2nd Edition*, are additional resources for individual practice.

## TIMETABLE FOR THE TOEFL iBT®

| Test Section | Questions | Time |
|---|---|---|
| Reading | 3–4 passages with 12–14 questions each | 60–80 minutes |
| Listening | 2–3 conversations with 5 questions each<br>2–3 lectures with 6 questions each<br>2–3 discussions with 6 questions each | 60–90 minutes |
| BREAK | | 10 minutes |
| Speaking | 2 independent tasks<br>4 integrated tasks | 20 minutes |
| Writing | 1 integrated task<br>1 independent task | 20 minutes<br>30 minutes |

# 2
# ORIENTATION

## ✔ *Inform yourself about the TOEFL iBT®*

## OVERVIEW OF THE TOEFL

The TOEFL iBT® tests your ability to understand and use English for academic purposes. There are four sections on the TOEFL, with special directions for each section.

## READING SECTION

The Reading Section tests your ability to understand reading passages like those in college textbooks. The short format has three passages and the long format has four passages. After each passage, you will answer 12–14 questions about it.

## LISTENING SECTION

The Listening Section tests your ability to understand spoken English that is typical of interactions and academic speech on college campuses. During the test, you will listen to conversations, lectures, and discussions, and answer questions about them. The short format has two conversations, two lectures, and two discussions and the long format has three conversations, three lectures, and three discussions.

## SPEAKING SECTION

The Speaking Section tests your ability to communicate in English in an academic setting. During the test, you will be presented with six speaking questions. The questions ask for a response to a single question; a reading passage and a conversation; a reading passage and a lecture; a conversation or a lecture.

## WRITING SECTION

The Writing Section tests your ability to write essays in English similar to those you would write in college courses. During the test, you will write one essay about an academic topic and one essay about a familiar topic.

# FAQs—FREQUENTLY ASKED QUESTIONS ABOUT THE TOEFL iBT®

## TOEFL PROGRAMS

### ➤ What is the purpose of the TOEFL?

The TOEFL is used by scholarship selection committees of governments, universities, and agencies such as Fulbright, the Agency for International Development, AMIDEAST, and Latin American Scholarship Programs as a standard measure of the English proficiency of their candidates. Some professional licensing and certification agencies also use TOEFL scores to evaluate English proficiency. Admissions officers at more than 10,000 colleges and universities in the United States, Canada, Australia, Great Britain, and 130 other countries worldwide require foreign applicants to submit TOEFL scores along with transcripts and recommendations in order to be considered for admission. In addition, workers applying for visas in English-speaking countries often use TOEFL scores as part of their applications.

### ➤ May I choose the format that I prefer—iBT or PBT?

The official TOEFL is offered in two formats—the Internet-Based TOEFL (iBT) or the Paper-Based TOEFL (PBT). The format that you take depends on the test center location for which you register. Only four percent of the sites continue to offer the PBT, which was revised in 2016. It is being phased out. To see a schedule of times and test centers, visit the TOEFL website or check the *TOEFL iBT® Registration and Information Bulletin* on the TOEFL website at *www.ets.org/toefl*. A revised timeline is continuously updated on the TOEFL website.

### ➤ What is the Institutional TOEFL Program (ITP)?

Many schools, colleges, universities, and private agencies administer the Institutional TOEFL (ITP). The Institutional TOEFL is used for admission, placement, eligibility, or employment *only* at the school or agency that offers the test. The dates for the Institutional TOEFL usually correspond to the beginning of an academic session on a college or university calendar. The fees are set by the institution administering the test. The format is paper-based. If you plan to use your TOEFL score for a different college, university, or agency, you should not take the Institutional TOEFL at another site. You should register for the official iBT.

### ➤ Which language skills are tested on the TOEFL?

| Institutional TOEFL (ITP) | Internet-Based TOEFL (iBT) | Revised Paper-Based TOEFL (PBT) |
|---|---|---|
| Listening | Listening | Listening |
| Structure | Speaking | Reading |
| Reading | Reading | Writing |
| Optional Essay | Writing | |

## ➤ Why was the Structure Section removed from the TOEFL iBT®?

Grammar is tested as part of the other sections. It is especially important to use good grammar in the Speaking and the Writing Sections. Chapter 6 will help you review specific problems to gain points on the TOEFL.

## ➤ Which keyboard will be used for the Writing Section?

A standard English language QWERTY keyboard will be used for the Writing Section on TOEFL iBT® examinations worldwide. QWERTY is the most common keyboard for English-language computers. Its name refers to the first six letters on the top row left. It is a good idea to practice on this type of keyboard when you prepare for the TOEFL, using the model tests in this book.

## ➤ Must I take all sections of the test?

The Speaking Section and the Writing Section are required on the Internet-Based TOEFL. You must take all sections of the TOEFL in order to receive a score.

# REGISTRATION

## ➤ How do I register for the TOEFL?

You can register for the Internet-Based TOEFL online, by mail, or by telephone.

Online    *www.ets.org/toefl* for testing worldwide

Phone    1-800-GO-TOEFL (1-800-468-6335) or 1-443-751-4862 for testing in the United States, U.S. territories, and Canada, or call your Regional Registration Center for testing outside the United States and Canada.

Mail    Download a registration form from the TOEFL website and mail it to the closest Regional Registration Center (addresses listed on the ETS website as well as in the Resources section on pages 808–809 of this book).

---

**NOTE: Mac® Users**

The TOEFL online registration system is not compatible with Safari. Please use Google Chrome or Mozilla Firefox.

---

## ➤ Where can I find a free *TOEFL iBT® Registration and Information Bulletin*?

This important bulletin includes the information that you will need to register for the TOEFL. It can be downloaded free from the TOEFL website *www.ets.org/toefl*. In addition, most Regional Registration Centers have copies of the bulletin, or it can be found at many libraries, universities, and educational counseling centers around the world.

## ➤ Where are the TOEFL iBT® Resource Centers?

Resource Centers support the test sites and counseling centers in each region. They are listed in Chapter 10 of this book. TOEFL iBT® Resource Centers cannot always assist with registration and information about the test results.

## ➤ Will my registration be confirmed?

Your registration number can be printed when you register online, and you will also receive your number by email.

## ➤ When should I register for the TOEFL?

You must register at least seven days before the test date. If there is space, you may register three days before the test date. The late fee for a three-day registration is $40. Because test centers fill rapidly during desirable times, it is a good idea to register three or four months in advance. If you are taking the TOEFL as part of the application process for college or university admission, you should plan to take the test early enough for your score to be received by the admissions office before the application deadline.

## ➤ May I change the date or cancel my registration?

To receive a refund, you must reschedule or cancel three full days before your test date. For example, if your test is on Friday, you must call to cancel your registration on Monday. If you cancel your registration, you will usually receive half of your test fee as a refund. Some countries have additional requirements.

## ➤ What are the fees for the TOEFL iBT®?

The fee for the test administration, including four score reports, depends on the location that your choose. Current testing fees range from $160 to $250 U.S. Other fees include late registration ($40) and rescheduling ($60).

## ➤ How may I pay the fees?

You may pay in U.S. dollars by credit card, e-check from bank accounts in the United States and its territories, Western Union, Quick Pay, PayPal, or money orders in U.S. dollars drawn on a bank in the United States, checks in Canadian dollars drawn on a bank in Canada, and euro checks drawn on a bank in the same country as the person writing the check.

## TEST ADMINISTRATION

### ➤ How is the TOEFL iBT® administered?

The TOEFL is offered on a schedule of dates in a network of test centers throughout the world. The room in which the TOEFL is administered is usually a computer lab. You will be assigned a seat. If you are late, you will probably not be admitted. The TOEFL website at *www.ets.org/ toefl* lists test centers and schedules.

### ➤ What should I do the day before I take the TOEFL?

View your order in your online TOEFL account. Check your confirmation, and look for announcements with changes in the time or location of the test center.

### ➤ When should I arrive at the test center?

You must arrive at least 30 minutes before your test is scheduled to begin so that you can complete the check-in procedures. You should allow plenty of time to travel to the center so that you are not feeling rushed and stressed before you begin your exam.

### ➤ What should I take with me to the test room?

Take your registration confirmation with your registration number on it and your valid identification to the test site. You are not permitted to take anything with you when you enter the test room except your identification. No cell phones, watches, paper, dictionaries, pens, or pencils are allowed. The test supervisor will give you a headset, paper, and pencils. Some of the sites have lockers for you to store your personal items, but some sites do not have secure storage spaces. You should not take anything to the test site that is too large for a small locker.

### ➤ What kind of identification is required?

In the United States, only your valid passport will be accepted for admission to the TOEFL. In other countries, your valid passport is still the best identification, but if you do not have a passport, you may refer to the TOEFL website for special directions. Your photograph will be taken at the test center and reproduced on all official score reports, along with your signature. Be sure to use the same spelling and order of your name on your registration materials, the test center log that you will sign when you enter and leave the test area, the forms on the computer screens, and any correspondence that you may have with the TOEFL office. You should also use the same spelling on applications for schools and documents for agencies that will receive your score reports. Even a small difference can cause serious delays or even denial of the applications.

### ➤ What are the procedures before testing?

You will be asked to copy a paragraph in which you agree not to share information about the test. Then you will have your photograph taken and other security procedures will be performed. At some centers, thumb prints, hand-held metal detectors, biometric voice identifications, and other forms of technology will be used to verify your identity.

## EXAMINATION

### ➤ How long is the testing session?

The TOEFL iBT® takes about four to four-and-a-half hours to administer, including the time required for giving directions and the break between the Listening and the Speaking Sections.

### ➤ Why are some of the Reading and Listening Sections longer?

Some of the tests include experimental questions that are being field tested for use in the Reading or Listening Section of future exams. Your answers to these experimental questions will not be calculated as part of your score, but you must do your best on all the questions because you will not know which questions are experimental and which are test questions that will be scored.

### ➤ May I take notes?

You are permitted to take notes and use them to answer the questions on the iBT. You will be given scratch paper for that purpose when you enter the test room. Your notes will not be graded. They will be collected and shredded after the test.

### ➤ May I change an answer?

The Reading Section is divided into passages. You can change your answer by clicking on a new answer. You can change your answer as many times as you wish, and you can go back to previous answers in the same passage or previous passages. On the Listening Section, you can change your answer by clicking on a new answer. You can change your answer as many times as you wish until you click on the **Confirm Answer (OK)** button. On the Speaking Section, you will be cued with a beep to begin and end speaking. Everything that you say during the recording time will be submitted. You cannot change an answer. On the Writing Section, you can revise your essays as much as you wish until the clock indicates that no time is remaining. If you submit your essays before time is up, you cannot return to them. The Internet model tests that supplement this book will provide you with practice in choosing and changing answers on the computer screen.

### ➤ If I am not sure of an answer, should I guess?

If you are not sure of an answer, you should guess. The number of incorrect answers is not subtracted from your score. First, eliminate all the possibilities that you know are NOT correct. Then, if you are almost sure of an answer, guess that one. If you have no idea of the correct answer for a question, choose one letter and use it for your "guess answer" throughout the entire examination. The "guess answer" is especially useful for finishing a section quickly.

## ➤ Do I need to wear headphones?

You will receive headphones with a microphone attached. Before the test begins, you will have an opportunity to adjust the volume. If there is a problem with your headset, raise your hand, and ask the test supervisor to provide you with another headset.

## ➤ Will everyone speak at the same time to record the answers for the Speaking Section?

Speakers will begin to record their answers at slightly different times. The problem is that you may be disturbed by the noise while you are trying to concentrate on your answers either on the Speaking Section or on other sections of the TOEFL. It is a good idea to keep your headphones on during the entire test in order to block out as much of the noise as possible.

## ➤ What can I do if there is a problem during the test?

If there is a problem with the Internet connection or the power that supplies the computers, and if the test must be discontinued, everyone who is taking the test at that site is entitled to a refund or a free test on another date. This does not happen very often.

## ➤ Are breaks scheduled during the TOEFL?

A mandatory 10-minute break is scheduled between the Listening and the Speaking Sections. If you need to use the restroom at another time during the test, you may, but the test clock will not stop while you are gone.

## ➤ How often may I take the TOEFL iBT®?

You may take the TOEFL iBT® as many times as you wish to score to your satisfaction, but only once within 12 days.

## ➤ If I have already taken the TOEFL, how will the previous scores affect my new score?

TOEFL scores are valid for two years. If you have taken the TOEFL more than once in the past two years, a report will be sent for the test date that you request.

## ➤ What happens to someone who cheats on the TOEFL iBT®?

Entering the room with false identification, tampering with the computer, using a camera, giving or receiving help, or trying to remove test materials or notes is considered cheating. Do not cheat. In spite of opportunity, knowledge that others are doing it, the desire to help a friend, or fear that you will not make a good score, *do not cheat*. On the TOEFL, cheating is a very serious matter. If you are discovered, you will be dismissed from the room, your score will be canceled, and you may not be able to take the test again on a future date.

## SCORE REPORTS

### ➤ How is the Speaking Section scored?

Trained raters listen to each of the speaking responses and assign them a number 0–4. The scores for all six responses are converted to a total section score 0–30. The raters grade the Speaking Section using checklists similar to those printed in this book.

### ➤ How is the Writing Section scored?

Trained raters read your essays and assign them a number 0–5. Automated machine scoring called e-rater complements the scores by human raters. If there is disagreement about your score, a team leader will also read your essays. The scores for each essay are combined and converted to a section score 0–30. Raters grade the Writing Section using checklists similar to those printed in this book. The combination of human raters for content and meaning and machine scoring for language and mechanics provides a more objective evaluation.

### ➤ How is the total TOEFL score calculated?

The iBT has converted section scores for each of the four sections. The range for each section score is 0–30. When the scores for the four sections are added together, the total score range is 0–120.

### ➤ When can I see my scores?

You will be able to see and download your score report online about 10–13 days after you take the TOEFL. You will receive an email to verify that the score has been posted. Official score reports will be mailed to you and to the schools and agencies that you designate a few days after they have been posted online. You should expect delivery by mail in ten days in the United States and as long as six weeks outside the United States. You are entitled to five copies of your test results, including one copy for you and four official score reports.

### ➤ Should I have my Speaking and Writing scores reviewed?

The TOEFL office will review either your Speaking score or your Writing score for $80, or both scores for $160. In very few cases, this will result in a higher score. Most of the time, your score will not be changed to a higher score. You should only do this if you are absolutely certain that the score you received is a mistake. To request a review, fill out the form on the website at *www.ets.org/toefl*.

### ➤ How do I interpret my score?

You cannot pass or fail the TOEFL. Each school or agency will evaluate the scores according to its own requirements. Even at the same university, the requirements may vary for different programs of study, levels of study (graduate or undergraduate), and degrees of responsibility (student or teaching assistant). To be certain of the requirements for your school or agency, contact them directly.

## ➤ May I cancel my scores?

If you choose to report your scores, you will choose four institutions or agencies to receive score reports. All of this is arranged by responding to questions on the computer screen at the end of the TOEFL exam. If you do not want your scores to be reported, click on **Cancel** when this option appears on the screen at the end of the test.

## ➤ How can I send additional score reports?

If you need more than four score reports, which are provided as part of your test fee, you may order more at $20 each. Order online or mail in the order form that you will find in your *TOEFL iBT® Registration and Information Bulletin.* You may also fax your order to 1-610-290-8972. Reports are sent in four to seven days when you order them online. Fax orders are mailed two weeks after payment.

## ➤ Is there a direct correspondence between proficiency in English and a TOEFL score?

There is not always a direct correspondence between proficiency in English and a score on the TOEFL. Many students who are proficient in English are not proficient in how to approach the examination. That is why it is important to prepare by using this book and the materials online.

## ➤ Will I succeed on the TOEFL?

You will receive from your study what you give to your study. The information is here. Now, it is up to you to devote the time and the effort. More than one million students have succeeded by using *Barron's TOEFL.* You can be successful, too.

# 3

# PRETEST FOR THE TOEFL iBT®

✔ *Evaluate your strengths and weaknesses*

# MODEL TEST 1: PRETEST

## READING SECTION

The Reading Section tests your ability to understand reading passages like those in college textbooks. The reading passages are presented in one complete section, which allows you to move to the next passage and return to a previous passage to change answers or answer questions that you may have left blank. The passages are about 700 words in length.

This is the short format for the Reading Section. On the short format, you will read three passages. After each passage, you will answer 12–14 questions about it. You may take notes while you read, but notes are not graded. You may use your notes to answer the questions. Some passages may include a word or phrase that is underlined in blue. Click on the word or phrase to see a glossary definition or explanation.

Choose the best answer for multiple-choice questions. Follow the directions on the page or on the screen for computer-assisted questions. Most questions are worth 1 point, but the last question in each passage is worth more than 1 point.

Click on **Next** to go to the next question. Click on **Back** to return to previous questions. You may return to previous questions for all of the passages.

You can click on **Review** to see a chart of the questions you have answered and the questions you have not answered. From this screen, you can return to the question you want to answer.

Although you can spend more time on one passage and less time on another passage, you should try to pace yourself so that you are spending about 20 minutes to read each passage and answer the questions for that passage. You will have 60 minutes to complete all of the passages and answer all of the questions on the short format. A clock on the screen will show you how much time you have to complete the Reading Section.

### Reading 1

The following reading passage was adapted from *World Mythology*, Third Edition by Donna Rosenberg, National Textbook-McGraw Hill Education, 1998.

### "Beowulf"

#### Historical Background

P1 ➔ The epic poem *Beowulf*, written in Old English, is the earliest existing Germanic epic and one of four surviving Anglo-Saxon manuscripts. Although *Beowulf* was written by an anonymous Englishman in Old English, the tale takes place in that part of Scandinavia from which Germanic tribes emigrated to England. Beowulf comes from Geatland, the southeastern part of what is now Sweden. Hrothgar, king of the Danes, lives near what is now Leire, on Zealand, Denmark's largest island. The *Beowulf* epic contains three major tales about Beowulf and several minor tales that reflect a rich Germanic oral tradition of myths, legends, and folklore.

P2 ➔ The *Beowulf* warriors have a foot in both the Bronze and Iron Ages. Their mead-halls reflect the wealthy living of the Bronze Age Northmen, and their wooden shields, wood-shafted spears, and bronze-hilted swords are those of the Bronze Age warrior. However, they carry iron-tipped spears, and their best swords have iron or iron-edged blades. Beowulf also orders an iron shield for his fight with a dragon. Iron replaced bronze because it produced a blade with a cutting edge that was stronger and sharper. The Northmen learned how to forge iron in about 500 B.C. Although they had been superior to the European Celts in bronze work, it was the Celts who taught them how to make and design iron work. Iron was accessible everywhere in Scandinavia, usually in the form of "bog-iron" found in the layers of peat in peat bogs.

P3 The *Beowulf* epic also reveals interesting aspects of the lives of the Anglo-Saxons who lived in England at the time of the anonymous *Beowulf* poet. The Germanic tribes, including the Angles, the Saxons, and the Jutes, invaded England from about A.D. 450 to 600. By the time of the Beowulf poet, Anglo-Saxon society in England was neither primitive nor uncultured. A

P4 ➔ Although the *Beowulf* manuscript was written in about A.D. 1000, it was not discovered until the seventeenth century. B Scholars do not know whether *Beowulf* is the sole surviving epic from a flourishing Anglo-Saxon literary period that produced other great epics or whether it was unique even in its own time. C Many scholars think that the epic was probably written sometime between the late seventh century and the early ninth century. If they are correct, the original manuscript was probably lost during the ninth-century Viking invasions of Anglia, in which the Danes destroyed the Anglo-Saxon monasteries and their great libraries. However, other scholars think that the poet's favorable attitude toward the Danes must place the epic's composition after the Viking invasions and at the start of the eleventh century, when this *Beowulf* manuscript was written.

→ The identity of the *Beowulf* poet is also uncertain. D He apparently was a Christian who loved the pagan heroic tradition of his ancestors and blended the values of the pagan hero with the Christian values of his own country and time. Because he wrote in the Anglian dialect, he probably was either a monk in a monastery or a poet in an Anglo-Saxon court located north of the Thames River.

**Appeal and Value**

*Beowulf* interests contemporary readers for many reasons. First, it is an outstanding adventure story. Grendel, Grendel's mother, and the dragon are marvelous characters, and each fight is unique, action-packed, and exciting. Second, Beowulf is a very appealing hero. He is the perfect warrior, combining extraordinary strength, skill, courage, and loyalty. Like Hercules, he devotes his life to making the world a safer place. He chooses to risk death in order to help other people, and he faces his inevitable death with heroism and dignity. Third, the *Beowulf* poet is interested in the psychological aspects of human behavior. For example, the Danish hero's welcoming speech illustrates his jealousy of Beowulf. The behavior of Beowulf's warriors in the dragon fight reveals their cowardice. Beowulf's attitudes toward heroism reflect his maturity and experience, while King Hrothgar's attitudes toward life show the experiences of an aged nobleman.

Finally, the *Beowulf* poet exhibits a mature appreciation of the transitory nature of human life and achievement. In *Beowulf*, as in the major epics of other cultures, the hero must create a meaningful life in a world that is often dangerous and uncaring. He must accept the inevitability of death. He chooses to reject despair; instead, he takes pride in himself and in his accomplishments, and he values human relationships.

1. According to paragraph 1, which of the following is true about *Beowulf*?

   Ⓐ It is the only manuscript from the Anglo-Saxon period.
   Ⓑ The original story was written in a German dialect.
   Ⓒ The author did not sign his name to the poem.
   Ⓓ It is one of several epics from the first century.

   Paragraph 1 is marked with an arrow [→].

2. The word major in the passage is closest in meaning to

   Ⓐ basic
   Ⓑ principal
   Ⓒ distinct
   Ⓓ current

3. Why does the author mention "bog-iron" in paragraph 2?

   Ⓐ To demonstrate the availability of iron in Scandinavia
   Ⓑ To prove that iron was better than bronze for weapons
   Ⓒ To argue that the Celts provided the materials to make iron
   Ⓓ To suggest that 500 B.C. was the date that the Iron Age began

   Paragraph 2 is marked with an arrow [➜].

4. Which of the sentences below best expresses the information in the highlighted statement in the passage? The other choices change the meaning or leave out important information.

   Ⓐ Society in Anglo-Saxon England was both advanced and cultured.
   Ⓑ The society of the Anglo-Saxons was not primitive or cultured.
   Ⓒ The Anglo-Saxons had a society that was primitive, not cultured.
   Ⓓ England during the Anglo-Saxon society was advanced, not cultured.

5. The word unique in the passage is closest in meaning to

   Ⓐ old
   Ⓑ rare
   Ⓒ perfect
   Ⓓ weak

6. According to paragraph 4, why do many scholars believe that the original manuscript for *Beowulf* was lost?

   Ⓐ Because it is not like other manuscripts
   Ⓑ Because many libraries were burned
   Ⓒ Because the Danes were allies of the Anglo-Saxons
   Ⓓ Because no copies were found in monasteries

   Paragraph 4 is marked with an arrow [➜].

7. In paragraph 4, the author suggests that *Beowulf* was discovered in which century?

   Ⓐ First century
   Ⓑ Ninth century
   Ⓒ Eleventh century
   Ⓓ Seventeenth century

   Paragraph 4 is marked with an arrow [➜].

8. Why does the author of this passage use the word "apparently" in paragraph 5?

    Ⓐ He is not certain that the author of *Beowulf* was a Christian.
    Ⓑ He is mentioning facts that are obvious to the readers.
    Ⓒ He is giving an example from a historical reference.
    Ⓓ He is introducing evidence about the author of *Beowulf*.

    Paragraph 5 is marked with an arrow [→].

9. Why did the author compare the Beowulf character to Hercules?

    Ⓐ They are both examples of the ideal hero.
    Ⓑ Their adventures with a dragon are very similar.
    Ⓒ The speeches that they make are inspiring.
    Ⓓ They lived at about the same time.

10. The word exhibits in the passage is closest in meaning to

    Ⓐ creates
    Ⓑ demonstrates
    Ⓒ assumes
    Ⓓ terminates

11. The word reject in the passage is closest in meaning to

    Ⓐ manage
    Ⓑ evaluate
    Ⓒ refuse
    Ⓓ confront

12. Look at the four squares [■] that show where the following sentence could be inserted in the passage.

    **Moreover, they disagree as to whether this *Beowulf* is a copy of an earlier manuscript.**

    Where could the sentence best be added?

    Click on a square [■] to insert the sentence in the passage.

13. **Directions:** An introduction for a short summary of the passage appears below. Complete the summary by selecting the THREE answer choices that mention the most important points in the passage. Some sentences do not belong in the summary because they express ideas that are not included in the passage or are minor points from the passage. ***This question is worth 2 points.***

***Beowulf* is the oldest Anglo-Saxon epic poem that has survived to the present day.**

- 
- 
- 

## Answer Choices

A  The Northmen were adept in crafting tools and weapons made of bronze, but the Celts were superior in designing and working in iron.

B  In the Viking invasions of England, the Danish armies destroyed monasteries, some of which contained extensive libraries.

C  King Hrothgar and Beowulf become friends at the end of their lives, after having spent decades opposing each other on the battlefield.

D  The poem chronicles life in Anglo-Saxon society during the Bronze and Iron Ages when Germanic tribes were invading England.

E  Although *Beowulf* was written by an anonymous poet, probably a Christian, about A.D. 1000, it was not found until the seventeenth century.

F  *Beowulf* is still interesting because it has engaging characters, an adventurous plot, and an appreciation for human behavior and relationships.

## Reading 2

The following reading passage was adapted from *Biology*, Eighth Edition by Neil A. Campbell et al., Pearson Education, Inc., 2008.

### *"Thermoregulation"*

P1 → Mammals and birds generally maintain body temperature within a narrow range (36–38°C for most mammals and 39–42°C for most birds) that is usually considerably warmer than the environment. Because heat always flows from a warm object to cooler surroundings, birds and mammals must counteract the constant heat loss. This maintenance of warm body temperature depends on several key adaptations. The most basic mechanism is the high metabolic rate of endothermy itself. Endotherms can produce large amounts of metabolic heat that replace the flow of heat to the environment, and they can vary heat production to match changing rates of heat loss. Heat production is increased by such muscle activity as moving or shivering. In some mammals, certain hormones can cause mitochondria to increase their metabolic activity and produce heat instead of ATP. This **nonshivering thermogenesis (NST)** takes place throughout the body, but some mammals also have a tissue called **brown fat** in the neck and between the shoulders that is specialized for rapid heat production. Through shivering and NST, mammals and birds in cold environments can increase their metabolic heat production by as much as 5 to 10 times above the minimal levels that occur in warm conditions.

P2 → Another major thermoregulatory adaptation that evolved in mammals and birds is insulation (hair, feathers, and fat layers), which reduces the flow of heat and lowers the energy cost of keeping warm. Most land mammals and birds react to cold by raising their fur or feathers, thereby trapping a thicker layer of air. Ⓐ Humans rely more on a layer of fat just beneath the skin as insulation; goose bumps are a vestige of hair-raising left over from our furry ancestors. Ⓑ Vasodilation and vasoconstriction also regulate heat exchange and may contribute to regional temperature differences within the animal. Ⓒ For example, heat loss from a human is reduced when arms and legs cool to several degrees below the temperature of the body core, where most vital organs are located. Ⓓ

P3 → Hair loses most of its insulating power when wet. Marine mammals such as whales and seals have a very thick layer of insulation fat called blubber, just under the skin. Marine mammals swim in water colder than their body core temperature, and many species spend at least part of the year in nearly freezing polar seas. The loss of heat to water occurs 50 to 100 times more rapidly than heat loss to air, and the skin temperature of a marine mammal is close to water temperature. Even so, the blubber insulation is so effective that marine mammals maintain body core temperatures of about 36–38°C with metabolic rates about the same as those of land mammals of similar size. The flippers or tail of a whale or seal lack insulating blubber, but countercurrent heat exchangers greatly reduce heat loss in these extremities, as they do in the legs of many birds.

P4    → Through metabolic heat production, insulation, and vascular adjustments, birds and mammals are capable of astonishing feats of thermoregulation. For example, small birds called chickadees, which weigh only 20 grams, can remain active and hold body temperature nearly constant at 40°C in environmental temperatures as low as –40°C—as long as they have enough food to supply the large amount of energy necessary for heat production.

P5    Many mammals and birds live in places where thermoregulation requires cooling off as well as warming. For example, when a marine mammal moves into warm seas, as many whales do when they reproduce, excess metabolic heat is removed by vasodilation of numerous blood vessels in the outer layer of the skin. In hot climates or when vigorous exercise adds large amounts of metabolic heat to the body, many terrestrial mammals and birds may allow body temperature to rise by several degrees, which enhances heat loss by increasing the temperature gradient between the body and a warm environment.

P6    → Evaporative cooling often plays a key role in dissipating the body heat. If environmental temperature is above body temperature, animals gain heat from the environment as well as from metabolism, and evaporation is the only way to keep body temperature from rising rapidly. Panting is important in birds and many mammals. Some birds have a pouch richly supplied with blood vessels in the floor of the mouth; fluttering the pouch increases evaporation. Pigeons can use evaporative cooling to keep body temperature close to 40°C in air temperatures as high as 60°C, as long as they have sufficient water. Many terrestrial mammals have sweat glands controlled by the nervous system. Other mechanisms that promote evaporative cooling include spreading saliva on body surfaces, an adaptation of some kangaroos and rodents for combating severe heat stress. Some bats use both saliva and urine to enhance evaporative cooling.

**Glossary**
ATP: energy that drives certain reactions in cells
mitochondria: a membrane of ATP

14. According to paragraph 1, what is the most fundamental adaptation to maintain body temperature?

   Ⓐ The heat generated by the metabolism
   Ⓑ A shivering reflex in the muscles
   Ⓒ Migration to a warmer environment
   Ⓓ Higher caloric intake to match heat loss

Paragraph 1 is marked with an arrow [→].

15. Based on information in paragraph 1, which of the following best explains the term "thermogenesis"?

    Ⓐ Heat loss that must be reversed
    Ⓑ The adaptation of brown fat tissue in the neck
    Ⓒ The maintenance of healthy environmental conditions
    Ⓓ Conditions that affect the metabolism

    Paragraph 1 is marked with an arrow [➔].

16. Which of the sentences below best expresses the information in the highlighted statement in the passage? The other choices change the meaning or leave out important information.

    Ⓐ An increase in heat production causes muscle activity such as moving or shivering.
    Ⓑ Muscle activity like moving and shivering will increase heat production.
    Ⓒ Moving and shivering are muscle activities that increase with heat.
    Ⓓ When heat increases, the production of muscle activity also increases.

17. The word minimal in the passage is closest in meaning to

    Ⓐ most recent
    Ⓑ most active
    Ⓒ newest
    Ⓓ smallest

18. In paragraph 2, how does the author explain the concept of vasodilation and vasoconstriction?

    Ⓐ Describing the evolution in our ancestors
    Ⓑ Giving an example of heat loss in the extremities
    Ⓒ Comparing the process in humans and animals
    Ⓓ Identifying various types of insulation

    Paragraph 2 is marked with an arrow [➔].

19. The word regulate in the passage is closest in meaning to

    Ⓐ protect
    Ⓑ create
    Ⓒ reduce
    Ⓓ control

20. According to paragraph 3, why do many marine animals require a layer of blubber?

    Ⓐ Because marine animals have lost their hair during evolution
    Ⓑ Because heat is lost in water much faster than it is in air
    Ⓒ Because dry hair does not insulate marine animals
    Ⓓ Because they are so large that they require more insulation

    Paragraph 3 is marked with an arrow [➔].

21. Why does the author mention "chickadees" in paragraph 4?

    Ⓐ To discuss an animal that regulates heat very well
    Ⓑ To demonstrate why chickadees have to eat so much
    Ⓒ To mention an exception to the rules of thermoregulation
    Ⓓ To give a reason for heat production in small animals

    Paragraph 4 is marked with an arrow [➔].

22. The word sufficient in the passage is closest in meaning to

    Ⓐ established
    Ⓑ valuable
    Ⓒ safe
    Ⓓ adequate

23. In paragraph 6, the author states that evaporative cooling is often accomplished by all of the following methods EXCEPT

    Ⓐ by spreading saliva over the area
    Ⓑ by urinating on the body
    Ⓒ by panting or fluttering a pouch
    Ⓓ by immersing themselves in water

    Paragraph 6 is marked with an arrow [➔].

24. The word enhance in the passage is closest in meaning to

    Ⓐ simplify
    Ⓑ improve
    Ⓒ replace
    Ⓓ interrupt

25. Look at the four squares [■] that show where the following sentence could be inserted in the passage.

    **The insulating power of a layer of fur or feathers mainly depends on how much still air the layer traps.**

    Where could the sentence best be added?

    Click on a square [■] to insert the sentence in the passage.

26. **Directions:** An introduction for a short summary of the passage appears below. Complete the summary by selecting the THREE answer choices that mention the most important points in the passage. Some sentences do not belong in the summary because they express ideas that are not included in the passage or are minor points from the passage. *This question is worth 2 points.*

    **Thermoregulation is the process by which animals control body temperatures within healthy limits.**

    - 
    - 
    - 

### Answer Choices

A Although hair can be a very efficient insulation when it is dry and it can be raised, hair becomes ineffective when it is submerged in cold water.

B Some animals with few adaptations for thermoregulation migrate to moderate climates to avoid the extreme weather in the polar regions and the tropics.

C Mammals and birds use insulation to mitigate heat loss, including hair and feathers that can be raised to trap air as well as fat or blubber under the skin.

D Some birds have a special pouch in the mouth, which can be fluttered to increase evaporation and decrease their body temperatures by as much as 20°C.

E Endotherms generate heat by increasing muscle activity, by releasing hormones into their blood streams, or by producing heat in brown fat tissues.

F Panting, sweating, and spreading saliva or urine on their bodies are all options for the evaporative cooling of animals in hot environmental conditions.

## *Reading 3*

The following reading passage was adapted from *Psychology Applied to Modern Life*, Ninth Edition by Wayne Weiten et.al., Wadsworth, 2009.

### *"Social Readjustment Scales"*

P1  → In 1967, Holmes and Rahe developed the Social Readjustment Rating Scale (SRRS) to measure life change as a form of stress. A The scale assigns numerical values to 43 major life events that are supposed to reflect the magnitude of the readjustment required by each change. In responding to the scale, respondents are asked to indicate how often they experienced any of these 43 events during a certain time period (typically, the past year). The person then adds up the numbers associated with each event checked. B

P2  → The SRRS and similar scales have been used in thousands of studies by researchers all over the world. C Overall, these studies have shown that people with higher scores on the SRRS tend to be more vulnerable to many kinds of physical illness—and many types of psychological problems as well. D More recently, however, experts have criticized this research, citing problems with the methods used and raising questions about the meaning of the findings.

P3    First, the assumption that the SRRS measures change exclusively has been shown to be inaccurate. We now have ample evidence that the desirability of events affects adaptational outcomes more than the amount of change that they require. Thus, it seems prudent to view the SRRS as a measure of diverse forms of stress, rather than as a measure of change-related stress.

P4  → Second, the SRRS fails to take into account differences among people in their subjective perception of how stressful an event is. For instance, while divorce may deserve a stress value of 73 for *most* people, a particular person's divorce might generate much less stress and merit a value of only 25.

P5  → Third, many of the events listed on the SRRS and similar scales are highly ambiguous, leading people to be inconsistent as to which events they report experiencing. For instance, what qualifies as "trouble with the boss"? Should you check that because you're sick and tired of your supervisor? What constitutes a "change in living conditions"? Does your purchase of a great new sound system qualify? As you can see, the SRRS includes many "events" that are described inadequately, producing considerable ambiguity about the meaning of one's response. Problems in recalling events over a period of a year also lead to inconsistent responding on stress scales, thus lowering their reliability.

P6    Fourth, the SRRS does not sample from the domain of stressful events very thoroughly. Do the 43 events listed on the SRRS exhaust all the major stresses that people typically experience? Studies designed to explore that question have found many significant omissions.

P7    → Fifth, the correlation between SRRS scores and health may be inflated because subjects' neuroticism affects both their responses to stress scales and their self-reports of health problems. Neurotic individuals have a tendency to recall more stress than others and to recall more symptoms of illness than others. These tendencies mean that some of the correlation between high stress and high illness may simply reflect the effects of subjects' neuroticism. The possible contaminating effects of neuroticism obscure the meaning of scores on the SRRS and similar measures of stress.

**The Life Experiences Survey**

P8    In the light of these problems, a number of researchers have attempted to develop improved versions of the SRRS. For example, the Life Experiences Survey (LES), assembled by Irwin Sarason and colleagues, has become a widely used measure of stress in contemporary research. The LES revises and builds on the SRRS survey in a variety of ways that correct, at least in part, most of the problems just discussed.

P9    → Specifically, the LES recognizes that stress involves more than mere change and asks respondents to indicate whether events had a positive or negative impact on them. This strategy permits the computation of positive change, negative change, and total change scores, which helps researchers gain much more insight into which facets of stress are most crucial. The LES also takes into consideration differences among people in their appraisal of stress, by dropping the normative weights and replacing them with personally assigned weightings of the impact of relevant events. Ambiguity in items is decreased by providing more elaborate descriptions of many items to clarify their meaning.

P10    The LES deals with the failure of the SRRS to sample the full domain of stressful events in several ways. First, some significant omissions from the SRRS have been added to the LES. Second, the LES allows the respondent to write in personally important events that are not included on the scale. Third, the LES has an extra section just for students. Sarason and colleagues suggest that special, tailored sections of this sort be added for specific populations whenever it is useful.

27. Based on the information in paragraph 1 and paragraph 2, what can be inferred about a person with a score of 30 on the SRRS?

    Ⓐ A person with a higher score will experience less stress than this person will.
    Ⓑ It is likely that this person has not suffered any major problems in the past year.
    Ⓒ The amount of positive change is greater than that of a person with a score of 40.
    Ⓓ This person has a greater probability to be ill than a person with a 20 score.

    Paragraph 1 and paragraph 2 are marked with arrows [→].

28. The word outcomes in the passage is closest in meaning to

    Ⓐ opportunities
    Ⓑ conditions
    Ⓒ results
    Ⓓ issues

29. The word diverse in the passage is closest in meaning to

    Ⓐ necessary
    Ⓑ steady
    Ⓒ limited
    Ⓓ different

30. In paragraph 4, why does the author use divorce as an example?

    Ⓐ To show how most people respond to high stress situations in their lives
    Ⓑ To demonstrate the serious nature of a situation that is listed as a stressful event
    Ⓒ To illustrate the subjective importance of a situation listed on the scale
    Ⓓ To identify the numerical value for a stressful event on the SRRS

Paragraph 4 is marked with an arrow [➔].

31. In paragraph 5, how does the author demonstrate that the response events on the SRRS are not consistent?

    Ⓐ By asking questions that could be answered in more than one way
    Ⓑ By giving examples of responses that are confusing
    Ⓒ By comparing several ways to score the stress scales
    Ⓓ By suggesting that people do not respond carefully

Paragraph 5 is marked with an arrow [➔].

32. According to paragraph 7, why is the SRRS inappropriate for people with neuroses?

    Ⓐ They are ill more often, which affects their scores on the scale.
    Ⓑ Their self-reporting on the scale is affected by their neuroses.
    Ⓒ They tend to suffer more stress than people without neuroses.
    Ⓓ Their response to stress will probably not be recorded on the scale.

Paragraph 7 is marked with an arrow [➔].

33. The word assembled in the passage is closest in meaning to

    Ⓐ announced
    Ⓑ influenced
    Ⓒ arranged
    Ⓓ distributed

34. The word relevant in the passage is closest in meaning to

   Ⓐ occasional
   Ⓑ modern
   Ⓒ related
   Ⓓ unusual

35. According to paragraph 9, why does the LES ask respondents to classify change as positive or negative?

   Ⓐ To analyze the long-term consequences of change
   Ⓑ To determine which aspects of change are personally significant
   Ⓒ To explain why some people handle stress better than others
   Ⓓ To introduce normative weighting of stress events

   Paragraph 9 is marked with an arrow [➔].

36. According to the passage, which of the following is true about the SRRS as compared with the LES?

   Ⓐ The SRRS includes a space to write in personal events that have not been listed.
   Ⓑ The SRRS features a section for specific populations such as students.
   Ⓒ The SRRS assigns numbers to calculate the stress associated with events.
   Ⓓ The SRRS has hints to help people recall events that happened over a year ago.

37. Which of the following statements most accurately reflects the author's opinion of the SRRS?

   Ⓐ There are many problems associated with it.
   Ⓑ It is superior to the LES.
   Ⓒ It should be studied more carefully.
   Ⓓ The scale is most useful for students.

38. Look at the four squares [■] that show where the following sentence could be inserted in the passage.

   **This sum is an index of the amount of change-related stress the person has recently experienced.**

   Where could the sentence best be added?

   Click on a square [■] to insert the sentence in the passage.

39. **Directions:** An introduction for a short summary of the passage appears below. Complete the summary by selecting the THREE answer choices that mention the most important points in the passage. Some sentences do not belong in the summary because they express ideas that are not included in the passage or are minor points from the passage. *This question is worth 2 points.*

**Several social readjustment scales have been developed to measure stress from life changing events.**

- 
- 
- 

**Answer Choices**

Ⓐ The Life Experiences Survey (LES) takes into consideration both positive and negative changes as well as the individual differences among people assigning values for stressful events.

Ⓑ The Life Experiences Survey (LES) was developed to correct a number of problems in the Social Readjustment Rating Scale (SRRS).

Ⓒ The Social Readjustment Rating Scale (SRRS) assigns mathematical values to major life events and collects data about the events that an individual has experienced during a specific time.

Ⓓ Researchers have called into question the usefulness of instruments like the Social Readjustment Rating Scale (SRRS) and the Life Experiences Survey (LES) and have begun to develop a new scale to measure stress.

Ⓔ People who have neurotic tendencies are not good candidates to take the Social Readjustment Scale (SRRS) because they may provide higher values for stressful events.

Ⓕ Positive events and negative events can both cause stress, according to social readjustment scales designed to measure them.

# LISTENING SECTION

**Reminder:** To access the audio for this section of the test, visit *http://bit.ly/Barrons-TOEFL*.

 **Model Test 1, Listening Section, Track 1**

The Listening Section tests your ability to understand spoken English that is typical of inter-actions and academic speech on college campuses. During the test, you will listen to conversations, lectures, and discussions, and you will answer questions about them.

This is the long format for the Listening Section. On the long format, you will listen to three conversations, three lectures, and three discussions. After each listening passage, you will answer 5–6 questions about it. Only two conversations, two lectures, and two discussions will be graded. The other passages are part of an experimental section for future tests. Because you will not know which conversations, lectures, and discussions will be graded, you must try to do your best on all of them.

You will hear each passage one time. You may take notes while you listen, but notes are not graded. You may use your notes to answer the questions.

Choose the best answer for multiple-choice questions. Follow the directions on the page or on the screen for computer-assisted questions. Click on **Next** and then on **OK** to go on to the next question. You cannot return to previous questions.

The Listening Section is divided into sets. Each set includes one conversation, one lecture, and one discussion. You have 10 minutes to answer all of the questions for each set. You will have 30 minutes to answer all of the questions on the long format. A clock on the screen will show you how much time you have to complete your answers for the section. The clock does NOT count the time you are listening to the conversations, lectures, and discussions.

### Listening 1 "Learning Center"

1.  What does the woman need?

    Ⓐ  A meeting with Professor Simpson
    Ⓑ  An English composition class
    Ⓒ  An appointment for tutoring
    Ⓓ  Information about the Learning Center

2.  Why does the woman say this:

    Ⓐ  She is worried that she cannot afford the service.
    Ⓑ  She is trying to negotiate the cost of the sessions.
    Ⓒ  She is showing particular interest in the man.
    Ⓓ  She is expressing surprise about the arrangement.

3.  Why is the man concerned about the woman's attendance?

    Ⓐ  If she is absent, her grade will be lowered.
    Ⓑ  He will not get a paycheck if she is absent.
    Ⓒ  She has been sick a lot during the semester.
    Ⓓ  Her grades need to be improved.

4. What does the man agree to do?

    Ⓐ He will show the woman how to use the library.
    Ⓑ He will write some compositions for the woman.
    Ⓒ He will talk with the woman's English professor.
    Ⓓ He will show the woman how to improve her writing.

5. What does the man imply about the woman's teacher?

    Ⓐ The professor is very difficult to understand.
    Ⓑ He does not know where she came from.
    Ⓒ Her students seem to like her teaching style.
    Ⓓ He is familiar with her requirements.

## Listening 2 "Geology Class"

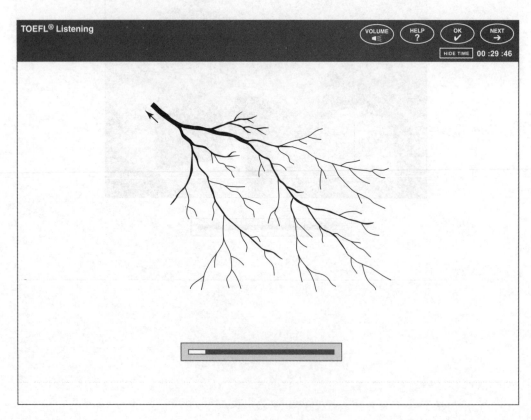

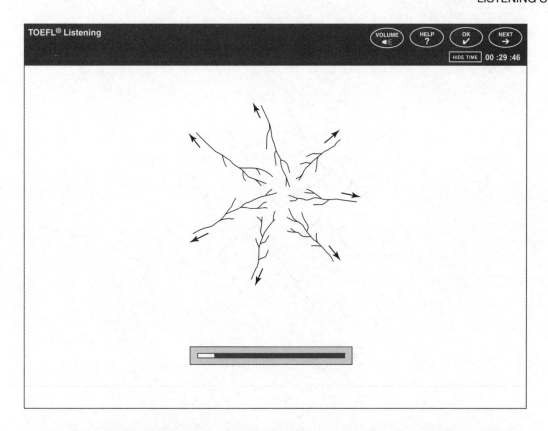

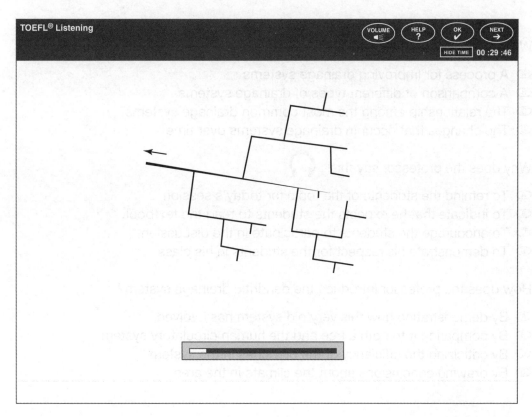

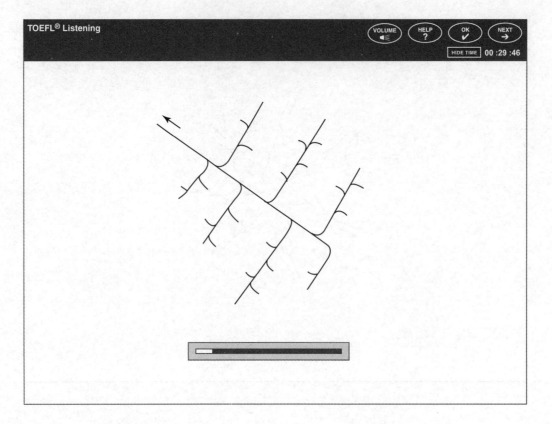

TOEFL® Listening

VOLUME    HELP ?    OK ✓    NEXT →

HIDE TIME   00 :29 :46

6. What is this lecture mainly about?

Ⓐ A process for improving drainage systems
Ⓑ A comparison of different types of drainage systems
Ⓒ The relationship among the most common drainage systems
Ⓓ The changes that occur in drainage systems over time

7. Why does the professor say this:

Ⓐ To remind the students of the topic for today's session
Ⓑ To indicate that he expects the students to read the textbook
Ⓒ To encourage the students to participate in the discussion
Ⓓ To demonstrate his respect for the students in his class

8. How does the professor introduce the dendritic drainage system?

Ⓐ By demonstrating how this very old system has evolved
Ⓑ By comparing it to both a tree and the human circulatory system
Ⓒ By criticizing the efficiency of the branches in the system
Ⓓ By drawing conclusions about the climate in the area

9. Why does the professor mention the spokes of a wheel?

&#9400; To make a point about the stream beds in a trellis pattern
&#9401; To contrast the formation with that of a rectangular one
&#9402; To explain the structure of a radial drainage system
&#9403; To give an example of a dendritic drainage system

10. In the lecture, the professor discusses the trellis drainage pattern. Indicate whether each of the following is typical of this pattern. Click in the correct box for each phrase.

|   |   | Yes | No |
|---|---|---|---|
| A | Parallel stream beds flowing beside each other |   |   |
| B | Stream beds with sharp 90 degree turns |   |   |
| C | Drainage from the top of a central peak |   |   |
| D | Hard rock formations on top of soft rock formations |   |   |
| E | Geological evidence of folding with outcroppings |   |   |

11. What does the professor imply when he says this:

&#9400; The test questions will be very difficult.
&#9401; The students should read their textbooks before the test.
&#9402; The basic patterns from the notes will be on the test.
&#9403; The test will influence the final grade.

*Listening 3 "Psychology Class"*

12. What is the discussion mainly about?

    Ⓐ The difference between suppression and repression
    Ⓑ Why Freud's theories of defense mechanisms are correct
    Ⓒ Some of the more common types of defense mechanisms
    Ⓓ How to solve a student's problem with an unfair professor

13. How does the student explain the term *repression*?

    Ⓐ He contrasts it with suppression.
    Ⓑ He identifies it as a conscious response.
    Ⓒ He gives several examples of it.
    Ⓓ He refers to a study by Freud.

14. Why does the professor say this:

    Ⓐ She is getting the class to pay attention.
    Ⓑ She is making a joke about herself.
    Ⓒ She is asking for a compliment.
    Ⓓ She is criticizing a colleague.

15. Which of the following is an example of *displacement* that was used in the discussion?

    Ⓐ Insisting that the professor dislikes you, when you really dislike him
    Ⓑ Defending the professor even when you are angry about his behavior
    Ⓒ Blaming someone in your study group instead of blaming the professor
    Ⓓ Refusing to acknowledge that a problem exists because of the low grade

16. According to the professor, what happened in the 1990s?

    Ⓐ The concept of defense mechanisms was abandoned.
    Ⓑ New terms were introduced for the same mechanisms.
    Ⓒ Modern researchers improved upon Freud's theory.
    Ⓓ Additional categories were introduced by researchers.

17. How does the professor organize the discussion?

    Ⓐ She has visual aids to explain each point.
    Ⓑ She uses a scenario that students can relate to.
    Ⓒ She provides a handout with an outline.
    Ⓓ She helps students read the textbook.

### Listening 4 "Professor's Office"

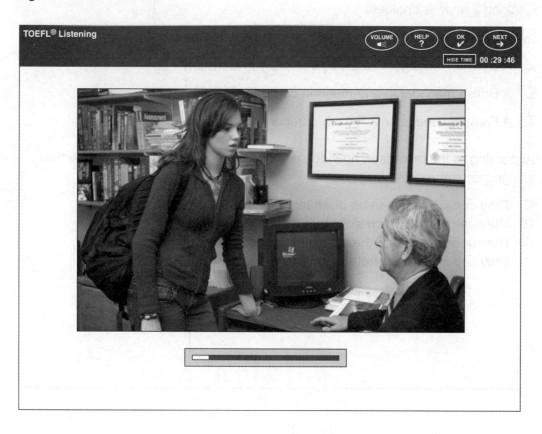

18. Why does the woman go to see her professor?

    Ⓐ To get notes from a class that she has missed

    Ⓑ To clarify some of the information from a lecture

    Ⓒ To talk about her career in international business

    Ⓓ To ask some questions about a paper she is writing

19. According to the professor, which factor causes staffing patterns to vary?

    Ⓐ The yearly earnings for all of the branch offices

    Ⓑ The number of employees in a multinational company

    Ⓒ The place where a company has its home office

    Ⓓ The number of years that a company has been in business

20. Why does the professor say this:

    Ⓐ To indicate that he is getting impatient

    Ⓑ To encourage the woman to continue

    Ⓒ To show that he does not understand

    Ⓓ To correct the woman's previous comment

21. Which of the following would be an example of a third-country pattern?

    <mark>Click on 2 answer choices.</mark>

    Ⓐ A Scottish manager in an American company in Africa

    Ⓑ A German manager in a Swiss company in Germany

    Ⓒ A British manager in an American company in India

    Ⓓ A French manager in a French company in Canada

22. According to the professor, how do senior-level Japanese managers view their assignments abroad?

    Ⓐ They consider them to be permanent career opportunities.

    Ⓑ They use them to learn skills that they will use in Japan.

    Ⓒ They understand that the assignment is only temporary.

    Ⓓ They see them as a strategy for their retirement.

## Listening 5 "Art Class"

TOEFL® Listening    VOLUME    HELP ?    OK ✓    NEXT →

HIDE TIME  00 :29 :46

23. What is the lecture mainly about?

    Ⓐ The way that drawing has influenced art
    Ⓑ The relationship between drawing and other art
    Ⓒ The distinct purposes of drawing
    Ⓓ The reason that artists prefer drawing

24. According to the professor, why do architects use sketches?

    Ⓐ Architects are not clear about the final design at the beginning.
    Ⓑ To design large buildings, architects must work in a smaller scale.
    Ⓒ Engineers use the architect's sketches to implement the details.
    Ⓓ Sketches are used as a record of the stages in development.

25. What does the professor mean when she says this:

    Ⓐ She is checking to be sure that the students understand.
    Ⓑ She is expressing uncertainty about the information.
    Ⓒ She is inviting the students to disagree with her.
    Ⓓ She is indicating that she is in a hurry to continue.

26. Why does the professor mention the drawing of Marie Antoinette?

    Ⓐ It is an example of a work copied in another medium.
    Ⓑ Drawing was typical of the way that artists were educated.
    Ⓒ The sketch was a historical account of an important event.
    Ⓓ The size of the drawing made it an exceptional work of art.

27. What is the professor's opinion of Picasso?

    Ⓐ Picasso was probably playing a joke by offering drawings for sale.
    Ⓑ At the end of his career, Picasso may have chosen drawing because it was easy.
    Ⓒ Picasso's drawings required the confidence and skill of a master artist.
    Ⓓ Cave drawings were the inspiration for many of Picasso's works.

28. According to the lecture, what are the major functions of drawing?

Click on 3 answer choices.

    Ⓐ A technique to remember parts of a large work

    Ⓑ A method to preserve a historical record

    Ⓒ An example of earlier forms of art

    Ⓓ An educational approach to train artists

    Ⓔ A process for experimenting with media

### Listening 6 "Astronomy Class"

29. What is the discussion mainly about?

        Ⓐ The discovery of the Alpha Centauri system
        Ⓑ The reason solar systems are confused with galaxies
        Ⓒ The vast expanse of the universe around us
        Ⓓ The model at the National Air and Space Museum

30. Why does the professor say this:

        Ⓐ The students can read the details in the textbook.
        Ⓑ The professor wants the students to concentrate on listening.
        Ⓒ The facts are probably already familiar to most of the class.
        Ⓓ This lecture is a review of material from a previous session.

31. Why wouldn't a photograph capture a true picture of the solar system walk?

        Ⓐ It would not show the distances between the bodies in space.
        Ⓑ The information on the markers would not be visible in a picture.
        Ⓒ The scale for the model was not large enough to be accurate.
        Ⓓ A photograph would make the exhibit appear much smaller.

32. How does the professor explain the term *solar system*?

    Ⓐ He identifies the key features of a solar system.
    Ⓑ He refers to the glossary in the textbook.
    Ⓒ He gives several examples of solar systems.
    Ⓓ He contrasts a solar system with a galaxy.

33. Why does the professor say this:

    Ⓐ He is trying to get the students to pay attention.
    Ⓑ He is correcting something that he said earlier in the discussion.
    Ⓒ He is beginning a summary of the important points.
    Ⓓ He is joking with the students about the lecture.

34. What can be inferred about the professor?

    Ⓐ The professor used to teach in Washington, D.C.
    Ⓑ The professor likes his students to participate in the discussion.
    Ⓒ The professor wants the students to take notes on every detail.
    Ⓓ The professor is not very interested in the subject of the discussion.

### Listening 7  "Bookstore"

35. What does the man need from the bookstore?

&#9398; A schedule of classes for next term
&#9399; A form to order books
&#9400; Specific books for his classes
&#9401; Information about employment

36. What does the man need if he wants a full refund?

Click on 2 answer choices.

A   Identification

B   His registration form

C   A receipt for the purchase

D   Proof of his deposit

37. What does the woman mean when she says this:

&#9398; She is not sure that the student employee will give her the form.
&#9399; She thinks that he will have to wait for the student employees.
&#9400; She does not want the man to bother her because she is busy.
&#9401; She is is not sure that the man understands what to do.

38. What does the woman imply about the used books she sells?

&#9398; They are purchased before new books.
&#9399; They do not have marks in them.
&#9400; She does not recommend buying them.
&#9401; She would rather sell new books.

39. What does the man need to do now?

&#9398; Go to the bank to get money for the deposit
&#9399; Sit down and fill out the form to order books
&#9400; Take his books back to the dormitory
&#9401; Locate the section numbers for his classes

## *Listening 8  "Environmental Science Class"*

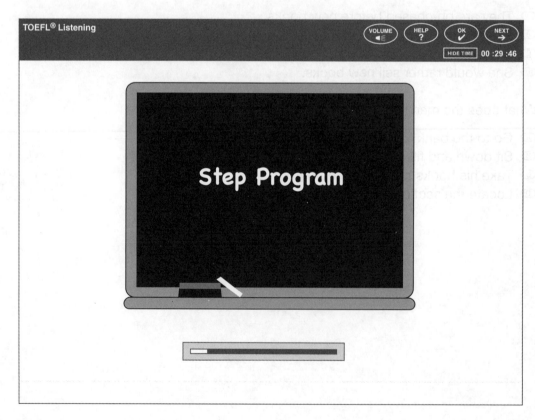

40. What is this lecture mainly about?

    &Ⓐ An overview of fuel cell technology
    Ⓑ A process for producing fuel cells
    Ⓒ A comparison of fuel cell models
    Ⓓ Some problems in fuel cell distribution

41. What does the professor mean when he says this:

    Ⓐ He wants the students to take notes.
    Ⓑ He would like the students to participate.
    Ⓒ He is impressed with these options.
    Ⓓ He does not plan to talk about the alternatives.

42. Why does the professor mention the STEP Program in Australia?

    Ⓐ He has personal experience in this project.
    Ⓑ He is referring to information from a previous discussion.
    Ⓒ He is comparing it to a successful program in Japan.
    Ⓓ He thinks it is a very good example of a project.

43. Why does the professor say this:

    Ⓐ To indicate that the date is not important
    Ⓑ To provide a specific date for the contract
    Ⓒ To correct a previous statement about the date
    Ⓓ To show that he is uncertain about the date

44. What are some of the problems associated with fuel cell technology?

    Click on 2 answer choices.

    Ⓐ Noise pollution

    Ⓑ Public acceptance

    Ⓒ Supplies of hydrogen

    Ⓓ Investment in infrastructures

45. What is the professor's attitude toward fuel cells?

    Ⓐ He thinks that the technology is not very efficient.
    Ⓑ He is hopeful about their development in the future.
    Ⓒ He is doubtful that fuel cells will replace fossil fuels.
    Ⓓ He is discouraged because of the delays in production.

*Listening 9  "Philosophy Class"*

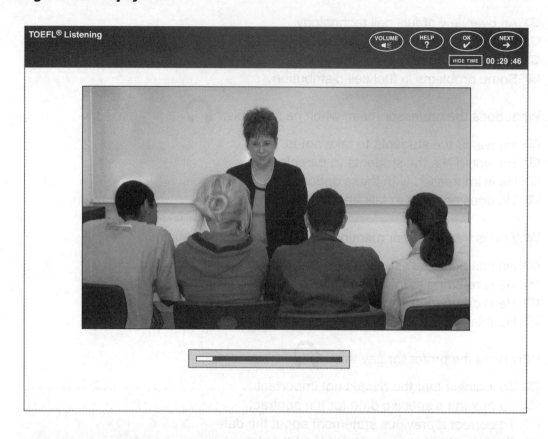

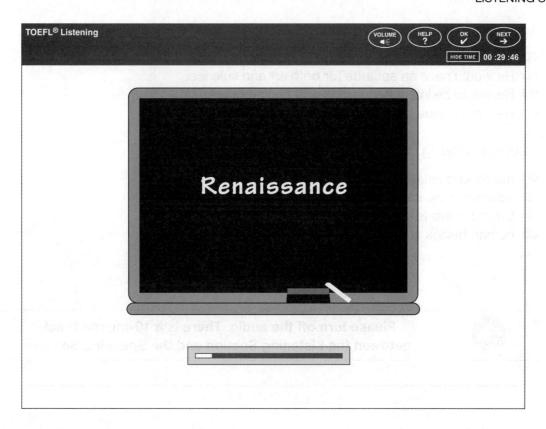

46. What is the main focus of this discussion?

    Ⓐ The Renaissance
    Ⓑ Important scholars
    Ⓒ Humanism
    Ⓓ Political reform

47. Why does the professor say this:

    Ⓐ She thinks that the spelling of the term is not important.
    Ⓑ She assumes that the students know how to spell the term.
    Ⓒ She knows that the term can be found in the textbook.
    Ⓓ She does not want to spend time explaining the term.

48. Why does the professor mention the drawing by Leonardo da Vinci?

    Ⓐ She wants the students to refer to their textbook more often.
    Ⓑ She uses it as an example of the union of art and science.
    Ⓒ She says that it is one of her personal favorites.
    Ⓓ She contrasts his work with that of other artists.

49. According to the professor, what was the effect of using Latin as a universal language of scholarship?

    Ⓐ It facilitated communication among intellectuals in many countries.
    Ⓑ It made Rome the capital of the world during the Renaissance.
    Ⓒ It caused class distinctions to be apparent throughout Europe.
    Ⓓ It created an environment in which new ideas were suppressed.

50. According to the professor, what can be inferred about a Renaissance man?

   Ⓐ He would probably be a master craftsman.
   Ⓑ He would have an aptitude for both art and science.
   Ⓒ He would be interested in classical philosophers.
   Ⓓ He would value logic at the expense of creativity.

51. All of the following characteristics are true of humanism EXCEPT

   Ⓐ mankind is innately good
   Ⓑ scholars must serve society
   Ⓒ the individual is important
   Ⓓ human beings are rational

---

**Please turn off the audio. There is a 10-minute break
between the Listening Section and the Speaking Section.**

# SPEAKING SECTION

 **Model Test 1, Speaking Section, Track 2**

The Speaking Section tests your ability to communicate in English in an academic setting. During the test, you will be presented with six speaking questions. The questions ask for a response to a single question, conversation, talk, or lecture. The prompts and questions are presented one time.

You may take notes as you listen, but notes are not graded. You may use your notes to answer the questions. Some of the questions ask for a response to a reading passage and a talk or a lecture. The reading passages and the questions are written, but the directions will be spoken.

Your speaking will be evaluated on both the fluency of the language and the accuracy of the content. You will have 15–20 seconds to prepare and 45–60 seconds to respond to each question. Typically, a good response will require all of the response time and the answer will be complete by the end of the response time.

You will have about 20 minutes to complete the Speaking Section. A clock on the screen will show you how much time you have to prepare each of your answers and how much time you have to record each response.

### *Independent Speaking Question 1 "Marriage Partner"*

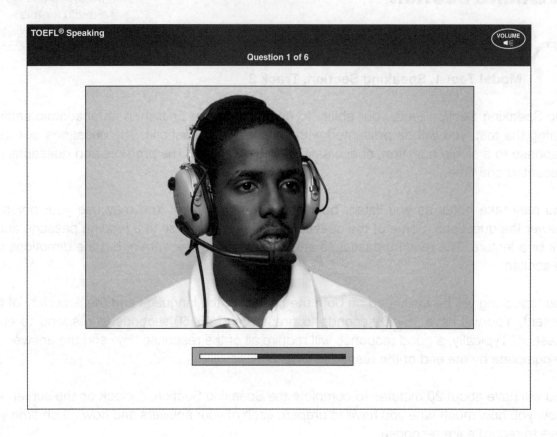

 Listen for a question about a familiar topic.

**Question**

Describe an ideal marriage partner. What qualities do you think are most important for a husband or wife? Use specific reasons and details to explain your choices.

Preparation Time: 15 seconds
Recording Time: 45 seconds

## *Independent Speaking Question 2 "News"*

TOEFL® Speaking

Question 2 of 6

VOLUME

 Listen for a question that asks your opinion about a familiar topic.

### Question

Agree or disagree with the following statement:

Getting news on TV or on a computer is better than reading it in a print newspaper.

Use specific reasons and examples to support your choice.

Preparation Time: 15 seconds
Recording Time: 45 seconds

### *Integrated Speaking Question 3 "Meal Plan"*

Read a short passage and listen to a talk on the same topic.

Reading Time: 45 seconds

---

Change in Meal Plans

Residence hall students are no longer required to purchase seven-day meal plans. Now two meal plan options will be offered. The traditional seven-day plan will still be available, including three meals every day at a cost of $168 per month. In addition, a five-day plan will be offered, including three meals Monday–Friday at a cost of $120 per month. Students who elect to use the five-day plan may purchase meals on the weekend at three dollars per meal. The food court in the College Union provides several fast-food alternatives. In addition to burgers and pizza, Chinese food, Mexican food, and a salad bar are also available.

---

 Now listen to two students who are talking about the plan.

**Question**
The man expresses his opinion of the new meal plan. Report his opinion, and explain the reasons that he gives for having that opinion.

Preparation Time: 30 seconds
Recording Time: 60 seconds

## Integrated Speaking Question 4  "Allegories"

Read a short passage and listen to part of a lecture on the same topic.

Reading Time: 45 seconds

<u>Allegories</u>

An allegory is a story, a poem, a play, or an image that can be understood on a deeper level by interpreting symbols or hidden meanings that the author or artist has embedded. Allegories exist on two levels—a literal level that is direct and a figurative level that is below the surface. Characters, settings, and events represent something quite different from those in the literal story. In an allegory, the author often writes about a moral or political theme. Stories to teach a moral lesson to children are often allegories because it is possible through this literary device to explain complicated, abstract ideas in concrete terms by representing them as characters or situations.

TOEFL® Speaking

Question 4 of 6

VOLUME

 Now listen to part of a lecture in a literature class. The professor is talking about a story by Dr. Seuss.

**Question**

Using the example from the lecture, explain why "The Sneetches" is an allegory. Draw upon information in both the reading and the lecture.

Preparation Time: 30 seconds
Recording Time: 60 seconds

## *Integrated Speaking Question 5 "Scheduling Conflict"*

 Now listen to a short conversation between a student and his friend.

**Question**
Describe the man's problem and the two suggestions that his friend makes about how to handle it. What do you think the man should do, and why?

Preparation Time: 20 seconds
Recording Time: 60 seconds

## *Integrated Speaking Question 6 "Laboratory Microscope"*

 Now listen to part of a talk in a biology laboratory. The teaching assistant is explaining how to use the microscope.

### Question
Using the main points and examples from the talk, describe the two major systems of the laboratory microscope, and then explain how to use it.

Preparation Time: 20 seconds
Recording Time: 60 seconds

# WRITING SECTION

The Writing Section tests your ability to write essays in English similar to those that you would write in college courses. During the test, you will write two essays.

**The Integrated Essay.** First you will read an academic passage and then you will listen to a lecture on the same topic. You may take notes as you read and listen, but notes are not graded. You may use your notes to write the essay. The reading passage will disappear while you are listening to the lecture, but the passage will return to the screen for reference when you begin to write your essay. You will have 20 minutes to plan, write, and revise your response. Typically, a good essay for the integrated topic will require that you write 150–225 words.

**The Independent Essay.** You will read a question on the screen. It usually asks for your opinion about a familiar topic. You will have 30 minutes to plan, write, and revise your response. Typically, a good essay for the independent topic will require that you write 300–350 words.

A clock on the screen will show you how much time you have left to complete each essay.

### *Integrated Essay "Online Graduate Programs"*

You have 20 minutes to plan, write, and revise your response to a reading passage and a lecture on the same topic. First, read the passage and take notes. Then, listen to the lecture and take notes. Finally, write your response to the writing question. Typically, a good response will require that you write 150–225 words.

**Reading Passage**
Time: 3 minutes

Online graduate degree programs are being offered worldwide. In many respects, the programs are like the same degree programs available in a traditional campus environment, but in several key aspects, they are very different.

First, online degree programs do not offer one-on-one time with the professors. On campus, professors hold regular office hours and expect to have conferences with their graduate students. In addition, many opportunities present themselves for informal interactions before and after class or in chance meetings on campus. Some professors invite their graduate students to their homes or otherwise make themselves available in semi-social settings. In contrast, online professors are unable to see their graduate students in person and, consequently, do not know them very well.

Second, many online graduate programs are not as challenging or as high quality as their on-campus counterparts. In fact, some courses are so easy that students are able to complete them online in one weekend. For the most part, senior faculty members refuse to teach the online courses, contributing to the difference in quality of the online and on-campus courses with the same titles. Many excellent professors view the huge numbers in the online classes as an impediment. Technology allows for more students to take the same course, and junior faculty or graders provide feedback on assignments that are graded by senior faculty teaching on campus.

Third, top schools do not offer online degree programs. Although non-credit courses or even a handful of credit courses may be available, the best schools still require that graduate students complete a more conventional program with most of their time spent in residence on campus. For students who want a graduate degree from a prestigious university, online options are not open to them.

**Model Test 1, Writing Section, Track 3**

TOEFL® Writing        VOLUME    HELP    NEXT

Now listen to a lecture on the same topic as the passage that you have just read.

**Question**
Summarize the main points in the lecture and then explain how they cast doubt on the ideas in the reading passage.

*Independent Essay "An Important Leader"*

**Question**

**Leaders like John F. Kennedy and Martin Luther King have made important contributions to the people of the United States. Name another world leader you think is important.**

Give specific reasons and examples for your choice.

# MODEL TEST 1

## ANSWER KEYS

Use the following Answer Keys to check your scores on the Reading and Listening Sections of Model Test 1.

### READING SECTION

| *Reading 1* | *Reading 2* | *Reading 3* |
|---|---|---|
| 1.  C | 14.  A | 27.  D |
| 2.  B | 15.  D | 28.  C |
| 3.  A | 16.  B | 29.  D |
| 4.  A | 17.  D | 30.  C |
| 5.  B | 18.  B | 31.  A |
| 6.  B | 19.  D | 32.  B |
| 7.  D | 20.  B | 33.  C |
| 8.  A | 21.  A | 34.  C |
| 9.  A | 22.  D | 35.  B |
| 10.  B | 23.  D | 36.  C |
| 11.  C | 24.  B | 37.  A |
| 12.  C | 25.  A | 38.  B |
| 13.  E, D, F | 26.  C, E, F | 39.  A, B, C |

## LISTENING SECTION

| Listening Set 1 | Listening Set 2 | Listening Set 3 |
|---|---|---|
| 1. C | 18. B | 35. B |
| 2. A | 19. D | 36. A, C |
| 3. B | 20. B | 37. A |
| 4. D | 21. A, C | 38. A |
| 5. D | 22. A | 39. D |
| 6. B | 23. C | 40. A |
| 7. B | 24. B | 41. D |
| 8. B | 25. A | 42. D |
| 9. C | 26. C | 43. D |
| 10. A, D, E: Yes | 27. C | 44. B, D |
| 11. C | 28. A, B, D | 45. B |
| 12. C | 29. C | 46. C |
| 13. A | 30. B | 47. B |
| 14. B | 31. A | 48. B |
| 15. C | 32. D | 49. A |
| 16. B | 33. C | 50. B |
| 17. B | 34. B | 51. B |

 # EXPLANATORY AND EXAMPLE ANSWERS, MODEL TEST 1

Go to the Barron's TOEFL site at *http://bit.ly.Barrons-TOEFL* to study detailed Explanatory Answers for the Reading and Listening Sections and Outlines, Example Answers, and Checklists for the Speaking and Writing Sections of Model Test 1.

# 4

# REVIEW OF TOEFL iBT® SECTIONS

## ✔ *Study the most frequent question types*

## READING

### OVERVIEW OF THE READING SECTION

The Reading Section tests your ability to understand reading passages like those in college textbooks. The reading passages are presented in one complete section, which allows you to move to the next passage and return to a previous passage to change questions or answers that you may have left blank throughout the entire section. The passages are about 700 words in length.

There are two formats for the Reading Section. On the short format, you will read three passages. On the long format, you will read four passages. After each passage, you will answer 12–14 questions about it. Only three passages will be graded. The other passage is part of an experimental section for future tests. Because you will not know which passages will be graded, you must try to do your best on all of them. You may take notes while you read, but notes are not graded. You may use your notes to answer the questions. Some passages may include a word or phrase that is underlined in blue. Click on the word or phrase to see a glossary definition or explanation.

Choose the best answer for multiple-choice questions. Follow the directions on the page or on the screen for computer-assisted questions. Most questions are worth 1 point, but the last question in each passage is worth more than 1 point.

Click on **Next** to go to the next question. Click on **Back** to return to previous questions. You may return to previous questions for all of the passages.

You can click on **Review** to see a chart of the questions you have answered and the questions you have not answered. From this screen, you can return to the question you want to answer.

Although you can spend more time on one passage and less time on another passage, you should try to pace yourself so that you are spending about 20 minutes to read each passage and answer the questions for that passage. You will have 60 minutes to complete all of the passages and answer all of the questions on the short format and 80 minutes to read all of the passages and answer all of the questions on the long format. A clock on the screen will show you how much time you have to complete the Reading Section.

# REVIEW OF QUESTIONS

 **Reading Passage**

Read the following passage in your book, and then go to the Barron's TOEFL site online to study the types of questions that are most frequently tested on the TOEFL iBT®. When you take the test, directions will appear with each question, but if you already recognize the type of question presented and you are familiar with the directions, you will save time. The less time you have to spend analyzing the question and reading the directions, the more time you will have to read the passages and answer the questions.

The following reading passage was adapted from *Geosystems: An Introduction to Physical Geography*, Seventh Edition by Robert W. Christopherson, Pearson Education, Inc., 2009.

## "Producers, Consumers, and Decomposers"

P1 → Organisms that are capable of using carbon dioxide as their sole source of carbon are called *autotrophs* (self-feeders), or **producers**. These are the plants. They chemically fix carbon through photosynthesis. Organisms that depend on producers as their carbon source are called *heterotrophs* (feed on others), or **consumers**. Generally, these are animals. From the producers, which manufacture their own food, energy flows through the system along a circuit called the **food chain**, reaching consumers and eventually *detritivores*. Organisms that share the same basic foods are said to be at the same *trophic* level. Ecosystems generally are structured in a **food web**, a complex network of interconnected food chains. In a food web, consumers participate in several different food chains, comprising both strong interactions and weak interactions between species in the food web.

P2    Primary consumers feed on producers. Ⓐ Because producers are always plants, the primary consumer is called an **herbivore**, or plant eater. A **carnivore** is a secondary consumer and primarily eats meat. Ⓑ A consumer that feeds on both producers (plants) and consumers (meat) is called an **omnivore.** Ⓒ

P3    Detritivores (detritus feeders and decomposers) are the final link in the endless chain. Ⓓ Detritivores renew the entire system by releasing simple inorganic compounds and nutrients with the breaking down of organic materials. Detritus refers to all the dead organic debris—remains, fallen leaves, and wastes—that living processes leave. Detritus feeders—worms, mites, termites, centipedes, snails, crabs, and even vultures, among others—work like an army to consume detritus and excrete nutrients that fuel an ecosystem. **Decomposers** are primarily bacteria and fungi that digest organic debris outside their bodies and absorb and release nutrients in the process. This metabolic work of microbial decomposers produces the rotting that breaks down detritus. Detritus feeders and decomposers, although different in operation, have a similar function in an ecosystem.

P4   → One example of a complex community is the oceanic food web that includes krill, a primary consumer. *Krill* is a shrimplike crustacean that is a major food for an interrelated group of organisms, including whales, fish, seabirds, seals, and squid in the Antarctic region. All of these organisms participate in numerous other food chains as well, some consuming and some being consumed. *Phytoplankton* begin this chain by harvesting solar energy in photosynthesis. *Herbivorous zooplankton* such as krill and other organisms eat phytoplankton. Consumers eat krill at the next trophic level. Because krill are a protein-rich, plentiful food, increasingly factory ships, such as those from Japan and Russia, seek them out. The annual krill harvest currently surpasses a million tons, principally as feed for chickens and livestock and as protein for human consumption.

## Efficiency in a Food Web

P5    Any assessment of world food resources depends on the level of consumer being targeted. Let us use humans as an example. Many people can be fed if wheat is eaten directly. However, if the grain is first fed to cattle (herbivores) and then we eat the beef, the yield of available food energy is cut by *90%* (810 kg of grain is reduced to 82 kg of meat); far fewer people can be fed from the same land area.

P6    In terms of energy, only about 10% of the kilocalories (food calories, not heat calories) in plant matter survive from the primary to the secondary trophic level. When humans consume meat instead of grain, there is a further loss of biomass and added inefficiency. More energy is lost to the environment at each progressive step in the food chain. You can see that an omnivorous diet such as that of an average North American and European is quite expensive in terms of biomass and energy.

P7   → Food web concepts are becoming politicized as world food issues grow more critical. Today, approximately half of the cultivated acreage in the United States and Canada is planted for animal consumption—beef and dairy cattle, hogs, chickens, and turkeys. Livestock feed includes approximately 80% of the annual corn and nonexported soybean harvest. In addition, some lands cleared of rainforest in Central and South America were converted to pasture to produce beef for export to restaurants, stores, and fast-food outlets in developed countries. Thus, lifestyle decisions and dietary patterns in North America and Europe are perpetuating inefficient food webs, not to mention the destruction of valuable resources, both here and overseas.

## Glossary
phytoplankton:  a plant that lives in the sea and produces its own energy source
trophic level:  category measured in steps away from the energy input in an ecosystem

## Vocabulary

A *vocabulary* question asks you to choose a synonym for a word that is highlighted in the passage.

 **Review, Reading Section, Vocabulary**

---

### 1  Quickly identify the vocabulary question

The word "------" in the passage is closest in meaning to

The phrase "------" in the passage is closest in meaning to

---

### 2  Focus on the question, not the passage

The word <u>sole</u> in the passage is closest in meaning to

o major

o steady

o only

o ideal

P 1  Organisms that are capable of using carbon dioxide as their <u>sole</u> source of carbon are called *autotrophs* (self-feeders), or **producers**. These are the plants.

---

### 3  Read the sentence with the synonym

If you are not sure of the answer, read the sentence with the answer choice that you are considering.

Organisms that are capable of using carbon dioxide as their <u>only</u> source of carbon are called *autotrophs* (self-feeders), or **producers**.

## Question

1.  The word <u>sole</u> in the passage is closest in meaning to
o major
o steady
o only
o ideal

## Answer

The word <u>sole</u> in the passage is closest in meaning to
o major
o steady
● only
o ideal

## Explanation

*Only* is a synonym for "sole." None of the other words are synonyms. You can answer this question without referring to the reading passage.

## Inference

An *inference* question asks you to draw a logical conclusion based on information in the passage. Think of the information as evidence for an idea that is not directly expressed in the passage.

 **Review, Reading Section, Inference**

---

### 1  Identify the inference question words

Which of the following can be *inferred* about-------?

What does paragraph-------*suggest* about-------?

The information in paragraph-------*implies* that

What can *be concluded* about-------?

---

### 2  Find the evidence in the passage

| It may be concluded that human beings are omnivores because... | P 2  Primary consumers feed on producers. Because producers are always plants, the primary consumer is called an **herbivore**, or plant eater. A **carnivore** is a secondary consumer and primarily eats meat. A consumer that feeds on both producers (plants) and consumers (meat) is called an **omnivore**. |

---

### 3  Draw a logical conclusion

*Directly stated in the passage*:  "A consumer that feeds on both producers (plants) and consumers (meat) is called an **omnivore**."

*Evidence not stated in the passage*: Most human beings eat both producers and consumers.

*Conclusion*: Human beings are omnivores.

## Question

It may be concluded from Paragraph 2 that human beings are omnivores for which reason?

o People feed on producers for the most part.

o People are usually tertiary consumers.

o People generally eat both producers and consumers.

o Most people are the top carnivores in the food chain.

Paragraph 2 is marked with an arrow ➜

## Answer

It may be concluded from Paragraph 2 that human beings are omnivores for which reason?

o People feed on producers for the most part.

o People are usually tertiary consumers.

● People generally eat both producers and consumers.

o Most people are the top carnivores in the food chain.

Paragraph 2 is marked with an arrow ➜

## Explanation

The evidence in the passage is that an omnivore feeds on both producers and consumers. We know that most human beings eat both plants (producers) and meat (consumers). Therefore, it may be concluded that human beings are omnivores.

## Reference

A *reference* question asks you to identify a word or phrase in the passage that refers to the word or phrase in the question. The word in the passage is usually a pronoun that refers to one of the nouns in the question choices.

 **Review, Reading Section, Reference**

---

### 1 Start by looking earlier in the passage

You are probably looking for a noun that is later replaced by a pronoun. That means you should look earlier in the passage for the noun.

---

### 2 Compare the pronoun and noun

**Number**
A singular pronoun (it) refers to a singular noun (consumer).
A plural pronoun (them) refers to a plural noun (consumers).

**Gender**
A masculine pronoun (his) refers to a masculine noun (man).
A feminine pronoun (her) refers to a feminine noun (woman).
A neutral pronoun (it) refers to a neutral noun (research).

---

### 3 Read the sentence with the noun

Detritus feeders—worms, mites, termites, centipedes, snails, crabs, and even vultures,  among <u>feeders</u>—work like an army to consume detritus and excrete nutrients that fuel an ecosystem.

## Question

The word <u>others</u> in the passage refers to

o debris

o feeders

o processes

o nutrients

## Answer

The word <u>others</u> in the passage refers to

o debris

● feeders

o processes

o nutrients

## Explanation

The word *others* is a pronoun that refers to "feeders." It agrees in number (plural) and in gender (neutral).

## Purpose

A *purpose* question asks you to look for the reason that a word, phrase, or sentence is included in the reading passage. Why did the author mention it?

  **Review, Reading Section, Purpose**

---

### 1  Identify the purpose question

Why does the author mention "krill" in Paragraph 4?

The author uses "krill" as an example of

The author discusses "krill" in order to

---

### 2  Find the word or phrase in the passage

Why does the author mention "krill" in paragraph 4?

P 4   One complex community is the oceanic food web that includes krill, a primary consumer. *Krill* is a shrimplike crustacean that is a major food for an interrelated group of organisms, including whales, fish, seabirds, seals, and squid in the Antarctic region. All of these organisms participate in numerous other food chains as well.

---

### 3  Read the first words in the answer choices

To *contradict*  OR  To *refute*
To *contrast*
To *criticize*
To *define*
To *explain*  OR  To *illustrate*
To *provide an example*  OR  To *provide evidence*
To *point out*  OR  To *note*
To *suggest* a solution

## Question

Why does the author mention "krill" in paragraph 4?
o To suggest a solution for a problem in the food chain
o To provide evidence that contradicts previously
  stated opinions
o To present an explanation for the killing of krill
o To give an example of a complex food web
Paragraph 4 is marked with an arrow ➜

## Answer

Why does the author mention "krill" in paragraph 4?
o To suggest a solution for a problem in the food chain
o To provide evidence that contradicts previously
  stated opinions
o To present an explanation for the killing of krill
● To give an example of a complex food web
Paragraph 4 is marked with an arrow ➜

## Explanation

The passage states that "One complex community is
the oceanic food web that includes krill, a primary
consumer."

This is one *example* of complex communities.

## Paraphrase

A *paraphrase* question asks you to choose the best restatement of an important sentence in the reading passage. The sentence will be highlighted in the passage.

The question will always be similar to this one: Which of the sentences below best expresses the information in the highlighted statement in the passage? The other choices change the meaning or leave out important information.

 **Review, Reading Section, Paraphrase**

---

### 1  Find the basic facts in the sentence

Make simple sentences to find the basic facts.

The annual krill harvest currently surpasses a million tons, principally as feed for chickens and livestock and as protein for human consumption.

The krill harvest is a million tons per year.
The krill is used principally to feed chickens and livestock.
The krill is also used to provide protein for humans.

---

### 2  Eliminate incorrect answer choices

| *Incomplete answer choices* | *False information choices* |
|---|---|
| Some of the choices will include correct information from the original sentence, but they will not restate *all* of the information. Do not choose an incomplete answer. | Some of the choices will include incorrect information. |

---

### 3  Check the basic facts in your choice

The krill harvest is a million tons per year.
The krill is used principally to feed chickens and livestock.
The krill is also used to provide protein for humans.

More than one million tons of krill is eaten by both animals and humans every year.

## Question
Which of the sentences below best expresses the information in the highlighted statement in the passage?

o Part of the one million tons of krill harvested annually is used for protein in animal feed.

o Both livestock and chickens as well as humans eat krill as a main part of their diet.

o The principal use of krill is for animal feed, although some of the one million tons is eaten by people.

o More than one million tons of krill is eaten by both animals and humans every year.

## Answer
Which of the sentences below best expresses the information in the highlighted statement in the passage?

o Part of the one million tons of krill harvested annually is used for protein in animal feed.

o Both livestock and chickens as well as humans eat krill as a main part of their diet.

o The principal use of krill is for animal feed, although some of the one million tons is eaten by people.

● More than one million tons of krill is eaten by both animals and humans every year.

## Explanation
Which of the sentences below best expresses the information in the highlighted statement in the passage?

o Part of the one million tons of krill harvested annually is used for protein in animal feed.  *Incomplete*

o Both livestock and chickens as well as humans eat krill as a main part of their diet.  *Incomplete*

o The principal use of krill is for animal feed, although some of the one million tons is eaten by people.  *Incorrect*

o More than one million tons of krill is eaten by both animals and humans every year.

## Exception

An *exception* question asks you to choose a statement that includes information not in the passage.

 **Review, Reading Section, Exception**

1  Look for the word EXCEPT or NOT in the question

The passage mentions all of the following EXCEPT

What is NOT true of-------

2  Scan the passage for information in each choice

For most of the questions, the text on the right side of the screen will show you the part of the passage in which you will find the answer to the question.

For Exception Questions, you will probably have to scroll through more than one paragraph in order to scan for the choices.

3  Keep track of the choices as you find them

On your scratch paper, make a quick list of the choices in a row that corresponds to the order of the choices on the screen. Then make a check mark beside the choices as you find them in the passage. The remaining choice is the correct answer.

*Note  Paper*

✓A

✓B

✓C

D

## Question

According to the passage, all of the following characteristics describe producers EXCEPT

o Producers serve as food for consumers.

o Producers make their own food.

o Producers form the first tropic level.

o Producers include bacteria and fungi.

## Answer

According to the passage, all of the following characteristics describe producers EXCEPT

o Producers serve as food for consumers.

o Producers make their own food.

o Producers form the first tropic level.

● Producers include bacteria and fungi.

## Explanation

✓A Paragraph 2, sentence 1.

✓B Paragraph 1, sentence 5.

✓C Paragraph 1, sentences 5, 6.

  D Contradicts the definition of *producers*. *Bacteria* and *fungi* are *decomposers*, according to Paragraph 3.

## Insert

An *insert* question asks you to locate a place in the passage to insert a sentence. Choose from four options marked with a square.

 **Review, Reading Section, Insert**

### 1  Identify key reference words and phrases

Look for key words in the sentences before and after the squares in the passage that refer to the key words in the insert sentence.

### 2  Look for words that logically connect sentences

**Addition:** *Furthermore, Moreover*
**Contrast:** *On the other hand, On the contrary, In contrast*
**Dates:** Check for chronological order as in *1900, 1925, 1932*
**Example:** *For instance, For example*
**Order:** *First, Second, Third, Finally*
**Restatement:** *In other words*
**Result:** *Therefore, As a result, Consequently*

### 3  Check for pronoun agreement

If an insert sentence includes a pronoun, make sure that it agrees with the noun in the previous sentence.

A <u>carnivore</u> is a secondary consumer. <u>It</u> primarily eats meat. <u>Carnivores</u> are secondary consumers. <u>They</u> primarily eat meat.

## Question

Look at the four squares [ ■ ] that show where the following sentence could be inserted.

**A tertiary consumer eats primary and secondary consumers and is referred to as a "top carnivore" in the food chain.**

Where could the sentence best be added?
Click on a square [ ■ ] to insert the sentence in the passage.

## Answer

A **carnivore** is a secondary consumer and primarily eats meat.

**A tertiary consumer eats primary and secondary consumers and is referred to as a "top carnivore" in the food chain.**

A consumer that feeds on both producers (plants) and consumers (meat) is called an **omnivore**.

## Explanation

Both reference words  and words that logically connect sentences show you which square to use for the insert sentence.

The sentence before the square includes the key word *carnivore* that refers to *"top carnivore"* in the insert sentence.

The word *secondary* appears in the sentence before the insert sentence. The insert sentence contains the word *tertiary* to continue the order.

## Detail

A *detail* question asks you to answer a question about a specific point in the passage. The question usually directs you to the paragraph where the answer is found.
According to paragraph 7…

 **Review, Reading Section, Detail**

### 1 Look for the answer in the reference paragraph

The question is probably not a main idea that you will remember from reading the passage. After you read the question, go back to the paragraph referred to in the question to look for the answer.

### 2 Read all of the answer choices

Detail questions may seem simple, but the wording in the answer choices can be confusing. Read *all* of the answer choices. Don't stop if you find a choice that looks correct. Remember, you are looking for the *best* answer, so you have to consider all of them.

### 3 Be sure to answer the question that is asked

Be sure to read the question carefully and look for the answer to that specific question. Some of the answer choices may be *true* according to information in the passage, but they may not be the answer to the question that is asked.

## Question

According to paragraph 7, how much land is used to grow crops for animal feed?

o 80 percent of the acreage in Europe

o Most of the rainforest in Central America

o 50 percent of the farm land in Canada and the United States

o Half of the land in North and South America

Paragraph 7 is marked with an arrow ➔

## Answer

According to paragraph 7, how much land is used to grow crops for animal feed?

o 80 percent of the acreage in Europe

o Most of the rainforest in Central America

● 50 percent of the farm land in Canada and the United States

o Half of the land in North and South America

Paragraph 7 is marked with an arrow ➔

## Explanation

The question asks about *growing crops*

50 % of the farm land in Canada and the United States is *planted* for animal consumption. 80% refers to corn and soybeans in the US, not Europe. The rainforest is pasture, not land for crops. 50% refers to North, but not South America.

Today, approximately half of the cultivated acreage in the United States and Canada is planted for animal consumption—beef and dairy cattle, hogs, chickens, and turkeys. Livestock feed includes approximately 80 % of the annual corn and nonexported soybean harvest. In addition, some lands cleared of rainforest in Central and South America were converted to pasture to produce beef...

## Classification

A *classification* question asks you to match phrases with the categories to which they refer. You click and drag the phrase under the category.

 **Review, Reading Section, Classification**

---

### 1  Find the first category in the passage

Review the major points.
Compare them with the answer choices.
Drag the choices to the category.

---

### 2  Find the next category in the passage

Review the major points.
Compare them with the answer choices.
Drag the choices to the category.

---

### 3  Eliminate answers

Exclude the following answer choices:
   **X**  Not correct according to the passage.
   **X**  Not mentioned in the passage.
   **X**  Not a major point from the passage.

## Question

| Producers | Consumers |
|---|---|

A  Depend upon photosynthesis to survive
B  Have a weak interaction among species
C  Generally consist of animal life forms
D  Include both herbivores and carnivores
E  Eat meat as one of their primary food sources
F  Are always some variety of plant life
G  Made exclusively of inorganic materials

## Answer

**Producers**
A  Depend upon photosynthesis to survive
F  Are always some variety of plant life

**Consumers**
C  Generally consist of animal life forms
D  Include both herbivores and carnivores
E  Eat meat as one of their primary food sources

## Explanation

**Producers**

A  Lines 2–3:
"They (**producers**) chemically fix carbon through photosynthesis."

F  Line 3:
"These (**producers**) are the plants."

**Consumers**

C  Line 5:
"Generally, these (consumers) are animals."

D  Lines 14–15:
"…the primary consumer is called an **herbivore**….
A **carnivore** is a secondary consumer…."

E  Lines 14–15:
"A **carnivore** is a secondary consumer and primarily eats meat."

## Summary

A *summary* question asks you to complete a summary of the reading passage by choosing three statements from a list of six statements.

 **Review, Reading Section, Summary**

### 1  Analyze the introductory sentence

The introductory sentence in bold is a one-sentence summary. Words that identify the main ideas are often in this sentence.

**The food web is comprised of <u>producers</u>, <u>consumers</u>, and <u>decomposers</u>, which interact in endless cycles.**

### 2  Eliminate new ideas or minor points

Some of the answer choices are ideas that are not found in the passage. *New* ideas should not be in the summary.

Some of the choices are minor points. Minor points are true and may be mentioned to support the main ideas in the passage. Remember that a minor point is often an example or an explanation of the main ideas. *Minor* points should not be in the summary.

### 3  Read all of the sentences

Read the introductory sentence and the three sentences in your answer choices. Do the four sentences sound like a summary of the passage you have just read?

## Question
**The food web is comprised of producers, consumers, and decomposers, which interact in endless cycles.**
o Consumers, primarily animals, feed on producers, plants that manufacture their own food source through photosynthesis.

oDecomposers digest and recycle dead plants and animals, releasing inorganic compounds into the food chain.

oSince more energy is depleted into the environment at each level in the food chain, dietary choices affect the efficiency of food webs.

---

o Among consumers, human beings are considered omnivores because they eat not only plants but also animals.

o An example of an undersea food web includes plankton, krill, and fish, as well as birds, seals, and whales.

o Rainforests are being cut down in order to clear pastureland for cattle that can be exported to countries with fast-food restaurants.

---

## Answer
**The food web is comprised of producers, consumers, and decomposers, which interact in endless cycles.**
● Consumers, primarily animals, feed on producers, plants that  manufacture their own food source through photosynthesis.
● Decomposers digest and recycle dead plants and animals, releasing inorganic compounds into the food chain.
● Since more energy is depleted into the environment at each level in the food chain, dietary choices affect the efficiency of food webs.

---

## Explanation

| | |
|---|---|
| oAmong consumers, human beings are considered omnivores because they eat not only plants but also animals. | A minor point that can be inferred but is not directly stated |
| o An example of an undersea food web includes plankton, krill, and fish, as well as birds, seals, and whales. | An extended example of a food web |
| o Rainforests are being cut down in order to clear pastureland for cattle that can be exported to countries with fast-food restaurants. | A minor point in one sentence in the passage |

## READING STRATEGIES

In addition to the academic skills that you will learn in Chapter 5, there are several reading strategies that will help you succeed on the TOEFL and after the TOEFL.

### ➤ Read on screen

Reading on a computer screen is different from reading on a page. First, generally less text is visible. Second, you must scroll instead of turning pages. Finally, icons or buttons may allow you to click through to other information. To become comfortable reading on a computer screen, you should take advantage of every opportunity to practice. Spend time reading on screen.

- Practice scrolling
- Read extensively

### ➤ Choose academic topics

The reading passages on the TOEFL are similar to those that you find in textbooks from general courses taught in colleges and universities during the first two years. If you can borrow English language textbooks, read passages from natural sciences, social sciences, the humanities, and the arts. Passages in encyclopedias are usually at a reading level slightly below that of textbooks, but they offer an inexpensive way to obtain a lot of reading material for different subject areas. If you have access to the Internet, free encyclopedias are available online. If you purchase an encyclopedia on CD-ROM, an edition from a previous year will be cheaper and just as useful for your purposes.

- Select textbook passages
- Read online encyclopedias

### ➤ Preview

Research shows that it is easier to understand what you are reading if you begin with a general idea of what the passage is about. Previewing helps you form a general idea of the topic. To preview, first read the title, the headings and subheadings, and any words in bold print or italics. You should do this as quickly as possible. You are reading not for specific information but for an impression of the topic. Next, read the first sentence of each paragraph and the last sentence of the passage. Again, this should take seconds, not minutes, to complete. This time you are looking for the main idea. Remember, to move to the questions, you must scroll to the bottom of the page.

- Look at the title and headings
- Read the first sentence of every paragraph
- Scroll to the last sentence of the passage

### ➤ Read faster

To read faster, read for meaning. Try to understand sentences or even paragraphs, not individual words. To do this, you should read phrases instead of reading word by word. Practice using the vision that allows you to see on either side of the word you are focusing on with your eyes. This is called *peripheral vision*. When you drive a car or ride a bike, you are looking ahead of you but you are really taking in the traffic situation on both sides. You are using peripheral vision to move forward. This is also important in learning to read faster. Your mind can take in more than one word at the same time. Just think if you stopped every time you wanted to know what was going on in the next lane! You would never get to your destination. To read faster, you have to read for ideas. If you don't know the meaning of a word but you understand the sentence, move on. Don't stop to look up the word in your dictionary. Don't stop your car or your bike.

- Use peripheral vision
- Read for meaning

## ➤ Use contexts

Before you can use a context, you must understand what a context is. In English, a *context* is the combination of vocabulary and grammar that surrounds a word. Context can be a sentence or a paragraph or a passage. Context helps you make a general prediction about meaning. If you know the general meaning of a sentence, you also know the general meaning of the words in the sentence. Making predictions from contexts is very important when you are reading a foreign language. In this way, you can read and understand the meaning of a passage without stopping to look up every new word in a dictionary. On an examination like the TOEFL, dictionaries are not permitted in the room. Of course, you have to know some of the words in order to have a context for the words that you don't know. That means that you need to work on learning a basic vocabulary, and then you can make an educated guess about the meaning of new words by using the context.

- Learn basic vocabulary
- Predict new words in context

## ➤ Skim and scan

To *scan* is to let your eyes travel quickly over a passage in order to find something specific that you are looking for. By scanning, you can find the place in a reading passage where the answer to a question is found. First, read the question and look for a reference. A reference in the TOEFL will identify a paragraph where the answer to the question is found. For example, you may read, *Paragraph 2 is marked with an arrow* [➔]. You know that you need to scan for the arrow at the beginning of paragraph 2 in the passage. The paraphrased sentences and the vocabulary words on the TOEFL are shaded to help you find them.

If a question does not have a reference like an arrow or shading, then you should find the important content words in the question. *Content words* are usually nouns, verbs, or adjectives. They are called content words because they contain the meaning of a sentence. Now scan the passage for the same content words or synonyms of the words in the questions. Finally, read those specific sentences carefully, and choose the answer that corresponds to the meaning of the sentences you have read.

- Refer to arrows and shading
- Locate the details
- Check for exceptions

## QUICK QUIZ FOR THE READING SECTION

This is a quiz for the Reading Section of the TOEFL iBT®. This section tests your ability to understand reading passages like those in college textbooks. During the quiz, you will read one reading passage and respond to 10 questions about it. You will have 20 minutes to read the passage and answer the questions. You may take notes while you read. You may use your notes to answer the questions.

The following reading passage was adapted from *Foundations of Education*, Tenth Edition by Allan Ornstein, Wadsworth, 2008.

### "The Heredity Versus Environment Debate"

P1   The past century has seen heated controversy about whether intelligence, which relates strongly to school achievement, is determined primarily by heredity or by environment. A When IQ tests were undergoing rapid development early in the twentieth century, many psychologists believed that intelligence was determined primarily by heredity. B

P2   → **Environmentalist view.** By the middle of the twentieth century, numerous studies had counteracted the hereditarian view, and most social scientists took the position that environment is as important as or even more important than heredity in determining intelligence. C Social scientists who stress the **environmentalist view of intelligence** generally emphasize the need for continual compensatory programs beginning in infancy. Many also criticize the use of IQ tests on the grounds that these tests are culturally biased. D

P3   James Flynn, who collected similar data on other countries, found that "massive" gains in the IQ scores of the population in fourteen nations have occurred during the twentieth century. These improvements, according to Flynn's analysis, largely stemmed not from genetic improvement in the population but from environmental changes that led to gains in the kinds of skills assessed by IQ tests. Torsten Husen and his colleagues also have concluded, after reviewing large amounts of data, that improvements in economic and social conditions, and particularly in the availability of schooling, can produce substantial gains in average IQ from one generation to the next. In general, educators committed to improving the performance of low-achieving students find these studies encouraging.

P4   → **Hereditarian view.** The **hereditarian view of intelligence** underwent a major revival in the 1970s and 1980s, based particularly on the writings of Arthur Jensen, Richard Herrnstein, and a group of researchers conducting the Minnesota Study of Twins. Summarizing previous research as well as their own studies, these researchers identified heredity as the major factor in determining intelligence—accounting for up to 80 percent of the variation in IQ scores.

|P5|     Jensen published a highly controversial study in the *Harvard Educational Review* in 1969. Pointing out that African-Americans averaged about 15 points below whites on IQ tests, Jensen attributed this gap to a genetic difference between the two races in learning abilities and patterns. Critics countered Jensen's arguments by contending that a host of environmental factors that affect IQ, including malnutrition and prenatal care are difficult to measure and impossible to separate from hereditary factors. IQ tests are biased, they said, and do not necessarily even measure intelligence. After his 1969 article, Jensen has continued to cite data that he believed link intelligence primarily to heredity. His critics continue to respond with evidence that environmental factors, and schooling in particular, have a major influence on IQ.

|P6| → **Synthesizers' view.** Certain social scientists have taken a middle, or "synthesizing," position in this controversy. The **synthesizers' view of intelligence** holds that both heredity and environment contribute to differences in measured intelligence. For example, Christopher Jencks, after reviewing a large amount of data, concluded that heredity is responsible for 45 percent of the IQ variance, environment accounts for 35 percent, and interaction between the two ("interaction" meaning that particular abilities thrive or wither in specific environments) accounts for 20 percent. Robert Nichols reviewed all these and other data and concluded that the true value for heredity may be anywhere between 0.40 and 0.80 but that the exact value has little importance for policy. In general, Nichols and other synthesizers maintain that heredity determines the fixed limits of a range; within those limits, the interaction between environment and heredity yields the individual's intelligence. In this view, even if interactions between heredity and environment limit our ability to specify exactly how much of a child's intelligence reflects environmental factors, teachers (and parents) should provide each child with a productive environment in which to realize her or his maximum potential.

**Glossary**
IQ:   intelligence quotient; a numerical value for intelligence

1. Which of the sentences below best expresses the information in the highlighted statement in the passage? The other choices change the meaning or leave out important information.

   Ⓐ Changes in the environment rather than genetic progress caused an increase in IQ scores, according to studies by Flynn.

   Ⓑ Flynn's studies were not conclusive in identifying the skills that resulted in improvements on IQ tests.

   Ⓒ IQ test results in research by Flynn did not improve because of genetics and environment.

   Ⓓ The reason that gains in IQ tests occurred was because of the changes in skills that were tested.

2. The word data in the passage is closest in meaning to

&#9398; experts
&#9399; advice
&#9400; arguments
&#9401; information

3. Why does the author mention the "Minnesota Study of Twins" in paragraph 4?

&#9398; To argue that environment is more important than heredity
&#9399; To prove the importance of heredity in measuring IQ
&#9400; To establish the synthesizer's view of intelligence
&#9401; To summarize previous research before designing a new study

Paragraph 4 is marked with an arrow [&#8594;].

4. According to Jensen's opponents, why are IQ tests unreliable?

&#9398; Heredity is not measured on the current forms of IQ tests.
&#9399; It is difficult to determine whether a factor is due to heredity or environment.
&#9400; Learning abilities and patterns are different for people of diverse racial heredity.
&#9401; They only measure intelligence and not many other important factors.

5. According to a synthesizer's view, how does heredity influence intelligence?

&#9398; Heredity is very important but not as influential as environment.
&#9399; Heredity sets limits on intelligence, but environment can overcome them.
&#9400; A productive environment influences intelligence more than any other factor.
&#9401; Heredity and environment interact within the limits set at birth.

6. According to the passage, all of the following are true of the hereditarian view EXCEPT

&#9398; Studies by Jensen and Herrnstein support this point of view.
&#9399; Many psychologists in the early twentieth century were hereditarians.
&#9400; Intelligence as measured by IQ tests is a result of genetic predisposition.
&#9401; Environmental factors are not able to be separated from heredity.

7. Which of the following statements most accurately reflects the author's opinion about IQ tests?

&#9398; The author believes that IQ tests should be used continuously from infancy.
&#9399; According to the author, there are too many disadvantages to IQ testing.
&#9400; The author maintains a neutral point of view about IQ tests in the discussion.
&#9401; IQ tests should be used in research studies but they should not be used in schools.

8. Look at the four squares [■] that show where the following sentence could be inserted in the passage.

**Those who took this *hereditarian* view of intelligence thought that IQ tests and similar instruments measured innate differences present from birth in people's capacity.**

Where could the sentence best be added?

Click on a square [■] to insert the sentence in the passage.

9. Complete the table by matching the phrases on the left with the headings on the right. Select the appropriate answer choices and drag them to the views of intelligence to which they relate. TWO of the answer choices will NOT be used.
   ***This question is worth 4 points.***

   To delete an answer choice, click on it. To see the passage, click on **View Text**.

**Answer Choices**

Ⓐ Proposed interaction between heredity and environment

Ⓑ Attributed lower IQ to malnutrition and lack of health care

Ⓒ Suggested an innate range of IQ was influenced by environment

Ⓓ Was supported by the Minnesota Twins study in the 1970s

Ⓔ Claimed racial composition was a factor in measured IQ

Ⓕ Maintained that IQ tests were often biased in favor of the majority culture

Ⓖ Cited schooling as a positive consideration in the gains in IQ

Ⓗ Stated that social improvements improve performance on IQ tests

Ⓘ Advanced this viewpoint when IQ tests were being developed

**Hereditarian**

- 
- 
- 

**Environmentalist**

- 
- 
- 
-

10. **Directions:** An introduction for a short summary of the passage appears below. Complete the summary by selecting the THREE answer choices that mention the most important points in the passage. Some sentences do not belong in the summary because they express ideas that are not included in the passage or are minor points from the passage. ***This question is worth 2 points.***

**Historically, psychologists have proposed three viewpoints to explain the influence of heredity and environment on IQ scores.**

- 
- 
- 

### Answer Choices

A Studies by James Flynn verified significant increases in IQ scores among populations in fourteen nations in the last century.

B By the 1970s, psychologists reversed their position, citing heredity as the primary determiner of intelligence as measured by IQ tests.

C Because IQ tests are unfair to minority cultures, the current view is to disregard previous studies that use them as a basis for measurement.

D In the mid-1900s, the popular view was that environment was the more important factor in the development of intelligence.

E Before the development of IQ tests, both heredity and environment were thought to influence the relative intelligence of children.

F Some modern psychologists have proposed a theory that relies on the interaction between heredity and environment to determine IQ.

# Progress Chart for the Reading Section

The chart below will help you evaluate your progress and determine what you need to read again. First, use the Correct Answer column to grade the quiz. Next, check the Problem Types to locate which ones you answered incorrectly. Review the lessons that correspond to the Reading Problem for each question that you missed.

| Quiz Question | Problem Type | Correct Answer |
| --- | --- | --- |
| 1 | Paraphrase | A |
| 2 | Vocabulary | D |
| 3 | Purpose | B |
| 4 | Detail | B |
| 5 | Detail | D |
| 6 | Exception | D |
| 7 | Inference | C |
| 8 | Insert | B |
| 9 | Classification: | |
| | Hereditarian | D E I |
| | Environmentalist | B F G H |
| 10 | Summary | D B F |

## ADVISOR'S OFFICE

If your body is relaxed, your mind can relax more easily. During the TOEFL examination, if you find yourself pursing your lips, frowning, and tightening your shoulders, then use a few seconds to stretch. Clasp your hands and put your arms over your head. Then turn your palms up to the ceiling and look up at your fingers. Pull your arms up as high as you can to stretch your muscles. Be sure not to look at anything but your own hands and the ceiling. That way, you won't be suspected of signaling to a friend. Even a two-second stretch can make a difference. Now, yawn or take a deep breath in and out, and you'll be more relaxed and ready to go on.

# LISTENING

## OVERVIEW OF THE LISTENING SECTION

> **Reminder:** To access the audio for this section of the test, visit *http://bit.ly/Barrons-TOEFL.*

The Listening Section tests your ability to understand spoken English that is typical of interactions and academic speech on college campuses. During the test, you will listen to conversations, lectures, and discussions, and you will answer questions about them.

There are two formats for the Listening Section. On the short format, you will listen to two conversations, two lectures, and two discussions. On the long format, you will listen to three conversations, three lectures, and three discussions. After each listening passage, you will answer 5–6 questions about it. Only two conversations, two lectures, and two discussions will be graded. The other passages are part of an experimental section for future tests. Because you will not know which conversations, lectures, and discussions will be graded, you must try to do your best on all of them.

You will hear each passage one time. You may take notes while you listen, but notes are not graded. You may use your notes to answer the questions.

Choose the best answer for multiple-choice questions. Follow the directions on the page or on the screen for computer-assisted questions. Click on **Next** and then on **OK** to go to the next question. You cannot return to previous questions.

The Listening Section is divided into sets. Each set includes one conversation, one lecture, and one discussion. You have 20 minutes to answer all of the questions on the short format and 30 minutes to answer all of the questions on the long format. A clock on the screen will show you how much time you have to complete your answers for the section. The clock does NOT count the time you are listening to the conversations, lectures, and discussions.

## REVIEW OF QUESTIONS

### Scripts for Listening Passages

Listen to the following passages in your book, and then go to the Barron's TOEFL site online to study the types of questions that are most frequently tested on the TOEFL iBT®. When you take the test, you will not be able to see the scripts, but they are printed in the book to help you study this review.

**CONVERSATION**

### Questions 1–4, Conversation, Track 4

Listen to a conversation on campus between a student and a teaching assistant.

| | |
|---|---|
| Man: | Wait up. I need to ask you about something. |
| Woman: | Oh, hi Jack. |
| Man: | Hi. Listen, I was just wondering whether you could explain what Professor Carson was saying about the review session next Monday? |
| Woman: | Sure. |
| Man: | Well, the way I get it, it's optional. |
| Woman: | Right. He said if you don't have any questions, you could just use the time to study on your own. |
| Man: | Okay. That's what I thought. Maybe I'll just skip it then. What do you think? |
| Woman: | Well, it's up to you, but the thing is . . . sometimes at a review session, someone else will ask a question, and, you know, the way the professor explains it, it's really helpful, I mean, to figure out what he wants on the test. |
| Man: | Oh I didn't think about it that way, but it makes sense. So, you think I should go then. |
| Woman: | Absolutely. Um, I've been a T.A. for Carson for awhile now, and the review sessions have always helped students gets organized for the test. |
| Man: | Oh. |
| Woman: | And, if you've missed any of the lectures, he usually has extra handouts from all the classes. So . . . |
| Man: | Well, I haven't missed any of the sessions. |
| Woman: | I know you're a serious student. I can see that. Look, uh, if it's like the other review sessions, the first hour he's going to go over the main points for each class, kind of like an outline of the course. Then from 5:30 to 6:30, he'll take questions. That's the best part. And the last half hour, he'll stay for individual conferences with people who need extra help. You probably won't need to stay for that. |
| Man: | Okay. So we just show up at the regular time and place for class? |
| Woman: | Or not, if you decide to study on your own. |
| Man: | Right. But, don't you think he'll notice who's there? |
| Woman: | He said he wasn't going to take attendance. |
| Man: | Yeah, but still . . . |
| Woman: | It's a fairly large class. |
| Man: | But if he's grading your final and he remembers you were at the review, it might make a difference. |
| Woman: | Maybe. I think the important thing is just to study really hard and do your best. But, the review sessions usually help. I think they're really good. |
| Man: | Okay. Thanks. I guess I'll go then. |
| Woman: | So I'll see you there. |
| Man: | Yeah, I think I . . . I'd better go. |

## Reason

A *reason* question asks you to explain the reason why the speakers are having the conversation. Why does the woman go to see her professor?

 **Review, Listening Section, Reason**

---

### 1  Listen carefully to the introduction

"Listen to a conversation between a student and a professor."

"Listen to a conversation between a student and a librarian."

"Listen to a conversation between a student and a teaching assistant."

---

### 2  Be ready for the answer to the question

The first question in a conversation is often a reason question. If you are listening for the reason that the student has gone to see the professor or another campus service person, then you will probably have the answer to the first question.

"Hi. Listen, I was just wondering whether you could explain what Professor Carson was saying about the review session next Monday?"

---

### 3  Click on **Next** and **Okay**

Clicking immediately on **Next** and **Okay** moves you quickly to the next question. Develop a rhythm for clicking on these two buttons to move through the Listening Section.

If you click on **Next** without clicking on **Okay**, you will go to a message screen, and you will lose several seconds.

## Question

Why does the man want to talk with the teaching assistant?

o To ask her to help him study for the exam
o To get some handouts for a class he has missed
o To clarify his understanding of the review session
o To find out her opinion of Professor Carson

## Answer

Why does the man want to talk with the teaching assistant?

o To ask her to help him study for the exam
o To get some handouts for a class he has missed
● To clarify his understanding of the review session
o To find out her opinion of Professor Carson

## Explanation

If you were listening for the reason that the man wanted to talk with the teaching assistant, you were ready to answer the first question. You heard and remembered his request to "...explain...about the review session...."

"Hi. Listen, I was just wondering whether you could explain what Professor Carson was saying about the review session next Monday?"

## Detail

A *detail* question asks you to answer a question about a specific point in the conversation or lecture. Choose one answer.

 **Review, Listening Section, Detail**

### 1  Include major details in your notes

The question is probably not a main idea that you will recall from memory. You will need to be able to find major details in your notes.

### 2  Read all of the answer choices

Detail questions in the Listening Section are like those in the Reading Section. They may seem simple, but the wording in the answer choices can be confusing. Read *all* of the answer choices. Don't stop if you find a choice that looks correct. Remember, you are looking for the *best* answer, so you have to consider all of them.

### 3  Be sure to answer the question that is asked

Be sure to read the question carefully and look for the answer to that specific question. Some of the answer choices may be *true* according to information in the passage, but they may not be the answer to the question that is asked.

## Question

Why does the woman think the review session will be helpful?

- ○ Because she has some questions that she wants to ask the professor
- ○ Because Professor Carson will tell them some of the test questions
- ○ Because it helps to hear the answers to questions that other people ask
- ○ Because she needs an individual conference with the professor

## Answer

Why does the woman think the review session will be helpful?

- ○ Because she has some questions that she wants to ask the professor
- ○ Because Professor Carson will tell them some of the test questions
- ● Because it helps to hear the answers to questions that other people ask
- ○ Because she needs an individual conference with the professor

## Explanation

The woman makes a direct statement, explaining why the review session will be helpful.

"...but the thing is...sometimes at a review session, someone else will ask a question, and, you know, the way the professor explains it, it's really helpful, I mean, to figure out what he wants on the test."

## Function

A *function* question asks you to understand and interpret meaning that is not directly stated. What does the professor mean when she says this?

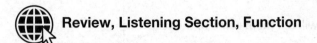 **Review, Listening Section, Function**

### 1  Listen carefully to a replay cue

Some of the questions provide you with a replay of sentences in the lecture or conversation. When you hear the cue, "Listen again," you should get ready to interpret the function of the sentences that you hear.

### 2  Learn to identify functions

Some of the most common examples of functions are agreement, apology, assumption, complaint, disagreement, doubt, interest, refusal, regret, request, and suggestion.

Sometimes the speaker is making a joke.

### 3  Focus on the speaker's purpose

Remember that a function is not the same as a direct statement or question. You must interpret the purpose of the words.

*Why* does the speaker say this?

## Question

Listen again to part of the conversation. Then answer the following question.  🔊

Woman: "He said he wasn't going to take attendance."
Man: "Yeah. But still…"
Woman: "It's a fairly large class."

Why does the man say this: "Yeah. But still…"

## Answer

Why does the man say this: "Yeah. But still…"?

● He thinks that the professor will notice if a student is absent.
○ He agrees with the T.A. about the attendance policy.
○ He wants to change the subject that they are discussing.
○ He tries to encourage the woman to explain her opinion.

## Explanation

The man agrees by saying, "Yeah." But the tone of his voice expresses uncertainty. He follows up by saying, "but still…" to show further doubt.

## Attitude and Opinion

An *attitude and an opinion* question asks you to recognize how the speakers feel or think about the conversation or lecture. Likes or dislikes, confidence, and certainty may also be expressed.

 **Review, Listening Section, Attitude and Opinion**

### 1 Listen for direct statements

Sometimes the speakers state their feelings or opinions directly.

### 2 Identify the tone that a speaker uses

A neutral tone expresses facts without emotion.

Emotions such as anger, fear, impatience, or uncertainty are usually expressed with a change in the volume (louder or softer) or the pitch (higher or lower).

### 3 Interpret humor and irony

When you say something and mean the opposite, it can be heard as humorous or ironic. For example, you might say, "That's great," when you mean that it isn't great at all!

The intonation usually falls at the end of an ironic statement, and the word or phrase that has the opposite meaning may be a littler louder.

## Question

What is the T.A.'s attitude toward the student?

o Critical
o Supportive
o Surprised
o Offended

## Answer

What is the T.A.'s attitude toward the student?

o Critical
● Supportive
o Surprised
o Offended

## Explanation

The T.A. makes direct statements that show support:
"I know you're a serious student."

The tone is friendly and positive.

No humor or ironic statements are made.

## Lecture

Listen to the following passage in your book, and then go to the Barron's TOEFL site online to study the types of questions that are most frequently tested on the TOEFL iBT®. When you take the test, you will not be able to see the script, but it is printed in the book to help you study this review.

### Questions 5–10, Lecture, Track 5

Listen to part of a lecture in a zoology class. The professor is talking about mimicry.

Professor:

As you know from the textbook, mimicry isn't limited to insects, but it's most common among them, and by mimicry, I'm referring to the likeness between two insects that aren't closely related but look very much alike. The insects that engage in mimicry are usually very brightly colored. One of the insects, the one that's characterized by an unpleasant taste, a bad smell, a sting or bite, that insect is called the *model*. The mimic looks like the model but doesn't share the characteristic that protects the model from predators. But, of course, the predators associate the color pattern or some other trait with the unpleasant characteristic and leave both insects alone.

Henry Bates was one of the first naturalists who noticed that some butterflies that closely resembled each other were actually unrelated. The phenomenon in which one species copies another is called Batesian mimicry. I have some lab specimens of a few common mimics in the cases in the front of the room, and I want you to have a chance to look at them before the end of the class, and I've also removed a few to show you as we talk about them. Here's a day flying moth with brown and white and yellow markings. And this moth is the model because it has a very unpleasant taste and tends to be avoided by moth eaters. But you'll notice that the swallowtail butterfly mounted beside it has very similar coloration, and actually the swallowtail doesn't have the unpleasant taste at all. Another example is this monarch butterfly, which is probably more familiar to you since they pass through this area when they're migrating. But you may not know that they have a very nasty taste because I seriously doubt that any of you have eaten one. But for the predators who *do* eat butterflies, this orange and black pattern on the monarch is a warning signal not to sample it. So, the viceroy butterfly here is a mimic. Same type of coloring but no nasty taste. Nevertheless, the viceroy isn't bothered by predators either, because it's mistaken for the monarch. So how does a predator know that the day flying moth and the monarch aren't good to eat? Well, a bird only has to eat one to start avoiding them all—models and mimics.

This stinging bumblebee is another model insect. The sting is painful and occasionally even fatal for predators. So there are a large number of mimics. For example, here's a beetle that mimics bumblebees by beating its wings to make noise, and the astonishing thing is that it's able to do this at the same rate as the bumblebee so exactly the same buzzing sound is created. I don't have a specimen of that beetle, but I do have a specimen of the hoverfly, which is a mimic of the honeybee, and it makes a similar buzzing sound, too. When you compare the bee with the fly, you'll notice that the honeybee has two sets of wings, and the hoverfly has only one set of wings, but as you can imagine, the noise and the more or less similar body and color will keep most predators from approaching closely enough to count the wings.

Some insects without stingers have body parts that mimic the sharp stinger of wasps or bees. Although the hawk moth is harmless, it has a bundle of hairs that protrudes from the rear of its body. The actual purpose of these hairs is to spread scent, but to predators, the bundle mimics a stinger closely enough to keep them away, especially if the hawk moth is moving in a threatening way as if it were about to sting. There's a hawk moth here in the case, and to me at least, it doesn't look that much like the wasp mounted beside it, but remember when you're looking at a specimen, it's stationary, and in nature the *movement* is also part of the mimicry.

Oh, here's a specimen of an ant, and this is interesting. Another naturalist, Fritz Muller, hypothesized that similarity among a large number of species could help protect *all* of them. Here's what he meant. After a few battles with a stinging or biting ant, especially when the entire colony comes to the aid of the ant being attacked, a predator will learn to avoid ants, even those that don't sting or bite, because they all look alike and the predator associates the bad experience with the group. And by extension, the predator will also avoid insects that mimic ants, like harmless beetles and spiders.

Look at this.

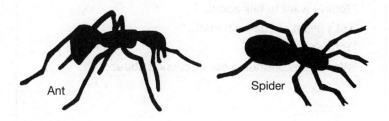

Ant          Spider

I have a drawing of a specimen of a stinging ant beside a specimen of a brownish spider and the front legs of the spider are mounted so they look more like antennae because that's just what the spider does to mimic an ant. That way it appears to have six legs like an ant instead of eight like a spider.

Okay, we only have about ten more minutes, and I want you to take this opportunity to look at the specimen cases here in the front of the room. The specimens are labeled, and the models are on the left. I'll be available for questions if you have them. How about forming two lines on either side of the cases so more of you can see at the same time?

## Main Idea

A *main idea* question asks you to identify the general topic of a lecture or discussion.
What is the main topic of the lecture? What is the lecture mainly about?

 **Review, Listening Section, Main Idea**

---

### 1  Listen to the introduction

"Listen to part of a lecture in a zoology class. The
professor is talking about mimicry."

---

### 2  Listen for key words

"Today I want to talk about..."
"Let's begin our discussion of..."
"Today's lecture is..."
"We will be continuing our discussion about..."

---

### 3  Distinguish a main idea from the major points

Major points are the big pieces in a lecture that support
the main idea. Professors often use two or three points.
Sometimes the professor will use *first*, *second*, *third*, or
other organization to signal a major point.

In your notes, these points will all relate to <u>one</u> main
idea.

## Question

What is the lecture mainly about?

o An explanation of mimicry among species in the insect world

o A comparison of the features of the viceroy and the monarch

o A hypothesis to explain why similarity among species protects them

o A response to questions about the specimens displayed in the cases

## Answer

What is the lecture mainly about?

● An explanation of mimicry among species in the insect world

o A comparison of the features of the viceroy and the monarch

o A hypothesis to explain why similarity among species protects them

o A response to questions about the specimens displayed in the cases

## Explanation

"Listen to part of a lecture in a zoology class. The professor is talking about mimicry."

"As you know from the textbook, mimicry isn't limited to insects, but it's most common among them, and by mimicry, I'm referring to…"

In this case, the answer is found in the introduction to the listening passage.

But the beginning of the lecture also identifies the main idea.

## Organization

An *organization* question asks you to recognize the way that the professor structures a lecture or discussion, for example, chronological order, steps in a sequence, cause and effect, comparison or contrast.

  **Review, Listening Section, Organization**

### 1  Recognize the options for organization

Some of the most common ways to organize a lecture are:

Chronological order
Steps in a sequence
Cause and effect
Comparison and contrast
Demonstration

### 2  Listen for key words

**Chronological order**: *dates*

**Steps in a sequence**: *first, second, third, etc.*

**Cause and effect**: *so, then, therefore, thus, because, due to*

**Comparison**: *like, similar, alike, the same*

**Contrast**: *different, differ, in contrast, on the other hand*

**Demonstration**: *examples, specimens*

### 3  Scan your notes

The way that you organize your notes will often show you how the lecture is organized.

## Question

How does the professor organize the lecture?

o He shows specimens to demonstrate his points.
o He compares the theories of two naturalists.
o He classifies different types of mimics.
o He puts the ideas in chronological order.

## Answer

How does the professor organize the lecture?

● He shows specimens to demonstrate his points.
o He compares the theories of two naturalists.
o He classifies different types of mimics.
o He puts the ideas in chronological order.

## Explanation

"I have some lab specimens of a few common mimics in the cases in the front of the room....and I've also removed a few to show you as we talk about them..."

During the lecture, the professor shows specimens as examples of the common mimics that he is referring to.

## Details

A *details* question asks you to answer a question about a specific point in a conversation or lecture. Choose 2 or 3 answers.

 **Review, Listening Section, Details**

---

### 1 Watch for answer choices with boxes

For most of the answer choices, you will click on ovals, but for details questions with more than one answer, you will click on boxes.

☐

☐

☐

☐

---

### 2  Choose the correct number of answers

The number of answers to choose will appear before the answer choices.  When you click on a box to choose an answer, an X will appear.

*Click on 2 answers.*

☐

☒

☒

☐

---

### 3 Move quickly to the next question

Don't waste time!

If you choose the wrong number of answers for a *details* question, you will see a message screen, and you will have to click to return to the question. Be sure to respond with the correct number of choices the first time.

## Question

According to the lecture, which of the following are characteristics of a model?

*Click on 3 answers.*

☐ A drab color
☐ A foul odor
☐ A bad taste
☐ A painful sting

## Answer

According to the lecture, which of the following are characteristics of a model?

*Click on 3 answers.*

☐ A drab color
☒ A foul odor
☒ A bad taste
☒ A painful sting

## Explanation

"One of the insects, the one that's characterized by an unpleasant taste, a bad smell, a sting or bite, that insect is called a *model*."

## Inference

An *inference* question asks you to draw a logical conclusion based on information in the conversation or lecture. Think of the information as evidence for an idea that is not directly expressed in the passage. This is very similar to the inference question in the Reading Section.

 **Review, Listening Section, Inference**

---

### 1  Identify the inference question words

What does the professor *imply*?

What can *be inferred* about-------?

---

### 2  Find the evidence in the listening passage

It may be concluded from the professor that Batesian mimicry was named for Henry Bates because...

"Henry Bates was one of the first naturalists who noticed that some butterflies that closely resembled each other were actually unrelated. The phenomenon in which one species copies another is called Batesian mimicry."

---

### 3  Draw a logical conclusion

*Directly stated in the passage*: "Henry Bates was one of the first naturalists who noticed that some butterflies that closely resembled each other were actually unrelated."

*Additional evidence in the passage*: "The phenomenon in which one species copies another is called Batesian mimicry."

*Conclusion*: Batesian mimicry was named for Henry Bates.

## Question

What does the professor imply about Batesian Mimicry?

o  It is a phenomenon limited to butterflies.
o  It is the course title of the zoology class.
o  It was originally Fritz Muller's idea.
o  It is named for Henry Bates, who first noticed it.

## Answer

What does the professor imply about Batesian mimicry?

o  It is a phenomenon limited to butterflies.
o  It is the course title of the zoology class.
o  It was originally Fritz Muller's idea.
●  It is named for Henry Bates, who first noticed it.

## Explanation

The evidence in the passage is that "Henry Bates was one of the first naturalists to notice [mimicry]" and "The phenomenon in which one species copies another is called Batesian mimicry." Therefore, it may be concluded that mimicry was named for Henry Bates.

## Technique

A *technique* question asks you to identify the way a professor makes a point or why a certain point is mentioned.

 **Review, Listening Section, Technique**

---

### 1 Notice how the professor explains a point

Some of the most common techniques for explaining a concept or an idea are providing a definition, giving an example, or a making a comparison.

---

### 2 Listen closely to examples

Examples are an important technique that professors use in their lectures. When a professor gives an example, the concept that is being explained is probably a main idea. Be sure that both the main idea and the example are in your notes.

---

### 3  Listen for a sudden change in topic

Ask yourself *why* the professor is mentioning a new topic. How does it relate to the general topic? What is the purpose?

A common way to present a technique question is: Why does the professor mention---?

## Question

How does the professor explain Batesian mimicry?

o By giving a precise definition
o By providing several examples
o By referring to the textbook
o By contrasting it with another hypothesis

## Answer

How does the professor explain Batesian mimicry?

o By giving a precise definition
● By providing several examples
o By referring to the textbook
o By contrasting it with another hypothesis

## Explanation

The professor mentions a number of examples of models and mimics to explain Batesian mimicry: the monarch and viceroy butterflies; the day flying moth and the swallowtail butterfly; the bumblebee and the beetle; the honeybee and the hoverfly; the wasp and the hawk moth.

## Connections

A *connections* question asks you to relate ideas in a lecture or discussion by filling in a chart. You will usually be asked to compare, classify, or identify a sequence.

 **Review, Listening Section, Connections**

---

### 1 Look for classifications in your notes

Mimicry – model/mimic

Model–bad taste, bad smell, sting, bite

| Model | Mimic |
|-------|-------|
| Monarch | Viceroy |
| Bumblebee | Beetle |
| Honeybee | Hoverfly |

---

### 2 Watch for a chart

| Insects | Mimic | Model |
|---------|-------|-------|
| Viceroy butterfly | | |
| Brown spider | | |
| Hawk moth | | |
| Bumblebee | | |
| Biting ant | | |

---

### 3  Fill in the answers that you know

| Insects | Mimic | Model |
|---------|-------|-------|
| Viceroy butterfly | X | |
| Brown spider | | |
| Hawk moth | | |
| Bumblebee | | X |
| Biting ant | | |

## Question

Indicate whether each insect below refers to a model or a mimic. Click in the correct box.

| Insects | Mimic | Model |
|---|---|---|
| Viceroy butterfly | | |
| Brown spider | | |
| Hawk moth | | |
| Bumblebee | | |
| Biting ant | | |

## Answer

| Insects | Mimic | Model |
|---|---|---|
| Viceroy butterfly | X | |
| Brown spider | X | |
| Hawk moth | X | |
| Bumblebee | | X |
| Biting ant | | X |

## Explanation

"So, the viceroy butterfly here is a mimic."

"...the hawk moth is harmless...bundle (of hairs) mimics a stinger."

"A stinging bumblebee is another model insect."

"...brownish spider mimic(s) an ant."

## LISTENING STRATEGIES

In addition to the academic skills that you will learn in Chapter 5, there are several listening strategies that will help you succeed on the TOEFL and after the TOEFL.

### ➤ Get organized

Before you begin the Listening Section on the official TOEFL, you will have an opportunity to adjust the volume on your headset. Be sure to do it before you dismiss the directions and begin the test. After the test has begun, you may not be able to adjust the volume without missing some of the information in the audio. When you practice using the model tests in this book, adjust the volume at the beginning. Learn to get it right without touching the volume button again during practice. Then, prepare to listen. The directions tend to be long and boring, especially if you have experience taking model tests and know what to do. Don't get distracted. Be ready to hear the first word in the introduction to the first listening passage.

- Adjust the volume first
- Prepare to listen

### ➤ Use visuals

The photographs and other visuals are there to provide a context for the conversations and lectures. In general, the pictures of people are for orientation to the conversations and lectures, whereas the visuals of objects, art, specimens, maps, charts, blackboards, and drawings support the meaning of the conversations and lectures. Do *not* focus on the pictures of people. *Do* focus on the other visuals that appear during the conversations and lectures. They could reappear in a question. When you take the model tests, practice selective attention. Look briefly at the pictures of the professor and the students, but be alert to the other visuals. If you become too involved in looking at the people, you may pay less attention to the audio, and you could miss part of the passage.

- Glance at the photos of people
- Focus on content visuals

### ➤ Read screen text

During the questions for conversations and lectures, watch the screen carefully. You will hear the questions, and you will also see them as text on the screen. If you find that it is to your advantage to close your eyes or look away from the photo during the short conversations, be sure to give your full attention to the screen again while the questions are being asked and the answer choices are presented. By using the model tests, you will be able to develop a rhythm that is best for your interaction with the screen.

- Read the questions
- Develop a rhythm

## ➤ Understand campus context

The conversations and lectures take place in a campus context. A glossary on the Barron's site online contains flashcards of campus vocabulary. These words and phrases will help you understand the conversations between campus personnel, professors, and students. The example sentences include pragmatic functions. A few examples of functions are an apology, an explanation, or a way to get the listener's attention or to change the topic. Pragmatic understanding will also help you interpret the speaker's attitude and the nature of the information—a fact or an opinion. Studying the online glossary is an important strategy for the Listening Section. Start now.

- Learn campus vocabulary
- Study pragmatic cues for lectures

## ➤ Listen to English

Take advantage of every opportunity to listen to English conversations and lectures, including international news broadcasts, educational television programs, and free lectures in English. Choose news channels that feature reporters from various English-speaking countries, especially Canada, the United States, Australia, and Great Britain. Don't take notes. Just listen and try to understand as much of the information as you can. If they are available on TV or online, watch the Learning Channel, Discovery, the Public Broadcasting Station, and National Geographic because their programming includes subjects that simulate lecture topics on the TOEFL. Take notes while you watch. During commercial breaks, mute the program and try to summarize the main points that you have heard, using your notes. Local colleges, clubs, and tourist attractions often have free lectures in English. In addition, several websites offer lectures and talks. Use the resources listed in Chapter 10. Select topics from natural science, social science, the humanities, and the arts.

- Listen to conversations for main ideas
- Take notes and summarize lectures

## ➤ Concentrate

Sometimes the environment for the TOEFL is not ideal. If the room is small, you may hear a very low hum from another headset, the scratch of pencils on paper when others are taking notes or even their spoken responses for questions on the Speaking Section. These sounds can be distracting, especially during the Listening Section. The earphones on your headset should suppress most of the noise, but it will be helpful if you have some strategies to help you concentrate. Some students press their earphones more tightly to their ears by holding them with their hands during long listening passages, but this may be clumsy for you when you reach for the mouse to answer questions. Other students train themselves to concentrate in a somewhat distracting environment by taking at least one model test in a small room where other people are studying, such as a library or a study lounge in a dormitory. Remember, you may not be able to control the test environment, but you can control your response to it. By keeping your eyes on the screen and the scratch paper and by remaining calm, you will be able to concentrate better. If the test situation is noisy, don't get angry and start negative talk in your mind. Don't let your emotions interfere with your concentration.

- Focus on the test materials
- Stay calm

## QUICK QUIZ FOR THE LISTENING SECTION

This is a quiz for the Listening Section of the TOEFL iBT®. This section tests your ability to understand campus conversations and academic lectures. During the quiz, you will listen to one conversation and one lecture. You will hear each conversation or lecture one time and respond to questions about them. You may take notes while you listen. You may use your notes to answer the questions. Once you begin, do not pause the audio. For your reference, the script for this quiz is on the Barron's TOEFL site.

### CONVERSATION

 **Questions 1–4, Conversation, Track 6**

Listen to a conversation on campus between a professor and a student.

1. Why does the man go to see his professor?

   Ⓐ To borrow a reference book that he needs
   Ⓑ To ask a question about the material
   Ⓒ To get advice about studying for a test
   Ⓓ To pick up some handouts from the class

2. Why does the student say this:

   Ⓐ To challenge the professor's idea
   Ⓑ To encourage the professor to explain
   Ⓒ To try to change the subject
   Ⓓ To interrupt the professor respectfully

3. How should Jack prepare for the test?

   Ⓐ He should memorize the material in the book.
   Ⓑ He should study the questions before the test.
   Ⓒ He should organize his notes by topic.
   Ⓓ He should not change his usual study plan.

4. What is the professor's attitude when the student asks her why she gives open-book tests?

   Ⓐ She feels offended that he would question her.
   Ⓑ She is surprised that he would want to know.
   Ⓒ She answers the question reluctantly.
   Ⓓ She does not mind explaining her reason.

## LECTURE

**Questions 5–12, Lecture, Track 6 continued**
Listen to part of a lecture in an economics class.

5. What is the lecture mainly about?

Ⓐ Changes in economic systems
Ⓑ Tax incentives for business
Ⓒ Supply-side economics
Ⓓ A favorable balance of trade

6. How does the professor organize the lecture?

Ⓐ By contrasting several economic systems
Ⓑ By taking a historical perspective
Ⓒ By arguing against Friedman and Asmus
Ⓓ By pointing out the benefits of Reaganomics

7. According to the lecturer, what did Kennedy and Reagan have in common?

Ⓐ They were both honored as Nobel laureates in economics.
Ⓑ They cut taxes to spur the economy during their administrations.
Ⓒ They identified themselves with supply-side economics.
Ⓓ They both taught at the Chicago School of Economics.

8. What would Milton Friedman most likely say about moving a manufacturing plant from the United States to a site abroad?

Ⓐ He would oppose it because it would cause people to lose their jobs.
Ⓑ He would consider it an opportunity for business to cut costs.
Ⓒ He would view it as a natural process in the shift to technology.
Ⓓ He would be concerned about the decrease in productivity.

9. According to Barry Asmus, what are two key ways that consumers contribute to the creation of new jobs?

Click on 2 answer choices.

Ⓐ By investing their tax savings

Ⓑ By purchasing cheaper goods

Ⓒ By moving on to better paying jobs

Ⓓ By spending more money

10. How does the professor explain the shift from manufacturing to technology?

      Ⓐ He points to the global economy as the explanation for it.
      Ⓑ He disagrees with most economists about the long-term effects.
      Ⓒ He compares it with the change from agriculture to manufacturing.
      Ⓓ He believes that it is too soon to draw any conclusions about it.

11. Why does the professor say this:

      Ⓐ He would like the students to answer the question.
      Ⓑ He is joking with the students about the supply-siders.
      Ⓒ He wants the students to follow his logical answer.
      Ⓓ He is impatient because the students aren't paying attention.

12. Put the following events in the correct order.

      Ⓐ Businesses hire more employees with the tax savings.     1. _____
      Ⓑ The government works to affect a reduction in taxes.     2. _____
      Ⓒ The businesses and their employees pay more taxes.     3. _____
      Ⓓ Profits increase because of the growth in businesses.     4. _____

To see the script and listen online, go to the Barron's TOEFL site and click on **Quick Quizzes**, **Listening Quiz**, then select **Script**.

# Progress Chart for the Listening Section

The chart below will help you evaluate your progress and determine what you need to read again. First use the Correct Answer column to grade the quiz. Next, check the Problem Types to locate which ones you answered incorrectly and review the lessons that correspond to the Listening Problem for each question that you missed.

| Quiz Question | Problem Types | Correct Answer |
|---|---|---|
| 1 | Reason | C |
| 2 | Function | B |
| 3 | Inference | C |
| 4 | Attitude and Opinion | D |
| 5 | Main Idea | C |
| 6 | Organization | B |
| 7 | Detail | B |
| 8 | Inference | C |
| 9 | Details | A D |
| 10 | Technique | C |
| 11 | Pragmatics | C |
| 12 | Connections | B A D C |

## ADVISOR'S OFFICE

There is usually a ten-minute break after the Listening Section. What you do during the break is important. If you start to talk in your language with friends who are nervous or negative, you will go back into the Speaking Section nervous and negative. If you are permitted to talk, choose a friend who is willing to speak English with you during the break. Use the time to encourage each other with positive talk. If you speak English, you will continue thinking in English, and you will make a smooth transition into the next section of the TOEFL. If you are also thinking positively, you will be ready to do your best. If you are instructed not to talk to others, then prepare some positive phrases in English to repeat in your mind or begin to rehearse some of the phrases that you have prepared for the first two tasks, page 142 and page 143 in this chapter.

# SPEAKING

## OVERVIEW OF THE SPEAKING SECTION

The Speaking Section tests your ability to communicate in English in an academic setting. During the test, you will be presented with six speaking questions. The questions ask for a response to a single question, a conversation, a talk, or a lecture. The prompts and questions are presented only one time.

You may take notes as you listen, but notes are not graded. You may use your notes to answer the questions. Some of the questions ask for a response to a reading passage and a talk or a lecture. The reading passages and the questions are written, but the directions will be spoken.

Your speaking will be evaluated on both the fluency of the language and the accuracy of the content. You will have 15–20 seconds to prepare and 45–60 seconds to respond to each question. Typically, a good response will require all of the response time, and the answer will be complete by the end of the response time.

You will have about 20 minutes to complete the Speaking Section. A clock on the screen will show you how much time you have to prepare each of your answers and how much time you have to record each response.

## REVIEW OF QUESTIONS

### Experiences

In Question 1, you will be asked to speak about a personal experience. This may be a place, a person, a possession, a situation, or an occasion. After you hear the question, you will have 15 seconds to plan and 45 seconds to talk about your experience and give examples or an explanation.

**Question**
Where would you like to study in the United States?

 **Review, Speaking Section, Experiences**

---

1  Write down a few words

You will not have enough time to make detailed notes before you are asked to speak. Write down only a few words or abbreviations to help you remember the main points you want to make.

**Example Notes**

Wash
• Fam—advice, help
• Intl—food, stores
• Tours
• U's

---

## 2 Change the question into a statement

A direct statement is a good way to begin. By changing the question into a statement, you are providing an introduction and answering the question at the same time.

**Example Question**
Where would you like to study in the United States?

**Example Statement**
"I'd like to study at a university in Washington, D.C."

## 3 Use the word *because* in the introduction

You are expected to include reasons, details, examples, and support for your response. By using the word *because* and providing a reason in the introduction, you are demonstrating that you understand what to do, and you are giving a complete answer.

**Example Introduction**
"I'd like to study at a university in Washington, D.C. *because* I have family in the area, and...."

## Example Answer

I'd like to study at a university in Washington, D.C. because I have family in the area, so I could visit them on holidays and in case I need help. I've been to Washington, and I like it. It's an international city with restaurants and stores where I can buy food from my country. And Washington is exciting. I've gone on tours, but I still have places to see. Also, um, there are trains to New York and Florida. Um, as for the universities, there are several, uh, excellent schools in Washington and...and I'd probably be accepted at one of them.

## Checklist 1

✓ The talk answers the question.
✓ The speaker communicates a main idea.
✓ Examples and details are included.
✓ The speaker uses different vocabulary words.
✓ The speaker makes few errors in grammar.
✓ The pronunciation is understandable.
✓ The talk does not include long pauses.
✓ The ideas in the talk are easy to follow.
✓ The talk is complete within the time limit.

## Preferences

In Question 2, you will be asked to speak about a personal choice. You may be asked to agree or disagree with a statement. After you hear the question, you will have 15 seconds to plan and 45 seconds to choose between the options presented and explain why you made that choice.

### Question

Some students live in dormitories on campus. Other students live in apartments off campus. Which living situation do you think is better, and why?

 **Review, Speaking Section, Preferences**

---

### 1  Choose the option that is easy to defend

Some choices are more difficult to defend. You are not being asked to choose an option that you really support. You are being asked to speak clearly and effectively. If you can think of 2 or 3 reasons to support one of the choices, then that is the one to choose for your talk.

**Example Question**

Some students live in dormitories on campus. Other students live in apartments off campus. Which living situation do you think is better, and why?

---

### 2  List 2 or 3 reasons in your notes

You won't have time to make more than 2 or 3 points in 45 seconds.

**Example Notes**

+ interact—Eng
- respons—meals, laund, clean
+ loca—lib, rec, class

---

## 3  Acknowledge the other position

When giving an opinion, speakers often acknowledge that the other position has merit. The acknowledgement usually happens in the introductory sentence.

**Example Introductions**

"Although living off campus has many advantages, I prefer..."
"Even though living off campus has many advantages, I prefer..."
"Despite the advantages of living off campus, I would rather..."
"In spite of the advantages of living off campus, I would rather..."
"Living off campus has many advantages, but I think..."
"Living off campus has many advantages; however, I think..."

## Example Answer

A lot of my friends live off campus, but I think living in a dormitory is better, especially for the first year. Dormitories provide opportunities for interaction and making friends. As a foreign student, it would be an advantage to practice English and find study groups in the dormitory. And dorm students have uh, less responsibility for meals, laundry, and, uh, cleaning because there are meal plans and services available as part of the fees. Besides, there's only one check so the bookkeeping ...it's minimal. And the dormitory offers an ideal location near the library and recreational facilities, and classroom buildings. ◄))

## Checklist 2

✓ The talk answers the question.
✓ The speaker states an opinion clearly.
✓ Reasons for the opinion are explained.
✓ The speaker uses different vocabulary words.
✓ The speaker makes few errors in grammar.
✓ The pronunciation is understandable.
✓ The talk does not include long pauses.
✓ The ideas in the talk are easy to follow.
✓ The talk is complete within the time limit.

## Reports

In Question 3, you will be asked to read a short passage about a campus topic and then listen to a speaker on the same topic. After you hear the question, you will have 30 seconds to plan and 60 seconds to report the speaker's opinion and relate it to the reading passage.

### Reading Passage
Time: 45 seconds

---

Annoucement concerning a proposal for a branch campus

The university is soliciting state and local funding to build a branch campus on the west side of the city where the I-19 expressway crosses the 201 loop. This location should provide convenient educational opportunities for students who live closer to the new campus as well as for those students who may choose to live on the west side once the campus is established. The city plan for the next ten years indicates that there will be major growth near the proposed site, including housing and a shopping area. By building a branch campus, some of the crowding on the main campus may be resolved.

---

### Script for Talk
Now listen to a student who is expressing an opinion about the proposal.

> I understand that a branch campus on the city's west side would be convenient for students who live near the proposed site, and it might attract more local students, but I oppose the plan because it will redirect funds from the main campus where several classroom buildings need repair. Hanover Hall for one. And, uh, a lot of equipment in the chemistry and physics labs should be replaced. In my lab classes, we don't do some of the experiments because we don't have enough equipment. And we need more teachers on the main campus. I'd like to see the branch campus funding allocated for teachers' salaries in order to decrease the student-teacher ratios. Most of the freshman classes are huge, and there's very little interaction with professors. A branch campus would be a good addition, but not until some of the problems on the main campus have been taken care of.

*On the official TOEFL iBT®, you will not have a script to read. The script is provided here to support your study.

### Question
The man expresses his opinion of the proposal in the announcement. Report his opinion and explain the reasons he gives for having that opinion.

**Review, Speaking Section, Reports**

## 1 Summarize the announcement quickly

Your summary should not take more than 10 seconds. The question is about the speaker's opinion, and you are expected to spend most of the time reporting the opinion. Sometimes a summary is only referred to in the context of the speaker's opinion.

**Example Summary**

"The university proposes that a branch campus be built on the west side of the city."
OR

"The man concedes that the branch campus might be advantageous for students living close to the new location, but he's concerned that…"

## 2 Report the speaker's opinion

Be careful. This question does not ask for *your* opinion. You are supposed to report the speaker's opinion and the reasons that the speaker gives for having that opinion. List the reasons in your notes.

## 3 Use strong verbs in your report

When you report someone else's opinion, it is easy to repeat the phrases, *He said* or *She said*. When you use strong verbs, the rater gives you points for a wide range of vocabulary.

Refer to Chapter 5, Activity 29 for a list of strong verbs.

## Example Notes

Plans to open a branch campus
• Convenient for students near
• Might attract more local students
• Relieve crowding on main campus
But will redirect funds from main campus
• Buildings need repair
• Equipment should be replaced
• More teachers—smaller classes

## Example Answer

The man concedes that the branch campus might be advantageous for students living close to the location, but he's concerned that the funding for a branch campus will affect funding on the main campus for important capital improvements such as classroom buildings in need of repair. Um, and equipment in the science labs needs to be replaced. He also points out that more teachers are needed for the main campus to reduce student-teacher ratios, which would improve the quality of teaching and interaction. So the man feels that funding should be directed to improve the main campus before a branch campus is considered.

## Checklist 3

✓ The speaker briefly summarizes the reading.
✓ The speaker states the opinion in the listening.
✓ Reasons for the opinion are explained.
✓ The speaker uses different vocabulary words.
✓ The speaker makes few errors in grammar.
✓ The pronunciation is understandable.
✓ The talk does not include long pauses.
✓ The ideas in the talk are easy to follow.
✓ The talk is complete within the time limit.

# Examples

In Question 4, you will be asked to read a short passage and then listen to a speaker on the same topic. The reading is usually about a general concept and the lecture is an example of it. After you hear the question, you will have 30 seconds to plan and 60 seconds to relate the lecture to the reading.

## Reading Passage
Time: 45 seconds

> The telegraphic nature of early sentences in child language is a result of the omission of grammatical words such as the article *the* and auxiliary verbs *is* and *are* as well as word endings such as *-ing*, *-ed*, or *-s*. By the end of the third year, these grammatical forms begin to appear in the speech of most children. It is evident that a great deal of grammatical knowledge is required before these structures can be used correctly, and errors are commonly observed. The correction of grammatical errors is a feature of the speech of preschoolers four and five years old. The study of the errors in child language is interesting because it demonstrates when and how grammar is acquired.

## Script for Lecture
Now listen to a lecture on the same topic.

> English uses a system of about a dozen word endings to express grammatical meaning—the *-ing* for present time, *-s* for possession and plurality, and, uh, the *-ed* for the past, to mention only a few. But . . . how and when do children learn them? Well, in a classic study by Berko in the 1950s, investigators . . . they elicited a series of forms that required the target endings. For example, a picture was shown of a bird, and . . . and the investigator identified it by saying, "This is a Wug." Then the children were shown two similar birds, to, uh, . . . to elicit the sentence, "There are two ___." And if the children completed the sentence by saying "Wugs," well, then it was inferred that they had learned the *-s* ending. Okay. Essential to that study was the use of nonsense words like "Wug," since the manipulation of the endings could have been supported by words that the children had . . . had already heard. In any case, charts were developed to demonstrate the gradual nature of grammatical acquisition. And the performance by children from eighteen months to four years confirmed the basic theory of child language that the gradual reduction of grammatical errors . . . that these are evidence of language acquisition.

*On the official TOEFL iBT®, you will not have a script to read. The script is provided here to support your study.

## Question
Describe the Wug experiment and explain why the results supported the basic theory of child language acquisition.

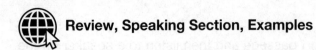

## Review, Speaking Section, Examples

### 1 Read for general information

You will have about 45 seconds to read 100 words. The topic will be an academic concept. You do not have to remember details. You need to be able to summarize the concept and the main points that characterize the concept.

To read the passage, return to your book. 📖

The script for the lecture is also printed in your book.
To listen to the lecture, click on the speaker. 🔊

### 2 Take notes on the reading

Since the passage will disappear after the time limit for reading it, you should take a few notes to help you summarize and characterize the concept in your talk.

**Example Notes**

Word endings—gram relationships
-ed past
-ing pres
-s plural

### 3 Relate the example in listening to the concept in reading

The question requires that you show how the example supports the concept.

**Example Notes**

Wug Experiment—Berko
Nonsense wds-not familiar
Manipulated endings
Data @ development

## Question

Describe the Wug experiment and explain why the results supported the basic theory of child language acquisition.

## Example Answer

In English, important word endings express grammatical relationships, for example, *-s* means "more than one," at the end of a noun. When children learn English, they make errors in endings, but they gradually master them. In the Wug Experiment, Berko created nonsense words to get children to use endings so the researchers could follow their development. So this experiment provided data about the time it takes and the age when endings are learned. It supported the theory of child language that sorting out grammatical errors is a feature of the speech of four-year-olds and a stage in language acquisition.

## Checklist 4

✓ The speaker summarizes the concept in the reading.
✓ The example in the lecture is related to the concept.
✓ The speaker paraphrases the wording.
✓ The information is accurate.
✓ The speaker uses different vocabulary words.
✓ The speaker makes few errors in grammar.
✓ The pronunciation is understandable.
✓ The talk does not include long pauses.
✓ The ideas in the talk are easy to follow.
✓ The talk is complete within the time limit.

## Problems

In Question 5, you will be asked to listen to a conversation and explain a problem, report the solutions that are proposed, and give your opinion about what the person should do. After you hear the question, you will have 20 seconds to plan and 60 seconds to summarize the problem and explain why you think that one solution is better than the other.

### Script for Conversation

Now listen to a conversation between two students.

| | |
|---|---|
| Student 1: | Did your scholarship check come yet? |
| Student 2: | Yeah, it came last week. Didn't yours? |
| Student 1: | No. That's the problem. And everything's due at the same time—tuition, my dorm fee, and let's not forget about books. I need about four hundred dollars just for books. |
| Student 2: | Well, do you have any money left from last semester, in your checking account, I mean? |
| Student 1: | Some, but not nearly enough. The check probably won't be here until the end of the month, and I won't get paid at work for two more weeks . . . I don't know what I'm going to do. |
| Student 2: | How about your credit card? Could you use that? |
| Student 1: | Maybe, but I'm afraid I'll get the credit card bill before I get the scholarship check and then I'll be in worse trouble because of, you know, the interest rate for the credit card on top of everything else. |
| Student 2: | I see your point. Still, the check might come before the credit card bill. You might have to gamble, unless . . . |
| Student 1: | I'm listening. |
| Student 2: | Well, unless you take out a student loan. A short-term loan. They have them set up at the Student Credit Union. Isn't that where you have your checking account? |
| Student 1: | Umhum. |
| Student 2: | So you could take out a short-term loan and pay it off on the day that you get your check. It wouldn't cost that much for interest because it would probably be only a few weeks. That's what I'd do. |

*On the official TOEFL iBT®, you will not have a script to read. The script is provided here to support your study.

### Question

Describe the woman's budgeting problem and the two suggestions that the man makes. What do you think that the woman should do, and why?

**Review, Speaking Section, Problems**

## 1 Organize notes in three sections

Even before you begin to listen to Speaking Question 5, you can organize your notes. Write the following three words on your scratch paper.

Problem

Solutions

Opinion

## 2 Fill in details as you listen to the conversation

Problem—not enough money
Scholarship check late
Books, tuition, dorm due

Solutions
Use credit card
Take out student loan

## 3 Report your opinion logically

This question asks for *your* opinion and for the reasons why you have that opinion. In order to make a logical response, you should use the first two sections of your notes to help you summarize the problem and the solutions that are presented in the conversation. You should do this quickly to reserve enough time to give your opinion and to explain why you have that opinion.

Opinion—support student loan
Paid same day
$ not much

## Example Answer

The woman doesn't have enough money to pay tuition and her dorm fee and books. So the problem is everything has to be paid now, and she won't get her scholarship check until the end of the month, and she won't get her paycheck for two weeks. The man suggests that she use her credit card, but the problem is the interest if the scholarship check is delayed. The other idea— to take out a student loan—seems better because the loan could be paid on the day the check arrives, and it wouldn't cost much to get a short-term loan. So . . . I support applying for a student loan.

## Checklist 5

✓ The talk summarizes the problem.
✓ The suggestions are presented.
✓ The speaker's opinion is clear.
✓ The speaker includes reasons for the opinion.
✓ Different vocabulary words are used.
✓ The speaker makes few errors in grammar.
✓ The pronunciation is understandable.
✓ The talk does not include long pauses.
✓ The ideas in the talk are easy to follow.
✓ The talk is complete within the time limit.

# Summaries

In Question 6, you will be asked to listen to part of an academic lecture and to give a summary of it. After you hear the question, you will have 20 seconds to plan and 60 seconds to summarize the lecture.

### Script for Lecture
Now listen to a short lecture.

> Two types of irrigation methods that are used worldwide are mentioned in your textbook. Flood irrigation—that's been a method in use since ancient times—and we still use it today where water's cheap. Basically, canals connect a water supply like a river or a reservoir to the fields where ditches are constructed with valves that allow farmers to siphon water from the canal, sending it down through the ditches. So that way the field can be totally flooded, or smaller, narrow ditches along the rows can be filled with water to irrigate the crop. But, this method does have quite a few disadvantages. Like I said, it's contingent upon cheap water because it isn't very efficient and the flooding isn't easy to control, I mean, the rows closer to the canal usually receive much more water, and of course, if the field isn't flat, then the water won't be evenly distributed. Not to mention the cost of building canals and ditches and maintaining the system. So let's consider the alternative—the sprinkler system. In this method of irrigation, it's easier to control the water and more efficient since the water's directed only on the plants. But, in hot climates, some of the water can evaporate in the air. Still, the main problem with sprinklers is the expense for installation and maintenance because there's a very complicated pipe system and that usually involves a lot more repair and even replacement of parts, and of course, we have to factor in the labor costs in feasibility studies for sprinklers.

*On the official TOEFL iBT®, you will not have a script to read. The script is provided here to support your study.

### Question
Using examples from the lecture, describe two general types of irrigation systems. Then explain the disadvantages of each type.

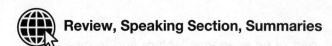 **Review, Speaking Section, Summaries**

## 1 Identify the organization of the lecture

Some of the most common ways to organize a short lecture in the Speaking Section are:

Theory and application
Concept and examples
Comparison and contrast
Cause and effect
Process and steps

By identifying the organization, you can prepare to take notes on the most important points.

## 2 Listen for numbers

Numbers in the introduction and in the transitions will help you to recognize the major points. When you hear "two types," you know that 2 main points will be made. When you hear "first," "second," and "third," you know that you should listen for 3 major points.

## 3 Mention all the major points

You will not receive full credit for your response if you leave out a major point. If you spend too much time on the first point, you may have to rush through the second point, and, if there is a third point, you may not have time to mention it at all.

If there are 3 points, spend about 15 seconds on each one. That will allow you time for a strong introduction and an optional conclusion. Glance at the clock on your screen to keep on track.

**Example Notes**

Flood
- Not efficient
- Difficult to control—flat fields
- Initial expense to build
- Requires maintenance

Sprinkler
- Complicated pipe system
- Expensive to install, maintain, repair, replace
- Labor cost

**Example Answer**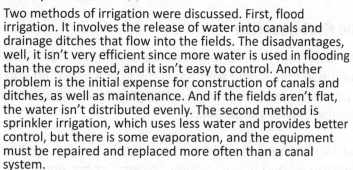

Two methods of irrigation were discussed. First, flood irrigation. It involves the release of water into canals and drainage ditches that flow into the fields. The disadvantages, well, it isn't very efficient since more water is used in flooding than the crops need, and it isn't easy to control. Another problem is the initial expense for construction of canals and ditches, as well as maintenance. And if the fields aren't flat, the water isn't distributed evenly. The second method is sprinkler irrigation, which uses less water and provides better control, but there is some evaporation, and the equipment must be repaired and replaced more often than a canal system.

**Checklist 6**

✓ The talk summarizes the lecture.
✓ All major points are included.
✓ Examples and details support the main idea.
✓ The speaker paraphrases the wording.
✓ The information is accurate.
✓ Different vocabulary words are used.
✓ The speaker makes few errors in grammar.
✓ The pronunciation is understandable.
✓ The talk does not include long pauses.
✓ The ideas in the talk are easy to follow.
✓ The talk is complete within the time limit.

## SPEAKING STRATEGIES

In addition to the academic skills that you will learn in Chapter 5, there are several speaking strategies that will help you succeed on the TOEFL and after the TOEFL.

### ➤ Pronounce to communicate

Everyone has an accent in English. People from Australia have an Australian accent. People from the United States have an American accent. People from Britain have a British accent. The important point is that your accent is okay as long as the listener can understand you. It is good to try to improve your pronunciation, but communication is more important for the TOEFL and for your academic and professional life.

- Accept your accent
- Improve communication

### ➤ Anticipate the first question

You will be asked to talk about familiar topics at the beginning of the Speaking Section. If you think about some of these topics, you will know how to answer when you hear the questions. A few seconds to prepare does not give you enough time to organize your thoughts unless you have the advantage of prior preparation.

You may be asked to choose a favorite person, place, activity, or item to talk about. To prepare for this question, spend a few minutes thinking about your personal favorites. Who is your favorite teacher? Person? What is your favorite city? Class? Book? Movie? Sport? Vacation place? Holiday? Music?

- Write down some answers
- Read them aloud

### ➤ Read 135 words per minute

Yes, this is a speaking strategy. To succeed on the Speaking Section, you will be asked to read short passages of about 100 words each, and you will have about 45 seconds in which to complete the reading. This reading speed is not impossibly fast, but you will have to avoid rereading phrases in order to finish within the time limit. When you take the quiz at the end of this section, you will hear a cue to start reading, and a question at the end of 45 seconds. This will help you time yourself. You probably already read 135 words per minute. If not, work on reading faster, using the reading strategies at the beginning of this chapter.

- Time yourself
- Increase speed to 135 words

# KEY PHRASES

Some key phrases are useful for each of the problems in the Speaking Section. Refer to pages 189–190 for additional words and phrases.

## Question 1: Experiences

My favorite _____ is _____ because _____ .

## Question 2: Preferences

Although some people _____ , I prefer _____ because _____ .

Although there are many good reasons why _____ , I favor _____ because _____ .

Although a good argument can be made for _____ , my preference is _____ because _____ .

## Question 3: Reports

The speaker supports _____ because _____ .

The speaker opposes _____ because _____ .

## Question 4: Examples

According to the (reading, lecture) _____ .

_____ is an example of _____ .

## Question 5: Problems

The problem is that _____ .

According to _____ , one solution is to _____ .

Another possibility is to _____ .

I think that the best solution is to _____ because _____ .

It seems to me that _____ is the best solution because _____ .

**Question 6: Summaries**

| | |
|---|---|
| **Definition:** | According to the lecturer, a _____ is _____ . |
| **Description:** | According to the lecturer, a _____ has (three) characteristics. |
| **Classification:** | (Two) types of _____ were discussed in the lecture. |
| **Chronology:** | The lecturer explained the sequence of events for _____ . |
| **Comparison:** | The lecturer compared _____ with _____ . |
| **Contrast:** | The lecturer contrasted _____ with _____ . |
| **Cause and Effect:** | The lecturer explains why _____ . |
| **Problem and Solution:** | The lecturer presents several solutions for the problem of _____ . |

- Study the key phrases
- Practice using them

## ➤ Use verbal pauses

If you get to a point where you don't know what to say, it is better to use some verbal pauses to think instead of stopping and thinking in silence. Silence on the tape is going to lose points for you. You can say, *Okay, Now, Um, And,* or *Uh*. All of these verbal pauses are very common in the speech of native speakers. Of course, if you use them too often, you will also lose points because they will distract the listener and you won't have enough time to answer the question completely.

- Learn verbal pauses
- Use them when necessary

## ➤ Listen to good models

Research is clearly on the side of those who advocate listening as a method to improve speaking. This means that one of the best ways to learn to speak well is to listen to good speakers. To improve your TOEFL score, you should listen to good speakers responding to the six question types in the Speaking Section. That is why this book has recorded example answers for the questions in this review chapter and on the model tests. For additional listening, ask a teacher or a tutor to respond to the speaking questions on the practice tests in Chapter 7. You ask the questions and listen to the answers. Don't give them the questions in advance. Use the same presentation and timing that you use when you take the practice tests yourself.

- Listen to example answers
- Test good speakers

## ➤ Speak to the criteria for evaluation

There are checklists for each question on the Speaking Section. Use these checklists to evaluate your speaking. If you do not know how to use the checklist, get some extra help. Resources for teachers and tutors are in Chapter 10.

- Keep the checklists in mind
- Take advantage of resources

## ➤ Sound confident

If you speak in a very low voice, hesitating and apologizing, the listener makes negative assumptions. This person is not confident. This person probably doesn't know the answer. Try to speak up and sound self-assured without being aggressive. It helps to start with a smile on your face.

- Speak up
- Be self-assured

## ➤ Stay positive

It is natural to be a little anxious about speaking in a second language, but it is important not to become negative and frightened. Negative thoughts can interfere with your concentration, and you may not hear the questions correctly. Take some deep breaths before each question and say this in your mind: "I am a good speaker. I am ready to speak." If you begin to have negative thoughts during the test, take another deep breath and think "confidence" as you breathe in. Focus on listening to the questions. Focus on taking notes.

- Take deep breaths
- Use positive self-talk

## QUICK QUIZ FOR THE SPEAKING SECTION

**Reminder:** To access the audio for this section of the test, visit *http://bit.ly/Barrons-TOEFL.*

This is a quiz for the Speaking Section of the TOEFL iBT®. This section tests your ability to communicate in English in an academic context. During the quiz, you will respond to six speaking questions. You may take notes as you listen. You may use your notes to answer the questions. The reading passages and the questions are written (printed in the book), but the directions will be spoken. Once you begin, do not pause the audio.

 **Quiz for the Speaking Section, Track 7**

### QUESTION 1

If you were asked to choose one movie that has influenced your thinking, which one would you choose? Why? What was especially impressive about the movie? Use specific reasons and details to explain your choice.

Preparation Time: 15 seconds
Recording Time: 45 seconds

### QUESTION 2

Some people think that teachers should be evaluated by the performance of their students on standardized tests at the end of the term. Other people maintain that teachers should be judged by their own performance in the classroom and not by the scores that their students achieve on tests. Which approach do you think is better, and why? Use specific reasons and examples to support your opinion.

Preparation Time: 15 seconds
Recording Time: 45 seconds

## QUESTION 3

Reading Time: 45 seconds

> ### Policy for Tuition
>
> In order to qualify for in-state tuition, a student must have lived within this state for a period of not less than one year. Furthermore, the in-state address must be the permanent residence of the student. College campus addresses may not be used as permanent residences. The student's driver's license and any vehicles must be registered in the state, and the previous year's state tax form must have been submitted to this state. Voter registration and a high school diploma may also be used as evidence of in-state status. Spouses and children of military personnel qualify for in-state tuition without residence requirements.

The student expresses his opinion of the policy for in-state tuition. Report his opinion and explain the reasons that he gives for having that opinion.

Preparation Time: 30 seconds
Recording Time: 60 seconds

## QUESTION 4

Reading Time: 45 seconds

> ### Communication with Primates
>
> Early experiments to teach primates to communicate with their voices failed because of the differences in their vocal organs, not their intellectual capacity. Dramatic progress was observed when researchers began to communicate by using American Sign Language. Some chimpanzees were able to learn several hundred signs that they put together to express a number of relationships similar to the initial language acqusition of children. In addition, success was achieved by using plastic symbols on a magnetic board, each of which represented a word. For example, a small blue triangle represented an apple. Chimpanzees were able to respond correctly to basic sequences and even to form some higher-level concepts by using the representative system.

Explain how the example of the Kanzi experiment demonstrates progress in research on primate communication.

Preparation Time: 30 seconds
Recording Time: 60 seconds

## QUESTION 5

Describe the woman's problem and the two suggestions that her friend makes about how to handle it. What do you think the woman should do, and why?

Preparation Time: 20 seconds
Recording Time: 60 seconds

## QUESTION 6

Using the main points and examples from the lecture, describe the habitable zone, and then explain how the definition has been expanded by modern scientists.

Preparation Time: 20 seconds
Recording Time: 60 seconds

 To see the script and listen online, go to the Barron's TOEFL site and click on **Quick Quizzes**, **Speaking Quiz**, then select **Script**. To listen to example answers, select **Example Answers**.

## ADVISOR'S OFFICE

When you face a challenge, "fake it until you can make it." This means that you should act as though everything were working out well, even when you have doubts. Put a smile on your face, even if it isn't real, and eventually it will be a real smile. Stand up straight with your head high and walk with purpose. You will start to actually feel more confident. If you are acting like a successful person, it may feel strange at first. But the more you practice your role as a successful person, the more comfortable you will be. Soon, when you reach your goals and you are truly successful, you will have practiced the role, and you will be the person you have been playing.

# WRITING

## OVERVIEW OF THE WRITING SECTION

The Writing Section tests your ability to write essays in English similar to those that you would write in college courses. During the test, you will write two essays.

**The Integrated Essay.** First you will read an academic passage and then you will listen to a lecture on the same topic. You may take notes as you read and listen, but notes are not graded. You may use your notes to write the essay. The reading passage will disappear while you are listening to the lecture, but the passage will return to the screen for reference when you begin to write your essay. You will have 20 minutes to plan, write, and revise your response. Typically, a good essay for the integrated topic will require that you write 150–225 words.

**The Independent Essay.** You will read a question on the screen. It usually asks for your opinion about a familiar topic. You will have 30 minutes to plan, write, and revise your response. Typically, a good essay for the independent topic will require that you write 300–350 words.

A clock on the screen will show you how much time you have left to complete each essay.

# REVIEW OF QUESTIONS

## Integrated Essay

In Question 1, the Integrated Essay, you will be asked to read a three-minute passage from a textbook and then listen to part of a short lecture about the same topic. The ideas in the lecture will usually challenge the ideas in the reading passage. After you read the question, you will have 20 minutes to plan and write an essay that includes information from both the reading passage and the lecture. The essay should be about 150–225 words.

### Reading Passage
Time: 3 minutes

> Global warming has become a hotly contested issue. Although they concede that changes will be different from one region to another globally, a consensus of scientists support the theory that greenhouse gases produced by human activities are causing unprecedented changes. According to the Intergovernmental Panel on Climate Change (IPCC), the warming of the climate system is evident from observations of increases in global average air and ocean temperatures, widespread melting of snow and ice, and rising global average sea levels. The panel cites 200 worldwide scientific organizations that hold the same position.
>
> Satellite data also supports the position on climate change. Earth orbiting satellites and other technological advances have enabled scientists to collect information about the planet and climate on a global scale. For example, we know that less $CO_2$ has been escaping to outer space at the specific wavelengths of greenhouse gases but increased long-wave radiation is measured at the surface of the Earth at the same wavelengths.
>
> Finally, in spite of the fact that the global annual temperature is lower than would have been expected by models of warming, supporters of the global warming model account for the missing heat by postulating that it can be found in the oceans. Variations in ocean temperatures occur on a 15- to 30-year cycle. In the positive phase, El Niño tends to warm the atmosphere. In the negative phase, La Niña brings cold waters up from the depths along the Equator and cools the planet. By inserting this cyclical factor into the climate change model, the lower temperatures fit the general pattern predicted.

## Script for Lecture

**Lecture, Track 8**

Now listen to a lecture on the same topic as the passage you have just read. When you take the test, you will not be able to see the script, but it is printed in the book to support your study.

Although the dominant argument for global warming is that a majority of scientists support the model, well, any scientist would have to agree that consensus is a false proof of a scientific theory. Why? Because only one contradictory piece of empirical evidence is sufficient to refute a theory. That is, to quote Richard Feynman, "The exception proves that the rule is wrong." That's the core of the scientific method. And many scientists with credentials equal to those of the proponents of global warming have put forward objections to the models that argue the global warming issue. To cite only one example, Lindzen and Choi have measured changes in the outgoing long-wave radiation from the top of the atmosphere during periods of warming, and their findings directly contradicted the global warming model because the increased carbon dioxide didn't block outgoing long-wave radiation. Even the latest IPCC report acknowledges that the models don't simulate clouds well, and that's where the main uncertainties lie. So there isn't a consensus, even among the proponents of the global warming models.

Now let's look at the satellite data, that supposedly proves the theory. In a joint study by the University of Alabama with NASA, . . . in their study, they found a huge discrepancy between the forecasts by the United Nations, using computer models and the actual amount of heat that's trapped, especially over the oceans. In fact, the NASA data shows that the models put forward for the past 25 years have consistently predicted more heat being trapped than real-world satellite data actually records.

Finally, we must examine the primary explanation for the difference between the climate change in global average temperature that global warming has predicted and the much lower change in global average temperature that we've experienced. Now according to a model by von Shuckmann, the missing heat is in the ocean at depths of about 2000 meters but the problem here is that the top of the ocean is cooling, so how can the bottom be warming? And furthermore, we should see a hot spot close to the tropics because more water should have evaporated to this part of the atmosphere and would have caused rapid warming if the models were accurate, but again this doesn't conform to the scientific data.

**Question**

Summarize the main points in the lecture, and explain how they cast doubt on the ideas in the reading passage.

 **Review, Writing Section, Synthesis of Opposing Ideas**

---

### 1  Present the ideas in the reading passage

This introduction should be very brief. Most of your essay will be devoted to explaining how the lecture casts doubt on the ideas in the reading passage.

**Example Introduction**

The lecturer refutes all three arguments for global warming presented in the reading passage. First...
OR
The reading passage claims that global warming is supported by a consensus of scientists, satellite data, and cyclical currents in the ocean. However, the lecturer refutes all three arguments.

---

### 2  Refute each point in the reading passage

Each point from the reading passage can be challenged in a separate paragraph. The argument in the lecture that refutes the point should be developed in the paragraph.

**Example Argument**

First, she [the lecturer] points out that a consensus does not prove a theory....Furthermore, the most recent IPCC report recognizes that the model doesn't simulate clouds well....

---

### 3  Include an optional conclusion

If you write a conclusion, it should not be lengthy.

**Example Conclusion**

*In short*, at this point, many highly regarded experts disagree with the model because the scientific data contradict it.

## Example Notes

**Global warming—data does not prove model**

### Consensus of scientists

| | |
|---|---|
| IPCC observations | 1 contradiction refutes |
| 200 organizations | Lindzen and Choi study |
| | IPCC—clouds ∅ simulated |

### Satellite data

| | |
|---|---|
| Satellite data supports | NASA w/U Al discrepancy |
| Less $CO_2$ escaping/ | 25 yrs predictions more heat |
| More long-wave @ surface | than data |

### Global average temps

| | |
|---|---|
| Missing heat in oceans | Von Shuckmann—top cooling |
| El Niño/La Niña cycle | No hot spots tropics |

## Checklist 1

✓ The essay answers the question.
✓ A topic sentence summarizes the main idea.
✓ An outline sentence previews the major points.
✓ Examples and details support the points.
✓ The information is accurate.
✓ Each lecture point is addressed.
✓ The writer paraphrases the wording.
✓ Different vocabulary words are used.
✓ The writer makes few mistakes in grammar.
✓ A variety of sentences are included.
✓ The essay is complete within the time limit.
✓ The essay is easy for someone to read.

## Integrated Essay

The lecturer refutes all three arguments for global warming presented in the reading passage. First, she points out that a consensus does not prove a theory. For scientific proof, all the evidence must support the hypothesis. However, many credible scientists disagree with those who champion the global warming issue. For example, the results of experiments by Lindzen and Choi contradicted the global warming model. Furthermore, the most recent IPCC report recognizes that the model doesn't simulate clouds well, which introduces uncertainty even among those who come down on the side of global warming.

Next, satellite data released by NASA in a joint study with the University of Alabama revealed a major inconsistency between the predictions by the United Nations, using computer models and actual data collected by satellites for the past 25 years. The models projected more heat, especially over the oceans, than the satellite data recorded.

Last, global warming proponents have offered a weak explanation for the lower average temperatures on Earth as compared with the expected temperatures in the model. According to von Schuckmann, for instance, the missing heat can be found in the ocean at depths of about 2000 meters. One flaw in this argument is the inconsistency of cooling on the surface and warming below it. A second problem is the absence of a hot spot near the tropics where more water should have evaporated, causing rapid warming, as predicted in the global warming model.

In short, at this point, many highly regarded experts disagree with the model because the scientific data contradict it.

## Evaluator's Comments

The essay answers the topic question and the content is accurate. The writer credits the researchers and paraphrases ideas. It is a well-organized essay with logically connected sentences. The meaning is clear.

# Independent Essay

In Question 2, the Independent Essay, you will be asked to write about a familiar topic. After you read the question, you will have 30 minutes to plan and write an essay that states your opinion, and explains why you have that opinion. The essay should be about 300 words.

## Question

Some students apply for admission only to their first-choice school, while others apply to several schools. Which plan do you agree with, and why? Be sure to include details and examples to support your opinion.

 **Review, Writing Section, Opinion**

---

### 1 State your opinion directly

A long introduction is not required for an opinion essay. It is correct to state your opinion in the first sentence. Acknowledging the opposite opinion in a clause before your opinion is also correct.

**Example Introduction**

I support making application to several different schools.
OR
Although I understand students who desire to concentrate all of their energy on applications to their first-choice school, I support making application to several different schools.

---

### 2 Write an outline sentence

An outline sentence provides the reader with an outline of the entire essay. Sometimes it is a very short statement that previews the number of major points that will follow. Sometimes it is a summary of the points themselves.

**Example Outline Sentence**

There are two reasons why I feel this is important.
OR
This is important because an application does not guarantee admission and because the application process is an opportunity to learn more about the schools.

## 3 Write a paragraph for each major point

Each paragraph should include reasons, details, examples, and support for the major point. In addition, transition words and phrases should connect the paragraphs and make the essay easier to read.

**Example Transition**

*First*, application does not...

*Another reason* to apply...

---

## Example Notes

Several schools
• Application Ø guarantee admission
competitive standards—no space—w/o school 1
semester--$ but saves time
• Learn about options
communications—discover advantages—
assistantships—negative experience
• I plan 3 schools
1 choice happy—options open

---

## Checklist 2

✓ The essay answers the question.
✓ A topic sentence summarizes the opinion.
✓ An outline sentence previews the major points.
✓ The writer's point of view is clear.
✓ Reasons and examples support the opinion.
✓ Different vocabulary words are used.
✓ The writer makes few mistakes in grammar.
✓ A variety of sentences are included.
✓ The essay is complete within the time limit.
✓ The essay is easy for someone to read.

**Independent Essay**

Although I understand students who desire to concentrate all of their energy on applications to their first-choice schools, I support making application to several different schools. There are two reasons why I feel this is important. First, application does not guarantee admission, even for a very highly qualified applicant. The school that a student prefers may have very competitive standards for acceptance. In spite excellent academic credentials, high scores on admissions tests such as the SAT and the TOEFL, and exceptional supporting documents, some qualified applicants may be turned away because of not enough space to accommodate them. If students apply to their first-choice schools, and they are not accepted for reasons that could not be anticipated, they may find themselves in the position of being without a school for at least a semester while they scramble to apply to the schools they had considered as second or third choices. It is expensive to apply to a large number of schools because of the application fees, but making applications to three schools can save time, which is also a valuable commodity.

Another reason to apply to several schools is the opportunity to learn more about each the educational options during the application process. While materials are being submitted and communication is occurring between the student and the school officials, advantages at the second- or third-choice school may be discovered as a result of the information exchanged. Scholarships, grants, and other opportunities may be extended when the committee is reviewing the application at one of the schools. For example, an unpublicized research assistantship may be available because of the prior work experience that an applicant has included on the application form. Conversely, the experience that the student has in applying to the first-choice school may be so negative that another school will be more attractive than the first-choice institution.

When I am ready to study at a university, I plan to apply to three schools—two with very competitive standards and one with moderate standards. If I am admitted at my first-choice school, I will be happy, but I will leave my options open during the application process just in case I discover some advantages at one of the other schools.

**Evaluator's Comments**

The writing sample is well-organized. It addresses the question and does not digress from the topic. There is a logical progression of ideas, and the writer uses good transitions. Opinions are supported by examples. The writer demonstrates excellent language proficiency, as evidenced by a variety of grammatical structures and acceptable vocabulary. The reader can understand this opinion without rereading. There are only a few grammatical errors that appear to have occurred because of time constraints. They have been corrected below:

| | |
|---|---|
| Line 5 | in spite of |
| Line 7 | because there is not enough space |
| Line 14 | each of the educational options |

## WRITING STRATEGIES

In addition to the academic skills that you will learn in Chapter 5, there are several writing strategies that will help you succeed on the TOEFL and after the TOEFL. Some of the strategies are more appropriate for the integrated essay and others are more useful for the independent essay.

### Integrated Essay

The integrated question asks for a synthesis of the content in a lecture and a reading passage. It is the first essay question.

### ➤ Report

When you are writing about content, it is important not to offer your opinions. To do this, you must distinguish between content and opinion. Content may include both facts and the ideas of the author or lecturer. Opinion is what *you* think. Your job in an integrated essay is to report the facts and ideas without making judgments and without expressing your opinions.

- State the facts and ideas
- Avoid expressing your opinions

### ➤ Combine Sentences

Essays with a variety of sentence structures are more interesting, and they receive higher scores. Complex sentence structures, achieved by combining simple sentences, also improve scores. Refer to Chapter 5, Activity 31 to review sentence combining.

- Vary sentence structures
- Include complex sentences

### ➤ Edit your writing

If you use all of your time to write, you won't have enough time to edit your writing. Students who take the time to read what they have written will find some of their own mistakes and can correct them before submitting the final essays. Be sure to edit both the independent essay and the integrated essay. To edit most effectively, use the grading checklist that raters will use to evaluate your writing.

- Reread your essay
- Edit with the checklist

### Independent Essay

The independent question on the TOEFL asks for your opinion. It is the second essay question.

### ➤ Respond to the topic

It is very important to read the question carefully and analyze the topic. Topics previously used for independent questions on the TOEFL Writing Section are listed in the *TOEFL iBT® Information*

*Bulletin* available free from Educational Testing Service. They are also listed on the website at *www.ets.org.* Read through the questions, and think about how you would respond to some of the topics. Since most of them require you to state an opinion, it is helpful to form a general opinion on each topic. If you write on a topic other than the one that you have been assigned, your essay will not be scored.

- Analyze the topic
- Write on the assigned topic

## ➤ Be direct

When you are asked for your *opinion*, it is appropriate to begin with a direct statement. Optional phrases and clauses introduce a direct statement.

| INTRODUCTION | OPINION |
|---|---|
| **Introductory phrase,** | **Direct statement = Subject + Verb** |
| In my opinion, | School uniforms are a good idea. |
| In my view, | |
| From my point of view, | |
| From my perspective, | |
| | |
| **Introductory clause** | **Direct statement = Subject + Verb** |
| I agree that | School uniforms are a good idea. |
| I disagree that | |
| I think that | |
| I believe that | |
| I support the idea that | |
| I am convinced that | |
| It is clear to me that | |

- Begin with an introductory phrase or clause
- Make a direct statement of opinion

## ➤ Use an outline sentence

Some books call the second sentence in an essay the *topic sentence,* the *controlling sentence,* the *thesis statement,* or the *organizing sentence.* The purpose of this sentence is to preview the main ideas of the essay for the reader. Here are some examples of outline sentences.

**First sentence:**
Although there are many advantages to living in the city, I prefer life in a small town.
**Outline sentence:**
Three personal experiences convince me that small towns provide a better lifestyle.

**First sentence:**
Despite the differences among cultures, I believe that peace is possible.
**Outline sentence:**
History provides several encouraging examples.

**First sentence:**
In spite of the benefits of studying in a group, I prefer to study alone.
**Outline sentence:**
There are three reasons why I have this preference.

- Write an outline sentence
- Preview the main ideas

## ➤ Think in English

How do English-speaking writers think? According to research by Robert Kaplan, they organize their thoughts in a linear pattern. This means that they think in a straight line. Details and examples must relate to the main points. Digressions are not included.

For essays that require an opinion, the organization would look like this:

| | |
|---|---|
| Opinion ↓ | In my view, school uniforms are a good idea. |
| Outline Sentence ↓ | Three reasons convince me that wearing uniforms will improve the educational experience of students. |
| Reason 1 ↓ | In the first place, uniforms are not as expensive as brand-name clothing. |
| Example/Detail | For example, a new school uniform costs about $30, but designer jeans and a name-brand shirt cost five times that amount. An expensive book would be a better investment. |
| Reason 2 ↓ | Second, it is easier to get ready for school. |
| Example/Detail | When there are five choices, it requires time and thought to decide what to wear. Uniforms simplify the problem of choosing a shirt to complement a certain pair of pants and, furthermore, selecting socks and shoes to go with them. All of these decisions take time and divert attention from preparing for classes. |
| Reason 3 ↓ | Finally, students who wear uniforms identify themselves with their school. |
| Example/Detail | Wearing the school colors establishes that each student is part of the group. |
| Conclusion | In conclusion, I think schools that require uniforms send a positive message to their students. They communicate that it is more important to be the best student than it is to have the best clothing. |

- Think in a straight line
- Connect each idea with the next

### ➤ Write a strong conclusion

In TOEFL essays, it is not appropriate to apologize for not having written enough, for not having enough time, or for not using good English skills. An apology will cause you to lose points. In addition, a good conclusion does not add new information. It does not introduce a new idea. A strong conclusion is more like a summary of the ideas in one last sentence.

- Summarize the main idea
- Avoid apologies and new topics

### ➤ Read good examples

Research confirms that reading is important to the development of writing. This means that one of the best ways to learn to write well is to read good models of writing. By being exposed to good writing, you will acquire good techniques. That is why this book contains examples of the answers that excellent writers might create in response to the questions in this review chapter and in the Writing Section of each model test. It is important to read these example answers carefully. Remember that you will be asked to produce expository, not literary, essays. For this reason, you should read opinion essays instead of short stories. It is also a good idea to read summaries of content material. Many popular college textbooks in English provide summaries at the end of the chapters. In general, these summaries are good models for you to read.

### ➤ Review topics

Topics previously used for independent questions on the TOEFL Writing Section are listed in the *TOEFL iBT® Information Bulletin* available free from Educational Testing Service. They are also listed on the website at *www.ets.org.* Read through the questions, and think about how you would respond to some of the topics. Since most of them require you to state an opinion, it is helpful to form a general opinion on each topic.

- Read questions
- Avoid apologies and new topics

### ➤ Read expository writing

Research confirms that reading is important to the development of writing. This means that one of the best ways to learn to write well is to read good models of writing. By being exposed to good writing, you will acquire good techniques. That is why this book contains examples of the answers that excellent writers might create in response to the questions in this review chapter and in the Writing Section of each model test. It is important to read these example answers carefully. Remember that you will be asked to produce expository, not literary, essays. For this reason, you should read opinion essays instead of short stories. It is also a good idea to read summaries of content material. Many popular college textbooks in English provide summaries at the end of the chapters. In general, these summaries are good models for you to read.

- Study example answers
- Read essays and summaries

## QUICK QUIZ FOR THE WRITING SECTION

This is a quiz for the Writing Section of the TOEFL iBT®. This section tests your ability to write essays in English. During the quiz, you will respond to two writing questions. You may take notes as you read and listen to academic information. You may use your notes to write the essays. Once you begin, you have 20 minutes to write the first essay and 30 minutes to write the second essay.

### QUESTION 1

**Reading Passage**
Time: 3 minutes

**Stonehenge**

Stonehenge, located on the Salisbury Plain in England, is a circular arrangement of bluestones and sarsen stones. Each bluestone weighs several tons and each sarsen stone weighs ten tons, or more. The question is, what was the original purpose of this monument?

Many theories have been put forward, the most popular being that ancient astronomers may have used Stonehenge as a solar calendar; however, excavations by researchers from the Stonehenge Riverside Project support a newer hypothesis. Evidence of burials and cremations dating back to 3000 B.C.E. influenced researchers involved in the Riverside Project to conclude that the real purpose of Stonehenge was to serve as a burial site. More than 50,000 cremated bone fragments of 63 individuals were excavated and studied by the team, including about equal numbers of men and women, as well as an infant.

In addition to cremated remains, chalk dust in several holes suggested that fifty-six bluestones once stood in the circular arrangement. According to the lead researcher, Professor Mike Parker Pearson, bluestones have been closely associated with burials from similar time periods, and their presence serves as further support for the burial ground hypothesis.

Finally, although few artifacts have been unearthed at Stonehenge, the head of a stone mace, an object similar to a scepter, supported the assumption that important persons were selected for burial in the site. A small bowl, burned on one side, may have held incense, further suggesting that the dead could have been religious and political leaders and their immediate families. Most prehistorical burials in England involved leaving the dead in the wild for animals to clean or throwing the bodies into the rivers, another indication that the Stonehenge burial site was reserved for leaders. Clearly, a possession like the stone mace would have belonged to someone of high rank and status among those who occupied the site and could have been buried with the body.

To see the script and listen online, go to the Barron's TOEFL site and click on **Quick Quizzes**, **Writing Quiz**, then select **Script**.

Now listen to a lecture on the same topic as the passage you have just read.

**Question 1**
Summarize the points in the lecture, and then explain how they cast doubt on the ideas in the reading passage.

Writing Time: 20 minutes
Typical Response: 150–225 words

**Question 2**
Some people like to communicate by email and voice mail. Other people like to communicate by telephone or face-to-face. Which type of communication do you prefer, and why? Be sure to include details and examples to support your opinion.

Writing Time: 30 minutes
Typical Response: 300–350 words

## QUESTION 1: EXAMPLE ESSAY

The lecturer refutes the three arguments presented in the reading passage, calling into question the new hypothesis to explain the purpose of Stonehenge. According to the hypothesis, the site was constructed as a burial ground for elite members of society in approximately 3000 B.C.E. The researchers in the Riverside Project cited the discovery of human remains, the presence of bluestones, and several important artifacts as evidence for their claim. However, the lecturer presents a counterargument for each assertion.

First, he maintains that the discovery of human remains is not unique to this project. Excavations as early as 200 years ago provided evidence of burials in Stonehenge. Although the remains prove that ritual burials were performed at Stonehenge, it does not necessarily follow that the monument was built for the purpose of burials. Previous researchers evaluating the same evidence have not come to the same conclusion.

Moreover, the bluestones could have been brought to the area for purposes other than burial rites. Since they have acoustical properties, ancient music could have been played on the stones. Some studies suggest that the stones may have had a magical purpose or could have been used for healing, in which case the burials could have been performed when healing was not successful.

In spite of the discovery of two significant artifacts that probably belonged to highly important people, the lecturer points out that the number of objects is insufficient to draw conclusions and, furthermore, that the current excavation may have been corrupted by previous digs and theft.

## QUESTION 2: EXAMPLE ESSAY

Although it can be argued that voice mail and email are more efficient, and in many ways, more convenient, I still prefer to communicate in person, or if that is not possible, by telephone. In my experience, face-to-face interactions are best for a number of reasons. In the first place, when you hear the speaker's tone of voice, you are better able to judge the attitude and emotions that can be easily hidden in a written reply. In addition, the exchange is more immediate. Even instant messaging isn't as fast as a verbal interaction in person or by phone. Email seems efficient; however, sometimes multiple messages over several days are required to clarify the information that a short phone call would have taken care of in one communication. We have all tried to return a voice mail only to hear a recording on the original caller's voice mail. Clearly, no real communication is possible in a situation that allows only one person to talk. Moreover, the body language and the expression on the speaker's face often communicate more than the words themselves. Research indicates that more than 80 percent of a message is nonverbal. The way that a speaker stands or sits can indicate interest or disagreement. The eye contact and the movement of the eyebrows and the mouth can actually communicate the opposite of the words that the speaker is saying. Finally, no technology has succeeded in duplicating a firm handshake to close a deal, a hug to encourage a friend, or a kiss goodbye. Until email and voice mail can provide the subtle communication, the immediate interaction, and the emotional satisfaction of a face-to-face conversation, complete with facial expressions and gestures, I will prefer to talk instead of to type.

## OPTIONS FOR EVALUATION

It is difficult to evaluate your own writing. If you are taking an English class, ask your teacher to use the checklists in this chapter to evaluate your writing. You need to know how you are progressing in relationship to the criteria on the checklists because that is how you will be evaluated on the TOEFL.

If you do not have a teacher, you may find an online tutor or an evaluation service, using the resources in Chapter 10.

### ADVISOR'S OFFICE

Keep your eyes on the destination, not on the road. There are short roads and long roads to the same destination, but the important point is to arrive where you want to be. Of course, there are several reasons why you prefer to achieve a successful score on the TOEFL the first time that you attempt it. It is costly to take the test again, and you are eager to begin your academic studies or professional life. Nevertheless, a goal is seldom destroyed by a delay, so don't destroy your positive attitude, either. If you take the time to prepare, you will probably be able to take the short road, but if you have not studied English very long, you may need more practice. Please don't compare yourself to anyone else. They are on their road, and you are on yours. Just keep going. You will get there.

# 5

# ACADEMIC SKILLS

## ✔ *Master the most important academic skills*

The TOEFL iBT® is a test of academic English. This means that you need more than English language proficiency to succeed. You need academic skills as well. You won't find a chapter like this in any other TOEFL preparation book. Campus Vocabulary, Taking Notes, Paraphrasing, Summarizing, and Synthesizing will help you succeed on the TOEFL and on campus in your college or university program.

## CAMPUS VOCABULARY

Many references provide a list of academic vocabulary, which contains words that are commonly found in textbooks and academic journals, but the *Glossary of Campus Vocabulary* at the end of this book is unique. It includes the most common vocabulary that you will hear and use in conversations on campus at English-speaking colleges and universities. There are three problems that you will confront when you are using campus vocabulary on the TOEFL and after the TOEFL when you are on an actual college or university campus.

1. **The meaning of the word is specific to a college or university campus.** This means that you have to understand the glossary meaning of campus vocabulary words.
2. **Intonation might change the meaning of the word.** This means that you also have to understand the meaning that is implied when the word is spoken in a conversation.
3. **You need to be able to pronounce the words so that you are understood.** This means that you have to be able to use campus vocabulary when you respond to some of the speaking tasks on the TOEFL and, afterward, when you are on campus.

This chapter will help you improve your campus vocabulary. You will learn how to

- **Become familiar with the definitions**
- **Recognize patterns of intonation**
- **Improve your pronunciation**

# BECOME FAMILIAR WITH THE DEFINITIONS

**Strategies to Use**
➤ Understand the meaning when you hear it
➤ Look up unfamiliar campus vocabulary

*How will these strategies help you on the TOEFL?* By learning campus vocabulary, you will be able to understand the conversations on the Listening Section and with professors, staff, and other students on campus.

## ➤ Understand the meaning when you hear it

### PRACTICAL STRATEGY

Using a pronouncing glossary is not like using a traditional dictionary. You can read the words and learn the meanings as you would when you use a dictionary, but you can also learn how the words are pronounced. The *Glossary of Campus Vocabulary* is on a dedicated Internet site, exclusively for those who have purchased this book. The site presents a flashcard for each vocabulary entry. Click on the speaker icon beside the word or phrase to hear the correct pronunciation. Then click on the speaker icon beside the example sentence to hear it again in a longer context.

### PRACTICE ACTIVITY 1

Did you understand? Listen to the words and example sentences from the *Glossary of Campus Vocabulary*, which you will find by accessing the Barron's TOEFL site online at *http://bit.ly/Barrons-TOEFL*. Click on **Flashcards**.

Identify five entries to practice every day. Repeat the word or phrase after the speaker. Then repeat the example sentence. Do you understand the meanings when you see them? When you hear them? The Example in Activity 1 shows you how to interact with the glossary.

**EXAMPLE**

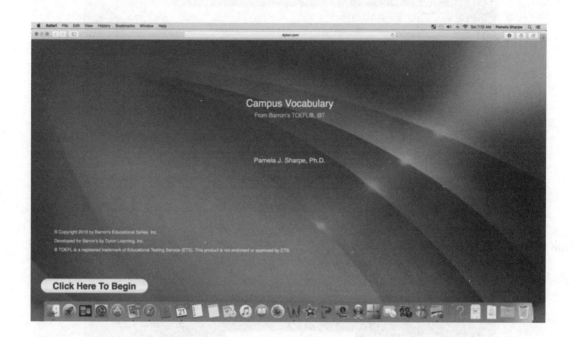

Click on **Click Here To Begin** to see the list of Campus Vocabulary words.

Click on a word to see the flashcard.

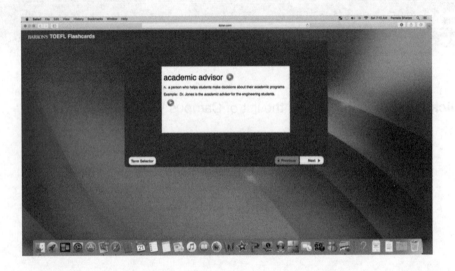

Click on the **Arrow** button beside the word to hear the pronunciation.

You can click more than one time to repeat it.

Click on the **Arrow** button under the Example to hear the word in the context of a sentence.

Click on the **Term Selector** button to see the list of all the Campus Vocabulary words.

Click on the **Previous** button to return to the flashcard for the previous word in the alphabetical list.

Click on the **Next** button to progress to the flashcard for the next word in the alphabetical list.

## ➤ Look up unfamiliar campus vocabulary

### PRACTICAL STRATEGY

Use the glossary online to look up unfamiliar vocabulary as you continue to prepare for the TOEFL with the model tests in the next chapter. Don't stop to search for a word or phrase while you are taking a model test, but when you are using the Answer Key and the Explanatory Answers, you can note campus vocabulary that you want to add to your list of five entries to practice every day.

## RECOGNIZE PATTERNS OF INTONATION

**Strategies to Use**
- ➤ Interpret expressions of surprise
- ➤ Comprehend requests for confirmation
- ➤ Become familiar with options for suggestions

## ➤ Interpret expressions of surprise

Two ways to express surprise are commonly used in conversation—question statements and emphatic statements.

### PRACTICAL STRATEGY

A rising intonation is usually heard at the end of a *question*. When a rising intonation is heard at the end of a *statement*, it usually shows surprise. The speaker had assumed the opposite.

### PRACTICE ACTIVITY 2

Did you understand? Listen to the following sentences from your glossary. Anticipate the rising intonation at the end, which expresses surprise. You may also hear emphasis and a rising intonation in a key word or phrase in the statement. Try to repeat each sentence after the speaker, using the same intonation. Notice that question statements include a question mark at the end.

 **Activity 2, Track 9**

### EXAMPLE

ace
Kathy aced her computer science class?

tuition
1. Tuition at private colleges is more?

prerequisites
2. You took the prerequisites last year?

handout
3. You lost the handouts?

laptop
4. Your laptop crashed?

article
5. You read the articles already?

skip class
6. Ron skipped class yesterday?

review session
7. The review session was productive?

call on
8. You sat in the front of the room and weren't called on?

curve
9. Dr. Graham grades his tests on the curve?

book bag
10. Your brand new book bag fell apart?

### PRACTICAL STRATEGY

Sometimes a statement of surprise is introduced by the phrase *You mean*.

## PRACTICE ACTIVITY 3

Did you understand? Listen to the following sentences from your glossary. Identify the intonation that signals surprise. Try to repeat each question after the speaker, using the same intonation.

 **Activity 3, Track 10**

EXAMPLE

off campus
You mean Carol doesn't want to live off campus?

notes
1. You mean you lent your notes to someone?

audit
2. You mean you're auditing the course?

turn in
3. You mean I could have turned in my paper tomorrow?

cram
4. You mean you crammed for the biology final?

draft
5. You mean you wrote the first draft in one night?

drop
6. You mean you dropped the class because it was too hard?

extension
7. You mean your request for an extension was denied?

lower division
8. You mean all the lower-division classes are full?

plagiarize
9. You mean you know someone who plagiarized?

sophomore
10. You mean Bill is only a sophomore?

## PRACTICAL STRATEGY

An auxiliary verb in a statement can express both emphasis and surprise. Usually the auxiliary verbs are *do, does,* and *did*. Sometimes the auxiliary verbs *is, are*, *has*, and *have* are also used. Often the statement begins with the word *So*. In these statements, the speaker had assumed the opposite.

## PRACTICE ACTIVITY 4

Did you understand? Listen to the following sentences from your glossary. Identify the auxiliary verbs that express emphasis and surprise. Try to repeat each sentence after the speaker, using the same intonation.

 **Activity 4, Track 11**

## EXAMPLE

T.A.
So Bill *did* apply to be a T.A.

degree
1. So you *did* graduate with a degree in music theory.

studies
2. So Jane *is* beginning her studies.

dean
3. So you *did* speak with the dean.

assignment
4. So you *do* read the assignments after all.

snack bar
5. So you *are* going to the snack bar after class.

report
6. So you *did* listen to Ken's report.

all-nighter
7. So your roommate *did* pull another all-nighter.

credit hour
8. So you *did* complete fifteen credit hours last summer.

makeup test
9. So Dr. Peterson *did* let you take a makeup test.

library card
10. So you *did* bring your library card with you.

## ➤ Comprehend requests for confirmation

### Practical Strategy

A statement that ends with the word *right* or a tag question with a rising intonation is a request for confirmation. These questions at the end mean that the speaker wants to confirm that he or she has understood correctly.

### Practice Activity 5

Did you understand? Listen to the following sentences from your glossary. Identify the question that signals a request for confirmation. Try to repeat each question after the speaker, using the same intonation.

 **Activity 5, Track 12**

### Example

elective
You're going to take an elective in art appreciation, right?

transfer
1. Dana transferred to State University, right?

student I.D. number
2. Pat has a student I.D. number, doesn't she?

transcript
3. You got your transcripts, didn't you?

incomplete
4. Bill took an incomplete in sociology last semester, didn't he?

undergrad
5. You're an undergrad, right?

cheat
6. Gary was expelled because he cheated, right?

extra credit
7. You signed up for extra credit, right?

get caught up
8. Sue got caught up over vacation, didn't she?

fill-in-the-blank(s)
9. The test was all fill-in-the-blanks, right?

hand back
10. Dr. Mitchell hasn't handed back your exam yet, has he?

## PRACTICAL STRATEGY

Sometimes the speaker asks for repetition to confirm that he or she has understood correctly. These sentences often begin with the phrase *Did you say*.

## PRACTICE ACTIVITY 6

Did you understand? Listen to the following sentences from your glossary. Identify the question that signals a request for confirmation. Try to repeat each question after the speaker, using the same intonation.

 **Activity 6, Track 13**

### EXAMPLE

probation
Did you say you're on probation?

fee
1. Did you say there are fees for using the recreational facilities?

admissions office
2. Did you say you couldn't find the admissions office?

flunk
3. Did you say you might have flunked the test?

fine
4. Did you say you were charged a fine for parking there?

tuition hike
5. Did you say you graduated before the tuition hike?

pop quiz
6. Did you say you passed all of the pop quizzes?

married student housing

7. Did you say there are no vacancies in married student housing?

shuttle

8. Did you say there's no shuttle on Sundays?

dorm

9. Did you say you've lived in a dorm for four years?

drop out

10. Did you say Diane dropped out after her junior year?

## ➤ Become familiar with options for suggestions

### PRACTICAL STRATEGY

The modal auxiliary words *should*, *could*, *would*, and *had better* are used for suggestions. Each auxiliary adds a different meaning to the suggestion. *Had better* means that it is necessary to follow the suggestion or some consequence will result. *Should* means that the speaker is presenting a strong suggestion. *Could* means that the speaker is presenting an option. *Could* is not as strong a suggestion as *should*. *Would* is used with the phrase *If I were you*. A speaker who makes a suggestion by beginning *If I were you* is presenting what he or she would do in similar circumstances.

### PRACTICE ACTIVITY 7

Did you understand? Listen to the following sentences from your glossary. Identify the words and phrases that signal a suggestion. Try to repeat each sentence after the speaker, using the same intonation.

**Activity 7, Track 14**

assistantship

1. If I were you, I'd apply for an assistantship.

audit

2. You could audit the course if you don't need the credit.

get behind

3. You'd better study this weekend or you'll get behind in English.

excused absence

4. You could take an excused absence in your Friday class so we could leave early.

**withdraw**

5. You should withdraw so you won't have failing grades on your transcript.

**student union**

6. You could meet Ken in the student union before the concert.

**work-study**

7. Dana should apply for the work-study position next fall.

**group project**

8. You should select your group project before midterm.

**check out**

9. If you want to check out books for your research paper, you'd better go to the library soon.

**room and board**

10. You should plan to include the price of room and board in your budget.

## IMPROVE YOUR PRONUNCIATION

Saying the word or phrase clearly

---

**Strategies to Use**
➤ Practice TOEFL listening tasks
➤ Practice TOEFL speaking tasks

---

## ➤ Practice campus vocabulary in TOEFL listening tasks

### PRACTICAL STRATEGY

Listen to an example of Listening Task 1 while you read along. Notice the campus vocabulary in the conversation. Listen for meaning, intonation, and pronunciation. Remember, this is a practice activity. You will not be able to read while you listen to a conversation on the actual TOEFL.

### PRACTICE ACTIVITY 8

Do you understand the general meaning of the conversation? Can you understand and pronounce each of the campus vocabulary words? Which speaker expresses surprise? Which speaker asks for confirmation? The answers are printed in Chapter 5 on page 278.

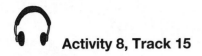

**Activity 8, Track 15**

## LISTENING TASK 1

| | |
|---|---|
| Man: | Hi Jane. How's it going? |
| Woman: | Good. You? |
| Man: | Same old problem. My roommate is driving me crazy. |
| Woman: | But I thought you lived in a dorm. |
| Man: | I do. |
| Woman: | Oh. Then why don't you see your resident advisor? |
| Man: | Been there, done that. I even went to the head resident. |
| Woman: | Really? And it didn't help? |
| Man: | Nope. He says that we should work it out between the two of us. |
| Woman: | Wow. How do you do that when he's always partying in the room? |
| Man: | I know. I keep waiting for him to flunk out. |
| Woman: | He's on probation, right? |
| Man: | Again. He cuts class, I never see him doing any homework, but he crams for his finals and always seems to just get by. |
| Woman: | I'm so sorry. I suppose you could go to the study lounge or the library to study, but you're probably already doing that. |
| Man: | I *am*, but it's not very convenient. I mean, I have all of my stuff in my room but now I have to pack it up every time I want to study . . . |
| Woman: | . . . and then you have to pack it all up again when you want to go back to your room. |
| Man: | That's about the size of it. |
| Woman: | Are you getting behind? |
| Man: | Not really. But I have a scholarship so I have to keep my G.P.A. up. And I'm a senior. |
| Woman: | You're a senior? Well then, you need to start thinking about graduate school. |
| Man: | I've already applied. But I need to submit this quarter's grades before they make a decision. |
| Woman: | So you really must be hitting the books. What can I do to help? |
| Man: | Not much. But thanks for listening. |

## ➤ Practice TOEFL speaking tasks

### PRACTICAL STRATEGY

Listen to an example of Speaking Task 3. Notice the campus vocabulary in the conversation. Listen for meaning, intonation, and pronunciation. Remember, this is a practice activity. You will not be able to read while you listen to a conversation on the actual TOEFL.

### PRACTICE ACTIVITY 9

Do you understand the general meaning of the conversation? Can you understand and pronounce each of the campus vocabulary words? Which speaker asks for confirmation? Which speaker makes a suggestion? The answers are printed on pages 278–279.

### SPEAKING TASK 3

Reading Time: 45 seconds

---

**Announcement from Student Services**
During spring break, County College will offer an alternative to the trips that many students plan to relax at beaches and resorts. Community service trips will be offered to assist low-income communities throughout the country. Students who sign up for these trips will be part of a team that will live and work with social service groups in the local area. Previous community service trips have provided tutoring for elementary school students in Texas and caregiving for senior citizens in Chicago. The trips are paid for by grants to the college.

---

 **Activity 9, Track 16**

| | |
|---|---|
| Man: | Are you going on the community service trip over spring break? |
| Woman: | I never go anywhere on break. I just visit my family for a few days and then come back and get ready for the next semester. |
| Man: | I know, but this is different. It seems made to order for *you*. |
| Woman: | Are you serious? I don't drink, I don't like the beach, and I don't have the money to waste on airfare and hotels. |
| Man: | That's what I mean. This spring break trip isn't about any of that. It's a community service trip. Look, you work with a team on a project in a low-income area. You're minoring in social work, aren't you? |
| Woman: | Yeah. |
| Man: | So you can see why I thought you might be interested. |

Woman:     Actually, that does sound interesting. And I think it's a great idea. Spring break is so wild and crazy for a lot of my friends. Maybe this kind of alternative will attract some of the people who just want to get away from campus and do something different before they start another term.

Man:       I was thinking about going or at least checking it out over at student services.

Woman:     Yeah, but it would be expensive . . . unless the community is close by.

Man:       No. Here's the thing: a grant pays for your transportation and your living expenses so there aren't any fees. You just have to be willing to work.

Woman:     What kind of work is it? Do you know?

Man:       Not exactly. Some of the projects that were funded in the past have served senior citizens and I'm pretty sure that there was tutoring for kids.

Woman:     Now you've really got me interested.

Man:       I thought you would be. We should go over to student services to get a few more details, like where they're planning to go and what projects are funded. I think Professor Keller has his office hours now, and he's the one who's organizing the trip.

Woman:     Well, sure. I'm free right now until my next class at two. That ought to give us plenty of time.

Man:       Okay then.

Woman:     And if it doesn't work out for me to go, I think it's a great idea to give people an alternative to . . . to . . . going crazy on some beach with a bunch of strangers from other colleges. That's never been my thing.

## PRACTICAL STRATEGY

Listen to an example of Speaking Task 5. Notice the campus vocabulary in the conversation. Listen for meaning, intonation, and pronunciation. Remember, this is a practice activity. You will not be able to read while you listen to a conversation on the actual TOEFL.

## PRACTICE ACTIVITY 10

Do you understand the general meaning of the conversation? Can you understand and pronounce each of the campus vocabulary words? Which speaker asks for confirmation? Which speaker makes a suggestion? The answers are printed on pages 279–280.

**Activity 10, Track 17**

## SPEAKING TASK 5

Man:       Hi Linda. I was hoping I might run into you today.

Woman:     Really?

Man:       Yeah. I wanted to ask you for . . . I wanted some advice.

Woman:    Oh, okay.

Man:    So you have Dr. Jackson for your academic advisor, don't you?

Woman:    Unhuh. He's the advisor for most of the biology majors.

Man:    I know. And he's *my* advisor, too. But I'm just having problems communicating with him. I mean, he's nice and everything, but I feel like he just doesn't listen to me, and I leave the meetings thinking that I didn't get done what I needed to do. Do you ever feel like that?

Woman:    I can't say that I do, but it's a problem for sure if that's what's happening to *you*. Have you ever just had a serious talk about this with him? That's what I'd do.

Man:    I've tried, but I'm just not getting through. I'm so frustrated.

Woman:    Well, you could request another advisor. I think Dr. Chee advises biology majors.

Man:    I thought about that, but if I change advisors then I'll have to sign up for a couple of my upper-division courses with Dr. Jackson, and he might resent it that I wanted a different advisor. Besides, he's on the committee for my thesis.

Woman:    I don't think he'd mind all that much. He has a lot of graduate students to advise. Listen, you could make an appointment to talk with him before he finds out about the change and you could give him some reason that isn't personal, like your schedule makes it hard to see him during his office hours or something.

Man:    I *could* say that, but what if he offers to see me at a different time?

Woman:    Right. Well, that could happen, but I don't think so.

# TAKING NOTES

Taking notes is writing down information while you are listening or reading. There are three problems that you will confront when you are taking notes.

1. **The professor determines the pace of a lecture.** This means that you have to take notes as quickly as the professor speaks.
2. **The notes must include all the main ideas and major facts.** This means that you have to know how to identify important information when you hear it or read it.
3. **The notes may be used for different reasons.** This means that you have to organize the notes to help you remember, to add to the information from another assignment, or to plan a speech or an essay.

This chapter will help you improve your note taking skills. You will learn how to

- **Organize your notes**
- **Identify important information**
- **Take notes quickly**

***How will these strategies help you on the TOEFL?*** By learning to take better notes when you hear lectures, you will have the information you need to respond to the listening comprehension questions and to prepare your speaking and writing questions. You will even improve your reading comprehension. Taking excellent notes is one of the most important academic skills for success on the TOEFL and after the TOEFL when you are enrolled in a college or university program.

## ORGANIZE YOUR NOTES

**Strategies to Use**
➤ Anticipate the purpose
➤ Divide the paper into columns
➤ Separate the major and minor points

## ➤ Anticipate the purpose

If you can anticipate the purpose of a reading or a lecture, you will be able to prepare your mind to receive the information, and you will already know how to organize your notes.

## PRACTICAL STRATEGY

The most common purposes for academic English are to provide the answers to basic questions. These questions are answered in textbooks and lectures to help you learn the academic subjects.

| Purpose | Question |
|---|---|
| Definition | What is it? |
| Description and Example | What are the characteristics? |
| Classification | Which group does it belong to? |
| Sequence | What is the order—first, second, and so on? |
| Comparison and Contrast | How is it the same as or different from something else? |
| Cause and Effect | How does it cause something? What happens? |
| Problem and Solution | Why is it a problem? What is the solution? |
| Persuasion or Evaluation | Why should it be supported or rejected? |

The headings and subheadings in textbooks help you anticipate the purpose of the chapter or the sections within a chapter. For example, a heading in an earth science textbook that includes only one noun, **The Atmosphere**, will probably be a definition or a description of the atmosphere. A heading such as **Forces Within the Atmosphere** implies that several forces will be discussed and further implies that this will be a classification or perhaps a comparison and contrast of the forces. **Atmospheric Patterns of Motion** introduces a process and could anticipate a sequence or even a cause and effect. **Problems in Predicting Weather** is a heading that contains the purpose in the word *problems*. You know that this is a problem and solution section. Persuasion can usually be identified because of words like *should* and *must* as well as subjective or judgmental phrases like *better* or *worse*, whereas evaluation contains both sides of an issue.

## PRACTICE ACTIVITY 11

Did you understand? Try to anticipate the purpose of each section in a textbook by reading the headings and subheadings. Here are some headings and subheadings for practice. The first one is completed to give you an example. The answers are printed in Chapter 5 on page 280.

Sometimes you will make a mistake anticipating the purpose. Your prediction will be different from the way that the reading or lecture proceeds. Don't worry. Trying to predict is still a good idea, and you will become more skilled as you practice using other activities and tests in this book.

## EXAMPLE

**Subheading:** The Enlightenment          **Purpose:** definition *or* description

1. Settlement Patterns

2. The Functions of Art

3. Language Development

4. How Important Is Relativity?

5. Causes of Schizophrenia

6. Evaluating Kohlberg's Theory

7. Types of Financial Services

8. A History of Plate Tectonics

9. Estimating Population

10. Black Holes

## PRACTICAL STRATEGY

The lectures on the TOEFL begin with an introductory screen followed by a narrator's introduction. They will give you a general direction for your listening. Most of the time, the narrator will tell you in which class the lecture is given. Sometimes the narrator will also provide the main topic.

## PRACTICE ACTIVITY 12

Did you understand? Try to anticipate part of the narrator's introduction by viewing the introductory screen. Here are some introductions to lectures for practice. The first one is completed to give you an example. The answers are printed on page 280.

**EXAMPLE**

| Astronomy |
| --- |

"Listen to part of a lecture in an astronomy class."

  **Activity 12, Track 18**

1.  | Business |
| --- |

    Listen to part of a lecture in _____.

2.  | Music Appreciation |
| --- |

    Listen to part of a lecture in _____.

3.  | Biology |
| --- |

    Listen to part of a lecture in _____.

4.  | Anthropology |
| --- |

    Listen to part of a lecture in _____.

5.  | Engineering |
| --- |

    Listen to part of a lecture in _____.

6.  | Linguistics |
| --- |

    Listen to part of a lecture in _____.

7.  | Art History |
| --- |

    Listen to part of a lecture in _____.

8.  | Psychology |
| --- |

    Listen to part of a lecture in _____.

9. | Geology |

Listen to part of a lecture in _____.

10. | History |

Listen to part of a lecture in _____.

## PRACTICAL STRATEGY

A good lecturer will also give you ways to anticipate the purpose of a lecture or part of a lecture with verbal cues. Sometimes the lecturer will announce the topic in such a way that the purpose is directly stated. Other times you will have to draw a conclusion. Although the topic is stated at the beginning of the lecture, there may be some references to previous lectures or some classroom business to conclude before the topic is announced. When the topic for a lecture is stated, the lecturer may either pause just before saying the topic or stress the topic by raising the volume or using very clear pronunciation.

To be a good listener, you should prepare your mind to accept the information. If you know which class the lecturer is teaching, you already know how to focus your attention. By hearing the cue that identifies the topic, you have a context for the rest of the lecture.

## PRACTICE ACTIVITY 13

Did you understand? Try to anticipate the purpose of a lecture by listening to the beginning of it. Here are some short introductions to lectures for practice. The first one is completed to give you an example. The answers are printed on page 281.

## EXAMPLE

"Okay then, let's get started. Uh, today we're going to talk about the *biosphere*."

 **Activity 13, Track 19**

1.

2.

3.

4.

5.

6.

7.

8.

9.

10.

## ➤ Divide the paper into columns

There are many variations of column note taking. This style is very simple and effective. Draw a line down your note paper from the top to the bottom about two inches from the left margin, as shown on the next page. This is called two-column notes. When you are taking notes, put the topics or main ideas in the left column and add details and examples in the right column. This system helps you take notes more quickly because you don't have to identify the main ideas and the details or examples by writing out words or by using a more complicated outline format that requires letters and numbers. Placement to the left or to the right of the line sorts the ideas in order of importance and shows their relationship.

### PRACTICAL STRATEGY

Draw a line across the paper from the left to the right about two inches from the top. This is a space for the main idea. Draw another line about two inches from the bottom, as shown. This is a space that you can use for your thoughts and ideas as you are taking notes. Later, when you look at your notes, you will know which ideas are from the textbook or lecture and which are yours.

Main Idea

| Major point 1 | Examples and details |
| Major point 2 | Examples and details |
| Major point 3 | Examples and details |

My Ideas

### PRACTICE ACTIVITY 14

Did you understand? Try to put the information in the following sentence outline into two-column notes. Refer to the two-column format above as an example. The answers are printed on page 281.

There are three arguments in support of protecting endangered species.

  I.  Aesthetic justification states that the various forms of nature influence the life experience of human beings in a positive way.
      A. Many endangered species are uniquely beautiful.
      B. They are appreciated universally in art and literature.
      C. Some are important to the religious community.

II.  Ecological self-interest assumes that a balance of nature benefits all species.
    A. All species perform essential functions.
        1. For example, an endangered species may be the unique carrier of a cure for a human disease.
    B. In order to protect ourselves, we must protect other species.

III. Moral justification asserts that the creatures themselves have rights.
    A. The United Nations World Charter for Nature declares that all species have the right to exist.
    B. Human beings have the responsibility to preserve all species.

IV.  The professor does not directly promote any argument, but advocacy for the protection of endangered species is implied in the lecture.

## ➤ Separate the major and minor points

In order to use two columns for notes, you must be able to classify the ideas into major and minor points. There are usually three or four major points in a short lecture or reading passage. Each of the major points is supported by examples and details. The examples and details are minor points.

### PRACTICAL STRATEGY

When you hear a major point, write it on the left. When you hear a minor point, write it on the right.

### PRACTICE ACTIVITY 15

Did you understand? Look at the notes under each topic. The sentences in the notes refer to either the major points or the minor points. Try to organize the notes under the topic by putting the major points in the left column and the minor points in the right column. Your answer is correct if the points are placed correctly on either the left or right. The points do not have to be in exactly the same order. The first one is completed to give you an example. The answers are printed on pages 282–283.

### EXAMPLE

There are three types of managers in addition to the general manager.

    The line manager is responsible for production.
    For example, a production manager is a line manager.
    A staff manager is in charge of support activities such as human resources.
    Information systems is also overseen by a staff manager.
    A functional manager is the head of a department.
    A department chair at a college is a functional manager.
    The manager of a sales department at a company is also a functional manager.

### 3 managers

| line manager<br>production | production manager |
|---|---|
| staff manager<br>support activities | human resources<br>information systems |
| functional manager<br>head dept | dept chair college<br>sales dept company |

1. According to Mead, the self has two sides: the "I" and the "me."

   It is predictable because social conformity is expected.
   This part of the self is less predictable because it is unique.
   This part of the self is formed through socialization by others.
   The "I" represents the individuality of a person.
   For instance, a spontaneous reaction might reveal the "I."
   The "me" represents the expectations and attitudes of others.

2. The mystery of pulsars was resolved in the 1960s.

   We see pulses of light each time the beam sweeps past the Earth.
   The pulsar in the Crab Nebula, for example, currently spins about thirty times per second.
   We also know that pulsars are not perfectly timed because each revolution of a pulsar takes a little longer.
   We know that pulsars are neutron stars, like lighthouses left by supernova explosions.
   It will probably spin about half as fast two thousand years from now.
   Like a lighthouse, the neutron star revolves.

3. Britain transported convicts to Australia in an effort to solve the problems of overcrowding in prisons.

   There were 11 ships with 750 prisoners aboard.
   Four companies of marines sailed with them as guards.
   They took enough supplies for two years.
   In 1787, the first fleet left for Botany Bay in New South Wales.
   Shortly after arriving in 1788, the colony was moved to Sydney Cove.
   In Sydney, the water supply and soil were better.
   Although Sydney was the new site, for many years it was called Botany Bay.

4.  Frederick Carl Frieseke was an American impressionist.

    In Normandy, he began to paint indoor settings.
    In 1905, Frieseke moved to Giverney where he lived until 1920.
    He studied with Whistler in the late 1800s.
    Born in Michigan, he went to Paris in 1897.
    In his later work, he began to use a darker palette.
    From Whistler, he learned the academic style of the salons.
    At Giverney, Frieseke was influenced by Monet.
    Monet was experimenting with the effects of sunlight.
    The style of Monet and his school is known as impressionism.
    By 1920, Frieseke had left Giverney for Normandy.

5.  Two types of weathering will break down rock masses into smaller particles.

    Interaction between surface or ground water and chemicals causes chemical weathering.
    With increased precipitation or temperature, chemicals tend to break down faster.
    Mechanical weathering occurs when force and pressure grind rocks down.
    A common example is the wearing away of granite facades on buildings.
    The weathering of feldspar in granite can be caused by a reaction to acids in rain.
    Pressure from freezing and thawing causes rocks to expand and contract.
    When a rock is broken in two by physical forces, it is more vulnerable to weathering.

## IDENTIFY IMPORTANT INFORMATION

> **Strategies to Use**
> ➤ Pay attention to key words
> ➤ Notice cues in speech and writing

## ➤ Pay attention to key words

Key words help you identify the important information in a textbook or a lecture. Certain key words appear more often in a reading passage or a lecture with a particular purpose.

### PRACTICAL STRATEGY

The key words below are listed under the purpose for which they are frequently used. These key words are not 100 percent accurate, but they do give you a starting point. Key words are especially important in lectures since the sentences that the professor uses in speech are not edited like the sentences in textbooks, and are, therefore, more difficult to follow.

## Definition

Is known as
Is called
Is
Refers to
Means

## Description and Example

Consists of
Adjective
For example
For instance
Namely
Specifically
That is

## Classification

Kinds of
Types of
Classes of
Groups of
Parts of
Properties of
Characteristics of
Varieties of

## Sequence—Chronology or Process

First, second, third
Next, then, last
Finally
Before
After
At the same time
Meanwhile
Now
As soon as
Later
Subsequently
Eventually
Step
Stage
Phase

## Comparison and Contrast

Like
Similar to
Differ from
Compared with
In comparison
Similarly
In the same way
In contrast
Whereas
Adjective + -er
Although
But
Conversely
In spite of
Even though
However
Instead
On the contrary
On the other hand
Despite

## Cause and Effect

As a consequence
As a result
Thus
Therefore
Because
Because of
For this reason
Consequently
Since
So

## Problem and Solution

Problem

## Persuasion or Evaluation

First, second, third
Should, must, ought to
Therefore
In conclusion, in summary

***PRACTICE ACTIVITY 16***

Did you understand? Try to identify the key words in the sentences. Underline them. Then decide in which kind of reading passage they might be found. Here are some sentences for practice. The first one is completed to give you an example. The answers are printed on page 283.

**EXAMPLE**

Mesopotamia <u>refers to</u> the land between two rivers. *Definition*

1. There are two types of mixtures—heterogeneous and homogeneous.

2. As a result, the litmus paper turns blue when the solution is a base.

3. In contrast, a counterculture exhibits behavior that is contrary to the dominant culture.

4. The first stage of sleep produces alpha waves.

5. The main properties of soil include color, texture, and structure.

6. Community service should be a requirement for graduation from the College of Education.

7. For example, the Navajo create sacred images in colored sand in order to restore the spiritual and physical health of the sick.

8. The maximum amount of water that air can hold at a given temperature and pressure is known as saturation.

9. Whereas an objective is specific and measurable, a goal is broader and is usually not time specific.

10. Dutch explorers in the early seventeenth century called the west coast of Australia "New Holland," a name that was used to describe the continent until the beginning of the nineteenth century.

## ➤ Notice cues in speech and writing

Sometimes professors will tell you that a point is important while they are presenting their lectures. Some phrases to listen for include the following:

> Pay particular attention to
> Be sure to
> Especially important is
> And this is important
> And this is the key point

Written cues will also appear in textbooks. Look for headings, bold letters, and italics.

## PRACTICAL STRATEGY

Underline the information or put a star beside it to indicate that the professor has identified it as an important point.

## PRACTICE ACTIVITY 17

Did you understand? Listen to the beginning of a lecture on language and try to identify the important information in the notes. Underline it or put a star beside it. A sentence from the lecture is shown here along with a star beside the corresponding point in the notes to give you an example. The answers are printed on pages 283–284.

### EXAMPLE

"And this is important—standard language is appropriate in both speech and writing."
Notes: *appropriate speech + writing

Listen to the beginning of a lecture in a linguistics class.

 **Activity 17, Track 20**

Definition + comparison = three types of language

| | |
|---|---|
| Standard usage | definitions   words + phrases found in dictionary |
| Permanent core | used formal + informal situations |
| | *appropriate speech + writing |
| | |
| Colloquial language | included in dictionary marked as colloquial idioms |
| Often evolves into standard | understood + used in informal situations, not formal |
| | more common in speech |
| | |
| Slang expressions | sometimes in dictionary marked as slang |
| Temporary phenomenon | used by some speakers in informal situations |
| | more common in speech |
| | |
| Continuum | most formal—least formal |
| | standard—colloquial—slang |

## TAKE NOTES QUICKLY

**Strategies to Use**
➤ Know what to ignore
➤ Use abbreviations and symbols
➤ Draw relationships

## ➤ Know what to ignore

Sometimes professors will pause to think before they continue their lectures. Some professors will use verbal pauses, for example, *uh* and *um*, as well as words like *now*, *so*, *okay*, *well*. Other professors will use repetition or restatement as a way to gather their thoughts or to clarify a previous point. In repetition, the professor will use the same words or phrases several times. In restatement, the professor will say the same thing in a slightly different way. Since repetition and restatement do not add to the meaning, you can ignore them.

### PRACTICAL STRATEGY

The time that the professor uses to think is advantageous to you because you can ignore these pauses, repetitions, and restatements and you can use the additional time to take notes.

### PRACTICE ACTIVITY 18

Did you understand? Try to identify the important information in the lecture. Cross out everything in the transcript that you could ignore. The first sentence from the lecture is shown to give you an example. The answers are printed on pages 284–285.

### EXAMPLE

Status ███████ position █ society ██████ group.

**Sociology**

Listen to the beginning of a lecture in a sociology class as you read the transcript. The professor is discussing status and roles.

### Activity 18, Track 21

Status refers to, uh, a position in society or . . . or in a group. But there are really two types of status—ascribed status and achieved status. Okay, in ascribed status, the status is automatic, so you don't have a choice. In other words, it's an involuntary status. And some examples that come to mind are status because of race or sex. Not much you can do about that. On the other hand, achieved status requires some effort, and there's a choice involved. For instance, a marriage partner, or the type of education, or, for that matter, the length of time in school. Well, these are choices, uh, achievements, and so they fall under the category of achieved status. So, that brings us to the status set. A status set is the combination of all statuses that an individual has. Me, for example. I'm a professor, but I'm also a husband and a father, and a son, since my mother is still living.

So, in each of these statuses I have certain behaviors that are expected because of the status. Okay, all of the behaviors are roles, I mean, a role is the behavior expected because of status. Okay, back to status set. All of the statuses—husband, father, son, professor—combine to form the status set, and each of the statuses have certain expectations. Let me use that professor status again. So, as a professor, I have a teaching role, and I have to prepare classes. That's expected. I also advise students, grade assignments, and evaluate my students. But this role has very different expectations. As a researcher, I, I have to design studies, raise funds for grants, and uh, then perform the research, and, and, finally, I write articles and reports. So, I think you see what I mean.

But, one more thing, and this is important, sometimes role conflict can occur. Let me say that again, *role conflict*. And that means that meeting the expectations for one role will cause problems for an individual who is trying to meet other expectations in a different role. Okay, let's say that one of my students is dating my daughter. I don't recommend this. But anyway, I may have role strain that could even develop into role conflict because it will be difficult for me to meet the expectations for my role as teacher and uh, when the student comes to my house, I'll have to remember my status as father and my role that requires me to welcome a guest into my home, and well, form an opinion about someone who wants to take my daughter out on a date. The textbook actually . . .

## ➤ Use abbreviations and symbols

Use abbreviations for important words and phrases that are repeated. There are two ways to do this. You can use capital letters that will remind you of the word or phrase. For example, in a lecture about Colonial America, you might use C A as an abbreviation for the phrase; in a lecture about the philosophy of John Dewey, you could use D as an abbreviation for the name. Or you can write the beginning of the word or phrase. For Colonial America, you could write Col Am; for John Dewey, J Dew. The abbreviation can be anything that will remind you of the word or phrase when you are reading your notes.

You should also use symbols and abbreviations for small words that are common in the language. The following list includes some of the most commonly used words in English. The abbreviations here are shortened forms for these frequently heard words.

| | |
|---|---|
| + | and |
| w/ | with |
| w/o | without |
| = | is, are, means, refers to, like, is called |
| Ø | different, not |
| # | number |
| X | example |
| → | results in, causes, produces, therefore |
| ← | comes from, derives from |
| ex | example |
| @ | about, approximately |
| 1, 2, 3 | first, second, third |
| < | less, smaller |
| > | more, larger |
| btw/ | between |
| ↑ | over, up |
| ↓ | under, down |

**Beyond the Book**
**Mini-Lesson for the TOEFL**
**Note Taking**

To view the lesson, visit the Barron's TOEFL site online. Click on **Academic Skills**, then click on **Mini-Lesson for Note Taking**.

## PRACTICAL STRATEGY

The abbreviations in the list printed above are part of my system for taking notes and some of my students use it, but I encourage you to create your own system because you will probably come up with symbols and abbreviations that will have meaning to you, and you will understand them later when you are reading your notes. There is space for additional words. Be sure to choose something that makes sense to you.

| *Symbol* | *Word* |
| --- | --- |
| | and |
| | with |
| | without |
| | is, are, means, refers to, like, is called |
| | different, not |
| | number |
| | times |
| | results in, causes, produces, therefore |
| | comes from, derives from |
| | example |
| | at |
| | first, second, third |
| | less, smaller |
| | more, larger |
| | between |

## PRACTICE ACTIVITY 19

Did you understand? Now practice taking notes with your system. First, listen to each of the sentences and write your notes here. When you are finished taking notes for all ten sentences, try to write the original sentences using only your notes. Then compare your sentences with the sentences printed in the Answer Key. An example is shown using my system. Your answer is correct if *you* can read it and if the meaning is the same as the original sentence. The words do not have to be exactly the same. Example answers are printed on page 286.

Listen to some sentences from college lectures. Take notes as quickly as you can.

 **Activity 19, Track 22**

### EXAMPLE

Friction between moving air and the ocean surface generates undulations of water called *waves.*

| Short: | Friction btw air + ocean surface → waves |
| --- | --- |
| Very short: | Fric btw air + Ø surf → waves |

Friction between air and the ocean surface causes *waves.*

1.

2.

3.

4.

5.

6.

7.

8.

9.

10.

## ➤ Draw relationships

To take notes, you can use symbols and diagrams. By using this system, you can reduce the number of words that you have to write. Here are some examples of notes for each of the common relationships.

### DEFINITION

Definitions are part of every academic subject because the vocabulary must be introduced in order to understand and learn new concepts. Definitions often appear in italic or bold print in textbooks. Many textbooks have a glossary of specialized vocabulary in the back of the book.

Professors often give new words special emphasis in their lectures by pausing after the word and before the definition or by stressing the word the first time it is introduced. Look at these examples of definitions and notice the diagrams that show the relationship between the word and the definition.

A *menu* is a list of computer functions that appears on the screen.
Menu = list /functions on screen

The *id* consists of instincts.
*Id* = instincts

### CLASSIFICATION

Classifications are also found in every subject. To classify means to organize into groups with similar characteristics. Look at these examples of classifications and notice how the diagrams show the relationship between the main category and the classification of types or kinds.

This chapter explores four highly specialized forms of fungus, which include molds, yeasts, lichens, and mycorrhizae.

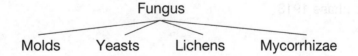

Two types of motivation have been identified by cognitive psychologists. *Intrinsic motivation* is based on internal factors, as for example curiosity or the challenge to succeed, whereas *extrinsic motivation* involves external incentives such as rewards or even punishments.

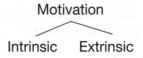

Sometimes this diagram is enough for you to remember other details, but a word or a brief phrase can help you recall a definition for each type.

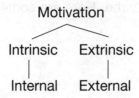

## SEQUENCE

Sequence is often found in narrations of historical events, in descriptions of research studies, and in directions for scientific experiments or processes.

The Roman Empire was built in three stages, which consisted of the conquest of Italy, the conflict with Carthage and expansion into the Western Mediterranean, and, finally, the domination of the Greek kingdoms and the Eastern Mediterranean.

Roman Empire

- Conquest Italy
- Conflict Carthage + expansion W Med
- Domination Greek + E Med

The history of Cubism falls into three phases—the Cezanne phase, which lasted only two years from 1907 to 1909, followed by the Analytical phase from 1910 to 1912, which, by the way, was the phase in which the most abstract purification of the form was realized, and finally, the Synthetic phase, beginning in 1913.

Cubism

- Cezanne phase 1907–9
- Analytical phase 1910–12
    abstract purification
- Synthetic phase 1913

## COMPARISON AND CONTRAST

Comparison and contrast identifies how two or more objects or ideas are the same or different. A side-by-side chart shows the relationships efficiently.

Cirrus clouds are the highest at altitudes between 17,000 and 50,000 feet, but they don't produce rain, in contrast with cumulonimbus clouds, which also penetrate the upper atmosphere, but cause lightning storms, rain, and tornadoes.

| Cirrus | Cumulonimbus |
| --- | --- |
| 17–50,000 ft | upper atmos |
| Ø rain | rain–lightning–tornadoes |

Although each person is responsible for one instrument in most sections of the orchestra, the members of the percussion section are required to play several instruments in one concert or even for one composition.

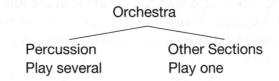

Orchestra

Percussion          Other Sections
Play several        Play one

## CAUSE AND EFFECT

Cause and effect or cause and result are found in research studies for all subjects, but the natural sciences contain many examples.

Mercantilism is an economic concept that assumes that the total volume of trade is unchangeable and, therefore, that trade causes conflict.

Mercantilism = total volume trade unchangeable
Trade → Conflict

When the temperatures on Earth dropped below the melting point of the rocks on the surface, the outer crust gradually solidified.

Temp Earth < melt pt rocks → crust solid

## PROBLEM AND SOLUTION

A problem and solution relationship is similar to a cause-and-effect relationship and can be represented by a similar drawing.

Because employees can begin to expect incentives simply for doing their jobs, and this can become a problem, it is better to reserve incentives for occasions that require exceptional effort.

Expect incentives/job → Reserve incentives/exceptional

The problem is that most populations of ginseng in Canada are too small to survive unless they are completely protected from harvesting by humans.

Ginseng survive → 0 human harvesting

## PRACTICAL STRATEGY

Sometimes it is faster to represent an idea with a symbol or a diagram than it is to write notes in words. This is especially true of relationships.

## PRACTICE ACTIVITY 20

Did you understand? Now practice drawing diagrams to represent relationships. First listen to each of the sentences from lectures on different topics. Then stop the audio and draw your diagram. Compare your drawings with the drawings in the Answer Key. The first one is completed to give you an example. Your answer is correct if it shows the same relationship as the drawings in the Answer Key, even if the diagram is not exactly the same. The answers are printed on pages 286–288.

### EXAMPLE

The nervous system is divided into two major parts: the central nervous system and the peripheral nervous system.

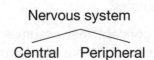

Listen to some sentences from college lectures. Take notes by drawing diagrams.

 **Activity 20, Track 23**

1.

2.

3.

4.

5.

6.

7.

8.

9.

10.

## ADVISOR'S OFFICE

This advice from Dr. Charles Swindell is framed on the wall of my office near my computer so that I can see it every day. I am happy to share it with you:

*The longer I live, the more I realize the impact of attitude on life. Attitude to me is more important than facts. It is more important than the past, than education, than money, than circumstances, than failures, than successes, than what other people think or say or do. It is more important than appearance, giftedness, or skill. The remarkable thing is, we have a choice every day regarding the attitude we embrace for that day. We cannot change our past. We cannot change the fact that people may act in a certain way. We cannot change the inevitable. The only thing we can do is play on the one string we have, and that is our attitude. I am convinced that life is 10 percent what happens to me and 90 percent how I react to it. And so it is with you. We are in charge of our attitudes.*

Henry Ford said it another way: *"If you think you can or you think you can't, you are probably right."*

# PARAPHRASING

Paraphrasing means using different words to express the same meaning. When you paraphrase, you express an idea that you have heard or read, but you say or write it in your own words. Because you are including all of the information when you paraphrase, the paraphrase is usually about the same length as the original. There are three problems that you will confront when you are paraphrasing.

1. **There is a natural tendency to repeat the same words instead of paraphrasing them.** This means that you need to listen and read for meaning instead of focusing on individual words and grammatical structures.
2. **Reference materials such as a thesaurus may not be used on the TOEFL.** This means that you have to know synonyms for words and phrases.
3. **Sometimes it is not possible to think of a paraphrase.** This means that you must learn how to give credit to sources when you use them in speaking or writing.

This chapter will help you improve your paraphrasing skills. You will learn how to

- **Choose synonyms for words and phrases**
- **Use alternative grammatical structures**
- **Cite expressions and ideas**

*How will these strategies help you on the TOEFL?*  By learning to paraphrase well, you will achieve a higher score on all four sections of the TOEFL. There are questions that require you to recognize or produce paraphrases on the Reading, Listening, Writing, and Speaking Sections. Paraphrasing is a very important academic skill for success in college or university classes as well. Using someone else's words is called *plagiarizing.* Plagiarizing is a very serious offense and can result in your being expelled from school.

## CHOOSE SYNONYMS FOR WORDS AND PHRASES

**Strategies to Use**
➤ Substitute multiple synonyms
➤ Use phrases
➤ Make an explanation

## ➤ Substitute multiple synonyms

When you use the strategy of substituting synonyms, you must substitute more than one word or phrase. An excellent paraphrase will also be expressed by a different grammatical structure. You will learn about using alternative structures later in this chapter.

### PRACTICAL STRATEGY

Paraphrases with synonyms must be restatements. Substituting only one vocabulary word in a sentence is not a restatement. It is so close to the original that it is not an acceptable paraphrase. Here is an example statement and an unacceptable paraphrase:

Original Statement:               The hardest woodwind instrument to learn is the oboe.

Unacceptable Paraphrase:     The *most difficult* woodwind instrument to learn is the oboe.

Why is the first paraphrase unacceptable? Did you notice that only one word was different from the original statement? Remember that substituting one synonym is not a restatement and not an acceptable paraphrase.

    Now look at an acceptable paraphrase:

Original Statement:               The hardest woodwind instrument to learn is the oboe.

Acceptable Paraphrase:         The *most difficult* woodwind instrument to *master* is the oboe.

Why is the second paraphrase acceptable? Did you notice that more than one synonym was different? The phrase *most difficult* was substituted for the word *hardest* and the word *master* was substituted for the word *learn*. But this paraphrase is still very close to the original sentence.

    This is an improvement in paraphrasing:

Original Statement:               The hardest woodwind instrument to learn is the oboe.

Excellent Paraphrase:          The oboe is the most difficult woodwind instrument to master.

Why is this paraphrase considered excellent? Like the acceptable paraphrase, more than one synonym was different. The phrase *most difficult* was substituted for the word *hardest* and the word *master* was substituted for the word *learn*. Did you also see how the structure of the sentence changed? The subject of the original statement was *the hardest woodwind instrument* and the complement was *the oboe.* In the excellent paraphrase, *the oboe* was the subject and *the hardest woodwind instrument* was the complement.

## PRACTICE ACTIVITY 21

Did you understand? Try to rewrite each sentence that you may see in a textbook by substituting synonyms for the underlined words and phrases. As you have learned, an excellent paraphrase will also change the structure of the sentence, but in this practice activity, let's begin by writing acceptable paraphrases. Substitute multiple synonyms. The first one is completed to give you an example. Your answer is correct if the words or phrases you use are synonyms for the underlined words or phrases and the meaning of the sentence is the same. The synonyms do not have to be the ones that are used in the Answer Key. Example answers are printed on page 288.

**EXAMPLE**

Original:     Thomas Edison was a very <u>curious</u> child, <u>performing</u> his first experiment when he was only three years old.

Paraphrase:   Thomas Edison was a very <u>inquisitive</u> child, <u>conducting</u> his first experiment <u>at the age of three</u>.

1. The copperhead, a snake that <u>strikes</u> without warning, is <u>considered</u> much more <u>dangerous</u> than the rattlesnake.

2. Because J. P. Morgan was known as a <u>reputable</u> and <u>prudent</u> businessman, he was able to <u>persuade</u> others to <u>remain</u> in the market even after the crash had <u>begun</u>.

3. Phosphorus is <u>used</u> in paint on highway signs and markers because it is <u>bright</u> <u>at night</u>.

4. Rain forests are <u>often</u> <u>located</u> <u>near</u> the equator.

5. By the <u>mid-nineteenth century</u>, land was so <u>expensive</u> in <u>large</u> cities that architects <u>began</u> to <u>conserve</u> space by <u>building</u> skyscrapers.

6. <u>Research</u> <u>studies</u> of vertebrates <u>show</u> <u>development</u> from a very <u>simple</u> heart in fish to a <u>complex</u> four-chamber heart in humans.

7. When two products are <u>fundamentally</u> <u>the same</u>, advertising can <u>influence</u> the <u>choice</u> that the public makes.

8. <u>As a whole</u>, in birds, the male of the species is <u>more brilliantly</u> colored.

9. The <u>price</u> of gold on the world market <u>is subject</u> to several <u>variables</u>, including but not <u>limited to</u> supply and demand.

10. The <u>idea</u> of a submarine is not <u>recent</u>, dating from the <u>1400s</u> when Drebbel and da Vinci <u>drew</u> <u>initial</u> sketches.

# ➤ Use phrases

There is a tendency to try to find one word to paraphrase, but phrases can be a useful alternative.

## PRACTICAL STRATEGY

The English language contains many phrasal verbs that express the same meaning as a one-word verb. In general, the phrasal verb is used for informal writing and speaking, and the one-word verb is used for more formal language. Some of the phrasal verbs that are common to academic language are listed here.

| | |
|---|---|
| Bring about | cause |
| Carry on | transact; continue |
| Carry out | complete; accomplish |
| Clear up | clarify |
| Come about | happen |
| Come across | find |
| Come by | find accidentally |
| Come out with | publish; produce |
| Come up with | create |
| Cut down on | reduce |
| Fall through | fail |
| Figure out | understand |
| Find out | discover |
| Give off | emit |
| Go after | follow |
| Go back | return |
| Go before | precede |
| Go down | decrease |
| Go on | continue; happen |
| Go over | review |
| Go through | experience; penetrate |
| Go up | increase |
| Keep on | continue |
| Keep up | remain current |
| Leave out | exclude; omit |
| Look for | seek |
| Look into | investigate |
| Look like | resemble |
| Look over | examine |
| Look up | locate information |
| Look up to | respect |
| Make out | understand with difficulty |
| Make up | invent; compose |
| Pick out | select |
| Point out | show; indicate |
| Put off | postpone |

| | |
|---|---|
| Put up with | tolerate |
| Rule out | eliminate |
| Run across | find accidentally |
| Run into | meet by accident |
| Set up | arrange |
| Show up | appear unexpectedly |
| Spell out | state in detail |
| Stand for | represent |
| Stick out | protrude |
| Take into account | consider |
| Take over | assume control |
| Take place | occur |
| Think through | reason |
| Throw away | discard |
| Touch on | mention briefly |
| Try out | test |
| Turn into | transform |
| Turn out | conclude |
| Turn up | discover |
| Wind up | finish |
| Work out | active |
| Write up | report |

## PRACTICE ACTIVITY 22

Did you understand? First read each sentence. Then try to say each sentence using a phrase instead of a one-word verb. The first one is completed to give you an example. Your answer is correct if the phrases that you use are synonyms for the underlined words and the meaning of the sentence is the same. The phrases do not have to be the ones that are used in the Answer Key. Spoken answers are recorded on Track 24 of the audio. Example answers are printed on pages 288–289.

### PHRASAL VERBS

#### EXAMPLE

Written:    A balance of international payment refers to the net result of the business that a nation <u>transacts</u> with other nations in a given period.

Spoken:    A balance of international payment refers to the net result of the business that a nation <u>carries on</u> with other nations in a given period.

**Activity 22, Track 24**

Listen to the example answers after you complete your answers.

1. Because light travels faster than sound, lightning appears to <u>precede</u> thunder.

2. Congress <u>respected</u> Jefferson because of his intelligence and creativity.

3. The lower teeth in crocodiles <u>protrude</u> when their mouths are closed.

4. Some sponges <u>resemble</u> plants.

5. The first census was <u>accomplished</u> in Great Britain in 1801.

6. People who have <u>experienced</u> a traumatic event may have recurring images of it.

7. In algebra, letters and other symbols <u>represent</u> numbers.

8. During periods of stress or excitement, the heart rate <u>increases</u> and airways to the lungs become dilated.

9. Theories of prehistory and early humans are constantly changing as we <u>consider</u> the new evidence from archeological finds.

10. Dreams may have been the inspiration for the Surrealists to <u>create</u> their works of art.

## ➤ Make an explanation

Sometimes even native speakers cannot retrieve a word from memory when they are paraphrasing, especially when they are speaking. When this happens to you, there are several ways to compensate for the word that has slipped your mind. Make an explanation.

### PRACTICAL STRATEGY

If it is an adjective, you can use an opposite adjective with the word *not*. For example, if a synonym for the adjective *large* slips your mind, you can say, *not small. The sum was not small.* If it is a verb, you can use a general verb instead of a specific synonym. For example, if you forget the synonym for the verb *rely on*, you can say, *use*, which is a very general verb that includes many meanings. Early traders *used* barter instead of money to exchange goods. If it is a noun, you can describe the noun with a descriptive phrase or clause. For example, if you forget the synonym for the noun *farmer* or if the word *farmer* slips your mind, you can describe it by saying, *the person who engages in agriculture.*

These compensatory strategies are used to get out of a problem when you are speaking. They should be used as a last resort instead of stopping when you are speaking.

## PRACTICE ACTIVITY 23

Did you understand? Try to restate each sentence that you may see in a textbook by explaining the meaning instead of substituting a synonym for the underlined word. The first one is completed to give you an example. Spoken answers are recorded on Track 25 of the audio. Example answers are printed on page 289.

### EXAMPLE

The Constitution guarantees that private homes will not be searched without a warrant. The Constitution guarantees that private homes will not be searched without written authorization.

 **Activity 23, Track 25**

Listen to the example answers after you complete your answers.

### ADJECTIVES

Use an opposite.

### EXAMPLE

The second movement of a symphony is usually slow.
The second movement of a symphony is usually not fast.

1.   The temperature in many desert regions is cold at night.

2.   Facial expressions may be common across cultures.

3.   Obsidian is shiny because it cools too quickly for crystals to form.

4.   Few musical instruments play louder than 100 decibels or softer than 20 decibels.

5.   The people who have adapted to life at very high altitudes are usually short.

### NOUNS

Use a phrase.

### EXAMPLE

Skyscrapers are representative of the International Style of architecture.
Tall buildings are representative of the International Style of architecture.

1.   In many cities, vendors must have a license to set up their booths in public places.

2.   Studies show that small pets are a positive influence in elderly people's lives.

3.   Staircases were an important feature of the palaces constructed during the Baroque period.

4.  Global wind patterns are affected by the <u>Earth's rotation</u>.

5.  <u>Bilingual education</u> is more common in regions where language minorities live.

## VERBS

Use a general verb.

### EXAMPLE

Many managers <u>employ</u> teams to accomplish complex goals.
Many managers <u>use</u> teams to accomplish complex goals.

1.  Unlike cast iron, pure wrought iron <u>contains</u> no carbon.

2.  Hypnosis <u>achieves</u> a heightened state of suggestibility in a willing participant.

3.  Productivity increases when fewer employees are required to <u>accomplish</u> the work.

4.  Normally, the plasma in human blood <u>constitutes</u> 50–60 percent of the total blood volume.

5.  Three-fourths of the goods <u>manufactured</u> in Canada for export are sold to the United States.

## USE ALTERNATIVE GRAMMATICAL STRUCTURES

> **Strategies to Use**
> ➤ Produce restatements
> ➤ Read and listen for meaning
> ➤ Edit problem paraphrases

## ➤ Produce restatements

Learning to identify possibilities for alternative structures will improve your paraphrasing skills. A restatement with an alternative structure is not a paraphrase because it uses too many of the same words and phrases. Later in this chapter, you will use restatements with synonyms to produce paraphrases.

### PRACTICAL STRATEGY

Study the examples of restatements in each of the categories below. Learn to make restatements using alternative structures. When you can use both synonyms and alternative structures, you will be able to paraphrase appropriately. For now, focus on alternative structures.

| Chronology | before/after/during |
| Coordination | not only-but also/neither-nor/not-but/both-and/as well as |
| Cause | because/because of/since/as a result |
| Comparison | similar/like/the same/differ/different/more/less |
| Concession | although/even though/despite/in spite of/but/whereas |
| Negatives | not + un-/not once/not one/very rarely/very seldom |
| Passives | BE + past participle |

## CHRONOLOGY

Original:    After the Missouri Compromise was abandoned by Congress, the Republican Party was formed in 1854, partly in opposition to the spread of slavery in the United States.

Restatement:    Before the Republican Party was formed in 1854, in part to oppose the spread of slavery in the United States, the Missouri Compromise had already been abandoned by Congress.

## COORDINATION

Original:    Byzantine art consisted not only of oriental style but also of Greek ideas that maintained its popularity for more than eleven centuries.

Restatement:    Popular for more than eleven hundred years, Byzantine art consisted of both oriental style and Greek ideas.

## CAUSE

Original:    In the classic experiment in operant conditioning, Pavlov's dog salivated when he heard a bell because he associated the sound with food.

Restatement:    Since Pavlov's dog associated the sound of a bell with being fed, he salivated when he heard it in the classic experiment in operant conditioning.

## COMPARISON

Original:    As a conductor of heat and electricity, aluminum exceeds all metals except silver, copper, and gold.

Restatement:    Silver, copper, and gold are better conductors of heat and electricity than aluminum is.

## CONCESSION

Original:               Despite the great differences in size, shape, and function, all human cells have the same forty-six chromosomes.

Restatement:            Although the forty-six chromosomes are the same in all human cells, there are differences in the size, shape, and function.

## NEGATIVE

Original:               It is not illegal in some cultures to be married to more than one woman at the same time, but the monogamous relationship is the most common.

Restatement:            In some cultures, it is legal to be married to several women at once, but it is more common to be married to just one woman.

## PASSIVE

Original:               The explosive properties of nitroglycerin, later one of the components of dynamite, were discovered by Ascanio Sobrero, an Italian chemistry professor.

Restatement:            Italian chemistry professor Ascanio Sobrero discovered that nitroglycerin, later used in the production of dynamite, had explosive properties.

## PRACTICE ACTIVITY 24

Did you understand? Try to restate each sentence that you may see in a textbook by writing an alternative grammatical structure. Make changes to the grammar but do not make changes in the meaning of the sentence. The first one for each structure is completed to give you an example. Example answers are printed on pages 289–290.

## CHRONOLOGY

### EXAMPLE

Chronology:             After the death of Queen Mary in 1558, her half-sister Elizabeth ascended the throne of England.

Chronology
Restatement:            Before Elizabeth ascended the throne of England in 1558, her half-sister Mary ruled.

1. Not until the Triassic Period did the first primitive mammals appear.

2. Glass became a major construction material during the late Middle Ages.

3. Helium replaced hydrogen as a power source for dirigibles because it was safer.

4. The Moriori people settled the Chatham Islands off the coast of New Zealand long before the Europeans arrived in 1791.

5. Always rinse your test tubes and pipettes with a small amount of distilled water before you store them in the lab cabinets.

## COORDINATION

### EXAMPLE

Coordination:       Before the introduction of the musical staff, composers preserved their work not only by writing it down but also by teaching it to a younger musician.

Coordination
Restatement:       Before the introduction of the musical staff, composers preserved their work by teaching it to a younger musician, as well as by writing it down in a book.

1. Both genes and viruses are made of essential chemicals called nucleoproteins.

2. Successful managers neither proceed without a plan nor ignore opportunities that arise.

3. Technically, not only glass but also water is considered a mineral.

4. Neither corn nor winter wheat is native to the Americas.

5. Ethnicity is usually based on race and religion as well as national origin.

## CAUSE

### EXAMPLE

Cause:       The diesel engine that runs on oil is more efficient than most other engines because it converts more of the useful energy stored in the fuel.

Cause
Restatement:       The diesel engine runs more efficiently than most other engines because of the oil that converts more useful energy.

1. Psychologists suggest that incentives cause workers to increase productivity.

2. Because many flakes have been found in excavations of Stone Age settlements, anthropologists conclude that they were used as tools for cutting and scraping.

3. Too much water can cause plants to turn brown on the edges.

4. Blood pressure can become elevated as a result of increased salt consumption.

5. Since the interstate highway system linking roads across the country was built in the 1930s, most of the roads in the system need to be repaired.

## COMPARISON

### EXAMPLE

Comparison:              Although they are smaller in size, for the most part, chipmunks are like most other ground squirrels.

Comparison
Restatement:              Chipmunks are mostly like other ground squirrels except for their smaller size.

1. Viruses and the first life forms that appeared on Earth millions of years ago have a similar structure.

2. The lungs have a higher oxygen concentration than the blood does.

3. The Indian Ocean is smaller but deeper than the Atlantic Ocean.

4. Picasso's work was not the same during various artistic periods.

5. The difference in the gravitational attraction of various places on the Earth's surface is the reason that the weight of objects is not the same.

## CONCESSION

### EXAMPLE

Concession:              Although oil paint tends to yellow with age, tempera colors retain their vibrancy for centuries.

Concession
Restatement:              Oil paint tends to yellow with age, but tempera colors retain their vibrancy for centuries.

1. Whereas insulin levels are close to or above normal in type 2 diabetes, target cells cannot respond adequately.

2. Although the idea of an English language academy is regularly proposed, the response has never been very positive.

3. Even though the Jovian planets are grouped together, each one has had a very different evolutionary history.

4. Despite the advantage that young people enjoy for recall in vocabulary studies, older people appear to be better at word recognition.

5. In spite of the fact that interviews are the most common strategy for assessing job applicants, they tend to have low validity.

## NEGATIVE

### EXAMPLE

Negative:            The addiction to gambling is not unlike the addiction to substances.

Affirmative
Restatement:        The addiction to gambling is like the addiction to substances.

1. Not once has the geyser known as Old Faithful failed to erupt on time.

2. Nonstandard dialects are not used as educational models in schools.

3. Never has there been such wide access to news from so many media.

4. The construction of a city on the ruins of a previous settlement is not uncommon.

5. Not until the Triassic Period did the first primitive mammals develop.

## PASSIVE

### EXAMPLE

Active statement:    Seagulls need either fresh or salt water for them to survive.

Passive
Restatement:        Either fresh or salt water is needed by seagulls for them to survive.

1. It is interesting that people over the age of sixty-five experience fewer mental health disorders.

2. In the stringed instruments, a bow produces the tones when it is played across a set of strings made of wire or gut.

3. High-frequency radiation from the Sun and other sources partly ionize gases in the ionosphere.

4. Architects can use a domed roof to conserve floor space.

5. The Egyptians used papyrus to make paper, sails, baskets, and clothing.

## ➤ Read and listen for meaning

When you read or listen for meaning, you learn to think about the ideas that the writer or speaker is communicating, not the individual words or grammar used.

### PRACTICAL STRATEGY

Practice reading and listening for meaning. By focusing on sentences or even paragraphs, you will train your mind to make connections and comprehend the ideas instead of trying to understand word by word. The important question is this: What does the author or the lecturer mean? What ideas are being expressed?

### PRACTICE ACTIVITY 25

Did you understand? Try to identify the sentences that express the same idea. The first one is completed to give you an example. Example answers are printed on page 291.

### EXAMPLE

What does the professor mean by the following statement:

Poet and humorist Ogden Nash tried but failed to adapt himself to the academic, and later, the business world.

&#9398; He was a better businessman than he was a teacher.
&#9899; He did not succeed in either teaching or business.
&#9400; He tried teaching before he finally succeeded in business.
&#9401; He made no effort to succeed in teaching and business.

1. What does the professor mean by the following statement:

After hitting a bar several times with similar results, an animal learns that it can get food by pressing the bar.

&#9398; An animal is able to press the bar more after it is fed three or four times.
&#9399; Three or four animals are used in the experiment with similar results.
&#9400; There are several trials by an animal before the food is released.
&#9401; An animal learns how to get food by hitting a bar.

2. What does the professor mean by the following statement:

Although he wrote many short stories, it was a poem, "The Raven," that brought Poe his greatest recognition as a writer.

&#9398; Poe is remembered more for a poem than for his short stories.
&#9399; "The Raven" is less well-known than Poe's short stories.
&#9400; Poe is famous for writing both short stories and poetry.
&#9401; Poe wrote more short stories than poems during his career.

3.  What does the professor mean by the following statement:

It was an atom that contained in the form of pure energy the fundamental components of the entire universe.

Ⓐ  The universe was made up of many atoms of pure energy.
Ⓑ  The effect of a pure atom in the universe was to produce energy.
Ⓒ  Everything in the universe was reduced to pure energy in one atom.
Ⓓ  The energy in the universe was stored in pure atoms.

4.  What does the professor mean by the following statement:

Although a bear does not eat during the winter, sustaining itself on body fat, its temperature remains almost normal, and it breathes regularly.

Ⓐ  When a bear survives on body fat instead of eating, its temperature and respiration are reduced.
Ⓑ  Not eating during the winter does not affect the bear's breathing, but it does affect its temperature.
Ⓒ  During the winter, the bear's temperature is normal and its respiration is regular, but it does not require food.
Ⓓ  The bear's diet of fat during the winter does not affect its temperature or respiration.

5.  What does the professor mean by the following statement:

It is generally true that as long as the CEO maintains the confidence of the board of directors, they will not intervene to dictate specific policies.

Ⓐ  Policies are dictated by the board with the approval of the CEO.
Ⓑ  The board will assume control only if they lose confidence in the CEO.
Ⓒ  The confidence of the CEO is important to decisions that the board makes.
Ⓓ  The intervention by the CEO in board policies does not occur often.

6.  What does the professor mean by the following statement:

Temperature variations cause pressure differences in the air.

Ⓐ  Fluctuations in the air pressure are a result of changes in temperature.
Ⓑ  Changes in the air pressure and temperature vary at different times.
Ⓒ  The temperature is usually different from the air pressure.
Ⓓ  Changeable temperatures are caused by reversals in the wind.

7.  What does the professor mean by the following statement:

To maintain a healthy body weight, an animal must balance energy intake with energy output, largely by metabolic activity and regular physical exertion.

Ⓐ  Metabolism regulates activity and exercise reduces body weight for a healthy lifestyle.
Ⓑ  A healthy lifestyle includes exercise in order to control weight gain that is caused by the metabolism.
Ⓒ  Metabolism and exercise are ways to stabilize consumption and production of energy for a healthy weight.
Ⓓ  Animals generally balance their metabolisms by healthy eating and exercise, which also controls their weight.

8. What does the professor mean by the following statement:

An example of children's literature that supports the natural inclination to play with language is the *nursery rhyme.*

Ⓐ The nursery rhyme is a good example of children's literature because it is fun.

Ⓑ Children like nursery rhymes because they enjoy them during playtime.

Ⓒ Children's literature is written in language that the child can understand.

Ⓓ The child's interest in playing with language is encouraged by the nursery rhyme.

9. What does the professor mean by the following statement:

For employees whose jobs involve sitting at a computer terminal entering data or typing reports, the location of the computer relative to the company is of no consequence.

Ⓐ Employees who work at their computers like to choose their locations.

Ⓑ It does not matter where employees work at their computers.

Ⓒ The location of their computers should be comfortable to employees.

Ⓓ Computer terminals must be located near each other in a company.

10. What does the professor mean by the following statement:

Ireland was first settled around 7500 B.C. by hunting tribes from Scotland, followed by people from the Mediterranean know as the Firbolgs.

Ⓐ The Firbolgs arrived in Ireland from the Mediterranean after the Scottish people had already settled there.

Ⓑ Irish tribes went to Scotland and then followed a hunting route all the way to the Mediterranean area called Firbolgs.

Ⓒ The Irish and Scottish people explored Europe, reaching as far as the Mediterranean where they settled.

Ⓓ Looking for a place to live, the Firbolgs went to Scotland and then to Ireland where they finally settled.

## ➤ Edit problem paraphrases

Here are some problems that you can learn to avoid:

- Don't change the meaning
- Don't leave out important information
- Don't use too much of the original wording
- Don't copy the original

Original Sentence:

Sometimes students plagiarize material from lectures and reading passages because they don't understand how to make the appropriate changes for an excellent paraphrase.

## DON'T CHANGE THE MEANING

This is not an excellent paraphrase because the meaning has been changed from the original:

> On occasion, students use paraphrases of excellent lectures and reading passages without understanding the purpose of the changes that they have made in them.

## DON'T LEAVE OUT IMPORTANT INFORMATION

This is not an excellent paraphrase because it does not include all of the important information in the original:

> On occasion, students use lecture and reading material verbatim.

## DON'T USE TOO MUCH OF THE ORIGINAL WORDING

This is not an excellent paraphrase because it looks and sounds too much like the original:

> On occasion, students plagiarize material from lectures and reading passages because they don't comprehend how to make the necessary changes for an excellent paraphrase.

## DON'T COPY THE ORIGINAL

This is not an excellent paraphrase because it is an exact copy of the original.

> Sometimes students plagiarize material from lectures and reading passages because they don't understand how to make the appropriate changes for an excellent paraphrase.

## PRACTICE ACTIVITY 26

Did you understand? Try to find the problem in each paraphrase and edit it. The first one is completed to give you an example. Example answers are printed on pages 291–292.

### EXAMPLE

| | |
|---|---|
| Original: | Tides are caused by the gravitational pull of both the Sun and the Moon. |
| Paraphrase: | Tides are produced by the gravitational pull of both the Sun and the Moon. |
| Problem: | The paraphrase is too much like the original. Only one word was changed. |
| Edited Paraphrase: | The combined gravitational effects of the Sun and Moon produce tides on Earth. |

Why is this better? Because synonyms have been substituted and an alternative grammatical structure has been used, but the meaning has not changed.

1. Original:      Proteins are molecules that regulate the movement of materials across cell walls.

   Paraphrase:   Molecules that regulate the movement of materials across cell walls are proteins.

2. Original:      The invention of the steam engine played a major role in the Industrial Revolution because it caused the factory system to extend itself to many areas of production apart from the cotton industry.

   Paraphrase:    The invention of the steam engine was a primary influence in the Industrial Revolution.

3. Original:      Although big companies are trying to maintain a balance between traditional advertising and some of the newer alternatives like blogging, it is often the smaller entrepreneurs who are using bloggers as an efficient way to stack their competition.

   Paraphrase:    Big companies are using bloggers to defeat their smaller rivals.

4. Original:      Fossils of bones have the appearance of stone, but the holes and pores are actually infused with mineral deposits from the surrounding sediments.

   Paraphrase:    Fossils of bones look like stone, but there are mineral deposits from the surrounding sediments in the holes and pores.

5. Original:      Pictograms found in many parts of the world about 1500 B.C. constitute the earliest system of writing, although written symbols have been discovered that date from as early as 3500 B.C.

   Paraphrase:    Pictograms found in various parts of the world are the earliest evidence of a written system despite the discovery of written symbols.

6. Original:      The modern atmosphere is probably the fourth atmosphere in the history of the Earth.

   Paraphrase:    The modern atmosphere is probably the fourth atmosphere in the history of the Earth.

7. Original:      Whereas alcohol is a depressant, coffee is a stimulant.
   Paraphrase:    Alcohol is not like coffee.

8. Original:      The Pacific Basin, which includes the continent of Australia and the thousands of islands grouped together as Oceania, covers one-third of the surface of the Earth.

   Paraphrase:    The Pacific Basin is also called Oceania because it encompasses one-third of the Pacific Ocean.

9. Original:      In fresco painting, the pigments may be mixed with water and applied to the plaster before it dries so that the lime in the plaster fuses with the pigments on the surface.

   Paraphrase:    The lime in wet plaster bonds with the pigments on the surface when the colors are mixed.

10. Original:     As Linnaeus originally conceived the biological classification chart, he segregated all living creatures solely according to their degree of physical similarity.

    Paraphrase:   Linnaeus originally created the biological classification chart by categorizing all living creatures according to their degree of physical similarity.

# CITE EXPRESSIONS AND IDEAS

**Strategies to Use**
➤ Introduce the source before quoting
➤ Mark quotations in writing and in speaking
➤ Use strong verbs to report ideas
➤ Mention the source appropriately

## ➤ Introduce the source before quoting

It is important to cite the expressions and ideas of others. To cite means to give credit to the source. This is especially true when the idea is a definition, an opinion, a unique expression, or research data that is not common knowledge.

### PRACTICAL STRATEGY

There are several phrases and clauses that can be used to introduce the source of your ideas. Let's say that Professor Thompson makes the following statement in a lecture: "The shift from manufacturing to service has resulted in lower paying jobs and a decline in the strength of labor unions." You may want to quote this opinion. If you do, the words in the quotation must be exactly the same as those in the original. Here are five ways to introduce the source before the quotation.

*According to Professor Thompson,* "The shift from manufacturing to service has resulted in lower paying jobs and a decline in the strength of labor unions."

*In the words of Professor Thompson,* "The shift from manufacturing to service has resulted in lower paying jobs and a decline in the strength of labor unions."

*To quote Professor Thompson,* "The shift from manufacturing to service has resulted in lower paying jobs and a decline in the strength of labor unions."

*As Professor Thompson puts it,* "The shift from manufacturing to service has resulted in lower paying jobs and a decline in the strength of labor unions."

*Professor Thompson said,* "The shift from manufacturing to service has resulted in lower paying jobs and a decline in the strength of labor unions."

On the TOEFL examination, sometimes the professor is not named. In that case, you can still introduce your source by changing the introductions slightly:

According to the professor,
In the words of the professor,
To quote the professor,
As the professor puts it,
The professor said,

## PRACTICE ACTIVITY 27

Did you understand? Try to quote each sentence that you hear in a lecture by an unnamed professor. Be sure to use one of the introductory phrases or clauses before you begin your quotation. The first one is completed to give you an example. Your answer is correct if you write any of the introductions and if the words in your quotations are exactly the same as those of the professor. Example answers are printed on page 293.

### EXAMPLE

"Communicating is the act of transmitting information."

> According to the professor, "Communicating is the act of transmitting information."

Also correct:

> In the words of the professor, "Communicating is the act of transmitting information."

> To quote the professor, "Communicating is the act of transmitting information."

> As the professor puts it, "Communicating is the act of transmitting information."

> The professor said, "Communicating is the act of transmitting information."

1. A stock is equity in a company, and, therefore, it represents ownership.

2. The desalination of the ocean is going to be a crucial aspect of water management.

3. The theme of a worldwide flood is found in the mythology of many cultures.

4. Psychology focuses on the individual, whereas sociology focuses on social groups.

5. The ethics of science will become more important in this decade.

6. I call my idea the simplification principle.

7. The three-domain system is superior to the five-domain system of classification in biology.

8. The term *relief* describes any printing method with a raised image.

9. Training programs must address the issue of technology in the workplace.

10. Quasars are difficult to study because they are so far away.

## ➤ Mark quotations in writing and in speaking

Quotation marks are used before and after the words that you are quoting. This is easy to see when you are quoting in the written language. But when you are quoting in the spoken language, you need to *hear* the quotation marks. Words and phrases must be used to mark quotations in speaking.

## PRACTICAL STRATEGY

There are several phrases and clauses that can be used to mark quotations. Let's say that Professor Smith makes the following statement in a lecture: "Additives are chemicals that manufacturers add to food and other products." You may want to quote this definition. If you use the quotation in writing, you must use quotation marks before and after the words that you are quoting. If you use the quotation in speaking, you must use words and phrases in place of the quotation marks. The words in the quotation must be exactly the same as those in the original. Here are several ways to mark the beginning and ending of a quotation in speaking:

According to Professor Smith, *and I am quoting here,* "Additives are chemicals that manufacturers add to food and other products." *End quote.*

According to Professor Smith, *and I quote,* "Additives are chemicals that manufacturers add to food and other products." *End quote.*

*To quote* Professor Smith, "Additives are chemicals that manufacturers add to food and other products." *End quote.*

## PRACTICE ACTIVITY 28

Did you understand? Try to quote each sentence. First, put the quotation marks around the written quote. Be sure to put them above the line, not on the line. Then use verbal quotation marks for a spoken quote. The first one is completed to give you an example. Your answer is correct if you use any of the verbal quotation marks and if the words in your quotation are exactly the same as those of the source. Spoken answers are recorded on Track 26 of the audio. Example answers are printed on pages 293–294.

### EXAMPLE

A mirage is an optical illusion in the atmosphere.

Written quote:    According to Professor Brown, "A mirage is an optical illusion in the atmosphere."

Spoken quotes:    According to Professor Brown, *and I quote,* "A mirage is an optical illusion in the atmosphere." *End quote.*

According to Professor Brown, *and I am quoting here,* "A mirage is an optical illusion in the atmosphere." *End quote.*

*To quote* Professor Brown, "A mirage is an optical illusion in the atmosphere." *End quote.*

**Activity 28, Track 26**

Listen to the example answers after you complete your answers.

1. According to a study by Professor Carter, patients can lower their blood pressure by losing weight and decreasing their intake of salt.

2. According to Professor Jones, over fourteen billion euros were introduced into the world economy in January 2002.

3. To quote a study in the *Journal of Psychology*, many people who have achieved their career ambitions by midlife are afflicted by depression.

4. According to the textbook, an organ is a group of tissues capable of performing some special function.

5. According to Professor Stephens, John Philip Sousa was the greatest composer of marches for bands.

6. In Professor Davison's opinion, Ben Johnson may be the author of several plays attributed to William Shakespeare.

7. Professor Davis said that statistical data can be very difficult to interpret because correlations are not causes.

8. As Professor Gray puts it, the prime minister serves at the pleasure of the parliament.

9. According to the reading passage, moving water is the single most important factor in determining the surface features of the Earth.

10. In Professor Russell's opinion, the most important quality for a scientist is the ability to make careful observations.

## ➤ Use strong verbs to report ideas

### PRACTICAL STRATEGY

Sometimes you will want to refer to the ideas and research of others without using a direct quotation. When the ideas are specific to an author or researcher, it is still necessary to cite the source. Choose verbs that report the idea and convey the meaning that you wish to attach to the idea. You may choose verbs that express doubt, neutrality, or certainty.

**Beyond the Book
Mini-Lesson for the TOEFL
Paraphrasing**

To view the lesson, visit the Barron's TOEFL site online. Click on **Academic Skills**, then click on **Mini-Lesson for Paraphrasing**.

| Doubtful | Neutral | Certain |
|----------|---------|---------|
| Allege | Explain | Argue |
| Assume | Indicate | Assert |
| Believe | Illustrate | Conclude |
| Claim | Mention | Confirm |
| Imply | Note | Contend |
| Predict | Observe | Demonstrate |
| Propose | Point out | Discover |
| Suggest | Report | Find |
| Suppose | Say | Insist |
| Suspect | Show | Maintain |
| Think | State | Verify |

## PRACTICE ACTIVITY 29

Did you understand? Try to report each quotation. Choose a verb to express doubt, neutrality, or certainty. The first one is completed to give you an example. Your answer is correct if you use any of the verbs listed under the correct heading—doubtful, neutral, certain. Notice that both verbs in reported language are in the past tense. Example answers are printed on page 294.

### EXAMPLE

Quotation:        Psychologist Carl Rogers said, "Negative feedback causes people to develop a poor self-concept."

Certain Report:   Carl Rogers <u>argued</u> that negative feedback <u>caused</u> people to develop a poor self-concept.

Also Correct:     Carl Rogers <u>maintained</u> that negative feedback <u>caused</u> people to develop a poor self-concept.

1. Sociologist Lee Clark said, "When danger arises, the rule is for people to help those next to them before they help themselves." "Panic: Myth or Reality," *Contexts I* (Fall 2002), p. 21.
   Neutral report:

2. Biological anthropologist Barry Bogin said, "We can use the average height of any group of people as a barometer of the health of their society." "The Tall and Short of It," *Applying Anthropology: An Introductory Reader,* Mountain View, California: Mayfield Publishing Company, 2001, p. 54.
   Doubtful report:

3. Physician Stanley Joel Reiser said, "Machines direct the attention of both doctor and patient to the measurable aspect of illness, but away from the human factors that are at least equally important." *Medicine and the Reign of Technology,* New York: Cambridge University Press, 1978, p. 229.
   Certain report:

4. Educator Harry Wong said, "There is but one correlation with success, and that is attitude." *The First Days of School: How to Be an Effective Teacher,* Sunnyvale, California: Harry K. Wong Publications, 1991, p. 35.
   Certain report:

5. Choreographer Martha Graham said, "Technique and training have never been a substitute for that condition of awareness which is talent." *Dance as a Theatre Art,* Hightstown, New Jersey: Princeton Book Company, 1974, p. 136.
   Doubtful report:

6. Psychologist Carl Jung said, "The collective unconscious seems to be something like an unceasing stream or perhaps an ocean of images and figures which drift into consciousness in our dreams." "The Basic Postulates of Analytical Psychology," *Modern Man in Search of a Soul,* Routledge and Kegan Paul, 1933.
   Doubtful report:

7. Computer entrepreneur Bill Gates said, "The key for Microsoft™ has always been hiring very smart people." Transcript of video history interview, National Museum of American History, January 11, 2005.
   Neutral report:

8. Geneticists James Watson and Francis Crick said, "DNA structure has two helical chains each coiled around the same axis." "A Structure for Deoxyribose Nucleic Acid," *Nature,* Volume 171 (April 2), 1953, p. 737.
   Doubtful report:

9. Environmentalist John Sinclair said, "Many politicians are hostile to the environmental movement because they see it in conflict with the economic model they support." "The Legacy of Voluntary Conservationists." 1998 Romeo Lahey Lecture for the National Parks Association of Queensland, Australia.
Neutral report:


10. Astrophysicist Carl Sagan said, "Even a relatively small nuclear war may be capable of producing a global climatic catastrophe." Speech before the Commonwealth Club, February 8, 1985.
Certain report:


## ➤ Mention the source appropriately

You already know how to introduce a source, but sometimes you need to mention the source more than one time. In that case, there is a pattern that is customarily used to mention the source appropriately.


### Practical Strategy

When you cite the source the first time, use the first and last name. The title is optional. When you cite the second time, use the last name only. If you cite a third time, use a pronoun, for example, *he* or *she.* After the third citation, you may use the pronoun again if the meaning is clear, or you may repeat the last name for clarity.

In the case of speakers or writers who are not named, the source should still be cited. You may be able to identify and cite the source as a professor, a speaker, an author, a writer, or a student, based on the context in which the information is presented. Use this general description the first time that you cite the source. If it is clear that the person is a man or woman, you can use the correct pronoun when you cite the source a second or third time. After the third citation, you may use the pronoun again if the meaning is clear, or you may repeat the general description for clarity.


### Practice Activity 30

Did you understand? Try to report the information in the notes. Cite the source appropriately. The first report is completed to give you an example. Spoken answers are recorded on Track 27 of the audio. Example answers are printed on pages 294–295.


### Example

Source: Edwin Hubble (man) astronomer

- demonstrated Andromeda nebula located outside our galaxy
- established the islands universe theory = galaxies exist outside our own
- study resulted in Hubble's constant = standard relationship/galaxy's distance from Earth and speed recession

Astronomer <u>Edwin Hubble</u> demonstrated that the Andromeda nebula was located outside our galaxy. <u>Hubble</u> established the islands universe theory, which states that galaxies exist outside our own. <u>He</u> published a study that resulted in what is now called Hubble's constant, a standard relationship between a galaxy's distance from Earth and its speed of recession.

**Activity 30, Track 27**

Listen to the example answers after you complete your answers.

1. Source: Theodore White (man)
   Book—*The Making of the President*

   - 1960 presidential debate—press conference
   - Nixon proceeded—personal debate
   - Kennedy spoke directly to TV viewers
   - estimated Kennedy gained 2 mil votes

2. Source: Paul Cezanne (man)

   - all forms in nature—based on geometric shapes
   - cone, sphere, cylinder primary
   - used outlining to emphasize shapes

3. Source: Marie Curie (woman)

   - won Nobel p physics 1903 w/husband—discovery of radium
   - won Nobel p chemistry 1911—isolation pure radium
   - 1st person 2 Nobel p

4. Source: Erik Erikson (man) psychologist

   - proposed eight stages/personal development
   - psychological crises/each stage shaped sense/self
   - lifelong process

5. Source: Margaret Mead (woman)

   - first fieldwork in Samoa 1925
   - book *Coming of Age in Samoa* best seller—translated many languages
   - still one/most well-known anthropologists
   - people/simple societies provide valuable lessons/industrialized

6. Source: Leonardo da Vinci (man)

   - quintessential Renaissance man
   - brilliant painter
   - interested in mechanics
   - work in math clear in perspective

7.  Source: Peter Drucker (man) author
    - *Management Challenges for the 21st Century*
    - five transforming forces
    - trends have major implications for long-term strategies of companies

8.  Source: Friedrich Mohs (man)

    - devised hardness scale/10 minerals
    - assigned 10 to diamond—hardest known
    - lesser values other min
    - scale still useful/relative hardness

9.  Source: Maria Montessori (woman)

    - proposed educational model
    - not transmission knowledge
    - free to develop
    - success child working independently

10. Source: Jane Goodall (woman)

    - collaboration Louis Leakey
    - years living w/chimpanzees—Gombe Reserve
    - imitated behaviors
    - discovered chimp complex social organization
    - first document chimp making/using tools
    - also identified 20 different sounds/communication

---

### ADVISOR'S OFFICE

Do you talk to yourself? Of course you do. Maybe not aloud, but all of us have mental conversations with ourselves. So the question is *how* do you talk to yourself?

| *Negative Talk* | *Positive Talk* |
|---|---|
| I can't study all of this. | I am studying every day. |
| My English is poor. | My English is improving. |
| I won't get a good score. | I will do my best. |
| If I fail, I will be so ashamed. | If I need a higher score, I can try again. |

How would you talk to good friends to encourage and support them? Be a good friend to yourself. When negative talk comes to mind, substitute positive talk. Encourage yourself to learn from mistakes.

# SUMMARIZING

Summarizing is related to paraphrasing because you are using your own words to express an idea that you have heard or read. Remember that when you paraphrase, you are including all of the information, but when you summarize, you are including only the main ideas. A paraphrase is about the same length as the original, but a summary is shorter than the original. There are three problems that you will confront when you are summarizing.

1. **A summary does not include everything in the original.** This means that you should not try to write too much.
2. **Details and examples that support the main points are usually not included in a summary.** This means that you have to be able to discriminate between the main points and the details or examples.
3. **The author's point of view must be maintained.** This means that you cannot express your opinion when you report the information.

This chapter will help you improve your summarizing skills. You will learn how to

- **Condense the ideas**
- **Identify the main points**
- **Report the information**

*How will these strategies help you on the TOEFL?* By learning to summarize, you will be able to answer the questions that are worth the most points on the Reading Section. There are also questions that require you to produce summaries on the Writing and Speaking Sections. Moreover, research demonstrates that students who understand how to summarize and use this skill when they prepare for tests will be able to remember information better.

## CONDENSE THE IDEAS

**Strategies to Use**
➤ Be brief
➤ Combine sentences

## ➤ Be brief

A summary is a shorter version of the original. For example, if the original is 1,000 words, a summary would be 200–500 words. A paraphrase is about the same number of words as the original, but a summary should be brief and concise.

### PRACTICAL STRATEGY

Details and examples are used to explain and extend the main points in a reading or a lecture. To be brief, delete the details and examples in a summary.

### PRACTICE ACTIVITY 31

Did you understand? Try to mark out all the example sentences in the following passage and lecture. Then recopy the remaining sentences below the originals. You will have a good start for writing your summaries. But remember that you cannot use someone else's words. You still need to paraphrase when you summarize. The answers are printed on pages 295–296. Your answers are correct if you have paraphrased the same ideas.

## 1. Reading

Although speech is the most advanced form of communication, there are many ways of communicating without using speech. Signals, signs, and symbols may be found in every known culture. The basic function of a signal is to impinge upon the environment in such a way that it attracts attention. For example, the flashing lights at an intersection are designed to direct the driver's attention to the road. Smoke from a distant fire can also send a message, as does the more detailed version in the dots and dashes of a telegraph. Unlike signals, which, in general, are coded to refer to speech, signs contain meaning in and of themselves. A barber pole or a picture of a loaf of bread can convey meaning quickly and conveniently when placed in front of a shop. A stop sign means *stop* even though the words may not be written out on the red octagon. Finally, gestures are actions, which are more difficult to describe because of their relationship with cultural perceptions. For instance, in some cultures, applauding in a theater provides performers with an auditory symbol of approval. In other cultures, applauding can mean that the performance was not well received.

## 2. Lecture

Listen to part of a lecture in a botany class. Write down the major points but do not take notes on the examples. Then write a summary.

  **Activity 31, Track 28**

## ➤ Combine sentences

Another good way to condense the ideas is to combine sentences. Connecting words put sentences together and show the relationships between them. There are several types of sentences with connecting words for each type. Connecting words for clauses introduce a subject and a verb. Connecting words for phrases introduce a noun.

**Clauses of Addition**

| | |
|---|---|
| and | addition |
| moreover | addition |

1. Penguins are the most highly specialized of all aquatic birds.
2. Penguins may live for twenty years.

Penguins are the most highly specialized of all aquatic birds, and they may live for twenty years.
*or*
Penguins are the most highly specialized of all aquatic birds; moreover, they may live for twenty years.

**Clauses of Reversal**

| but | reversal |
|-----|----------|
| however | reversal |

1. Penguins may live for twenty years.
2. Penguins have several obstacles to their survival.

Penguins may live for twenty years, but they have several obstacles to their survival.
*or*
Penguins may live for twenty years; however, they have several obstacles to their survival.

**Clauses of Result**                           **Phrase of Result**

| although | unexpected result | because of + noun | expected result |
|----------|-------------------|-------------------|-----------------|
| even though | unexpected result | | |
| because | expected result | | |
| since | expected result | | |
| when | absolute scientific result | | |

1. Both parents have brown eyes.
2. Their children may be born with blue eyes.

Although both parents have brown eyes, their children may be born with blue eyes.
*or*
Their children may be born with blue eyes although both parents have brown eyes.

Even though both parents have brown eyes, their children may be born with blue eyes.
*or*
Their children may be born with blue eyes even though both parents have brown eyes.

1. Their children are born with blue eyes.
2. Both brown-eyed parents have recessive genes for blue eyes.

Because both brown-eyed parents have recessive genes for blue eyes, their children are born with blue eyes.
*or*
Their children are born with blue eyes because both brown-eyed parents have recessive genes for blue eyes.

Since both brown-eyed parents have recessive genes for blue eyes, their children are born with blue eyes.
*or*
Their children are born with blue eyes since both brown-eyed parents have recessive genes for blue eyes.

Because of recessive genes, their children are born with blue eyes.
*or*
Their children are born with blue eyes because of recessive genes.

When both brown-eyed parents have recessive genes for blue eyes, their children are born with blue eyes.
*or*
Their children are born with blue eyes when both brown-eyed parents have recessive genes.

| **Clauses of Contrast** | | **Phrases of Contrast** | |
|---|---|---|---|
| whereas | on the contrary | in spite of + noun | contradiction |
| | | despite | |

1.  Many Native American tribes waged isolated battles against white settlers.
2.  Under Chief Tecumseh, the Shawnees tried to establish a confederacy to unify resistance against white settlers.

Whereas many Native American tribes waged isolated battles against white settlers, under Chief Tecumseh the Shawnees tried to establish a confederacy to unify resistance against them.

1.  Tecumseh's fearless opposition.
2.  Tecumseh's coalition was defeated at the Battle of Fallen Timbers.

In spite of Tecumseh's fearless opposition, his coalition was defeated at the Battle of Fallen Timbers.
*or*
Despite Tecumseh's fearless opposition, his coalition was defeated at the Battle of Fallen Timbers.

| **Descriptive Clauses** | |
|---|---|
| which | not human |
| who | human |

1.  Magnesium is the lightest of the structural metals.
2.  Magnesium is important in engineering industries.

Magnesium, which is the lightest of the structural metals, is important in engineering industries.

1.  Engineers often need lightweight metals.
2.  Engineers use magnesium for their designs.

Engineers, who often need lightweight metals, use magnesium for their designs.

**More Descriptive Clauses**
that                               human or not human

1. The bill was not passed until 1920.
2. The bill allowed women the right to vote in the United States.

The bill that granted women the right to vote in the United States was not passed until 1920.

| **Chronology Clauses** | | **Chronology Phrases** | |
| --- | --- | --- | --- |
| while | same time | during | same time |
| before | earlier time | | |
| after | later time | | |

1. The Romans invaded England.
2. The Celts were living in England.

The Romans invaded England while the Celts were living there.
*or*
The Romans invaded England during the Celtic occupation.

1. First the Iberians had been living in England.
2. Then the Angles and Saxons came to England.

The Iberians had been living in England before the Angles and Saxons came there.
*or*
The Angles and Saxons came to England after the Iberians had been living there.

**Conclusion Clauses**
therefore               logical conclusion
thus                    logical conclusion

1. The amount of land cannot be increased.
2. The amount of water cannot be increased.
3. Efficient agricultural methods must be employed.

The amount of land and water cannot be increased; therefore, efficient agricultural methods must be employed.
*or*
The amount of land and water cannot be increased; thus, efficient agricultural methods must be employed.

**Parallel Structures**
Similar structures connected by commas
Nouns
Verbs
Adjectives

1.  Best known for creating the Sherlock Holmes mysteries, British author Sir Arthur Conan Doyle was a physician.
2.  Sir Arthur Conan Doyle was also a world traveler.
3.  Sir Arthur Conan Doyle wrote numerous adventure stories.

Best known for creating the Sherlock Holmes mysteries, British author Sir Arthur Conan Doyle was a physician, a world traveler, and a writer of numerous adventure stories.
*or*
Best known for creating the Sherlock Holmes mysteries, British author Sir Arthur Conan Doyle practiced medicine, traveled the world, and wrote numerous adventure stories.
*or*
Best known for creating the Sherlock Holmes mysteries, British author Sir Arthur Conan Doyle was well educated, adventurous, and prolific.

### Introductory Verbal Modifiers (-*ing* and -*ed*)

-*ing* forms and -*ed* forms may be used as verbals. Verbals function as modifiers. An introductory verbal modifier with -*ing* or -*ed* should immediately precede the noun it modifies. Otherwise, the relationship between the noun and the modifier is unclear, and the sentence is illogical.

1.  Lindbergh designed his own plane, the *Spirit of St. Louis.*
2.  Lindbergh flew from Roosevelt Field in New York to Le Bourget Field outside Paris.

Having designed his own plane, the *Spirit of St. Louis*, Lindbergh flew from Roosevelt Field in New York to Le Bourget Field outside Paris.

The plane was designed by Lindbergh.
The plane flew across the ocean with few problems.

Designed by Lindbergh, the plane flew across the ocean with few problems.

## PRACTICE ACTIVITY 32

Did you understand? Try to combine the sentences. Copy the combined sentences below the originals. The first sentence is completed to give you an example. The answers are printed on pages 296–297.

### EXAMPLE

An attitude is a positive or negative evaluation.
A positive or negative attitude may affect behavior.
An attitude may play an important role in perception.
which

An attitude, which is a positive or negative evaluation, may affect behavior and play an important role in perception.

1. Charlie Chaplin was a comedian.
   Charlie Chaplin was best known for his work in silent movies.
   who

2. Water is heated to 212 degrees F.
   Water becomes steam.
   when

3. Quasars are relatively small objects.
   Quasars emit an enormous amount of energy.
   which

4. The Earth moves into the shadow of the Moon.
   A total eclipse occurs.
   during

5. The Jamestown colony was founded by John Smith.
   Jamestown became the first successful English colony in America.
   *-ed* introductory verbal modifier

6. Many of the names of cities in California are adapted from the Spanish language.
   Early missionaries and settlers from Spain had extended their influence in the area.
   since/because/because of

7. The oceans cover two-thirds of the Earth's surface.
   The oceans are the object of study for oceanographers.
   which

8. A chameleon is a tree lizard.
   The chameleon can change colors to conceal itself in vegetation.
   that

9. First cultural nationalism arose among people with similar languages and traditions.
   Then political nationalism threatened the existing order.
   before/after

10. Empowerment increases the autonomy of employees in organizations.
    Empowerment improves communication between workers and management.
    and/moreover

11. Monogamy means being married to one spouse.
    Serial monogamy involves marriage, divorce, and remarriage.
    whereas

12. Humor is associated with fun.
    Humor is also used as a coping strategy to relieve stress.
    but/however

13. Solar panels can convert sunlight into electricity.
    Solar panels are still not being exploited fully.
    although/even though

14. The root system of the alfalfa plant allows it to survive.
    Drought conditions do not kill alfalfa.
    despite/in spite of

15. Pain warns the victim before further damage is done.
    Pain has a positive function.
    therefore/thus

## IDENTIFY THE MAIN POINTS

**Strategies to Use**
➤ Find a topic sentence
➤ Identify the major points
➤ Identify the minor points

## ➤ Find a topic sentence

The topic answers the question: What is this reading or lecture about? A topic sentence is a very general statement that includes the subject of the reading or lecture and also the way that the author or speaker plans to develop the topic. For example, a topic might be *management strategies in business*. This topic could be developed in a number of different ways. For example, *management strategies* could be developed by listing several types of strategies or by comparing different strategies. When you are looking for the topic, you should look for a sentence that includes a subject and a verb. *Management strategies in business* is a subject, but without a verb in the sentence, we still don't know how the topic will be developed. Some books call this kind of topic sentence *a controlling idea*.

### PRACTICAL STRATEGY

The first sentence in a summary should be a direct statement. It should give the reader or listener a general idea of the topic for the reading or lecture and the way that the topic will be developed. Sometimes you can paraphrase a topic sentence from the original reading or lecture, but sometimes you must create it yourself from several sentences in the original.

### PRACTICE ACTIVITY 33

Did you understand? Try to write one sentence that summarizes the entire reading or lecture. Example answers are printed on pages 297–298. Your answers are correct if your ideas are the same as the example answers.

## 1. Reading

The nuclear family, consisting of a mother, father, and their children, may be more an ideal than a reality. Although the so-called traditional family was always more varied than we had been led to believe, reflecting the very different racial, ethnic, class, and religious customs among different American groups, today the diversity is even more obvious.

The most recent government census statistics reveal that only about one-third of all current American families fits the traditional mold of two parents and their children, and another third consists of married couples who either have no children or have none still living at home. An analysis of the remaining one-third of the population reveals that about 20 percent of the total number of American households are single people, the most common descriptor being women over 65 years of age. A small percentage, about 3 percent of the total, consists of unmarried people who choose to live together, and the rest, about 7 percent, are single parents, with at least one child.

There are several easily identifiable reasons for the growing number of single-parent households. First, the sociological phenomenon of single-parent households reflects changes in cultural attitudes toward divorce and also toward unmarried mothers. A substantial number of adults become single parents as a result of divorce. In addition, the number of children born to unmarried women who choose to keep their babies and rear them by themselves has increased dramatically. Finally, there is a small percentage of single-parent families that have resulted from untimely death. Today, these varied family types are typical and, therefore, normal.

Moreover, because many families live far from relatives, close friends have become a more important part of family life than ever before. The vast majority of Americans claim that they have people in their lives whom they regard as family although they are not related. A view of family that only accepts the traditional nuclear arrangement not only ignores the reality of modern American family life but also undervalues the familial bonds created in alternative family arrangements. Apparently, many Americans are achieving supportive relationships in family forms other than the traditional one.

## 2. Lecture

Listen to part of a lecture in a chemistry class. Then summarize the lecture in one sentence.

**Activity 33, Track 29**

## ➤ Identify the major points

### PRACTICAL STRATEGY

A major point is almost always directly stated. A major point has examples and details that refer to it. A major point is often found at the beginning of a new paragraph. Inferences and conclusions or examples and details are usually NOT major points.

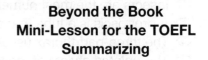

**Beyond the Book
Mini-Lesson for the TOEFL
Summarizing**

To view the lesson, visit the Barron's TOEFL site online. Click on **Academic Skills**, then click on **Mini-Lesson for Summarizing**.

## PRACTICE ACTIVITY 34

Did you understand? Try to identify the major points. The answers are printed in Chapter 5 on pages 298–300.

### 1. Reading

The body of an adult insect is subdivided into three sections, including a head, a three-segment thorax, and a segmented abdomen. Ordinarily, the thorax bears three pairs of legs and a single or double pair of wings. The vision of most adult insects is specialized through two large compound eyes and multiple simple eyes.

Features of an insect's mouth parts are used in classifying insects into types. Biting mouth parts called mandibles, such as the mouth parts found in grasshoppers and beetles, are common among insects. Behind the mandibles are located the maxillae or lower jaw parts, which serve to direct food into the mouth between the jaws. A labrum above and one below are similar to another animal's upper and lower lips. In an insect with a sucking mouth function, the mandibles, maxillae, labrum, and labium are modified in such a way that they constitute a tube through which liquid such as water, blood, or flower nectar can be drawn. In a butterfly or moth, this coiled drinking tube is called the proboscis because of its resemblance, in miniature, to the trunk of an elephant or a very large nose. Composed chiefly of modified maxillae fitted together, the insect's proboscis can be flexed and extended to reach nectar deep in a flower. In mosquitoes or aphids, mandibles and maxillae are modified to sharp stylets with which the insect can drill through surfaces like human or vegetable membranes to reach juice. In a housefly, the expanding labium forms a spongelike mouth pad that it can use to stamp over the surface of food, sopping up food particles and juices.

- Ⓐ An adult insect has a three-section body that includes a head, a thorax, and an abdomen.
- Ⓑ Mandibles are mouth parts that facilitate biting and usually include upper and lower labrum.
- Ⓒ A mouth pad similar to a sponge allows flies to attract crumbs and juice on the surface of food.
- Ⓓ Insects are classified according to their mouth parts, which are specialized for feeding.
- Ⓔ Insects are the most numerous creatures on the planet and also the most adaptable.
- Ⓕ A proboscis Is a tube that stretches to penetrate flowers where nectar is stored.
- Ⓖ The three-part thorax usually has six legs and two or four wings attached to it.
- Ⓗ The pointed stylets of mosquitoes and aphids facilitate drilling through skin on plants and humans.

### 2. Lecture

Listen to part of a lecture in an English class. Then identify the major points from the options on page 239.

**Activity 34, Track 30**

Ⓐ Noah Webster had a degree in law and practiced for a short time before he became a school teacher.

Ⓑ *The American Spelling Book*, Webster's first successful textbook, afforded him an income while he was writing his dictionary.

Ⓒ *An American Dictionary of the English Language* was written to demonstrate the unique usage of English in the United States.

Ⓓ *An American Dictionary of the English Language* has had many revised editions.

Ⓔ *The Compendious Dictionary of the English Language*, published in 1807, provided Webster with practice in compiling a dictionary.

Ⓕ Although he had a copyright for *The American Spelling Book*, ironically Webster did not have a copyright for the original dictionary and subsequent editions that bear his name.

Ⓖ Webster graduated from Yale only two years after the end of the Revolution that won independence for the United States from England.

## ➤ Identify the minor points

A minor point can be an example or a detail that supports a major point, or it can be a point that is not very well developed. A minor point may be mentioned without supporting examples or details in the original reading or lecture.

### PRACTICAL STRATEGY

Minor points are usually not included in a summary. If you can identify the minor points, you can eliminate them. You can shorten your summary.

### PRACTICE ACTIVITY 35

Did you understand? Try to identify the minor points. Then write a summary that includes only the major points. The answers are printed on pages 300–301. Your summary is correct if it includes the same ideas.

### 1. Reading

In the fifteenth century, two important advances in painting were introduced. Prior to that time, most paintings were created on wood panels; however, in the second half of the century, many artists began to prefer linen canvas. The canvas offered several important advantages. Whereas wood panels were heavy and difficult to transport and hang, the lighter linen canvas could be rolled up for shipment and was relatively easy to transport, frame, and mount. Moreover, if patrons were at a distance from the artist, the finished work might have to be hauled in a cart. It was difficult to protect it from damage as it bumped along the primitive roads. In addition, the patrons were demanding larger and larger works and the large wood pieces had a tendency to crack. In contrast, the linen canvases could be stretched to almost any size and remained perfectly smooth.

The oil paints themselves were also superior to previous paints. One of the most obvious improvements was the fact that the paint dried slowly, and thus, layers of paint could be brushed on top of previously applied layers, allowing the artist to erase a section that was not perfect. Another refinement was the range of consistencies possible with oils. Thin oil paints take on the characteristics of a glaze, but thick oils look like paste and can be layered to create a three-dimensional aspect.

## 2. Lecture

Listen to part of a lecture in an engineering class. Then write a summary. Do not include the minor points.

 **Activity 35, Track 31**

# REPORT THE INFORMATION

**Strategies to Use**
➤ Use the same organization as the original
➤ Report the content accurately
➤ Retain the original emphasis
➤ Maintain an objective point of view
➤ Check the summary

## ➤ Use the same organization as the original

A summary should retain the same organization as the original reading or lecture. For example, if the passage identifies three different types of evergreen trees, then the organization is classification. Your summary should also be organized to classify the three different types of trees. If the passage explains the cause of deforestation in Canada, then the organization of the passage is cause and effect. Your summary should also be organized to demonstrate cause and effect. If the passage explains the life cycle of a pine tree, then the organization is chronological. Your summary should also be organized in chronological order. It is also important NOT to rearrange the order. A good summary begins with the first major point and follows with each major point in the order that it appears in the original.

### PRACTICAL STRATEGY

First, determine the organization of the reading or lecture. Then list the major points in the order in which you read or heard them. This list gives you an outline for your summary.

### PRACTICE ACTIVITY 36

Did you understand? Put the major points in the order that they should appear in a summary. The answers are printed on pages 301–302. Your answers are correct if they are in the same order as the original.

## 1. Reading

Although stage plays have been set to music since the era of the ancient Greeks when the dramas of Sophocles and Aeschylus were accompanied by lyres and flutes, the usually accepted date for the beginning of opera as we know it is 1600. As part of the celebration of the marriage of King Henry IV of France to the Italian aristocrat Maria de Medici, the Florentine composer Jacopo Peri produced his famous *Euridice*, generally considered to be the first opera. Following his example, a group of Italian musicians, poets, and noblemen called the Camerata revived the style of musical story that had been used in Greek tragedy. Taking most of the plots for their operas from Greek and Roman history and mythology, they began the process of creating an opera by writing a libretto or drama that could be used to establish the framework for the music. They called their compositions *opera in musica* or musical works. It is from this phrase that the word *opera* was borrowed and abbreviated.

For several years, the center of opera was Florence in northern Italy, but gradually, during the Baroque period, it spread throughout Italy. By the late 1600s, operas were being written and performed in many places throughout Europe, especially in England, France, and Germany. However, for many years, the Italian opera was considered the ideal, and many non-Italian composers continued to use Italian librettos. The European form de-emphasized the dramatic aspect of the Italian model, however, introducing new orchestral effects and even some ballet.

Furthermore, composers acquiesced to the demands of singers, writing many operas that were little more than a succession of brilliant tricks for the voice, designed to showcase the splendid vocal talent of the singers who had requested them. It was thus that complicated arias, recitatives, and duets evolved. The aria, which is a long solo, may be compared to a song in which the characters express their thoughts and feelings. The recitative, which is also a solo of sorts, is a recitation set to music, the purpose of which is to continue the story line. The duet is a musical piece written for two voices, a musical device that may serve the function of either an aria or a recitative within the opera.

### Major Points

  Ⓐ Three types of musical pieces in opera
  Ⓑ The first opera in Italy
  Ⓒ The growth of opera throughout Europe

## 2. Lecture

Listen to part of a lecture in a biology class. Then put the major points in the same order as the lecture.

  **Activity 36, Track 32**

### Major Points

  Ⓐ A method of classification for protozoans—the three types motility
  Ⓑ Current research—questions, redefinitions
  Ⓒ Similarity to plants—make food from water/$CO_2$
  Ⓓ A definition of protozoans—single cell
  Ⓔ Considered animals—eating, breathing, reproducing

## ➤ Report the content accurately

You will be evaluated not only on how well you use language to write a summary but also on how accurately you understand and report the content of the original.

### PRACTICAL STRATEGY

Read and listen for meaning. When you have finished reading or listening, review the content. Ask yourself some basic questions. Include the questions that reporters use in their writing—*who, what, when, where, why, how?* The content may not include answers to all of the questions, but, with practice, you will be able to identify the questions that are important to the content you have read or heard.

### PRACTICE ACTIVITY 37

Did you understand? Answer the content questions. Then, copy the answers to the questions in paragraph form to make a summary. The answers and the example summaries are printed on pages 302–303.

### 1. Reading

According to the controversial sunspot theory, great storms on the surface of the Sun hurl streams of solar particles into space and eventually into the atmosphere of our planet, causing shifts in the weather on the Earth and interference with radio and television communications.

A typical sunspot consists of a dark central umbra, a word derived from the Latin word for shadow, which is surrounded by a lighter penumbra of light and dark threads extending out from the center like the spokes of a wheel. Actually, the sunspots are cooler than the rest of the photosphere, which may account for their apparently darker color. Typically, the temperature in a sunspot umbra is about 4000 K, whereas the temperature in a penumbra registers 5500 K, and the granules outside the spot are 6000 K.

Sunspots range in size from tiny grains to complex structures with areas stretching for billions of square miles. About 5 percent of all sunspots are large enough so that they can be seen from Earth without instruments; consequently, observations of sunspots have been recorded for thousands of years. They have been observed in arrangements of one to more than 100 spots, but they tend to occur in pairs. There is also a marked tendency for the two spots of a pair to have opposite magnetic polarities. Furthermore, the strength of the magnetic field associated with any given sunspot is closely related to the spot's size.

Sunspots have also been observed to occur in cycles, over a period of eleven years. At the beginning of a cycle, the storms occur between 20 and 40 degrees north and south of the equator on the Sun. As the cycle continues, some of the storms move closer to the equator. As the cycle diminishes, the number of sunspots decreases to a minimum, and they cluster between 5 and 15 degrees north and south latitude.

Although there is no theory that completely explains the nature and function of sunspots, several models show scientists' attempts to relate the phenomenon to magnetic field lines along the lines of longitude from the north and south poles of the Sun.

1.  What is the author's main purpose in the passage?

    ⓐ To describe the nature of sunspots
    ⓑ To propose a model for cycles in the solar year
    ⓒ To compare the umbra and the penumbra in sunspots
    ⓓ To argue for the existence of magnetic fields in sunspots

2.  Why are solar particles hurled into space?

    ⓐ Undetermined causes on Earth
    ⓑ Disturbances of wind on the Sun
    ⓒ Small rivers on the surface of the Sun
    ⓓ Changes in the Earth's atmosphere

3.  How can we describe the effect of matter from the Sun that enters the Earth's atmosphere?

    ⓐ It causes volcanic eruptions on the surface of the Earth.
    ⓑ It affects changes in the weather patterns on Earth.
    ⓒ It results in shadows across the Earth's surface.
    ⓓ It produces higher temperatures on the Earth.

4.  How would you describe most sunspots?

    ⓐ A shadow encircled by bright and dark lines extending out like spokes in a wheel
    ⓑ A bright wheel with a dark shadow that covers part of the spokes that extend out
    ⓒ A wheel with alternating spokes of dark shadows and bright spaces in between
    ⓓ A spoke of a wheel with a bright trail partially covered by a dark shadow

5.  What does the author mean by the statement "Actually, the sunspots are cooler than the rest of the photosphere, which may account for their apparently darker color"?

    ⓐ Neither sunspots nor the photosphere is hot.
    ⓑ Sunspots in the photosphere do not have any color.
    ⓒ The color of sunspots could be affected by their temperature.
    ⓓ The size of a sunspot affects its temperature.

6.  In which configuration do sunspots usually occur?

    ⓐ In one spot of varying size
    ⓑ In a configuration of two spots
    ⓒ In arrangements of 100 or more spots
    ⓓ In groups of several thousand spots

7.  How are sunspots explained?

    ⓐ Sunspots appear to be related to the pull of highly magnetic fields on the Earth.
    ⓑ Sunspots may be related to magnetic fields that follow longitudinal lines on the Sun.
    ⓒ Sunspots are explained by large storms that occur on the surface of the Earth.
    ⓓ Sunspots have no theory or model to explain their occurrence or reappearance.

8. The sunspot theory is

    Ⓐ not very important
    Ⓑ widely accepted
    Ⓒ subject to debate
    Ⓓ relatively new

## *2. Lecture*

Listen to part of a lecture in an anthropology class. Then answer the questions and use the answers to write a summary.

 **Activity 37, Track 33**

1. According to the lecturer, fossils are considered valuable for all of the following reasons EXCEPT

    Ⓐ they suggest how the climate may have been
    Ⓑ they provide information about migration
    Ⓒ they document the evolution of the horse
    Ⓓ they maintain a record of life prior to the Miocene

2. What does the lecturer mean by the statement, "Geologists believe that the first horses appeared on Earth about 60 million years ago as compared with only 2 million years ago for the appearance of human beings."

    Ⓐ Geologists claim that horses appeared on Earth millions of years before human beings.
    Ⓑ Both horses and human beings appeared several million years ago, if we believe geologists.
    Ⓒ The geological records for the appearance of horses and human beings are not very accurate.
    Ⓓ Horses and human beings cannot be compared by geologists because they appeared too long ago.

3. According to the lecture, the anchitheres

    Ⓐ never lived in the North American continent
    Ⓑ had migrated to Europe in the Miocene Period from North America
    Ⓒ developed larger bodies than the hipparion from North America
    Ⓓ were only about the size of a small dog when they invaded North America

4. Which of the following conclusions may be made on the basis of information in the lecture?

    Ⓐ Following the same route, the hipparion migrated to Europe in the Pliocene.
    Ⓑ There are no fossil remains of either the anchitheres or the hipparion in Europe.
    Ⓒ Both horses were in North America when the first European colonists arrived.
    Ⓓ Very little is conclusively known about the evolution of the horse in Europe.

5.  What happened to the anchitheres when the hipparion invaded Europe?

    Ⓐ  They interbred with the hipparion.
    Ⓑ  They migrated into Asia.
    Ⓒ  They did not survive.
    Ⓓ  They evolved into large horses.

6.  What do we know about horses in North America during the Pleistocene?

    Ⓐ  They were very large and strong.
    Ⓑ  They were already extinct.
    Ⓒ  They lived in the Bering Strait.
    Ⓓ  They migrated south from Alaska.

7.  What happened to the hipparion in Europe?

    Ⓐ  They developed into a sturdy animal, like modern breeds of horses.
    Ⓑ  They were replaced by other larger, stronger animals.
    Ⓒ  They evolved into modern ponies instead of modern horses.
    Ⓓ  They disappeared because they were hunted into extinction.

8.  How was the domesticated horse introduced in North America?

    Ⓐ  Early hunting tribes from Europe herded them across the Bering Strait.
    Ⓑ  They were used as transportation by immigrants who used a land route.
    Ⓒ  Europeans returned the horse to the American colonies on ships.
    Ⓓ  They migrated to find better grasslands than they had in Europe and Asia.

## ➤ Retain the original emphasis

The emphasis should be the same in both the original and the summary. For example, a passage about the three different types of leaves may include all three types, but it may dedicate half of the passage to one type—palmate leaves. In this case, your summary should retain the same emphasis by dedicating half of the summary to palmate leaves.

### PRACTICAL STRATEGY

When you read, think in terms of space. How much space does the author devote to each point? When you listen, think in terms of time. How much time does the speaker devote to each point? When you do this, you are determining the emphasis for each point in the original, and you will know how much emphasis to give to these points in your summary.

### PRACTICE ACTIVITY 38

Did you understand? Try to identify the emphasis for each part of the original and assign percentages. Then write a summary that retains the original emphasis. The answers and example summaries are printed on pages 303–304.

## 1. Reading

The Federal Reserve System, commonly called the Fed, is an independent agency of the United States government charged with overseeing the national banking system. Since 1913, the Federal Reserve System has served as the central bank for the United States. The Fed's primary function is to control monetary policy by influencing the cost and availability of money and credit through the purchase and sale of government securities. If the Federal Reserve provides too little money, interest rates tend to be high, borrowing is expensive, business activity slows down, unemployment goes up, and the danger of a recession is augmented. On the other hand, if there is too much money, interest rates decline, and borrowing can lead to excess demand, pushing up prices and fueling inflation. In addition to controlling the money supply, the Fed has several other responsibilities. In collaboration with the U.S. Department of the Treasury, the Fed puts new coins and paper currency into circulation by issuing them to banks. It also supervises the activities of member banks abroad and regulates certain aspects of international finance.

The Federal Reserve System consists of 12 district reserve banks and their branch offices along with several committees and councils. All national commercial banks are required by law to be members of the Fed, and all deposit-taking institutions like credit unions are subject to regulation by the Fed regarding the amount of deposited funds that must be held in reserve and that, by definition, therefore, are not available for loans. The most powerful body is the seven-member board of governors in Washington, appointed by the president and confirmed by the Senate. Although it is true that the Federal Reserve does not depend on Congress for budget allocations, and therefore is free from the partisan politics that influence most of the other governmental bodies, it is still responsible for frequent reports to the Congress on the conduct of monetary policies.

In many ways, the Federal Reserve is like a fourth branch of the United States government because it is composed of national policy makers. However, in practice, the Fed does not stray from the financial policies established by the executive branch of the government.

### Major Points

- The function and responsibilities of the Fed
- The composition of the Fed
- A comparison of the Fed to a fourth branch of government

## 2. Lecture

Listen to part of a lecture in a psychology class. Then assign a percentage to each of the following points from the lecture and write a summary using the percentages to determine how much to write on each point.

 **Activity 38, Track 34**

### Major Points

- The level of sophistication for human memory
- The memory trace
- Working memory

## ➤ Maintain an objective point of view

An objective point of view is a neutral position. A summary is not an analysis or a commentary. A summary does not invite an opinion.

### PRACTICAL STRATEGY

In your summary, you should not agree or disagree with the author's or the speaker's ideas. Don't make judgments. Don't add information. When you report, you should not include *your* opinions or comments. The conclusion should be the author's or the speaker's conclusion, not yours.

### PRACTICE ACTIVITY 39

Did you understand? Try to find the opinions in the summary and delete them. Use the original reading to compare the content. The answers are printed on pages 305–306.

### 1. Reading

Charles Ives, who is now acclaimed as the first great American composer of the twentieth century, had to wait many years for the public recognition he deserved. Born to music as the son of a bandmaster, Ives played drums in his father's community band and organ at the local church. He entered Yale University at twenty to study musical composition with Horatio Parker, but after graduation he chose not to pursue a career in music. He suspected correctly that the public would not accept the music he wrote because Ives did not follow the musical fashion of his times. While his contemporaries wrote lyrical songs, Ives transfigured music and musical form. He quoted, combined, insinuated, and distorted familiar hymns, marches, and battle songs, while experimenting with the effects of polytonality, or the simultaneous use of keys with conflicting rhythms and time. Even when he could convince some musicians to show some interest in his compositions, after assessing them conductors and performers said that they were essentially unplayable.

Ives turned his attention to business. He became a successful insurance executive, building his company into the largest agency in the country in only two decades. Although he occasionally hired musicians to play one of his works privately for him, he usually heard his music only in his imagination. After he recovered from a serious heart attack, he became reconciled to the fact that his ideas, especially the use of dissonance and special effects, were just too different for the musical mainstream to accept. Determined to share his music with the few people who might appreciate it, he published his work privately and distributed it free.

In 1939, when Ives was 65, American pianist John Kirkpatrick played *Concord Sonata* in Town Hall. The reviews were laudatory. One reviewer proclaimed it "the greatest music composed by an American." By 1947, Ives was famous. His *Second Symphony* was presented to the public in a performance by the New York Philharmonic, 50 years after it had been written. The same year, Ives received the Pulitzer Prize. He was 73.

### Summary

Charles Ives started his musical career as a member of his father's band and received a degree from Yale University in music, but he became a businessman instead because he was afraid that his music would not be well accepted. His music was very different from the popular songs of his era because he used small phrases from well-known music with unusual rhythms and tones. Fifty years after he wrote his *Second Symphony*, it was performed by the New York Philharmonic, and he was awarded the Pulitzer Prize.

I think that Charles Ives was wrong not to pursue his musical career from the beginning. If he had continued writing music instead of selling insurance, we would have more pieces now.

### 2. Lecture

Listen to part of a lecture in a geology class. Then delete the opinions from the summary.

 **Activity 39, Track 35**

In my opinion, geysers are interesting. They happen when underground water gets hot and pressure from above causes the water to get hotter and lighter so it goes up to the surface and explodes out. Then, the water runs back into the ground and starts all over again. Geysers have to have heat, a place to store water, an opening where the water can shoot up, and cracks in the ground for the water to go back down into a pool. Geysers are in New Zealand, Iceland, and the United States. Old Faithful in Yellowstone is the most famous geyser, but the best place to see geysers is in New Zealand. I saw the Pohutu Geyser there on my vacation two years ago, and it was awesome.

### ➤ Check the summary

If you know how your summary will be evaluated, you can use the same criteria to check it before you submit it.

#### PRACTICAL STRATEGY

Save some time at the end of your written summary to re-read it and check it. Keep a short checklist in mind as you review your content and organization.

#### PRACTICE ACTIVITY 40

Did you understand? Try to find the problems in the following summaries. Use the original reading to compare the content and the short checklist to identify which problems to correct. The answers are printed on page 306.

#### Short Checklist for Summaries

✔ Be brief
✔ Use the same organization as the original
✔ Include the major points
✔ Report the content accurately
✔ Retain the original emphasis
✔ Paraphrase using your own words
✔ Maintain an objective point of view

## Reading

Very few people in the modern world obtain their food supply by hunting and gathering in the natural environment surrounding their homes. This method of harvesting from nature's provision, however, is not only the oldest known subsistence strategy but also the one that has been practiced continuously in some parts of the world for at least the last 2 million years. It was, indeed, the only way to obtain food until rudimentary farming and very crude methods for the domestication of animals were introduced about 10,000 years ago.

Because hunter-gatherers have fared poorly in comparison with their agricultural cousins, their numbers have dwindled, and they have been forced to live in the marginal wastelands. In higher latitudes, the shorter growing season has restricted the availability of plant life. Such conditions have caused a greater dependence on hunting and, along the coasts and waterways, on fishing. The abundance of vegetation in the lower latitudes of the tropics, on the other hand, has provided a greater opportunity for gathering a variety of plants. In short, the environmental differences have restricted the diet and have limited possibilities for the development of subsistence societies.

Contemporary hunter-gatherers may help us understand our prehistoric ancestors. We know from observation of modern hunter-gatherers in both Africa and Alaska that a society based on hunting and gathering must be very mobile. Following the food supply can be a way of life. If a particular kind of wild herding animal is the basis of the food for a group of people, those people must move to stay within reach of those animals. For many of the native people of the great central plains of North America, following the buffalo, who were in turn following the growth of grazing foods, determined their way of life.

For gathering societies, seasonal changes mean a great deal. While the entire community camps in a central location, a smaller party harvests the food within a reasonable distance from the camp. When the food in the area is exhausted, the community moves on to exploit another site. We also notice a seasonal migration pattern evolving for most hunter-gatherers, along with a strict division of labor between the sexes. These patterns of behavior may be similar to those practiced by humankind during the Paleolithic Period.

## Summary 1

By studying hunter-gatherers in today's world, we can better understand the people from prehistoric times. In a hunter-gatherer society, the surrounding vegetation limits the dietary options. In addition, the length of the growing season restricts the amount of gathering that can be done and requires more hunting and fishing for groups to survive. We note that groups must follow the herds and travel to new sites where edible plants are in season. Although few people are now dependent upon hunting and gathering, it is the most ancient lifestyle, and perhaps the only way to subsist before agricultural communities arose during the past 10,000 years. Furthermore, men and women have specialized tasks. Competition with agricultural societies has crowded hunter-gatherers into harsh terrains.

## Summary 2

Although few people are now dependent upon hunting and gathering, it is the most ancient lifestyle, and perhaps the only way to subsist before agricultural communities arose during the past 10,000 years. Competition with agricultural societies has crowded hunter-gatherers into harsh terrains. In a hunter-gatherer society, the surrounding vegetation limits the dietary options. In addition, the length of the growing season restricts the amount of gathering that can be done and requires more hunting and fishing for groups to survive. By studying hunter-gatherers in today's world, we can better understand the people from prehistoric times. We note that groups must follow the herds and travel to new sites where edible plants are in season. Furthermore, men and women have specialized tasks.

### Summary 3

Few people are now dependent upon hunting and gathering; however, it is the most ancient lifestyle, and perhaps the only way to subsist before agricultural communities arose during the past 10,000 years. Competition with agricultural societies has crowded hunter-gatherers into harsh terrains. In my opinion, we should help these groups to learn how to grow their own crops so that they will not have to have limited diets and will not have to move to new sites where edible plants are in season. By studying hunter-gatherers in today's world, we can better understand the people from prehistoric times, and that is good, but we should help them, too.

### Summary 4

Although very few people in the modern world obtain their food supply by hunting and gathering, this method is the oldest known subsistence strategy. Because hunter-gatherers have fared poorly, they have been forced to live in harsh environments with limited possibilities for their diet. By observation of modern hunter-gatherers, we know that people must move to stay within reach of the herds they hunt. When the food in the area is exhausted, the community moves on to exploit another site.

### Summary 5

Few people are now dependent upon hunting and gathering, but it is the most ancient lifestyle, and perhaps the only way to subsist before agricultural communities arose during the past 10,000 years. It has been part of human cultures beginning two million years ago and continues to the present in some parts of the world. Modern hunter-gatherers provide us with information about prehistoric people. They probably moved to stay close to the herds they hunted and moved to take advantage of seasonal plants.

---

## ADVISOR'S OFFICE

Why are you preparing for the TOEFL? What goal is motivating you to study and improve your score? Do you want to attend a university in an English-speaking country? Do you want to try for a scholarship from a sponsor in your country or region? Is the TOEFL required for graduation from your high school? Do you plan to apply for an assistantship at a graduate school? Do you need the score for a professional license?

Goals can be experienced as mental images. You can close your eyes and imagine everything, just like a movie. See yourself achieving your goal. Watch yourself as you attend school or practice your profession in your ideal environment. See other people congratulating you. Enjoy the success.

Understand that you cannot control reality with visualization. However, it does change your attitude, it helps you to focus, provides motivation, and reduces stress. Positive visualization is an excellent way to take a short break from studying.

# SYNTHESIZING

Synthesizing means to combine two or more sources in order to create something new. It is probably the most complex academic skill because it includes the other academic skills that you have studied—taking notes, paraphrasing, and summarizing. In addition, the result of a synthesis should be more than the sum of the parts. There are three problems that you will confront when you are synthesizing.

1. **The relationship between the sources may not be obvious.** This means that you may have to figure out the connection.
2. **One source appears to contain all of the necessary information.** This means that you need to be sure to balance the information so that all of the sources are used.
3. **Synthesis requires a high level of thinking.** This means that you should have a plan in order to create a synthesis.

This chapter will help you improve your synthesizing. You will learn how to

- **Analyze the task**
- **Include information from both sources**
- **Follow a plan**

*How will these strategies help you on the TOEFL?* By learning to synthesize information from readings and lectures or talks, you will develop ways of thinking that will help you prepare important integrated speaking and writing questions. The ability to synthesize is also required for success in making presentations, taking exams, and writing research papers for college or university classes.

## ANALYZE THE TASK

---

**Strategies to Use**
➤ Identify the question
➤ Clarify the relationships

---

## ➤ Identify the question

At least two sources are required for a synthesis. The primary source presents the major points, and the secondary source provides additional information. The wording of the question or the assignment will direct your thinking.

## PRACTICAL STRATEGY

Questions found in Task 4 of the Speaking Section often, but not always, include agreement words because you are usually asked to show how the lecture clarifies or extends the information in the reading passage. The reading passage typically introduces a general concept, theory, definition, or idea and the lecture that follows provides an example, a case study, a research study, a model, or an illustration. Start your thinking by recognizing words in the question or assignment as *agreement* words.

### Agreement/Extension/Clarification

| | |
|---|---|
| Adds to | includes more evidence |
| Affirms | maintains to be true |
| Agrees with | has the same opinion |
| Clarifies | makes easy to understand |
| Concurs with | has the same opinion |
| Confirms | establishes that something is true |
| Corroborates | shows the same evidence |
| Demonstrates | shows with proof or evidence |
| Endorses | gives approval |
| Explains | makes clear |
| Proves | shows that something is true |
| Provides an example of | gives an illustration |
| Provides evidence for | gives proof |
| Reinforces | makes stronger |
| Substantiates | offers proof |
| Supports | maintains a position |
| Validates | shows the facts |
| Verifies | shows the truth |

### EXAMPLE

Summarize the points that the lecturer makes, explaining how they <u>support</u> the information in the reading.

Show how the points in the lecture agree with the information in the reading passage.

## PRACTICE ACTIVITY 41

Did you understand? Without looking at the list above, underline the agreement words. Then write a short explanation of the question. The answers are printed on page 307.

1. Referring to the main points in the reading passage, show how the example in the professor's lecture demonstrates the principle of Occam's razor.

2. Explain how the lecturer's view substantiates the opinions expressed in the reading passage.

3. The professor describes the behavior of dolphins. Explain why this behavior provides an example of higher-level intelligence, as defined in the reading passage.

4. Explain how the example of learning to drive clarifies the automaticity of learning.

5. Using the case study discussed by the professor, explain how the results reinforce the argument in favor of direct mail marketing presented in the reading passage.

## PRACTICAL STRATEGY

Questions found in the Integrated Writing Task often, but not always, include disagreement words. The reading passage generally presents a position or a point of view and the lecture that follows provides an opposing or contrasting position or point of view. Start your thinking by recognizing words in the question or assignment as *disagreement* words.

### Disagreement/Contrast/Opposition

| | |
|---|---|
| Casts doubt on | Shows uncertainty |
| Challenges | Makes doubtful |
| Contradicts | Maintains the opposite |
| Contrasts with | Shows differences |
| Counters | Shows the opposite |
| Differs from | Shows difference |
| Disagrees with | Gives a different opinion |
| Discredits | Shows that something is probably not true |
| Disproves | Establishes that something is not true |
| Disputes | Argues that something is wrong |
| Opposes | Argues the opposite |
| Provides an alternative to | Gives a different option |
| Refutes | Proves false |

### EXAMPLE

Summarize the points that the lecturer makes, explaining how they <u>cast doubt on</u> the information in the reading.

Show how the points in the lecture make the points presented in the reading passage less certain.

### PRACTICE ACTIVITY 42

Did you understand? Without looking at the list above, underline the disagreement words. Then write a short explanation of the question. Example answers are printed on pages 307–308.

1. Summarize the main points made in the lecture, being sure to explain how they challenge the specific claims made in the reading passage.

2. Summarize the main points in the lecture, showing how they discredit the specific arguments in the reading passage.

3. Summarize the points made in the lecture, being sure to explain how they oppose specific points made in the reading passage.

4. Summarize the major points made in the lecture, being sure to explain how they contrast with the specific problems presented in the reading passage.

5. Summarize the main points in the lecture, showing how they cast doubt on the point of view in the reading passage. Be sure to address each point in the passage.

## ➤ Clarify the relationships

You already know how to identify the question, and you know that, whether you are speaking or writing, your first task is to clarify the relationship between the lecture and the reading passage. After reading the passage and listening to the lecture, you will know whether the relationship between them is agreement or disagreement. You should usually express this relationship in the first sentence that you speak or write on an integrated task. Let's think of this first sentence as a *relationship sentence* that begins your response. A good relationship sentence states agreement or disagreement. A better relationship sentence uses a strong verb to signal agreement or disagreement. The best relationship sentence includes a strong verb *and* detail about the relationship between the information in the reading and in the lecture.

### PRACTICAL STRATEGY

Using the lists of words that signal agreement or disagreement on pages 252 and 253, use one of the strong verbs to rewrite relationship sentences. Then try to add detail to the sentences.

### EXAMPLE

Reading passage: Solutions to eradicating disease on a worldwide basis

Lecture: World Health Organization's successful campaign against smallpox
Relationship: Agreement

*Basic*: The example in the lecture <u>agrees with</u> the suggestions for eradicating disease in the reading passage.

*Better*: The example in the lecture <u>clarifies</u> the suggestions for eradicating disease in the reading passage.

*Best*: The example in the lecture of the World Health Organization's successful campaign against smallpox clarifies the suggestions for eradicating disease on a worldwide basis listed in the reading passage.

### PRACTICAL STRATEGY

In Task 3 on the Speaking Section, you will read a short passage and then hear a conversation about the passage. The reading passage is usually an announcement about a policy on campus. The conversation includes opinions about the policy. First, determine whether the speakers agree or disagree with the policy. Then write a relationship sentence that expresses the opinion. The three verbs listed below are commonly used for opinions in conversational English. A basic relationship sentence will state an opinion that shows agreement or disagreement with the passage. A better relationship sentence will state agreement or disagreement and will also include a summary of the reasons for the opinion. Remember that you are not being asked for *your* opinion. You are being asked to summarize *the speaker's* opinion.

### Opinion Verbs

Believes
Says
Thinks

## PRACTICE ACTIVITY 43

Did you understand? First, state the speaker's opinion. Next, identify the reasons for the opinion. Finally, write a relationship sentence that includes both the opinion and the reasons. Example answers are printed on page 308.

### EXAMPLE

| | |
|---|---|
| Reading passage: | A change in the bus schedule |
| Conversation: | The man is giving his opinion |
| Relationship: | Disagreement |
| Reasons: | Fewer stops, inconvenient times, more expensive |

Basic sentence:   The man believes that the change in the bus schedule is a bad idea.

Better sentence:   The man believes that the change in the bus schedule is a bad idea because there are fewer stops, the new times are inconvenient, and the passes are more expensive.

**Also good examples:**

The man says that the change in the bus schedule is a bad idea because there are fewer stops, the new times are inconvenient, and the passes are more expensive.

The man thinks that the change in the bus schedule is a bad idea because there are fewer stops, the new times are inconvenient, and the passes are more expensive.

1.  Reading passage:   A new location for the cafeteria
    Conversation:   The woman is giving her opinion
    Relationship:   Disagreement
    Reasons:   Farther from the dorm, smaller space

    Basic sentence:

    Better sentence:

2.  Reading passage:   A change in the final exam schedule
    Conversation:   The man is giving his opinion
    Relationship:   Agreement
    Reasons:   More time to study, fewer conflicts with other exams

    Basic sentence:

    Better sentence:

3.  Reading passage:   More lighting around the square
    Conversation:   The woman is giving her opinion
    Relationship:   Agreement
    Reasons:   Safer for bikers, better security for walkers, will look nicer

    Basic sentence:

    Better sentence:

4.  Reading passage:     Closing the post office on campus
    Conversation:        The woman is giving her opinion
    Relationship:        Disagreement
    Reasons:             The campus post office is always busy, the closest post office off
                         campus is not within walking distance

    Basic sentence:

    Better sentence:

5.  Reading passage:     Eliminating all single rooms in the graduate dorms
    Conversation:        The man is giving his opinion
    Relationship:        Disagreement
    Reasons:             No inexpensive alternative on campus, no adjustment in fees,
                         and no opportunity to provide input

    Basic sentence:

    Better sentence:

## PRACTICE ACTIVITY 44

Did you understand? First, read the summary of the main ideas in the reading passage
and the lecture and the relationship between them. Next, study the basic relationship sentence. Then try to substitute a stronger verb to make the relationship sentence better. Finally,
include more detail to make the relationship sentence the best. Example answers are printed
on pages 309–310.

1.  Reading passage:     Advantages of cooperative learning in education
    Lecture:             Research study in Chicago schools
    Relationship:        Agreement

2.  Reading passage:     Methods to solve the problem of noise pollution in technological
                         societies
    Lecture:             European noise ordinances
    Relationship:        Agreement

3.  Reading passage:     Nuclear power is too dangerous
    Lecture:             Opposing view—three points
    Relationship:        Disagreement

4.  Reading passage:     Ideas for successful international advertising campaigns
    Lecture:             Toyota's marketing plan in the United States
    Relationship:        Agreement

5.  Reading passage:     Meteor impact caused the disappearance of dinosaurs
    Lecture:             Opposing view—three points
    Relationship:        Disagreement

6. Reading passage: More than 40 van Gogh paintings are fakes
   Lecture: Opposing view—three points
   Relationship: Disagreement

7. Reading passage: The theory of flow
   Lecture: A Harvard University study on flow
   Relationship: Agreement

8. Reading passage: Successful marriages require similarities
   Lecture: Opposing view—three points
   Relationship: Disagreement

9. Reading passage: Definition of a biogeographic realm
   Lecture: A biome
   Relationship: Agreement

10. Reading passage: Censorship is necessary in the media
    Lecture: Opposing view—three points
    Relationship: Disagreement

## INCLUDE INFORMATION FROM BOTH SOURCES

**Strategies to Use**
➤ Get organized
➤ Discuss each point

## ➤ Get organized

### PRACTICAL STRATEGY

Even before you read the passage, you can begin to get organized. First, quickly draw a chart for your notes like the one below. Then, as you begin reading, note the main points in the passage and write them under **Reading** in the chart. Next, listen to the **Conversation** or **Lecture** and take notes. Listen carefully for information that relates to *each point* from the reading passage. Finally, decide whether the speaker agrees or disagrees with the general information in the reading passage. Write a **Relationship sentence** at the top of the chart. Remember, three points are usually included, but sometimes only two are mentioned.

Relationship sentence: _____.

| Reading | Conversation/Lecture |
|---------|---------------------|
| Point 1 | Point 1 |
| Point 2 | Point 2 |
| Point 3 | Point 3 |

### PRACTICE ACTIVITY 45

Did you understand? Read a passage and then listen to a conversation on the same topic. Get organized, using a chart like the one in the example above. Draw it quickly on your scratch paper before you begin reading. Then fill it in as you read the passage and listen to the conversation. Compare your chart with the example chart on pages 310–311.

### INTEGRATED SPEAKING TASK 3

SCRATCH PAPER

Reading Time: 45 seconds

---

**Summer School Announcement**

In an effort to conserve energy during summer session, all classes will be held Monday through Thursday to allow for air conditioning and lights to be shut down completely for three days per week. During the four-day school week, thermostats will be set at 78 degrees for air conditioning units, and all units will be automatically switched off at eight o'clock at night and switched on at eight o'clock in the morning. In addition, motion-sensitive light panels will replace current manual switches in all buildings, including classrooms, offices, meeting rooms, and bathrooms. When no motion is detected in a room for more than one minute, the lights will turn off until motion reactivates them.

---

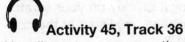
**Activity 45, Track 36**
Now listen to a conversation on the same topic.

### PRACTICE ACTIVITY 46

Did you understand? Read a passage and then listen to a lecture on the same topic. Get organized, using a chart like the one in the example above. Draw it quickly on your scratch paper before you begin reading. Then fill it in as you read the passage and listen to the lecture. Compare your chart with the example chart on page 311.

## Integrated Speaking Task 4

SCRATCH PAPER

Reading Time: 45 seconds

---

**Marsupials**

   Marsupials are a group of mammals that are born alive after a very short gestation period. In order to survive, the young, underdeveloped marsupial must crawl from the exit of the reproductive tract over its mother's body to attach itself to a nipple inside a fold of skin called the *marsupium* or pouch. During embryonic development, a marsupial stays with the mother, climbing in and out of the pouch to nurse or sleep.

   Like other mammals, marsupials are covered with hair. Auditory and olfactory senses are highly developed in marsupials because they are nocturnal creatures that depend on their ears and eyes to locate food at night.

---

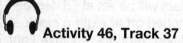**Activity 46, Track 37**

Now listen to part of a lecture in a biology class.

## Practice Activity 47

Did you understand? Read a passage and then listen to a lecture on the same topic. Get organized, using a chart like the one in the example above. Draw it quickly on your scratch paper before you begin reading. Then fill it in as you read the passage and listen to the conversation. Compare your chart with the example chart on page 312.

SCRATCH PAPER

## INTEGRATED WRITING TASK 1: INTEGRATED ESSAY

Reading Time: 3 minutes

Although bottled water was an alternative during even the earliest civilizations, it has become more popular in the past few decades, for a variety of reasons. First, it is a healthier choice. In the United States, bottled water is comprehensively regulated by the Food and Drug Administration as a packaged food product. Minerals such as magnesium and chloride have been removed, along with salt. In contrast, the potential for heavy metals exists in public water supplies, such as copper and lead from storage tanks and industrial chemicals like dry-cleaning toxins. Of course, these issues are not a concern for bottled water, which is pure and free of contamination.

Furthermore, bottled water tastes better. Most bottled water comes from natural springs and wells, whereas local water supplies come from ground water that is trapped in aquifers or from wells drilled near rivers and streams. To make these water supplies safe to drink, water treatment plants remove contaminants and disinfect their tap water with chemicals, usually chlorine, which smells and leaves an aftertaste.

Finally, bottled water is convenient, and the packaging is, for the most part, reusable and recyclable. In fact, most plastic water bottles are 100 percent recyclable and are among the most recycled packaged products in the recycle system. In recent years, campaigns have raised public awareness and the recycling of water bottles has increased by as much as 6 percent per year. The introduction of lighter-weight plastics has also allowed the bottling industry to further reduce its environmental footprint.

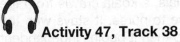

### Activity 47, Track 38

Now listen to part of a lecture in a general science class. The professor is talking about bottled water.

## ➤ Discuss each point

### PRACTICAL STRATEGY

You will receive a lower score for your integrated speaking and writing tasks if you do not relate all of the main points in the reading to the conversation or lecture. Be sure to refer to the main points in your notes while you are speaking and read your essay after you have written it. Check to make sure that you have a complete response.

### EXAMPLE

These responses refer to the integrated speaking and writing tasks in Activities 45, 46, and 47, Tracks 36, 37, and 38. When you compare the example responses and example essay with the notes, you find the relationship sentence. You also find all three points from the reading passage and ideas that the speaker or lecturer presented to support or refute each point.

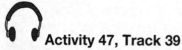

**Activity 47, Track 39**

## Question
The woman expresses her opinion of the announcement. State her opinion and give the reasons that she gives for the opinion.

## Example Response
The woman doesn't agree with the idea to shut down the campus for three days every week in order to conserve energy. Although she supports the conservation of resources, she thinks that the intensive weekend courses that will be cancelled are important, especially for working people like her sister. The online courses replacing them won't provide the personal interaction that weekend courses do for those who are already taking online classes. She concedes that the idea of motion sensors for lighting makes sense, but she's not sure that turning off the power completely is an energy efficient plan because power outages could occur when the power is turned on in all the buildings on campus at eight o'clock Monday morning.

## Question
The professor describes a koala. Using information from both the reading and the lecture, explain why a koala would be considered a marsupial.

## Example Response
A koala is a good example of a marsupial because it completes its embryotic development in its mother's pouch, it's hairy like other mammals, and it has a keen sense of smell and hearing, which are important to its nocturnal nature. Like all marsupials, a koala crawls from the birth canal to the mother's pouch and attaches itself to a nipple to nurse. It stays with the mother for about eight months until it's too big for the pouch and then it begins independent life in trees, using its sensitive nose to feed on eucalyptus leaves at night.

## Question
Using the main points in the reading passage, show how the lecturer contradicts the claims.

## Example Essay
The lecturer discredits the claim in the reading passage that bottled water is better than tap water. First, she refutes the assertion that bottled water is healthier by pointing out that 40 percent of all water in bottles comes from city water sources. In other words, it is just tap water in a bottle. Furthermore, she contends that bottled water is actually less healthy than tap water because it contains a lower level of fluoride, a mineral that retards tooth decay.

Second, she maintains that minerals actually make the water taste better. Sodium, calcium, magnesium, and fluoride keep water from tasting flat. She backs up this statement by citing a taste test by *Good Morning America* in which 45 percent of the participants chose New York City tap water over bottled water.

Third, she concedes that it would be possible to recycle the plastic bottles used for bottled water, but she points out that only 15 percent of all water bottles are ever recycled, which means that 59.5 million of the 70 million bottles used daily in the United States are thrown into landfills.

## PRACTICE ACTIVITY 48

Did you understand? Read a passage and listen to a conversation or lecture on the same topic. Then listen to the example response or read the example essay. Is it complete? Are all of the points in the reading passage mentioned? Are all of the same points from the conversation or lecture included? Compare your answer with the example answers on pages 313–315.

## SPEAKING TASK 3

SCRATCH PAPER

Reading Time: 45 seconds

---

**Announcement from the Office of the President**
The Board of Trustees approved tuition, mandatory fees, and room and board rates during its June meeting on Friday. The plan provides for tuition for in-state students to be frozen at $12,000, the same rate as last year. Out-of-state tuition is scheduled to increase 3 percent over the last academic year. Tuition for current international students will also increase by 3 percent; however, the tuition for new international students will increase by 5 percent over the last academic year. In-state students make up approximately 80 percent of undergraduate students, out-of-state students 12 percent, and international students 8 percent.

---

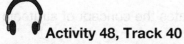 **Activity 48, Track 40**
Now listen to a conversation on the same topic.

**Question**
The man expresses his opinion of the announcement. State his opinion and give the reasons he has for holding that opinion.

**Example Response**

## SPEAKING TASK 4

SCRATCH PAPER

Reading Time: 45 seconds

---

**Strategic Alliances**

In a global economy, collaboration and strategic alliances may be essential to success. Although there are a number of ways to cooperate, including mergers in which two companies form a legal union, or a joint venture where several companies pool resources to create a separate entity, a strategic alliance is much less involved than either one. Quite simply, a strategic alliance is a mutual agreement between two or more companies in order to work more effectively toward their goals. This usually involves a plan to share resources for mutual benefit. The major advantages of strategic alliances are that each company retains its separate identity and that the alliances may be easily formed and easily dissolved, which makes them a perfect vehicle in a rapidly changing business environment.

---

**Activity 48, Track 41**

Now that you have read the explanation of strategic business alliances in the reading, listen to part of a lecture on a similar topic.

**Question**

Explain how the example that the professor provides demonstrates the concept of strategic alliances defined in the reading passage.

**Example Response**

## INTEGRATED ESSAY

SCRATCH PAPER

Reading Time: 3 minutes

In a recent survey of developed nations, it was found that workers in the United States receive the least number of paid vacation days in the world. Although many Americans are paid for ten national holidays, they are not legally entitled to any paid vacation time in spite of the fact that paid vacations bring benefits not only to the employee but also to the company.

Employees with paid vacation are less likely to call in unexpectedly. Companies with paid vacation benefits have more control over unscheduled absenteeism, which allows for a more predictable coverage of responsibilities. Being able to plan is critical to most companies.

Moreover, time off from the work environment assures the company of a workforce that is healthier and more productive after the break. People who take vacations exhibit lower stress levels, less risk of heart disease, a more positive attitude, and higher motivation to achieve goals. Surprisingly, the effects of a vacation appear to be beneficial for as long as eight weeks before the actual leave from work. Employees looking forward to a break tend to tie up loose ends on their jobs before they go. After they return, they are rested and their productivity is significantly higher than it was before their time away from work.

Vacation time also has the advantage of attracting more highly qualified employees. Those employees with the best qualifications can select from among several offers. Candidates who are the most difficult to recruit will be more likely to sign on when a company provides an attractive vacation plan. For a company to be most competitive, it is advantageous to appeal to a highly qualified team.

Companies that do not choose to offer paid vacation time may save money in the short term; however, an investment in time off for their employees would probably be smarter in the long run.

**Activity 48, Track 42**

Now listen to part of a lecture in a business class. The professor is talking about vacation time.

## Question

Summarize the main points in the lecture, and then explain how they cast doubt on the ideas in the reading passage.

### Example Essay

The lecturer contradicts the points in the reading passage that make a case for more paid vacation time for employees. First, he disagrees with the assumption that companies will have more control over absenteeism because employees will schedule their time around vacation days. He explains that emergencies cannot be predicted or arranged around a vacation schedule; therefore, the company is not able to control or plan for absences at critical times in spite of generous paid vacations.

Second, he concedes that some evidence suggests a relationship between vacations and good health as well as productivity. However, he argues that many employees do not use their vacation days to rest and relax. In fact, many employees use the time to participate in stressful activities that they are unable to accomplish during the usual workweek. Instead of taking a break, they rush to do as much as possible in a short time, leaving them exhausted by the time that they return to the work schedule.

Third, although paid vacation days could be attractive to some employees that a company may wish to recruit, the lecturer points out that contract negotiation is a highly individual process. Whereas some candidates would like more paid vacation days, others would prefer other benefits such as health care, higher salaries, or a fast track to promotion.

In short, the lecturer does not believe that more paid vacation days would be in the best interest of American companies.

## FOLLOW A PLAN

**Strategies to Use**
➤ Memorize the steps
➤ Practice with the plan

## ➤ Memorize the steps

### *PRACTICAL STRATEGY*

Three tasks on the TOEFL require synthesis: Task 3 and Task 4 in the Speaking Section and Task 1 in the Writing Section. Each task requires a slightly different approach, but in general, you follow the same steps for all of them:

1 Draw a chart with space for a relationship sentence at the top and 3 points underneath.

2 Read a short passage and take notes on the chart.

3 Listen to a conversation or a lecture on the same topic and take notes on the chart.

4 Write a relationship sentence on the chart.

5 Respond using information from both the reading and the conversation or lecture.

6 Use the points on the chart to check for a complete response.

## PRACTICE ACTIVITY 49

The examples below will show you specific steps for each of the integrated tasks. Take your time as you study each example. You will have an opportunity to practice the steps in Activity 50.

## EXAMPLE SPEAKING TASK 3

Be careful! This task does NOT ask you for your opinion, although you will be asked about the opinions of the speakers in the conversation or talk.

1 Draw a chart with space for a relationship sentence at the top and 3 points underneath.

Relationship sentence: _____

| Reading | Conversation |
|---------|--------------|
| Point 1 | Point 1 |
| Point 2 | Point 2 |
| Point 3 | Point 3 |

2 Read a short passage about a campus-related topic and take notes on the chart.

Reading Time: 45 seconds

> **Announcement from Campus Security**
> On Monday, all State University residence halls will begin requiring students to scan their fingerprints at the door in order to gain access to their building. As part of a continuing effort to make residence halls safer, fingerprint scanners have been installed at every building entry point. To prepare for this, students must scan their fingerprints at the campus security office in the student union. Guests are still allowed into residence halls but must now leave a valid ID in exchange for a guest pass.

Relationship sentence: _____

| Reading | Conversation |
|---------|--------------|
| Point 1<br>Mon scan prints<br>Access dorms | Point 1 |
| Point 2<br>Prepare scan at<br>Campus Security<br>S Union | Point 2 |
| Point 3<br>Guests ID-pass | Point 3 |

③ Listen to a conversation on the same topic and take notes on the chart.

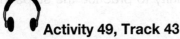

**Activity 49, Track 43**

Now listen to a conversation on the same topic.

<u>Relationship sentence:</u> The woman approves of the security policy because it is a serious plan, it will be easy to use, and it should be a deterrent to theft and safety.

<u>Reading</u>

Point 1
Mon scan prints
Access dorms

Point 2
Prepare scan at
Campus Security
S Union

Point 3
Guests ID-pass

<u>Conversation</u>

Point 1
Current plan not enforced
New plan serious

Point 2
Easy—devices secure
Students too

Point 3
Deterrent crime

## Question

The woman expresses her opinion of the announcement. State her opinion and the reasons that she has for having that opinion.

④ Write a relationship sentence on the chart.

⑤ Respond using information from both the reading and the conversation.

## Example Response

The woman approves of the new security policy because it's a serious plan, it will be easy to use, and it should be a deterrent to crime. She explains that the previous system that required a pass to enter the dorm wasn't enforced. But now, without a scan, it won't be possible to go in the door. She also points out that it's really easy, like scanning to access a secure mobile device. She argues that scanning a fingerprint will be a deterrent to theft and the dorms will be safer because it'll be better than a guest pass to keep track of everyone who's in the buildings.

⑥ Use the points on the chart to check for a complete response.

This is a complete response because it includes all three points that the woman makes to explain her opinion that the security policy is a good idea: It is a serious plan, easy to use, and will be a deterrent to crime.

### EXAMPLE SPEAKING TASK 4

Be careful! The reading usually presents the definition of a term, a concept, a principle, or a theory, and the lecture usually provides an example, evidence, a case study, a research study, or a specific instance. In other words, this task is usually a synthesis of agreement, extension, and clarification. But sometimes, it can be a synthesis of disagreement and opposition.

1 Draw a chart with space for a relationship sentence at the top and 3 points underneath.

Relationship sentence: _____

| Reading | Lecture |
|---------|---------|
| Point 1 | Point 1 |
| Point 2 | Point 2 |
| Point 3 | Point 3 |

2 Read a short passage about an academic topic and take notes on the chart.

Reading Time: 45 seconds

---

**Endangered Languages**

   Recent estimates of language populations indicate that half of the world's languages will likely become extinct in the twenty-first century. Three main criteria are used as guidelines for considering a language endangered: the number of speakers currently living, the average age of native speakers, and the percentage of the youngest generation acquiring fluency.

   Given these criteria, it is obvious that language extinction occurs gradually across generations. Fewer and fewer speakers use the traditional language until only the older generation is familiar enough with the grammar to understand and express themselves in it.

---

Relationship sentence: _____

| Reading | Lecture |
|---------|---------|
| Point 1<br>Number speakers | Point 1 |
| Point 2<br>Average age native | Point 2 |
| Point 3<br>Percent youngest gen | Point 3 |

3 Listen to a lecture on the same topic and take notes on the chart.

**Activity 49, Track 44**

Now listen to part of a lecture in a linguistics class. The professor is talking about endangered languages.

<u>Relationship sentence:</u> The Christensen study in 1995 provided evidence that Ojibwa should be on the endangered language list.

| Reading | Lecture |
|---------|---------|
| Point 1<br>Number speakers | Point 1<br>500–3 states |
| Point 2<br>Average age native | Point 2<br>elders 80+ |
| Point 3<br>Percent youngest gen | Point 3<br>Almost no children |

## Question

The professor reports a study of the Ojibwa language. Explain why the study confirms that Ojibwa is an endangered language.

4 Write a relationship sentence on the chart.

5 Respond using information from both the reading and the lecture.

## Example Response

Ojibwa is considered an endangered language because it meets all three criteria for that classification. First, few speakers are fluent in the language. In Christensen's study in 1995, only about 500 of the tribal members in the tri-state area studied were fluent speakers. Second, the average age of native speakers is older. Among the 500 fluent speakers, most were elders 80 years of age or older. Finally, the percentage of speakers in the youngest generation is small. Among Ojibwa speakers, almost *no* children were fluent. Unfortunately, this study confirmed that Ojibwa is endangered, and despite efforts to teach the language in federally funded preschools, its future is very uncertain.

6 Use the points on the chart to check for a complete response.

The response is complete because it includes all three criteria for a language to be considered endangered and provides evidence from the Christensen study to prove that Ojibwa meets all three criteria.

## EXAMPLE WRITING TASK 1: INTEGRATED ESSAY

The reading usually presents a position or argument in favor of a topic. The lecture presents information that calls into question the position or a counterargument. In other words, this task is usually a synthesis of disagreement, contrast, or opposition.

1 Draw a chart with space for a relationship sentence at the top and 3 points underneath.

Relationship sentence: _____

Reading
Point 1

Point 2

Point 3

Lecture
Point 1

Point 2

Point 3

2 Read a short passage about an academic topic and take notes on the chart.

Reading Time: 3 minutes

Homeownership is a goal for many people because they see it as a sound investment with many other positive outcomes as well.

Although it is true that the housing market can be volatile, from an individual perspective, buying a home to live in is still one of the best ways to acquire wealth. In the first place, homes appreciate. Over the long term, even initial losses reverse themselves and property values rise. Moreover, the cost for a rental tends to go up every year, whereas the cost of a 30-year mortgage is fixed. If the purchase is made when financing costs are low, then the investment is even more attractive. Traditionally, tax advantages have been offered to homeowners, providing additional financial incentives to enter the real estate market.

Another positive aspect of homeownership is the control that owners have over their living situation. Landlords can change the terms of rental agreements at the end of a short contract, forcing tenants to increase their expenditure or move. In contrast, homeowners have a sense of security and stability. By owning a home in a community, it is possible to maintain a stable environment without being compelled to make changes that may not be advantageous or well timed.

Finally, there are some unexpected social benefits for homeowners. In general, research supports positive outcomes in education, health, and crime. Specifically, the children of homeowners tend to achieve higher grades in school, both adults and children living in their own homes report better health and higher self-esteem, and crime rates are significantly lower in neighborhoods with a high percentage of resident homeowners.

Relationship sentence: _____

Reading                                  Lecture

Point 1 wealth creation—              Point 1
homes appreciate, fixed
mortgage, tax incentives

Point 2 control over living           Point 2
situation—rental contracts
change

Point 3 social benefits—              Point 3
health, education, crime

3  Listen to a lecture on the same topic and take notes on the chart.

**Activity 49, Track 45**

Now listen to part of a lecture in an economics class. The professor is talking about home-ownership.

Relationship sentence: The lecturer refutes the idea in the reading passage that homeownership is a goal promising positive outcomes.

Reading                                  Lecture

Point 1 wealth creation—   Point 1   recession—high mortgage, half value
homes appreciate,
fixed mortgage
tax incentives

Point 2 control over living   Point 2   foreclosure—insecurity, loss control
situation—rental contracts
change

Point 3 social benefits—   Point 3   one paycheck from losing home—stress,
health, education, crime   children lower grades, less involved in school

4  Write a relationship sentence on the chart.

5  Respond using information from both the reading and the lecture.

**Question**

Summarize the main points in the lecture, and then explain how they cast doubt on the ideas in the reading passage.

**Example Essay**

The lecturer refutes the idea in the reading passage that homeownership is a goal promising positive outcomes. He makes a case for a reversal of this trend in the current economy, addressing the three assumptions in the passage.

First, he questions whether a home is a good way to create wealth. Although homes appreciated in the past, in today's market, homes are, in fact, depreciating to such a low that some homeowners are paying a high fixed mortgage for a home that is worth about half the value of its purchase price.

Second, the lecturer disagrees that homeownership provides control over one's living situation. During the recession, foreclosures and forced sales created a loss of control and a climate of insecurity in the market. He points out that many first-time homeowners would rather rent but cannot solve the problem of how to return to a rental without losing a significant investment in the home that they now own.

Third, studies confirm that many owners are only one paycheck away from losing their homes, a situation that creates stress for all family members, reversing the social benefits that homeownership once assured, including lower grades and less involvement in school activities on the part of the children.

Clearly, economic instability has affected the value of homeownership in serious ways.

6 Use the points on the chart to check for a complete response.

*The essay is complete because it includes all three arguments proposed in the reading passage with the opposing argument for each one presented in the lecture.*

## ➤ Practice with the plan

### PRACTICAL STRATEGY

Remember that three tasks on the TOEFL require synthesis: Task 3 and Task 4 in the Speaking Section and Task 1 in the Writing Section. Now that you have memorized the steps, practice using them. Don't worry! The model tests in this book and on the CD-ROM will give you more practice, and soon you will be able to respond with confidence within the time limits on the iBT. For now, don't worry about timing yourself.

### PRACTICE ACTIVITY 50

First, write the step after the number. Then practice the step to complete the task. Compare your answers with the example answers on pages 318–322.

## SPEAKING TASK 3

⬜1

Reading Time: 45 seconds

---

### Announcement from the Office of the President

After five months of remodeling, the Faculty Club will move into a new space on the top floor of Anderson Hall. The facilities, open to all full-time faculty, will include a restaurant open for breakfast, lunch, and dinner, a private dining area that seats twenty, and a bar that will serve beer and wine. The Club will be open next Monday. The Honors Program that formerly occupied the Anderson Hall space has moved to a smaller suite of offices and a lounge in the basement of Harkins Hall. The offices are already open and the lounge will be available for honors students to use next month.

---

⬜3

**Activity 50, Track 46**

Now listen to a conversation on the same topic.

### Question

The man expresses his opinion of the announcement. State his opinion and give the reasons that he gives for the opinion.

⬜4

### Response

⬜5

⬜6

*After you have completed your response, listen to the example response for Speaking Task 3 on page 319.*

**SPEAKING TASK 4**

1

2

Reading Time: 45 seconds

---

<u>Courtship Display</u>
    A courtship display is a series of behaviors that an animal might use to attract a mate, and occasionally to warn rivals who may intrude. In general, the males initiate the courtship displays to arouse a female's interest and to win her selection among competing males. These behaviors may include ritualized dances or vocalizations that showcase the beauty or strength of the potential mate. In birds, these courtship displays often include postures by males to expose their plumage. Fanning and shaking the tail feathers, turning them to catch the light, and strutting around the female bird are common elements of the display.

---

3

 **Activity 50, Track 47**
Now listen to a lecture in a biology class about the same topic.

**Question**
The professor discusses peacocks. Explain how their behavior conforms to the usual rituals for courtship displays.

4

5

**Response**

6

*After you have completed your response, listen to the example response for Speaking Task 4 on page 320.*

## WRITING TASK 1

1️⃣

2️⃣

Reading Time: 3 minutes

> Government censorship of the Internet benefits society in three ways. First, like other forms of mass media, including television and movies, censorship protects children. Restricting adult content and providing punitive measures for pornographic websites discourages the exposure of young children to inappropriate images and explicit language. Since children are growing up in an environment in which they can easily access the Internet, some restrictions should be in place to protect them.
>
> Second, censorship curtails criminal activities. Censorship discovers and discourages financial frauds, theft, and harassment, or even potentially violent encounters. Because the Internet affords criminals a high degree of anonymity, unless their activities are monitored, they can sell illegal substances, threaten or bully individuals, or intrude into the lives of large numbers of people with spam advertising. Censorship reduces the instances of these disturbing contacts.
>
> Finally, censorship assures personal privacy. Censorship laws establish standards for websites and security measures to protect identity, financial records, and personal information. Censorship restricts access to credit cards and bank accounts, as well as medical and employment records, and it reduces the incidents of identity theft.

3️⃣

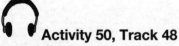 **Activity 50, Track 48**
Now listen to a lecture about the same topic.

**Question**
Summarize the main points in the lecture, and then explain how they cast doubt on the ideas in the reading passage.

## Question
The professor talks about censorship on the Internet. Explain how the lecture casts doubt on the information in the reading passage.

④

⑤

## Essay

⑥

*After you have completed your response, read the example essay for Writing Task 1 on page 322.*

**Beyond the Book
Mini-Lesson for the TOEFL
Synthesis**

To view the lesson, visit the
Barron's TOEFL site online. Click
on **Academic Skills**, then click on
**Mini-Lesson for Synthesis.**

# ANSWERS AND AUDIO SCRIPTS

## PRACTICE ACTIVITY 8

 Activity 8, Track 15

**Listening Task 1**

| | |
|---|---|
| Man: | Hi Jane. How's it going? |
| Woman: | Good. You? |
| Man: | Same old problem. My roommate is driving me crazy. |
| Woman: | But I thought you lived in a dorm. [*Surprise*] |
| Man: | I do. |
| Woman: | Oh. Then why don't you see your resident advisor? |
| Man: | Been there, done that. I even went to the head resident. |
| Woman: | Really? And it didn't help? |
| Man: | Nope. He says that we should work it out between the two of us. |
| Woman: | Wow. How do you do that when he's always partying in the room? |
| Man: | I know. I keep waiting for him to flunk out. |
| Woman: | He's on probation, right? [*Confirmation*] |
| Man: | Again. He cuts class, I never see him doing any homework, but he crams for his finals and always seems to just get by. |
| Woman: | I'm so sorry. I suppose you could go to the study lounge or the library to study, but you're probably already doing that. |
| Man: | I *am*, but it's not very convenient. I mean, I have all of my stuff in my room but now I have to pack it up every time I want to study . . . |
| Woman: | . . . and then you have to pack it all up again when you want to go back to your room. |
| Man: | That's about the size of it. |
| Woman: | Are you getting behind? |
| Man: | Not really. But I have a scholarship so I have to keep my G.P.A. up. And I'm a senior. |
| Woman: | You're a senior? [*Surprise*] Well then, you need to start thinking about graduate school. |
| Man: | I've already applied. But I need to submit this quarter's grades before they make a decision. |
| Woman: | So you really must be hitting the books. What can I do to help? |
| Man: | Not much. But thanks for listening. |

## PRACTICE ACTIVITY 9

 Activity 9, Track 16

**Speaking Task 3**

| | |
|---|---|
| Man: | Are you going on the community service trip over spring break? |
| Woman: | I never go anywhere on break. I just visit my family for a few days and then come back and get ready for the next semester. |
| Man: | I know, but this is different. It seems made to order for you. |

| Woman: | Are you serious? I don't drink, I don't like the beach, and I don't have the money to waste on airfare and hotels. |
|---|---|
| Man: | That's what I mean. This spring break trip isn't about any of that. It's a community service trip. Look, you work with a team on a project in a low-income area. You're minoring in social work, aren't you? [*Confirmation*] |
| Woman: | Yeah. |
| Man: | So you can see why I thought you might be interested. |
| Woman: | Actually, that does sound interesting. And I think it's a great idea. Spring break is so wild and crazy for a lot of my friends. Maybe this kind of alternative will attract some of the people who just want to get away from campus and do something different before they start another term. |
| Man: | I was thinking about going or at least checking it out over at student services. |
| Woman: | Yeah, but it would be expensive . . . unless the community is close by. |
| Man: | No. Here's the thing: a grant pays for your transportation and your living expenses so there aren't any fees. You just have to be willing to work. |
| Woman: | What kind of work is it? Do you know? |
| Man: | Not exactly. Some of the projects that were funded in the past have served senior citizens, and I'm pretty sure that there was tutoring for kids. |
| Woman: | Now you've really got me interested. |
| Man: | I thought you would be. We should go over to student services to get a few more details, like where they're planning to go and what projects are funded. [*Suggestion*] I think Professor Keller has his office hours now, and he's the one who's organizing the trip. |
| Woman: | Well, sure. I'm free right now until my next class at two. That ought to give us plenty of time. |
| Man: | Okay then. |
| Woman: | And even if it doesn't work out for me to go, I think it's a great idea to give people an alternative to . . . to . . . going crazy on some beach with a bunch of strangers from other colleges. That's never been my thing. |

## PRACTICE ACTIVITY 10

 **Activity 10, Track 17**

**Speaking Task 5**

| Man: | Hi Linda. I was hoping I might run into you today. |
|---|---|
| Woman: | Really? |
| Man: | Yeah. I wanted to ask you for . . . I wanted some advice. |
| Woman: | Oh, okay. |
| Man: | So you have Dr. Jackson for your academic advisor, don't you? [*Confirmation*] |
| Woman: | Unhuh. He's the advisor for most of the biology majors. |
| Man: | I know. And he's *my* advisor, too. But I'm just having problems communicating with him. I mean, he's nice and everything, but I feel like he just doesn't listen to me, and I leave the meetings thinking that I didn't get done what I needed to do. Do you ever feel like that? |
| Woman: | I can't say that I do, but it's a problem for sure if that's what's happening to *you*. Have you ever just had a serious talk about this with him? That's what I'd do. [*Suggestion*] |
| Man: | I've tried, but I'm just not getting through. I'm so frustrated. |
| Woman: | Well, you could request another advisor. I think Dr. Chee advises biology majors. [*Suggestion*] |

Man:         I thought about that, but if I change advisors, then I'll still have to sign up for a couple of my upper-division courses with Dr. Jackson, and he might resent it that I wanted a different advisor. Besides, he's on the committee for my thesis.

Woman:      I don't think he'd mind all that much. He has a lot of graduate students to advise. Listen, you could make an appointment to talk with him before he finds out about the change, and you could give him some reason that isn't personal, like your schedule makes it hard to see him during his office hours or something. [*Suggestion*]

Man:         I *could* say that, but what if he offers to see me at a different time?

Woman:      Right. Well, that could happen, but I don't think so.

## PRACTICE ACTIVITY 11

1.  Settlement Patterns                classification *or* comparison and contrast
2.  The Functions of Art               classification
3.  Language Development               sequence
4.  How Important Is Relativity?       persuasion *or* evaluation
5.  Causes of Schizophrenia            cause and effect
6.  Evaluating Kohlberg's Theory       persuasion *or* evaluation
7.  Types of Financial Services        classification
8.  A History of Plate Tectonics       sequence
9.  Estimating Population              cause and effect *or* problem and solution
10. Black Holes                        definition *or* description

## PRACTICE ACTIVITY 12

**Activity 12, Track 18**
**Example**
Listen to part of a lecture in an astronomy class.

1.  Listen to part of a lecture in a business class.
2.  Listen to part of a lecture in a music appreciation class.
3.  Listen to part of a lecture in a biology class.
4.  Listen to part of a lecture in an anthropology class.
5.  Listen to part of a lecture in an engineering class.
6.  Listen to part of a lecture in a linguistics class.
7.  Listen to part of a lecture in an art history class.
8.  Listen to part of a lecture in a psychology class.
9.  Listen to part of a lecture in a geology class.
10. Listen to part of a lecture in a history class.

## PRACTICE ACTIVITY 13

 **Activity 13, Track 19**

1. I have several slides of *mosaic art*, mostly from the fifth century.
2. Right. So last time we were discussing uh, multinational companies. Today we're going to look at *global companies*.
3. Well, today's lecture is about *light-years*.
4. So, if you read the chapter in your textbook, the one about *insurance*, then you have some background for today's lecture.
5. Although Malthus's theory of population is still important, I'm going to share a different approach with you today called *demographic transition*.
6. Okay then, let's begin our discussion of *marshland habitats*.
7. Sorry about the mixup with our classroom on the schedule. I'm glad you found us. So this will be the room we'll be using for the rest of the semester. Okay, then, let's get on with our discussion of *igneous rocks*.
8. From your syllabus, you know that today we're talking about *adobe construction*, specifically, how it can be adapted to modern architecture.
9. Let's ask ourselves this simple question: how does an *antibiotic* make you well?
10. All right. We've been talking about *reptiles*. Now let's turn our attention to *amphibians*.

## PRACTICE ACTIVITY 14

There are three arguments in support of protecting endangered species.

| | |
|---|---|
| Aesthetic justification<br>Various forms of nature influence<br>the life experience of human beings<br>in a positive way. | uniquely beautiful<br>appreciated universally in art and literature<br>important to the religious community |
| Ecological self-interest assumes<br>that a balance of nature benefits<br>all species. | perform essential functions<br>ex. unique carrier of a cure for a human<br>disease<br>to protect ourselves, we must protect other species |
| Moral justification asserts that<br>the creatures themselves have rights. | United Nations World Charter for Nature—<br>all species have the right to exist<br>human beings have the responsibility to preserve<br>all species |

The professor does not directly promote any argument, but advocacy for the protection of endangered species is implied in the lecture.

## PRACTICE ACTIVITY 15

1. According to Mead, the self has two sides: the "I" and the "me."

| | |
|---|---|
| The "I" represents the individuality of a person. | For instance, a spontaneous reaction might reveal the "I." This part of the self is less predictable because it is unique. |
| The "me" represents the expectations and attitudes of others. | This part of the self is formed through socialization by others. It is predictable because social conformity is expected. |

2. The mystery of pulsars was resolved in the 1960s.

| | |
|---|---|
| We know that pulsars are neutron stars, like lighthouses left by supernova explosions. | Like a lighthouse, the neutron star revolves. We see pulses of light each time the beam sweeps past the Earth. |
| We also know that pulsars are not perfectly timed because each revolution of a pulsar takes a little longer. | The pulsar in the Crab Nebula, for example, currently spins about thirty times per second. It will probably spin about half as fast 2,000 years from now. |

3. Britain transported convicts to Australia in an effort to solve the problems of overcrowding in prisons.

| | |
|---|---|
| In 1787, the first fleet left for Botany Bay in New South Wales. | There were 11 ships with 750 prisoners aboard. Four companies of marines sailed with them as guards. They took enough supplies for two years. |
| Shortly after arriving in 1788, the colony was moved to Sydney Cove. | In Sydney, the water supply and soil were better. Although Sydney was the new site, for many years it was called Botany Bay. |

4. Frederick Carl Frieseke was an American impressionist.

| | |
|---|---|
| Born in Michigan, he went to Paris in 1897. | He studied with Whistler in the late 1800s. From Whistler, he learned the academic style of the salons. |
| In 1905, Frieseke moved to Giverney where he lived until 1920. | At Giverney, Frieseke was influenced by Monet. Monet was experimenting with the effects of sunlight. The style of Monet and his school is known as impressionism. |
| By 1920, Frieseke had left Giverney for Normandy. | In Normandy, he began to paint indoor settings. In his later work, he began to use a darker palette. |

5. Two types of weathering will break down rock masses into smaller particles.

| | |
|---|---|
| Interaction between surface or ground water and chemicals causes chemical weathering. | With increased precipitation or temperature, chemicals tend to break down faster. The weathering of feldspar in granite can be caused by a reaction to acids in rain. A common example is the wearing away of granite facades on buildings. |
| Mechanical weathering occurs when force and pressure grind rocks down. | Pressure from freezing and thawing causes rocks to expand and contract. When a rock is broken in two by physical forces, it is more vulnerable to weathering. |

## PRACTICE ACTIVITY 16

1. There are two <u>types</u> of mixtures—heterogeneous and homogeneous. *Classification*
2. <u>As a result</u>, the litmus paper turns blue when the solution is a base. *Cause and Effect*
3. <u>In contrast</u>, a counterculture exhibits behavior that is contrary to the dominant culture. *Contrast*
4. The first <u>stage</u> of sleep produces alpha waves. *Sequence*
5. The main <u>properties</u> of soil include color, texture, and structure. *Description and Example*
6. Community service <u>should</u> be a requirement for graduation from the College of Education. *Persuasion and Evaluation*
7. <u>For example</u>, the Navajo create sacred images in colored sand in order to restore the spiritual and physical health of the sick. *Description and Example*
8. The maximum amount of water that air can hold at a given temperature and pressure <u>is known as</u> saturation. *Definition*
9. <u>Whereas</u> an objective is specific and measurable, a goal is broader and is usually not time specific. *Comparison and Contrast*
10. Dutch explorers in the early <u>seventeenth century</u> called the west coast of Australia "New Holland," a name that was used to describe the continent until the beginning of the <u>nineteenth century</u>. *Sequence*

## PRACTICE ACTIVITY 17

 **Activity 17, Track 20**
Listen to the beginning of a lecture in a linguistics class.

Good morning. Well, we have a lot to do today, so let's get going. If you're caught up with your . . . your reading assignments, you've already read the article on the three types of language, but before we go on with the discussion, I want to take a few minutes to compare them. Okay, standard language first. That's language that's comprehended, used, and considered acceptable by most speakers, I mean, native speakers. So definitions of words and phrases in standard language . . . they're found in the dictionary. They can be used in both formal and informal, . . . situations . . . settings. And this is important—standard language is appropriate in both speech and writing. I'd say that all of these characteristics combine to make standard language, well, let's just say that it's the permanent core of a language.

That brings us to colloquial language, which is included in dictionaries but colloquial language is marked, and usually it's a colloquial idiom. So these patterns of colloquial language are understood and used and accepted in informal exchanges and in, well . . . people use them in informal situations, but they're not really considered appropriate in formal settings. Did I say that colloquial language is more prevalent in speech than in writing? That's important and the key point in the article was that colloquial language becomes so much a part of the culture that at some point, it often . . . evolves . . . into standard language. So you can compare an earlier dictionary with a recent dictionary and that will . . . you can see how some phrases that are marked as colloquial language lose that designation in later editions of the same dictionary.

Okay, so you can see that colloquial idioms last a long time, either remaining popular in colloquial speech or, as I said, it can evolve into standard language and become a permanent part of the language. But that's very different from slang expressions because . . . and this is the key point . . . slang is usually a *temporary* phenomenon. It's used by some speakers or groups in informal situations and they're much more common in speech than they are in writing. Sometimes they're included in a dictionary but, uh, they're always clearly marked as slang, and when you check later editions of the dictionary, quite often the slang expression is no longer included because it's out of style.

Now, let's consider the three types of language together and uh . . . I want you to think of them on a continuum from most to least formal. So, if we do that, colloquial language would have to go between standard and slang. So the slang is often relegated to a temporary fad, and standard language contains the stable elements of the language and colloquial language has the potential to become a permanent part of a language, but . . . it might not.

I think it's interesting that most native speakers will use all three types of language and they'll use them all appropriately without thinking about it. In fact, only a few speakers will be able to analyze their speech and writing using the labels that the author identified in the article.

That said, let's get out the article for today's discussion and . . .

**Notes**

Definition + comparison = three types of language

| | |
|---|---|
| Standard usage<br>*Permanent core | definitions words + phrases found in dictionary<br>*used formal + informal situations<br>appropriate speech + writing |
| Colloquial language<br>*Often evolves into standard | included in dictionary marked as colloquial idioms<br>understood + used in informal situations, not formal more common in speech |
| Slang expressions<br>*Temporary phenomenon | sometimes in dictionary marked as slang<br>used by some speakers in informal situations<br>more common in speech |
| Continuum | most formal—least formal<br>standard—colloquial—slang |

## PRACTICE ACTIVITY 18

   **Activity 18, Track 21**
Listen to the beginning of a lecture in a sociology class as you read the transcript.
The professor is discussing status and roles.

Status refers to, uh, a position in society or . . . or in a group. But there are really two types of status—ascribed status and achieved status. Okay, in ascribed status, the status is automatic so you don't have a choice. In other words, it's an involuntary status. And some examples that come to mind are status because of race or sex. Not much you can do about that. On the other hand, achieved status requires some effort, and there's a choice involved. For instance, a marriage partner, or the type of education, or, for that matter, . . . the length of time in school. Well, these are choices, uh, achievements, and so they fall under the category of achieved status. So, that brings us to the status set. A status set is the combination of all statuses that an individual has. Me, for example. I'm a professor, but I'm also a husband and a father, and, . . . a son, since my mother is still living.

So, in each of these statuses I have certain behaviors that are expected because of the status. Okay, all of the behaviors are roles, I mean, a role is the behavior expected because of status. Okay, back to status set. All of the statuses—husband, father, son, professor—combine to form the status set, and each of the statuses have certain expectations. Let me use that professor status again. So, as a professor, I have a teaching role, and I have to prepare classes. That's expected. I also advise students, grade assignments, and evaluate my students. But this role has very different expectations. As a researcher, I, I have to design studies, raise funds for grants, and uh, then perform the research, and, and, finally, I write articles and reports. So, I think you see what I mean.

But, one more thing, and this is important, sometimes role conflict can occur. Let me say that again, role conflict. And that means that meeting the expectations for one role will cause problems for an individual who is trying to meet other expectations in a different role. Okay, let's say that one of my students is dating my daughter. I don't recommend this. But anyway, I may have role strain that could even develop into role conflict because it will be difficult for me to meet the expectations for my role as teacher and, uh, when the student comes to my house, I'll have to remember my status as father and my role that requires me to welcome a guest into my home, and well, form an opinion about someone who wants to take my daughter out on a date. The textbook actually . . .

## Notes

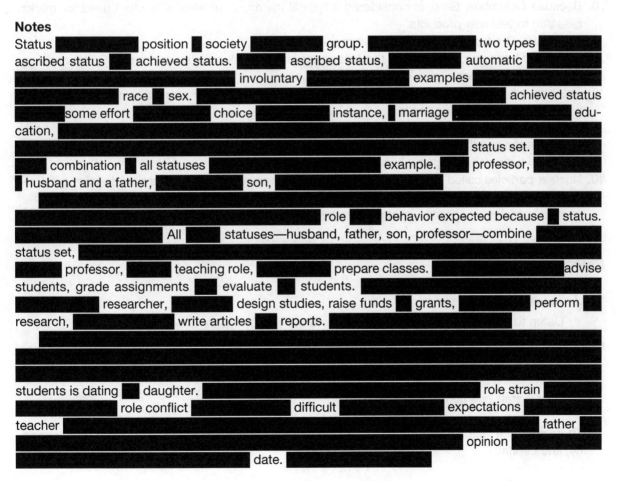

Status ▮▮▮▮▮▮ position ▮ society ▮▮▮▮▮ group. ▮▮▮▮▮▮▮▮ two types ▮▮▮▮▮ ascribed status ▮ achieved status. ▮▮▮▮ ascribed status, ▮▮▮▮▮ automatic ▮▮▮▮▮▮▮▮▮▮▮▮▮▮ involuntary ▮▮▮▮▮ examples ▮▮▮▮▮▮▮ ▮▮▮▮▮▮▮ race ▮ sex. ▮▮▮▮▮▮▮▮▮▮▮ achieved status ▮▮▮▮ some effort ▮▮▮▮ choice ▮▮▮▮ instance, ▮ marriage ▮ ▮▮▮▮▮ education, ▮▮▮▮▮▮▮▮▮▮▮▮▮▮▮▮▮▮▮ status set. ▮▮▮ ▮▮▮ combination ▮ all statuses ▮▮▮▮▮▮▮▮ example. ▮▮ professor, ▮▮▮▮ ▮ husband and a father, ▮▮▮▮▮ son, ▮▮▮▮▮▮▮▮▮ ▮▮▮▮▮▮▮▮▮ role ▮▮ behavior expected because ▮ status. ▮▮▮▮▮▮▮ All ▮▮ statuses—husband, father, son, professor—combine ▮▮ status set, ▮▮▮▮ professor, ▮▮▮▮ teaching role, ▮▮▮▮▮ prepare classes. ▮▮▮▮▮▮▮▮ advise students, grade assignments ▮ evaluate ▮ students. ▮▮▮▮▮▮▮▮ ▮▮▮▮▮ researcher, ▮▮▮▮▮ design studies, raise funds ▮ grants, ▮▮▮▮▮ perform ▮ research, ▮▮▮▮▮▮ write articles ▮ reports. ▮▮▮▮▮▮▮ ▮▮▮▮▮▮▮▮▮▮▮ ▮▮▮▮▮▮▮▮▮▮▮ ▮▮▮▮▮▮▮▮▮▮▮ students is dating ▮ daughter. ▮▮▮▮▮▮▮▮ role strain ▮▮▮ ▮▮▮▮ role conflict ▮▮▮▮▮ difficult ▮▮▮▮ expectations ▮▮▮ teacher ▮▮▮▮▮▮▮▮▮▮ father ▮ ▮▮▮▮▮▮▮▮▮▮▮▮ opinion ▮▮▮ ▮▮▮▮▮▮▮ date. ▮▮▮▮▮▮

## PRACTICE ACTIVITY 19

  **Activity 19, Track 22**

Listen to some sentences from college lectures. Take notes as quickly as you can.

1. The Nineteenth Amendment to the U.S. Constitution gave women the right to vote, beginning with the elections of 1920.

   19 → women vote/1920

2. In a suspension bridge, there are two towers with one or more flexible cables firmly attached at each end.

   suspension = 2 towers w/flex cables @ ends

3. A perennial is any plant that continues to grow for more than two years, as, for example, trees and shrubs.

   perennial = plant 2+ yrs ex. trees, shrubs

4. Famous for innovations in punctuation, typography, and language, Edward Estlin Cummings, known to us as e.e. cummings, published his collected poems in 1954.

   ee. cummings → innovations punct, typo, lang 1954 poems

5. Absolute zero, the temperature at which all substances have zero thermal energy, and thus the lowest possible temperatures, is unattainable in practice.

   absolute zero = temp. all subs 0 therm en → lowest temps

6. Because Columbus, Ohio, is considered a typical metropolitan area, it is often used for market research to test new products.

   Columbus, O = typical metro → market res new prod

7. The cacao bean was cultivated by the Aztecs not only to drink but also as currency in their society.

   cacao bean ← Aztecs = curr

8. The blue whale is the largest known animal, reaching a length of more than one hundred feet, which is five times its size at birth.

   blue whale = largest an 100′ = 5× birth size

9. Ontario is the heartland of Canada, both geographically and, I would say, historically as well.

   Ontario = heartland Can geo + hist

10. Nuclear particles called hadrons, which include the proton and neutron, are made from quarks—very odd particles that have a slight electrical charge but that cannot exist alone in nature.

    nuclear particles = hadrons = proton + neutron ← quarks = part slight elec charge 0 nature

## PRACTICE ACTIVITY 20

  **Activity 20, Track 23**

Listen to some sentences from college lectures. Take notes by drawing diagrams.

**Notes**

1. A *filament* is the stalk of a stamen.

   filament = stalk /stamen

2. There are three factors that determine whether a credit applicant is a good risk—character, capacity, and capital.

   Credit risk
   character   capacity   capital

3. In photosynthesis, the chloroplasts in the leaf absorb energy from the Sun and then convert carbon dioxide from the atmosphere and water into carbohydrates.

photosynthesis = chloroplasts ← energy/ Sun → $CO_2$ → carbohydrates

4. It was in the Cenozoic Era that *Homo sapiens* first appeared, which was only about 1.8 million years ago, long after the Mesozoic Era, perhaps 200 million years ago, when the dinosaurs were roaming the Earth, and even earlier, approximately 540 million years ago, well, that was the Paleozoic Era when there was an explosive evolution of marine life.

- Cenozoic 1.8 m/yrs    *Homo sapiens*
- Mesozoic 200          dinosaurs
- Paleozoic 540         marine life

5. In the sense that it is used among sociologists, the overwhelming feeling or need to escape a situation immediately is known as *panic*.

Feeling/need to escape = panic

6. The difference between slate and phyllite is the coarseness of the grain and the color—slate being much more fine, often gray and easily split along the cleavage, whereas phyllite tends to be more coarsely grained, rather lustrous in appearance and feel, and, oh yes, it can be gray, green, or even red.

| Slate | Phyllite |
|---|---|
| fine | coarse |
| split/cleavage | lustrous |
| gray | gray, green, red |

7. Regulatory genes called homeotic genes cause the body parts of animals to develop appropriately.

homeotic genes → body parts/animals develop

8. There were two types of decorations on Renaissance structures—the *cartouche*, which was an ornamental panel in the form of a scroll or some type of document, and the *graffito*, which was a white surface with a black undercoating, and uh, the . . . the design was made by scraping the white to reveal the black.

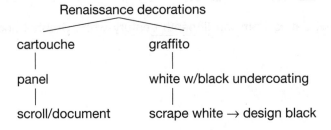

Renaissance decorations

cartouche          graffito

panel              white w/black undercoating

scroll/document    scrape white → design black

9. Ptolemy, a Greek living in Alexandria in the second century A.D. . . . Ptolemy assumed that the Earth was at the center of the universe, a theory that was accepted until 1543 when Copernicus, a Polish cleric, proposed that the Sun was at the center and the planets, including the Earth, revolved around it.

Ptolemy/Greek in Alexandria    Copernicus/Polish cleric
2 Cent A.D.                     1543
Earth center                   Sun center

10. The brain consistently sends out electrical waves during sleep, and there are two basic types—slow waves, which are larger and more often occur at the beginning of the sleep cycle and . . . and may be more important for physical recuperation . . . as compared with REM or "rapid eye movement" waves that are faster and probably occur three to five times in an eight-hour period, usually later in the sleep cycle, and we think that REM may be more effective in resting the brain than slow waves.

Slow waves            <u>REM</u>
larger                rapid eye movement
beginning sleep       later 3–5/8 hrs
physical recuperation rests brain

## Practice Activity 21

1. The copperhead, a snake that <u>attacks</u> without warning, is <u>regarded</u> as much more <u>treacherous</u> than the rattlesnake.
2. Because J. P. Morgan was known as a <u>trustworthy</u> and <u>careful</u> businessman, he was able to <u>convince</u> others to <u>stay</u> in the market even after the crash had <u>started</u>.
3. Phosphorus is <u>employed</u> in paint on highway signs and markers because it is <u>luminous in the dark</u>.
4. Rain forests are <u>frequently</u> <u>situated</u> <u>close</u> to the equator.
5. By the <u>mid-1800s</u>, land was so <u>costly</u> in <u>big</u> cities that architects <u>started</u> <u>to save</u> space by <u>constructing</u> skyscrapers.
6. <u>Investigations</u> of vertebrates <u>demonstrate</u> evolution from a very <u>basic</u> heart in fish to a <u>complicated</u> four-chamber heart in humans.
7. When two products are <u>essentially</u> <u>identical</u>, advertising can <u>affect</u> the <u>decision</u> that the public makes.
8. <u>In general</u>, in birds, the male of the species is <u>more vividly</u> colored.
9. The <u>value</u> of gold on the world market <u>depends on</u> several <u>factors</u>, including, but not <u>restricted to</u>, supply and demand.
10. The <u>concept</u> of a submarine is not <u>new</u>, dating from the <u>fifteenth century</u> when Drebbel and da Vinci <u>made</u> <u>preliminary</u> drawings.

## Practice Activity 22

 **Activity 22, Track 24**

1. Because light travels faster than sound, lightning appears to <u>go before</u> thunder.
2. Congress <u>looked up to</u> Jefferson because of his intelligence and creativity.
3. The lower teeth in crocodiles <u>stick out</u> when their mouths are closed.
4. Some sponges <u>look like</u> plants.
5. The first census was <u>carried out</u> in Great Britain in 1801.
6. People who have <u>gone through</u> a traumatic event may have recurring images of it.

7. In algebra, letters and other symbols <u>stand for</u> numbers.
8. During periods of stress or excitement, the heart rate <u>goes up</u> and airways to the lungs become dilated.
9. Theories of prehistory and early humans are constantly changing as we <u>take into account</u> the new evidence from archeological finds.
10. Dreams may have been the inspiration for the Surrealists to <u>come up with</u> their works of art.

## Practice Activity 23

 **Activity 23, Track 25**

### ADJECTIVES
1. The temperature in many desert regions is <u>not hot</u> at night.
2. Facial expressions may <u>not</u> be <u>unique</u> across cultures.
3. Obsidian is <u>not dull</u> because it cools too quickly for crystals to form.
4. <u>Not many</u> musical instruments play louder than 100 decibels or softer than 20 decibels.
5. The people who have adapted to life at very high altitudes are usually <u>not tall</u>.

### NOUNS
1. In many cities, <u>people who are trying to sell their goods</u> must have a license to set up their booths in public areas.
2. Studies show that small <u>animals that live indoors</u> are a positive influence in elderly people's lives.
3. Staircases were an important feature of the <u>palaces where the aristocracy lived</u> constructed during the Baroque period.
4. Global wind patterns are affected by the <u>way that the Earth turns</u>.
5. <u>Education that includes two languages</u> is more common in regions where language minorities live.

### VERBS
1. Unlike cast iron, pure wrought iron <u>has</u> no carbon.
2. Hypnosis <u>causes</u> a heightened state of suggestibility in a willing participant.
3. Productivity increases when fewer employees are required to <u>do</u> the work.
4. Normally, the plasma in human blood <u>is</u> 50–60 percent of the total blood volume.
5. Three-fourths of the goods <u>made</u> in Canada for export are sold to the United States.

## Practice Activity 24

### CHRONOLOGY
1. The first primitive mammals appeared in the Triassic Period.
2. Before the late Middle Ages, glass was not a major construction material.
3. Hydrogen was used as a power source for dirigibles before helium, which was safer.
4. The Europeans arrived in 1791, long after the Moriori people settled the Chatham Islands off the coast of New Zealand.
5. Store your test tubes and pipettes in the lab cabinets after you rinse them with a small amount of distilled water.

### COORDINATION
1. Not only genes but also viruses are made of essential chemicals called nucleoproteins.
2. Successful managers don't proceed without a plan, but they don't ignore opportunities that arise either.

3. Technically, both glass and water are considered minerals.
4. Corn and winter wheat are not native to the Americas.
5. Ethnicity is usually based on race, religion, and national origin.

## CAUSE

1. According to psychologists, workers increase productivity because of incentives.
2. Anthropologists conclude that flakes were used as tools for cutting and scraping since many of them have been found in excavations of Stone Age settlements.
3. Plants can turn brown on the edges because of too much water.
4. Increasing the consumption of salt can cause higher blood pressure.
5. Most of the roads in the interstate highway system linking roads across the country need to be repaired because they were built in the 1930s.

## COMPARISON

1. Viruses have a structure that is like that of the first life forms that appeared on Earth millions of years ago.
2. The oxygen concentration in the blood is lower than that in the lungs.
3. The Atlantic Ocean is larger but it is not deeper than the Indian Ocean.
4. Picasso's works during various artistic periods differ quite a lot from each other.
5. The weight of one object cannot be the same as that of another because the gravitational attraction differs from place to place on the surface of the Earth.

## CONCESSION

1. Even though insulin levels are close to or above normal in type 2 diabetes, target cells cannot respond adequately.
2. The idea of an English language academy is regularly proposed, but the response has never been very positive.
3. The Jovian planets are grouped together; however, each one has had a very different evolutionary history.
4. Even though young people enjoy an advantage for recall in vocabulary studies, older people appear to be better at word recognition.
5. Although interviews are the most common strategy for assessing job applicants, they tend to have low validity.

## NEGATIVE

1. The geyser known as Old Faithful has never failed to erupt on time.
2. Only standard dialects are used as educational models in schools.
3. There has never been such wide access to news from so many media.
4. The construction of a city on the ruins of a previous settlement is common.
5. The first primitive mammals did not develop until the Triassic Period.

## PASSIVE

1. It is interesting that fewer mental health disorders are experienced by people over the age of 65.
2. In the stringed instruments, the tones are produced by a bow when it is played across a set of strings made of wire or gut.
3. Gases in the ionosphere are partly ionized by high-frequency radiation from the Sun and other sources.
4. A domed roof can be used by architects to conserve floor space.
5. Papyrus was used by the Egyptians to make paper, sails, baskets, and clothing.

## PRACTICE ACTIVITY 25

1. **D**  An animal learns how to get food by hitting a bar.
2. **A**  Poe is remembered more for a poem than for his short stories.
3. **C**  Everything in the universe was reduced to pure energy in one atom.
4. **C**  During the winter, the bear's temperature is normal and its respiration is regular, but it does not require food.
5. **B**  The board will assume control only if they lose confidence in the CEO.
6. **A**  Fluctuations in the air pressure are a result of changes in temperature.
7. **C**  Metabolism and exercise are ways to stabilize consumption and production of energy for a healthy weight.
8. **D**  The child's interest in playing with language is encouraged by the nursery rhyme.
9. **B**  It does not matter where employees work at their computers.
10. **A**  The Firbolgs arrived in Ireland from the Mediterranean after the Scottish people had already settled there.

## PRACTICE ACTIVITY 26

1. Problem:  The paraphrase is too much like the original. Only the subject and complement have been reversed in this alternative grammatical structure.
   Edited
   Paraphrase:  Molecules that function as regulators in the transmission of substances across cell walls are known as proteins.

Why is this better? Because synonyms have been substituted for all the nontechnical vocabulary and the subject and complement are reversed in an alternative grammatical structure.

2. Problem:  The paraphrase is not complete. Information about the factory system and the cotton industry are not included.
   Edited
   Paraphrase:  The factory system spread across a large number of enterprises in addition to cotton manufacturing as a result of the introduction of steam engines.

Why is this better? Because the relationship between cause and effect has been retained using different vocabulary and grammar, and both the factory system and the cotton industry are included.

3. Problem:  The paraphrase is not correct. The meaning has been changed.
   Edited
   Paraphrase:  Small enterprises are frequently using bloggers to compete effectively with large businesses that are still employing more conventional marketing strategies as well as some of the more recent options.

Why is this better? Because the meaning of the original sentence has been retained.

4. Problem:  The paraphrase is too much like the original. Too many words and phrases are the same, and the grammatical structure is too similar.
   Edited
   Paraphrase:  Although fossilized bones may look like stone, minerals from sedimentary material fill the spaces.

Why is this better? Because synonyms have been substituted for all the nontechnical vocabulary, and the subject and complement are reversed in an alternative grammatical structure.

5.  Problem:         The paraphrase is incomplete. The dates are important here.
    Edited
    Paraphrase:      About 3500 B.C., two thousand years before written symbols were introduced in
                     1500 B.C., the first pictographic writing system appeared simultaneously in vari-
                     ous regions of the known world.

    Why is this better? Because the chronology is not clear without a time frame. The date solves this
    problem.

6.  Problem:         This is not a paraphrase. It is copied directly from the original.
    Edited
    Paraphrase:      In all likelihood, the Earth's current atmosphere was preceded by three earlier
                     atmospheres.

    Why is this better? Because copying directly from a source is the worst kind of plagiarism. Even
    when you are in a hurry, be sure that you are not copying.

7.  Problem:         This is not a paraphrase. It is too general.
    Edited
    Paraphrase:      Alcohol depresses the central nervous system, but coffee increases neural trans-
                     mission.

    Why is this better? Because details are necessary for a paraphrase to be specific. A general state-
    ment does not include enough information.

8.  Problem:         This paraphrase changes the meaning of the original statement.
    Edited
    Paraphrase:      Australia and the islands of Oceania comprise the Pacific Basin, an area that
                     encompasses about 33 percent of the Earth's surface.

    Why is this better? Because this paraphrase retains the original meaning. The area is one third of
    the surface of the Earth, not one-third of the Pacific Ocean.

9.  Problem:         The paraphrase is incomplete. It does not identify the process as fresco painting.
    Edited
    Paraphrase:      The lime in wet plaster bonds with the colors on the surface when the paints are
                     mixed for frescos.

    Why is this better? Because the process described in the paraphrase is identified as fresco painting.

10. Problem:         The paraphrase is too much like the original. Too many words and phrases are
                     repeated.
    Edited
    Paraphrase:      The Linnaean chart used to classify all biological species was initially created to
                     categorize each specimen in conformity with its resemblance to other organisms.

    Why is this better? Because the edited paraphrase retains the meaning of the original, but the
    words and phrases are different, and the grammatical structure is changed.

## PRACTICE ACTIVITY 27

1. According to the professor, "A stock is equity in a company, and, therefore, it represents ownership."
2. According to the professor, "The desalination of the ocean is going to be a crucial aspect of water management."
3. According to the professor, "The theme of a worldwide flood is found in the mythology of many cultures."
4. According to the professor, "Psychology focuses on the individual, whereas sociology focuses on social groups."
5. According to the professor, "The ethics of science will become more important in this decade."
6. According to the professor, her idea is called "the simplification principle."
7. According to the professor, "The three-domain system is superior to the five-domain system of classification in biology."
8. According to the professor, "The term *relief* describes any printing method with a raised image."
9. According to the professor, "Training programs must address the issue of technology in the workplace."
10. According to the professor, "Quasars are difficult to study because they are so far away."

## PRACTICE ACTIVITY 28

 **Activity 28, Track 26**

1. Written:  According to a study by Professor Carter, "patients can lower their blood pressure by losing weight and decreasing their intake of salt."

   Spoken:  According to a study by Professor Carter, and I quote, "patients can lower their blood pressure by losing weight and decreasing their intake of salt." End quote.

2. Written:  According to Professor Jones, "over fourteen billion euros were introduced into the world economy in January 2002."

   Spoken:  According to Professor Jones, and I'm quoting here, "over fourteen billion euros were introduced into the world economy in January 2002." End quote.

3. Written:  To quote a study in the *Journal of Psychology*, "many people who have achieved their career ambitions by midlife are afflicted by depression."

   Spoken:  To quote a study in the *Journal of Psychology*, "many people who have achieved their career ambitions by midlife are afflicted by depression." End quote.

4. Written:  According to the textbook, "an organ is a group of tissues capable of performing some special function."

   Spoken:  According to the textbook, and I am quoting here, "an organ is a group of tissues capable of performing some special function." End quote.

5. Written:  According to Professor Stephens, "John Philip Sousa was the greatest composer of marches for bands."

   Spoken:  According to Professor Stephens, and I quote, "John Philip Sousa was the greatest composer of marches for bands." End Quote.

6. Written:  In Professor Davison's opinion, "Ben Johnson may be the author of several plays attributed to William Shakespeare."

   Spoken:  In Professor Davison's opinion, and I quote, "Ben Johnson may be the author of several plays attributed to William Shakespeare." End quote.

7. Written:  Professor Davis said that, "statistical data can be very difficult to interpret because correlations are not causes."

   Spoken:  Professor Davis said that, and I am quoting here, "statistical data can be very difficult to interpret because correlations are not causes." End quote.

8. Written:  As Professor Gray puts it, "the prime minister serves at the pleasure of the parliament."

   Spoken:  As Professor Gray puts it, and I quote, "the prime minister serves at the pleasure of the parliament." End quote.

9. Written:    According to the reading passage, "moving water is the single most important factor in determining the surface features of the Earth."

   Spoken:    According to the reading passage, and I quote, "moving water is the single most important factor in determining the surface features of the Earth." End quote.

10. Written:   In Professor Russell's opinion, "the most important quality for a scientist is the ability to make careful observations."

    Spoken:   In Professor Russell's opinion, and I am quoting here, "the most important quality for a scientist is the ability to make careful observations." End quote.

## PRACTICE ACTIVITY 29

1. Neutral report: Sociologist Lee Clark observed that when danger arose, the rule was for people to help those next to them before they helped themselves.

2. Doubtful report: Biological Anthropologist Barry Bogin claimed that we could use the average height of any group of people as a barometer of the health of their society.

3. Certain report: Physician Stanley Joel Reiser maintained that machines directed the attention of both doctor and patient to the measurable aspect of illness, but away from the human factors that are at least equally important.

4. Certain report: Educator Harry Wong concluded that there was but one correlation with success, and that was attitude.

5. Doubtful report: Choreographer Martha Graham suggested that technique and training had never been a substitute for that condition of awareness which was talent.

6. Doubtful report: Psychologist Carl Jung believed that the collective unconscious seemed to be something like an unceasing stream or perhaps an ocean of images and figures which drifted into consciousness in our dreams.

7. Neutral report: Computer entrepreneur Bill Gates indicated that the key for Microsoft™ had always been hiring very smart people.

8. Doubtful report: Geneticists James Watson and Francis Crick proposed that DNA structure had two helical chains each coiled around the same axis.

9. Neutral report: Environmentalist John Sinclair pointed out that many politicians were hostile to the environmental movement because they saw it in conflict with the economic model they supported.

10. Certain report: Astrophysicist Carl Sagan argued that even a relatively small nuclear war might be capable of producing a global climatic catastrophe.

## PRACTICE ACTIVITY 30

 Activity 30, Track 27

1. In his book, *The Making of the President,* Theodore White noted that the 1960 presidential debate was more like a press conference. According to White, Nixon proceeded as though he were engaged in a personal debate. In contrast, Kennedy spoke directly to the TV viewers. He estimated that Kennedy gained two million votes as a result.

2. Paul Cezanne believed that all forms in nature were based on geometric shapes. Cezanne identified the cone, sphere, and cylinder as the primary forms. He used outlining to emphasize these shapes.

3. Along with her husband, Marie Curie won the Nobel Prize for physics in 1903 for the discovery of radium. Curie then received the Nobel Prize for chemistry in 1911 for the isolation of pure radium. She was the first person to be awarded two Nobel Prizes.

4. Psychologist Erik Erikson proposed eight stages of personal development. Erikson claimed that psychological crises at each stage shaped the sense of self. He believed that development was a lifelong process.

5. Margaret Mead did her first fieldwork in Samoa in 1925. Mead's book, *Coming of Age in Samoa*, was a best seller that was translated into many languages. She is still one of the most well-known anthropologists in the world. Mead believed that people in simple societies could provide valuable lessons for the industrialized world.

6. Leonardo da Vinci was the quintessential Renaissance man. A brilliant painter, da Vinci was perhaps best remembered for his art. But he was also interested in mechanics, and his understanding of mathematics is clear in his use of perspective.

7. Author Peter Drucker wrote *Management Challenges for the 21st Century*. In this book, Drucker proposed five transforming forces. He predicted that these trends will have major implications for the long-term strategies of companies.

8. Friedrich Mohs devised a scale of hardness for ten minerals. By assigning 10 to diamond, the hardest known mineral, Mohs was able to attribute relative values to all the other minerals. His scale is still useful in the study of minerals today.

9. Maria Montessori proposed an educational model that has become known as the Montessori Method. Montessori insisted that education should not be merely the transmission of knowledge but the freedom to develop as a person. She felt her greatest success was achieved when a child began working independently.

10. In collaboration with Louis Leakey, Jane Goodall spent years living with chimpanzees on the Gombe Reserve. Goodall imitated their behaviors and discovered that chimpanzees lived within a complex social organization. She was the first to document chimpanzees making and using tools, and she also identified twenty different sounds that were part of a communication system.

## PRACTICE ACTIVITY 31

### 1. Reading

**Step 1: Examples Deleted**

    Although speech is the most advanced form of communication, there are many ways of communicating without using speech. Signals, signs, and symbols may be found in every known culture. The basic function of a signal is to impinge upon the environment in such a way that it attracts attention. Unlike signals, which are coded to refer to speech, signs contain meaning in and of themselves. Finally, gestures are actions, which are more difficult to describe because of their relationship with cultural perceptions.

**Step 2: Paraphrased Summary**

    Found in every culture, signals, signs, and symbols are examples of alternatives to speech communication. A signal, which is referenced to speech, intrudes upon the environment so that it is noticed. In contrast, a sign does not refer to speech because it displays a general message. Last, gestures, which are culturally defined, consist of actions.

### 2. Lecture

 **Activity 31, Track 28**

    Listen to part of a lecture in a botany class.

The *Acacia* is a genus of trees and shrubs of the Mimosa family that originated in Australia and has long been used in building simple mud and stick structures there. The acacia is called a *wattle* in Australia, and the structures are made of wattle stuck together with daub, which is a kind of mud adobe. Now this is interesting—the acacia is related to the family of plants known as legumes, and I'm sure you remember that legumes include peas, beans, lentils, peanuts, and pods with beanlike seeds. Some acacias actually produce edible crops. But other acacia varieties are valued for the sticky resin, called *gum Arabic* or *gum acacia*, and that is used widely in medicines, foods, and perfumes. A few varieties are grown for the dark, dense wood, which is just excellent for making pianos, or for the bark that is very rich in tannin, a dark, acidic substance used to cure the hides of animals to make leather.

Let's see. Nearly five hundred species of *Acacia* have been identified and categorized and proven capable of survival in hot and generally arid parts of the world, but only a dozen of the three hundred Australian varieties seem to thrive in the southern United States. Most acacia imports are low, spreading trees, but of these, only three flower. The Bailey Acacia has fernlike silver leaves and small, fragrant flowers arranged in, uh, in sort of rounded clusters. The Silver Wattle is similar to the Bailey Acacia, but it grows about twice as high, and the Sydney Golden Wattle is bushy with broad, flat leaves, and it's the Golden Wattle with the showy bright yellow blossoms. Okay. The Black Acacia is also called the Blackwood. It has dark green foliage and the blossoms are rather ordinary, but besides being a popular ornamental tree, the Black Acacia is considered valuable for its dark wood, which is used in making furniture and musical instruments. I think I mentioned that acacias are used to make pianos. Well, a piano made of Black Acacia is highly prized in the musical world.

Now, some of you may have heard that the acacia's unique custom of blossoming in February in the United States has something to do with its Australian origins, but that just isn't so. It isn't the date. It's the quality of light that makes the difference for the flowering cycle of a tree. As you know, in the Southern Hemisphere, the seasons are reversed, and February, which is wintertime in the United States, is summertime in Australia. Actually, however, the pale, yellow blossoms appear in August in Australia. So, whether it grows in the Northern or the Southern Hemisphere, the acacia blossoms in winter.

### Step 1: Examples Deleted

The *Acacia*, a genus of trees and shrubs of the Mimosa family that originated in Australia, is called a *wattle* in Australia. The acacia is related to the family of plants known as legumes. Some acacias actually produce edible crops. Other acacia varieties are valued for the sticky resin, dense wood, or bark. Nearly five hundred species of *Acacia* are capable of survival in hot and generally arid parts of the world. A dozen of the three hundred Australian varieties survive in the southern United States. Whether it grows in the Northern or Southern Hemisphere, the acacia blossoms in winter.

### Step 2: Paraphrased Summary

The *Acacia*, called a *wattle* in its native Australia, is a member of the Mimosa family and a relative of the family of plants that includes legumes. Acacias are valuable for wood, resin, and even food crops. Of the five hundred species of *Acacia* that grow in hot, dry climates, three hundred are found in Australia, but only twelve flourish in the southern United States. One of its unusual characteristics is that it typically flowers in the winter, whether it is planted in the Northern or Southern Hemisphere.

## PRACTICE ACTIVITY 32

1. Charlie Chaplin was a comedian who was best known for his work in silent movies.
2. Water becomes steam when it is heated to 212 degrees F.
3. Quasars, which are relatively small objects, emit an enormous amount of energy.
4. The Earth moves into the shadow of the Moon during a total eclipse. *or*
   During a total eclipse, the Earth moves into the shadow of the Moon.
5. Founded by John Smith, Jamestown became the first successful English colony in America.
6. Many of the names of cities in California are adapted from the Spanish language since early missionaries and settlers from Spain had extended their influence in the area. *or*
   Since early missionaries and settlers from Spain had extended their influence in the area, many of the names of cities in California are adapted from the Spanish language. *or*
   Many of the names of cities in California are adapted from the Spanish language because early missionaries and settlers from Spain had extended their influence in the area. *or*

Because early missionaries and settlers from Spain had extended their influence in the area, many of the names of cities in California are adapted from the Spanish language. *or*

Many of the names of cities in California are adapted from the Spanish language because of the influence in the area of early missionaries and settlers from Spain.

7. The oceans, which cover two-thirds of the Earth's surface, are the object of study for oceanographers. *or*

The oceans, which are the object of study for oceanographers, cover two thirds of the Earth's surface.

8. A chameleon is a tree lizard that can change colors to conceal itself in vegetation.

9. Cultural nationalism arose among people with similar languages and traditions before political nationalism threatened the existing order. *or*

Before political nationalism threatened the existing order, cultural nationalism arose among people with similar languages and traditions. *or*

Political nationalism threatened the existing order after cultural nationalism arose among people with similar languages and traditions. *or*

After cultural nationalism arose among people with similar languages and tradition, political nationalism threatened the existing order.

10. Empowerment increases the autonomy of employees in organizations and improves communication between workers and management. *or*

Empowerment increases the autonomy of employees in organizations; moreover, it improves communication between workers and management.

11. Monogamy means being married to one spouse, whereas serial monogamy involves marriage to one spouse, divorce, and remarriage to another spouse. *or*

Whereas serial monogamy involves marriage to one spouse, divorce, and remarriage to another spouse, monogamy means being married to one spouse.

12. Humor is associated with fun, but it is also used as a coping strategy to relieve stress. *or*

Humor is associated with fun; however, it is also used as a coping strategy to relieve stress.

13. Although solar panels can convert sunlight into electricity, they are still not being exploited fully. *or*

Solar panels are still not being exploited fully, although they can convert sunlight into electricity. *or*

Even though solar panels can convert sunlight into electricity, they are still not being exploited fully. *or*

Solar panels are still not being exploited fully, even though they can convert sunlight into electricity.

14. The root system of the alfalfa plant allows it to survive despite drought conditions. *or*

The root system of the alfalfa plant allows it to survive in spite of drought conditions.

15. Pain warns the victim before further damage is done; therefore, pain has a positive function. *or*

Pain warns the victim before further damage is done; thus, pain has a positive function.

## PRACTICE ACTIVITY 33

### 1. Reading

### Summary

Whereas one-third of the population consists of the traditional nuclear family of two parents and their children, most Americans are either married couples with no children at home, single people, or single-parent households, many of whom have developed close friendships to replace extended family living at a distance.

## 2. Lecture

 **Activity 33, Track 29**

Listen to part of a lecture in a chemistry class.

Although the purpose and techniques were often magical, alchemy was, in many ways, the predecessor of the modern science of chemistry. The fundamental premise of alchemy derived from the best philosophical dogma and scientific practice of the time, and the majority of educated persons between 1400 and 1600 believed that alchemy had great merit.

The earliest authentic works on European alchemy are those of the English monk Roger Bacon and the German philosopher St. Albertus Magnus. In their treatises, they maintained that gold was the perfect metal and that inferior metals such as lead and mercury were removed by various degrees of imperfection from gold. They further asserted that these base metals could be transmuted to gold by blending them with a substance more perfect than gold. This elusive substance was referred to as the "Philosopher's Stone." The process was called transmutation.

Most of the early alchemists were artisans who were accustomed to keeping trade secrets and often resorted to cryptic terminology to record the progress of their work. The term *Sun* was used for gold, *Moon* for silver, and the five known planets for the base metals. This convention of substituting symbolic language attracted some mystical philosophers who compared the search for the perfect metal with the struggle of humankind for the perfection of the soul. The philosophers began to use the artisan's terms in the mystical literature that they produced. Thus, by the fourteenth century, alchemy had developed two distinct groups of practitioners—the laboratory alchemist and the literary alchemist. Both groups of alchemists continued to work throughout the history of alchemy, but, of course, it was the literary alchemist who was more likely to produce a written record; therefore, much of what is known about the science of alchemy is derived from philosophers rather than from the alchemists who labored in laboratories.

Despite centuries of experimentation, laboratory alchemists failed to produce gold from other materials. However, they gained wide knowledge of chemical substances, discovered chemical properties, and invented many of the tools and techniques that are used by chemists today. Many laboratory chemists earnestly devoted themselves to the scientific discovery of new compounds and reactions and, therefore, must be considered the legitimate forefathers of modern chemistry. They continued to call themselves alchemists, but they were becoming true chemists.

### Summary

Laboratory alchemists failed to refine base metals to produce gold, but they discovered chemical substances, properties, compounds, reactions, tools, and techniques that helped to establish the field of modern chemistry.

## Practice Activity 34

### 1. Reading

Choice A is a major point because the paragraph that follows includes details about each section.

Choice B is a detail that describes one of the types of mouth parts. It refers to the major point about how insects are classified.

Choice C is a detail that describes one of the adaptations of mouth parts. It refers to the major point about how insects are classified.

Choice D is a major point because several types of mouth parts are explained in reference to this point.

Choice E is true but it is not mentioned in the passage.

Choice F is a detail that defines the term *proboscis*. It refers to the major point about how insects are classified.

Choice G is a detail that refers to one of the body parts in the major point about the three-section body.

Choice H is a detail that explains the purpose of one of the adaptations of mouth parts. It refers to the major point about how insects are classified.

## 2. Lecture

 **Activity 34, Track 30**
Listen to part of a lecture in an English class.

Few have influenced the development of American English to the extent that Noah Webster did. After a short career in law, he turned to teaching, but he discovered how inadequate the available schoolbooks were for the children of a new and independent nation.

In response to the need for truly American textbooks, Webster published *A Grammatical Institute of the English Language*, a three-volume work that consisted of a speller, a grammar, and a reader. The first volume, which was generally known as *The American Spelling Book*, was so popular that eventually it sold more than eighty million copies and provided him with a considerable income for the rest of his life. Can you imagine that?

Anyway, in 1807, Noah Webster began his greatest work, *An American Dictionary of the English Language*. In preparing the manuscript, he devoted ten years to the study of English and its relationship to other languages, and seven more years to the writing itself. Published in two volumes in 1828, *An American Dictionary of the English Language* has become the recognized authority for usage in the United States. Webster's purpose in writing it was to demonstrate that the American language was developing distinct meanings, pronunciations, and spellings from those of British English. He is responsible for advancing many of the simplified spelling forms that distinguish American English from British.

Webster was the first author to gain copyright protection in the United States by being awarded a copyright for *The American Spelling Book* and he continued to lobby over the next fifty years for the protection of intellectual properties, that is, for author's rights. By the time that Webster brought out the second edition of his dictionary, which included 70,000 entries instead of the original 38,000, the name Webster had become synonymous with American dictionaries. It was this second edition that served as the basis for the many revisions that have been produced by others, ironically, under the uncopyrighted Webster name.

### Summary

*The American Spelling Book*, Webster's first successful textbook, afforded him an income while he was writing his dictionary. *An American Dictionary of the English Language* was written to demonstrate the unique usage of English in the United States. Although he had a copyright for *The American Spelling Book*, ironically, Webster did not have a copyright for the original dictionary and subsequent editions that bear his name.

Choice A is a detail that refers to Webster's life before he began to write.

Choice B is a major point because the spelling book allowed Webster to continue his writing career.

Choice C is a major point because several examples refer to the unique usage.

Choice D is a detail because the revisions refer to the major point about copyrights.

Choice E is probably true but it is not mentioned in the lecture.

Choice F is a major point because about one-third of the lecture is on the topic of copyright protection.

Choice G is a detail that relates to Webster's early life.

## PRACTICE ACTIVITY 35

### 1. Reading

Both oil paints and canvas were artistic improvements introduced in the fifteenth century. Canvas was superior to the wood panels that predated it because it could be stretched to accommodate the huge works that were then popular and then rolled up to ship. When it arrived, it was light enough to be easily framed and hung and, unlike wood, it didn't crack. Oil paints were preferable because they dried slowly, allowing the artist to rework on top of a previously painted section. Furthermore, it was possible to mix the oils to either a thin or thick consistency from a glaze to a paste.

### 2. Lecture

**Activity 35, Track 31**

Listen to part of a lecture in an engineering class.

The question has often been posed: Why were the Wright brothers able to succeed in an effort at which so many others had failed? Well, many explanations have been mentioned, but, uh, three reasons are most often cited, and I tend to agree with them. First, the Wright brothers were a team. Both men worked congenially and cooperatively, read the same books, located and shared information, talked incessantly about the possibility of manned flight, and, . . . and served as consistent sources of inspiration and encouragement to each other. So, to put it quite simply, two geniuses are better than one genius.

Second, both the brothers were glider pilots. So, unlike some other engineers who experimented with the theories of flight, Orville and Wilbur Wright experienced the practical aspects of aerodynamics by building and flying gliders, and this may surprise you, they even flew in kites. Now, each craft they built was slightly superior to the last because they incorporated the knowledge that they had gained from previous failures to adjust the next design. They had realized fairly early on from their experiments that the most serious challenge in manned flight would be stabilizing and maneuvering the aircraft once it was airborne. So, um, while others concentrated their efforts on the problem of achieving lift for take-off, the Wright brothers were focusing on developing a three-axis control for guiding their aircraft. By the time that the brothers started to build an airplane, they were already among the world's best glider pilots and they knew about the problems of riding the air firsthand.

In addition, the Wright brothers had designed more effective wings for their airplane than anyone else had been able to engineer. Using a wind tunnel, they tested more than two hundred different wing designs, recording the effects of slight variations in shape on the pressure of air on the wings. The data from these experiments allowed the Wright brothers to construct a superior wing for their aircraft.

But, you know, in spite of these advantages, the Wright brothers still might not have succeeded if they hadn't been born at precisely the right time in history. Attempts to achieve manned flight in the early nineteenth century were doomed because the steam engines that powered the aircrafts were just too heavy in proportion to the power that they produced. But by the end of the nineteenth century, when the brothers were experimenting with engineering options, a relatively light internal combustion engine had already been invented, and they were able to bring the ratio of weight to power within acceptable limits for flight.

### Summary

The Wright brothers were successful in achieving the first manned flight because they worked collaboratively; they were both glider pilots who recognized the importance of stabilization and control in an aircraft; they were able to design, test, and engineer the best wings for the plane; and they were able to take advantage of the relatively light internal combustion engine.

### PRACTICE ACTIVITY 36

### 1. Reading

1. **B**   The first opera in Italy
2. **C**   The growth of opera throughout Europe
3. **A**   Three types of musical pieces in opera

### 2. Lecture

   **Activity 36, Track 32**
Listen to part of a lecture in a biology class.

The protozoans, minute aquatic creatures, each of which consists of a single cell of protoplasm, constitute a classification of the most primitive forms of animal life. The very name protozoan indicates the scientific understanding of the animals. *Proto* means "first" or "primitive" and *zoa* refers to the animal.

They are fantastically diverse, but three major groups may be identified on the basis of their motility. The Mastigophora have one or more long tails that they use to propel themselves forward. The Ciliata, which use the same basic means for locomotion as the Mastigophora, have a larger number of short tails. The Sarcodina, which include amoebae, float or row themselves about on their crusted bodies.

In addition to their form of movement, several other features discriminate among the three groups of protozoans. For example, at least two nuclei per cell have been identified in the Ciliata, usually a large nucleus that regulates growth but decomposes during reproduction, and a smaller one that contains the genetic code necessary to generate the large nucleus.

So all of this seems very straightforward to this point, but now we are going to complicate the picture. Chlorophyll, which is the green substance in plants, is also found in the bodies of some protozoans, enabling them to make at least some of their own food from water and carbon dioxide. Sounds like photosynthesis, doesn't it? But protozoans are animals, right? And plants are the life forms that use photosynthesis. Okay. Well, protozoans are not considered plants because, unlike pigmented plants to which some protozoans are otherwise almost identical, they don't live on simple organic compounds. Their cells demonstrate all of the major characteristics of the cells of higher animals, such as eating, breathing, and reproducing.

Now many species of protozoans collect into colonies, physically connected to one another and responding uniformly to outside stimuli. Current research into this phenomenon along with investigations carried out with advanced microscopes may necessitate a redefinition of what constitutes protozoans, even calling into question the basic premise that they have only one cell. Nevertheless, with the current data available, almost 40,000 species of protozoans have been identified. No doubt, as technology improves methods of observation, better models of classification of these simple single cells will be proposed.

1. **D**   A definition of protozoans—single cell
2. **A**   A method of classification for protozoans—the three types motility
3. **C**   Similarity to plants—make food from water + $CO_2$
4. **E**   Considered animals—eating, breathing, reproducing
5. **B**   Current research—questions, redefinitions

## PRACTICE ACTIVITY 37

### 1. Reading

1. **A**
2. **B**
3. **B**
4. **A**
5. **C**
6. **B**
7. **B**
8. **C**

### Summary

The author's main purpose in the passage is to describe the nature of sunspots. Sunspots are solar particles that are hurled into space by disturbances of wind on the Sun. Matter from the Sun that enters the Earth's atmosphere affects changes in the weather patterns on Earth. Most sunspots appear as a shadow encircled by bright and dark lines extending out like spokes in a wheel. Sunspots usually occur in a configuration of two spots. The color of sunspots could be affected by their temperature. Sunspots may be related to magnetic fields that follow longitudinal lines on the Sun. The sunspot theory is subject to debate, however.

### 2. Lecture

**Activity 37, Track 33**
Listen to part of a lecture in an anthropology class.

The development of the horse has been recorded from the beginning, through all of its evolutionary stages, to the modern form. It is, perhaps, one of the most complete and well-documented chapters of paleontological history. Fossil finds provide us not only with detailed information about the horse itself but also with valuable insights into the migration of herds and even evidence for the speculation about the climatic conditions that could have instigated their migratory behavior.

Now geologists believe that the first horses appeared on Earth about sixty million years ago as compared with only two million years ago for the appearance of human beings. There is evidence of early horses on both the American and European continents, but it has been documented that, almost twelve million years ago at the beginning of the Pliocene Age, a horse about midway through its evolutionary development crossed a land bridge where the Bering Strait is now located. It traveled from Alaska into the grasslands of Asia and all the way to Europe. So, this early horse was a hipparion, about the size of a modern-day pony with three toes and specialized cheek teeth for grazing. In Europe, the hipparion encountered another less advanced horse called the anchitheres, which had previously invaded Europe by the same route, probably during the Miocene Period. Less developed and smaller than the hipparion, the anchitheres was eventually completely replaced by it.

By the end of the Pleistocene Age, both the anchitheres and the hipparion had become extinct in North America where they originated, as fossil evidence clearly demonstrates. In Europe, they evolved into the larger and stronger animal that is very similar to the horse as we know it today. For many years, this horse was probably hunted for food by early tribes of human beings. Then the qualities of the horse that would have made it a good servant were recognized—mainly its strength and speed. It was time for the horse to be tamed, used as a draft animal at the dawning of agriculture, and then ridden as need for transportation increased. It was the descendant of this domesticated horse that was brought back across the ocean to the Americas by European colonists.

1. **D**
2. **A**
3. **B**
4. **A**
5. **C**
6. **B**
7. **A**
8. **C**

## Summary

According to the lecturer, fossils document the evolution of the horse, providing information about the climate and migration patterns. Geologists claim that horses appeared on Earth millions of years before human beings. A horse known as the anchitheres had migrated to Europe in the Miocene from North America. Following the same route, the hipparion migrated to Europe later in the Pliocene. When the hipparion invaded Europe, the anchitheres did not survive. In contrast, the hipparion developed into a sturdy animal, like modern breeds of horses. Ironically, horses were already extinct in North America by the Pleistocene, and Europeans returned the horse to the American colonies on ships.

## PRACTICE ACTIVITY 38

### 1. Reading

50%   The function and responsibilities of the Fed
40%   The composition of the Fed
10%   A comparison of the Fed to a fourth branch of government

Although the summary below is actually closer to 50%, 30%, 20%, it still maintains a reasonably accurate emphasis.

### Summary

The function of the Federal Reserve System is to regulate money and credit by buying and selling government securities, thereby influencing periods of recession and inflation. Moreover, the Fed cooperates with the Department of the Treasury to issue new coins and paper notes to banks and participates in international financial policies through member banks overseas.

The Fed includes twelve district reserve banks and branches, all national commercial banks and credit unions, as well as several committees and councils, including the powerful board of governors appointed by the president.

Because of its powerful membership, the Fed has been compared to a fourth branch of government, but the president's policies are usually implemented.

## 2. Lecture

 **Activity 38, Track 34**

Listen to part of a lecture in a psychology class.

Okay then, let's talk about human memory, which was formerly believed to be rather inefficient as compared with, for example, computers. But we are finding that we probably have a much more sophisticated mechanism than we had originally assumed. Researchers approaching the problem from a variety of points of view have all concluded that there is a great deal more stored in our minds than has been generally supposed. Here's what I mean—Dr. Wilder Penfield, a Canadian neurosurgeon, proved that by stimulating their brains electrically, he could elicit the total recall of complex events in his subjects' lives. Even dreams and other minor events supposedly forgotten for many years suddenly emerged in detail.

The *memory trace* is the term for whatever forms the internal representation of the specific information about an event stored in the memory. So, the trace is probably made by structural changes in the brain, but the problem is that the memory trace isn't really subject to direct observation because it's . . . it's . . . more a theoretical construct that we use to speculate about how information presented at a particular time can cause performance at a later time. So most theories include the strength of the memory trace as a variable in the degree of learning, retention, and retrieval possible for a memory. One theory is that the fantastic capacity for storage in the brain is the result of an almost unlimited combination of interconnections between brain cells, stimulated by patterns of activity. And repeated references to the same information supports recall. Or, to say that another way, improved performance is the result of strengthening the chemical bonds in the memory.

Now here's the interesting part. Psychologists generally divide memory into at least two types—short-term memory and long-term memory, which combine to form what we call *working memory*. Short-term memory contains what we are actively focusing on at any particular time but items aren't retained longer than twenty or thirty seconds without verbal rehearsal. We use short-term memory when we look up a telephone number and repeat it to ourselves until we can place the call. In contrast, long-term memory can store facts, concepts, and experiences after we stop thinking about them. All conscious processing of information, as in problem solving, for example, involves both short-term and long-term memory. As we repeat, rehearse, and recycle information, the memory trace is strengthened, allowing that information to move from short-term memory to long-term memory.

25%    The level of sophistication for human memory
40%    The memory trace
35%    Working memory

Although the summary below is actually closer to 25%, 35%, 40%, it still maintains a reasonably accurate emphasis.

### Summary

Human memory is more highly developed than previously thought. Penfield's experiments prove that detailed memories can be recalled when the brain is stimulated electrically. Using the memory trace, a theoretical model, we can conjecture how facts are retrieved and used at a later time. Current thinking assumes that chemical bonds can be improved by repeated exposure to the same information. The concept of working memory includes both short-term memory, which includes recall for twenty or thirty seconds, and long-term memory, which stores facts and experiences more permanently. Information is transferred from short-term to long-term memory when the memory trace is reinforced.

## PRACTICE ACTIVITY 39

### 1. Reading

#### Summary

Charles Ives started his musical career as a member of his father's band and received a degree from Yale University in music, but he became a businessman instead because he was afraid that his music would not be well accepted. His music was very different from the popular songs of his era because he used small phrases from well-known music with unusual rhythms and tones. Fifty years after he wrote his *Second Symphony*, it was performed by the New York Philharmonic, and he was awarded the Pulitzer Prize. I think that Charles Ives was wrong not to pursue his musical career from the beginning. If he had continued writing music instead of selling insurance, we would have more pieces now.

### 2. Lecture

### Activity 39, Track 35

Listen to part of a lecture in a geology class.

A geyser is the result of underground water under the combined conditions of high temperatures and increased pressure beneath the surface of the Earth. Now, temperature rises about maybe 1 degree Fahrenheit for every 60 feet under the Earth's surface, and we know that pressure also increases with depth, water that seeps down in cracks and fissures, so when the water, . . . when the water reaches very hot rocks in the Earth's interior, it becomes heated to the temperature of, let's say, 290 degrees.

Okay, then, water under pressure can remain liquid at temperatures above the normal boiling point, but in a geyser, the weight of the water nearer the surface exerts so much pressure on the deeper water that the water at the bottom of the geyser reaches much higher temperatures than the water at the top. And as the deep water becomes hotter, and consequently lighter, it suddenly rises to the surface and shoots out of the ground in the form of steam and hot water. In turn, the explosion agitates all of the water in the geyser reservoir, and what do you think happens then? More explosions. So immediately afterward, the water goes back into the underground reservoir, it starts to heat up again, and the whole process repeats itself.

So, in order to function, then, a geyser must have a source of heat, a reservoir where water can be stored until the temperature rises to an unstable point, an opening through which the hot water and steam can escape, and underground channels for resupplying water after an eruption.

Now, favorable conditions for geysers exist in regions of geologically recent volcanic activity, especially in areas of more than average precipitation. For the most part, geysers are located in three regions of the world—New Zealand, Iceland, and the Yellowstone Park area of the United States. I'd say that the most famous geyser in the world is Old Faithful in Yellowstone. It erupts every hour, rising to a height of 125 to 170 feet and expelling more than ten thousand gallons of hot water during each eruption. Old Faithful earned its name, because unlike most geysers, it has never failed to erupt on schedule even once in eighty years of observation.

## Summary

In my opinion, geysers are interesting. They happen when underground water gets hot and pressure from above causes the water to get hotter and lighter so it goes up to the surface and explodes out. Then, the water runs back into the ground and starts all over again. Geysers have to have heat, a place to store water, an opening where the water can shoot up, and cracks in the ground for the water to go back down into a pool. Geysers are in New Zealand, Iceland, and the United States. Old Faithful in Yellowstone is the most famous geyser, but the best place to see geysers is in New Zealand. I saw the Pohutu Geyser there on my vacation two years ago, and it was awesome.

## PRACTICE ACTIVITY 40

### Summary 1

This is a good summary. The content is accurate, and all the major points are included. The problem here is that the writer did not follow the order in the original so the points are not in the same sequence and they are difficult to follow.

### Summary 2

This is a good summary because it is brief, uses the same organization as the original, includes the major points, reports the content accurately, paraphrases using the summarizer's own words, and maintains an objective point of view that does not include the opinions of the person summarizing the original.

### Summary 3

This is not really a summary of the original passage. Instead of a factual report, this paragraph includes opinions and judgments that the original author did not express.

### Summary 4

This summary is not paraphrased. Sentences are copied from the original. The summary would not be scored, and no credit would be assigned. This is the most serious problem in summarizing.

### Summary 5

The problem in this summary is the emphasis. Too much attention is given to information in the first paragraph of the original reading, whereas points from the second paragraph are not included. Facts from the third and fourth paragraphs are only briefly mentioned.

## *Practice Activity 41*

1. Referring to the main points in the reading passage, show how the example in the professor's lecture <u>demonstrates</u> the principle of Occam's razor.

   *Show how the example in the lecture shows proof of the principle of Occam's razor presented in the reading passage.*

2. Explain how the lecturer's view <u>substantiates</u> the opinions expressed in the reading passage.

   *Show how the lecture offers proof of the views in the reading passage.*

3. The professor describes the behavior of dolphins. Explain why this behavior <u>provides an example of</u> higher-level intelligence, as defined in the reading passage.

   *Show how the professor's example of dolphin behavior illustrates the concept of higher-level intelligence.*

4. Explain how the example of learning to drive <u>clarifies</u> the automaticity of learning.

   *Show how the professor's example of learning to drive makes the notion of the automaticity of learning easier to understand.*

5. Using the case study discussed by the professor, explain how the results <u>reinforce</u> the argument in favor of direct mail marketing presented in the reading passage.

   *Show how the professor's case study makes the argument for direct mail marketing in the reading stronger.*

## *Practice Activity 42*

1. Summarize the main points made in the lecture, being sure to explain how they <u>challenge</u> the specific claims made in the reading passage.

   *Show how the lecture makes each of the points presented in the reading passage doubtful.*

2. Summarize the main points in the lecture, showing how they <u>discredit</u> the specific arguments in the reading passage.

   *Show how the lecture demonstrates that each argument in the reading passage is not true.*

3. Summarize the points made in the lecture, being sure to explain how they <u>oppose</u> specific points made in the reading passage.

   *Show how the lecture argues the opposite of each point in the reading passage.*

4. Summarize the major points made in the lecture, being sure to explain how they <u>contrast with</u> the specific problems presented in the reading passage.

*Show how the lecture presents a different point of view for each problem in the reading passage.*

5. Summarize the main points in the lecture, showing how they <u>cast doubt on</u> the point of view in the reading passage. Be sure to address each point in the passage.

*Show how each point in the lecture makes the point of view in the reading less certain.*

## *Practice Activity 43*

1. Basic sentence:   The woman thinks that moving the cafeteria is going to be a problem.
   Better sentence:   The woman thinks that moving the cafeteria is going to be a problem because it will be farther from the dorm and the space is smaller than that of the current location.

2. Basic sentence:   The man believes that the change in the final exam schedule is a good idea.
   Better sentence:   The man believes that the change in the final exam schedule is a good idea because students will have more time to study and experience fewer conflicts with other exams.

3. Basic sentence:   The woman thinks that installing more lighting around the square is a good plan.
   Better sentence:   The woman thinks that installing more lighting around the square is a good plan because it will make the pathways safer for bikers, provide better security for walkers, and make the central campus look nicer.

4. Basic sentence:   The woman says that closing the post office on campus is a mistake.
   Better sentence:   The woman says that closing the post office on campus is a mistake because the campus post office is always busy and the closest post office off campus is not within walking distance.

5. Basic sentence:   The man believes that eliminating all single rooms in the graduate dorms is a bad policy decision.
   Better sentence:   The man believes that eliminating all single rooms in the graduate dorms is a bad policy decision because there is no inexpensive alternative on campus for a private room, no adjustment in fees for moving from a single to a double room, and no opportunity to provide input before a final decision is made.

## Practice Activity 44

1. The research study in the lecture <u>agrees with</u> the advantages of cooperative learning in the reading passage.

   The research study in the lecture <u>corroborates</u> the advantages of cooperative learning in the reading passage.

   The results of the research study in the Chicago schools reported in the lecture corroborate the advantages of cooperative learning in education described in the reading passage.

2. The summary in the lecture <u>agrees with</u> the methods to solve the problem of noise pollution.

   The summary in the lecture <u>substantiates</u> the methods to solve the problem of noise pollution in the reading passage.

   The summary of European noise ordinances in the lecture substantiates the methods to solve the problem of noise pollution in technological societies outlined in the reading passage.

3. The lecturer <u>disagrees with</u> the argument in the reading passage.

   The lecturer <u>challenges</u> the argument in the reading passage.

   The lecturer challenges the argument in the reading passage that nuclear power is too dangerous.

4. The example in the lecture <u>agrees with</u> the three ideas for successful international advertising campaigns.

   The example in the lecture <u>supports</u> the three ideas for successful international advertising campaigns in the reading passage.

   The example of Toyota's marketing plan in the United States in the lecture supports the three ideas for successful international advertising campaigns listed in the reading passage.

5. The lecturer <u>disagrees with</u> the viewpoint in the reading passage.

   The lecturer <u>refutes</u> the viewpoint in the reading passage.

   The lecturer refutes the viewpoint in the reading passage that a meteor impact caused the disappearance of dinosaurs.

6. The lecturer <u>disagrees with</u> the claim in the reading passage.

   The lecturer <u>disputes</u> the claim in the reading passage.

   The lecturer disputes the claim in the reading passage that more than 40 van Gogh paintings are fakes.

7. The study in the lecture <u>agrees with</u> the theory of flow in the reading passage.

   The study in the lecture <u>validates</u> the theory of flow in the reading passage.

   The Harvard University study in the lecture validates the theory of flow explained in the reading passage.

8. The lecturer <u>disagrees with</u> the premise in the reading passage.

   The lecturer <u>discredits</u> the premise in the reading passage.

   The lecturer discredits the premise in the reading passage that successful marriages require similarities.

9. The illustration in the lecture <u>agrees with</u> the definition in the reading passage.

   The illustration in the lecture <u>provides an example of</u> the definition for a biogeographic realm in the reading passage.

   The illustration of a biome in the lecture provides an example of a biogeographic realm as defined in the reading passage.

10. The lecturer <u>disagrees with</u> the assumption in the reading passage.

    The lecturer <u>contradicts</u> the assumption in the reading passage.

    The lecturer contradicts the assumption in the reading passage that censorship is necessary in the media.

## Practice Activity 45

   **Activity 45, Track 36**
Now listen to a conversation on the same topic.

Man:      Hi Jan. Have you heard about the new summer schedule?

Woman:   No. Is there a change?

Man:      Just saw it in the *Campus News* this morning. No Friday or weekend classes.

Woman:   Really? Why's that?

Man:      Energy. The lights and air conditioning will be turned off for three days to cut down on energy consumption during the hottest months.

Woman:   Well, I'm the first one in line to support conservation of resources, but what about the people who are working during the summer and depend on weekend courses to keep on track with their part-time degree programs? I know my sister always takes those intensive weekend classes. She starts Friday after work and gets out about ten at night. Then she's in class all day Saturday and Sunday from eight till eight, with breaks of course. It works out to be about 24 hours on campus, and then she has 12 hours of online activities for each three-hour course. I think she actually took three courses like that last summer.

Man:      Not this year. I wonder what they'll do about that?

Woman:   Probably move those classes into the online curriculum. But that's really too bad for the people who are already taking a lot of online courses, because it's good to interact one-on-one with the professor and the other students.

Man:      Sure. I can see that. Then when you take the online courses, you kind of know people, and . . . and . . . it's more like being in a regular class.

Woman:   Exactly.

Man:      Oh, and did I mention the motion-sensitive lighting, and that thermostats will be set at 78 during the day and air conditioning will be turned off completely at eight o'clock at night?

Woman:   I get the motion-sensitive lighting, but wonder if the shut off is really efficient.

Man:      My thought exactly. It takes a lot of power to crank up the air conditioner after the building has heated up. I mean, I know it'll be cooler during the night, but still, it'll require a power surge to get going in the morning.

Woman:   Well, you know more about this than I do since you're an engineering student, but won't that put a lot of pressure on the system campus wide if everything starts up at eight? Not just for one building, but for the whole campus power system?

Man:      I'm not sure. You'd think that they would've considered that problem, but you never know till you actually try it out.

Woman:    So our energy conservation plan could cause power outages when everything starts up again after the weekend.

Man:    Monday morning is going to be interesting around here this summer.

Relationship sentence: The woman does not agree with the changes in the summer schedule that will offer classes Monday through Thursday.

| Reading | Conversation |
|---|---|
| Point 1 | Point 1 |
| Conserve energy | Weekend courses—part time students |
| lights/air 3 days | Fri to 10 |
| | Sat/Sun 8-8 |
| | 12 hrs online |
| | |
| Point 2 | Point 2 |
| Therm 78 | Not efficient |
| 8-8 off | Power surge am |
| | Outages Mon 8 |
| | |
| Point 3 | Point 3 |
| Motion detect | OK |
| 1 min = off | |

## Practice Activity 46

 **Activity 46, Track 37**
Now listen to part of a lecture in a biology class.

People call it a bear, but the koala is really a marsupial. So, it's much more like a kangaroo than it is like a bear. Here's what I mean. First, the koala has a gestation period of only about 35 days before it's born. Then, a tiny pink, furless creature about 19 millimeters long makes its way from the birth canal into the mother's pouch, where it attaches itself to one of two nipples. So it stays in the pouch to complete its development, and six to seven months later, it pokes its head out and explores a short distance from the mother, jumping back into the pouch until it reaches eight months when it's too big to fit, and for another four months it rides on the mother's back or hangs from her stomach until it finally becomes independent at about one year old. By then, it's about the same size as a Teddy Bear and looks remarkably like one, with a furry coat, rounded ears, and a large nose to support its keen senses of smell and hearing. Native to Australia, the koala lives in trees and is a skillful climber. It sleeps in the branches during the day, and at night, it combs the trees for its favorite meal—eucalyptus leaves.

Relationship sentence: The koala discussed in the lecture provides an example of marsupials.

| Reading | | Lecture | |
|---|---|---|---|
| Point 1 | short gestation | Point 1 | embryo in pouch |
| Point 2 | hair | Point 2 | furry coat |
| Point 3 | auditory/olfactory | Point 3 | ears/nose keen senses |

## Practice Activity 47

**Activity 47, Track 38**
Now listen to part of a lecture in a general science class. The professor is talking about bottled water.

Let's go through each of the points that were presented to promote the drinking of bottled water. Bottled water is healthier. Not always. In fact, as much as 40 percent of bottled water comes from city water supplies. Granted, the bottling companies filter the water and occasionally add some minerals, but just because the water is in a bottle or because it has an exotic name that evokes mountain streams and icebergs, that doesn't mean that the water is necessarily from a healthier source. It could be, but it's not guaranteed. And another thing, bottled water usually doesn't contain a high enough level of fluoride to improve dental health. In contrast, people who get their water from public water systems receive fluoridated water, which has been proven to reduce tooth decay.

Bottled water tastes better. Really? Well, the purest water is distilled water because all of the minerals and salts are removed. But without them, the water tastes flat. It's the sodium, calcium, magnesium, and chlorides that give water its good taste. The reason that tap water may taste funny is the higher level of chlorine, but if you put it in the refrigerator for a few hours without a lid, the chlorine taste will dissipate. And here's the real surprise: A recent study administered by the Swiss-based World Wildlife Fund asked the studio audience at the popular TV show *Good Morning America* to participate in a blind tasting that included two of the best-selling bottled waters, oxygenated water, and tap water from the New York City water system. And tap water received 45 percent of the vote.

Yes, it's true that the plastic bottles—all 70 million per day in the United States alone—all of those bottles *could* be recycled because they're made of recyclable plastic, but unfortunately, only about 15 percent of them actually make it into the recycle bins, which leaves a whopping 85 percent or 59.5 million bottles per day that end up in landfills.

Relationship sentence: The lecturer discredits the claim in the reading passage that bottled water is better than tap water.

| Reading | Lecture |
|---|---|
| Point 1 healthier | Point 1 40% city water/low fluoride |
| Point 2 tastes better | Point 2 flat w/o minerals<br>sodium, calcium, magnesium, chlorides<br>tap 45% vote GMA |
| Point 3 recyclable | Point 3 70 m US 15% recycled<br>59.5/day landfills |

## *Practice Activity 48*

## *SPEAKING TASK 3*

 **Activity 48, Track 40**
Now listen to a conversation on the same topic.

| | |
|---|---|
| Man: | Have you heard about the fee hike? |
| Woman: | Sure. Everybody's talking about it. |
| Man: | But it won't affect you, right? Because you're from Florida. |
| Woman: | Right. My fees will be the same as last year. But you're an out-of-state student so that will mean . . . |
| Man: | $360. That's 3 percent. |
| Woman: | Oh. |
| Man: | Per semester. So really it's $720 for the year. |
| Woman: | Just be glad you aren't an international student. |
| Man: | Isn't their fee increase the same as out-of-state students? |
| Woman: | It *is*, if they're already enrolled, but if they're applying, as new students I mean, then they have to pay 5 percent more than last year. |
| Man: | Well, I think this whole idea is *not* well thought out because part of your education is supposed to be exposure to new people as well as to new ideas, and if you punish out-of-state students and international students, then, naturally, fewer of us will apply and attend. And that means that in-state students like you will have a very different experience. You'll just have a lot of people with the same background on campus. |
| Woman: | That's a really good point. My roommate is from India, and it's been great learning about her customs and her point of view on issues and events. |
| Man: | Well her fees will go up, but at the same rate as mine because she's already a student here. But I'll bet her family will give it some thought before they send her younger brothers and sisters. Five percent is a lot. |

### Question
The man expresses his opinion of the announcement. State his opinion and give the reasons he has for holding that opinion.

### Example Response

The man disagrees with the increases in tuition and fees for out-of-state students and international students. As an out-of-state student, he'll have to pay 3 percent more, that is, the same increase as continuing international students, but he emphasizes the fact that *new* international students will have to pay 5 percent more . . . so there will probably be a serious decline in that population on campus. And he says that it won't be good for the campus environment because so many students will have the same background.

*The response is incomplete because it does not include the fee structure for in-state students. It will be frozen at the same amount as last year.*

## SPEAKING TASK 4

 **Activity 48, Track 41**

Now that you have read the explanation of strategic business alliances in the reading, listen to part of a lecture on a similar topic.

Okay, now I want you to think about two companies that have historically been in competition for the package delivery service in the United States. Well, the first to come to mind has to be the U.S. Postal Service, right? But now think *fast* delivery. For that, Federal Express is at the top of the list. But, instead of viewing their relationship as totally competitive, these two companies struck an unprecedented strategic alliance several years ago. The U.S. Postal Service agreed to let Federal Express place package collection boxes at thousands of post offices throughout the United States, which was great for Fed Ex because they achieved an immediate national presence. But in exchange, Fed Ex allowed the Postal Service to buy unused space on the Federal Express airplanes in order to carry first-class, priority, and, most importantly, express mail envelopes and packages, increasing the speed with which they could deliver the mail without purchasing aircraft. Moreover, by sharing websites to track their deliveries, both companies have been able to create a larger Internet presence.

So why would these companies be willing to help each other? Probably the most commonly espoused explanation is that they're both battling fax, email, and other emerging messaging technologies and their combined resources may result in survival and success for both of them against a common threat. And that fits in nicely with the whole concept of strategic alliances. But, besides that, many countries—New Zealand, Sweden, Germany, and the Netherlands, to name only a few—these countries have ended the special government status that postal services have traditionally enjoyed, with all the benefits, including tax advantages and subsidies. So, it may be that the U.S. Postal Service is trying to find alternatives to show progress before privatization ends its chance of survival. And Federal Express might be positioning itself to be the really big winner if the Postal Service goes up on the auction block at some time in the future. In other words, the real purpose of strategic alliances like this one may be to serve competing interests in the long run in an agreement that allows each company to retain its identity and dissolve the association when it's no longer advantageous.

### Question

Explain how the example that the professor provides demonstrates the concept of strategic alliances defined in the reading passage.

### Example Response

An example of a strategic alliance is the agreement between the U.S. Postal Service and Federal Express in which the Postal Service allowed Fed Ex to place its depositories in a large number of post offices in exchange for the opportunity to buy space on Fed Ex airplanes. The Postal Service obtained transportation for their first-class, priority, and express mail without purchasing aircraft. Fed Ex secured a national presence for their brand. All three key features of a strategic alliance were present in the agreement. First, both entities retained their individual identities. Second, the alliance provided for the companies to share resources for their mutual benefit and cooperate in the competitive arena against newer technologies. Third, the alliance, easily organized and easily terminated, could place each company in a more favorable position when business conditions change.

*The response is complete because it includes the definition of a strategic alliance, the concept presented in the reading passage, and it demonstrates how the example of the agreement between the U.S. Postal Service and Federal Express includes all three key features of a strategic alliance: individual identity, shared resources, and a simple procedure to form and dissolve the association.*

## *INTEGRATED ESSAY*

**Activity 48, Track 42**
Now listen to part of a lecture in a business class. The professor is talking about vacation time.

Many advantages have been cited for companies that offer paid vacation time to their employees, but when we look more closely at each of these arguments, they start to fall apart. In the first place, companies who give generous vacation time to employees are supposed to receive more control over absenteeism, especially the unexpected absence of an employee at a critical time. In reality, unexpected absences occur at about the same rate in companies with paid vacation time and in those without that benefit. Unfortunately, it's simply not possible to plan for the unexpected or to schedule emergencies around a planned vacation period.

Next, let's look at the issues of health and productivity. Although there's some evidence that people who take vacations tend to be healthier, both mentally and physically, there's no assurance that the paid time away from work will be used for a refreshing holiday. More often than not, employees with paid vacation will use that time to accomplish a project at home, schedule an elective surgery, take care of an ailing relative, or some other activity that doesn't lend itself to returning rested and restored from the so-called vacation. In fact, in some studies, employees returning from paid vacations reported feeling more tired and stressed than before leaving.

Okay then, what about vacation time as a recruitment strategy? That seems to be rather straightforward, but again, it really isn't. Because like most other contractual issues, one size doesn't fit all when it comes to offering benefits. Some highly talented employees are less interested in time off than they are in better health care for themselves and their families. Others want more money and fewer perks. And still others are just looking for a clear path for advancement and promotion, and being gone from the workplace isn't a good way to make *that* happen.

So, yes, workers in the United States are at the bottom of the chart for paid vacation days, but it's hard to make the argument that giving employees time off is better for American companies.

**Example Essay**
*The essay on page 266 is complete because it includes all three arguments that the lecturer makes, contradicting the points in the reading passage, including control over absenteeism, the relationship between health and vacation time, and the advantage of a good vacation plan as part of a recruitment package.*

## *Practice Activity 49*

1. Draw a chart with space for a relationship sentence at the top and three points underneath.

2. Read a short passage and take notes on the chart.

3. Listen to a conversation or a lecture on the same topic and take notes on the chart.

4. Write a relationship sentence on the chart.

5. Respond, using information from both the reading and the conversation or lecture.

6. Use the chart to check for a complete response.

## EXAMPLE SPEAKING TASK 3

 **Activity 49, Track 43**
Now listen to a conversation on the same topic.

Woman:   I know you think it's a hassle, but I'm really happy about the new security measures. You wouldn't believe the people who parade through our dorm in the middle of the night.

Man:   And the scans will help that?

Woman:   Maybe. At least we'll know who's there. And people who just walk in from who-knows-where will have to get guest passes.

Man:   Don't they have to do that now?

Woman:   Well, yes, but it isn't really enforced. And this looks like a serious plan.

Man:   I'll give you that.

Woman:   And for students—well, how long does it take to scan a fingerprint at the door?

Man:   True.

Woman:   It won't be any different from opening up your phone or tablet with your fingerprint.

Man:   I hadn't thought about that. I guess it's just the time to go get your fingerprint scanned at the security office.

Woman:   Look, back to the issue of phones and tablets. You want to keep those secure. Why wouldn't you want to keep students secure?

Man:   That's a point.

Woman:   It stands to reason that someone who wants to steal something or even hurt someone, well, maybe they'll think about it if they have to scan their prints or leave their ID at the desk. I know I'm going to feel better about living in the dorm.

Man:   Okay. I'm convinced. It isn't such a big deal to go to the security office. I can just stop by there when I'm in the student union the next time. But . . . I hope there isn't a line a mile long.

### Question
The woman expresses her opinion of the announcement. State her opinion and the reasons that she has for having that opinion.

### Example Response
The woman approves of the new security policy because it's a serious plan, it will be easy to use, and it should be a deterrent to crime. She explains that the previous system that required a pass to enter the dorm wasn't enforced, but now, without a scan, it won't be possible to go in the door. She also points out that it's really easy, like scanning to access a secure mobile device. She argues that scanning a fingerprint will be a deterrent to theft and the dorms will be safer because it'll be better than a guest pass to keep track of everyone who's in the buildings.

## EXAMPLE SPEAKING TASK 4

 **Activity 49, Track 44**
Now listen to part of a lecture in a linguistics class. The professor is talking about endangered languages.

Today I want to give you an example of a language that, unfortunately, meets all the criteria to be considered an endangered language. Like many other Native American languages, Ojibwa, also known as Chippewa, is struggling to survive. A North American indigenous language of the Algonquian language family, Ojibwa has traditionally been spoken in Canada and along the Northern border of the United States. It was very important during the fur-trading era in the Great Lakes region—to such an extent, in fact, that French traders often used Ojibwa to speak with other tribes. But although the total ethnic population still includes more than 200 thousand people, and that number comes from self-identification—the people who claim Ojibwa tribal membership—well, of those 200 thousand, only about 30 thousand still speak Ojibwa on any level of proficiency. And the number of children in the youngest generation who are fluent in Ojibwa is almost nonexistent.

In a study in 1995 of Ojibwa language usage in a three-state area consisting of Michigan, Wisconsin, and Minnesota, Rosemary Christensen was able to locate only 500 fluent Ojibwa speakers. Of those speakers, most were elders, over the age of 80, and none were under the age of 45. She found no children who were fluent in Ojibwa.

Partly in response to this study, and with funding from the Department of Health and Human Services, four preschools were opened in Minneapolis in 2006. In cooperation with the 100 remaining Ojibwa speakers in the area, immersion classrooms in Ojibwa began teaching young children in their ancestral language. Will it be too little too late? Only time will tell. As for now, Ojibwa remains on the endangered list, a language with an uncertain future.

## Question

The professor reports a study of the Ojibwa language. Explain why the study confirms that Ojibwa is an endangered language.

## Example Response

Ojibwa is considered an endangered language because it meets all three criteria for that classification. First, few speakers are fluent in the language. In Christensen's study in 1995, only about 500 of the tribal members in the tri-state area studied were fluent speakers. Second, the average age of native speakers is older. Among the 500 fluent speakers, most were elders 80 years of age or older. Finally, the percentage of speakers in the youngest generation is small. Among Ojibwa speakers, almost *no* children were fluent. Unfortunately, this study confirmed that Ojibwa is endangered, and despite efforts to teach the language in federally funded preschools, its future is very uncertain.

## EXAMPLE WRITING TASK 1: INTEGRATED ESSAY

 **Activity 49, Track 45**

Now listen to part of a lecture in an economics class. The professor is talking about home ownership.

The reading passage lists three reasons to own a home, but recent changes in the economy persuade us to reassess the assumptions.

First, we have to question whether owning a home is a sound investment in today's economy. Although it was once considered a strategy in the creation of wealth, it is now being reexamined. During recessions like the one recently experienced, the value of homes has dramatically fallen. So much so that many homeowners were paying a high mortgage for a home that was worth only half of its value at the time of the purchase. Whether owning a home that has depreciated in value so rapidly will be a sound investment long term—well, the verdict will have to wait for a decade to give us that kind of data. But short term, for many homeowners, the plan to create wealth is a disappointment.

The sharp increase in foreclosures and forced sales has also decreased the sense of security that homeowners once experienced. Struggling to pay a mortgage and a looming possibility that the property will be foreclosed leads to a loss of control and a sense of insecurity—the exact opposite of the anticipated stability that homeowners used to enjoy. A significant number of first-time owners report that they would prefer to rent but don't know how to reverse their situation without losing their initial investment.

As for the social benefits, the pressures associated with owning and maintaining a home are taking a toll on the psychological and physical health of homeowners. Many homeowners report that they're only one paycheck away from being unable to pay the costs of owning a home. The stress affects *all* of the family members, even the children, who seem to respond to the pressures by bringing home lower grades and by being less involved in school activities than was previously reported. So, as you see, times have changed.

## *Practice Activity 50*

### *SPEAKING TASK 3*

☐1  Draw a chart with space for a relationship sentence at the top and three points underneath.

Relationship sentence: The man is not happy about the relocation of the honors program to Harkins Hall because the other location in Anderson Hall was larger and had a better view.

| Point 1 | Harkins to Anderson | Point 1 | inferior space—smaller, no view, dark |
| Point 2 | Faculty Club | Point 2 | uses lounge more |
| Point 3 | Honors smaller suite | Point 3 | honors program not important |

☐2  Read a short passage about a campus-related topic and take notes on the chart.

☐3  Listen to a conversation on the same topic and take notes on the chart.

 **Activity 50, Track 46**
Now listen to a conversation on the same topic.

Man: You're an honors student, aren't you?

Woman: Yes.

Man: So I guess you've been over to Harkins Hall.

Woman: Umhum. It's pretty grim. But they aren't done yet, so maybe it will be okay.

Man: Always the optimist. How can a basement be better than the top floor of Anderson Hall? That was really a nice place to hang out. The view was phenomenal.

Woman: It still is. It's just not our view anymore. That's why the faculty wanted it.

Man: Right.

Woman: But you spend more time there than I do so it doesn't matter so much to me. I just go over there when I need my advisor's signature for something. I haven't used the lounge that much.

Man: Well, since I live off campus, I'm there between classes and I even eat my lunch there sometimes. There's always a chess game going, and I'm friends with a lot of the regulars.

Woman: Then it's a big change for you.

Man: It *is*. And it bugs me that the new space is so inferior to what we had. I think they should have tried harder to find something better than a basement. It just communicates that the Honors Program isn't important.

Woman:  Oh, I don't know about that. I feel lucky to be in smaller classes and to be able to take graduate courses while I'm still an undergrad, don't you?

Man:    Sure. Of course I do. But the lounge is supposed to be our place to meet up with other honors students, and, besides, how do you think the advisors feel? Their offices are cramped and dark compared with the program offices that they had in Anderson.

Woman:  Of course, they can always use the Faculty Club when they want to.

Man:    Unlike us. Listen, are you always so upbeat? It seems like you just take everything in stride.

Woman:  Pretty much. Especially when it's something I can't change anyway.

[4] Write a relationship sentence on the chart.

[5] Respond, using information from both the reading and the conversation.

**Example Response**

The man isn't happy about the relocation of the Honors Program to Harkins Hall because the other location in Anderson Hall was larger and had a better view. He uses the lounge to hang out with friends and eat lunch because he lives off campus, and the new space isn't as nice. It's dark, small, and it doesn't have a view because it's in a basement. He feels that moving the Honors Program to an inferior space indicates that the program isn't very important to the college.

[6] Use the chart to check for a complete response.

*All three points in the chart are included in the response.*

## SPEAKING TASK 4

[1] Draw a chart with space for a relationship sentence at the top and three points underneath.

Relationship sentence: Peacocks are a good example of animals that use courtship displays to compete with other males and attract a mate.

Point 1  ritualized dances        Point 1  strut and dance around female

Point 2  postures tail-feathers   Point 2  large fan w/ many eyespots

Point 3  vocalization             Point 3  mating calls–vibrations train 20 hertz

[2] Read a short passage about an academic topic and take notes on the chart.

[3] Listen to a lecture on the same topic and take notes on the chart.

**Activity 50, Track 47**
Now listen to a lecture in a biology class about the same topic.

Peacocks are large, colorful birds, known for their beautiful blue-green tail feathers, which they spread out in a distinctive fan. When extended, the fantail represents more than 60 percent of the peacock's total body weight. Arched into a magnificent train, it surrounds the bird's back and spreads out onto the ground on either side. Female birds choose their mates according to the size, color, and quality of the feathered trains. In addition to the blue-green feathers, colorful eye markings of red and gold and many other colors enhance the beauty of individual birds and form very different patterns from one bird to another.

Although the term *peacock* is commonly used to refer to both males and females, technically only the male is a peacock. The *peahens* watch the display in order to make a selection. In general, the more eyespots and the more evenly spaced their pattern, the more attractive a male peacock appears to the female. A large fan is also appealing; however, tails that are too big are considered too burdensome for mating. And as though the beautiful feathers and the graceful movements of the males were not enough, as they strut and perform an elaborate dance in front of their potential mates, well, these beautiful birds also communicate in very low-pitched mating calls that are produced by the vibrations of the feather train at a level of 20 hertz, far too low to be heard by the human ear, but just right for a peahen to notice.

4  Write a relationship sentence on the chart.

5  Respond, using information from both the reading and the lecture.

**Example Response**
Peacocks are a good example of animals that use courtship displays to compete with other males and attract a mate. Like other birds, peacocks engage in ritualized dances, strutting gracefully around the female. In addition, they display their magnificent fan of blue-green tail feathers, posturing to show the eyespots and beautiful colors to their advantage. They also use vocalizations, in this case, mating calls that are generated by vibrations when they shake their feathers.

6  Use the chart to check for a complete response.

*All three points in the chart are included in the response.*

## WRITING TASK 1

1. Draw a chart with space for a relationship sentence at the top and three points underneath.

Relationship sentence: The lecturer refutes the idea that government censorship of the Internet should be instituted to protect children, curtail crime, and assure personal privacy.

Point 1  Protects children

Point 2  Curtails crime

Point 3  Assures personal privacy

Point 1  Parents, guardians monitor

Point 2  Personal responsibility better—passwords, firewalls, anti-virus, no attach, good judgment

Point 3  Laws not enforced—take care ourselves—separate email, don't disclose personal info social media

2. Read a short passage about an academic topic and take notes on the chart.

Reading Time: 3 minutes

> Government censorship of the Internet benefits society in three ways. First, like other forms of mass media, including television and movies, censorship protects children. Restricting adult content and providing punitive measures for pornographic websites discourages the exposure of young children to inappropriate images and explicit language. Since children are growing up in an environment in which they can easily access the Internet, some restrictions should be in place to protect them.
>
> Second, censorship curtails criminal activities. Censorship discovers and discourages financial frauds, theft, and harassment, or even potentially violent encounters. Because the Internet affords criminals a high degree of anonymity, unless their activities are monitored, they can sell illegal substances, threaten or bully individuals, or intrude into the lives of large numbers of people with spam advertising. Censorship reduces the instances of these disturbing contacts.
>
> Finally, censorship assures personal privacy. Censorship laws establish standards for websites and security measures to protect identity, financial records, and personal information. Censorship restricts access to credit cards and bank accounts, as well as medical and employment records, and it reduces the incidents of identity theft.

3. Listen to a lecture on the same topic and take notes on the chart.

 **Activity 50, Track 48**
Now listen to a lecture about the same topic.

Although it may be true that government censorship has the potential to benefit society, realistically, it's just not possible to enforce. That aside, let's look at each of the advantages that are mentioned in the reading passage. Hardly anyone would disagree that children should be protected from pornography and other inappropriate websites. The issue is, *who* should protect them—the government or their parents? Software that installs parental controls is readily available and relatively cheap. My position is that responsible adults should monitor their children's Internet access. Even if censorship *does* restrict some viewing, it's still up to the parents or guardians to take care of their children.

Now, as for criminal activities, no one wants to deal with this, especially since the Internet intrudes into our workspaces and our homes. And censorship helps somewhat. But again, personal responsibility is a better deterrent. Everyone needs to choose and use strong passwords, install firewalls and antivirus software, avoid opening attachments from unidentified sources, and use good judgment when interacting with unfamiliar people or businesses—but, of course, that's true for face-to-face encounters and purchases as well. And we don't want the government to censor those, that's for sure.

So last, of course, we want to guard our identities and our personal and financial information. And censorship laws may establish standards. But, as I said in the beginning, the laws are very difficult, even impossible to enforce. So in the long run, it comes down to taking care of ourselves. How can we do that? Well, first we should establish a separate email account for Internet transactions—one that we can close down easily if we need to. In other words, we have a disposable identity in cyberspace. Second, never give out personal information like a social security number, credit card or bank account numbers unless *you* initiate the interaction. And this is important—don't divulge too much personal information on social media. If we want to protect ourselves even more, we have the option to subscribe to an identity theft plan.

The bottom line is this: To keep our children safe and to avoid being victims of crime or identity theft, we have to take personal responsibility. Censorship on the Internet isn't necessary, and it doesn't work.

4 Write a relationship sentence on the chart.

5 Respond, using information from both the reading and the lecture.

**Example Essay**

The lecturer refutes the idea that government censorship of the Internet should be instituted to protect children, curtail crime, and assure personal privacy. He contends that censorship cannot be enforced, and that, in any case, personal responsibility is better than censorship.

According to the lecturer, parents and guardians, not the government, should monitor their children's Internet use to protect them from inappropriate sites and images.

Moreover, users should assume individual responsibility to avoid becoming victims of crime. We can do this by using strong passwords and by installing firewalls and antivirus software, as well as by using good judgment about opening attachments and interacting with unfamiliar people and businesses online.

Furthermore, he claims that we should take care of our own identities by using email accounts that can be closed if they are breached by intrusive sources. Finally, he recommends that we not disclose too much personal information on social media.

In short, the lecturer is an advocate for personal responsibility instead of for government censorship.

6 Use the chart to check for a complete response.

*All three points in the chart are included in the response.*

# 6
# USAGE AND STYLE FOR TOEFL iBT®

## ✔ *Learn the grammar that adds points*

Although the TOEFL iBT® does not test grammar in a separate section, you can add points to your Speaking and Writing scores by using correct grammatical structures in your answers. *Usage* is customary practice in spoken or written language. *Style* is the way that the parts of a sentence relate to each other and to other sentences in speech or writing. This is a short review of usage and style with grammar charts. It is organized to help you improve your English for a specific purpose, in this case, to increase your score on the Speaking and Writing Sections of the TOEFL. In order for you to use the charts in this chapter, you must understand five kinds of symbols.

**Abbreviations.** An *abbreviation* is a shortened form. In the charts, four abbreviations are used. S for Subject, V for Verb, C for Complement, and M for Modifier.

**Small Letters.** *Small letters* are lowercase letters. In the charts, a verb written in small (lowercase) letters may not change form. For example, the verb *have* may not change to *has* or *had* when it is written in small letters.

**Capital Letters.** *Capital letters* are uppercase letters. In the charts, a verb written in capital (uppercase) letters may change form. For example, the verb *HAVE* may remain as *have*, or may change to *has*, or *had*, depending on agreement with the subject and choice of tense.

**Parentheses.** *Parentheses* are curved lines that enclose information. In the charts, the words in parentheses provide specific information about the abbreviation or word that precedes them. For example, *V (dictionary)* means that the verb must be the form in the dictionary, without endings. *N (count)* means that the noun must be a countable noun.

**Alternatives.** *Alternatives* are different ways to express the same idea. In the charts, alternatives are shown in a vertical column. For example, in the following chart, there are three alternatives. All three are correct.

| S | had<br>would have<br>could have | participle | C |
|---|---|---|---|
| The students | had<br>would have<br>could have | understood | the charts |

## USAGE PROBLEMS

1     Descriptions—Infinitive and *-ing* subjects
2     Descriptions—*Enjoy* + *-ing*
3     Descriptions—*Plan* + infinitive
4     Descriptions—*Used to* and *BE used to*
5     Descriptions—Descriptive clauses
6     Reasons and Examples—*Because* and *because of*
7     Reasons and Examples—*For example, for instance,* and *such as*
8     Reasons and Examples—Examples of concepts
9     Purposes—*So* and *so that*
10    Purposes—Infinitives
11    Opinions—Direct statements
12    Opinions—Opinion verbs
13    Opinions—Introductory phrases
14    Opinions—Importance
15    Preferences—*Prefer* and *would prefer*
16    Preferences—*Instead of* and *instead*
17    Preferences—*Would rather*
18    Preferences—*Like better than*
19    Concessions—*Although* and *even though*
20    Concessions—*Despite* and *in spite of*
21    Definitions—Noncount nouns
22    Definitions—Count nouns in other languages
23    Definitions—Ø meaning *all*
24    Definitions—Qualifying phrases
25    Reports—Reported speech
26    Reports—Past verbs
27    Reports—Preferences *would rather that*
28    Reports—Suggestions and recommendations
29    Suggestions and Recommendations—*Should* and *could*
30    Suggestions and Recommendations—*Had better*
31    Suggestions and Recommendations—Verbs
32    Summaries—Narrations with passive statements
33    Summaries—Classifications *kind* and *type*
34    Summaries—Comparisons of general similarity *similar to* and *similar/like* and *alike*
35    Summaries—Comparisons of general difference *different from* and *different*
36    Summaries—Consecutive order *one, another, the other*
37    Summaries—Consecutive order s*ome, other, the other/some, others, the others (the rest)*
38    Hypothetical Situations—Imagined (possible) results
39    Hypothetical Situations—Imagined (impossible) results
40    Hypothetical Situations—Scientific (absolute) results

# USAGE

## DESCRIPTIONS

You may be asked to describe a familiar person, object, place, or event in both the Speaking and the Writing Sections. Speaking Question 1 and Writing Question 2 may ask you for a description. The following grammatical structures will support your responses.

## Problem 1: Descriptions—Infinitive and *-ing* subjects

Either an infinitive or an *-ing* form may be used as the subject of a sentence or a clause.

| S (infinitive) | V | |
|---|---|---|
| To read a foreign language well | requires | practice |

| S (*-ing* form) | V | |
|---|---|---|
| Reading a foreign language well | requires | practice |

### *Improve Your Speaking*

 Read the question silently. Then read the answer aloud and record it.

Question: Describe a perfect day. What would you do? Be sure to include reasons or examples in your answer.

Answer: "<u>Relaxing</u> with my family would be my idea of a perfect day. We would cook together and go for a walk after dinner."

### *Edit Your Essays*

Draft: To planting trees is a custom that we have in my country to recognize an important occasion.

Edit: <u>Planting</u> trees is a custom that we have in my country to recognize an important occasion.

OR

<u>To plant</u> trees is a custom that we have in my country to recognize an important occasion.

## Problem 2: Descriptions—*Enjoy + -ing*

The verb *enjoy* introduces an *-ing* form.

| S | enjoy | *-ing* | |
|---|-------|--------|---|
| I | enjoy | reading | |

Other verbs that require an *-ing* form include *admit, appreciate, avoid, complete, consider, delay, deny, discuss, finish, keep, mention, miss, postpone, practice, quit, recall, recommend, regret, stop,* and *suggest*. Verb phrases that require an *-ing* form include *approve of, be better off, can't help, count on, do not mind, forget about, get through, insist on, keep on, look forward to, object to, recall,* and *think about*.

### Improve Your Speaking

 Read the question silently. Then read the answer aloud and record it.

Question: Talk about a hobby you enjoy. Why do you like this hobby? Be sure to include reasons or examples in your answer.

Answer: "I enjoy playing golf because it's relaxing, it gives me an opportunity to be outside, and it's good exercise."

### Edit Your Essays

Draft: I enjoy the travel because I meet interesting people, see new sights, and learn about the world.

Edit: I enjoy traveling because I meet interesting people, see new sights, and learn about the world.

## Problem 3: Descriptions—*Plan* + infinitive

The verb *plan* introduces an infinitive.

| S | plan | infinitive | |
|---|------|-----------|---|
| I | plan | to study | engineering |

Other verbs that require an infinitive include *agree, ask, decide, expect, forget, hope, intend, learn, need, prepare, promise, refuse, tend,* and *want.*

### *Improve Your Speaking*

 Read the question silently. Then read the answer aloud and record it.

Question: Talk about a good decision that you made. Why was it beneficial to you? Be sure to include reasons or examples in your answer.

Answer: "I decided to work for one year before going abroad to study. It was beneficial because I improved my English language skills and gained experience in my profession."

### *Edit Your Essays*

Draft: When I decided choosing friends who are serious students, it made a difference in my life.

Edit: When I decided to choose friends who are serious students, it made a difference in my life.

## Problem 4: Descriptions—*Used to* and *BE used to*

*Used to* expresses a custom in the past that has not continued into the present. *BE used to* means *be accustomed to* as a habit or routine.

| S | used to | V (dictionary) | |
|---|---------|----------------|---|
| I | used to | exercise | every day |

### Improve Your Speaking

    Read the question silently. Then read the answer aloud and record it.

Question: Talk about a good memory that you have of your childhood. Explain why it was such a warm recollection.

Answer: "When I was a child, I <u>used to go</u> to the park with my mother. It makes me happy to think of it because I remember my mother, my childhood friends, and the place with affection."

### Edit Your Essays

Draft: My aunt used to reading with me when I was a child.

Edit: My aunt <u>used to read</u> with me when I was a child. She introduced me to books and encouraged me to become an avid reader.

| S | BE | used to | *-ing* | |
|---|----|---------|--------|---|
| I | was | used to | exercising | every day |

### Improve Your Speaking

    Read the question silently. Then read the answer aloud and record it.

Question: Talk about a good routine that you have developed. Explain why it is helpful to you.

Answer: "I <u>am</u> used to <u>getting up</u> early in the morning and starting my day. This routine helps me get a lot done before my classes."

### Edit Your Essays

Draft: Although young people used to writing abbreviations in text messages, essays still require formal spellings.

Edit: Although young people <u>are used to</u> <u>writing</u> abbreviations in text messages, essays still require formal spellings.

# Problem 5: Descriptions—Descriptive clauses

*Who* is used for people and refers to the subject of the main clause. *That* is used for things and refers to the subject of the main clause. *Whom* is used for people and refers to the subject of the main clause, but serves as the object of the descriptive clause. *Which* is used for things, and is in a descriptive clause separated by commas. The descriptive clause between the commas is not necessary for the meaning of the sentence.

| | | MAIN CLAUSE | | | |
| | | DESCRIPTIVE CLAUSE | | | |
| S (Main) | that who | V | | V (Main) | (Name a thing) (Name a person) |
|---|---|---|---|---|---|
| The movie | that | has influenced | me the most | is | Ghandi |
| The person | who | has inspired | me the most | is | my math teacher |

## *Improve Your Speaking*

 Read the question silently. Then read the answer aloud and record it.

Question: Choose a book that has influenced you and explain why and how you were affected. Be sure to include reasons or examples in your answer.

Answer: "The book that has influenced me the most is Dale Carnegie's *How to Win Friends and Influence People* because it has been helpful both personally and professionally."

## *Edit Your Essays*

Draft: The person has inspired me the most is my older brother because he is very successful.

Edit: The person who has inspired me the most is my older brother because he is very successful.

| | | MAIN CLAUSE | | | |
| | | DESCRIPTIVE CLAUSE | | | |
| S (Main) The thing The person | that whom | S | V | V (Main) | (Name a thing) (Name a person) |
|---|---|---|---|---|---|
| The possession | that | I | value | the most | is | my wedding ring |
| The person | whom | I | admire | the most | is | my grandfather |

The words *that* and *whom* are optional in informal conversation.

### Improve Your Speaking

 Read the question silently. Then read the answer aloud and record it.

Question: Choose a person you admire and explain why you admire him or her. Be sure to include reasons or examples in your answer.

Answer: "The person <u>whom</u> <u>I</u> <u>admire</u> most is my neighbor because he does so much for the people on our street."

### Edit Your Essays

Draft: The person which I would like to meet is the president of my country because I would like to ask him a few questions about his policies.

Edit: The person <u>whom</u> <u>I</u> <u>would like to meet</u> is the president of my country because I would like to ask him a few questions about his policies.

| | | MAIN CLAUSE | | | | | |
|---|---|---|---|---|---|---|---|
| | | DESCRIPTIVE CLAUSE | | | | | |
| **The thing** | , | which | S | V | | , | |
| The gift | , | which | I | received | for graduation | , | is | very special to me |

The word *which* is optional in informal conversation. Commas are deleted if *which* is deleted.

### Improve Your Speaking

 Read the question silently. Then read the answer aloud and record it.

Question: Describe your favorite city and explain why. Be sure to include reasons or examples in your answer.

Answer: "New York, which I visit regularly, is my favorite city because there is always something new to see."

### Edit Your Essays

Draft: The class what I took when I was in England helped me improve my English.

Edit: The class, <u>which</u> <u>I</u> <u>took</u> when I was in England, helped me improve my English.

## REASONS AND EXAMPLES

You will be asked to provide reasons and examples for your answers. The following grammatical structures will support your responses when you are asked *why*.

### Problem 6: Reasons and Examples—*Because* and *because of*

*Because* is a conjunction that introduces a subject and a verb. *Because of* is a prepositional phrase that introduces a noun or noun phrase.

| S | V | | because | S | V | |
|---|---|---|---------|---|---|---|
| My sister | is | my favorite person | because | she | has | many outstanding qualities |

#### *Improve Your Speaking*

 Read the question silently. Then read the answer aloud and record it.

Question: Think about a movie that made an impression on you. Be sure to mention why you chose it.

Answer: "The Star Wars movies made an impression on me <u>because</u> the special effects for each one <u>used</u> the latest technology and the characters clearly represented good and evil."

#### *Edit Your Essays*

Draft: I like hiking because of it is good exercise and I enjoy nature.

Edit: I like hiking <u>because</u> it <u>is</u> good exercise and I enjoy nature.

| S | V | | because of | N phrase |
|---|---|---|------------|----------|
| Florida | is | my favorite vacation place | because of | the weather and Disney World |

#### *Improve Your Speaking*

 Read the question silently. Then read the answer aloud and record it.

Question: What makes you homesick? Please include specific reasons in your response.

Answer: "I get homesick <u>because of</u> <u>the absence</u> of my friends and family <u>and</u> <u>the differences</u> in the culture, especially the food."

#### *Edit Your Essays*

Draft: I prefer to live in the country because the health benefits and the peaceful surroundings beneficial to physical and mental health.

Edit: I prefer to live in the country <u>because of</u> <u>the health benefits and the peaceful surroundings</u>, which are beneficial to physical and mental health.

## Problem 7: Reasons and Examples—*For example, for instance,* and *such as*

Example phrases introduce an example.

| S | , | for example<br>for instance | , | subject reference | , | V |
|---|---|---|---|---|---|---|
| Team sports | , | for example | , | baseball and basketball | , | do not require much equipment |

| For example<br>For instance | , | S | V |
|---|---|---|---|
| For instance | , | baseball and basketball | do not require much equipment |

### Improve Your Speaking

 Read the question silently. Then read the answer aloud and record it.

Question: Think about a character in a children's book that you admired when you were a child. Why did you like that character? Include specific details and examples to support your answer.

Answer: "When I was young, I admired Anne of Green Gables because she was a strong character and a role model for girls. For example, she stood up for her beliefs and protected her friends."

### Edit Your Essays

Draft: According to the lecturer, some birds, example cardinals, do not migrate.

Edit: According to the lecturer, some birds, for example, cardinals, do not migrate.

| S | such as | subject reference | V |
|---|---|---|---|
| Individual sports | such as | golf and swimming | are popular electives for physical education |

### *Improve Your Speaking*

 Read the question silently. Then read the answer aloud and record it.

Question: Besides English, what language would you enjoy learning? State your reasons for choosing it.

Answer: "I would like to learn a number of languages, such as Chinese and Spanish, because they are two of the most widely spoken languages in the world."

### *Edit Your Essays*

Draft: On the other hand, coniferous trees, as such pine and spruce, grow in colder climates.

Edit: On the other hand, coniferous trees, <u>such as</u> pine and spruce, grow in colder climates.

## Problem 8: Reasons and Examples—Examples of concepts

Concepts are explained by providing examples.

| EXAMPLE | is | an example | of | CONCEPT |
|---|---|---|---|---|
| The Mohave | is | an example | of | a subtropical desert |

| EXAMPLE | demonstrates | the | CONCEPT | of | |
|---|---|---|---|---|---|
| The example of basketball practice | demonstrates | the | concept | of | visualization |
| | clearly shows | | law<br>principle<br>theory | | |

### *Improve Your Speaking*

 Read the question silently. Then read the answer aloud and record it.

Question: Explain why the example of baby ducks demonstrates the concept of imprinting. Include specific details and examples to support your answer.

Answer: "<u>The example</u> of baby ducks <u>demonstrates</u> <u>the concept</u> of imprinting because the young birds identify with and form an attachment very soon after hatching."

### *Edit Your Essays*

Draft: Texting and email are examples the principle of least effort.

Edit: Texting and email <u>are examples of</u> the principle of least effort.

## PURPOSES

You may be asked to explain the purpose of a statement to support your answer.

### Problem 9: Purposes—*So* and *so that*

*So* and *so that* introduce a subject and verb. *So* is commonly used in speech and *so that* is preferred in writing.

| S | V | | | so (that) | S | V | |
|---|---|---|---|---|---|---|---|
| All students | should have | a free education | | so (that) | they | can learn | a profession or skill |

### *Improve Your Speaking*

 Read the question silently. Then read the answer aloud and record it.

Question: Do you agree or disagree with this statement: Exploration of outer space should be postponed until the problems on Earth have been solved. Please include specific reasons in your response.

Answer: "I agree that space exploration should be postponed <u>so the huge expenditure</u> <u>can</u> <u>be</u> <u>used</u> to solve problems on Earth, specifically <u>so famine and unhealthy water supplies</u> <u>can</u> <u>be addressed</u>."

### *Edit Your Essays*

Draft: Our country should try to preserve its ancient monuments that the younger generations can better understand and appreciate their culture and history.

Edit: Our country should try to preserve its ancient monuments <u>so that</u> the younger generations can better understand and appreciate their culture and history.

## Problem 10: Purposes—Infinitives

An infinitive can express purpose. It is a short form of the phrase *in order to.*

| S | V | | infinitive | |
|---|---|---|---|---|
| I | read | my lecture notes | to prepare | for a test |

### *Improve Your Speaking*

 Read the question silently. Then read the answer aloud and record it.

Question: What do you do to relax when you are stressed out? Be sure to include details and examples in your response.

Answer: "I practice yoga <u>to relax</u> because it is good for my body and my mind."

### *Edit Your Essays*

Draft: The reading passage states that animals engage in characteristic behavior for to attract a mate, including rituals and gifts of food and nesting materials.

Edit: The reading passage states that animals engage in characteristic behavior <u>to attract</u> a mate, including rituals and gifts of food and nesting materials.

## OPINIONS

You may be asked to give your opinion in both the Speaking and the Writing Sections. Speaking Question 2, Speaking Question 5, and Writing Question 2 may ask for your opinion. The following grammatical structures will support your responses when you are asked for your opinion.

## Problem 11: Opinions—Direct statements

Direct statements make a good introduction. They express your opinion. When you are making a direct statement, remember that every English sentence must have a subject and a main verb. Always edit your writing to be sure that the main verb is in your sentence. A complement and a modifier may or may not follow.

| S | V | C | M |
|---|---|---|---|
| Pets | improve | their owners' lives | in many ways |

### *Improve Your Speaking*

 Read the question silently. Then read the answer aloud and record it.

Question: What is the best way to succeed when you set a goal?

Answer: "A positive attitude is the first step when you set a goal."

### *Edit Your Essays*

Draft: Recent technological advances more benefits than disadvantages.

Edit: Recent technological advances have more benefits than disadvantages.

## Problem 12: Opinions—Opinion verbs

The three common verbs that are used to express opinions are *think*, *believe*, and *feel*. Many native speakers use these words interchangeably, but they are not exactly the same. *Think* implies that you have thought about it; it is the strongest opinion. *Believe* implies that you are committed to it, but can't prove it. *Feel* implies that you have a general impression.

| I | think<br>believe<br>feel | that | S | V |
|---|---|---|---|---|
| I | think | that | swimming | is the best sport |

The word *that* is optional in informal conversation.

### Improve Your Speaking

 Read the question silently. Then read the answer aloud and record it.

Question: In your opinion, should attendance be a requirement for a college class?

Answer: "I think that attendance should be optional in college classes because some students can succeed without attending."

### Edit Your Essays

Draft: I believe that social skills important in a world that is dominated by technological interactions.

Edit: I believe that social skills are important in a world that is dominated by technological interactions.

## Problem 13: Opinions—Introductory phrases

When you are introducing your opinion, you have several options. The introductory phrases listed here are appropriate for both informal speaking and formal writing situations. *If you ask me* is appropriate on the Speaking Section.

| Introductory phrases | S | V | |
|---|---|---|---|
| In my opinion, | a group project | has | many disadvantages |
| In my view, | the professor | speaks | too fast |
| In my experience, | tutors | are | helpful |
| From my perspective, | open-book tests | can be | very difficult |

### *Improve Your Speaking*

 Read the question silently. Then read the answer aloud and record it.

Question: Do you think that smoking should be allowed in public areas outside of buildings and in outdoor recreational areas? Why or why not?

Answer: "If you ask me, people should be able to smoke outside if they wish because the smoke is only harmful to the person smoking outdoors."

### *Edit Your Essays*

Draft: My opinion, women should be allowed to serve in combat situations if they can meet the requirements.

Edit: In my opinion, women should be allowed to serve in combat situations if they can meet the requirements.

## Problem 14: Opinions—Importance

The following adjectives are used to express importance: essential, imperative, important, necessary.

| It is | adjective | infinitive | |
|---|---|---|---|
| It is | important | to verify | the data |

| It is | adjective | that | S | V (dictionary) | |
|---|---|---|---|---|---|
| It is | important | that | the researcher | verify | the data |

| It is | adjective | that | S | be (dictionary) | participle |
|---|---|---|---|---|---|
| It is | important | that | the data | be | verified |

### *Improve Your Speaking*

 Read the question silently. Then read the answer aloud and record it.

Question: The woman expresses her opinion of the announcement. State her opinion and the reasons that she has for having that opinion.

Answer: "According to the woman, it is important that the university policy on designated drivers be taken seriously at all campus restaurants and bars. She provides three reasons."

### *Edit Your Essays*

Draft: It is important that a college has special programs for international students.

Edit: It is important that a college have special programs for international students. OR
It is important for a college to have special programs for international students.

## PREFERENCES

You may be asked to give your preference in both the Speaking and the Writing Sections. Speaking Question 2 and Writing Question 2 may ask for your preference. The following grammatical structures will support your responses when you are asked for your preference.

### Problem 15: Preferences—*Prefer* and *would prefer*

The verb *prefer* introduces either an infinitive or an *-ing* form. In American English, the more common usage is the infinitive. *Would prefer* is slightly more polite. Although *would prefer* is in past tense, it expresses preference for something that happens in present or future time.

| S | prefer | infinitive | Option 1 |
|---|--------|------------|----------|
| I | prefer | to give | a report |

#### *Improve Your Speaking*

Read the question silently. Then read the answer aloud and record it.

Question: Some students like to prepare for a test alone, but other students like to prepare with a study group. How do you prefer to study for a test, and why? Be sure to include reasons or examples in your answer.

Answer: "I <u>prefer</u> <u>to study</u> for a test alone because I can focus on the material that I need to review and I can work at my own pace."

#### *Edit Your Essays*

Draft: I prefer live in a dormitory with a roommate for several reasons.
Edit: I <u>prefer</u> <u>to live</u> in a dormitory with a roommate for several reasons.

| S | would prefer | (infinitive) | Option 1 |
|---|--------------|--------------|----------|
| I | would prefer | to listen to | classical music |

#### *Improve Your Speaking*

Read the question silently. Then read the answer aloud and record it.

Question: How do you learn new important information? Do you like to read new information in a book or hear it in a lecture? Use specific reasons to support your response.

Answer: "I <u>would prefer</u> <u>to learn</u> new important information in a lecture because the teacher is available to repeat difficult concepts and to answer questions."

### Edit Your Essays

Draft: I had prefer to have one or two close friends instead of a large number of them because I can get to know a few friends on a deeper level and I can give them more of my time.

Edit: I <u>would prefer to have</u> one or two close friends instead of a large number of them because I can get to know a few friends on a deeper level and I can give them more of my time.

## Problem 16: Preferences—*Instead of* and *instead*

Sometimes your preference replaces another option.

| S | prefer | infinitive | Option 1 | instead of | *-ing* | Option 2 |
|---|--------|-----------|----------|-----------|--------|----------|
| I | prefer | to take | a test | instead of | writing | a paper |
| I | prefer | | a test | instead of | | a paper |

### Improve Your Speaking

 Read the question silently. Then read the answer aloud and record it.

Question: Some students like to ride a bike on campus. Others prefer to walk. Still others want to drive their cars. How do you prefer to get around on campus, and why? Be sure to include reasons or examples in your answer.

Answer: "I <u>prefer</u> <u>to ride</u> my bike to get around on campus <u>instead of</u> <u>driving</u> or <u>walking</u> because it is easier to park and faster than walking."

### Edit Your Essays

Draft: Unlike lions, tigers prefer to live and hunt alone instead in social groups.

Edit: Unlike lions, tigers <u>prefer</u> <u>to live and hunt</u> alone <u>instead of</u> <u>living and hunting</u> in social groups.

| S | prefer | infinitive | Option 1 | instead |
|---|--------|-----------|----------|---------|
| I | prefer | to write | a paper | instead |

*Instead* is also a replacement, but it is used at the end of a sentence.

### Improve Your Speaking

 Read the question silently. Then read the answer aloud and record it.

Question: Some students like to take classes early in the morning. Others prefer to go to class in the afternoon. Still others want to have classes at night. How do you prefer to schedule your classes, and why? Be sure to include reasons or examples in your answer.

Answer: "Although many students like to take classes during the day, I <u>prefer</u> to <u>schedule</u> my classes at night <u>instead</u>."

### Edit Your Essays

Draft: According to the passage, some students should draw diagrams to connect information instead making an outline. Visual learners understand better when they are given images instead.

Edit: According to the passage, some students should draw diagrams to connect information <u>instead of</u> <u>making</u> an outline. Visual learners understand better when they are given images <u>instead</u>.

## Problem 17: Preferences—*Would rather*

*Would rather* is similar to a modal. Although *would rather* is in past tense, it expresses preference for something that happens in present or future time.

| S | would rather | V (dictionary) | Option 1 | than | Option 2 |
|---|---|---|---|---|---|
| I | would rather | be | the group leader | than | a group member |

### Improve Your Speaking

 Read the question silently. Then read the answer aloud and record it.

Question: Some students like to make presentations, but other students prefer to write a report. Which assignment do you prefer and why? Be sure to include reasons or examples in your answer.

Answer: "I <u>would rather</u> <u>make</u> a presentation than a report."

### Edit Your Essays

Draft: I would rather to get the news on my computer than in the newspaper because it is more up to date, it is easier to access while I am working, and it is free.

Edit: I <u>would rather</u> <u>get</u> the news on my computer than in the newspaper because it is more up to date, it is easier to access while I am working, and it is free.

# Problem 18: Preferences—*Like better than*

The verb phrase *like better than* expresses preference for an option. *Better* is also a replacement, but it is used at the end of a sentence.

| S | like | Option 1 | better | than | Option 2 |
|---|------|----------|--------|------|----------|
| I | like | sports | better | than | music |

| S | like | Option 1 | better |
|---|------|----------|--------|
| I | like | sports | better |

### *Improve Your Speaking*

 Read the question silently. Then read the answer aloud and record it.

Question: Some students enjoy going to museums. Other students would rather watch a ballgame. Which activity would you prefer, and why?

Answer: "I <u>like</u> <u>going</u> to museums <u>better than</u> <u>watching</u> ballgames."

### *Edit Your Essays*

Draft: I like seeing movies more better than reading the books that inspire them.

Edit: I <u>like</u> <u>seeing</u> movies <u>better than</u> <u>reading</u> the books that inspire them.

## CONCESSIONS

A concession shows respect for the other opinion without agreeing. After the concession, you express your opinion.

### Problem 19: Concessions—*Although* and *even though*

*Although* and *even though* have the same meaning. They introduce an opposite opinion.

| Although | S | V | | , | S | V | |
|---|---|---|---|---|---|---|---|
| Although | traveling alone | has | many advantages | , | I | think | a tour group is a better option |

### Improve Your Speaking

 Read the question silently. Then read the answer aloud and record it.

Question: In your opinion, should students prepare for a test alone or in a study group, and why? Be sure to include reasons or examples in your answer.

Answer: "Although preparing for a test in a group has many benefits, I think that studying alone makes more sense because you can focus on the material you need to review."

### Edit Your Essays

Draft: Living off campus has its appeal, in my opinion, living in a dormitory with a roommate is better for several reasons.

Edit: Although living off campus has its appeal, in my opinion, living in a dormitory with a roommate is better for several reasons.

| Even though | S | V | | , | S | V | |
|---|---|---|---|---|---|---|---|
| Even though | many students | work | while they are in school | , | I | think | it is a distraction |

*Improve Your Speaking*

   Read the question silently. Then read the answer aloud and record it.

Question: In your opinion, is a large university or a small college a better choice, and why? Be sure to include reasons or examples in your answer.

Answer: "Even though a small college has many benefits, I think that a large university is a better choice because, in general, the facilities are better."

*Edit Your Essays*

Draft: Even although language classes abroad are often excellent, in my opinion, learning a language in the country where it is spoken has more advantages.

Edit: Even though language classes abroad are often excellent, in my opinion, learning a language in the country where it is spoken has more advantages.

## Problem 20: Concessions—*Despite* and *in spite of*

*Despite* and *in spite of* have the same meaning, but they are used in different grammatical structures. They introduce an opposite opinion.

| Despite | N | , | S | V | that | S | V | |
|---|---|---|---|---|---|---|---|---|
| Despite | the benefits of e-books | , | I | think | that | traditional books | are | easier to read |

*Improve Your Speaking*

   Read the question silently. Then read the answer aloud and record it.

Question: You have a choice between working an eight-hour day, five days a week or a ten-hour day, four days a week. In your opinion, which schedule is better, and why? Be sure to include reasons or examples in your answer.

Answer: "Despite the attraction of working a four-day week, I think working five days a week for eight hours a day would be better because I wouldn't work as efficiently at the end of a ten-hour day, and I would probably be contacted on my day off by other people who were working on that day."

### *Edit Your Essays*

Draft: Despite of several convincing arguments for uniforms, I think that students should be able to choose what they wear to school.

Edit: <u>Despite</u> several convincing <u>arguments</u> for uniforms, I think that students should be able to choose what they wear to school.

| In spite of | N | , | S | V | that | S | V | |
|---|---|---|---|---|---|---|---|---|
| In spite of | the problems | , | I | believe | that | studying abroad | is | a worthwhile experience |

### *Improve Your Speaking*

 Read the question silently. Then read the answer aloud and record it.

Question: In your opinion, should space exploration be funded or should the money be spent to solve problems on Earth? Be sure to include reasons or examples in your answer.

Answer: "<u>In spite of</u> valid <u>reasons</u> to support space exploration, I believe that we should use the money to solve problems on Earth."

### *Edit Your Essays*

Draft: In spite convincing arguments in favor of them, I believe that first impressions are not useful.

Edit: <u>In spite of</u> convincing <u>arguments</u> in favor of them, I believe that first impressions are not useful.

# DEFINITIONS

A definition clarifies or explains the meaning.

## Problem 21: Definitions—Noncount nouns

Noncount nouns have only one form. They are used in agreement with singular verbs. The word *the* is not used with noncount nouns. Categories of noncount nouns can help you organize your study.

1. ***Food staples that can be purchased in various forms***: bread, meat, butter
2. ***Construction materials that change shape, depending on what is made:*** wood, iron, glass
3. ***Liquids that change shape, depending on the container:*** oil, tea, milk
4. ***Natural substances that change shape, due to natural laws***: steam, water, ice; smoke, ashes
5. ***Substances with small parts too numerous to count:*** rice, salt, sand, sugar
6. ***Groups of things with different sizes and shapes:*** clothing—a coat, a shirt, a sock; furniture—a table, a chair, a bed; luggage—a suitcase, a trunk, a box; homework—a paper, a reading assignment, a project
7. ***Languages:*** Arabic, Chinese, English, Japanese, Korean, Spanish
8. ***Subjects:*** Anthropology, Biology, Math, Psychology, Science, Sociology
9. ***Abstract concepts often with endings -ance, -ence, -ity, -ness:*** beauty, ignorance, peace
10. ***Most -ing nouns***: learning, shopping, working

| Noncount N | V | |
|---|---|---|
| Homework | should be | relevant |

### Improve Your Speaking

 Read the question silently. Then read the answer aloud and record it.

Question: Define happiness and explain what it means to you. Be sure to include examples and details in your answer.

Answer: "<u>Happiness</u> is a choice that we make. To me, it means that I choose to be grateful for what I have."

### Edit Your Essays

Draft: A glass has been made into both decorative and utilitarian objects for at least 4,500 years.

Edit: <u>Glass</u> has been made into both decorative and utilitarian objects for at least 4,500 years.

## Problem 22: Definitions—Count nouns in other languages

Many nouns are count nouns in other languages but noncount nouns in English. Don't use *a* or *an* before these nouns.

| | | | |
|---|---|---|---|
| advice | fun | leisure | patience |
| anger | homework | luck | permission |
| courage | ignorance | money | poetry |
| damage | information | music | poverty |
| equipment | knowledge | news | progress |

| S | V | Noncount | |
|---|---|---|---|
| You | need | permission | to miss class |

### Improve Your Speaking

 Read the question silently. Then read the answer aloud and record it.

Question: State the problem and the two solutions that are offered. Which solution do you think is better, and why?

Answer: "The man does not understand how to study for the midterm. I think he should make an appointment with his professor to ask for <u>advice</u>."

### Edit Your Essays

Draft: I think that a good luck is important to success.

Edit: I think that <u>good luck</u> is important to success.

## Problem 23: Definitions—∅ meaning all

When no article is used before a noncount or a plural count noun, it means *all*.

| ∅ | Noncount N | V (singular) | |
|---|---|---|---|
| | Homework | is due | at the beginning of the class |

| ∅ | Count N (plural) | V (plural) | |
|---|---|---|---|
| | Projects | are due | next week |

### *Improve Your Speaking*

 Read the question silently. Then read the answer aloud and record it.

Question: Using the two examples in the lecture, talk about energy in the ancient world.

Answer: "<u>Wind</u> is an ancient source of energy."

### *Edit Your Essays*

Draft: The soil is composed of a mixture of organic matter called *humus* and inorganic matter derived from rocks.

Edit: <u>Soil</u> is composed of a mixture of organic matter called *humus* and inorganic matter derived from rocks.

## Problem 24: Definitions—Qualifying phrases

When *the* is used before a noncount noun, a specific qualifying phrase is required after it to explain the noun.

| The | Noncount N | Qualifying Phrase | V | |
|-----|------------|-------------------|-----|------------|
| The | homework | that was assigned last week | is | due today |
| The | art | of the Middle Ages | is | on display |

### Improve Your Speaking

 Read the question silently. Then read the answer aloud and record it.

Question: The professor describes old English ballads. Explain how they may be related to traditional ballads.

Answer: "The music of country Western singers is probably a combination of old English ballads and cowboy songs."

### Edit Your Essays

Draft: Poverty of people in rural areas is not as visible as that of people in the city.

Edit: The poverty of people in rural areas is not as visible as that of people in the city.

# REPORTS

You may be asked to report another person's opinion or recommendation in both the Speaking and the Writing Sections. Speaking Question 3, Speaking Question 5, and Writing Question 1 may ask you to make a report. The following grammatical structures will support your responses when you are asked to report.

## Problem 25: Reports—Reported speech

The following verbs are commonly used to report past events: *asked, believed, forgot, knew, remembered, reported, said, thought, told*. Don't use a present verb in the report.

| S | V (past) | that | S | V (past) | C |
|---|---|---|---|---|---|
| The professor | said | that | insects | could solve | the food shortage |

A list of strong verbs to report ideas is found in Chapter 5, Activity 29.

### *Improve Your Speaking*

  Read the question silently. Then read the answer aloud and record it.

Question: What does the man think about the change in the fees? State the man's opinion and the reason that he has for having that opinion.

Answer: "The man <u>thought</u> that the change <u>was</u> unfair because only new students <u>had</u> to pay."

### *Edit Your Essays*

Draft: According to the reading passage, ancient people believed that the Earth is the center of the universe and the Sun and Moon rotated around it.

Edit: According to the reading passage, ancient people <u>believed</u> that the Earth <u>was</u> the center of the universe and the Sun and Moon <u>rotated</u> around it.

## Problem 26: Reports—Past verbs

The forty most common verbs with an irregular past form are listed here for your reference. The past form is not the same as the participle:

| Dictionary Verb | Past Form | Participle |
| --- | --- | --- |
| be | was/were | been |
| become | became | become |
| begin | began | begun |
| blow | blew | blown |
| break | broke | broken |
| choose | chose | chosen |
| come | went | gone |
| do | did | done |
| draw | drew | drawn |
| drink | drank | drunk |
| drive | drove | driven |
| eat | ate | eaten |
| fall | fell | fallen |
| fly | flew | flown |
| forget | forgot | forgotten |
| forgive | forgave | forgiven |
| freeze | froze | frozen |
| get | got | gotten |
| give | gave | given |
| go | went | gone |
| grow | grew | grown |
| hide | hid | hidden |
| know | knew | known |
| ride | rode | ridden |
| run | ran | run |
| see | saw | seen |
| shake | shook | shaken |
| show | showed | shown |
| shrink | shrank | shrunk |
| sing | sang | sung |
| speak | spoke | spoken |
| steal | stole | stolen |
| swim | swam | swum |
| take | took | taken |
| tear | tore | torn |
| throw | threw | thrown |
| wear | wore | worn |
| weave | wove | woven |
| withdraw | withdrew | withdrawn |
| write | wrote | written |

| S | V (irregular past) | |
|---|---|---|
| I | went | to California on spring break |

| S | HAVE | participle | |
|---|---|---|---|
| I | had | gone | to California when I was a child |

### Improve Your Speaking

 Read the question silently. Then read the answer aloud and record it.

Question: Using the main points from the lecture, explain why the Vikings settled in Newfoundland.

Answer: "The Vikings <u>began</u> to settle in Newfoundland because they were interested in exploiting the natural resources, especially animal furs and lumber."

### Edit Your Essays

Draft: According to the reading passage, before the Angles and the Saxons come to England, the Iberians had lived there.

Edit: According to the reading passage, before the Angles and the Saxons <u>came</u> to England, the Iberians <u>had lived</u> there.

## Problem 27: Reports—Preferences *Would rather that*

When you are reporting someone else's preference, you need a clause after *would rather that*. Notice the dictionary form of the verb in the clause.

| S | would rather | that | S | V (dictionary) | | |
|---|---|---|---|---|---|---|
| The man | would rather | that | the university | use | the fees | for parking lots |

### Improve Your Speaking

 Read the question silently. Then read the answer aloud and record it.

Question: The woman expresses her opinion of the decision to close the library at six o'clock during finals week. State her opinion and the reasons that she has for having that opinion.

Answer: "The woman would rather that the library stay open late during finals week because many students need a quiet place to study for their exams."

### Edit Your Essays

Draft: Those who responded to the survey would rather that a friend texts them instead of calling.

Edit: Those who responded to the survey would rather that a friend text them instead of calling.

## Problem 28: Reports—Suggestions and recommendations

The verbs *suggest* and *recommend* require the dictionary form of the verb in the clause that follows when reporting a suggestion or recommendation that has been made by another person.

| S | suggest recommend | that | S | Verb (dictionary) | |
|---|---|---|---|---|---|
| The man | suggested | that | his friend | study | in the library |
| The woman | recommended | that | Joe | take | a break |

### Improve Your Speaking

 Read the question silently. Then read the answer aloud and record it.

Question: Describe the man's problem and the two possible solutions that the woman suggests.

Which solution do you prefer, and why?

Answer: "The woman <u>suggested</u> <u>that</u> <u>the man</u> <u>talk</u> with his professor. As an alternative, she recommended that he make an appointment with the teaching assistant."

### Edit Your Essays

Draft: The lecturer recommends that every job applicant changes the resume and cover letter to specifically address the requirements for the position.

Edit: The lecturer <u>recommends</u> <u>that</u> every job <u>applicant</u> <u>change</u> the resume and cover letter to specifically address the requirements for the position.

## SUGGESTIONS AND RECOMMENDATIONS

You may be asked to report a suggestion or make a recommendation in both the Speaking and the Writing Sections. Speaking Question 5 and Writing Question 2 may ask you to suggest or recommend a plan of action. The following grammatical structures will support your responses when you are asked to report or make suggestions and recommendations.

### Problem 29: Suggestions and Recommendations—*Should* and *could*

*Should* and *could* both express a suggestion or recommendation. *Should* is stronger than *could*.

| S | should could | V (dictionary) | |
|---|---|---|---|
| You | should could | join | a club |

| S | should could | not | V (dictionary) | |
|---|---|---|---|---|
| You | should could | not -n't | study | all the time |

#### *Improve Your Speaking*

 Read the question silently. Then read the answer aloud and record it.

Question: Describe the man's problem and the two possible solutions that the woman suggests.

Which solution do you prefer, and why?

Answer: "I think the man <u>should</u> <u>drop</u> the course because a failing grade will lower his GPA."

#### *Edit Your Essays*

Draft: Students should to choose the courses that they need to take because some of the requirements do not support their career goals.

Edit: Students <u>should</u> <u>choose</u> the courses that they need to take because some of the requirements do not support their career goals.

# Problem 30: Suggestions and Recommendations—*Had better*

*Had better* is like a modal. Although *had* is a past verb, *had better* expresses a strong suggestion for the future.

| S | had better | V (dictionary) | |
|---|---|---|---|
| She | had better | declare | a major |

| S | had better | not | V (dictionary) |
|---|---|---|---|
| She | had better | not | wait |

## *Improve Your Speaking*

 Read the question silently. Then read the answer aloud and record it.

Question: Describe the man's problem and the two possible solutions that the woman suggests.

Which solution do you prefer, and why?

Answer: "The man <u>had better</u> <u>take</u> his friend's advice because he could have serious problems if he doesn't meet the deadline."

## *Edit Your Essays*

Draft: International students had better don't take too many courses the first semester because they will have many things to learn outside of the classroom.

Edit: International students <u>had better</u> <u>not</u> <u>take</u> too many courses the first semester because they will have many things to learn outside of the classroom.

## Problem 31: Suggestions and Recommendations—Verbs

Subjunctive verb clauses are used for recommendations. The most common subjunctive verbs are: *ask, demand, insist, prefer, propose, recommend, request, require, suggest,* and *urge.*

| S | V (subjunctive) | that | person | V (dictionary) | |
|---|---|---|---|---|---|
| I | recommend | that | she | drop | the course |

| S | V (subjunctive) | that | person | not | V (dictionary) | |
|---|---|---|---|---|---|---|
| I | recommend | that | she | not | drop | the course |

| S | V (subjunctive) | that | person thing | (not) | be | participle | |
|---|---|---|---|---|---|---|---|
| I | recommend | that | she | (not) | be | given | a failing grade |
| I | recommend | that | the grade | | be | changed | |

### Improve Your Speaking

 Read the question silently. Then read the answer aloud and record it.

Question: Describe the man's problem and the two possible solutions that the woman suggests.

Which solution do you prefer and why?

Answer: "The woman <u>suggests</u> <u>that</u> the man <u>accept</u> the work study position in the admissions office."

### Edit Your Essays

Draft: The lecturer proposed that the experiments were repeated.

Edit: The lecturer <u>proposed</u> that the experiments <u>be</u> repeated.

## SUMMARIES

Summaries of academic topics require grammar that supports the purpose of the passage. The most common purposes are narration, classification, comparison, consecutive order, and cause and result.

## Problem 32: Summaries—Narrations with passive statements

The passive changes the emphasis of a sentence. The event or the result is more important than the person who causes it to happen. The passive is often used in narrations for history or science.

| S | BE | participle | |
|---|---|---|---|
| The TOEFL iBT® | was | introduced | in 2005 |

The people who introduced the TOEFL are not as important as the TOEFL iBT®. That is why the emphasis is on the TOEFL. "The TOEFL" is the subject of the sentence, and the passive is correct.

### *Improve Your Speaking*

    Read the question silently. Then read the answer aloud and record it.

Question: Using points from the lecture, explain how the experiment was conducted.

Answer: "The experiment to test extrasensory perception <u>was</u> <u>called</u> the checkerboard test."

### *Edit Your Essays*

Draft: Ethanol been used to power engines since the 1800s.

Edit: Ethanol <u>has been</u> <u>used</u> to power engines since the 1800s.

## Problem 33: Summaries—Classifications *kind* and *type*

*Kind* and *type* classify similar groups within a larger group.

|  | 2 or more | kinds types | of | Noun (plural count) |
|---|---|---|---|---|
| The Speaking Section has | six | kinds | of | tasks |
| The Writing Section has | two | types | of | essay questions |

| One | kind type | of | Noun (singular count) |  |  |
|---|---|---|---|---|---|
| One | kind | of | task | is | a summary |
| One | type | of | essay | is | an integrated essay |

### Improve Your Speaking

 Read the question silently. Then read the answer aloud and record it.

Question: Using the main points and examples from the lecture, describe the two main types of floods.

Answer: "The <u>two</u> main <u>types</u> <u>of</u> <u>floods</u> explained in the lecture are flash floods and river floods."

### Edit Your Essays

Draft: The three kind of neurons described in the reading passage are sensory neurons, motor neurons, and interneurons.

Edit: The <u>three</u> <u>kinds</u> <u>of</u> <u>neurons</u> described in the reading passage are sensory neurons, motor neurons, and interneurons.

## Problem 34: Summaries—Comparisons of general similarity *similar to* and *similar/like* and *alike*

*Similar to* and *similar* have the same meaning, but *similar to* is used between the two nouns compared, and *similar* is used after the two nouns or a plural noun. *Like* and *alike* have the same meaning, but *like* is used between the two nouns compared, and *alike* is used after the two nouns or a plural noun.

| Noun | | similar to | Noun |
|---|---|---|---|
| The online class | is | similar to | the class on campus |

| Noun | and | Noun | | similar |
|---|---|---|---|---|
| The online class | and | the class on campus | are | similar |

| Noun (plural) | | similar |
|---|---|---|
| All the classes | are | similar |

| Noun | | like | Noun |
|---|---|---|---|
| Professor Clark's lectures | are | like | Professor Martin's lectures |

| Noun | and | Noun | | alike |
|---|---|---|---|---|
| Professor Clark's lectures | and | Professor Martin's lectures | are | alike |

| Noun (plural) | | alike |
|---|---|---|
| The history professors' lectures | are | alike |

### Improve Your Speaking

   Read the question silently. Then read the answer aloud and record it.

Question: The professor describes early Mars. Using information from both the reading and the lecture, explain how it was like early Earth.

Answer: "According to a new study, the topography and the climate of early Mars and early Earth may have been <u>similar</u>."

### Edit Your Essays

Draft: The vegetation in temperate zones all around the world is like.

Edit: The vegetation in temperate zones all around the world is <u>alike</u>. OR
The vegetation in temperate zones all around the world is <u>similar</u>.

## Problem 35: Summaries—Comparisons of general difference *different from* and *different*

*Different from* and *different* have the same meaning, but *different from* is used between the two nouns compared, and *different* is used after the two nouns or a plural noun.

| Noun | V | different from | Noun |
|---|---|---|---|
| The new edition | is | different from | the previous edition |

| Noun | and | Noun | V | different |
|---|---|---|---|---|
| The new edition | and | the previous edition | are | different |

| Noun (plural) | V | different |
|---|---|---|
| The editions | are | different |

### Improve Your Speaking

 Read the question silently. Then read the answer aloud and record it.

Question: Using points and examples from the lecture, explain how cold-blooded and warm-blooded animals are different.

Answer: "Cold-blooded <u>animals</u> <u>are</u> different from warm-blooded <u>animals</u> in a number of important ways."

### Edit Your Essays

Draft: An ocean and a sea are difference.

Edit: An ocean and a sea are <u>different</u>.

# Problem 36: Summaries—Consecutive order *one, another, the other*

*One* and *the other* organize two nouns consecutively. *One, another*, and *the other* organize three nouns consecutively. When the nouns are the same, they do not have to be repeated because *one, another*, and *the other* are used in reference to and in place of the noun.

| One | Noun (singular count) | | | the other | Noun (singular count) | | |
|---|---|---|---|---|---|---|---|
| One | suggestion | is | to get a job | and the other | suggestion | is | to apply for a loan |
| One | suggestion | is | to get a job | and the other | | is | to apply for a loan |

| One | Noun (singular count) | | , | another | Noun (singular count) | | , | and |
|---|---|---|---|---|---|---|---|---|
| One | recommendation | is | to text, | another | recommendation | is | to call, | and |
| One | recommendation | Is | to text, | another | | is | to call, | and |

| the other | Noun (singular count) | | |
|---|---|---|---|
| the other | recommendation | is | to go in person |
| the other | | is | to go in person |

## Improve Your Speaking

 Read the question silently. Then read the answer aloud and record it.

Question: The students are discussing two possible solutions to the woman's problem. Describe her problem and then state which of the solutions you prefer.

Answer: "The woman is not doing well in her math class. <u>One</u> suggestion is to hire a tutor. <u>The other</u> suggestion is to ask the professor for help."

## Edit Your Essays

Draft: There are three types of solar eclipses described in the lecture. One is total, another is annular, and other is partial.

Edit: There are three types of solar eclipses described in the lecture. <u>One</u> is total, <u>another</u> is annular, and <u>the other</u> is partial.

## Problem 37: Summaries—Consecutive order *some, other, the other/ Some, others, the other(s)* or *the rest*

*Some* and *other* organize two nouns consecutively. *Some, other,* and *the other* organize three nouns consecutively. *Others* and *the others* can be used in reference to a noun without repeating the noun.

| Some | Noun (plural count) | | | and | other | Noun (plural count) | | |
|---|---|---|---|---|---|---|---|---|
| Some | schools | are | colleges | and | other | schools | are | universities |

| Some | Noun (plural count) | | other others | Noun (plural count) | | and |
|---|---|---|---|---|---|---|
| Some | specimens | will be black, | other | specimens | will be green, | and |
| Some | specimens | will be black, | others | | will be green, | and |

| the other the others | Noun (plural count) | |
|---|---|---|
| the other | specimens | will be red |
| the others | | will be red |
| the rest | | will be red |

### Improve Your Speaking

    Read the question silently. Then read the answer aloud and record it.

Question: Explain the new proposal for residence halls, and report the man's opinion of it. Be sure to include his reasons for the opinion.

Answer: "In the new proposal, <u>some</u> residence halls will be designated for undergraduate students, <u>others</u> will be designated for graduate students, and <u>the others</u> will be available for married students. The man disagrees with the plan because dormitories will no longer be provided for honors students."

### Edit Your Essays

Draft: Some plants are annuals, the anothers are biennials, and the rest are perennials.

Edit: <u>Some</u> plants are annuals, <u>others</u> are biennials, and <u>the rest</u> are perennials.

## HYPOTHETICAL SITUATIONS

Hypothetical situations are situations that we imagine. You may be asked to respond to a hypothetical situation in both the Speaking and the Writing Sections. Speaking Question 1 and Writing Question 2 may ask you to use your imagination. The following grammatical structures will support your responses when you are asked about a hypothetical situation.

### Problem 38: Hypothetical Situations—Imagined (possible) results

A past tense verb in the condition introduces a possible result that can be imagined in the future.

| CONDITION | | | | , | | RESULT | | |
|---|---|---|---|---|---|---|---|---|
| **If** | **S** | **V (past)** | | **,** | **S** | **would<br>could<br>might** | **V (dictionary)** | |
| If | I | won | the lottery | , | I | would | establish | scholarships |

***Improve Your Speaking***

    Read the question silently. Then read the answer aloud and record it.

Question: Imagine that you have one free day every week. How would you spend the time?

Answer: "If I had a free day every week, I would volunteer at a school."

***Edit Your Essays***

Draft: If I took only one backpack with me to move to a foreign country, I put three items in it.

Edit: If I took only one backpack with me to move to a foreign country, I would put three items in it.

## Problem 39: Hypothetical Situations—Imagined (impossible) results

The verb *BE* is always *were* when the condition is not a logical possibility.

| CONDITION | | | | , | RESULT | | | |
|---|---|---|---|---|---|---|---|---|
| If | S | were | | , | S | would<br>could<br>might | V (dictionary) | |
| If | I | were | a man | , | I | would | wear | comfortable shoes |

### *Improve Your Speaking*

 Read the question silently. Then read the answer aloud and record it.

Question: Imagine that you are the head of state in your country. What changes would you make?

Answer: "If I were the head of state in Canada, I would change the health care system."

### *Edit Your Essays*

Draft: If I were a teacher, I offer opportunities for extra credit.

Edit: If I were a teacher, I would offer opportunities for extra credit.

# Problem 40: Hypothetical Situations—Scientific (absolute) results

Scientific facts have absolute results when certain conditions are met.

| | | CONDITION | | | , | | RESULT |
|---|---|---|---|---|---|---|---|
| **If** | **S** | **V (present)** | | | **,** | **S** | **V (present)**<br>**will + V (dictionary)** |
| If | light | strikes | a rough surface | | , | it | diffuses |
| If | light | strikes | a rough surface | | , | it | will diffuse |

## *Improve Your Speaking*

 Read the question silently. Then read the answer aloud and record it.

Question: Using the main points and examples from the talk, explain the way that a salamander inspired research into growing human body parts.

Answer: "If a salamander loses a limb or a tail, it regenerates the lost body part."

## *Edit Your Essays*

Draft: According to the lecturer, if the trajectory of a satellite will be slightly off at launch, it will get worse as the flight progresses.

Edit: According to the lecturer, if the trajectory of a satellite is slightly off at launch, it gets worse as the flight progresses.

OR

According to the lecturer, if the trajectory of a satellite is slightly off at launch, it will get worse as the flight progresses.

## STYLE PROBLEMS

| | |
|---|---|
| 1 | Agreement—Modified subject and verb |
| 2 | Agreement—Noun and pronoun |
| 3 | Point of View—Present or past |
| 4 | Point of View—Verbs and adverbs |
| 5 | Redundancy—Repetition of noun by pronoun |
| 6 | Redundancy—Unnecessary phrases |
| 7 | Redundancy—Repetition by synonyms |
| 8 | Redundancy—Redundant pause word—Like |
| 9 | Word Choice—Similar meanings *Tell* and *say* |
| 10 | Word Choice—Similar meanings *Make* and *do* |
| 11 | Word Choice—Homophones |
| 12 | Word Choice—Word families |
| 13 | Parallel Structure—In a series |
| 14 | Parallel Structure—After correlative conjunctions |
| 15 | Formality—Informal spellings |
| 16 | Formality—Informal introductory words |
| 17 | Formality—Slang |
| 18 | Gender Inclusive Language—Generic nouns |
| 19 | Gender Inclusive Language—Plural pronouns |
| 20 | Variety—Subject variation |
| 21 | Variety—Sentence length |
| 22 | Complete Sentences—Fragments without a main verb |
| 23 | Complete Sentences—Fragments without an auxiliary verb |
| 24 | Complete Sentences—Run-ons without connections |
| 25 | Mechanics—Indentation, capitalization, punctuation |

# STYLE

## AGREEMENT

Agreement means subjects and verbs in a sentence must agree—either singular or plural. Nouns and the pronouns that refer to them must agree—either singular or plural; masculine, feminine, or neutral.

## Problem 1: Agreement—Modified subject and verb

The verb in a sentence must agree with the subject. When the subject is modified, then there are words between the subject and verb. Don't use a verb that agrees with the modifier of a subject instead of the subject.

| S (singular) | , | Modifier | , | V (singular) | |
|---|---|---|---|---|---|
| The human body | , | which contains 100 trillion cells | , | has | five vital organs |

### *Improve Your Speaking*

 Read the question silently. Then read the answer aloud and record it.

Question: Talk about a city that you have visited. Describe what impressed you about the place, and why you remember being there.

Answer: "Toronto, in my opinion, one of the world's most beautiful cities, is impressive because of the international ambience."

### *Edit Your Essays*

Draft: The ozone layer, at an altitude of about ten kilometers, absorb most of the ultraviolet rays.

Edit: The ozone layer, at an altitude of about ten kilometers, absorbs most of the ultraviolet rays.

## Problem 2: Agreement—Noun and pronoun

The pronoun in a sentence must agree with the noun to which it refers. Don't use a pronoun that does not agree in number (singular or plural) or does not agree in gender (masculine, feminine, or neutral) with the noun to which it refers.

| Noun (singular) | V | Pronoun (singular) | C |
|---|---|---|---|
| The college | should change | its | policies |

| Noun (plural) | V | Pronoun (plural) | C |
|---|---|---|---|
| The colleges | should change | their | policies |

### Improve Your Speaking

    Read the question silently. Then read the answer aloud and record it.

Question: Agree or disagree with this statement: Women and men should attend separate schools before they enroll in college.

Answer: "I think that a <u>woman's</u> educational experience in the lower grades will affect <u>her</u> success in a coeducational environment when <u>she</u> enrolls in college."

### Edit Your Essays

Draft: The Gray Wolf, a species reintroduced into their native habitat in Yellowstone National Park, has begun to breed there naturally.

Edit: The Gray Wolf, <u>a species</u> reintroduced into <u>its</u> native habitat in Yellowstone National Park, has begun to breed there naturally.

## POINT OF VIEW

Point of view means that verb tenses and time phrases in a sentence are the same.

## Problem 3: Point of View—Present or past

Maintain a point of view, either present or past.
Don't change from present verbs to past or from past verbs to present in the same sentence.

| S | V (present) | | S | V (present) | |
|---|---|---|---|---|---|
| Applications | are not considered | unless | they | include | a personal essay |

| S | V (past) | | S | V (past) | |
|---|---|---|---|---|---|
| Applications | were not considered | unless | they | included | a personal essay |

### *Improve Your Speaking*

 Read the question silently. Then read the answer aloud and record it.

Question: Talk about a vacation that was especially memorable. Why do you remember it?

Answer: "My family and I <u>took</u> many vacations, but the best <u>was</u> when we <u>went</u> to Disney World."

### *Edit Your Essays*

Draft: For example, the chestnut tree was an important species in the eastern forests of the United States until a blight kills a large number of trees.

Edit: For example, the chestnut tree <u>was</u> an important species in the eastern forests of the United States until a blight <u>killed</u> a large number of trees.

## Problem 4: Point of View—Verbs and adverbs

Maintain a point of view, either present or past. Be careful that time modifiers, for example, *now*, *ten years ago*, or *when I was a child*, correspond to the present or past point of view.

| S | V (present) | | M (present) |
|---|---|---|---|
| People | are using | more energy | now |

| S | V (past) | M (past) |
|---|---|---|
| The world population | doubled | in the last fifty years |

### *Improve Your Speaking*

 Read the question silently. Then read the answer aloud and record it.

Question: Talk about an experience from your childhood that has affected your life. Be sure to include details and examples.

Answer: "<u>When I was a child</u>, I <u>took</u> English classes on Saturday mornings."

### *Edit Your Essays*

Draft: Because early balloons were at the mercy of shifting winds, they are not considered a practical means of transportation until the 1850s.

Edit: Because early balloons <u>were</u> at the mercy of shifting winds, they <u>were</u> not considered a practical means of transportation <u>until the 1850s</u>.

# REDUNDANCY

Redundancy means using more words than you need.

## Problem 5: Redundancy—Repetition of noun by pronoun

Don't use a noun and the pronoun that refers to it one after the other.

Don't use a noun, *that*, and the pronoun consecutively.

| S | V | C | M |
|---|---|---|---|
| Advertising ~~it~~ | provides | most of the income | for Internet sites |

| S | V | C | M |
|---|---|---|---|
| Advertising ~~that it~~ | provides | most of the income | for Internet sites |

### *Improve Your Speaking*

 Read the question silently. Then read the answer aloud and record it.

Question: Talk about someone you would consider a hero. Explain why you think so.

Answer: "My father ~~he~~ is my hero because he has taught me so many things."

### *Edit Your Essays*

Draft: A perennial is any plant that it continues to grow for more than two years, such as trees and shrubs.

Edit: A perennial is any plant that ~~it~~ continues to grow for more than two years, such as trees and shrubs.

## Problem 6: Redundancy—Unnecessary phrases

Don't use an adjective with the phrases "in nature," "in character," or "in a way."

Use an adverb instead.

| S | V | C | Adverb | |
|---|---|---|---|---|
| Collectors | judge | art | ~~in a subjective way~~ | subjectively |

### Improve Your Speaking

 Read the question silently. Then read the answer aloud and record it.

Question: Using the examples from the lecture, explain the kinetic theory of matter.

Answer: "According to the theory, all of the molecules in the human body are moving constantly."

### Edit Your Essays

Draft: The lecturer points out that hummingbirds move their wings in so rapid a way that they can fly backward and even hang in the air.

Edit: The lecturer points out that hummingbirds move their wings so rapidly that they can fly backward and even hang in the air.

## Problem 7: Redundancy—Repetition by synonyms

Don't use words with the same meaning one after the other.

The most common errors occur with these words and phrases:

| *Redundant* | *Correct* |
|---|---|
| advance rapidly | advance OR proceed rapidly |
| almost nearly | almost OR nearly |
| close proximity | close OR in proximity to |
| new innovation | an innovation |
| not hardly | hardly |
| originally first | originally |
| repeat again | repeat OR say again |
| return back | return OR go back |
| simultaneously at the same time | simultaneously OR at the same time |
| sufficient enough | sufficient OR enough |

| S | V | C | M |
|---|---|---|---|
| The budget | includes | sufficient ~~enough~~ funds | to hire additional employees |
| The budget | Includes | ~~sufficient~~ enough funds | to hire additional employees |

### Improve Your Speaking

 Read the question silently. Then read the answer aloud and record it.

Question: Talk about your plans after you graduate from college.

Answer: "After I graduate from college, I plan to <u>return</u> to my hometown."

OR

"After I graduate from college, I plan to <u>go back</u> to my hometown."

### Edit Your Essays

Draft: Famous for his new innovations in punctuation and language, Edward Estlin Cummings published his collected poems in 1954.

Edit: Famous for his ~~new~~ innovations in punctuation and language, Edward Estlin Cummings published his collected poems in 1954.

## Problem 8: Redundancy—Redundant pause word—Like

English speakers use pause words like *uh* and *um* when they are thinking about what to say next. However, the word *like* is a pause word that is overused by young people and not appropriate on the TOEFL Speaking Section.

| S | V | ~~like~~ | C |
|---|---|---|---|
| It | was | ~~like~~ | a new experience |

| S | V | ~~like~~ | M |
|---|---|---|---|
| It | took | ~~like~~ | a long time |

| ~~Like~~ | S | V |
|---|---|---|
| ~~Like~~ | I | didn't understand |

| S | ~~like~~ | V |
|---|---|---|
| I | ~~like~~ | didn't understand |

### Improve Your Speaking

 Read the question silently. Then read the answer aloud and record it.

Question: Talk about a goal that you have achieved. Explain how you were able to accomplish it. Include specific examples in your answer.

Answer: "When I was ~~like~~ a freshman in high school, I ~~like~~ set a goal to study at a university in Canada. Then I made a list of things I had to do to accomplish my goal."

### Edit Your Essays

Draft: According to the reading, elephants, rhinoceroses, and gorillas could like face extinction.

Edit: According to the reading, elephants, rhinoceroses, and gorillas could ~~like~~ face extinction.

# WORD CHOICE

Word choice means choosing between similar words to express precise meanings.

## Problem 9: Word Choice—Similar meanings *Tell* and *say*

The verbs *tell* and *say* have similar meanings, but *tell* is often used before complements, especially persons. *Say* is usually followed by a clause introduced by *that*.

| S | TELL | C | M |
|---|---|---|---|
| The teacher | tells | us | where to sit |

| S | SAY | that | S + V |
|---|---|---|---|
| The teacher | says | that | we should sit in front |

Collocations are words that go together. **Say** *hello, goodbye, yes, no, prayers.* **Tell** *a joke, a story, the truth, a secret, the time.*

### Improve Your Speaking

 Read the question silently. Then read the answer aloud and record it.

Question: Summarize the problem and choose one of the solutions that the man proposes. Explain the reasons for your recommendation.

Answer: "The woman <u>says</u> <u>that</u> she has two final exams on the same day. The man <u>tells</u> <u>her</u> to ask her sociology professor whether she can take the sociology exam on another day."

### Edit Your Essays

Draft: The lecturer tells that smart cars have several disadvantages.

Edit: The lecturer <u>says</u> <u>that</u> smart cars have several disadvantages.

## Problem 10: Word Choice—Similar meanings *Make* and *do*

The main verbs *make* and *do* have similar meanings, but *do* is often used before complements that describe work and chores. *Make* is usually used before complements that are derived from verbs. *Do* also functions as an auxiliary verb for questions, but *make* is not an auxiliary verb.

| Do | Make | |
|---|---|---|
| an assignment | an agreement | (to agree) |
| a favor | an announcement | (to announce) |
| homework | an attempt | (to attempt) |
| a paper | a decision | (to decide) |
| research | a discovery | (to discover) |
| work | an offer | (to offer) |
| | a presentation | (to present) |
| | a profit | (to profit) |
| | a promise | (to promise) |
| | a speech | (to speak) |

| S | DO | C | M |
|---|---|---|---|
| I | have to do | a paper | in my psychology class |

| S | MAKE | C | M |
|---|---|---|---|
| I | have to make | a presentation | in my history class |

### Improve Your Speaking

 Read the question silently. Then read the answer aloud and record it.

Question: Talk about a promise that you kept. Include details about the situation.

Answer: "When my mother was very ill, I made a promise. I promised to help my father in our family business."

### Edit Your Essays

Draft: While they were working in the lab on a completely different line of investigation, they did a revolutionary discovery.

Edit: While they were working in the lab on a completely different line of investigation, they made a revolutionary discovery.

# Problem 11: Word Choice—Homophones

Homophones are words that sound the same but are not spelled the same. The following homophones are often confused. *Your*, *its*, and *their* are possessive pronouns. *You're*, *it's*, and *they're* are contractions of a subject pronoun and a *BE* verb. *There* is an adverb of place. The meanings are compared here.

| | |
|---|---|
| your | belongs or refers to you |
| you're | you are |
| | |
| its | belongs or refers to it |
| it's | it is |
| | |
| there | in that place |
| their | belongs or refers to them |
| they're | they are |

| S | V | | possessive | N |
|---|---|---|---|---|
| You | are | recording | your | answer |
| | You're | | | |

| S | V | | possessive | N |
|---|---|---|---|---|
| It | is | within | its | time limit |
| | It's | | | |

| S | V | | possessive | N |
|---|---|---|---|---|
| They | are | waiting for | their | scores |
| | They're | | | |

## *Improve Your Speaking*

 Read the question silently. Then read the answer aloud and record it.

Question: What is the student's opinion of the policy that is being proposed by the university?

Answer: "The student thinks that the university should retain its current policy (the university's policy) because it's (it is) more equitable."

## *Edit Your Essays*

Draft: As the lecturer explained, groups of tissues, each with there separate functions, make up the organs in the human body.

Edit: As the lecturer explained, groups of tissues, each with their separate functions, make up the organs in the human body.

## Problem 12: Word Choice—Word families

Word families are groups of words with similar meanings and spellings. Each word in the family is a different part of speech. For example, *agreement* is a noun; *agreeable* is an adjective; *agree* is a verb. The endings of words can help you identify the part of speech.

### NOUNS DERIVED FROM VERBS

| Verb | Noun Ending | Noun |
|---|---|---|
| store | -age | storage |
| accept | -ance | acceptance |
| insist | -ence | insistence |
| agree | -ment | agreement |
| authorize | -sion/-tion | authorization |
| research | -er | researcher |

### NOUNS DERIVED FROM ADJECTIVES

| Adjective | Noun Ending | Noun |
|---|---|---|
| convenient | -ce | convenience |
| redundant | -cy | redundancy |
| opposite | -tion | opposition |
| soft | -ness | softness |
| durable | -ity | durability |

### ADJECTIVES DERIVED FROM NOUNS

| Noun | Adjective Ending | Adjective |
|---|---|---|
| possibility | -able/-ible | possible |
| intention | -al | intentional |
| distance | -ant | distant |
| frequency | -ent | frequent |
| juice | -y | juicy |

### ADVERBS DERIVED FROM ADJECTIVES

| Adjective | Adverb Ending | Adverb |
|---|---|---|
| efficient | -ly | efficiently |

### *Improve Your Speaking*

  Read the question silently. Then read the answer aloud and record it.

Question: The passage describes the properties of ice. Using information from the lecture, explain how these properties affect glaciers at various depths.

Answer: "According to the reading passage, the density of water varies according to the temperature."

### *Edit Your Essays*

Draft: The professor maintains that many animals on the endangered species list do not really face the possible of extinction.

Edit: The professor maintains that many animals on the endangered species list do not really face <u>the possibility</u> of extinction.

## PARALLEL STRUCTURE

Parallel structure is the expression of ideas of equal importance with the same grammatical structures.

## Problem 13: Parallel Structure—In a series

Lists of ideas should be expressed with the same grammatical structures.

| S | V | C |
|---|---|---|
| Plants and animals | have | digestive systems, respiratory systems, and reproductive systems |

### *Improve Your Speaking*

    Read the question silently. Then read the answer aloud and record it.

Question: Agree or disagree with this statement. Use specific reasons to support your answer.

Notebook technology should replace paper textbooks in schools.

Answer: "I agree that notebooks and tablets should replace textbooks in schools because they are <u>cheaper</u> to buy, <u>lighter</u> to carry, and <u>easier</u> to use."

### *Edit Your Essays*

Draft: Microwaves have changed our lives in many ways because they are used for cooking, telecommunications, and also medical diagnosis is made from them.

Edit: Microwaves have changed our lives in many ways because they are used for <u>cooking</u>, <u>telecommunications</u>, and <u>medical diagnosis</u>.

## Problem 14: Parallel Structure—After correlative conjunctions

Ideas after correlative conjunctions should be expressed with the same grammatical structures.

*both...and...*
*not only...but also...*
*either...or...*
*neither...nor...*

| correlative | Noun | correlative | Noun | V | C |
|---|---|---|---|---|---|
| Both | dieting | and | exercising | contribute to | good health |

| correlative | Noun | correlative | Noun | V | C |
|---|---|---|---|---|---|
| Not only | dieting | but also | exercising | contribute to | good health |

| S | V | correlative | Adjective | correlative | Adjective | |
|---|---|---|---|---|---|---|
| Stars that are visible without a telescope | are | either | very bright | or | relatively close | to Earth |

| S | V | correlative | Adjective | correlative | Adjective | |
|---|---|---|---|---|---|---|
| Stars that are visible without a telescope | are | neither | dim | nor | far | from Earth |

### Improve Your Speaking

 Read the question silently. Then read the answer aloud and record it.

Question: Talk about your hometown.

Answer: "My hometown is in Ontario, which is the heart of Canada, both historically and geographically."

### Edit Your Essays

Draft: The cacao bean was cultivated by the Aztecs not only to drink but also currency.

Edit: The cacao bean was cultivated by the Aztecs not only to drink but also to use as currency.

## FORMALITY

In general, writing is more formal than speaking.

## Problem 15: Formality—Informal spellings

Informal pronunciation for spoken contractions is correct in the Speaking Section.

Don't use the informal spellings common to texts and emails when you are writing your essays.

The most common spoken contractions are listed here:

| *Written* | *Spoken Contractions* |
|---|---|
| Going to | [gonna] |
| Want to | [wanna] |
| Have to | [hafta] |
| Ought to | [oughta] |
| Should have | [shoulda] |
| Would have | [woulda] |
| Could have | [coulda] |
| Must have | [musta] |
| Might have | [mighta] |
| Have got to | [gotta] |
| A lot of | [alotta] |
| Kind of | [kinda] |

| S | V | C |
|---|---|---|
| The university | is ~~gonna~~ to change | the policy |
| The university | is going to change | the policy |

### Improve Your Speaking

 Read the question silently. Then read the answer aloud and record it.

Question: Explain the man's opinion of the fees and the reason that he has for it.

*Answer: "The man thinks that the increase in fees is unfair because even those students who don't use the new gym have got to [pronounced gotta] pay for it."

*Speaking only

### Edit Your Essays

Draft: After I receive my degree, I'm gonna work in my family's business.

Edit: After I receive my degree, I'm going to work in my family's business.

## Problem 16: Formality—Informal introductory words

Informal introductory words are correct in the Speaking Section.

Don't use the informal introductions when you are writing your essays. Use the formal connecting words for longer sentences.

| *Informal introductory words* | *Formal connecting words* |
|---|---|
| ***Addition*** | ***Addition*** |
| And | ; moreover, |
| And | ; furthermore, |
| ***Contrast*** | ***Contrast*** |
| But | ; however, |
| ***Conclusion*** | ***Conclusion*** |
| So | ; therefore, |

| ~~And~~ ~~But~~ ~~So~~ | S Chords | V must include | C three or more pitches | played simultaneously |
|---|---|---|---|---|
| *And | chords | must include | three or more pitches | played simultaneously |
| *But | chords | must include | three or more pitches | played simultaneously |
| *So | chords | must include | three or more pitches | played simultaneously |

*Speaking only

### Improve Your Speaking

   Read the question silently. Then read the answer aloud and record it.

Question: Using the examples in the lecture, explain the concept of scarcity in economics.

*Answer: "Desires may be unlimited. But resources are not."

*Speaking only

### Edit Your Essays

Draft: A vintage item can be 50 years old. But an object must be at least 100 years old to qualify as an antique.

Edit: A vintage item can be 50 years old; however, an object must be at least 100 years old to qualify as an antique.

# Problem 17: Formality—Slang

You may hear slang in the conversations on the TOEFL, but don't use slang in your responses on the Speaking Section and in your essays. Colloquial speech is between formal English and slang. Use colloquial expressions instead of slang expressions. The most common slang expressions to avoid are listed here:

| **Slang Expressions** | **Colloquial Expressions** |
| --- | --- |
| ***For people*** | |
| bunch | group |
| dude | man, friend |
| ***For things*** | |
| junk | things (without value) |
| stuff | things (in general) |
| ***For approval*** | |
| awesome | impressive, great |
| cool | good, nice, interesting |
| no big deal | not a problem |
| ***For emphasis*** | |
| real | very, quite, really |
| ***Verbs*** | |
| freak out | be upset |
| gross out | disgust |
| hang out | spend time |
| mess up | make a mistake |
| screw up | make a mistake |
| be bummed | be disappointed |
| be burned out | be exhausted |

| S | V | | M |
| --- | --- | --- | --- |
| I | ~~hang out~~ | | with my friends |
| I | spend | time | with my friends |

## *Improve Your Speaking*

 Read the question silently. Then read the answer aloud and record it.

Question: Talk about a mistake that you made and how you corrected it. Be sure to include details and examples to explain your answer.

Answer: "~~I messed up bigtime~~ I made a big mistake when I chose my major field of study."

## *Edit Your Essays*

Draft: I think it would be very cool to have a job that required overseas travel.

Edit: I think it would be very <u>interesting</u> to have a job that required overseas travel.

# GENDER INCLUSIVE LANGUAGE

Writing without gender bias can be achieved by replacing gender-biased language with generic nouns and by avoiding masculine pronouns to refer to both men and women. The most common avoidance strategy for pronouns is to use plural references and plural pronouns.

## Problem 18: Gender Inclusive Language—Generic nouns

| *Generic* | *Sexist* |
|---|---|
| humanity, humankind, people, or human beings | mankind |
| machine-made or manufactured | man-made |
| the average person or ordinary people | the common man |
| chair, head, or presiding officer | chairman |
| business executive or business person | businessman |
| congressional representative | congressman |
| mail carrier, fire fighter, police officer | mailman, fireman, policeman |

| S | V | |
|---|---|---|
| ~~Businessmen~~ | are responsible | for goals, policies, and procedures |
| Business executives | are responsible | for goals, policies, and procedures |

### Improve Your Speaking

 Read the question silently. Then read the answer aloud and record it.

Question: Talk about a technological advance that has benefited the world. Be sure to include details and examples in your response.

Answer: "The invention of writing, which was introduced independently in China and Mesopotamia, was perhaps the most important technological advance for <u>humanity</u>."

### Edit Your Essays

Draft: If I were the chairman of the United Nations finance committee, I would designate more money for health care for children.

Edit: If I were the <u>presiding officer</u> of the United Nations finance committee, I would designate more money for health care for children.

## Problem 19: Gender Inclusive Language—Plural pronouns

Many native speakers of English now avoid using singular references because they require a masculine pronoun or a clumsy "his or her" option. Plural pronouns are gender inclusive.

| S | Modifier | V | Pronoun | Noun | |
|---|----------|---|---------|------|---|
| ~~Every student~~ | ~~who applies to a selective school~~ | should send | ~~his~~ | ~~application~~ | ~~early~~ |
| All students | who apply to selective schools | should send | their | applications | early |

### Improve Your Speaking

 Read the question silently. Then read the answer aloud and record it.

Question: Talk about an important holiday in your country. Describe it and explain why it is important.

Answer: "All Australians enjoy celebrating Australia Day by cooking on their barbies and watching fireworks."

### Edit Your Essays

Draft: The reading passage argues that every resident should receive a universal basic income from his government.

Edit: The reading passage argues that all residents should receive universal basic incomes from their governments.

## VARIETY

Variety means using different types of sentences in a talk or an essay. Different grammar and different length add interest and gain points on the TOEFL.

## Problem 20: Variety—Subject variation

Don't use the same noun subject in consecutive sentences. Use a pronoun instead.

***No subject variation***: My hometown is in Hawaii. My hometown is small and everyone knows the neighbors. My hometown was a good place to grow up for a number of reasons.

***Subject variation***: My hometown is in Hawaii. ~~My hometown~~ Kahuku is a small town, and everyone knows the neighbors. ~~My hometown~~ It was a good place to grow up for a number of reasons.

### Improve Your Speaking

 Read the question silently. Then read the answer aloud and record it.

Question: Talk about your hobby. Explain why you chose it and provide details about it.

Answer: "My hobby is music. I enjoy playing several instruments and I like to sing. A number of people influenced my love of music, including my father, my music teacher in high school, and several friends."

### Edit Your Essays

Draft: A gap year delays college for one year. A gap year is a good idea. A gap year after high school can be used for several options.

Edit: A gap year delays college for one year. It is a good idea. Travel or work are two options for a gap year after high school.

# Problem 21: Variety—Sentence length

Don't use the same structure and length in a series of sentences. Variation provides rhythm and increases interest.

*Same sentence length*: Domestic animals are tame. They live with humans. They can be pets or livestock.  Wild animals are not tame. They live in the wild or in zoos.

*Variety of sentences*: Domestic animals are tame pets or livestock. They live with humans. Wild animals, on the other hand, are not tame. Unlike their domestic counterparts, they live in the wild or in zoos.

## Improve Your Speaking

 Read the question silently. Then read the answer aloud and record it.

Question: Describe the qualities of excellent teachers. Be specific and include examples.

Answer: "Excellent teachers are knowledgeable; that is, they understand their subject matter. They are also good communicators who know how to explain difficult concepts so that their students can comprehend them. Furthermore, excellent teachers have the ability to encourage interest on the part of their students. And finally, although it is not generally discussed, the really inspirational teachers develop a loving relationship with their students. Long after the class is over, these teachers are still mentoring and helping their former students to succeed."

## Edit Your Essays

Draft: Lying is sometimes advisable. A lie can protect another person. A lie can harm someone. You have to decide. You have to think about your motives. You should lie to help people.

Edit: Lying is sometimes advisable when you are doing it to protect or help another person. If you are lying to harm someone, then I do not agree with your motives and do not support lying.

## COMPLETE SENTENCES

Every English sentence or clause must have a subject and a main verb.

### Problem 22: Complete Sentences—Fragments without a main verb

A fragment is an incomplete sentence. Some common fragments omit the main verb.

| S | V | that | S | V | |
|---|---|------|---|---|---|
| The woman | says | that | the proposal | is | too expensive |

***Incorrect Fragment***: The woman says that the proposal too expensive.

### *Improve Your Speaking*

   Read the question silently. Then read the answer aloud and record it.

Question: Agree or disagree with the following statement:

> Pets are good for the people who own them.

Answer: "Pets <u>improve</u> their owners' lives in many ways."
*Incorrect fragment:* "Pets improvement their owners' lives in many ways."

### *Edit Your Essays*

Draft: Managing time well a problem for many college students.

Edit: <u>Managing time well</u> <u>is</u> a problem for many college students.

# Problem 23: Complete Sentences—Fragments without an auxiliary verb

When you are making a direct statement, remember that main verbs may require auxiliary verbs. BE + -ing, HAVE + participle, modal + dictionary verb.

| S | V (Auxiliary) | V (Main) | |
|---|---|---|---|
| | **BE** | **-ing** | |
| I | am | preparing | for the TOEFL |

| S | V (Auxiliary) | V (Main) | |
|---|---|---|---|
| | **HAVE** | **participle** | |
| My roommate | has | begun | to prepare for the TOEFL |

| S | V (Auxiliary) | V (Main) | |
|---|---|---|---|
| | **MODAL** | **V (dictionary)** | |
| He | will | take | the TOEFL soon |

***Incorrect Fragments***: I preparing for the TOEFL. My roommate begun to prepare for the TOEFL. He take the TOEFL soon.

## Improve Your Speaking

    Read the question silently. Then read the answer aloud and record it.

Question: Some students prefer online classes and others like to study on campus. Which experience do you prefer, and why?

Answer: "I have taken several online classes, but now I am studying on campus because I think that interacting with professors will help me."

## Edit Your Essays

Draft: According to some scientists, the Earth losing its outer atmosphere because of pollutants.

Edit: According to some scientists, the Earth is losing its outer atmosphere because of pollutants.

## Problem 24: Complete Sentences—Run-ons without connections

A run-on sentence is really two sentences that are not connected correctly. Sometimes a comma is incorrectly substituted for a connecting word. Refer to Style Problem 16 for more on formal connecting words for writing.

| Sentence 1 | | | |
|---|---|---|---|
| S | V | C | Connection word |
| | | | ; |
| Students | should wait | to take the TOEFL | because |
| Students | should wait | to take the TOEFL | ; |

| Sentence 2 | | |
|---|---|---|
| S | V | C |
| they | need | to have basic English skills first |

***Incorrect Run-on:*** ~~Students should wait to take the TOEFL, they need to have basic English skills first.~~

***Incorrect Run-on:*** ~~Students should wait to take the TOEFL they need to have basic English skills first.~~

### *Improve Your Speaking*

 Read the question silently. Then read the answer aloud and record it.

Question: Recall an embarrassing experience. Describe what happened and why you were embarrassed.

Answer: "I was embarrassed when I <u>forgot</u> my wallet <u>and</u> I <u>couldn't pay</u> for dinner."

OR

"I was embarrassed when I <u>forgot</u> my wallet; I <u>couldn't pay</u> for dinner."

### *Edit Your Essays*

Draft: According to the lecturer, the bronze artifacts are not real, they have the appropriate patina.

Edit: According to the lecturer, the bronze <u>artifacts</u> <u>are not</u> real, <u>but</u> <u>they</u> <u>have</u> the appropriate patina.

OR

According to the lecturer, the bronze <u>artifacts</u> <u>are not</u> real; <u>however,</u> <u>they</u> <u>have</u> the appropriate patina.

# MECHANICS

The mechanics of writing refers to written conventions that are used to help the reader. The most common ones are listed here as a reference for you as you edit your writing.

## Problem 25: Mechanics—Indentation, capitalization, punctuation

### INDENTATION

Indent the beginning of every paragraph.

### CAPITALIZATION

| | | |
|---|---|---|
| 1. | The first word in a sentence | The last step in writing is correcting minor errors. |
| 2. | Names and titles of people | Professor Williams |
| 3. | Names of places | Boston, Massachusetts, United States |
| 4. | Names of languages and nationalities | French, Hindi, Portuguese <br> French, Indian, Brazilian |
| 5. | Names of universities | Oxford University |

### PUNCTUATION

| | | |
|---|---|---|
| 1. | Period at the end of a sentence | Good writing is logically organized. |
| 2. | Comma to separate items in a series | An essay has an introduction, body, and conclusion. |
| 3. | Comma after sequence words | First,…Second,…Third,…Finally,…. |
| 4. | Comma before the following words that connect two clauses: | |

**Addition: and**

The first essay is an integrated question, and the second essay is an independent question.

**Contrast: but**

The integrated question includes a reading passage and a short lecture, but the independent question is a response to a topic question.

5.  Semicolon before and comma after
    the following words that connect
    two clauses:

| | |
|---|---|
| ***Addition: moreover and furthermore*** | Good writers begin with a thesis sentence; moreover, they often include an outline sentence. |
| | An outline sentence lists the main points; furthermore, it gives the reader a preview of the essay. |
| ***Contrast: however*** | Some writers use an outline to organize their essays; however, diagrams and maps are equally useful. |
| ***Conclusion: therefore*** | All writers need time to read their essays; therefore, they have to finish writing a few minutes before the time limit. |

# 7

# ONE-HOUR TOEFL iBT®
# PRACTICE TESTS

## ✔ *Practice taking short tests*

Like the official TOEFL iBT®, these Practice Tests include four sections: Reading, Listening, Speaking, and Writing. The questions are designed at the same level of difficulty as the TOEFL iBT®. Unlike the official TOEFL iBT®, which is an Internet-based test that requires 4 hours to complete, the Barron's TOEFL Practice Tests are paper-based tests, and all four sections can be completed in 1 hour.

> **Reminder:** To access the audio for this section of the test, visit *http://bit.ly/Barrons-TOEFL.*

# BARRON'S TOEFL PRACTICE TEST 1

## READING SECTION

The following reading passage was adapted from *Experience Sociology*, Second Edition by David Croteau and William Hoynes, McGraw-Hill, 2015.

**Directions:** Read the passage and answer the questions that follow. You will have 20 minutes to complete this Reading Section.

### Advertising to Target Children

P1   A great deal of thought, money, and effort goes into encouraging people to be consumers. Advertisers must make people unhappy with what they have and lead them to believe that a purchase will improve their condition. They cultivate dissatisfaction by encouraging consumers to feel insecure, bored, anxious, envious, or frustrated about the life they lead and then evoke an image or a lifestyle that consumers supposedly want to emulate, a process called "emotional obsolescence." The changes in fashion, the new car models, and the constant upgrades of media devices are all techniques designed to promote dissatisfaction with the older version of a product and plant the seed of desire for the new product. This endless cycle of consumption, dissatisfaction, and consumption is an inherent part of consumer culture.

P2   Increasingly, advertisers are exploiting the emotional vulnerabilities of children, and, to a greater extent, advertisers are using the media to target them. For example, children in laboratories are studied for their reactions to various kinds of advertising; marketers even measure their eye movements and physiological responses. Children fill out marketing surveys in schools, and sponsored classroom materials sometimes include brand-name acknowledgments that serve as advertisements for youth-oriented products. Marketers also employ psychologists who help craft messages to exploit the vulnerabilities of children, especially their feelings that they are "uncool," a "loser," or simply "left out" if they don't have the latest product. Children are even being hired for "stealth advertising" efforts, for example, by participating in slumber parties at which the children try to learn about and influence their friends' tastes and habits.

P3   Once a tiny portion of the advertising industry, children's advertising has grown dramatically in recent years. Today's children are being inundated with many more ads than any other generation has ever experienced. In the 1970s, children watched an estimated 55 television commercials a day. By the 1990s, this figure had doubled to 110, or 40,000 a year, and continues to increase. In 2010, the American Academy of Pediatrics reaffirmed its concern about the effect of advertising. It noted that young people see ads everywhere—on television, online, in magazines, and on billboards—and that the average child in the United States views more than 3,000 advertisements per day. In recent years, ads have become increasingly prevalent in other youth-oriented media, including video games and social networking websites.

P4 Ⓐ Children have a keen awareness of themselves as consumers and are often the first to try new technology. As Schor points out, "Children have become conduits from the consumer marketplace into the household, the link between advertisers and the family purse." Ⓑ Advertisers understand this process and target children accordingly. Ⓒ

P5 In addition to increased spending, this barrage of ad messages, says sociologist Juliet Schor, is causing an array of health and psychological problems. Ⓓ Schor has used sociological inquiry to study the inside operations of advertising agencies that target children, and she has explored the effects of advertising on children. Her findings are alarming. An epidemic in childhood obesity can be traced in part to a sedentary lifestyle often spent watching television and playing video games, coupled with a spike in the consumption of high-fat and high-sugar junk food advertised on children's programs. Recent studies found that television commercials for fast-food restaurants routinely target children by highlighting toy giveaways and movie tie-ins and that ads for foods with minimal nutritional value are common in schools. More broadly, Schor's research suggests that the more children are caught up in the consumer culture, the more likely they are to suffer from depression, anxiety, low self-esteem, and a variety of physical complaints brought on by emotional distress. The ability of advertising to promote dissatisfaction and envy can take a toll on young psyches.

P6 Surveys show that four out of five Americans think that there should be more restrictions on children's advertising, and nearly nine out of ten think that our consumer culture makes it more difficult to instill positive values in children. Even many of the marketers that Schor interviewed for her study spontaneously expressed ambivalence and guilt about what their work was doing to children.

1. According to paragraph 1, which of the following statements is true of "emotional obsolescence"?

Ⓐ The problem stops when the consumer buys a new product.
Ⓑ The advertiser must cause the consumer to feel dissatisfied.
Ⓒ The consumer culture is a result of increased income.
Ⓓ Most older consumers keep their products longer.

2. The phrase to a greater extent in paragraph 2 is closest in meaning to

    Ⓐ more than ever
    Ⓑ with better results
    Ⓒ by less exposure
    Ⓓ for major investment

3. Which of the sentences below best expresses the information in the highlighted statement in the passage? The other choices change the meaning or leave out important information.

    Ⓐ Ads that are made specifically for children have changed greatly during the past several years.
    Ⓑ Advertising for children has increased more than other similar industries in modern times.
    Ⓒ Formerly a small segment of the industry, advertising for children has greatly expanded recently.
    Ⓓ Children's ads have increased but are still a small part of the advertising industry today.

4. The word prevalent in the passage is closest in meaning to

    Ⓐ widespread
    Ⓑ expensive
    Ⓒ desirable
    Ⓓ contemporary

5. Look at the four squares [A] [B] [C] [D] that show where the following sentence could be inserted in the passage.

    **As such, children drive many forms of household consumption, often by nagging parents until they give in or using their own allowance to purchase products.**

    Where could the sentence best be added?

    Click on a square [■] to insert the sentence in the passage.

    Ⓐ
    Ⓑ
    Ⓒ
    Ⓓ

6. Why does the author mention "childhood obesity" in paragraph 5?

    Ⓐ To encourage children to eat in the school cafeteria
    Ⓑ To question the results of Schor's research studies
    Ⓒ To contrast fast-food meals with school lunches
    Ⓓ To connect health problems with advertising

7. The word routinely in the passage is closest in meaning to

    Ⓐ immediately
    Ⓑ frequently
    Ⓒ finally
    Ⓓ quickly

8. According to the passage, all of the following are mentioned as ways that advertisers promote their products to young people EXCEPT

    Ⓐ using children to find out what their friends want to buy
    Ⓑ influencing legislation to gain access to schools
    Ⓒ providing free toys with purchases
    Ⓓ sponsoring materials in classrooms

9. According to paragraph 6, what do the majority of Americans think about advertising that is directed to children?

    Ⓐ It should represent the culture.
    Ⓑ It needs to include positive values.
    Ⓒ It ought to be subject to limitations.
    Ⓓ It is a difficult problem to solve.

10. **Directions:** An introduction for a short summary of the passage appears below. Complete the summary by selecting the THREE answer choices that mention the most important points in the passage. Some sentences do not belong in the summary because they express ideas that are not included in the passage or are minor points from the passage. *This question is worth 2 points.*

    **Advertisers create dissatisfaction and a desire for new products.**

    Ⓐ Advertising and marketing strategies are directed toward children.
    Ⓑ Consumerism is causing psychological and physical problems for children.
    Ⓒ Consumers want upgrades as soon as they become available.
    Ⓓ Parents must be careful about the kind of advertising that their children watch.
    Ⓔ Brand-name products often promote self-esteem in children.
    Ⓕ The number of ads that children are exposed to continues to increase.

# LISTENING SECTION

   **Track 49**

**Directions:** Listen to the passages and answer the questions that follow. You may take notes as you listen, but notes will not be graded.

### *Listening 1: Campus Conversation*

1. What is the purpose of the appointment?

   Ⓐ The woman came to apologize for being late to class.
   Ⓑ The woman wants the professor to be her advisor.
   Ⓒ The woman would like help filing forms.
   Ⓓ The woman needs advice about choosing her major.

2. Listen again to part of the conversation. Then answer the question.

   What did the professor mean when he said this:

   Ⓐ He thinks that they should take a break before they continue.
   Ⓑ He wants the woman to explain more about her previous ideas.
   Ⓒ He is asking the woman to get to the point more quickly.
   Ⓓ He would like to know what Dr. Stephens has advised.

3. What is the professor's opinion of the woman's choice?

   Ⓐ She will have to follow a career path.
   Ⓑ Her undergraduate degree will determine her graduate program.
   Ⓒ She must decide whether earning a large salary is important.
   Ⓓ Her decision will probably not limit her opportunities.

4. Why does the professor mention communications?

   Ⓐ It is a general field that would provide many options for a career.
   Ⓑ He thinks the woman needs to choose a major that does not require math.
   Ⓒ The woman's courses in languages could be used in a communications major.
   Ⓓ It was the first idea that the woman had for a major field of study.

## Listening 2: Biology Class

5. What is this lecture mainly about?

    Ⓐ Extreme and hostile environments on the planet
    Ⓑ Fish that have adapted to hydrogen sulfide
    Ⓒ Genetic mutations in fish
    Ⓓ The Resch and Plath study

6. According to the Resch and Plath study, what has helped fish to survive in sulfidic water?

    Choose 2 answers.

    Ⓐ Genetic mutations over time
    Ⓑ Sulfide-free waters nearby
    Ⓒ Changes in behavior for survival
    Ⓓ Experimental conditions

7. What does the professor imply about larger fish?

    Ⓐ They need more oxygen to survive.
    Ⓑ They have relatively less exposure to toxins.
    Ⓒ They are not found in creeks and rivers.
    Ⓓ They live near the bottom of the water.

8. How do survivor fish detoxify the water?

    Ⓐ By swimming on the surface of the water to increase the oxygen
    Ⓑ By producing an enzyme that changes the chemistry of sulfides
    Ⓒ By reproducing and introducing large numbers of fish in the water
    Ⓓ By filtering the toxins through their large, expanded gills

9. Why does the professor mention survivor fish from different species and locations?

    Ⓐ To emphasize that they have developed in similar ways
    Ⓑ To encourage further research on survivor fish
    Ⓒ To propose that all survivor fish evolved from the same ancestor
    Ⓓ To categorize them into groups based on their traits

10. What point does the professor make about the reasons for fish to live in extreme habitats?

    Ⓐ Fish that populate extreme habitats could live in any environment.
    Ⓑ Pollution occurs slowly and fish make small changes without noticing them.
    Ⓒ More food is available in harsh habitats because fewer fish are competing for it.
    Ⓓ They have been forced out of fresh waters by the predators who live there.

# SPEAKING SECTION

  **Track 50**

*Directions:* Follow the narrator's directions for each question. You may take notes as you listen, but notes will not be graded.

### *Independent Speaking Question: Difficult Situation*

Listen for a question about a familiar topic. After you hear the question, you have 15 seconds to prepare and 45 seconds to record your answer.

### Question

Talk about a difficult situation that you have had to overcome in your life. Describe the situation and explain why it was difficult and what you had to do to rise above it.

Preparation Time: 15 seconds
Recording Time: 45 seconds

### *Integrated Speaking Question: Bike Share*

Read a short passage and listen to a talk on the same topic. After you hear the question, you have 30 seconds to prepare and 60 seconds to record your answer.

### Reading Passage
Reading Time: 45 seconds

> Bike Share
>
> Because many State University students use bikes to get to classes, a shared system of bicycles, similar to the one downtown, is being considered for campus. To support the system, a bike lane would be built through the campus and bike docking stations would be installed along the route. To use the system, students would purchase a membership for $30 per month or $90 per semester. The member key would unlock any bike. At the destination station, students would return and lock the bike. Bike Share is one of several ideas being presented to the governing board to alleviate the transportation and parking issues on campus.

  **Listening Passage**

Now listen to a student who is speaking at the meeting.

### Question

The student expresses his opinion about the plan for Bike Share. Report his opinion and explain the reasons that he has for having that opinion.

Preparation Time: 30 seconds
Recording Time: 60 seconds

# WRITING SECTION

 **Track 51**

*Directions:* You have 20 minutes to plan, write, and revise your response to a reading passage and a lecture on the same topic. First, read the passage and take notes. Then listen to the lecture and take notes. Finally, write your response to the question. Typically, a good response will require that you write 150–225 words.

### *Integrated Essay: Reading Passage*

Reading Time: 3 minutes

> Although technically, any unmanned spacecraft could be referred to as a robot, a more precise definition is usually employed. A *robot* is a system that is mobile and can manipulate objects and perform tasks either autonomously or by remote control. The main functions of a robot for space exploration are to position instruments, collect samples, or assemble structures on bodies and objects in outer space.
>
> Robots are superior to human astronauts in a number of ways. First, they are more productive. They don't get tired, they work faster, and continue to function for longer hours without a break. Second, robots can be deployed into extreme or even very hazardous conditions because there is no concern for injury or health issues that may present themselves during the mission. They don't require food or water to stay at peak performance, which makes space exploration much easier. In addition, rescue operations do not have to be factored into the mission. Furthermore, it is not mandatory that robots be returned to Earth when their tasks are completed unless the data cannot be transmitted. In contrast, it is expected that humans will be able to make a round-trip voyage. Third, robots are particularly well-suited to repetitive work that does not really require a superior intelligence. Moreover, they don't suffer from boredom or inattention, both of which can cause errors.

 **Listening Passage**

Now listen to a lecture on the same topic that you have just read.

### Question

Summarize the main points in the lecture and then explain how they cast doubt on the ideas in the reading passage.

# PRACTICE TEST 1

| *Reading* | *Listening* | *Speaking* | *Writing* |
|---|---|---|---|
| 1. B | 1. D | **INDEPENDENT QUESTION** | **INTEGRATED ESSAY** |
| 2. A | 2. B | Did your talk answer the question? | Did you answer the topic question? |
| 3. C | 3. D | Did you communicate a main idea? | Did you have a topic sentence? |
| 4. A | 4. A | Did you include examples or details? | Did you have an outline sentence? |
| 5. B | 5. B | Did you use different vocabulary words? | Did you include examples or details? |
| 6. D | 6. A, C | Did you make few mistakes in grammar? | Was the information accurate? |
| 7. B | 7. B | Did you finish your talk in the time limit? | Did you address each lecture point? |
| 8. B | 8. B | Was your pronunciation understandable? | Did you paraphrase in your own words? |
| 9. C | 9. A | Did you speak without long pauses? | Did you use different vocabulary words? |
| 10. A, B, F | 10. C | Were the ideas in the talk easy to follow? | Did you make few mistakes in grammar? |
| | | | Did you use a variety of sentences? |
| | | **INTEGRATED QUESTION** | Did you save time to edit and correct? |
| | | Did you briefly summarize the reading? | Was the essay easy for someone to read? |
| | | Did you state the speaker's opinion? | |
| | | Did you include reasons for the opinion? | |
| | | Did you use different vocabulary words? | |
| | | Did you make few mistakes in grammar? | |
| | | Was your pronunciation understandable? | |
| | | Did you speak without long pauses? | |
| | | Were the ideas in the talk easy to follow? | |
| | | Did you finish your talk in the time limit? | |

# BARRON'S TOEFL PRACTICE TEST 2

## READING SECTION

The following reading passage was adapted from *The Changing Earth*, Seventh Edition by James S. Monroe and Reed Wicander, Brooks Cole, 2014.

**Directions:** Read the passage and answer the questions that follow. You will have 20 minutes to complete this Reading Section.

### Amphibians

P1    The transition from water to land required vertebrate animals to surmount several barriers. Among the most critical were desiccation, reproduction, the effects of gravity, and the extraction of oxygen from the atmosphere by lungs rather than from water by gills. At the core of the evolutionary issue, however, is the development of limbs and, even more intriguing, why limbs evolved in the first place.

P2    *Eusthenopteron* is the classic example of a transitional form between fish and amphibians. It had an elongate body that helped it move swiftly in the water and paired muscular fins that many scientists thought could be used for moving on land. [A] The structural similarity between these fish and the earliest amphibians is striking and one of the most widely cited examples of a transition from one major group to another.

P3    [B] Many scientists believe, however, that the development of aquatic limbs was probably not for walking on land. [C] The fossil evidence seems to support this hypothesis.

P4    Fossils of *Acanthostega*, a tetrapod found in 360-million-year-old rocks from Greenland, reveal an animal that had limbs but was clearly unable to walk on land. [D] Paleontologist Jennifer Clack, who has recovered and analyzed hundreds of specimens of *Acanthostega*, points out that its limbs were not strong enough to support its weight on land, and its rib cage was too small for the necessary muscles needed to hold its body off the ground. In addition, *Acanthostega* had both gills and lungs, meaning that it could survive on land, but was more suited for the water. Clack thinks that *Acanthostega* used its limbs to maneuver around in swampy, plant-filled waters, where swimming would be difficult and limbs were an advantage. Fragmentary fossils from other tetrapods living at about the same time suggest, however, that some of these early tetrapods may have spent more time on dry land than in the water.

P5    In 2006, the exciting discovery of a 375-million-year-old "fishapod" from the late Devonian was announced. Discovered on Ellesmere Island, Canada, *Tiktaalik roseae*, from the Inuktitut language meaning "large fish in a stream," was hailed as the intermediary between lobe-finned fish like *Eusthenopteron* and the earliest tetrapod, *Acanthostega*.

P6    *Tiktaalik roseae* is truly a "fishapod" in that it has a mixture of both fish and tetrapod characteristics. For example, it has gills and fish scales, but also a broad skull, eyes on the top of its head, a flexible neck, a large rib cage that could support its body on land or in shallow water, and lungs, all of which are tetrapod features. What really excited scientists, however, was that *Tiktaalik roseae* has the beginnings of a true tetrapod forelimb, complete with functional wrist bones and five digits, as well as a modified ear region. Evidence suggests that *Tiktaalik roseae* lived in a shallow-water habitat associated with the late Devonian floodplains of Laurasia, which was the Northern Hemisphere including North America, Europe, and Northern Asia.

P7    The oldest known true amphibian, *Ichthyostega*, had skeletal features that allowed it to spend its life on land, growing to a length of about one meter. It had a streamlined body, a long tail, and fins along its back. In addition to four legs, it had a strong backbone, a rib cage, and pelvic and pectoral girdles, all of which were structural adaptations for walking on land.

P8    Like other groups that moved into new and previously unoccupied niches, early amphibians underwent rapid adaptive radiation and became abundant, even though they were limited in colonizing the land because they had to return to water to lay their gelatinous eggs and, therefore, could not venture too far from streams, lakes, or swamps. These early amphibians did not at all resemble the familiar frogs and salamanders that make up the modern amphibian fauna. In general, they were larger, but fossil remains suggest that they displayed a broad spectrum of sizes, shapes, and modes of life.

1. The phrase the classic example in paragraph 2 is closest in meaning to

   Ⓐ an old case study
   Ⓑ a typical illustration
   Ⓒ an unusual specimen
   Ⓓ a questionable sample

2. The word striking in the passage is closest in meaning to

   Ⓐ difficult to understand
   Ⓑ under investigation
   Ⓒ very remarkable
   Ⓓ well known

3. Look at the four squares [A] [B] [C] [D] that show where the following sentence could be inserted in the passage.

   **In fact, they think that the muscular fins and even actual limbs made it easier for animals to move around in streams, lakes, or swamps that were choked with water plants or other debris.**

   Where could the sentence best be added?

   Click on a square [■] to insert the sentence in the passage.

   [A]
   [B]
   [C]
   [D]

4. How did Jennifer Clack prove that *Acanthostega* could not walk on land?

   Ⓐ She experimented with them in her lab.
   Ⓑ She observed them in their habitat.
   Ⓒ She studied fossil evidence.
   Ⓓ She discovered a "fishapod."

5. Which of the sentences below best expresses the information in the highlighted statement in the passage? The other choices change the meaning or leave out important information.

   Ⓐ Early tetrapods lived on land instead of in the water like others from that time period.
   Ⓑ According to the fossil evidence, some early tetrapods spent less time in the water than they did on land.
   Ⓒ Early fossils suggest that tetrapods that lived on dry land did not go in the water.
   Ⓓ Information about tetrapods was not conclusive because whole fossils were not found.

6. The word hailed in the passage is closest in meaning to

   Ⓐ acknowledged
   Ⓑ dominated
   Ⓒ concealed
   Ⓓ classified

7. All of the following characteristics can be attributed to *Tiktaalik roseae* EXCEPT

   Ⓐ a rib cage strong enough to allow it to walk on land
   Ⓑ five digits at the end of its wrist
   Ⓒ both gills like fish and lungs like land animals
   Ⓓ large skulls with well-developed brains

8. According to paragraph 8, what was true of early amphibians?

   Ⓐ They had to stay close to the water.
   Ⓑ In general, they were very small.
   Ⓒ Only a limited number survived.
   Ⓓ Most of them were very similar.

9. Why does the author mention "frogs and salamanders" in paragraph 8?

    Ⓐ To contrast them with "fishapods" and early amphibians
    Ⓑ To provide an example of smaller early amphibians
    Ⓒ To explain why amphibians became so widespread
    Ⓓ To demonstrate the importance of fossil evidence

10. **Directions:** An introduction for a short summary of the passage appears below. Complete the summary by selecting the THREE answer choices that mention the most important points in the passage. Some sentences do not belong in the summary because they express ideas that are not included in the passage or are minor points from the passage. *This question is worth 2 points.*

**The most important evolutionary transition from water to land was the development of limbs.**

Ⓐ Research evidence supports the theory that limbs first developed to help animals swim through water plants.

Ⓑ Vertebrate animals had to replace their gills with lungs in order to breathe air from the atmosphere.

Ⓒ The extinction of tetrapods allowed amphibians to occupy their habitat in swamps and streams.

Ⓓ Intermediary animals known as "fishapods" had developed limbs with digits at the end of a flexible wrist.

Ⓔ The earliest amphibians had four legs as well as a sturdy skeleton that could support it on land.

Ⓕ Fossils from the Devonian era provide the best evidence for scholars like paleontologist Jennifer Clack.

# LISTENING SECTION

 **Track 52**

*Directions:* Listen to the passages and answer the questions that follow. You may take notes as you listen, but notes will not be graded.

## Listening 1: Campus Conversation

1. What is this conversation mainly about?

   Ⓐ The woman is thinking about changing her major to art.
   Ⓑ The professor wants the woman to enter her pottery in an exhibition.
   Ⓒ The professor wants the woman to help him with an art sale.
   Ⓓ The woman is interested in experimenting with interesting shapes.

2. How did the woman feel about her pottery before this conversation?

   Ⓐ She did not think that her pottery was worth very much.
   Ⓑ She did not plan to keep any of the pieces that she made.
   Ⓒ She thought that she could use her pottery to decorate buildings.
   Ⓓ She wanted to sell some of the pieces to the art department.

3. What did the professor especially appreciate about the woman's glazes?

   Choose 2 answers.

   Ⓐ The combinations from mixing different colors
   Ⓑ The effects from dipping the pieces in the glaze
   Ⓒ The techniques for painting glaze on the pieces
   Ⓓ The designs that had drips on the rims

4. What will the woman probably do?

   Ⓐ Take another art class
   Ⓑ Collect some pottery
   Ⓒ Make two more pieces
   Ⓓ Work at the exhibition

## Listening 2: Zoology Class

5. What is the discussion mainly about?

   Ⓐ The evolution of predators
   Ⓑ Strategies for hunting animals
   Ⓒ The shape of animal eyes
   Ⓓ The domestication of animals

6. What was demonstrated by the Banks and Love study on the shape of pupils?

&#9398; Animals can control the amount of light in their eyes.

&#9399; Domestic animals do not have good vision in the dark.

&#9400; Horizontal eye slits are more efficient than vertical slits.

&#9401; Predators and prey can be categorized by their pupils.

7. Why does the student say this:

&#9398; He is trying to understand the categories.

&#9399; He is suggesting that humans are predators.

&#9400; He is arguing with the professor.

&#9401; He is agreeing with the research study.

8. According to the professor, what is the difference between ambush predators and hunters?

&#9398; Hunters are taller than ambush predators.

&#9399; Only ambush predators are color blind.

&#9400; Ambush predators are stronger than hunters.

&#9401; Only hunters have forward-facing eyes.

9. What are the characteristics of grazing animals?

Choose 2 answers.

&#9398; They have forward facing eyes.

&#9399; They have horizontal pupils.

&#9400; Their eyes rotate when they graze.

&#9401; Their eyes are perpendicular to the ground.

10. How does the professor feel about the critics of the research that she is presenting?

&#9398; She disagrees completely with the criticism of the study.

&#9399; She acknowledges that the general premise has exceptions.

&#9400; She ignores the point of view that criticizes the research.

&#9401; She thinks that the research has been perfectly presented.

# SPEAKING SECTION

 **Track 53**

*Directions:* Follow the narrator's directions for each question. You may take notes as you listen, but notes will not be graded.

### *Integrated Speaking Question: Total Motivation*

Listen to part of a lecture in a business class. Then listen for a question about it. After you hear the question, you have 20 seconds to prepare and 60 seconds to record your answer.

**Question**
Using the main points and examples from the lecture, explain the difference between the two types of performance.

Preparation Time: 20 seconds
Recording Time: 60 seconds

### *Integrated Speaking Question: Critical Mass*

Read a short passage and listen to a talk on the same topic. After you hear the question, you have 30 seconds to prepare and 60 seconds to record your answer.

**Reading Passage**
Reading Time: 45 seconds

---

Critical Mass

Originally the term *critical mass* was used to represent the smallest mass of material that could sustain a nuclear reaction at a constant level. However, recent usage in the field of business has identified critical mass as a crucial stage in a company's development when the business reaches a point when it is viable without further investment. In other words, it refers to the size that a company must reach in order to compete efficiently. The size is determined by the number of employees, resources, revenue streams, and total market share. When all of these factors combine, a business operates at optimal efficiency and profitability.

---

 **Listening Passage**
Now listen to a professor who is discussing the same topic.

**Question**
Using the example from the talk, explain why Facebook is an example of *critical mass*.

Preparation Time: 30 seconds
Recording Time: 60 seconds

# WRITING SECTION

*Directions:* You have 30 minutes to plan, write, and revise your response to a question about a familiar topic. Typically, a good response will require that you write 300–350 words.

### Independent Essay: Question

Agree or disagree with the following statement:

*Students should be able to take notes in classes, using their laptop computers.*

Give reasons and examples to support your opinion.

# PRACTICE TEST 2

| Reading | Listening | Speaking |
|---------|-----------|----------|
| 1. B | 1. B | **INTEGRATED QUESTION** |
| 2. C | 2. A | Did you summarize the lecture? |
| 3. C | 3. A, D | Did you include all major points? |
| 4. C | 4. C | Did you give examples or details? |
| 5. B | 5. C | Did you paraphrase in your own words? |
| 6. A | 6. D | Was the information accurate? |
| 7. D | 7. A | Did you use different vocabulary words? |
| 8. A | 8. A | Did you make few mistakes in grammar? |
| 9. A | 9. B, C | Was your pronunciation understandable? |
| 10. A, D, E | 10. B | Did you speak without long pauses? |
|  |  | Were the ideas in the talk easy to follow? |
|  |  | Did you finish your talk in the time limit? |

**Writing**

**INDEPENDENT ESSAY**

Did you answer the topic question?

Did you have a topic sentence?

Did you have an outline sentence?

Was your point of view clear?

Did you include reasons for your opinion?

Did you use different vocabulary words?

Did you make few mistakes in grammar?

Did you use a variety of sentences?

Did you save time to edit and correct?

Did you finish your essay in the time limit?

Was the essay easy for someone to read?

**INTEGRATED QUESTION**

Did you briefly summarize the reading?

Did you relate the lecture to the reading?

Did you paraphrase in your own words?

Was the information accurate?

Did you use different vocabulary words?

Did you make few mistakes in grammar?

Was your pronunciation understandable?

Did you speak without long pauses?

Were the ideas in the talk easy to follow?

Did you finish your talk in the time limit?

# BARRON'S TOEFL PRACTICE TEST 3

## READING SECTION

The following reading passage was adapted from *Archaeology*, Sixth Edition by Robert L. Kelly and David Hurst Thomas, Wadsworth, 2013.

**Directions:** Read the passage and answer the questions that follow. You will have 20 minutes to complete this Reading Section.

### *Tree-Ring Dating*

P1    Tree-ring dating, also called *dendrochronology*, was developed by Andrew E. Douglass, an astronomer studying the effect of sunspots on the Earth's climate. Douglass knew that trees growing in temperate and arctic areas remain dormant during the winter and then burst into activity in the spring, resulting in the formation of familiar concentric growth rings. Trees have alternating dark and light rings. The light rings are a year's spring and summer growth, and the dark rings are that year's late summer and fall growth. Because each ring represents a single year, it is a simple matter to determine the age of a newly felled tree by counting the rings. In practice, the sample must contain at least 20 rings, which must be measured individually.

P2    For many tree species, ring width varies, and young trees grow more quickly than old ones. Therefore, absolute tree-ring width is a function of both seasonal growth and a tree's age. Furthermore, Douglass reasoned that tree rings might preserve information about past climates. Because climate affects all of the trees in a forest, Douglass reasoned, year-by-year patterns of tree growth manifested as variable ring widths should produce a long-term chronological sequence.

P3    Douglass began his research on living trees, mostly yellow pines in central Arizona. He studied recent stumps and cores taken from still-living trees, counted the rings, and recorded the pattern of light and dark ring widths. To extend this chronology backward in time, he searched for an overlap between the early portion of young trees with the final years of growth of an old tree or stump. This way, he created a master sequence of tree rings, but the stumps and living trees went back only about 500 years.

P4    Fortunately, Douglass worked in the American Southwest, where arid conditions enhance preservation. Sampling ancient beams in pueblo sites, he slowly built up a prehistoric "floating chronology" that spanned several centuries, and eventually linked it to the modern tree chronology, giving Southwestern archaeology a reliable, year-by-year dating tool.

P5    In August 1927, Douglass visited Betatakin, an impressive cliff dwelling in northeastern Arizona. A He collected two dozen samples that bracketed the construction of Betatakin within a decade of 1270 A.D. Accuracy to this degree was stunning back then, and still is, compared with every other technique.

P6    B Jeffery Dean of the University of Arizona's Laboratory of Tree-Ring Research collected more samples at Betatakin in the 1960s. He took the samples using a hand or power drill equipped with a bit that removed only a quarter-inch diameter cylinder of wood, a technique that does not harm living trees and is minimally destructive of archaeological materials. The total collection grew to 292 individual beams, allowing Dean to document the growth of Betatakin literally room by room. C

P7    Dean found that Betatakin was first occupied about 1250 A.D. by a small group who built a few structures that were soon destroyed. D This occupation was probably transient, with a rock shelter providing a seasonal camping spot for people traveling to plant fields at some distance from their home.

P8    The actual village at Betatakin was founded in 1267 A.D. when three-room clusters were constructed; a fourth cluster was added in 1268 A.D. The next year, a group of perhaps 20 to 25 people felled several trees, cut them to standard lengths, and stockpiled the lumber, in all likelihood, for future immigrants to the village. Inhabitants stockpiled additional beams in 1272 A.D., but they did not use them until 1275, which signaled a three-year immigration period during which more than ten room clusters and a kiva were added. Population growth at Betatakin slowed after 1277, reaching a peak of about 125 people in the mid-1280s. The village was abandoned sometime between 1286 A.D. and 1300 A.D. for unknown reasons. This is a remarkably precise reconstruction for a 700-year-old settlement.

P9    Today, computer programs can help, but exact measuring often requires visual comparison because some samples have oddities, such as missing rings or partial rings, that only a trained technician can detect. In fact, although Willard F. Libby's radiocarbon dating introduced in 1949 is more commonly used in modern archaeology, dendrochronology is still a more precise technique.

**Glossary**
kiva: a chamber for religious rites

1. What can be inferred about tree rings during the winter?

     Ⓐ They are darker than the rings from other seasons.
     Ⓑ They do not show growth during the wintertime.
     Ⓒ They represent an entire year's growth pattern.
     Ⓓ They will produce only one individual ring.

2. Which of the sentences below best expresses the information in the highlighted statement in the passage? The other choices change the meaning or leave out important information.

     Ⓐ The width of tree rings depends not only on the age of the tree but also on the growth pattern for the season.
     Ⓑ It is true that young tree rings are wider when a season is warmer because of the length of the growing season.
     Ⓒ Measuring tree rings is not exact because older trees do not grow as fast as younger trees every season.
     Ⓓ The age of trees is uncertain when tree rings are used to determine them in different seasons.

3. The word stunning in the passage is closest in meaning to

     Ⓐ difficult
     Ⓑ unimportant
     Ⓒ surprising
     Ⓓ normal

4. Look at the four squares [A] [B] [C] [D] that show where the following sentence could be inserted in the passage.

**However, tree-ring dating can be even more accurate and provide greater detail.**

Where could the sentence best be added?

Click on a [■] square to insert the sentence in the passage.

     Ⓐ
     Ⓑ
     Ⓒ
     Ⓓ

5. According to paragraph 4, what advantage did Douglass have?

     Ⓐ Modern tools
     Ⓑ A dry climate
     Ⓒ Previous studies
     Ⓓ Ancient beams

6. All of the following are true of Betatakin EXCEPT

    Ⓐ Betatakin is the site of a cliff dwelling in Arizona.
    Ⓑ People began living in Betatakin in the thirteenth century.
    Ⓒ The settlement of Betatakin was occupied for 700 years.
    Ⓓ When the forests disappeared, settlers deserted Betatakin.

7. The phrase in all likelihood in the passage is closest in meaning to

    Ⓐ favorably
    Ⓑ actually
    Ⓒ presumably
    Ⓓ primarily

8. The word detect in the passage is closest in meaning to

    Ⓐ record
    Ⓑ identify
    Ⓒ study
    Ⓓ compare

9. Why is "computer programming" mentioned in paragraph 9?

    Ⓐ To demonstrate the effectiveness of digital methods
    Ⓑ To introduce techniques for modern archaeology
    Ⓒ To promote the use of radiocarbon dating
    Ⓓ To contrast computers with human evaluators

10. **Directions:** An introduction for a short summary of the passage appears below. Complete the summary by selecting the THREE answer choices that mention the most important points in the passage. Some sentences do not belong in the summary because they express ideas that are not included in the passage or are minor points from the passage. *This question is worth 2 points.*

    **Dendrochronology remains the most effective way to date trees.**

    Ⓐ Douglass produced a master sequence of tree rings using living trees, stumps, and samples from early settlements.
    Ⓑ Dendrochronology is still the most accurate method in spite of advances in computer programs and radiocarbon dating.
    Ⓒ Leonardo da Vinci is probably the first person to identify growth rings in trees as an annual phenomenon.
    Ⓓ Stumps and living trees only provided a chronology of 500 years, which was not long enough as a dating tool.
    Ⓔ Dean continued Douglass's work at Betatakin, creating a very complete reconstruction of the site over 700 years.
    Ⓕ A power drill advanced the work at Betatakin because it did not damage the trees and the archaeological site.

# LISTENING SECTION

 **Track 54**

**Directions:** Listen to the passages and answer the questions that follow. You may take notes as you listen, but notes will not be graded.

### Listening 1: Campus Conversation

1. Why does the student go to see the professor?

   Ⓐ He wants to apply for a job in the lab.
   Ⓑ He needs help choosing a topic for his paper.
   Ⓒ He wants permission to use the professor's data.
   Ⓓ He wants more time to finish his experiment.

2. Why did the professor advise the man to use the data from the lab?

   Ⓐ She does not agree with the conclusions that the man has made.
   Ⓑ She does not think the man has considered the problems with field research.
   Ⓒ She is concerned that the man may gather too much data for the report.
   Ⓓ She doubts that the man can finish the field research in time.

3. Listen again to part of the conversation. Then answer the question.

   What did the professor mean when she said this:

   Ⓐ The man should ask his supervisor for permission to use the data.
   Ⓑ She agrees with the results of the data from the laboratory.
   Ⓒ She thinks that the man should use the data for his paper.
   Ⓓ The man should be more interested in the topic that he chooses.

4. What does the professor imply when she reminds the man that the paper is ten pages long?

   Ⓐ He needs to do more research.
   Ⓑ He should begin working on it now.
   Ⓒ He can narrow his topic to habitats.
   Ⓓ He should refer to the assignment.

### Listening 2: Political Science Class

5. What is this lecture mainly about?

   Ⓐ The first thirteen states
   Ⓑ The Continental Congress
   Ⓒ The electoral college
   Ⓓ Political parties

6. According to the professor, what was the situation immediately before the election of the first president?

   Ⓐ The country was still fighting a disastrous war.
   Ⓑ Transportation and communication were unreliable.
   Ⓒ National political parties had corrupt leaders.
   Ⓓ Only gentlemen were allowed to run for office.

7. Why didn't the Continental Congress approve a popular vote to elect the president?

   Ⓐ The larger states would have had too much influence.
   Ⓑ The president would have been obligated to the states.
   Ⓒ The Continental Congress wanted to retain their power.
   Ⓓ The qualifications to vote had not been determined.

8. What two factors determine the number of votes that each state has in the electoral college?

   Choose 2 answers.

   Ⓐ The number of senators from the state
   Ⓑ The number of representatives from the state
   Ⓒ The number of people registered to vote in the state
   Ⓓ The number of people elected to the state legislature

9. Why did the professor mention Florida?

   Ⓐ To prove that the electoral college has changed
   Ⓑ To demonstrate the disadvantage of the electoral college
   Ⓒ To offer an example of how the electoral college is organized
   Ⓓ To point out a problem in the electoral college procedure

10. What is the professor's opinion of the electoral college?

   Ⓐ She thinks it is a good compromise.
   Ⓑ She would prefer a balance of power.
   Ⓒ She doesn't have enough information.
   Ⓓ She is in favor of a popular vote.

# SPEAKING SECTION

 **Track 55**

**Directions:** Follow the narrator's directions for each question. You may take notes as you listen, but notes will not be graded.

### *Integrated Speaking Question: Cheating*

Listen to a short conversation. Then listen for a question about it. After you hear the question, you have 20 seconds to prepare and 60 seconds to record your answer.

**Question**

Describe the man's problem and the two suggestions that his friend makes about how to handle it. What do you think the man should do and why?

Preparation Time: 20 seconds
Recording Time: 60 seconds

### *Integrated Speaking Question: Faculty Review*

Read a short passage and listen to a talk on the same topic. After you hear the question, you have 30 seconds to prepare and 60 seconds to record your answer.

**Reading Passage**
Reading Time: 45 seconds

> Faculty Reviews
>
> Because it is helpful to compare instructors for courses with multiple sections or investigate the performance of instructors before registering for classes, State University is considering the development of an Internet site where students can access the teacher evaluation surveys submitted by students at the end of a course. If the project proceeds, students will be able to search the site by instructor name. The faculty senate supports the plan, alluding to the unofficial Internet review sites that students are currently using to make decisions. An open meeting will be held on Thursday at 4:00 P.M. in the auditorium of the Student Union before finalizing the plan.

 **Listening Passage**
Now listen to two students who are talking about the proposed site.

**Question**
The man expresses his opinion about the new website for faculty reviews. Report his opinion and explain the reasons that he has for having that opinion.

Preparation Time: 30 seconds
Recording Time: 60 seconds

# WRITING SECTION

*Directions:* You have 30 minutes to plan, write, and revise your response to a question about a familiar topic. Typically, a good response will require that you write 300–350 words.

## *Independent Essay: Question*

Agree or disagree with this statement:

***Employers should provide childcare at the workplace for employees with small children.***

Give reasons and examples to support your opinion.

# PRACTICE TEST 3

| *Reading* | *Listening* |
|---|---|
| 1. B | 1. B |
| 2. A | 2. D |
| 3. C | 3. C |
| 4. B | 4. C |
| 5. B | 5. C |
| 6. D | 6. B |
| 7. C | 7. A |
| 8. B | 8. A, B |
| 9. D | 9. C |
| 10. A, B, E | 10. A |

## *Speaking*

### INTEGRATED QUESTION

Did you summarize the problem?
Did you present the speaker's suggestions?
Did you state a clear opinion?
Did you include reasons for your opinion?
Did you use different vocabulary words?
Did you make few mistakes in grammar?
Was your pronunciation understandable?
Did you speak without long pauses?
Were the ideas in the talk easy to follow?
Did you finish your talk in the time limit?

### INTEGRATED QUESTION

Did you briefly summarize the reading?
Did you state the speaker's opinion?
Did you include reasons for the opinion?
Did you use different vocabulary words?
Did you make few mistakes in grammar?
Was your pronunciation understandable?
Did you speak without long pauses?
Were the ideas in the talk easy to follow?
Did you finish your talk in the time limit?

## *Writing*

### INDEPENDENT ESSAY

Did you answer the topic question?
Did you have a topic sentence?
Did you have an outline sentence?
Was your point of view clear?
Did you include reasons for your opinion?
Did you use different vocabulary words?
Did you paraphrase in your own words?
Did you make few mistakes in grammar?
Did you use a variety of sentences?
Did you save time to edit and correct?
Did you finish your essay in the time limit?
Was the essay easy for someone to read?

# BARRON'S TOEFL PRACTICE TEST 4

## READING SECTION

The following reading passage was adapted from *Marine Biology*, Fourth Edition by Jeffrey S. Levinton, Oxford University Press, 2014.

**Directions:** Read the passage and answer the questions that follow. You will have 20 minutes to complete this Reading Section.

### Ocean Migrations

P1    Until recently, we simply had no idea of the extent and fidelity of ocean-scale migrations. A This changed with the advent of satellite tags, and the results were startling. For example, a recent study confirmed that the great white shark moved between the waters of South Africa and western Australia, a distance of over 20,000 kilometers. However, because a far more sophisticated approach to tracking was needed, the TOPP group was formed (Tagging of Pacific Predators) by marine biologists. For more than a decade, this group of more than 90 scientists had followed the movements of 23 predatory species in the North Pacific Ocean using implanted pop-up archival tags that recorded data, including temperature, water pressure and depth, and GPS location. Unfortunately, each tag cost several thousand dollars and could be lost either by malfunction or by being swallowed by another giant predator. B Therefore, the TOPP group now relies on Argos tags that transmit data continuously to the Argos satellite system. C The results of the first decade's watch of the Pacific, using over 4,000 tags to follow approximately 1,800 tracks of 23 species, has produced the beginnings of a map of major North Pacific migration routes. Taken individually, many species of predators have somewhat different patterns. For example, the Pacific white shark shows a consistent homing migration between the Hawaiian Islands and California, but salmon sharks move between the waters of the Pacific subtropical ocean and Prince William Sound, Alaska. When combined with other species, we see that this great system is not exactly like major land migrations, for example, the relentless clockwise migration of herbivores on the grasslands of eastern Africa. D The African roundtrip is about 600 kilometers, which, as great as it is, is dwarfed by the journey of the great white shark. The Pacific is a larger and more diverse theater within which the ecological play is performed.

P2    The great marine predators are associated with highly localized and often spatially changing sources of food driven from the base of the oceanic food web. This association is quite evident with tuna, which are usually concentrated in upwelling regions where nutrients and plankton are abundant. Plankton-eating baleen whales may be found in a very localized upwelling zone with abundant zooplankton and then move hundreds of kilometers away after the resource is exhausted. These movements demonstrate that roving predators have been able to map the locations of a large number of areas with predictable, abundant but shifting food sources. Even seabirds that rove large expanses of the ocean for prey can smell zooplankton blooms, which allows them to find upwelling centers where zooplankton and fish are both abundant.

P3   On a grand scale, there are two great belts of predatory activity and migration in the North Pacific Ocean. First, the California Current Large Marine Ecosystem along the west coast of North America includes a large number of tuna, whale, seabirds, and other large fish species that move over tracks stretching hundreds to thousands of kilometers, usually in annual migrations, often related to upwelling. Overall, many species are migrating seasonally between the eastern and central North Pacific and the Gulf of Alaska.

P4   In only four months, another large group of species moves across the Pacific through the North Pacific Transition Zone that extends as an approximate east-west belt across the Pacific Ocean to California.

P5   These two major realms capture only part of the diversity of migrations, but a statistical analysis shows strong relationships between predator abundance and chlorophyll concentrations. Temperature is inevitably the major correlative factor in most distributions, since current structure, upwelling, and, therefore, food abundance are strongly linked to ocean climate. The major features of a large geographic scale of migration and the general rule of fidelity to multiple sites are shared by large Pacific marine predators. We are now beginning to have the tools needed to track oceanic predators wherever they swim or dive. Many other current systems in the world oceans, for example, the Canary Current off northwest Africa, are also being investigated on this oceanic megascale.

1. Which of the sentences below best expresses the information in the highlighted statement in the passage? The other choices change the meaning or leave out important information.

  Ⓐ The approach to tracking Pacific predators that the TOPP group advanced was used by marine biologists who were sophisticated.
  Ⓑ Marine biologists established the TOPP group because their research on Pacific predators required a more complex and precise tracking system.
  Ⓒ The TOPP group was an association of marine biologists who were interested in forming an exclusive organization to track predators in the Pacific.
  Ⓓ Tracking Pacific predators was not as simple as the TOPP group of marine biologists thought when they first formed their association.

2. What can be inferred about the Argos tags?

    Ⓐ They are less expensive than archival tags that were used previously.
    Ⓑ They are now being used to map land migration as well as ocean migration.
    Ⓒ They are a relatively new tool for researchers in marine science.
    Ⓓ They are active for about ten years before they must be replaced.

3. Look at the four squares [A] [B] [C] [D] that show where the following sentence could be inserted in the passage.

    **Because marine animals and sea turtles spend much of their time at the surface, they are ideal for such tags.**

    Where could the sentence best be added?

    Click on a square [■] to insert the sentence in the passage.

    Ⓐ
    Ⓑ
    Ⓒ
    Ⓓ

4. The word somewhat in the passage is closest in meaning to

    Ⓐ probably
    Ⓑ slightly
    Ⓒ commonly
    Ⓓ easily

5. Why does the author mention migration in Africa?

    Ⓐ To demonstrate the size of the ocean migrations
    Ⓑ To compare African wildlife with that of the Americas
    Ⓒ To prove that migration is a global phenomenon
    Ⓓ To emphasize the importance of land animals

6. The phrase associated with in the passage is closest in meaning to

    Ⓐ limited to
    Ⓑ related to
    Ⓒ supported by
    Ⓓ named for

7. The word Overall in the passage is closest in meaning to

    Ⓐ By itself
    Ⓑ Most likely
    Ⓒ Of late
    Ⓓ In general

8. According to paragraph 5, what does the analysis suggest?

   Ⓐ The water temperature is a key factor in the migratory system.
   Ⓑ Only the Pacific migration is large enough to be studied.
   Ⓒ Better tracking devices are needed to follow marine life under water.
   Ⓓ Statistics are inconclusive regarding the presence of chlorophyll.

9. According to the passage, all of the following are mentioned as migratory marine life EXCEPT

   Ⓐ baleen whales
   Ⓑ salmon sharks
   Ⓒ tuna
   Ⓓ dolphins

10. **Directions:** An introduction for a short summary of the passage appears below. Complete the summary by selecting the THREE answer choices that mention the most important points in the passage. Some sentences do not belong in the summary because they express ideas that are not included in the passage or are minor points from the passage. *This question is worth 2 points.*

   **Marine biologists are now able to study large-scale ocean migrations more accurately.**

   Ⓐ The migration through the Canary Current off northwest Africa has been researched.
   Ⓑ Tagging by marine biologists has allowed them to map major North Pacific migration patterns.
   Ⓒ Marine predators follow habitual food sources in upwelling areas during their migrations.
   Ⓓ Oceanic migrations occur when Pacific predators return to a familiar location to breed.
   Ⓔ The California Current and the North Pacific Transition Zone are the areas with the largest migratory movements.
   Ⓕ A serious problem in tracking is the loss of the tags because of technical failure or damage by a predator.

# LISTENING SECTION

 **Track 56**

**Directions:** Listen to the passages and answer the questions that follow. You may take notes as you listen, but notes will not be graded.

### Listening 1: Campus Conversation

1.  Why does the student go to the bookstore?

    Ⓐ To sell back her used textbooks
    Ⓑ To find out about renting textbooks
    Ⓒ To purchase the textbooks she rented
    Ⓓ To return textbooks she doesn't need

2.  What does the man infer about the woman?

    Ⓐ She will not buy her books today.
    Ⓑ She must be a part-time student.
    Ⓒ She is probably studying engineering.
    Ⓓ She does not mark in her books.

3.  What does the clerk say about the green tags?

    Ⓐ All engineering books should have green tags.
    Ⓑ The books with green tags are already sold.
    Ⓒ Rental books are marked with green tags.
    Ⓓ Green tags identify books that are in good condition.

4.  Why does the student have to give the clerk a credit card number?

    Ⓐ To pay for renting the book for the semester
    Ⓑ To buy the book at the end of the rental period
    Ⓒ To authorize a charge for an unreturned rental
    Ⓓ To hold a book until the beginning of the term

### Listening 2: Art Appreciation Class

5. What is the discussion mainly about?

  Ⓐ The problems of painting in a natural environment
  Ⓑ The rise of a new market for art in the 1800s
  Ⓒ The French influence in landscape painting
  Ⓓ The preference of artists for painting outdoors

6. What two reasons does the professor mention for the popularity of *plein air* painting?

   Choose 2 answers.

  Ⓐ New materials were introduced in the art world.
  Ⓑ The middle class could afford to have their portraits painted.
  Ⓒ *Plein air* painting had fewer problems than studio art.
  Ⓓ Artists considered natural daylight best for landscapes.

7. Why was the metal tube an important innovation for artists?

  Ⓐ Cheaper paints in metal tubes meant more artists could afford them.
  Ⓑ Metal tubes kept paints fresh and allowed artists to paint anywhere.
  Ⓒ Artists could mix the paints more easily using the metal tubes.
  Ⓓ Oil paints in metal tubes replaced the premixed tins of watercolors.

8. Why does the student say this:

  Ⓐ To make sure that he understands the professor's explanation
  Ⓑ To provide another example of the professor's premise
  Ⓒ To indicate that he is not in agreement with the professor
  Ⓓ To demonstrate his surprise about the professor's statement

9. Why does the professor mention "the studio" in reference to *plein air* painters?

  Ⓐ Sometimes it was not possible to find a suitable location outdoors.
  Ⓑ Studio painters used their imaginations to paint landscapes.
  Ⓒ Occasionally unfinished paintings had to be completed in a studio.
  Ⓓ Studios were often better locations for rapid composition.

10. What point did the professor make about the style of *plein air* painting?

  Ⓐ The *plein air* painters tried to copy Monet and Renoir.
  Ⓑ *Plein air* style required the painter to include sharp details.
  Ⓒ The style of the Hudson River School was more popular.
  Ⓓ Artists associated with *plein air* painting used different styles.

# SPEAKING SECTION

 **Track 57**

*Directions:* Follow the narrator's directions for each question. You may take notes as you listen, but notes will not be graded.

### *Independent Speaking Question: Planning a Trip*

Listen for a question about a familiar topic. After you hear the question, you have 15 seconds to prepare and 45 seconds to record your answer.

### Question

You are planning a cross-country trip at the end of your first year as a student in the United States. Which of the following options for travel will you choose? State your reasons for choosing that option.

> A multi-city airline ticket for five cities
> A railroad sleeping compartment
> A rental car and a GPS

Preparation Time: 15 seconds
Recording Time: 45 seconds

### *Integrated Speaking Question: Cryovolcanoes*

Read a short passage and listen to a talk on the same topic.

### Reading Passage
Reading Time: 45 seconds

---

Cryovolcanoes

   A cryovolcano or ice volcano erupts, expelling cryomagma in the form of water, ammonia, or methane instead of the lava or molten rock that is associated with volcanoes on rocky planets like Earth. The plumes that are produced may be a hundred or more degrees hotter than the frozen surface matter. After eruption, cryomagma condenses to a solid form because of its exposure to very low surrounding temperatures.

   Cryovolcanoes form on icy moons and other bodies, including some Kuiper belt objects. Heat from the core of the bodies supplies the energy that causes eruptions. The ice cap traps the heat and creates pressure that is strong enough to escape the inner surface, forming a volcano.

---

**Listening Passage**

Now listen to a professor who is discussing the same topic. After you hear the question, you have 30 seconds to prepare and 60 seconds to record your answer.

**Question**

Using examples from the talk, explain why scientists believe that formations on Pluto may be cryovolcanoes.

Preparation Time: 30 seconds
Recording Time: 60 seconds

# WRITING SECTION

 **Track 58**

**Directions:** You have 20 minutes to plan, write, and revise your response to a reading passage and a lecture on the same topic. First, read the passage and take notes. Then listen to the lecture and take notes. Finally, write your response to the question. Typically, a good response will require that you write 150–225 words.

### *Integrated Essay: Reading Passage*

Reading Time: 3 minutes

Beginning in the 1960s and 1970s, Walter Mischel, then a psychologist and professor at Stanford University, conducted a series of experiments collectively called the "Marshmallow Study." The purpose of the original research was to understand at what age children developed the ability to exercise delayed gratification, which is the willingness to wait in order to receive a reward. The original test and follow-up studies are among the most famous experiments in the history of psychology.

The subjects were children aged four or five who were attending the Bing Nursery School at Stanford. In the study, the children were offered one marshmallow immediately, or, if they were willing to wait for fifteen to twenty minutes by themselves in a room, then they could have two marshmallows. The researchers promised to return with two treats at the end of the time period.

As expected, two of every three children ate one marshmallow right away and one waited. Those who waited used a number of strategies to distract themselves, including playing with the marshmallows, covering their eyes, or singing.

In follow-up studies over a period of 40 years, the ability of children to delay gratification in the marshmallow study correlated with better grades, higher SAT scores, and, by middle age, lower levels of substance abuse, lower likelihood of obesity, and higher success in their relationships and careers. The series of experiments has been used to identify delayed gratification and self-control as critical factors for success in life. According to researchers, success often comes down to choosing discipline over immediate gratification.

 **Listening Passage**

Now listen to a lecture on the same topic that you have just read.

**Question**

Summarize the main points in the lecture and then explain how they cast doubt on the ideas in the reading passage.

# PRACTICE TEST 4

| Reading | Listening | Speaking | Writing |
|---|---|---|---|

**Reading**

1. B
2. A
3. C
4. B
5. A
6. B
7. D
8. A
9. D
10. B, C, E

**Listening**

1. B
2. C
3. C
4. C
5. D
6. A, D
7. B
8. A
9. C
10. D

**Speaking**

**INDEPENDENT QUESTION**

Did your talk answer the question?

Did you state a clear opinion?

Did you include reasons for your opinion?

Did you use different vocabulary words?

Did you make few mistakes in grammar?

Was your pronunciation understandable?

Did you speak without long pauses?

Were the ideas in the talk easy to follow?

Did you finish your talk in the time limit?

**INTEGRATED QUESTION**

Did you briefly summarize the reading?

Did you relate the lecture to the reading?

Did you paraphrase in your own words?

Was the information accurate?

Did you use different vocabulary words?

Did you make few mistakes in grammar?

Was your pronunciation understandable?

Did you speak without long pauses?

Were the ideas in the talk easy to follow?

Did you finish your talk in the time limit?

**Writing**

**INTEGRATED ESSAY**

Did you answer the topic question?

Did you have a topic sentence?

Did you have an outline sentence?

Did you include examples or details?

Was the information accurate?

Did you address each lecture point?

Did you paraphrase in your own words?

Did you use different vocabulary words?

Did you make few mistakes in grammar?

Did you use a variety of sentences?

Did you save time to edit and correct?

Was the essay easy for someone to read?

# BARRON'S TOEFL PRACTICE TEST 5

## READING SECTION

The following reading passage was adapted from *Astronomy Today*, Eighth Edition by Eric Chaisson and Steve McMillan, Pearson, 2014.

**Directions:** Read the passage and answer the questions that follow. You will have 20 minutes to complete this Reading Section.

### Meteors

P1    In general, meteors can be classified as either *meteoroids* or *meteorites*. Smaller *meteoroids* are mainly the rocky remains of broken up comets. Each time a comet passes near the Sun, some cometary fragments travel in dust or pebble-sized objects called a *meteoroid swarm,* moving in nearly the same orbit as the parent comet. Over time, the swarm gradually disperses along the orbit. If Earth's orbit happens to intersect the orbit of a cluster of meteoroids, a spectacular meteor shower can result. Earth's motion takes our planet across a given comet's orbit at most twice a year, depending on the precise orbit of each body. Intersection occurs at the same time each year so the appearance of certain meteor showers is a regular and fairly predictable event.

P2    Large meteoroids—more than a few centimeters in diameter—are usually *not* associated with swarms of cometary debris. Generally regarded as small bodies that have strayed from the asteroid belt, possibly as a result of collisions with or between asteroids, these objects have produced most of the cratering on the surfaces of the Moon, Mercury, Venus, Mars, and some of the moons of the Jovian planets. When these large meteoroids enter Earth's atmosphere, they produce energetic shock waves audible as sonic booms. Even more spectacularly, they heat the air, producing bright streaks in the sky and dusty trails of discarded debris. Such large meteors are sometimes known as *fireballs*. The greater the speed of the incoming object, the hotter its surface becomes and the faster it burns up. In any case, this brief flash, as impressive as it is, is in no way similar to the broad, steady arch of light associated with a comet's tail.

P3    A few large meteoroids enter the atmosphere at such high speed that they either break into pieces or disperse entirely at high altitudes; however, any piece of interplanetary debris that survives its fiery passage through our atmosphere and finds its way to the ground is called a *meteorite*. Some massive meteorites, at least a ton in mass and a meter across, make it to Earth's surface, producing craters such as the kilometer-wide Barringer Crater near Winslow, Arizona.

From the size of the crater, it is estimated that the meteoroid responsible for its formation must have had a mass of about 200,000 tons.

P4    Currently, Earth is scarred with nearly 100 craters larger than 0.1 km in diameter, most of which are so heavily eroded by weather and distorted by crustal activity that they can be identified only in satellite photography. Fortunately, such major collisions between Earth and large meteoroids are thought to be rare events now. Researchers estimate that, on average, they occur only once every few hundred thousand years.

P5    One feature that distinguishes small meteoroids, which burn up in Earth's atmosphere, from larger meteorites that reach the ground, is their strikingly different densities. Meteoric fireballs that are too small to reach the ground are low-density objects like comets, made of loosely packed ice and dust. In contrast, meteorites that reach Earth's surface are often much denser, suggesting a composition more like that of the asteroids.

P6    A Most meteorites are rocky, although a small percent is composed mainly of iron and nickel. The basic composition of the rocky meteorites is much like that of the inner planets and the Moon except that some of their lighter elements like hydrogen and oxygen appear to have boiled away long ago when the bodies from which the meteorites originated were molten. B Some meteorites show clear evidence of strong heating at some time in their past, most likely indicating that they originated on a larger body that either underwent some geological activity or was partially melted during the collision that liberated the fragments that eventually became the meteorites. C Others show no such evidence and probably date from the formation of the solar system. D

P7    Direct carbon dating shows most meteorites to be between 4.4 and 4.6 billion years old, roughly the age of the oldest lunar rocks. Meteorites, along with lunar rocks, comets, and Kuiper belt objects provide essential clues to the original state of matter in the solar neighborhood.

1. What is the main idea of this passage?

   Ⓐ The relationship of comets and meteors
   Ⓑ The major types of meteors
   Ⓒ The orbits of meteors in the solar system
   Ⓓ The composition of ancient meteors

2. According to paragraph 1, what causes a meteor shower?

   Ⓐ A comet passes near the Sun's orbit.
   Ⓑ A comet explodes when it is near Earth.
   Ⓒ A cluster of meteoroids crosses Earth's orbit.
   Ⓓ Large meteors cause shock waves.

3. Which of the sentences below best expresses the information in the highlighted statement in the passage? The other choices change the meaning or leave out important information.

   Ⓐ Objects that burn up in the atmosphere increase their velocities before they disappear.

   Ⓑ Objects that enter the atmosphere at high velocities get hotter and burn up faster.

   Ⓒ Objects that are hotter enter the atmosphere and burn up.

   Ⓓ Objects that enter the atmosphere faster increase their velocities as they burn up.

4. The word fragments in the passage is closest in meaning to

   Ⓐ explosions
   Ⓑ pieces
   Ⓒ lights
   Ⓓ sources

5. The word distorted in the passage is closest in meaning to

   Ⓐ enlarged
   Ⓑ softened
   Ⓒ reduced
   Ⓓ deformed

6. Look at the four squares [A] [B] [C] [D] that show where the following sentence could be inserted in the passage.

   **Most primitive of all are the black or dark gray meteorites with a relatively high carbon content.**

   Where could the sentence best be added?

   Click on a square [■] to insert the sentence in the passage.

   Ⓐ
   Ⓑ
   Ⓒ
   Ⓓ

7. The word roughly in the passage is closest in meaning to

   Ⓐ approximately
   Ⓑ principally
   Ⓒ finally
   Ⓓ individually

8. Why are "lunar rocks" mentioned in the last paragraph?

    Ⓐ They may have been meteors that collided with the moon.

    Ⓑ Their age compares with that of most meteors.

    Ⓒ They are very common objects in the solar system.

    Ⓓ Most lunar rocks have been carbon dated.

9. All of the following characteristics of small meteoroids are mentioned in the passage EXCEPT

    Ⓐ They often crash into asteroids at a very high velocity.

    Ⓑ They usually burn up before reaching the Earth's surface.

    Ⓒ They collect in swarms that accompany a comet's orbit.

    Ⓓ They are composed for the most part of rocky debris.

10. **Directions:** An introduction for a short summary of the passage appears below. Complete the summary by selecting the THREE answer choices that mention the most important points in the passage. Some sentences do not belong in the summary because they express ideas that are not included in the passage or are minor points from the passage. *This question is worth 2 points.*

**In general, meteors can be classified as either *meteoroids* or *meteorites*.**

    Ⓐ Objects that have strayed from the Asteroid Belt are referred to as large meteoroids.

    Ⓑ Several large meteors collide with the Earth on a daily basis.

    Ⓒ More than 100 craters on Earth have been formed by a meteorite collision.

    Ⓓ Small meteoroids are usually the residue of comets that have fragmented.

    Ⓔ Very old black or gray meteorites have a high carbon content.

    Ⓕ Meteorites are distinguishable because they reach the surface of the Earth.

# LISTENING SECTION

 **Track 59**

*Directions:* Listen to the passages and answer the questions that follow. You may take notes as you listen, but notes will not be graded.

### *Listening 1: Campus Conversation*

1. Why does the student go to see her professor?

   Ⓐ To get a syllabus because she was not at the first session
   Ⓑ To clarify the procedure for the group assignment
   Ⓒ To ask the professor to change one of the requirements
   Ⓓ To get permission to be added to the class roster

2. Why does the professor give two grades for the group project?

   Ⓐ The assignment is worth 25 percent of the final grade.
   Ⓑ The evaluation encourages both team and personal effort.
   Ⓒ The written work and the presentation are graded separately.
   Ⓓ The rehearsal and the class presentation are both considered.

3. How will the groups be organized?

   Ⓐ The professor will assign students to each of the groups.
   Ⓑ The groups will include students who know each other well.
   Ⓒ The names will be selected randomly for each group.
   Ⓓ The students will choose which group they prefer to join.

4. According to the professor, what is important in forming a group?

   Choose 2 answers.

   Ⓐ Experience communicating on social media
   Ⓑ Schedules that facilitate group meetings
   Ⓒ Finding members who want to do different jobs
   Ⓓ Rehearsing a presentation to get to know each other

### *Listening 2: Anthropology Class*

5. What is this lecture mainly about?

    Ⓐ Trade routes on the Great Plains
    Ⓑ The Spiro Mound site
    Ⓒ Rituals in Mississippian culture
    Ⓓ Early seasonal calendars

6. Why does the professor say this:

    Ⓐ He does not want to digress from the main topic now.
    Ⓑ He is trying to keep the students interested by previewing.
    Ⓒ He plans to demonstrate the game after the lecture.
    Ⓓ He is not familiar with that aspect of the Spiro culture.

7. According to the professor, what do we know about the Spiro Mound?

Choose 2 answers.

    Ⓐ It was the largest mound in the site.
    Ⓑ Evidence of burials was found inside.
    Ⓒ Many artifacts were preserved in it.
    Ⓓ The walls collapsed causing a mound.

8. What do archaeologists assume about the construction of the mounds?

    Ⓐ They were probably elevated for defensive purposes.
    Ⓑ Religious structures may have been built on top of them.
    Ⓒ The most important leaders in the community lived inside them.
    Ⓓ The platform was designed for sports and other events.

9. According to the professor, why were the Spiro Mound artifacts so well preserved?

    Ⓐ The important artifacts were removed before they could decay.
    Ⓑ The cedar logs that supported the earthen walls were very strong.
    Ⓒ Most of the artifacts were hidden and remained undisturbed.
    Ⓓ The most fragile objects were covered with earth to protect them.

10. What was the professor's opinion of the excavation in the 1930s?

    Ⓐ He was disappointed that more objects were not sold to collectors.
    Ⓑ He thought that the company did not pay a fair price for the artifacts.
    Ⓒ He was glad that the Oklahoma Historical Society led the excavation.
    Ⓓ He objected to the agreement by a private company to recover works of art.

# SPEAKING SECTION

 **Track 60**

*Directions:* Follow the narrator's directions for each question. You may take notes as you listen, but notes will not be graded.

## *Integrated Speaking Question: Smart Plants*

Listen to part of a lecture in a biology class. Then listen for a question about it. After you hear the question, you have 20 seconds to prepare and 60 seconds to record your answer.

**Question**
Using the main points and examples from the lecture, explain the ways that plants demonstrated learning.

Preparation Time: 20 seconds
Recording Time: 60 seconds

## *Integrated Speaking Question: Graduation*

Read a short passage and listen to a conversation on the same topic. After you hear the question, you have 30 seconds to prepare and 60 seconds to record your answer.

**Reading Passage**
Reading Time: 45 seconds

Graduation

The traditional commencement ceremony will be held on May 13 at the State University stadium at 10 o'clock A.M. At this event, no tickets will be required for graduates and their guests. The ceremony will feature a processional of graduates and faculty, remarks from the president, and a keynote speaker. At commencement, all graduating students will have their degrees conferred. For those unable to attend, the ceremony will be streamed live on the university website. That afternoon, each college will hold a more personal celebration to allow students to go on stage to receive their diplomas when their names are called. Graduating students can obtain an unlimited number of tickets online at the State University website.

 **Listening Passage**
Now listen to two students who are talking about the new graduation policy.

**Question**
The woman expresses her opinion about the new graduation policy. Report her opinion and explain the reasons that she has for having that opinion.

Preparation Time: 30 seconds
Recording Time: 60 seconds

# WRITING SECTION

**Directions:** You have 30 minutes to plan, write, and revise your response to a question about a familiar topic. Typically, a good response will require that you write 300–350 words.

### Independent Essay: Question

*Some people believe that couples should marry at a young age and begin their families. Others think that it is better to wait until they are older and more established. Which choice do you think is better, and why?*

Use specific reasons and examples to support your opinion.

# PRACTICE TEST 5

| *Reading* | *Listening* | *Speaking* | *Writing* |
|---|---|---|---|
| 1. B | 1. B | **INTEGRATED QUESTION** | **INDEPENDENT ESSAY** |
| 2. C | 2. B | Did you summarize the lecture? | Did you answer the topic question? |
| 3. B | 3. D | Did you include all major points? | Did you have a topic sentence? |
| 4. B | 4. B, C | Did you give examples or details? | Did you have an outline sentence? |
| 5. D | 5. B | Did you paraphrase in your own words? | Was your point of view clear? |
| 6. D | 6. A | Was the information accurate? | Did you include reasons for your opinion? |
| 7. A | 7. B, C | Did you use different vocabulary words? | Did you use different vocabulary words? |
| 8. B | 8. B | Did you make few mistakes in grammar? | Did you make few mistakes in grammar? |
| 9. A | 9. B | Was your pronunciation understandable? | Did you use a variety of sentences? |
| 10. A, D, F | 10. D | Did you speak without long pauses? | Did you save time to edit and correct? |
|  |  | Were the ideas in the talk easy to follow? | Did you finish your essay in the time limit? |
|  |  | Did you finish your talk in the time limit? | Was the essay easy for someone to read? |

**INTEGRATED QUESTION**

Did you briefly summarize the reading?

Did you state the speaker's opinion?

Did you include reasons for the opinion?

Did you use different vocabulary words?

Did you make few mistakes in grammar?

Was your pronunciation understandable?

Did you speak without long pauses?

Were the ideas in the talk easy to follow?

Did you finish your talk in the time limit?

# BARRON'S TOEFL PRACTICE TEST 6

## READING SECTION

The following reading passage was adapted from *Introduction to Psychology: Gateways to Mind and Behavior,* Fourteenth Edition by Dennis Coon and John O. Mitterer, Cengage Learning, 2016.

**Directions:** Read the passage and answer the questions that follow. You will have 20 minutes to complete this Reading Section.

### Environmental Stress

P1    Large cities are often thought of as stressful places to live. Traffic, congestion, pollution, crime, and impersonality are urban problems that immediately come to mind. To this list, psychologists have added crowding, overstimulation, and noise as major sources of urban stress.

P2    Nowhere are the effects of urbanization more evident than in the teeming cities of many developing nations. Conversely, the jammed busses, subways, and living quarters of large cities in developed countries also provide many opportunities to witness the stresses of crowding. One approach to assess the effects of crowding on people is to study the effects of overcrowding among animals. Although the results of animal experiments cannot be considered conclusive for humans, they point to some disturbing effects.

P3    For example, in an influential classic experiment, John Calhoun let a group of laboratory rats breed without limit in a confined space. Calhoun provided plenty of food, water, and nesting material for the rats. All that the rats lacked was space. At its peak, the colony numbered 80 rats; yet it was housed in a cage designed to comfortably hold about 50. Overcrowding in the cage was heightened by the actions of the two most dominant males. These rascals staked out private territory at opposite ends of the cage, gathered harems of eight to ten females, and prospered. Their actions forced the remaining rats into a small, severely crowded middle area.

P4    A high rate of pathological behavior developed in both males and females. Females gave up nest building and caring for their young. Pregnancies decreased, and infant mortality ran extremely high. Many of the animals became indiscriminately aggressive and went on campaigning attacks against others. Abnormal sexual behavior was rampant, with some animals displaying hypersexuality and others total sexual passivity. Many of the animals died, apparently from stress-caused diseases. The link between these problems and overcrowding was unmistakable.

P5    It can be argued that many of the same pathological behaviors can be observed in crowded inner city ghettos. It is, therefore, tempting to assume that violence, disorganization, and declining birthrates, as seen in these areas, are directly related to crowding. However, the connection has not been so clearly demonstrated with humans. People in the inner city suffer disadvantages in nutrition, education, income, and health care. These conditions, more than crowding, may deserve the blame for pathological behaviors. In fact, most laboratory studies using human subjects have failed to produce any serious ill effects by crowding people into small spaces. Most likely, this is because crowding is a psychological condition that is separate from density, that is, the number of people in a given space.

P6    Crowding refers to the objective feelings of being overstimulated by social inputs or a loss of privacy. Whether high density is experienced as crowding may depend on the relationships among those involved. In an elevator, subway, or prison, high densities may be uncomfortable. In contrast, a musical concert, party, or reunion may be most pleasant at high density levels. Thus, physical crowding may interact with situations to intensify existing stresses or pleasures. However, when crowding causes a loss of control over one's immediate social environment, stress and health problems are likely to result.

P7    Stress probably explains why death rates increase among prison inmates and mental hospital patients who live in crowded conditions in a state that psychologist Stanley Milgram called *attentional overload.* This is a stressful condition that occurs when sensory stimulation, information, and social contacts make excessive demands on attention. Large cities, in particular, tend to bombard residents with continuous input. The resulting sensory and cognitive overload can be quite stressful. Milgram believed that city dwellers learn to prevent attentional overload by engaging only in brief, superficial social contacts, by ignoring nonessential events, and by fending off others with cold and unfriendly expressions. In short, many city dwellers find that a degree of callousness is essential for survival. Thus, a blunting of sensitivity to the needs of others may be one of the more serious costs of urban stresses and crowding.

P8    Noise also contributes to the sensory assault that many people endure in urban environments. A A classic study of children attending schools near Los Angeles International Airport suggests that constant noise can be quite damaging. Children from the noisy schools were compared with similar students attending schools farther away from the airport. B Testing showed that children attending the noisy schools had higher blood pressure, were more likely to give up attempts to solve a difficult puzzle, and did a poorer job proofreading a printed paragraph, a task that requires close attention and concentration. C Even if such damage proves to be temporary, it is clear that noise pollution—annoying and intrusive sound—is a major cause of environmental stress. D

1. The word Conversely in the passage is closest in meaning to

   Ⓐ On the other hand
   Ⓑ Without a doubt
   Ⓒ By all means
   Ⓓ For the most part

2. The word assess in the passage is closest in meaning to

   Ⓐ evaluate
   Ⓑ confirm
   Ⓒ approach
   Ⓓ prevent

3. All of the following statements about the Calhoun study are true EXCEPT

   Ⓐ Dominant individuals threatened the group.
   Ⓑ Stress contributed to death rates in adults.
   Ⓒ Fewer of the young lived to adulthood.
   Ⓓ Pregnancy increased due to sexual behavior.

4. According to paragraph 6, what is the difference between crowding and density?

   Ⓐ Density can be pleasant in some circumstances, but crowding is stressful.
   Ⓑ Crowding suggests higher numbers of people than density does.
   Ⓒ Density is used with people, whereas crowding refers to animals.
   Ⓓ Crowding does not usually cause the health problems that density does.

5. Which of the sentences below best expresses the information in the highlighted statement in the passage? The other choices change the meaning or leave out important information.

   Ⓐ Laboratory studies with humans are more likely to fail when they are crowded.
   Ⓑ Humans tolerate crowding in the majority of laboratory studies conducted.
   Ⓒ Small spaces in laboratories are not successful for experiments with humans.
   Ⓓ Failure of laboratory studies with humans is a result of crowding into small spaces.

6. Why does the author mention "a musical concert"?

   Ⓐ To give an example of a situation in which loss of control causes stress
   Ⓑ To compare reunions with other situations that cause health risks
   Ⓒ To explain social contact in pleasant situations that involve high density
   Ⓓ To provide evidence of insensitivity to other people who are crowded

7. The word immediate in the passage is closest in meaning to

   Ⓐ exclusive
   Ⓑ closest
   Ⓒ normal
   Ⓓ safe

8. According to Milgram, why do city dwellers engage in superficial social interactions?

    Ⓐ They do not want friendships with people they rarely see.
    Ⓑ They are protecting themselves from too much stimulation.
    Ⓒ They are usually unfriendly because they are very busy.
    Ⓓ They do not feel safe with people on the streets of a city.

9. Look at the four squares [A] [B] [C] [D] that show where the following sentence could be inserted in the passage.

**The comparison students were from families of similar social and economic makeup.**

Where could the sentence best be added?

Click on a square [■] to insert the sentence in the passage.

    Ⓐ
    Ⓑ
    Ⓒ
    Ⓓ

10. **Directions:** An introduction for a short summary of the passage appears below. Complete the summary by selecting the THREE answer choices that mention the most important points in the passage. Some sentences do not belong in the summary because they express ideas that are not included in the passage or are minor points from the passage. ***This question is worth 2 points.***

**Crowding, overstimulation, and noise are major causes of stress in urban environments.**

    Ⓐ People who live in cities have higher mortality rates than people who live in less stressful environments.
    Ⓑ When crowding causes people to lose control over their situations, stress causes health problems.
    Ⓒ An excessive amount of sensory stimulation causes city dwellers to develop protective responses.
    Ⓓ Airports are very noisy environments for the people in residential neighborhoods surrounding them.
    Ⓔ Noise pollution in urban environments contributes to physical ailments and inhibits mental concentration.
    Ⓕ Experiments with laboratory rats in crowded conditions cause pathological behavior in the animals.

# LISTENING SECTION

  **Track 61**

**Directions:** Listen to the passages and answer the questions that follow. You may take notes as you listen, but notes will not be graded.

### *Listening 1: Campus Conversation*

1. Why does the student go to the professor's office?

   Ⓐ To get a handout from a lecture that he missed
   Ⓑ To ask the professor some questions about a lecture
   Ⓒ To talk about the baseball game that was played last Friday
   Ⓓ To borrow some notes from the last class session

2. According to the professor, which waves are called *compression waves*?

   Ⓐ Primary waves
   Ⓑ Secondary waves
   Ⓒ Surface waves
   Ⓓ Body waves

3. What was surprising to the student?

   Ⓐ He did not know that the professor liked baseball.
   Ⓑ He was not aware that there would be a quiz.
   Ⓒ He thought that his friend's notes were more accurate.
   Ⓓ He did not think P waves and S waves were body waves.

4. What does the professor suggest that the student do before the next class?

   Ⓐ Tell the baseball coach that he will be late.
   Ⓑ Go over the handouts from the class sessions.
   Ⓒ Look at the drawings in the book and online.
   Ⓓ Get notes from another student in the class.

### *Listening 2: Sociology Class*

5. What are the students mainly discussing?

   (A) The topic that one of the students chose for a paper
   (B) Violence in the games that children play with each other
   (C) How children learn by watching the behavior of others
   (D) Social learning in both animals and human beings

6. According to the study in England, what two conclusions were made about video games?

   Choose 2 answers.

   A  Playing more than three hours every day may have contributed to aggressive behavior.
   B  Playing less than one hour may have released some of the aggressive behavior.
   C  Not playing games at all may be the best way to prevent aggressive behavior.
   D  The games that players liked best were those that encouraged aggressive behavior.

7. What problem did the professor find in the study of video games?

   (A) The study was done with children who were having fun playing.
   (B) The researchers did not identify the ages of the children in the study.
   (C) The gamers in the study may have been playing for different reasons.
   (D) Only a small number of children were studied in the investigation.

8. Listen again to part of the conversation. Then answer the question.

   Why does the professor say this:

   (A) She would like the student to explain his question.
   (B) She disagrees with the student's comments.
   (C) She does not want the student to leave class early.
   (D) She admits that the student's idea is possible.

9. According to the student, what is the difference between TV and video games?

   (A) Children who watch TV are participating by using their imaginations.
   (B) Watching TV requires less participation than playing video games.
   (C) Neither TV nor video games are good examples of observational learning.
   (D) Observing the actions of others on TV is a good way to learn.

10. Why does the professor say this:

   (A) To change the student's topic for his paper
   (B) To clarify the idea that the student proposes
   (C) To encourage the student to consider both sides
   (D) To answer the question that the student asked

# SPEAKING SECTION

    Track 62

*Directions:* Follow the narrator's directions for each question. You may take notes as you listen, but notes will not be graded.

### *Integrated Speaking Question: Homesickness*

Listen to a conversation between two students. Then listen for a question about it. After you hear the question, you have 20 seconds to prepare and 60 seconds to record your answer.

**Question**
Describe the woman's problem and the suggestions that her friend makes about how to handle it. What do you think the woman should do, and why?

Preparation Time: 20 seconds
Recording Time: 60 seconds

### *Integrated Speaking Question: Automaticity*

Read a short passage and listen to a talk on the same topic.

**Reading Passage**
Reading Time: 45 seconds

---

Automaticity

*Automaticity* is the ability to complete tasks without engaging the mind in the low-level details required to accomplish them. The task becomes an automatic response. Automaticity usually occurs as a result of repetition and practice. By executing a task again and again, it requires less attention. The process for developing automaticity is *overlearning*, which requires new skills to be practiced beyond initial mastery. When tasks become automatic, it is possible to complete them while simultaneously thinking about or doing something else. The classic example of automaticity is driving a car, which initially requires attention to details, but, over time, becomes so automatic that little thought is given to activating turn signals and braking for a safe turn.

---

    **Listening Passage**
Now listen to a professor who is discussing the same topic.

**Question**
Using information from the talk, explain why language learning is an example of automaticity.

Preparation Time: 30 seconds
Recording Time: 60 seconds

# WRITING SECTION

*Directions:* You have 30 minutes to plan, write, and revise your response to a question about a familiar topic. Typically, a good response will require that you write 300–350 words.

## *Independent Essay: Question*

Agree or disagree with the following statement:

*It is important for all children to participate in team sports because it teaches them life lessons.*

Give reasons and examples to support your opinion.

# PRACTICE TEST 6

| Reading | Listening | Speaking | Writing |
|---|---|---|---|

**Reading**

1. A
2. A
3. D
4. A
5. B
6. C
7. B
8. B
9. B
10. B, C, E

**Listening**

1. B
2. A
3. B
4. C
5. C
6. A, B
7. C
8. A
9. B
10. B

**Speaking**

**INTEGRATED QUESTION**

Did you summarize the problem?
Did you present the speaker's suggestions?
Did you state a clear opinion?
Did you use different vocabulary words?
Did you make few mistakes in grammar?
Was your pronunciation understandable?
Did you speak without long pauses?
Were the ideas in the talk easy to follow?
Did you finish your talk in the time limit?

**INTEGRATED SPEAKING**

Did you briefly summarize the reading?
Did you relate the lecture to the reading?
Did you paraphrase in your own words?
Was the information accurate?
Did you use different vocabulary words?
Did you make few mistakes in grammar?
Was your pronunciation understandable?
Did you speak without long pauses?
Were the ideas in the talk easy to follow?
Did you finish your talk in the time limit?

**Writing**

**INDEPENDENT ESSAY**

Did you answer the topic question?
Did you have a topic sentence?
Did you have an outline sentence?
Was your point of view clear?
Did you include reasons for your opinion?
Did you use different vocabulary words?
Did you make few mistakes in grammar?
Did you use a variety of sentences?
Did you save time to edit and correct?
Did you finish your essay in the time limit?
Was the essay easy for someone to read?

# BARRON'S TOEFL PRACTICE TEST 7

## READING SECTION

The following reading passage was adapted from *Earth Science*, Fourteenth Edition by Edward J. Tarbuck and Frederick K. Lutgens, Pearson, 2015.

**Directions:** Read the passage and answer the questions that follow. You will have 20 minutes to complete this Reading Section.

### America's Coastlines

P1    The shoreline along the Pacific coast of the United States is strikingly different from that of the Atlantic and Gulf coast regions. Some of the differences are related to plate tectonics. The west coast represents the leading edge of the North American plate; therefore, it experiences active uplift and deformation. In contrast, the east coast is a tectonically quiet region that is far from any active plate margin. Because of this basic geologic difference, the nature of shoreline erosion problems along America's opposite coasts is different.

### *Atlantic and Gulf Coasts*

P2    Much of the coastal development along the Atlantic and Gulf coasts has occurred on barrier islands. A Typically, a barrier island consists of a wide beach that is backed by dunes and separated from the mainland by marshy lagoons. The broad expanses of sand and exposure to the ocean have made barrier islands exceedingly attractive sites for development. B

P3    Because barrier islands face the open ocean, they receive the full force of major storms that strike the coast. C When a storm occurs, the barriers absorb the energy of the waves primarily through the movement of sand. Waves may move sand from the beach to offshore areas or they may wash into the dunes, depositing sand onto the beach or carrying it out to sea. D In a process known as *overwash*, sometimes waves even carry sand from the beach and the dunes into marshes behind the barrier where water birds feed and nest.

P4    When a barrier is developed for homes or a resort, storm waves that previously ran harmlessly through the dunes now encounter buildings and highways. When damage occurs to their properties, homeowners tend to attribute it to a specific storm, rather than to the natural process along coastal barriers. Local residents and businesses are more likely to build barricades for the sand and the waves than to admit that development was inappropriately situated to begin with.

### Pacific Coast

P5   In contrast to the broad, gently sloping coastal plains of the Atlantic and Gulf coasts, much of the Pacific coast is characterized by relatively narrow beaches that are backed by steep cliffs and mountain ranges. America's western margin is a more rugged and tectonically active region than the eastern margin. Because uplift continues, the rise in sea level in the West is not so readily apparent. Nevertheless, like the shoreline erosion problems facing the East's barrier islands, west coast difficulties also stem largely from the alteration of natural systems by people.

P6   A major problem facing the Pacific shoreline, particularly along southern California, is a significant narrowing of many beaches. The bulk of the sand on many of these beaches is supplied by rivers that transport it from the mountainous regions to the coast. Over the years, this natural flow of material to the coast has been interrupted by dams built for irrigation and flood control. The reservoirs effectively trap the sand that would otherwise nourish the beach environment. When the beaches were wider, they protected the cliffs behind them from the force of storm waves. Now, however, the waves move across the narrowed beaches without losing much energy and cause more rapid erosion of the cliffs.

P7   Although the retreat of the cliffs provides material to replace some of the sand impounded behind dams, it also endangers homes and roads built on the bluffs. In addition, development atop the cliffs aggravates the problem. Urbanization increases runoff, which, if not carefully controlled, can result in serious bluff erosion. Watering lawns and gardens adds significant quantities of water to the slope. This water percolates downward toward the base of the cliff where it may emerge in small seeps, reducing the slope's stability and facilitating mass wasting.

P8   Shoreline erosion along the Pacific coast varies considerably from one year to the next, by and large because of the sporadic occurrence of storms. As a result, when the infrequent but serious episodes of erosion occur, the damage is often blamed on unusual storms and not on coastal development or the sediment-trapping dams that may be great distances away. If, as predicted, sea level experiences a significant rise, increased shoreline erosion and sea cliff retreat should be expected along many parts of the Pacific coast.

1. The word Typically in the passage is closest in meaning to

   Ⓐ Suddenly
   Ⓑ Usually
   Ⓒ Partially
   Ⓓ Fortunately

2. According to paragraphs 3 and 4, which of the following is true of barrier islands?

    &#9398; Barrier islands are a habitat for wildlife during severe storms.
    &#9399; Developers have identified barrier islands as inappropriate building sites.
    &#9400; Barrier islands protect the coastline by moving sand onto the beach.
    &#9401; Buildings and highways have replaced barrier islands as protection from waves.

3. Look at the four squares [A] [B] [C] [D] that show where the following sentence could be inserted in the passage.

**However, development has grown more rapidly than has our understanding of barrier island dynamics.**

Where could the sentence best be added?

Click on a square [■] to insert the sentence in the passage.

    &#9398;⃞ A
    &#9399;⃞ B
    &#9400;⃞ C
    &#9401;⃞ D

4. Which of the sentences below best expresses the information in the highlighted statement in the passage? The other choices change the meaning or leave out important information.

    &#9398; Unlike the narrow shore on the mountainous Pacific coast, the Atlantic and Gulf coasts have broad beaches with gradual inclines.
    &#9399; The Atlantic and Gulf coasts are not as broad as the beaches on the Pacific coast because of the mountains and cliffs.
    &#9400; The mountains on the Pacific coast are higher than the low hills that distinguish the Atlantic and Gulf coastlines.
    &#9401; The Pacific coastline and the Atlantic coastline as well as the Gulf coast have beaches that contrast with the mountains and cliffs.

5. The word apparent in the passage is closest in meaning to

    &#9398; studied
    &#9399; changing
    &#9400; serious
    &#9401; noticeable

6. Why are "lawns and gardens" mentioned in the passage?

    &#9398; To suggest a way for homeowners to prevent erosion
    &#9399; To identify a reason that the cliffs become unstable
    &#9400; To contrast rainwater with water that developers use
    &#9401; To predict a rise in sea levels on beaches nearby

7. The phrase by and large in the passage is closest in meaning to

&#9398; to some degree

&#9399; for the most part

&#9400; in all likelihood

&#9401; on purpose

8. According to paragraph 8, people would probably identify which of the following as the cause of coastal erosion?

&#9398; Dams on rivers that empty into the ocean

&#9399; Homes that are built on the cliffs above the beach

&#9400; Storms that bring heavy rain onto the land

&#9401; A significant rise in the sea levels near the coast

9. All of the following are mentioned in the passage as differences in the Atlantic and Pacific coastlines EXCEPT

&#9398; The width of the sandy beaches

&#9399; The activity of the tectonic plates

&#9400; The influence of barrier islands

&#9401; The development of resorts and homes

10. **Directions:** An introduction for a short summary of the passage appears below. Complete the summary by selecting the THREE answer choices that mention the most important points in the passage. Some sentences do not belong in the summary because they express ideas that are not included in the passage or are minor points from the passage. *This question is worth 2 points.*

**The Pacific coast of the United States is remarkably different from the shoreline of the Atlantic and Gulf coasts.**

A The Atlantic is characterized by barrier islands, dunes, and marshes, whereas the Pacific is typified by mountain ranges and cliffs.

B Development on both the Atlantic shore and the Pacific coast contributes to erosion, which in turn causes the destruction of property.

C When storms can be predicted, barriers can be erected on the Atlantic, Pacific, and Gulf shores to protect homes and resorts.

D Barrier islands are assaulted by the most violent waves because they face the open ocean where storms move in to the shore.

E Dams for irrigation and flood control have interrupted the natural flow of water and sand to the ocean and the beach.

F Property owners on both coasts attribute problems to natural disasters instead of to the choices they made for building sites.

# LISTENING SECTION

 **Track 63**

*Directions:* Listen to the passages and answer the questions that follow. You may take notes as you listen, but notes will not be graded.

### *Listening 1: Campus Conversation*

1. Why does the woman go to see the resident advisor?

  Ⓐ To try to change roommates
  Ⓑ To report alcohol in the dorm
  Ⓒ To find a quiet place to study
  Ⓓ To ask about other dorms

2. How did the woman choose her roommate?

  Ⓐ Her advisor matched her with a roommate.
  Ⓑ She used the school's online service.
  Ⓒ They had known each other for a long time.
  Ⓓ Her roommate met her at a party on campus.

3. What does the resident advisor imply when he says this:

  Ⓐ The woman's roommate does not have very many friends.
  Ⓑ He will not tell the woman's roommate that she complained.
  Ⓒ The woman is doing the right thing by reporting her roommate.
  Ⓓ This is not the only complaint that he has received about the problem.

4. What does the resident advisor plan to do about the situation?

  Ⓐ He will help the woman change roommates if the situation doesn't change.
  Ⓑ He will issue a warning every time he sees a party during the semester.
  Ⓒ He will have to talk with the woman about her unacceptable behavior.
  Ⓓ He will suspend the woman's roommate immediately for breaking the law.

### Listening 2: Western Civilization Class

5. What does the professor mainly discuss?

&#9398; The rule of Hadrian, Emperor of the Roman Empire
&#9399; Trade in Great Britain during the Roman occupation
&#9400; The wall and forts that were built across Britannia
&#9401; Modern methods for archaeological excavation

6. According to the lecture, what is NOT true of the earliest wall?

&#9398; The wall was about 12 feet high.
&#9399; Roman soldiers built the wall.
&#9400; It was mostly finished in six years.
&#9401; Only earth and wood were used.

7. What was the purpose of the *vallum*?

Choose 2 answers.

&#9398; To provide security
&#9399; To control travel
&#9400; To house soldiers
&#9401; To store goods

8. According to archaeological investigations, what occurred as a result of the wall's construction?

&#9398; Trade developed between the Roman military and the local people.
&#9399; Towns near the wall were moved farther away from the construction site.
&#9400; Necessities were in short supply because of the increase in population.
&#9401; Fewer wars were fought after the wall separated aggressive tribes.

9. What did the professor imply about the wall?

&#9398; Britons benefited from the wall.
&#9399; The wall was a new military idea.
&#9400; The plan for the wall was very costly.
&#9401; Many people died during construction.

10. Why did the wall fall into ruin after the Romans left Britain?

&#9398; The Celts demolished the wall during an invasion.
&#9399; The original wall was not very well built.
&#9400; The stone was used to build newer structures.
&#9401; The lumber and earth were damaged by the weather.

# SPEAKING SECTION

   Track 64

**Directions:** Follow the narrator's directions for each question. You may take notes as you listen, but notes will not be graded.

### Independent Speaking Question: Important Lesson

Listen for a question about a familiar topic. After you hear the question, you have 15 seconds to prepare and 45 seconds to record your answer.

**Question**

Talk about a person who has taught you an important lesson. Be sure to include details about the person and the lesson that you learned.

Preparation Time: 15 seconds
Recording Time: 45 seconds

### Integrated Speaking Question: Passwords

Read a short passage and listen to a talk on the same topic. After you hear the question, you have 30 seconds to prepare and 60 seconds to record your answer.

**Reading Passage**
Reading Time: 45 seconds

---

Passwords

In compliance with a new policy, Community College is requiring a mandatory password reset for students and faculty. When users sign in to the college website, they will be prompted to reset their passwords and update them on all mobile devices. After one week, the previous password will expire. If the password is not changed within the one-week period, the user will be locked out and will have to go to Student Services in order to be reinstated. Users will be prompted to change passwords every semester. The college administration understands that these changes will create a minor inconvenience, but they are necessary to increase account security.

---

   **Listening Passage**
Now listen to two students who are talking about the new password policy.

**Question**

The woman expresses her opinion about the new password policy. Report her opinion and explain the reasons that she has for having that opinion.

Preparation Time: 30 seconds
Recording Time: 60 seconds

# WRITING SECTION

   **Track 65**

*Directions:* You have 20 minutes to plan, write, and revise your response to a reading passage and a lecture on the same topic. First, read the passage and take notes. Then listen to the lecture and take notes. Finally, write your response to the question. Typically, a good response will require that you write 150–225 words.

## *Integrated Essay: Reading Passage*

Reading Time: 3 minutes

> Grading on the curve is a common practice that college professors use to encourage competition and motivate students to work harder for their grades. In this system, letter grades in a class are distributed along a bell curve, that is, a normal distribution shaped like a bell with a bulge in the middle. When an assignment or test is scored, the average score is given an average grade, usually a C. The scores above and below the average are distributed so that a few students receive As and a few Fs, with Bs and Ds distributed along the curve accordingly. Professors argue that the curve is a good practice because it motivates students to compete. With a limited number of A grades, students whose goal is to earn an A will have to work to score better than others in the class because very few A grades will be given.
>
> Professors also maintain that grading on the curve helps them evaluate their tests and adjust for any problems in the difficulty level of the questions. For example, if no one in the class scores above 80 percent on a test, and 40 percent is the average, then the test may have been too difficult. To adjust for this problem, the student with a 40 percent score at the middle of the curve will receive a C, and the student with an 80 percent score at the smallest part of the curve to the left will receive an A. On a standard grading system, no one would have received an A because no scores were above 90, and the average students would have failed the test.
>
> Another benefit of grading on the curve is to minimize the variation between different professors teaching sections of the same course because there will be a balanced distribution of grades among all sections.

   **Listening Passage**

Now listen to a lecture on the same topic that you have just read.

## Question

Summarize the main points in the lecture, and then explain how they cast doubt on the ideas in the reading passage.

# PRACTICE TEST 7

| *Reading* | *Listening* | *Speaking* | *Writing* |
|---|---|---|---|
| 1. B | 1. A | **INDEPENDENT QUESTION** | **INTEGRATED ESSAY** |
| 2. C | 2. B | Did your talk answer the question? | Did you answer the topic question? |
| 3. B | 3. B | Did you communicate a main idea? | Did you have a topic sentence? |
| 4. A | 4. A | Did you include examples or details? | Did you have an outline sentence? |
| 5. D | 5. C | Did you use different vocabulary words? | Did you include examples or details? |
| 6. B | 6. D | Did you make few mistakes in grammar? | Was the information accurate? |
| 7. B | 7. A, B | Was your pronunciation understandable? | Did you address each lecture point? |
| 8. C | 8. A | Did you speak without long pauses? | Did you paraphrase in your own words? |
| 9. D | 9. A | Were the ideas in the talk easy to follow? | Did you use different vocabulary words? |
| 10. A, B, F | 10. C | Did you finish your talk in the time limit? | Did you make few mistakes in grammar? |
| | | | Did you use a variety of sentences? |
| | | **INTEGRATED QUESTION** | Did you save time to edit and correct? |
| | | Did you briefly summarize the reading? | Was the essay easy for someone to read? |
| | | Did you state the speaker's opinion? | |
| | | Did you include reasons for the opinion? | |
| | | Did you use different vocabulary words? | |
| | | Did you make few mistakes in grammar? | |
| | | Was your pronunciation understandable? | |
| | | Did you speak without long pauses? | |
| | | Were the ideas in the talk easy to follow? | |
| | | Did you finish your talk in the time limit? | |

# BARRON'S TOEFL PRACTICE TEST 8

## READING SECTION

The following reading passage was adapted from *Western Civilizations: Their History and Their Culture*, Seventeenth Edition, Volume 2 by Judith Coffin, Robert Stacey, Joshua Cole, and Carol Symes, Norton, 2011.

**Directions:** Read the passage and answer the questions that follow. You will have 20 minutes to complete this Reading Section.

### Naval Technology and Navigation

P1   The new European empires of the fifteenth and sixteenth centuries rested on mastery of the oceans. The Portuguese *caraval*, the workhorse ship of the fifteenth-century voyages to Africa, was based on ship and sail designs that had been in use among Portuguese fishermen since the thirteenth century. Starting in the 1440s, however, Portuguese shipwrights began building larger caravals of about 50 tons of displacement with two masts, each carrying a triangular sail. Columbus's ship *Nina* was of this design, having been refitted with two square sails in the Canary Islands to enable it to sail more efficiently before the wind during the Atlantic crossing. Such ships required much smaller crews than did the multi-oared galleys that were still commonly used in the Mediterranean. By the end of the fifteenth century, even larger caravals of around 200 tons were being constructed, with a third mast and a combination of square and triangular sails.

P2   Europeans were also making significant advances in navigation during the fifteenth and sixteenth centuries. Ⓐ Quadrants, which could calculate latitude in the Northern Hemisphere by the height of the North Star above the horizon, were in widespread use by the 1450s. Ⓑ Like quadrants, astrolabes had been known in western Europe for centuries. But it was not until the 1480s that the astrolabe became a useful instrument for seaborne navigation, with the preparation of standard tables sponsored by the Portuguese crown. Ⓒ Compasses, too, were coming into more widespread use during the fifteenth century. Ⓓ Longitude, however, remained impossible to calculate accurately until the eighteenth century when the invention of the marine chronometer finally made it possible to keep accurate time at sea. In the sixteenth century, Europeans sailing east or west across the oceans generally had to rely on their skill at estimating to determine where they were on the globe.

P3    Additionally, European sailors benefited from a new interest in maps and navigational charts. Especially important to Atlantic sailors were books known as *rutters* or *routiers*. These references contained detailed sailing instructions and descriptions of the coastal landmarks a pilot could expect to encounter en route to a variety of destinations. Mediterranean sailors had used similar books since at least the fourteenth century. Known as *portolani* or portolan charts, they mapped the ports along the coastlines, tracked prevailing winds and tides, and warned of reefs and shallow harbors. In the fifteenth century, these map-making techniques were extended to the Atlantic Ocean; by the end of the sixteenth century, the accumulated knowledge contained in rutters spanned the globe.

P4    Larger, more maneuverable ships and improved navigational aids made it possible for the Portuguese and other European mariners to reach Africa, Asia, and the Americas by sea, but fundamentally, these sixteenth-century European commercial empires were a military achievement. As such, they reflected what Europeans had learned in their wars against each other during the fourteenth and fifteenth centuries. Perhaps the most critical military advance was increasingly sophisticated artillery, a development made possible not only by gunpowder but also by improved metallurgical techniques for casting cannon barrels.

P5    Indeed, the new ship designs of the first caravals, and the larger galleons, were important in part because their larger size made it possible to mount more effective artillery pieces on them. European vessels were now conceived as floating artillery platforms with scores of guns mounted in fixed positions along their sides and swivel guns mounted fore and aft. These guns were vastly expensive, as were the ships that carried them, but for rulers who could afford them, such ships made it possible to project military power around the world. Portuguese trading outposts in Africa and Asia were also fortifications, built not so much to guard against the attacks of native peoples as to ward off assaults from other Europeans. Without this essential military component, the European maritime empires of the sixteenth century could not have existed.

1. According to paragraph 1, all of the following were true of the Portuguese caravals in the fifteenth century EXCEPT

   Ⓐ Fewer crewmen were needed to maneuver them as compared with the older galley ships.
   Ⓑ Both square and triangular sails were used on two or three masts to sail more effectively.
   Ⓒ Portuguese fishermen used the new designs to sail farther into the ocean for their catch.
   Ⓓ Larger ships were designed for longer ocean voyages to the islands off the coast of Africa.

2. The phrase based on in the passage is closest in meaning to

   Ⓐ made like
   Ⓑ better than
   Ⓒ purchased from
   Ⓓ starting in

3. Why does the author mention "Columbus" in paragraph 1?

   Ⓐ To explain the reason why the Portuguese ships were built
   Ⓑ To prove that the ships could sail as far as the African coast
   Ⓒ To illustrate some of the technological advances of the era
   Ⓓ To describe one of the early voyages in the Mediterranean

4. The word standard in the passage is closest in meaning to

   Ⓐ universal
   Ⓑ expensive
   Ⓒ modern
   Ⓓ advanced

5. Look at the four squares [A] [B] [C] [D] that show where the following sentence could be inserted in the passage.

   **As sailors approached the equator, however, the quadrant became less and less useful, and navigators instead made use of astrolabes, which calculated latitude by the height of the Sun.**

   Where could the sentence best be added?

   Click on a square [■] to insert the sentence in the passage.

   Ⓐ
   Ⓑ
   Ⓒ
   Ⓓ

6. According to paragraph 3, which of the following is NOT true of rutters?

   Ⓐ They were developed and used during the fourteenth century.
   Ⓑ They provided facts about Mediterranean ports and harbors.
   Ⓒ They included navigational information about the Atlantic Ocean.
   Ⓓ They were not needed after more detailed maps were available.

7. Which of the sentences below best expresses the information in the highlighted statement in the passage? The other choices change the meaning or leave out important information.

   Ⓐ Neither gunpowder nor cannons were very well developed until improvements in technology made it possible to invent them.

   Ⓑ Both new technology that improved cannons and the invention of gunpowder resulted in better weapons, the most important military development.

   Ⓒ It was very important for military weapons to be developed so that the techniques for warfare could be more sophisticated.

   Ⓓ The gunpowder used in cannons was a complex development that advanced military techniques significantly.

8. The word conceived in the passage is closest in meaning to

   Ⓐ changed
   Ⓑ destroyed
   Ⓒ abandoned
   Ⓓ regarded

9. What can be inferred about the European empires?

   Ⓐ European empires shared trade routes and trading partners.
   Ⓑ Portugal was the only European power with forts in Asia and Africa.
   Ⓒ Military strength was not as important as commercial dominance.
   Ⓓ Naval battles to defend commercial interests were common.

10. **Directions:** An introduction for a short summary of the passage appears below. Complete the summary by selecting the THREE answer choices that mention the most important points in the passage. Some sentences do not belong in the summary because they express ideas that are not included in the passage or are minor points from the passage. *This question is worth 2 points.*

    **The European maritime empires in the sixteenth century were supported by improvements in ship building and better navigational aids as well as military advances.**

    Ⓐ Many ships were lost at sea before maps and charts of the oceans were commonly available.

    Ⓑ Larger ships with more masts and improvements in the designs of their sails supported ocean voyages.

    Ⓒ The marine chronometer gave sailors the advantage of accurate time keeping on board their ships.

    Ⓓ Forts and large ships with guns mounted on platforms protected trading outposts and cargo.

    Ⓔ Better navigational instruments and charts made longer journeys safer and more efficient.

    Ⓕ Local populations often attacked the trading outposts that European powers had established.

# LISTENING SECTION

    **Track 66**

***Directions:*** Listen to the passages and answer the questions that follow. You may take notes as you listen, but notes will not be graded.

### *Listening 1: Campus Conversation*

1.  Why does the student go to the office?

    Ⓐ To get his class schedule
    Ⓑ To have his photo taken
    Ⓒ To replace his student ID
    Ⓓ To renew his driver's license

2.  What does the woman need to process the student's request?

    Choose 2 answers.

    Ⓐ A $20-processing fee
    Ⓑ His current class schedule
    Ⓒ A digital photo
    Ⓓ His old student ID

3.  What does the woman suggest that the student do first?

    Ⓐ Go to the post office in the student services building
    Ⓑ Bring her the photograph from his original ID
    Ⓒ Come back to her office tomorrow morning
    Ⓓ Get his class schedule from his apartment

4.  What does the woman imply when she says this:

    Ⓐ She cannot help him a second time.
    Ⓑ He will have to have another photo taken.
    Ⓒ He will have to pay for this replacement.
    Ⓓ She cannot give him a class schedule.

## *Listening 2: General Science Class*

5. What is the purpose of this discussion?

    Ⓐ To answer questions about the information in the book
    Ⓑ To introduce the topic of global weather patterns
    Ⓒ To prepare the students for a general science test
    Ⓓ To debate the importance of monsoon seasons

6. According to the lecture, what defines a monsoon?

    Ⓐ Weather in India
    Ⓑ Changes in rainfall
    Ⓒ A shift in the wind
    Ⓓ High altitudes

7. Why does the professor say this:

    Ⓐ He has made an error, and needs to correct it before continuing.
    Ⓑ He wants to repeat information because he is not sure that it is clear.
    Ⓒ He needs to talk about something that should have been explained previously.
    Ⓓ He is going to ask the students to review information from yesterday's lecture.

8. What is the professor's opinion of the North American monsoon?

    Ⓐ The North American weather pattern is not a true example of a monsoon.
    Ⓑ It is a partial monsoon because the wind reversal is not complete.
    Ⓒ Although it is not as strong as others, it meets the conditions for a monsoon.
    Ⓓ He disagrees with the student's interpretation because it is not clearly stated.

9. According to the professor, how does the monsoon season in India compare with that of North America?

    Ⓐ The Indian monsoon season is much longer than the monsoon in North America.
    Ⓑ The mountain ranges that cause the two monsoon weather patterns are very similar.
    Ⓒ The monsoons in India and North America do not have the same general features.
    Ⓓ The Indian monsoon has a complete reversal of wind but the North American does not.

10. What is true about El Niño?

    Ⓐ A strong El Niño usually brings an earlier monsoon season.
    Ⓑ The presence of El Niño has very little influence on a monsoon.
    Ⓒ El Niño sometimes causes warmer weather without much rain.
    Ⓓ The effect of El Niño on monsoon weather is still being investigated.

# SPEAKING SECTION

    **Track 67**

*Directions:* Follow the narrator's directions for each question. You may take notes as you listen, but notes will not be graded.

### Independent Speaking Question: Advice

Listen for a question about a familiar topic. After you hear the question, you have 15 seconds to prepare and 45 seconds to record your answer.

### Question

Your friend is trying to decide whether to get a part-time job while attending college or take out a loan to pay for his last year. What advice would you give him?

Preparation Time: 15 seconds
Recording Time: 45 seconds

### Integrated Speaking Question: Kaleidoscopic Discovery

Read a short passage and listen to a talk on the same topic. After you hear the question, you have 30 seconds to prepare and 60 seconds to record your answer.

### Reading Passage
Reading Time: 45 seconds

---

Kaleidoscopic Discovery

The kaleidoscopic discovery engine asserts that all scientific discoveries are the result of many people working across generations, developing ideas and methods that are too complex for any one individual to develop during a lifetime. To put that another way, we learn from others, and when an accumulation of knowledge and practice is available, insights and inventions are introduced to the public. For this reason, we often find that if one scientist had not made a particular discovery, another scientist would have made it within a short time. As Newton observed, most scientists have stood on the shoulders of giants to see the world a bit further along the horizon.

---

    **Listening Passage**

Now listen to a professor who is discussing the same topic.

### Question
Referring to the professor's examples in the talk, explain *kaleidoscopic discovery*.

Preparation Time: 30 seconds
Recording Time: 60 seconds

# WRITING SECTION

 **Track 68**

**Directions:** You have 20 minutes to plan, write, and revise your response to a reading passage and a lecture on the same topic. First, read the passage and take notes. Then listen to the lecture and take notes. Finally, write your response to the question. Typically, a good response will require that you write 150–225 words.

### *Integrated Essay: Reading Passage*

Reading Time: 3 minutes

An ancient Greek parable explains that a fox knows many small things but a hedgehog knows only one big thing. In the parable, the fox tries to catch the hedgehog, using a variety of strategies, but the fox can never succeed because the big thing that the hedgehog knows is how to defend itself. Hundreds of years later, philosopher Isaiah Berlin applied the parable to people in a modern world. In his essay, "The Hedgehog and the Fox," Berlin divided people into two groups: foxes and hedgehogs, arguing that foxes pursue many goals at the same time and become unfocused and limited in their long-term achievements, whereas hedgehogs have one overarching goal that guides their thinking and assures their success against all odds.

In his seminal book, *Good to Great*, American business consultant Jim Collins proposed what he called the "hedgehog principle." According to Collins, organizations are most likely to succeed when their leaders focus on the one thing it does best. To find that out, they have to ask three questions: What can we do better than any other company? What are our people passionate about? And what drives the profit? In figuring out what an organization does best, it is also important to identify what it does not do well so that those distractions can be eliminated. In answering the question about passion, it is also necessary to keep only those people who demonstrate passion. And finding what drives the profit means that unprofitable aspects of a company have to go.

 **Listening Passage**

Now listen to a lecture on the same topic that you have just read.

### Question

Summarize the main points in the lecture, and then explain how they cast doubt on the ideas in the reading passage.

# PRACTICE TEST 8

| Reading | Listening | Speaking | Writing |
|---------|-----------|----------|---------|
| 1. C | 1. C | **INDEPENDENT QUESTION** | **INTEGRATED ESSAY** |
| 2. A | 2. B, C | Did your talk answer the question? | Did you answer the topic question? |
| 3. C | 3. D | Did you state a clear opinion? | Did you have a topic sentence? |
| 4. A | 4. A | Did you include reasons for your opinion? | Did you have an outline sentence? |
| 5. B | 5. A | Did you use different vocabulary words? | Did you include examples or details? |
| 6. D | 6. C | Did you make few mistakes in grammar? | Was the information accurate? |
| 7. B | 7. C | Was your pronunciation understandable? | Did you address each lecture point? |
| 8. D | 8. C | Did you speak without long pauses? | Did you paraphrase in your own words? |
| 9. D | 9. D | Were the ideas in the talk easy to follow? | Did you use different vocabulary words? |
| 10. B, D, E | 10. D | Did you finish your talk in the time limit? | Did you make few mistakes in grammar? |
| | | | Did you use a variety of sentences? |
| | | **INTEGRATED QUESTION** | Did you save time to edit and correct? |
| | | Did you briefly summarize the reading? | Was the essay easy for someone to read? |
| | | Did you relate the lecture to the reading? | |
| | | Did you paraphrase in your own words? | |
| | | Was the information accurate? | |
| | | Did you use different vocabulary words? | |
| | | Did you make few mistakes in grammar? | |
| | | Was your pronunciation understandable? | |
| | | Did you speak without long pauses? | |
| | | Were the ideas in the talk easy to follow? | |
| | | Did you finish your talk in the time limit? | |

# 8

# PROGRESS TESTS FOR THE TOEFL iBT®

---

## ✔ *Practice taking full-length model tests*

Taking the TOEFL iBT® is like running a marathon. You have to train in order to make it to the finish line. The one-hour practice tests were good training, but now you need to practice taking full-length model tests. You need to be able to go the distance by taking a four-hour test.

> **Reminder:** To access the audio for this section of the test, visit *http://bit.ly/Barrons-TOEFL.*

# MODEL TEST 2: PROGRESS TEST

## READING SECTION

The Reading Section tests your ability to understand reading passages like those in college textbooks. The reading passages are presented in one complete section, which allows you to move to the next passage and return to a previous passage to change answers or answer questions that you may have left blank. The passages are about 700 words in length.

This is the long format for the Reading Section. On the long format, you will read four passages. After each passage, you will answer 12–14 questions about it. You may take notes while you read, but notes are not graded. You may use your notes to answer the questions. Some passages may include a word or phrase that is underlined in blue. Click on the word or phrase to see a glossary definition or explanation. Only three passages will be graded. The other passage is part of an experimental section for future tests. Because you will not know which passages will be graded, you must try to do your best on all of them.

Choose the best answer for multiple-choice questions. Follow the directions on the page or on the screen for computer-assisted questions. Most questions are worth 1 point, but the last question in each passage is worth more than 1 point.

Click on **Next** to go to the next question. Click on **Back** to return to previous questions. You may return to previous questions for all of the passages.

You can click on **Review** to see a chart of the questions you have answered and the questions you have not answered. From this screen, you can return to the question you want to answer.

Although you can spend more time on one passage and less time on another passage, you should try to pace yourself so that you are spending about 20 minutes to read each passage and answer the questions for that passage. You will have 80 minutes to complete all of the passages and answer all of the questions on the long format. A clock on the screen will show you how much time you have to complete the Reading Section.

## *Reading 1*

The following reading passage was adapted from *A Brief History of Canada*, Second Edition by Roger Riendeau, Facts on File, Inc., 2007.

### *"Resources and Industrialism in Canada"*

P1 → While the much-anticipated expansion of the western frontier was unfolding in accordance with the design of the National Policy, a new northern frontier was opening up to enhance the prospects of Canadian industrial development. A Long the preserve of the fur trade, the Canadian Shield and the western Cordilleras became a treasury of minerals, timber and hydroelectric power in the late 19th and early 20th centuries. As early as 1883, CPR [Canadian Pacific Railway] construction crews blasting through the rugged terrain of northern Ontario discovered copper and nickel deposits in the vicinity of Sudbury. B As refining processes, uses, and markets for the metal developed, Sudbury became the world's largest nickel producer. The building of the Temiskaming and Northern Ontario Railway led to the discovery of rich silver deposits around Cobalt north of Lake Nipissing in 1903 and touched off a mining boom that spread northward to Kirkland Lake and the Porcupine district. C Although the economic importance of these mining operations was enduring, they did not capture the public imagination to the same extent as the Klondike gold rush of the late 1890s. D

P2 → Fortune-seekers from all parts of the world flocked to the Klondike and Yukon River valleys to pan for gold starting in 1896. At the height of the gold rush in 1898, the previously unsettled subarctic frontier had a population of about 30,000, more than half of which was concentrated in the newly estab-lished town of Dawson. In the same year, the federal government created the Yukon Territory, administered by an appointed commissioner, in an effort to ward off the prospect of annexation to Alaska. Even if the economic signifi-cance of the Klondike strike was somewhat exaggerated and short-lived, the tales of sudden riches, heroic and tragic exploits, and the rowdiness and law-lessness of the mining frontier were immortalized through popular fiction and folklore, notably the poetic verses of Robert W. Service.

P3 → Perhaps less romantic than the mining booms, the exploitation of forest and water resources was just as vital to national development. The Douglas fir, spruce, and cedar stands of British Columbia along with the white pine forests of Ontario satisfied construction demands on the treeless prairies as well as in the growing cities and towns of central Canada and the United States. British Columbia's forests also supplied lumber to Asia. In addition, the softwood for-est wealth of the Cordilleras and the Shield was a valuable source of pulpwood for the development of the pulp and paper industry, which made Canada one of the world's leading exporters of newsprint. Furthermore, the fast flowing rivers of the Shield and Cordilleras could readily be harnessed as sources of hydroelectric power, replacing coal in the booming factories of central Canada as well as in the evolving mining and pulp and paper industries. The age of electricity under public ownership and control was ushered in by the creation of the Ontario Hydro-Electric Power Commission (now Ontario Hydro) in 1906 to distribute and eventually to produce this vital source of energy.

P4    → Western settlement and the opening of the northern resource frontier stimulated industrial expansion, particularly in central Canada. As the National Policy had intended, a growing agricultural population in the West increased the demand for eastern manufactured goods, thereby giving rise to agricultural implements works, iron and steel foundries, machine shops, railway yards, textile mills, boot and shoe factories, and numerous smaller manufacturing enterprises that supplied consumer goods. By keeping out lower-priced foreign manufactured goods, the high tariff policies of the federal government received much credit for protecting existing industries and encouraging the creation of new enterprises. To climb the tariff wall, large American industrial firms opened branches in Canada, and the governments of Ontario and Quebec aggressively urged them on by offering bonuses, subsidies, and guarantees to locate new plants within their borders. Canadian industrial enterprises became increasingly attractive to foreign investors, especially from the United States and Great Britain. Much of the over $600 million of American capital that flowed into Canada from 1900 to 1913 was earmarked for mining and the pulp and paper industry, while British investors contributed near $1.8 billion, mostly in railway building, business development, and the construction of urban infrastructure. As a result, the gross value of Canadian manufactured products quadrupled from 1891 to 1916.

1. Why does the author mention "the railroads" in paragraph 1?

   Ⓐ Because miners were traveling to camps in the West
   Ⓑ Because mineral deposits were discovered when the railroads were built
   Ⓒ Because the western frontier was being settled by families
   Ⓓ Because traders used the railroads to transport their goods

   Paragraph 1 is marked with an arrow [→].

2. In paragraph 1, how does the author identify Sudbury?

   Ⓐ An important stop on the new railroad line
   Ⓑ A large market for the metals produced in Ontario
   Ⓒ A major industrial center for the production of nickel
   Ⓓ A mining town in the Klondike region

   Paragraph 1 is marked with an arrow [→].

3. The word enduring in the passage is closest in meaning to

   Ⓐ disruptive
   Ⓑ restored
   Ⓒ identifiable
   Ⓓ lasting

4. According to paragraph 2, why was the Yukon Territory created?

    Ⓐ To encourage people to settle the region
    Ⓑ To prevent Alaska from acquiring it
    Ⓒ To establish law and order in the area
    Ⓓ To legalize the mining claims

    Paragraph 2 is marked with an arrow [➜].

5. The word previously in the passage is closest in meaning to

    Ⓐ frequently
    Ⓑ suddenly
    Ⓒ routinely
    Ⓓ formerly

6. How did the poetry by Robert Service contribute to the development of Canada?

    Ⓐ It made the Klondike gold rush famous.
    Ⓑ It encouraged families to settle in the Klondike.
    Ⓒ It captured the beauty of the western Klondike.
    Ⓓ It prevented the Klondike's annexation to Alaska.

7. According to paragraph 3, the forest industry supported the development of Canada in all of the following ways EXCEPT

    Ⓐ by supplying wood for the construction of homes and buildings
    Ⓑ by clearing the land for expanded agricultural uses
    Ⓒ by producing the power for the hydroelectric plants
    Ⓓ by exporting wood and newsprint to foreign markets

    Paragraph 3 is marked with an arrow [➜].

8. The word Furthermore in the passage is closest in meaning to

    Ⓐ Although
    Ⓑ Because
    Ⓒ Therefore
    Ⓓ Moreover

9. The word distribute in the passage is closest in meaning to

    Ⓐ develop
    Ⓑ recognize
    Ⓒ supply
    Ⓓ continue

10. Which of the sentences below best expresses the information in the highlighted statement in the passage? The other choices change the meaning or leave out important information.

    Ⓐ New businesses and industries were created by the federal government to keep the prices of manufactured goods low.
    Ⓑ The lower price of manufacturing attracted many foreign businesses and new industries to the area.
    Ⓒ Federal taxes on cheaper imported goods were responsible for protecting domestic industries and supporting new businesses.
    Ⓓ The federal tax laws made it difficult for manufacturers to sell their goods to foreign markets.

11. According to paragraph 4, why did British and American businesses open affiliates in Canada?

    Ⓐ The Canadian government offered incentives.
    Ⓑ The raw materials were available in Canada.
    Ⓒ The consumers in Canada were eager to buy their goods.
    Ⓓ The infrastructure was attractive to investors.

Paragraph 4 is marked with an arrow [→].

12. Look at the four squares [■] that show where the following sentence could be inserted in the passage.

**Railway construction through the Kootenay region of southeastern British Columbia also led to significant discoveries of gold, silver, copper, lead, and zinc.**

Where could the sentence best be added?

Click on a square [■] to insert the sentence in the passage.

13. **Directions:** An introduction for a short summary of the passage appears below. Complete the summary by selecting the THREE answer choices that mention the most important points in the passage. Some sentences do not belong in the summary because they express ideas that are not included in the passage or are minor points from the passage. *This question is worth 2 points.*

**The northern frontier provided many natural resources that contributed to the industrial expansion of Canada.**

- 
- 
- 

### Answer Choices

A  The Yukon Territory was created in 1898 during the gold rush in the Klondike and Yukon River valleys.

B  The frontier was documented in the popular press, which published tales of heroes and gold strikes.

C  Significant discoveries of mineral deposits encouraged prospectors and settlers to move into the territories.

D  Wheat and other agricultural crops were planted after the forests were cleared, creating the central plains.

E  Powered by hydroelectricity, lumber and paper mills exploited the forests for both domestic and foreign markets.

F  Incentives encouraged American and British investors to help expand manufacturing plants in Canada.

## Reading 2

The following reading passage was adapted from *History of the Theatre*, Tenth Editon by Oscar G. Grockett and Franklin J. Hildy, Allyn and Bacon-Merrill Education, 2008.

### *"Looking at Theatre History"*

P1  → One of the primary ways of approaching the Greek theatre is through archeology, the systematic study of material remains such as architecture, inscriptions, sculpture, vase painting, and other forms of decorative art. A Serious on-site excavations began in Greece around 1870, but W. Dörpfeld did not begin the first extensive study of the Theatre of Dionysus until 1886. B Since that time, more than 167 other Greek theatres have been identified and many of them have been excavated. Ⓒ Nevertheless, they still do not permit us to describe the precise appearance of the *skene* (illustrations printed in books are conjectural reconstructions), since many pieces are irrevocably lost because the buildings in later periods became sources of stone for other projects and what remains is usually broken and scattered. Ⓓ That most of the buildings were remodeled many times has created great problems for those seeking to date the successive versions. Despite these drawbacks, archeology provides the most concrete evidence we have about the theatre structures of ancient Greece. But, if they have told us much, archeologists have not completed their work, and many sites have scarcely been touched.

P2  → Perhaps the most controversial use of archeological evidence in theatre history is vase paintings, thousands of which have survived from ancient Greece. (Most of those used by theatre scholars are reproduced in Margarete Bieber's *The History of the Greek and Roman Theatre*.) Depicting scenes from mythology and daily life, the vases are the most graphic pictorial evidence we have. But they are also easy to misinterpret. Some scholars have considered any vase that depicts a subject treated in a surviving drama or any scene showing masks, flute players, or ceremonials to be valid evidence of theatrical practice. This is a highly questionable assumption, since the Greeks made widespread use of masks, dances, and music outside the theatre and since the myths on which dramatists drew were known to everyone, including vase painters, who might well depict the same subjects as dramatists without being indebted to them. Those vases showing scenes unquestionably theatrical are few in number.

P3  → The texts to classical Greek plays were written down soon after the performance and possibly even before, though it is not always clear when or by whom. By 400 B.C.E., there was a flourishing book trade in Greece, but the texts for plays were a challenge. Hellenistic scholars dedicated years to sorting out the text and removing what they believed to be corruptions generally added by actors, but each time a text was copied there were new possibilities for errors.

P4  → The oldest surviving manuscripts of Greek plays date from around the tenth century C.E., some 1,500 years after they were first performed. Nevertheless, the scripts offer us our readiest access to the cultural and theatrical conditions out of which they came. But these scripts, like other kinds of evidence, are subject to varying interpretations. Certainly performances embodied a male perspective, for example, since the plays were written, selected, staged, and acted by men. Yet the existing plays feature numerous choruses of women and many feature strong female characters. Because these characters often seem victims of their own powerlessness and appear to be governed, especially in the comedies, by sexual desire, some critics have seen these plays as rationalizations by the male-dominated culture for keeping women segregated and cloistered. Other critics, however, have seen in these same plays an attempt by male authors to force their male audiences to examine and call into question this segregation and cloistering of Athenian women.

P5   → By far the majority of written references to Greek theatre date from several hundred years after the events they report. The writers seldom mention their sources of evidence, and thus we do not know what credence to give them. In the absence of material nearer in time to the events, however, historians have used the accounts and have been grateful to have them. Overall, historical treatment of the Greek theatre is something like assembling a jigsaw puzzle from which many pieces are missing: historians arrange what they have and imagine (with the aid of the remaining evidence and logic) what has been lost. As a result, though the broad outlines of Greek theatre history are reasonably clear, many of the details remain open to doubt.

**Glossary**

skene: a stage building where actors store their masks and change their costumes

14. According to paragraph 1, why is it impossible to identify the time period for theatres in Greece?

    Ⓐ There are too few sites that have been excavated and very little data collected about them.
    Ⓑ The archeologists from earlier periods were not careful, and many artifacts were broken.
    Ⓒ It is confusing because stones from early sites were used to build later structures.
    Ⓓ Because it is very difficult to date the concrete that was used in construction during early periods.

    Paragraph 1 is marked with an arrow [→].

15. What can be inferred from paragraph 1 about the *skene* in theatre history?

    Ⓐ Drawings in books are the only accurate visual records.
    Ⓑ Not enough evidence is available to make a precise model.
    Ⓒ Archeologists have excavated a large number of them.
    Ⓓ It was not identified or studied until the early 1800s.

    Paragraph 1 is marked with an arrow [→].

16. The word primary in the passage is closest in meaning to

    Ⓐ reliable
    Ⓑ important
    Ⓒ unusual
    Ⓓ accepted

17. The word precise in the passage is closest in meaning to

    Ⓐ attractive
    Ⓑ simple
    Ⓒ difficult
    Ⓓ exact

18. In paragraph 2, how does the author explain that all vases with paintings of masks or musicians may not be evidence of theatrical subjects?

    Ⓐ By arguing that the subjects could have been used by artists without reference to a drama

    Ⓑ By identifying some of the vases as reproductions that were painted years after the originals

    Ⓒ By casting doubt on the qualifications of the scholars who produced the vases as evidence

    Ⓓ By pointing out that there are very few vases that have survived from the time of early dramas

    Paragraph 2 is marked with an arrow [➜].

19. The word controversial in the passage is closest in meaning to

    Ⓐ accepted

    Ⓑ debated

    Ⓒ limited

    Ⓓ complicated

20. Which of the following statements most accurately reflects the author's opinion about vase paintings?

    Ⓐ Evidence from written documents is older than evidence from vase paintings.

    Ⓑ The sources for vase paintings are clear because of the images on them.

    Ⓒ The details in vase paintings are not obvious because of their age.

    Ⓓ There is disagreement among scholars regarding vase paintings.

21. According to paragraph 3, scripts of plays may not be accurate for which reason?

    Ⓐ The sources cited are not well known.

    Ⓑ Copies by hand may contain many errors.

    Ⓒ They are written in very old language.

    Ⓓ The printing is difficult to read.

    Paragraph 3 is marked with an arrow [➜].

22. In paragraph 4, what does the author state about female characters in Greek theatre?

    Ⓐ They had no featured parts in plays.

    Ⓑ They were mostly ignored by critics.

    Ⓒ They did not participate in the chorus.

    Ⓓ They frequently played the part of victims.

    Paragraph 4 is marked with an arrow [➜].

23. The word Overall in the passage is closest in meaning to

    Ⓐ Supposedly

    Ⓑ Generally

    Ⓒ Occasionally

    Ⓓ Finally

24. Why does the author mention a "jigsaw puzzle" in paragraph 5?

  Ⓐ To demonstrate the difficulty in drawing conclusions from partial evidence
  Ⓑ To compare the written references for plays to the paintings on vases
  Ⓒ To justify using accounts and records that historians have located
  Ⓓ To introduce the topic for the next reading passage in the textbook

  Paragraph 5 is marked with an arrow [→].

25. Look at the four squares [■] that show where the following sentence could be inserted in the passage.

**These excavations have revealed much that was previously unknown, especially about the dimensions and layout of theatres.**

Where could the sentence best be added?

Click on a square [■] to insert the sentence in the passage.

26. **Directions:** An introduction for a short summary of the passage appears below. Complete the summary by selecting the THREE answer choices that mention the most important points in the passage. Some sentences do not belong in the summary because they express ideas that are not included in the passage or are minor points from the passage. *This question is worth 2 points.*

**Greek theatre has been studied by a variety of methods.**

  ●

  ●

  ●

**Answer Choices**

Ⓐ Because the Greeks enjoyed dancing and music for entertainment outside of the theatre, many scenes on vases are ambiguous.

Ⓑ Historical accounts assembled many years after the actual theatrical works were presented give us a broad perspective of the earlier theatre.

Ⓒ Although considered less reliable, written records, including scripts, provide insights into the cultural aspects of theatre.

Ⓓ Archeological excavations have uncovered buildings and artifacts, many of which were vases with theatrical scenes painted on them.

Ⓔ For the most part, men wrote the plays for Greek theatre, but choruses and even strong roles were played by women.

Ⓕ Computer simulations can recreate the image of a building that is crumbling as long as the dimensions and layout are known.

### Reading 3

The following reading passage was adapted from *Environmental Science: Earth as a Living Planet*, Sixth Edition by Daniel B. Botkin and Edward A. Keller, John Wiley and Sons, 2007.

### "Geothermal Energy"

**P1** → Geothermal energy is natural heat from the interior of the Earth that is converted to heat buildings and generate electricity. The idea of harnessing Earth's internal heat is not new. As early as 1904, geothermal power was used in Italy. Today, Earth's natural internal heat is being used to generate electricity in 21 countries, including Russia, Japan, New Zealand, Iceland, Mexico, Ethiopia, Guatemala, El Salvador, the Philippines, and the United States. Total worldwide production is approaching 9,000 MW (equivalent to nine large modern coal-burning or nuclear power plants)—double the amount in 1980. Some 40 million people today receive their electricity from geothermal energy at a cost competitive with that of alternative energy sources. In El Salvador, geothermal energy is supplying 30% of the total electric energy used. However, at the global level, geothermal energy supplies less than 0.15% of the total energy supply.

**P2** → Geothermal energy may be considered a nonrenewable energy source when rates of extraction are greater than rates of natural replenishment. However, geothermal energy has its origin in the natural heat production within Earth, and only a small fraction of the vast total resource base is being utilized today. Although most geothermal energy production involves the tapping of high heat sources, people are also using the low-temperature geothermal energy of groundwater in some applications.

### Geothermal Systems

**P3** → A The average heat flow from the interior of the Earth is very low, about 0.06 W/m$^2$. B This amount is trivial compared with the 177 W/m$^2$ from solar heat at the surface in the United States. However, in some areas, heat flow is sufficiently high to be useful for producing energy. For the most part, areas of high heat flow are associated with plate tectonic boundaries. Oceanic ridge systems (divergent plate boundaries) and areas where mountains are being uplifted and volcanic island arcs are forming (convergent plate boundaries) are areas where this natural heat flow is anomalously high. C

**P4** On the basis of geological criteria, several types of hot geothermal systems (with temperatures greater than about 80°C, or 176°F) have been defined, and the resource base is larger than that of fossil fuels and nuclear energy combined. A common system for energy development is hydrothermal convection, characterized by the circulation of steam and/or hot water that transfers heat from depths to the surface. D

### Geothermal Energy and the Environment

**P5** → The environmental impact of geothermal energy may not be as extensive as that of other sources of energy. When geothermal energy is developed at a particular site, environmental problems include on-site noise, emissions of gas, and disturbance of the land at drilling sites, disposal sites, roads and pipelines, and power plants. Development of geothermal energy does not require large-scale transportation of raw materials or refining of chemicals, as development of fossil fuels does. Furthermore, geothermal energy does not produce the atmospheric pollutants associated with burning fossil fuels or the radioactive waste associated with nuclear energy. However, geothermal development often does produce considerable thermal pollution from hot waste-waters, which may be saline or highly corrosive.

P6    → Geothermal power is not always popular. For instance, geothermal energy has been produced for years on the island of Hawaii, where active volcanic processes provide abundant near-surface heat. There is controversy, however, over further exploration and development. Native Hawaiians and others have argued that the exploration and development of geothermal energy degrade the tropical forest as developers construct roads, build facilities, and drill wells. In addition, religious and cultural issues in Hawaii relate to the use of geothermal energy. For example, some people are offended by using the "breath and water of Pele" (the volcano goddess) to make electricity. This issue points out the importance of being sensitive to the values and cultures of people where development is planned.

**Future of Geothermal Energy**

P7    At present, the United States produces only 2,800 MN of geothermal energy. However, if developed, known geothermal resources in the United States could produce about 20,000 MW, which is about 10% of the electricity needed for the western states. Geohydrothermal resources not yet discovered could conservatively provide four times that amount (approximately 10% of total U.S. electric capacity), about equivalent to the electricity produced from water power today.

27. In paragraph 1, how does the author introduce the concept of geothermal energy?

    Ⓐ By explaining the history of this energy source worldwide
    Ⓑ By arguing that this energy source has been tried unsuccessfully
    Ⓒ By comparing the production with that of other energy sources
    Ⓓ By describing the alternatives for generating electric power

    Paragraph 1 is marked with an arrow [→].

28. What is true about geothermal energy production worldwide?

    Ⓐ Because it is a new idea, very few countries are developing geothermal energy sources.
    Ⓑ Only countries in the Southern Hemisphere are using geothermal energy on a large scale.
    Ⓒ Until the cost of geothermal energy becomes competitive, it will not be used globally.
    Ⓓ Geothermal energy is already being used in a number of nations, but it is not yet a major source of power.

29. The word approaching in the passage is closest in meaning to

    (A) hardly
    (B) mostly
    (C) nearly
    (D) briefly

30. The word alternative in the passage is closest in meaning to

    (A) numerous
    (B) optional
    (C) nearby
    (D) equivalent

31. In paragraph 2, why does the author state that geothermal energy is considered a nonrenewable resource?

    (A) The production of geothermal energy is a natural process.
    (B) Geothermal energy comes from the Earth.
    (C) We are not using very much geothermal energy now.
    (D) We could use more geothermal energy than is naturally replaced.

Paragraph 2 is marked with an arrow [→].

32. Which of the sentences below best expresses the information in the highlighted statement in the passage? The other choices change the meaning or leave out important information.

    (A) High heat is the source of most of the geothermal energy but low heat groundwater is also used sometimes.
    (B) Even though low temperatures are possible, high heat is the best resource for energy production for groundwater.
    (C) Both high heat and low heat sources are used for the production of geothermal energy from groundwater.
    (D) Most high heat sources for geothermal energy are tapped from applications that involve low heat in groundwater.

33. According to paragraph 3, which statement is true about the heat flow necessary for the production of geothermal energy?

    (A) It is like solar heat on the Earth's surface.
    (B) It happens near tectonic plate boundaries.
    (C) It must always be artificially increased.
    (D) It may be impractical because of its location.

Paragraph 3 is marked with an arrow [→].

34. The word considerable in the passage is closest in meaning to

    Ⓐ large
    Ⓑ dangerous
    Ⓒ steady
    Ⓓ unexpected

35. In paragraph 5, why does the author mention the "atmospheric pollution" and "waste" for fossil fuel and nuclear power?

    Ⓐ To introduce the discussion of pollution caused by geothermal energy development and production
    Ⓑ To contrast pollution caused by fossil fuels and nuclear power with pollution caused by geothermal energy
    Ⓒ To argue that geothermal production does not cause pollution like other sources of energy do
    Ⓓ To discourage the use of raw materials and chemicals in the production of energy because of pollution

    Paragraph 5 is marked with an arrow [➜].

36. According to paragraph 6, the production of geothermal energy in Hawaii is controversial for all of the following reasons EXCEPT

    Ⓐ the volcanoes in Hawaii could be disrupted by the rapid release of geothermal energy.
    Ⓑ the rainforest might be damaged during the construction of the geothermal energy plant
    Ⓒ the native people are concerned that geothermal energy is disrespectful to their cultural traditions
    Ⓓ some Hawaiians oppose using geothermal energy because of their religious beliefs

    Paragraph 6 is marked with an arrow [➜].

37. What is the author's opinion of geothermal energy?

    Ⓐ Geothermal energy has some disadvantages, but it is probably going to be used in the future.
    Ⓑ Geothermal energy is a source that should be explored further before large-scale production begins.
    Ⓒ Geothermal energy offers an opportunity to supply a significant amount of power in the future.
    Ⓓ Geothermal energy should replace water power in the production of electricity for the United States.

38. Look at the four squares [■] that show where the following sentence could be inserted in the passage.

**One such region is located in the western United States, where recent tectonic and volcanic activity has occurred.**

Where could the sentence best be added?

Click on a square [■] to insert the sentence in the passage.

39. **Directions:** An introduction for a short summary of the passage appears below. Complete the summary by selecting the THREE answer choices that mention the most important points in the passage. Some sentences do not belong in the summary because they express ideas that are not included in the passage or are minor points from the passage. *This question is worth 2 points.*

**Geothermal energy is natural heat from the interior of the Earth that is converted to electricity.**

- 
- 
- 

## Answer Choices

A Geothermal energy sources that convert natural heat to electricity account for 30% of the total energy supply in El Salvador at relatively competitive cost to the consumers.

B Although geothermal energy is nonrenewable when more is used than can be replaced naturally, only a small amount of the potential energy is being exploited worldwide.

C The heat from geothermal sites is thought to be the breath and water of the volcanic goddess Pele, worshiped by some native groups on the Hawaiian Islands.

D Hot geothermal systems at both divergent plate boundaries and convergent plate boundaries could provide more energy than fossil fuels and nuclear power.

E Some groups oppose the exploitation of geothermal sources because of pollution and other environmental problems or because of their cultural values.

F Thermal waste water can be very corrosive or can contain high levels of saline, which causes problems in disposal and water treatment at development sites.

### Reading 4

The following reading passage was adapted from *Out of Many: A History of the American People, Combined Volume*, Fifth Edition by John Mack Faragher, et. al., Pearson Education, Inc., 2006.

### *"Migration from Asia"*

P1    The Asian migration hypothesis is today supported by most of the scientific evidence. The first "hard" data linking American Indians with Asians appeared in the 1980s with the finding that Indians and northeast Asians share a common and distinctive pattern in the arrangement of the teeth. But perhaps the most compelling support for the hypothesis comes from genetic research. Studies comparing the DNA variation of populations around the world consistently demonstrate the close genetic relationship of the two populations, and recently geneticists studying a virus sequestered in the kidneys of all humans found that the strain of virus carried by Navajos and Japanese is nearly identical, while that carried by Europeans and Africans is quite different.

P2    → The migration could have begun over a land bridge connecting the continents. During the last Ice Age 70,000 to 10,000 years ago, huge glaciers locked up massive volumes of water and sea levels were as much as 300 feet lower than today. Asia and North America were joined by a huge subcontinent of ice-free, treeless grassland, 750 miles wide. Geologists have named this area Beringia, from the Bering Strait. Summers there were warm; winters were cold, dry, and almost snow-free. This was a perfect environment for large mammals—mammoth and mastodon, bison, horse, reindeer, camel, and saiga (a goatlike antelope). Small bands of Stone Age hunter-gatherers were attracted by these animal populations, which provided them not only with food but also with hides for clothing and shelter, dung for fuel, and bones for tools and weapons. Accompanied by a husky-like species of dog, hunting bands gradually moved as far east as the Yukon River basin of northern Canada, where field excavations have uncovered the fossilized jawbones of several dogs and bone tools estimated to be about 27,000 years old.

P3    → Other evidence suggests that the migration from Asia began about 30,000 years ago—around the same time that Japan and Scandinavia were being settled. This evidence is based on blood type. The vast majority of modern Native Americans have type O blood and a few have type A, but almost none have type B. Because modern Asian populations include all three blood types, however, the migrations must have begun before the evolution of type B, which geneticists believe occurred about 30,000 years ago.

P4    By 25,000 years ago human communities were established in western Beringia, which is present-day Alaska. Ⓐ But access to the south was blocked by a huge glacial sheet covering much of what is today Canada. How did the hunters get over those 2,000 miles of deep ice? The argument is that the climate began to warm with the passing of the Ice Age, and about 13,000 B.C.E. glacial melting created an ice-free corridor along the eastern front range of the Rocky Mountains. Ⓑ Soon hunters of big game had reached the Great Plains.

P5    → In the past several years, however, new archaeological finds along the Pacific coast of North and South America have thrown this theory into question. C The most spectacular find, at Monte Verde in southern Chile, produced striking evidence of tool making, house building, rock painting, and human footprints conservatively dated long before the highway had been cleared of ice. D Many archaeologists now believe that migrants moved south in boats along a coastal route rather than overland. These people were probably gatherers and fishers rather than hunters of big game.

P6    → There were two later migrations into North America. About 5000 B.C.E. the Athapascan or Na-Dene people began to settle the forests in the northwestern area of the continent. Eventually Athapascan speakers, the ancestors of the Navajos and Apaches, migrated across the Great Plains to the Southwest. The final migration began about 3000 B.C.E. after Beringia had been submerged, when a maritime hunting people crossed the Bering Strait in small boats. The Inuits (also known as the Eskimos) colonized the polar coasts of the Arctic, the Yupiks the coast of southwestern Alaska, and the Aleuts the Aleutian Islands.

P7    While scientists debate the timing and mapping of these migrations, many Indian people hold to oral traditions that include a long journey from a distant place of origin to a new homeland.

40. The word distinctive in the passage is closest in meaning to

   Ⓐ new
   Ⓑ simple
   Ⓒ different
   Ⓓ particular

41. According to paragraph 2, why did Stone Age tribes begin to migrate into Beringia?

   Ⓐ To intermarry with tribes living there
   Ⓑ To trade with tribes that made tools
   Ⓒ To hunt for animals in the area
   Ⓓ To capture domesticated dogs

   Paragraph 2 is marked with an arrow [→].

42. The phrase Accompanied by in the passage is closest in meaning to

   Ⓐ Found with
   Ⓑ Joined by
   Ⓒ Threatened by
   Ⓓ Detoured with

43. The word estimated in the passage is closest in meaning to

    Ⓐ clarified
    Ⓑ judged
    Ⓒ changed
    Ⓓ noticed

44. Why does the author mention "blood types" in paragraph 3?

    Ⓐ Blood types offered proof that the migration had come from Scandinavia.
    Ⓑ The presence of type B in Native Americans was evidence of the migration.
    Ⓒ The blood typing was similar to data from both Japan and Scandinavia.
    Ⓓ Comparisons of blood types in Asia and North America established the date of migration.

Paragraph 3 is marked with an arrow [➜].

45. How did groups migrate into the Great Plains?

    Ⓐ By walking on a corridor covered with ice
    Ⓑ By using the path that big game had made
    Ⓒ By detouring around a huge ice sheet
    Ⓓ By following a mountain trail

46. Why does the author mention the settlement at Monte Verde, Chile, in paragraph 5?

    Ⓐ The remains of boats suggest that people may have lived there.
    Ⓑ Artifacts suggest that humans reached this area before the ice melted on land.
    Ⓒ Bones and footprints from large animals confirm that the people were hunters.
    Ⓓ The houses and tools excavated prove that the early humans were intelligent.

Paragraph 5 is marked with an arrow [➜].

47. The word Eventually in the passage is closest in meaning to

    Ⓐ In the end
    Ⓑ Nevertheless
    Ⓒ Without doubt
    Ⓓ In this way

48. Which of the sentences below best expresses the information in the highlighted statement in the passage? The other choices change the meaning or leave out important information.

   Ⓐ Beringia was under water when the last people crossed the straits in boats about 3000 B.C.E.
   Ⓑ Beringia sank after the last people had crossed the straits in their boats about 3000 B.C.E.
   Ⓒ About 3000 B.C.E., the final migration of people in small boats across Beringia had ended.
   Ⓓ About 3000 B.C.E., Beringia was flooded, preventing the last people from migrating in small boats.

49. According to paragraph 6, all of the following are true about the later migrations EXCEPT

   Ⓐ the Athapascans traveled into the Southwest United States
   Ⓑ the Inuit established homes in the Arctic polar region
   Ⓒ the Aleuts migrated in small boats to settle coastal islands
   Ⓓ the Yupiks established settlements on the Great Plains

   Paragraph 6 is marked with an arrow [➔].

50. Which of the following statements most accurately reflects the author's opinion about the settlement of the North American continent?

   Ⓐ The oral traditions do not support the migration theory.
   Ⓑ The anthropological evidence for migration should be reexamined.
   Ⓒ Migration theories are probably not valid explanations for the physical evidence.
   Ⓓ Genetic markers are the best evidence of a migration from Asia.

51. Look at the four squares [■] that show where the following sentence could be inserted in the passage.

   **Newly excavated early human sites in Washington State, California, and Peru have been radiocarbon dated to be 11,000 to 12,000 years old.**

   Where could the sentence best be added?

   Click on a square [■] to insert the sentence in the passage.

52. **Directions:** An introduction for a short summary of the passage appears below. Complete the summary by selecting the THREE answer choices that mention the most important points in the passage. Some sentences do not belong in the summary because they express ideas that are not included in the passage or are minor points from the passage. **This question is worth 2 points.**

**There is considerable evidence supporting a theory of multiple migrations from Asia to the Americas.**

- 
- 
- 

### Answer Choices

Ⓐ Ancient stories of migrations from a far-away place are common in the cultures of many Native American nations.

Ⓑ The people who inhabited Monte Verde in southern Chile were a highly evolved culture as evidenced by their tools and homes.

Ⓒ Genetic similarities between Native American peoples and Asians include the arrangement of teeth, viruses, and blood types.

Ⓓ Hunters followed the herds of big game from Beringia south along the Rocky Mountains into what is now called the Great Plains.

Ⓔ Excavations at archaeological sites provide artifacts that can be used to date the various migrations that occurred by land and sea.

Ⓕ The climate began to get warmer and warmer, melting the glacial ice about 13,000 B.C.E.

# LISTENING SECTION

 **Model Test 2, Listening Section, Track 69**

The Listening Section tests your ability to understand spoken English that is typical of inter-actions and academic speech on college campuses. During the test, you will listen to conver-sations, lectures, and discussions, and you will answer questions about them.

This is the short format for the Listening Section. On the short format, you will listen to two conversations, two lectures, and two discussions. After each listening passage, you will answer 5–6 questions about it.

You will hear each passage one time. You may take notes while you listen, but notes are not graded. You may use your notes to answer the questions.

Choose the best answer for multiple-choice questions. Follow the directions on the page or on the screen for computer-assisted questions. Click on **Next** and then on **OK** to go on to the next question. You cannot return to previous questions.

The Listening Section is divided into sets. Each set includes one conversation, one lecture, and one discussion. You will have 10 minutes to answer all of the questions for each set. You will have 20 minutes to answer all of the questions on the short format. A clock on the screen will show you how much time you have to complete your answers for the section. The clock does NOT count the time you are listening to the conversations, lectures, and discussions.

## *Listening 1 "Professor's Office"*

1. Why does the man go to see his professor?

   Ⓐ To prepare for the next midterm
   Ⓑ To clarify a question from the midterm
   Ⓒ To find out his grade on the midterm
   Ⓓ To complain about his grade on the midterm

2. Why does the man say this:

   Ⓐ He is giving something to the professor.
   Ⓑ He is trying to justify his position.
   Ⓒ He is apologizing because he does not understand.
   Ⓓ He is signaling that he will explain his problem.

3. What did the man do wrong?

   Ⓐ He did not finish the test within the time limit.
   Ⓑ He did not study enough before the test.
   Ⓒ He did not answer one question completely.
   Ⓓ He did not understand a major concept.

4. According to the student, what is *divergent evolution*?

     Ⓐ A population that evolves differently does not have a common ancestor.
     Ⓑ A similar environment can affect the evolution of different species.
     Ⓒ A similar group that is separated may develop different characteristics.
     Ⓓ The climate of an area will allow scientists to predict the life forms.

5. What will Jerry probably do on the next test?

     Ⓐ He will look for questions with several parts.
     Ⓑ He will read the entire test before he begins.
     Ⓒ He will ask for more time to finish.
     Ⓓ He will write an outline for each essay.

## *Listening 2 "Art History Class"*

6. What is the main topic of this lecture?

Ⓐ The process of fixing a photograph
Ⓑ The problem of exposure time
Ⓒ The experiments by Louis Daguerre
Ⓓ The history of early photography

7. According to the professor, what two limitations were noted in Daguerre's process for developing and fixing latent images?

Click on 2 answer choices.

Ⓐ The photograph disappeared after a few minutes.

Ⓑ The images were very delicate and easily fell apart.

Ⓒ Multiple images could not be made from the plate.

Ⓓ The exposure time was still several hours long.

8. Why does the professor say this:

Ⓐ He is trying to generate interest in the topic.
Ⓑ He makes reference to a story in the textbook.
Ⓒ He is not sure whether the information is accurate.
Ⓓ He wants the students to use their imaginations.

9. What substance was first used to fix the images?

    Ⓐ Copper powder
    Ⓑ Table salt
    Ⓒ Mercury vapor
    Ⓓ Hot water

10. What can we assume about photographers in the 1800s?

    Ⓐ Most of them had originally been painters before they became interested in photography.
    Ⓑ Portrait photographers were in the highest demand since people wanted images of their families.
    Ⓒ There were only a few photographers who were willing to work in such a new profession.
    Ⓓ Some of them must have experienced health problems as a result of their laboratory work.

11. In what order does the professor explain photographic principles?

    Ⓐ From the least to the most important facts
    Ⓑ In a chronological sequence of events
    Ⓒ The order of the steps in the photographic process
    Ⓓ The advantages before the disadvantages

### Listening 3 "Linguistics Class"

12. What is the discussion mainly about?

&#9398; The history of the English language
&#9399; Different types of grammar
&#9400; A linguistic perspective for Latin
&#9401; Standard language in schools

13. How does the professor make his point about *native intuition*?

&#9398; He explains how to perform an easy experiment.
&#9399; He tells the class about his personal experience.
&#9400; He provides several examples of sentences.
&#9401; He contrasts it with non-native intuition.

14. What are two key problems for descriptive grammar?

Click on 2 answer choices.

&#9398; The information is very complicated and subject to change.

&#9399; The formal language must be enforced in all situations.

&#9400; The language can be organized correctly in more than one way.

&#9401; The description takes time because linguists must agree.

15. Why does the student say this: 🎧

    Ⓐ She is disagreeing with the professor.
    Ⓑ She is confirming that she has understood.
    Ⓒ She is trying to impress the other students.
    Ⓓ She is adding information to the lecture.

16. According to the professor, why were Latin rules used for English grammar?

    Ⓐ Latin was a written language with rules that did not change.
    Ⓑ The Romans had conquered England and enforced using Latin.
    Ⓒ English and Latin had many vocabulary words in common.
    Ⓓ English was taking the place of Latin among educated Europeans.

17. Why does the professor discuss the rule to avoid ending a sentence with a preposition?

    Ⓐ It is a good example of the way that descriptive grammar is used.
    Ⓑ It shows the students how to use formal grammar in their speech.
    Ⓒ It is a way to introduce a humorous story into the lecture.
    Ⓓ It demonstrates the problem in using Latin rules for English.

## Listening 4 "Admissions Office"

18. Why is the woman on campus?

    Ⓐ She works in one of the offices.
    Ⓑ She is training to be a group leader.
    Ⓒ She is taking a tour of the college.
    Ⓓ She is being interviewed for admission.

19. What is the admissions officer's opinion of the woman's group leader?

    Ⓐ He believes that the group leader is very good.
    Ⓑ He thinks the group leader should answer questions.
    Ⓒ He does not remember the group leader's name.
    Ⓓ He says that the group leader has too many students.

20. What are the woman's concerns about the school?

    Click on 2 answer choices.

    Ⓐ Class size

    Ⓑ Teaching assistants

    Ⓒ Major fields

    Ⓓ Admission requirements

21. Why do some students take more than four years to graduate?

    Ⓐ Their advisor does not approve their programs.
    Ⓑ They do not take courses in the summer.
    Ⓒ Graduate students teach the classes.
    Ⓓ They change their major fields of study.

22. Why does the student say this:

    Ⓐ She is agreeing with the admissions officer.
    Ⓑ She is worried that a full load will be too much.
    Ⓒ She is surprised that students don't study full time.
    Ⓓ She is doubtful that the information is correct.

## Listening 5 "Zoology Class"

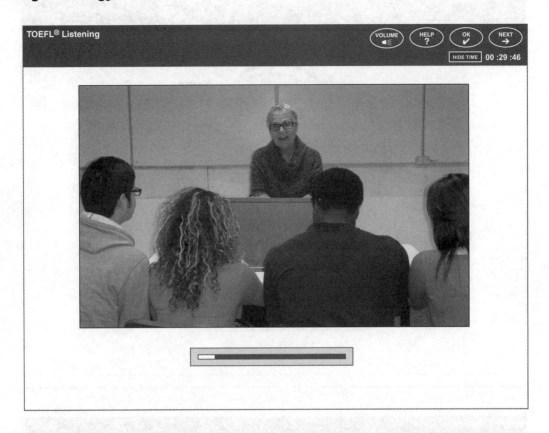

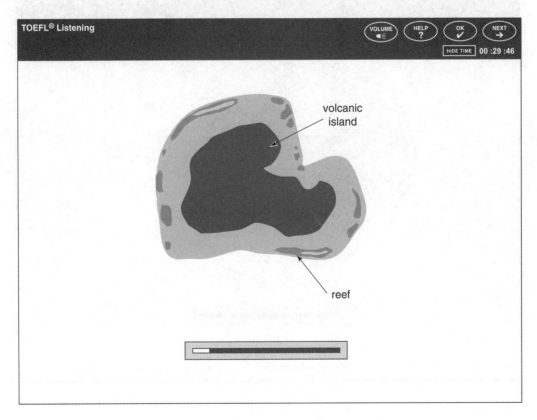

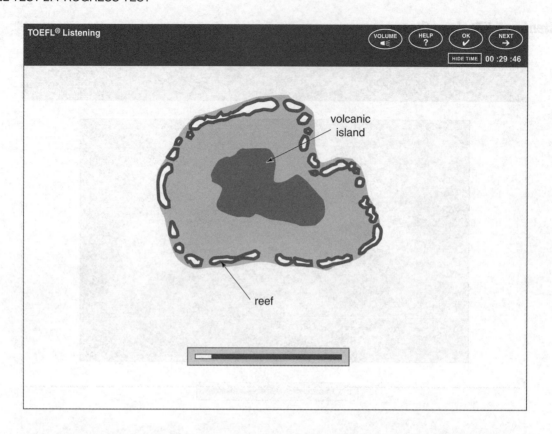

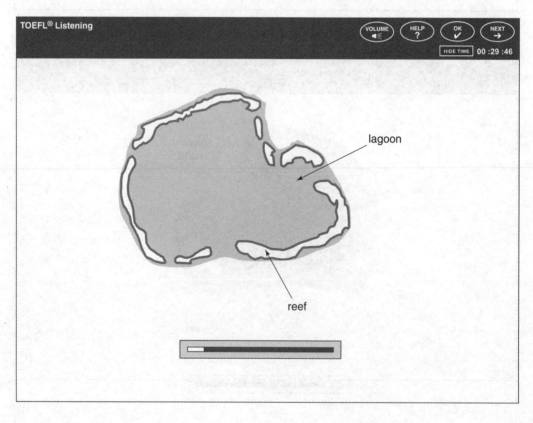

23. According to the professor, how do coral reefs grow?

    Ⓐ They become very large by eating other species.
    Ⓑ They connect corralite shells to build structures.
    Ⓒ They fill with ocean water to expand their size.
    Ⓓ They collect debris from ocean life in their habitat.

24. Why are so many egg bundles released during mass spawning?

    Ⓐ Some of the egg bundles will not be fertilized.
    Ⓑ Half of the egg bundles will not float.
    Ⓒ A number of the egg bundles will be eaten.
    Ⓓ Most of the egg bundles will break open.

25. According to the professor, what is *budding*?

    Ⓐ The division of a polyp in half to reproduce itself
    Ⓑ The growth of limestone between the shells of polyps
    Ⓒ The diversity that occurs within a coral reef
    Ⓓ The increase in size of a polyp as it matures

26. What is the relationship between zooxanthella and coral polyps?

Click on 2 answer choices.

    A  The coral and the zooxanthella compete for the same food.

    B  The zooxanthella uses the coral for a shelter from enemies.

    C  The coral eats food produced by the zooxanthella.

    D  The same predators attack both coral and zooxanthella.

27. Which of the following reefs is probably an atoll?

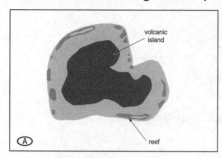

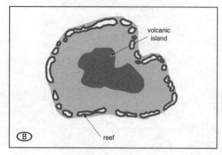

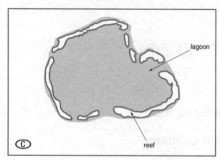

28. In the lecture, the professor explains coral reefs. Indicate whether each of the following is a true statement about coral reefs. Click in the correct box for each phrase.

| | | Yes | No |
|---|---|---|---|
| A | In general, the organism is quite simple. | | |
| B | The structure of a reef can be very large. | | |
| C | The living coral grows on top of dead shells. | | |
| D | Mass spawning is not very effective. | | |

## *Listening 6 "Business Class"*

29. What is the discussion mainly about?

    Ⓐ Global marketing of food products
    Ⓑ International business in Europe
    Ⓒ Surprises in food preferences abroad
    Ⓓ Packaging food for exportation

30. How does the professor organize the discussion?

    Ⓐ He compares domestic and foreign products.
    Ⓑ He relates the textbook to his professional experience.
    Ⓒ He refers to case studies from the textbook.
    Ⓓ He presents information from most to least important.

31. Why does the student say this:

    Ⓐ She is asking the professor a question about his previous point.
    Ⓑ She is offering a possible answer to the professor's question.
    Ⓒ She is changing the subject of the class discussion.
    Ⓓ She is checking her comprehension of the professor's opinion.

32. What technique does the professor use to encourage student discussion?

    Ⓐ He gives students positive reinforcement by praising their efforts.
    Ⓑ He asks the students to talk among themselves in small groups.
    Ⓒ He assigns a different part of the textbook to each student.
    Ⓓ He calls on each student by name to contribute to the discussion.

33. What did Ted Levitt mean by "the pluralization of consumption"?

     Ⓐ More people would begin to travel.
     Ⓑ More multinational corporations would produce brands.
     Ⓒ More consumers will have the means to afford goods.
     Ⓓ More people will want the same products.

34. What does the professor say about television and movie companies?

     Ⓐ He indicates that some companies hire foreign marketing experts.
     Ⓑ He criticizes the way that they advertise their programs and films.
     Ⓒ He notes that they are one of the most widely distributed exports.
     Ⓓ He points out that they are paid to display brand-name products.

 **Please turn off the audio. There is a 10-minute break between the Listening Section and the Speaking Section.**

# SPEAKING SECTION

 **Model Test 2, Speaking Section, Track 70**

The Speaking Section tests your ability to communicate in English in an academic setting. During the test, you will be presented with six speaking questions. The questions ask for a response to a single question, a conversation, a talk, or a lecture. The prompts and questions are presented only one time.

You may take notes as you listen, but notes are not graded. You may use your notes to answer the questions. Some of the questions ask for a response to a reading passage and a talk or a lecture. The reading passages and the questions are written, but the directions will be spoken.

Your speaking will be evaluated on both the fluency of the language and the accuracy of the content. You will have 15–20 seconds to prepare and 45–60 seconds to respond to each question. Typically, a good response will require all of the response time and the answer will be complete by the end of the response time.

You will have about 20 minutes to complete the Speaking Section. A clock on the screen will show you how much time you have to prepare each of your answers and how much time you have to record each response.

## *Independent Speaking Question 1 "Regret"*

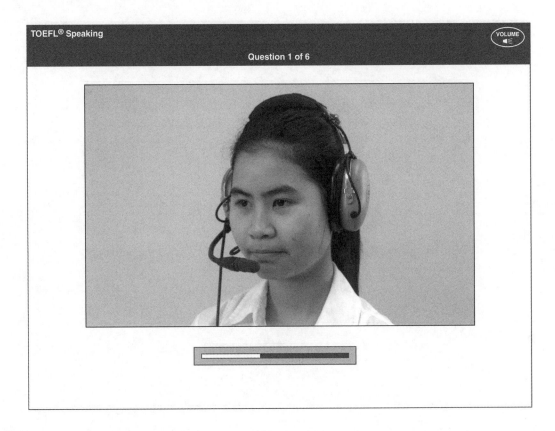

  Listen for a question about a familiar topic.

**Question**

Explain a situation in the past when you have regretted your decision. What would you do differently?

Preparation Time: 15 seconds
Recording Time: 45 seconds

*Independent Speaking Question 2 "Course Requirements"*

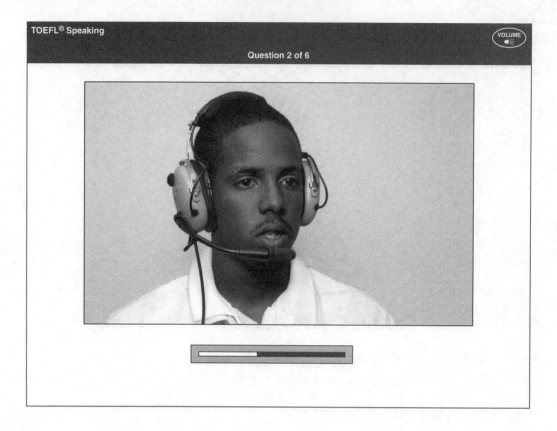

 Listen for a question that asks your opinion about a familiar topic.

**Question**
Some students would rather write a paper than take a test. Other students would rather take a test instead of writing a paper. Which option do you prefer, and why? Use specific reasons and examples to support your opinion.

Preparation Time: 15 seconds
Recording Time: 45 seconds

## *Integrated Speaking Question 3 "Health Insurance"*

Read a short passage and listen to a talk on the same topic.

Reading Time: 45 seconds

---

Health Insurance

All students may purchase health insurance at the time of registration by marking the insurance box on the course request form. Those students who choose not to use the health insurance option may still use the services of the Student Health Center, but their accounts must be settled at the time of each visit, and the alternative health insurance carrier must be billed directly by the students for reimbursement. International students are required to purchase student health insurance from the university and will be charged automatically at registration. Alternative health insurance carriers may not be substituted. No exceptions will be made.

---

 Now listen to the foreign student advisor. He is explaining the policy and expressing his opinion about it.

**Question**

The foreign student advisor expresses his opinion of the policy for health insurance. Report his opinion and explain the reasons that he gives for having that opinion.

Preparation Time: 30 seconds
Recording Time: 60 seconds

### *Integrated Speaking Question 4 "Choice"*

Read a short passage and then listen to part of a lecture on the same topic.

Reading Time: 45 seconds

---

<u>Paradox of Choice</u>

   It seems reasonable that more choices should lead to greater satisfaction; however, Barry Schwartz argues the opposite. According to Schwartz's book *Paradox of Choice* and the large number of research studies that were undertaken as a result, too many choices can actually cause unreasonably high expectations, uncertainty, and even paralysis, that is, the inability to arrive at any decision. According to Schwartz, an abundance of choices is exhausting to the human psyche and can undermine happiness, which may explain why, in societies that offer personal, professional, and material freedom of choice, so many people experience depression.

---

 Now listen to part of a lecture in a psychology class. The professor is talking about choice.

**Question**
Using the study from the lecture, explain the paradox of choice.

Preparation Time: 30 seconds
Recording Time: 60 seconds

## Integrated Speaking Question 5 "Extra Money"

 Now listen to a conversation between a student and her friend.

**Question**

Describe the woman's problem and the two suggestions that her friend makes about how to handle it. What do you think the woman should do, and why?

Preparation Time: 20 seconds
Recording Time: 60 seconds

## *Integrated Speaking Question 6 "Research References"*

 Now listen to part of a lecture in a sociology class. The professor is discussing the criteria for using older research references.

**Question**

Using the main points and examples from the lecture, describe the two criteria for using an older research reference presented by the professor.

Preparation Time: 20 seconds
Recording Time: 60 seconds

# WRITING SECTION

The Writing Section tests your ability to write essays in English similar to those that you would write in college courses. During the test, you will write two essays.

**The Integrated Essay.** First you will read an academic passage and then you will listen to a lecture on the same topic. You may take notes as you read and listen, but notes are not graded. You may use your notes to write the essay. The reading passage will disappear while you are listening to the lecture, but the passage will return to the screen for reference when you begin to write your essay. You will have 20 minutes to plan, write, and revise your response. Typically, a good essay for the integrated topic will require that you write 150–225 words.

**The Independent Essay.** You will read a question on the screen. It usually asks for your opinion about a familiar topic. You will have 30 minutes to plan, write, and revise your response. Typically, a good essay for the independent topic will require that you write 300–350 words.

A clock on the screen will show you how much time you have left to complete each essay.

### Integrated Essay "Collapse of Easter Island"

You have 20 minutes to plan, write, and revise your response to a reading passage and a lecture on the same topic. First, read the passage and take notes. Then, listen to the lecture and take notes. Finally, write your response to the writing question. Typically, a good response will require that you write 150–225 words.

**Reading Passage**
Time: 3 minutes

Because of its remote location, only a few species of plants and animals thrived on Easter Island, and the water surrounding it contained very few fish. Nevertheless, beginning with extremely limited resources on an isolated island, the native people achieved a very advanced culture, as evidenced by the gigantic monolithic human figures that line the coasts, as well as by other artifacts. The complete collapse of this civilization is still a mystery, but several theories have been put forward.

One theory suggests that the natives of Easter Island cut down large palm forests to clear land for agricultural purposes, fuel for heating and cooking, construction material for pole and thatch houses, and canoes for transportation. In addition, hundreds of *ahu*, or large stone monuments, were constructed and moved to the coast on rollers made of tree trunks. Assuming that the trees could regenerate quickly enough to sustain the environment, they continued the deforestation, which, in turn, caused serious erosion.

Another theory presents a very different explanation for the decline in the population. Since there were few predators on the island, and an abundance of food, it is thought that rats may have hidden in the canoes of the earliest settlers. When the native people cut and burned trees, the rats prevented regrowth by eating the fresh shoots before they could grow into large plants. With little food and no wood to build canoes to escape, the people perished.

A third theory contends that the population was decimated by a war between short-eared and long-eared people on the island. According to oral history, a plot by the long-eared people to kill the short-eared people was discovered and the short-eared people struck first, driving the long-eared people to a ditch where they were killed and burned.

**Model Test 2, Writing Section, Track 71**

 Now listen to a lecture on the same topic as the passage that you have just read.

## Question
Summarize the main points in the lecture, and then explain how they cast doubt on the ideas in the reading passage.

### *Independent Essay "Family Pets"*

#### Question
Agree or disagree with the following statement:

**Pets should be treated like family members.**

Give reasons and examples to support your opinion.

# MODEL TEST 2

## ANSWER KEYS

Use the following Answer Keys to check your scores on the Reading and Listening Sections of Model Test 2.

### READING SECTION

| *Reading 1* | *Reading 2* | *Reading 3* | *Reading 4* |
|---|---|---|---|
| 1.  B | 14.  C | 27.  A | 40.  D |
| 2.  C | 15.  B | 28.  D | 41.  C |
| 3.  D | 16.  B | 29.  C | 42.  B |
| 4.  B | 17.  D | 30.  B | 43.  B |
| 5.  D | 18.  A | 31.  D | 44.  D |
| 6.  A | 19.  B | 32.  A | 45.  D |
| 7.  B | 20.  D | 33.  B | 46.  B |
| 8.  D | 21.  B | 34.  A | 47.  A |
| 9.  C | 22.  D | 35.  B | 48.  A |
| 10.  C | 23.  B | 36.  A | 49.  D |
| 11.  A | 24.  A | 37.  C | 50.  D |
| 12.  C | 25.  C | 38.  C | 51.  C |
| 13.  C, E, F | 26.  B, C, D | 39.  B, D, E | 52.  C, D, E |

## LISTENING SECTION

| *Listening Set 1* | *Listening Set 2* |
|---|---|
| 1.  B | 18.  C |
| 2.  D | 19.  A |
| 3.  C | 20.  A, B |
| 4.  C | 21.  D |
| 5.  A | 22.  C |
| 6.  D | 23.  B |
| 7.  B, C | 24.  C |
| 8.  C | 25.  A |
| 9.  B | 26.  B, C |
| 10.  D | 27.  C |
| 11.  B | 28.  A, B, C: Yes |
| 12.  B | 29.  A |
| 13.  A | 30.  C |
| 14.  A, C | 31.  B |
| 15.  B | 32.  A |
| 16.  A | 33.  D |
| 17.  D | 34.  D |

 # EXPLANATORY AND EXAMPLE ANSWERS, MODEL TEST 2

Go to the Barron's TOEFL site to study detailed Explanatory Answers for the Reading and Listening Sections, and Outlines, Example Answers, and Checklists for the Speaking and Writing Sections of Model Test 2.

# MODEL TEST 3: PROGRESS TEST

## READING SECTION

The Reading Section tests your ability to understand reading passages like those in college textbooks. The reading passages are presented in one complete section, which allows you to move to the next passage and return to a previous passage to change answers or answer questions that you may have left blank. The passages are about 700 words in length.

This is the short format for the Reading Section. On the short format, you will read three passages. After each passage, you will answer 12–14 questions about it. You may take notes while you read, but notes are not graded. You may use your notes to answer the questions. Some passages may include a word or phrase that is underlined in blue. Click on the word or phrase to see a glossary definition or explanation.

Choose the best answer for multiple-choice questions. Follow the directions on the page or on the screen for computer-assisted questions. Most questions are worth 1 point, but the last question in each passage is worth more than 1 point.

Click on **Next** to go to the next question. Click on **Back** to return to previous questions. You may return to previous questions for all of the passages.

You can click on **Review** to see a chart of the questions you have answered and the questions you have not answered. From this screen, you can return to the question you want to answer.

Although you can spend more time on one passage and less time on another passage, you should try to pace yourself so that you are spending about 20 minutes to read each passage and answer the questions for that passage. You will have 60 minutes to complete all of the passages and answer all of the questions on the short format. A clock on the screen will show you how much time you have to complete the Reading Section.

## Reading 1

The following reading passage was adapted from *Environmental Science—A Study of Interrelationships*, Eleventh Edition by Elson D. Enger and Bradley F. Smith, McGraw-Hill Companies, 2008.

### "Symbiotic Relationships"

P1    **Symbiosis** is a close, long-lasting physical relationship between two different species. In other words, the two species are usually in physical contact and at least one of them derives some sort of benefit from this contact. There are three different categories of symbiotic relationships: parasitism, commensalism, and mutualism.

P2    **Parasitism** is a relationship in which one organism, known as the parasite, lives in or on another organism, known as the host, from which it derives nourishment. Generally, the parasite is much smaller than the host. Although the host is harmed by the interaction, it is generally not killed immediately by the parasite, and some host individuals may live a long time and be relatively little affected by their parasites. Some parasites are much more destructive than others, however. Newly established parasite-host relationships are likely to be more destructive than those that have a long evolutionary history. With a longstanding interaction between the parasite and the host, the two species generally evolve in such a way that they can accommodate one another. It is not in the parasite's best interest to kill its host. If it does, it must find another. Likewise, the host evolves defenses against the parasite, often reducing the harm done by the parasite to a level the host can tolerate.

P3    → Parasites that live on the surface of their hosts are known as **ectoparasites**. Fleas, lice, and some molds and mildews are examples of ectoparasites. Ⓐ Many other parasites, such as tapeworms, malaria parasites, many kinds of bacteria, and some fungi, are called **endoparasites** because they live inside the bodies of their hosts. Ⓑ A tapeworm lives in the intestines of its host where it is able to resist being digested and makes use of the nutrients in the intestine. Ⓒ

P4    Even plants can be parasites. Mistletoe is a flowering plant that is parasitic on trees. It establishes itself on the surface of a tree when a bird transfers the seed to the tree. It then grows down into the water-conducting tissues of the tree and uses the water and minerals it obtains from these tissues to support its own growth. Ⓓ

P5    **Commensalism** is a relationship between organisms in which one organism benefits while the other is not affected. It is possible to visualize a parasitic relationship evolving into a commensal one. Since parasites generally evolve to do as little harm to their host as possible and the host is combating the negative effects of the parasite, they might eventually evolve to the point where the host is not harmed at all.

P6       Many examples of commensal relationships exist. Many orchids use trees as a surface upon which to grow. The tree is not harmed or helped, but the orchid needs a surface upon which to establish itself and also benefits by being close to the top of the tree, where it can get more sunlight and rain. Some mosses, ferns, and many vines also make use of the surfaces of trees in this way.

P7       In the ocean, many sharks have a smaller fish known as a remora attached to them. Remoras have a <u>sucker</u> on the top of their heads that they can use to attach to the shark. In this way, they can hitchhike a ride as the shark swims along. When the shark feeds, the remora frees itself and obtains small bits of food that the shark misses. Then, the remora reattaches. The shark does not appear to be positively or negatively affected by remoras.

P8   →  **Mutualism** is another kind of symbiotic relationship and is actually beneficial to both species involved. In many mutualistic relationships, the relationship is obligatory; the species cannot live without each other. In others, the species can exist separately but are more successful when they are involved in a mutualistic relationship. Some species of Acacia, a thorny tree, provide food in the form of sugar solutions in little structures on their stems. Certain species of ants feed on the solutions and live in the tree, which they will protect from other animals by attacking any animal that begins to feed on the tree. Both organisms benefit; the ants receive food and a place to live, and the tree is protected from animals that would use it as food.

P9   →  One soil nutrient that is usually a limiting factor for plant growth is nitrogen. Many kinds of plants, such as legumes, beans, clover, Acacia trees, and Alder trees, have bacteria that live in their roots in little <u>nodules</u>. The roots form these nodules when they are infected with certain kinds of bacteria. The bacteria do not cause disease but provide the plants with nitrogen-containing molecules that the plants can use for growth. The nitrogen-fixing bacteria benefit from the living site and nutrients that the plants provide, and the plants benefit from the nitrogen they receive.

**Glossary**
sucker: an adaptation for sucking nourishment or sticking to a surface
nodules:  growths in the form of knots

1. The word derives in the passage is closest in meaning to

    Ⓐ  requests
    Ⓑ  pursues
    Ⓒ  obtains
    Ⓓ  rejects

2. The word categories in the passage is closest in meaning to

    Ⓐ  sources
    Ⓑ  ideas
    Ⓒ  classifications
    Ⓓ  problems

3. The word relatively in the passage is closest in meaning to

    Ⓐ comparatively
    Ⓑ routinely
    Ⓒ adversely
    Ⓓ frequently

4. Which of the sentences below best expresses the information in the highlighted statement in the passage? The other choices change the meaning or leave out important information.

    Ⓐ A parasite is less likely to destroy the host when it attaches itself at first.
    Ⓑ Parasites that have lived on a host for a long time have probably done a lot of damage.
    Ⓒ The most destructive phase for a host is when the parasite first invades it.
    Ⓓ The relationship between a parasite and a host will evolve over time.

5. The word tolerate in the passage is closest in meaning to

    Ⓐ permit
    Ⓑ oppose
    Ⓒ profit
    Ⓓ avoid

6. According to paragraph 3, how do ectoparasites survive?

    Ⓐ They live in mold and mildew on their hosts.
    Ⓑ They digest food in the intestines of their hosts.
    Ⓒ They live on the nutrients in their bacterial hosts.
    Ⓓ They inhabit the outside parts of their hosts.

    Paragraph 3 is marked with an arrow [➔].

7. Which of the following is mentioned as an example of a commensal relationship?

    Ⓐ Orchids
    Ⓑ Mistletoe
    Ⓒ Ants
    Ⓓ Fungus

8. The word actually in the passage is closest in meaning to

    Ⓐ frequently
    Ⓑ initially
    Ⓒ really
    Ⓓ usually

9. In paragraph 8, why does the author use the example of the *Acacia* tree?

    &#9400; To demonstrate how ants survive by living in trees
    &#9401; To explain how two species can benefit from contact
    &#9402; To show the relationship between plants and animals
    &#9403; To present a problem that occurs often in nature

Paragraph 8 is marked with an arrow [➔].

10. According to paragraph 9, how does bacteria affect beans and clover?

    &#9400; It causes many of the plants to die.
    &#9401; It limits the growth of young plants.
    &#9402; It supplies nitrogen to the crops.
    &#9403; It infects the roots with harmful nodules.

Paragraph 9 is marked with an arrow [➔].

11. Look at the four squares [■] that show where the following sentence could be inserted in the passage.

**They live on the feathers of birds or the fur of animals.**

Where could the sentence best be added?

Click on a square [■] to insert the sentence in the passage.

12. In which of the following chapters would this passage most probably appear?

    &#9400; Environment and Organisms
    &#9401; Pollution and Policies
    &#9402; Human Influences on Ecosystems
    &#9403; Energy Resources

13. **Directions:** An introduction for a short summary of the passage appears below. Complete the summary by selecting the THREE answer choices that mention the most important points in the passage. Some sentences do not belong in the summary because they express ideas that are not included in the passage or are minor points from the passage. *This question is worth 2 points.*

**Symbiosis is a close, continuing physical relationship between two species.**

- 
- 
- 

### Answer Choices

Ⓐ Parasitic species will feed on the host species, causing varying degrees of damage to the host as a result of the relationship.

Ⓑ Orchids benefit from being near the top of a tree where they can be exposed to more sunlight and rain.

Ⓒ Nodules in the roots of plants supply nitrogen from bacteria, thereby enriching the soil.

Ⓓ In commensalism, one species will benefit from the relationship, but the other species is not affected by it.

Ⓔ Certain species form mutualistic relationships in which both species benefit from the physical contact.

Ⓕ Evolutionary changes in species may allow them to live in close physical contact with little damage to each other.

## Reading 2 "Civilization"

The following reading passage was adapted from *Western Civilization*, Seventh Edition by Jackson J. Spielvogel, Wadsworth, 2009.

P1    Between 4000 and 3000 B.C., significant technological developments began to transform the Neolithic towns. The invention of writing enabled records to be kept, and the use of metals marked a new level of human control over the environment and its resources. Already before 4000 B.C., craftspeople had discovered that metal-bearing rocks could be heated to liquefy metals, which could then be cast in molds to produce tools and weapons that were more useful than stone instruments. Although copper was the first metal to be utilized in producing tools, after 4000 B.C. craftspeople in western Asia discovered that a combination of copper and tin produced bronze, a much harder and more durable metal than copper. Its widespread use has led historians to call the period the Bronze Age; thereafter, from around 3000 to 1200 B.C., bronze was increasingly replaced by iron.

P2 → At first, Neolithic settlements were hardly more than villages. But as their inhabitants mastered the art of farming, more complex human societies emerged. As wealth increased, these societies began to develop armies and to build walled cities. By the beginning of the Bronze Age, the concentration of larger numbers of people in the river valleys of Southwest Asia and Egypt was leading to a whole new pattern for human life.

P3 → As we have seen, early human beings formed small groups that developed a simple culture that enabled them to survive. As human societies grew and developed greater complexity, a new form of human existence—called civilization—came into being. A civilization is a complex culture in which large numbers of human beings share a number of common elements. Historians have identified a number of basic characteristics of civilization, most of which are evident in the Southwest Asian and Egyptian civilizations. These include (1) an urban focus: cities became the centers of political, economic, social, cultural, and religious development; (2) a distinct religious structure: the gods were deemed crucial to the community's success, and professional priestly classes, as stewards of the gods' property, regulated relations with the gods; (3) new political and military structures: an organized government bureaucracy arose to meet the administrative demands of the growing population while armies were organized to gain land and power and for defense; (4) a new social structure based on economic power: while kings and an upper class of priests, political leaders, and warriors dominated, there also existed large groups of free people (farmers, artisans, craftspeople) and at the very bottom, socially, a class of slaves; (5) the development of writing: kings, priests, merchants, and artisans used writing to keep records; and (6) new forms of significant artistic and intellectual activity: monumental architectural structures, usually religious, occupied a prominent place in urban environments.

P4 → Why early civilizations developed remains difficult to explain. Ⓐ Since civilizations developed independently in India, China, Mesopotamia, and Egypt, can general causes be identified that would explain why all of these civilizations emerged? Ⓑ A number of possible explanations of the beginning of civilization have been suggested. A theory of challenge and response maintains that challenges forced human beings to make efforts that resulted in the rise of civilization. Some scholars have adhered to a material explanation. Ⓒ Material forces, such as the growth of food surpluses, made possible the specialization of labor and development of large communities with bureaucratic organization. Ⓓ But the area of the Fertile Crescent, in which civilization emerged in Southwest Asia, was not naturally conducive to agriculture. Abundant food could be produced only with a massive human effort to carefully manage the water, an effort that created the need for organization and bureaucratic control and led to civilized cities. Some historians have argued that nonmaterial forces, primarily religious, provided the sense of unity and purpose that made such organized activities possible. Finally, some scholars doubt that we are capable of ever discovering the actual causes of early civilization.

14. Which of the following is the best definition of a "civilization"?

  Ⓐ Neolithic towns and cities
  Ⓑ Types of complex cultures
  Ⓒ An agricultural community
  Ⓓ Large population centers

15. The word utilized in the passage is closest in meaning to

  Ⓐ located
  Ⓑ used
  Ⓒ described
  Ⓓ improved

16. According to paragraph 2, what happens as societies become more prosperous?

  Ⓐ More goods are produced.
  Ⓑ Walled cities are built.
  Ⓒ Laws are instituted.
  Ⓓ The size of families increase.

  Paragraph 2 is marked with an arrow [➔].

17. The word hardly in the passage is closest in meaning to

  Ⓐ frequently
  Ⓑ likely
  Ⓒ barely
  Ⓓ obviously

18. Why does the author mention "Neolithic settlements" in paragraph 2?

  Ⓐ To give an example of a civilization
  Ⓑ To explain the invention of writing systems
  Ⓒ To argue that they should be classified as villages
  Ⓓ To contrast them with the civilizations that evolved

  Paragraph 2 is marked with an arrow [➔].

19. According to paragraph 3, how was the class system structured?

  Ⓐ An upper class and a lower class
  Ⓑ Slaves, free people, and a ruling class
  Ⓒ A king, an army, and slaves
  Ⓓ Intellectuals and uneducated farmers and workers

  Paragraph 3 is marked with an arrow [➔].

20. Which of the sentences below best expresses the information in the highlighted statement in the passage? The other choices change the meaning or leave out important information.

Ⓐ Southwest Asian and Egyptian civilizations exhibit the majority of the characteristics identified by historians.
Ⓑ The characteristics that historians have identified are not found in the Egyptian and Southwest Asian cultures.
Ⓒ Civilizations in Southwest Asia and Egypt were identified by historians who were studying the characteristics of early cultures.
Ⓓ The identification of most historical civilizations includes either Egypt or Southwest Asia on the list.

21. The word crucial in the passage is closest in meaning to

Ⓐ fundamental
Ⓑ arbitrary
Ⓒ disruptive
Ⓓ suitable

22. The word prominent in the passage is closest in meaning to

Ⓐ weak
Ⓑ important
Ⓒ small
Ⓓ new

23. According to paragraph 4, how can the independent development of civilization in different geographic regions be explained?

Ⓐ Scholars agree that food surpluses encouraged populations to be concentrated in certain areas.
Ⓑ There are several theories that explain the rise of civilization in the ancient world.
Ⓒ The model of civilization was probably carried from one region to another along trade routes.
Ⓓ Historians attribute the emergence of early cities at about the same time as a coincidence.

Paragraph 4 is marked with an arrow [→].

24. All of the following are cited as reasons why civilizations developed EXCEPT

Ⓐ religious practices unified the population.
Ⓑ the management of water required organization.
Ⓒ a major climate change made living in groups necessary.
Ⓓ extra food resulted in the expansion of population centers.

25. Look at the four squares [■] that show where the following sentence could be inserted in the passage.

    **Some historians believe they can be established.**

    Where could the sentence best be added?

    Click on a square [■] to insert the sentence in the passage.

26. **Directions:** An introduction for a short summary of the passage appears below. Complete the summary by selecting the THREE answer choices that mention the most important points in the passage. Some sentences do not belong in the summary because they express ideas that are not included in the passage or they are minor points from the passage. *This question is worth 2 points.*

    **Certain qualities appear to define a civilization.**

    - 
    - 
    - 

    **Answer Choices**

    A  Free citizens who work in professions for pay

    B  Bureaucracies for the government and armies

    C  Libraries to house art and written records

    D  A strategic location near rivers or the sea

    E  Organized religion, writing, and art

    F  A densely populated group with a class structure

## *Reading 3*

The following reading passage was adapted from *Horizons*, Eleventh Edition by Michael A. Seeds, Brooks-Cole, 2010.

### *"Life in Our Solar System"*

P1    Although we can imagine life based on something other than carbon chemistry, we know of no examples to tell us how such life might arise and survive. We must limit our discussion to life as we know it and the conditions it requires. The most important requirement is the presence of liquid water, not only as part of the chemical reactions of life, but also as a medium to transport nutrients and wastes within the organism.

P2    The water requirement automatically eliminates many worlds in our solar system. The moon is airless, and although some data suggest ice frozen in the soil at its poles, it has never had liquid water on its surface. In the vacuum of the lunar surface, liquid water would boil away rapidly. Mercury too is airless and cannot have had liquid water on its surface for long periods of time. Venus has some traces of water vapor in its atmosphere, but it is much too hot for liquid water to survive. If there were any lakes or oceans of water on its surface when it was young, they must have evaporated quickly. Even if life began there, no traces would be left now.

P3    The inner solar system seems too hot, and the outer solar system seems too cold. The Jovian planets have deep atmospheres, and, at a certain level, they have moderate temperatures where water might condense into liquid droplets. But it seems unlikely that life could begin there. The Jovian planets have no surfaces where oceans could nurture the beginning of life, and currents in the atmosphere seem destined to circulate gas and water droplets from regions of moderate temperature to other levels that are much too hot or too cold for life to survive.

P4    A few of the satellites of the Jovian planets might have suitable conditions for life. Jupiter's moon Europa seems to have a liquid-water ocean below its icy crust, and minerals dissolved in that water would provide a rich broth of possibilities for chemical evolution. Ⓐ Nevertheless, Europa is not a promising site to search for life because conditions may not have remained stable for the billions of years needed for life to evolve beyond the microscopic stage. Ⓑ If Jupiter's moons interact gravitationally and modify their orbits, Europa may have been frozen solid at some points in history. Ⓒ

P5    ➜ Saturn's moon Titan has an atmosphere of nitrogen, argon, and methane and may have oceans of liquid methane and ethane on its surface. Ⓓ The chemistry of life that might crawl or swim on such a world is unknown, but life there may be unlikely because of the temperature. The surface of Titan is a deadly –179°C (–290°F). Chemical reactions occur slowly or not at all at such low temperatures, so the chemical evolution needed to begin life may never have occurred on Titan.

P6    ➜ Mars is the most likely place for life in our solar system. The evidence, however, is not encouraging. Meteorite ALH84001 was found on the Antarctic ice in 1984. It was probably part of debris ejected into space by a large impact on Mars. ALH84001 is important because a team of scientists studied it and announced in 1996 that it contained chemical and physical traces of ancient life on Mars.

P7    Scientists were excited too, but being professionally skeptical, they began testing the results immediately. In many cases, the results did not confirm the conclusion that life once existed on Mars. Some chemical contamination from water on Earth has occurred, and some chemicals in the meteorite may have originated without the presence of life. The physical features that look like fossil bacteria may be mineral formations in the rock.

P8   Spacecraft now visiting Mars may help us understand the past history of water there and paint a more detailed picture of present conditions. Nevertheless, conclusive evidence may have to wait until a geologist in a space suit can wander the dry streambeds of Mars cracking open rocks and searching for fossils.

P9   We are left to conclude that, so far as we know, our solar system is bare of life except for Earth. Consequently, our search for life in the universe takes us to other planetary systems.

27. The word automatically in the passage is closest in meaning to

   Ⓐ partially
   Ⓑ actually
   Ⓒ occasionally
   Ⓓ naturally

28. The word data in the passage is closest in meaning to

   Ⓐ improvements
   Ⓑ agreements
   Ⓒ facts
   Ⓓ methods

29. Which of the following statements about the water on Venus is true?

   Ⓐ The water evaporated because of the high temperatures.
   Ⓑ The water became frozen in the polar regions.
   Ⓒ Only a little water is left in small lakes on the surface.
   Ⓓ Rain does not fall because there is no atmosphere.

30. The word stable in the passage is closest in meaning to

   Ⓐ visible
   Ⓑ active
   Ⓒ constant
   Ⓓ strong

31. What can be inferred from the passage about the Jovian planets?

   Ⓐ Some of the Jovian planets may have conditions that could support life.
   Ⓑ Jupiter is classified as one of the Jovian planets.
   Ⓒ Europa is the largest of the moons that revolve around Jupiter.
   Ⓓ The orbits of the Jovian planets have changed over time.

32. According to paragraph 5, why would life on Titan be improbable?

    Ⓐ It does not have an ocean.
    Ⓑ It is not a planet.
    Ⓒ It is too cold.
    Ⓓ It has a low atmosphere.

    Paragraph 5 is marked with an arrow [→].

33. Which of the sentences below best expresses the information in the highlighted statement in the passage? The other choices change the meaning or leave out important information.

    Ⓐ Life on Mars was found as a result of research in many cases.
    Ⓑ The evidence did not demonstrate that there was life on Mars in the past.
    Ⓒ Many cases of life were concluded in the history of Mars.
    Ⓓ The conclusion was that only one instance of life on Mars was verified.

34. The word originated in the passage is closest in meaning to

    Ⓐ turned
    Ⓑ changed
    Ⓒ begun
    Ⓓ disappeared

35. Why does the author mention the meteorite "ALH84001" in paragraph 6?

    Ⓐ Because it was found in Antarctica about fifty years ago
    Ⓑ Because it was evidence of a recent impact on Mars
    Ⓒ Because scientists thought that it contained evidence of life on Mars
    Ⓓ Because the meteorite probably came from Mars a long time ago

    Paragraph 6 is marked with an arrow [→].

36. How will scientists confirm the existence of life on Mars?

    Ⓐ By sending unmanned spacecraft to Mars
    Ⓑ By looking at fossils on Mars
    Ⓒ By viewing pictures taken of Mars
    Ⓓ By studying the present conditions on Mars

37. Which of the following statements most accurately reflects the author's opinion about life in our solar system?

    Ⓐ Life is probably limited to planets in the inner solar system.
    Ⓑ There is a large body of evidence supporting life on Mars.
    Ⓒ There is little probability of life on other planets.
    Ⓓ We should explore our solar system for conditions that support life.

38. Look at the four squares [■] that show where the following sentence could be inserted in the passage.

   **Such periods of freezing would probably prevent life from developing.**

   Where could the sentence best be added?

   Click on a square [■] to insert the sentence in the passage.

39. **Directions:** An introduction for a short summary of the passage appears below. Complete the summary by selecting the THREE answer choices that mention the most important points in the passage. Some sentences do not belong in the summary because they express ideas that are not included in the passage or are minor points from the passage. **This question is worth 2 points.**

   **Current evidence does not support the theory of life in our solar system.**

   ● 

   ● 

   ● 

### Answer Choices

A The meteorite that was discovered in the Antarctic in the 1980s was thought to contain evidence of early life on Mars, but it was later disputed.

B The planet that has the greatest probability for life in the past or now is Mars, but more investigation is required to draw conclusions.

C Europa has an ocean under the ice on the surface of the moon, which may contain the chemical combinations required for life to evolve.

D Although some of the moons that revolve around Saturn and Jupiter have conditions that might support life, the evidence contradicts this possibility.

E Other planetary systems must have life that is similar to that which has evolved on Earth because of the principles of carbon chemistry.

F It is too hot for life on the planets near the Sun in the inner solar system and too cold on the planets most removed from the Sun in the outer solar system.

# LISTENING SECTION

 **Model Test 3, Listening Section, Track 72**

The Listening Section tests your ability to understand spoken English that is typical of inter-actions and academic speech on college campuses. During the test, you will listen to conver-sations, lectures, and discussions, and you will answer questions about them.

This is the long format for the Listening Section. On the long format, you will listen to three conversations, three lectures, and three discussions. After each listening passage, you will answer 5–6 questions about it. Only two conversations, two lectures, and two discussions will be graded. The other passages are part of an experimental section for future tests. Because you will not know which conversations, lectures, and discussions will be graded, you must try to do your best on all of them.

You will hear each passage one time. You may take notes while you listen, but notes are not graded. You may use your notes to answer the questions.

Choose the best answer for multiple-choice questions. Follow the directions on the page or on the screen for computer-assisted questions. Click on **Next** and then on **OK** to go on to the next question. You cannot return to previous questions.

The Listening Section is divided into sets. Each set includes one conversation, one lecture, and one discussion. You have 10 minutes to answer all of the questions for each set. You will have 30 minutes to answer all of the questions on the long format. A clock on the screen will show you how much time you have to complete your answers for the section. The clock does NOT count the time you are listening to the conversations, lectures, and discussions.

## Listening 1 "Professor's Office"

1. Why does the student go to see his professor?

   Ⓐ To prepare for a field trip to a gold mine
   Ⓑ To clarify some points in his notes
   Ⓒ To see what he missed when he was absent
   Ⓓ To ask about a question on the last test

2. According to the professor, what is an *aquifer*?

   Ⓐ An underground cave filled with water
   Ⓑ Groundwater that forms a lake
   Ⓒ Layers of sediment that trap water
   Ⓓ Water pumped out from under rocks

3. How are porosity and permeability related?

   Ⓐ Highly porous sediment is usually also highly permeable.
   Ⓑ Clay is an example of low porosity and permeability.
   Ⓒ No generalities may be made about porosity and permeability.
   Ⓓ Space between layers is a measure of porosity and permeability.

4. Why does the professor say this:

    Ⓐ She does not have a very good answer.
    Ⓑ The terms have changed recently.
    Ⓒ The student's statement is true in part.
    Ⓓ She is impatient with the student.

5. Why does the professor mention "gold mining"?

    Ⓐ To compare the value of water with that of gold
    Ⓑ To demonstrate that water is a nonrenewable resource
    Ⓒ To explain where fossil water is usually found
    Ⓓ To contrast mines with man-made water reservoirs

### *Listening 2 "Sociology Class"*

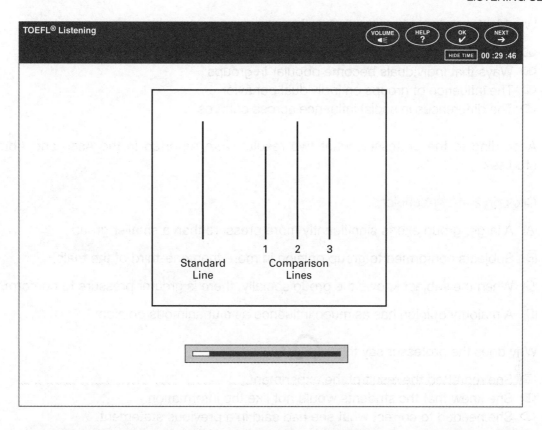

6. What is the main topic of the lecture?

    Ⓐ The problems inherent in group decisions
    Ⓑ Ways that individuals become popular in groups
    Ⓒ The influence of groups on individual behavior
    Ⓓ The differences in social influence across cultures

7. According to the professor, what two results were reported in the Asch and Abrams studies?

    Click on 2 answer choices.

    Ⓐ A larger group exerts significantly more pressure than a smaller group.

    Ⓑ Subjects conformed to group opinion in more than one-third of the trials.

    Ⓒ When the subject knows the group socially, there is greater pressure to conform.

    Ⓓ A majority opinion has as much influence as a unanimous opinion.

8. Why does the professor say this:

    Ⓐ She regretted the result of the experiment.
    Ⓑ She knew that the students would not like the information.
    Ⓒ She needed to correct what she had said in a previous statement.
    Ⓓ She neglected to mention important facts.

9. What generally happens after a group makes a decision?

    Ⓐ Some group members regret their decision.
    Ⓑ At least one group member presents a new idea.
    Ⓒ As a whole, the group is even more united in its judgment.
    Ⓓ The popular group members compete for leadership.

10. Based on information in the lecture, indicate whether the statements describe the Asch study.

    For each sentence, click in the Yes or No column.

    |   |   | Yes | No |
    | --- | --- | --- | --- |
    | A | Only one subject is being tested. |   |   |
    | B | The cards can be interpreted several ways. |   |   |
    | C | Some of the group collaborate with the experimenter. |   |   |

11. What is the professor's attitude about the studies on social influence?

    Ⓐ She seems surprised by the results.
    Ⓑ She appears to be very interested in them.
    Ⓒ She needs more information about them.
    Ⓓ She doubts that there is practical application.

## Listening 3 "Art History Class"

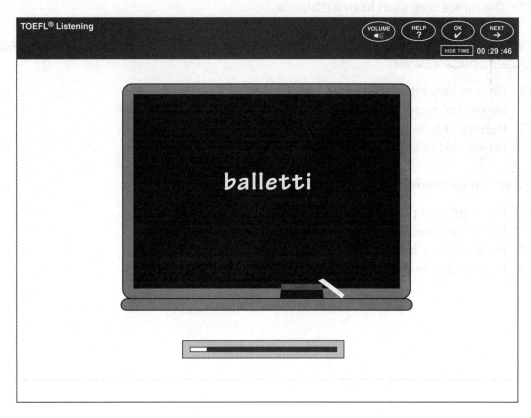

12. What is the discussion mainly about?

 Ⓐ Catherine de Medici's entertainments
 Ⓑ The figures for court dancing
 Ⓒ The development of the ballet
 Ⓓ The relationship between dance and meals

13. Why does the professor say this:

 Ⓐ To end his explanation and begin the lecture
 Ⓑ To apologize to the students about their tests
 Ⓒ To comment about the students' grades
 Ⓓ To regain the attention of the class

14. According to the professor, what does the term *balletti* mean?

 Ⓐ A dramatic story
 Ⓑ A parade of horses
 Ⓒ A dance done in figures
 Ⓓ An outdoor entertainment

15. How did the early choreographers accommodate the abilities of amateur performers?

 Ⓐ The steps were quite simple.
 Ⓑ The same performance was repeated.
 Ⓒ Practice sessions were lengthy.
 Ⓓ The dance was seen from a distance.

16. Why does the professor mention that he checked several references about the length of *Queen Louise's Ballet*?

 Ⓐ He was very interested in the ballet.
 Ⓑ He did not know much about it.
 Ⓒ He wasn't sure that it was accurate.
 Ⓓ He wanted to impress the class.

17. What can be inferred about the professor?

 Ⓐ He is not very polite to his class.
 Ⓑ He encourages the students to participate.
 Ⓒ He is not very interested in the topic.
 Ⓓ He is probably a good dancer.

*Listening 4 "Admissions Office"*

18. Why does the student go to the admissions office?

    (A) He is applying for financial aid.
    (B) He is requesting an official transcript.
    (C) He is transferring to another college.
    (D) He is trying to enroll in classes.

19. What is missing from the student's file?

    (A) A financial aid application
    (B) A transcript from County Community College
    (C) Grades from Regional College
    (D) An official copy of the application

20. Why does the woman say this:

    (A) She is asking the man to finish explaining the situation.
    (B) She is confirming that she understands the problem.
    (C) She is expressing impatience with the man's explanation.
    (D) She is trying to comprehend a difficult question.

21. What does the woman suggest that the man do?

    Ⓐ Make a copy of his transcripts for his personal file
    Ⓑ Complete all of the admissions forms as soon as possible
    Ⓒ Change his provisional status to regular status before registering
    Ⓓ Continue to request an official transcript from County Community College

22. What will the student most probably do now?

    Ⓐ Return later in the day to see the woman in the admissions office
    Ⓑ Go to the office for transfer students to be assigned an advisor
    Ⓒ Enter information in the computer to complete the application process
    Ⓓ See the woman's superior to get a provisional admission to State University

## Listening 5 "Geology Class"

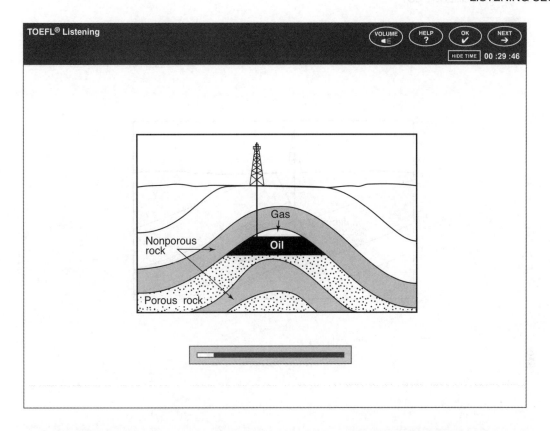

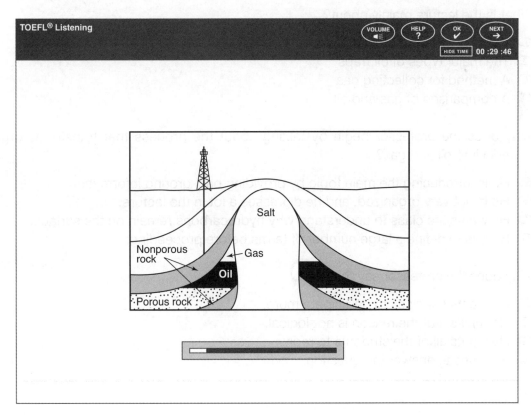

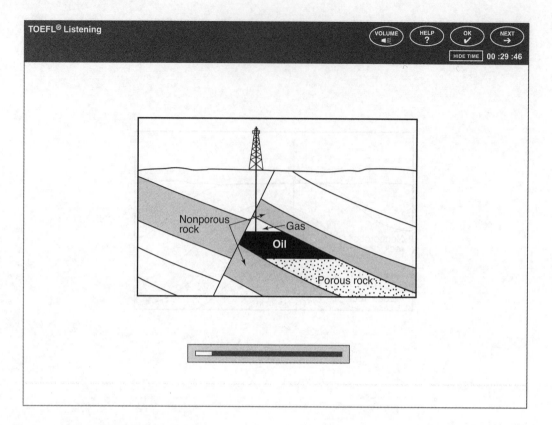

23. What is the lecture mainly about?

 (A) The process of photosynthesis
 (B) The major types of oil traps
 (C) A method for collecting gas
 (D) A comparison of gas and oil

24. Why does the professor begin by talking about the process that transforms organic material into oil and gas?

 (A) He is introducing the main topic by providing background information.
 (B) He is not very organized, and he digresses a lot in the lecture.
 (C) He wants the class to understand why hydrocarbons remain on the surface.
 (D) He has to define a large number of terms before proceeding.

25. Why does the professor say this:

 (A) He wants the class to participate more.
 (B) He thinks that the reason is not logical.
 (C) He wants all of the students to reply.
 (D) He plans to answer the question.

26.  Select the diagram of the anticline trap that was described in the lecture.

Click on the correct diagram.

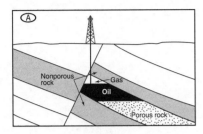

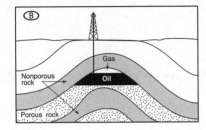

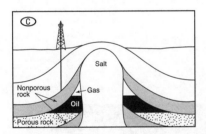

27.  Identify the nonporous rock in the diagram.

Click on the correct letter.

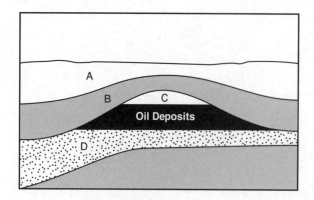

28.  According to the professor, what do geologists look for when they are trying to locate a salt dome?

Ⓐ  A bulge in an otherwise flat area
Ⓑ  Underground rocks shaped like an arch
Ⓒ  Salt on the surface of a large area
Ⓓ  A deep crack in the Earth

## Listening 6 "Anthropology Class"

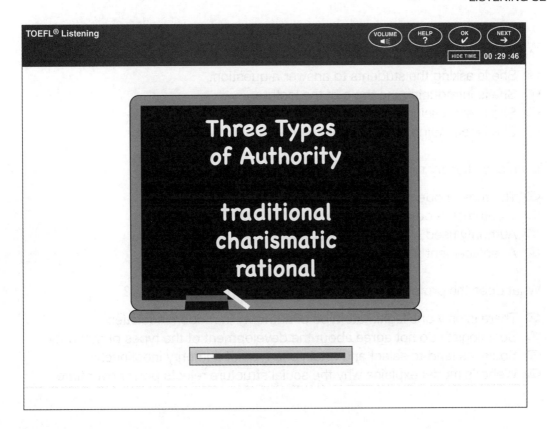

29. What is the main purpose of this discussion?

&#9312; To discuss three types of authority
&#9313; To distinguish between power and authority
&#9314; To examine alternatives to Weber's model
&#9315; To argue in favor of a legal rational system

30. Why do the students mention Kennedy and Reagan?

&#9312; They were founders of political movements.
&#9313; They were examples of charismatic leaders.
&#9314; They were attorneys who led by the law.
&#9315; They had contrasting types of authority.

31. According to the professor, what two factors are associated with charismatic authority?

Click on 2 answer choices.

&#9398; Sacred customs

&#9399; An attractive leader

&#9400; A social cause

&#9401; Legal elections

32. Why does the professor say this: 🎧

  Ⓐ She is asking the students to answer a question.
  Ⓑ She is introducing the topic of the lecture.
  Ⓒ She is expressing an opinion about the subject.
  Ⓓ She is reminding students of a previous point.

33. In an evolutionary model, how is rational legal authority viewed?

  Ⓐ The most modern form of authority
  Ⓑ A common type of authority in the industrial age
  Ⓒ Authority used by traditional leaders
  Ⓓ A replacement for the three ideal types of authority

34. What does the professor imply about the three types of authority?

  Ⓐ There is only one legitimate type of authority in modern societies.
  Ⓑ Sociologists do not agree about the development of the types of authority.
  Ⓒ Societies tend to select and retain one type of authority indefinitely.
  Ⓓ Weber's model explains why the social structure rejects power over time.

*Listening 7 "Library"*

35. What does the man need from the librarian?

    Ⓐ A DVD player
    Ⓑ Material for a class
    Ⓒ Research by Dr. Parsons
    Ⓓ His student ID

36. What is the man's problem?

    Ⓐ He has to study for an important exam.
    Ⓑ He needs to prepare for a class discussion.
    Ⓒ He owes a fine at the library.
    Ⓓ He does not own a DVD player.

37. What does the man feel when he says this:

    Ⓐ Amused
    Ⓑ Worried
    Ⓒ Confused
    Ⓓ Interested

38. What is the policy for materials on reserve?

    Ⓐ The materials cannot leave the library without exception.
    Ⓑ There is a ten-dollar fine for each hour the materials are late.
    Ⓒ Students must show the professor's signature to use the materials.
    Ⓓ Materials may be checked out overnight two hours before closing.

39. What does the librarian imply when she tells the man to return at nine o'clock?

    Ⓐ She will see the man after work.
    Ⓑ The library probably closes at eleven.
    Ⓒ She is too busy to help the man now.
    Ⓓ Her supervisor will be there at that time.

## *Listening 8 "Literature Class"*

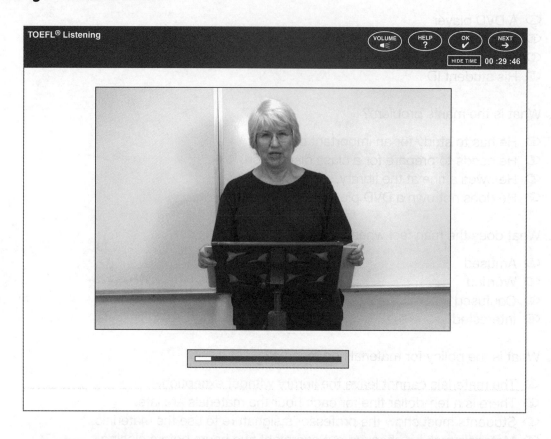

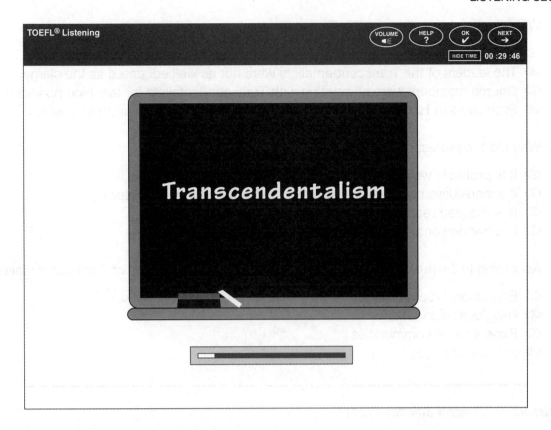

40. What does this lecturer mainly discuss?

    Ⓐ Transcendentalism
    Ⓑ Puritanism
    Ⓒ Ralph Waldo Emerson
    Ⓓ Nature

41. Why does the professor say this:

    Ⓐ She is joking with the students.
    Ⓑ She is drawing a conclusion.
    Ⓒ She is correcting the students' behavior.
    Ⓓ She is reasoning aloud.

42. According to the professor, what was true about the Puritans?

    Ⓐ They stressed the essential importance of the individual.
    Ⓑ They supported the ideals of the Transcendental Club.
    Ⓒ They believed that society should be respected above persons.
    Ⓓ They thought that people should live in communes like Brook Farm.

43. Why did the church oppose the Transcendental movement?

    Ⓐ The authority of the church would be challenged by a code of personal ethics.
    Ⓑ The leaders of the Transcendentalists were not as well educated as the clergy.
    Ⓒ Church members were competing with Transcendentalists for teaching positions.
    Ⓓ Professors at Harvard College convinced the church to support their position.

44. Why did the professor mention *Walden*?

    Ⓐ It is probably well-known to many of the students in the class.
    Ⓑ It is considered an excellent example of Transcendental literature.
    Ⓒ It is required reading for the course that she is teaching.
    Ⓓ It is her personal favorite of nineteenth-century essays.

45. According to the professor, what was the most lasting contribution of Transcendentalism?

    Ⓐ Educational reorganization
    Ⓑ Religious reformation
    Ⓒ Experimental communities
    Ⓓ Political changes

### Listening 9 "General Science Class"

46. What is this discussion mainly about?

    Ⓐ A model of the universe
    Ⓑ Interpretations of facts
    Ⓒ A definition of a hypothesis
    Ⓓ The scientific method

47. Why did the professor give the example of the ancient Egyptians?

    Ⓐ To explain the rotation of the Earth and the Sun
    Ⓑ To prove that facts may be interpreted differently
    Ⓒ To present a fact that can be verified by the students
    Ⓓ To discard a model that was widely accepted

48. Why did the professor say this:

    Ⓐ He is asking whether students need repetition.
    Ⓑ He is beginning a review of the process.
    Ⓒ He is complaining because students don't understand.
    Ⓓ He is making a suggestion before he proceeds.

49. According to the professor, what did Kepler do to verify his theory of planetary motion?

    Ⓐ He made predictions based on the model.
    Ⓑ He asked other scientists to make predictions.
    Ⓒ He used prior observations to test the model.
    Ⓓ He relied on insight to verify the theory.

50. What can be concluded from information in this discussion?

    Ⓐ A model does not always reflect observations.
    Ⓑ A model is not subject to change like a theory is.
    Ⓒ A model is considered true without doubt.
    Ⓓ A model does not require further experimentation.

51. What technique does the professor use to explain the practical application of the scientific method?

    Ⓐ A summary
    Ⓑ An example
    Ⓒ A prediction
    Ⓓ A formula

 **Please turn off the audio. There is a 10-minute break between the Listening Section and the Speaking Section.**

# SPEAKING SECTION

 **Model Test 3, Speaking Section, Track 73**

The Speaking Section tests your ability to communicate in English in an academic setting. During the test, you will be presented with six speaking questions. The questions ask for a response to a single question, a conversation, a talk, or a lecture. The prompts and questions are presented only one time.

You may take notes as you listen, but notes are not graded. You may use your notes to answer the questions. Some of the questions ask for a response to a reading passage and a talk or a lecture. The reading passages and the questions are written, but the directions will be spoken.

Your speaking will be evaluated on both the fluency of the language and the accuracy of the content. You will have 15–20 seconds to prepare and 45–60 seconds to respond to each question. Typically, a good response will require all of the response time and the answer will be complete by the end of the response time.

You will have about 20 minutes to complete the Speaking Section. A clock on the screen will show you how much time you have to prepare each of your answers and how much time you have to record each response.

## *Independent Speaking Question 1 "Advice"*

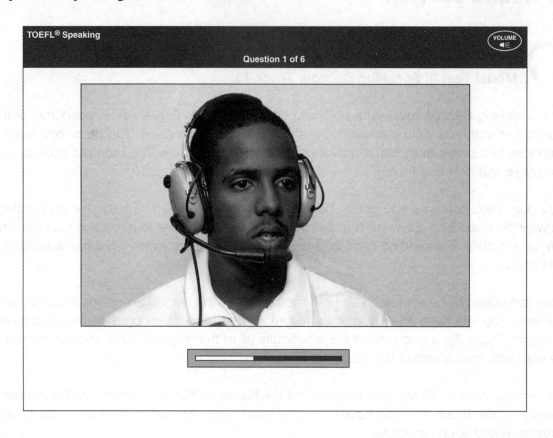

 Listen for a question about a familiar topic.

**Question**

The older generation often gives advice to younger family members. Describe a valuable piece of advice that an older person gave you. Why did it help you?

Preparation Time: 15 seconds
Recording Time: 45 seconds

## Independent Speaking Question 2 "Climate"

 Listen for a question that asks your opinion about a familiar topic.

### Question

Some people enjoy living in a location that has a warm climate all year. Other people like to live in a place where the seasons change. Which type of climate do you prefer and why? Use specific reasons and examples to support your opinion.

Preparation Time: 15 seconds
Recording Time: 45 seconds

### *Integrated Speaking Question 3 "Withdrawal from Classes"*

Read a short passage and listen to a talk on the same topic.

Reading Time: 45 seconds

---

Withdrawal from Classes

In order to qualify for a refund of 100 percent at any time during the semester, you must first establish eligibility. Serious illness or injury must be verified by a written statement signed by a doctor or a psychologist. The death of a family member must be verified by a death certificate. Military duty must be verified by a copy of the orders. Students who wish to withdraw without submitting official documentation may do so before the end of the drop-add period without penalty. After the end of the second week of classes, students may petition for a 90 percent reimbursement. After the end of the fourth week, students are eligible for a 50 percent refund.

---

 Now listen to the students discuss the policy with each other.

**Question**
The student expresses her opinion of the policy for reimbursement. Report her opinion and explain the reasons that she gives for having that opinion.

Preparation Time: 30 seconds
Recording Time: 60 seconds

### Integrated Speaking Question 4 "Ballads"

Read a short passage and then listen to part of a lecture on the same topic.

Reading Time: 45 seconds

> Ballads
>
> A *ballad* is a poem that tells a story and is sung to music. Usually the story is of unknown origin and a number of versions may be found for one song, a characteristic that stems from the oral tradition. As the song is passed on from one singer to another, a word is changed or a slight alteration is made in the tune. In short, ballads represent a living tradition that evolves as the song is performed and passed to the next musician. A collection of ballads has been preserved in written form in *English and Scottish Popular Ballads* by Francis James Child, and many ballads are still referred to by their "Child number."

TOEFL® Speaking

VOLUME

Question 4 of 6

Now listen to part of a lecture in a music appreciation class. The professor is talking about the ballad of "Barbara Allen."

**Question**
Define a ballad and then explain why "Barbara Allen" can be classified as a ballad.

Preparation Time: 30 seconds
Recording Time: 60 seconds

## *Integrated Speaking Question 5 "The Assignment"*

 Now listen to a conversation between a student and her friend.

**Question**

Describe the woman's problem and the two suggestions that her friend makes about how to handle it. What do you think the woman should do, and why?

Preparation Time: 20 seconds
Recording Time: 60 seconds

## *Integrated Speaking Question 6 "Ultrasound"*

 Now listen to part of a lecture in a general science class. The professor is discussing the way that ultrasound works.

### Question

Using the main points and examples from the lecture, describe the kind of information that ultrasound can provide and then explain the way that ultrasound is used in medical diagnosis.

Preparation Time: 20 seconds
Recording Time: 60 seconds

# WRITING SECTION

The Writing Section tests your ability to write essays in English similar to those that you would write in college courses. During the test, you will write two essays.

**The Integrated Essay.** First you will read an academic passage and then you will listen to a lecture on the same topic. You may take notes as you read and listen, but notes are not graded. You may use your notes to write the essay. The reading passage will disappear while you are listening to the lecture, but the passage will return to the screen for reference when you begin to write your essay. You will have 20 minutes to plan, write, and revise your response. Typically, a good essay for the integrated topic will require that you write 150–225 words.

**The Independent Essay.** You will read a question on the screen. It usually asks for your opinion about a familiar topic. You will have 30 minutes to plan, write, and revise your response. Typically, a good essay for the independent topic will require that you write 300–350 words.

A clock on the screen will show you how much time you have left to complete each essay.

### Integrated Essay "Emperor Penguins"

You have 20 minutes to plan, write, and revise your response to a reading passage and a lecture on the same topic. First, read the passage and take notes. Then, listen to the lecture and take notes. Finally, write your response to the writing question. Typically, a good response will require that you write 150–225 words.

**Reading Passage**
Time: 3 minutes

Emperor penguins are not only the largest species of penguin in the world but also one of the most unique. They are very social, living in colonies that can include hundreds of thousands of individuals. Nevertheless, emperor penguins are monogamous. Having selected a mate, emperor penguins remain faithful to each other for life, using vocal calls to find one another when they return to their breeding site on the compacted ice of the Antarctic continent. It is believed that different frequencies alert mates to the sound of their partner's call.

Another interesting aspect of emperor penguins is that they return to the same site, called a rookery, to nest each year. Although their path to the rookery is different every year due to the shifting sea ice, in general, the penguins continue to use the rookery where they were hatched. Their loyalty to a particular breeding ground results in increasingly larger penguin colonies, some with more than a million birds. Males tend to arrive first to reestablish and defend their preferred nesting sites and females return a day or so later.

Emperor penguins are not considered endangered and are not currently protected under international law. In fact, in areas where reliable population counts have been conducted, the evidence suggests that populations are stable. However, due to harsh environmental conditions, some colonies have not been monitored on a consistent basis. Estimates of population sizes are at about 240,000 breeding pairs. Taking into consideration the nonbreeding birds as well, the total translates into about 600,000 adult birds. Emperor chicks that reach adulthood can survive for 20 years.

**Model Test 3, Writing Section, Track 74**

 Now listen to a lecture on the same topic as the passage that you have just read.

**Question**

Summarize the main points in the lecture, and then explain how they cast doubt on the ideas in the reading passage.

### Independent Essay "The College Years"

**Question**

Agree or disagree with the following statement:

**The college years are the best time in a person's life.**

Give reasons and examples to support your opinion.

# MODEL TEST 3

## ANSWER KEYS

Use the following Answer Keys to check your scores on the Reading and Listening Sections of Model Test 3.

### READING SECTION

| *Reading 1* | *Reading 2* | *Reading 3* |
|---|---|---|
| 1. C | 14. B | 27. D |
| 2. C | 15. B | 28. C |
| 3. A | 16. B | 29. A |
| 4. C | 17. C | 30. C |
| 5. A | 18. D | 31. B |
| 6. D | 19. B | 32. C |
| 7. A | 20. A | 33. B |
| 8. C | 21. A | 34. C |
| 9. B | 22. B | 35. C |
| 10. C | 23. B | 36. B |
| 11. A | 24. C | 37. C |
| 12. A | 25. B | 38. C |
| 13. A, D, E | 26. B, E, F | 39. B, D, F |

## LISTENING SECTION

| *Listening Set 1* | *Listening Set 2* | *Listening Set 3* |
|---|---|---|
| 1.  B | 18.  D | 35.  B |
| 2.  C | 19.  B | 36.  B |
| 3.  A | 20.  B | 37.  D |
| 4.  C | 21.  D | 38.  D |
| 5.  B | 22.  B | 39.  B |
| 6.  C | 23.  B | 40.  A |
| 7.  B, C | 24.  A | 41.  A |
| 8.  C | 25.  D | 42.  C |
| 9.  C | 26.  B | 43.  A |
| 10.  A, C: Yes | 27.  B | 44.  B |
| 11.  B | 28.  A | 45.  D |
| 12.  C | 29.  A | 46.  D |
| 13.  A | 30.  B | 47.  B |
| 14.  C | 31.  B, C | 48.  B |
| 15.  A | 32.  B | 49.  C |
| 16.  C | 33.  A | 50.  A |
| 17.  B | 34.  B | 51.  B |

 # EXPLANATORY AND EXAMPLE ANSWERS, MODEL TEST 3

Go to the Barron's TOEFL site to study detailed Explanatory Answers for the Reading and Listening Sections, and Outlines, Example Answers, and Checklists for the Speaking and Writing Sections of Model Test 3.

# MODEL TEST 4: PROGRESS TEST

## READING SECTION

The Reading Section tests your ability to understand reading passages like those in college textbooks. The reading passages are presented in one complete section, which allows you to move to the next passage and return to a previous passage to change answers or answer questions that you may have left blank. The passages are about 700 words in length.

This is the long format for the Reading Section. On the long format, you will read four passages. After each passage, you will answer 12–14 questions about it. You may take notes while you read, but notes are not graded. You may use your notes to answer the questions. Some passages may include a word or phrase that is underlined in blue. Click on the word or phrase to see a glossary definition or explanation. Only three passages will be graded. The other passage is part of an experimental section for future tests. Because you will not know which passages will be graded, you must try to do your best on all of them.

Choose the best answer for multiple-choice questions. Follow the directions on the page or on the screen for computer-assisted questions. Most questions are worth 1 point, but the last question in each passage is worth more than 1 point.

Click on **Next** to go to the next question. Click on **Back** to return to previous questions. You may return to previous questions for all of the passages.

You can click on **Review** to see a chart of the questions you have answered and the questions you have not answered. From this screen, you can return to the question you want to answer.

Although you can spend more time on one passage and less time on another passage, you should try to pace yourself so that you are spending about 20 minutes to read each passage and answer the questions for that passage. You will have 80 minutes to complete all of the passages and answer all of the questions on the long format. A clock on the screen will show you how much time you have to complete the Reading Section.

### *Reading 1*

The following reading passage was adapted from *Sociology*, Fifth Edition by Margaret L. Andersen and Howard F. Taylor, Wadsworth, 2009.

### *"Layers of Social Class"*

P1    Taken together, income, occupation, and education are good measures of people's social standing. Using a layered model of stratification, most sociologists describe the class system in the United States as divided into several classes: upper, upper middle, middle, lower middle, and lower class. The different classes are arrayed along a continuum with those with the most money, education, and prestige at the top and those with the least at the bottom.

P2    In the United States, the *upper class* owns the major share of corporate and personal wealth; it includes those who have held wealth for generations as well as those who have recently become rich. Only a very small proportion of people actually constitute the upper class, but they control vast amounts of wealth and power in the United States. Those in this class exercise enormous control throughout society. Some wealthy individuals can wield as much power as entire nations.

P3    → Despite social myths to the contrary, the best predictor of future wealth is the family into which you are born. Each year, the business magazine *Forbes* publishes a list of the 400 wealthiest families and individuals in the country. Of all the wealth represented on the *Forbes 400* list, most is inherited, although, since the 1990s, there has been some increase in the number of people on the list with self-created wealth. Those in the upper class with newly acquired wealth are known as the *nouveau riche*. Luxury vehicles, high-priced real estate, and exclusive vacations may mark the lifestyle of the newly rich. However, although they may have vast amounts of money, they are often not accepted into "old rich" circles.

P4    → The *upper middle class* includes those with high incomes and high social prestige. They tend to be well-educated professionals or business executives. Their earnings can be quite high indeed—successful business executives can earn millions of dollars a year. It is difficult to estimate exactly how many people fall into this group because of the difficulty of drawing lines between the upper, upper middle, and middle classes. Indeed, the upper middle class is often thought of as "middle class" because their lifestyle sets the standard to which many aspire, but this lifestyle is actually unattainable by most.

P5    → The *middle class* is hard to define, in part because being "middle class" is more than just economic position. A very large portion of Americans identify themselves as middle class even though they vary widely in lifestyle and in resources at their disposal. But the idea that the United States is an open-class system leads many to think that the majority have a middle-class lifestyle; thus, the middle class becomes the ubiquitous norm even though many who call themselves middle class have a tenuous hold on this class position.

P6    The *lower middle class* includes workers in the skilled trades and low-income bureaucratic workers, many of whom may actually define themselves as middle class. Also known as the working class, this class includes blue-collar workers (those in skilled trades who do manual labor) and many service workers, such as secretaries, hair stylists, food servers, police, and firefighters. Medium to low income, education, and occupational prestige define the lower middle class relative to the class groups above it. The term *lower* in this class designation refers to the relative position of the group in the stratification system, but it has a pejorative sound to many people, especially to people who are members of this class, many of whom think of themselves as middle class.

P7    → The *lower class* is composed primarily of the displaced and poor. People in this class have little formal education and are often unemployed or working in minimum-wage jobs. A People of color and women make up a disproportionate part of this class. B The working poor include those who work at least 27 hours a week but whose wages fall below the federal poverty level. Six percent of all working people now live below the poverty line. The concept of the *underclass* has been added to the lower class. C The underclass includes those who are likely to be permanently unemployed and without means of economic support. D Rejected from the economic system, those in the under-class may become dependent on public assistance or illegal activities.

1. The word constitute in the passage is closest in meaning to

   Ⓐ explain
   Ⓑ reject
   Ⓒ form
   Ⓓ modify

2. The word enormous in the passage is closest in meaning to

   Ⓐ very large
   Ⓑ very new
   Ⓒ very early
   Ⓓ very good

3. Which of the sentences below best expresses the information in the highlighted statement in the passage? The other choices change the meaning or leave out important information.

   Ⓐ Although it is not generally accepted, your family provides the best prediction of your future wealth.
   Ⓑ You can achieve great future wealth in spite of the family in which you may have been born.
   Ⓒ It is not true that your family will restrict the acquisition of your future wealth and level of social status.
   Ⓓ Social myths are contrary to the facts about the future wealth and social status of your family.

4. Why does the author mention the *Forbes 400* in paragraph 3?

   Ⓐ To explain the meaning of the listing that appears every year
   Ⓑ To support the statement that most wealthy people inherit their money
   Ⓒ To cast doubt on the claim that family income predicts individual wealth
   Ⓓ To give examples of successful people who have modest family connections

   Paragraph 3 is marked with an arrow [→].

5. The word exclusive in the passage is closest in meaning to

   Ⓐ long
   Ⓑ expensive
   Ⓒ frequent
   Ⓓ relaxing

6. In paragraph 4, the author states that business and professional people with educational advantages are most often members of which class?

   Ⓐ lower middle class
   Ⓑ upper middle class
   Ⓒ *nouveau riche*
   Ⓓ upper class

   Paragraph 4 is marked with an arrow [→].

7. According to paragraph 5, why do most people identify themselves as middle class in the United States?

   Ⓐ They have about the same lifestyle as everyone else in the country.
   Ⓑ They prefer not to admit that there are class distinctions in the United States.
   Ⓒ They don't really know how to define their status because it is unclear.
   Ⓓ They identify themselves with the majority who have normal lifestyles.

   Paragraph 5 is marked with an arrow [→].

8. The word primarily in the passage is closest in meaning to

   ⓐ mostly
   ⓑ somewhat
   ⓒ finally
   ⓓ always

9. What can be inferred about the working class in the United States?

   ⓐ They are often not able to find entry-level jobs.
   ⓑ They work in jobs that pay minimum wage.
   ⓒ They are service workers and manual laborers.
   ⓓ They are considered lower class.

10. According to paragraph 7, why has the underclass emerged?

   ⓐ The new term was necessary because the lower class enjoyed a higher lifestyle than it had previously.
   ⓑ The increase in crime has supported a new class of people who live by engaging in illegal activities.
   ⓒ Changes in the economy have caused an entire class of people to survive by welfare or crime.
   ⓓ Minimum-wage jobs no longer support a class of people at a standard level in the economic system.

   Paragraph 7 is marked with an arrow [→].

11. All of the following are indicators of prestige in the United States EXCEPT

   ⓐ the level of education that a person has achieved
   ⓑ the amount of money that an individual has acquired
   ⓒ the type of employment that someone pursues
   ⓓ the hard work that a person does on a consistent basis

12. Look at the four squares [■] that show where the following sentence could be inserted in the passage.

   **In addition, working people constitute a surprising portion of those who are poor.**

   Where could the sentence best be added?

   Click on a square [■] to insert the sentence in the passage.

13. **Directions:** An introduction for a short summary of the passage appears below. Complete the summary by selecting the THREE answer choices that mention the most important points in the passage. Some sentences do not belong in the summary because they express ideas that are not included in the passage or are minor points from the passage. **This question is worth 2 points.**

**The levels of education, the acquisition of wealth, and occupational prestige determine social status in the United States.**

- ●

- ●

- ●

## Answer Choices

A People who have made their money more recently tend not to be accepted by those who have inherited their wealth from family holdings.

B The lower class includes working people with low incomes and a new underclass of people who are dependent on welfare or engage in crime.

C The upper class tends to acquire wealth through inheritance, whereas the upper middle class has a high income that they earn in their professions.

D Although the lifestyle of the upper middle class is the goal for the majority, it is difficult for many people to maintain this standard of living.

E Most people identify themselves as middle class, including blue-collar workers and service workers as well as bureaucratic employees.

F It is still possible to move from one social class to another in the United States by working your way up the ladder in a corporate environment.

## Reading 2

The following reading passage was adapted from *The Cosmic Perspective*, Fifth Edition by Jeffrey Bennett, et al., Addison Wesley, 2008.

### "Weather and Chaotic Systems"

P1    Weather and climate are closely related, but they are not quite the same thing. In any particular location, some days may be hotter or cooler, clearer or cloudier, calmer or stormier than others. The ever-varying combination of winds, clouds, temperature, and pressure is what we call *weather*. *Climate* is the long-term average of weather, which means it can change only on much longer time scales. The complexity of weather makes it difficult to predict, and at best, the local weather can be predicted only a week or so in advance.

P2     Scientists today have a very good understanding of the physical laws and mathematical equations that govern the behavior and motion of atoms in the air, oceans, and land. Why, then, do we have so much trouble predicting the weather? To understand why the weather is so unpredictable we must look at the nature of scientific prediction.

P3     → Suppose you want to predict the location of a car on a road 1 minute from now. You need two basic pieces of information: where the car is now, and how fast it is moving. If the car is now passing Smith Road and heading north at 1 mile per minute, it will be 1 mile north of Smith Road in 1 minute.

P4     Now, suppose you want to predict the weather. Again, you need two basic types of information: (1) the current weather and (2) how weather changes from one moment to the next. You could attempt to predict the weather by creating a "model world." For example, you could overlay a globe of the Earth with graph paper and then specify the current temperature, pressure, cloud cover, and wind within each square. These are your starting points, or initial conditions. Next, you could input all the initial conditions into a computer, along with a set of equations (physical laws) that describe the processes that can change weather from one moment to the next.

P5     → Suppose the initial conditions represent the weather around the Earth at this very moment and you run your computer model to predict the weather for the next month in New York City. The model might tell you that tomorrow will be warm and sunny, with cooling during the next week and a major storm passing through a month from now. But suppose you run the model again, making one minor change in the initial conditions—say, a small change in the wind speed somewhere over Brazil. A This slightly different initial condition will not change the weather prediction for tomorrow in New York City. B But for next month's weather, the two predictions may not agree at all! C

P6     The disagreement between the two predictions arises because the laws governing weather can cause very tiny changes in initial conditions to be greatly magnified over time. D This extreme sensitivity to initial conditions is sometimes called the *butterfly effect*: If initial conditions change by as much as the flap of a butterfly's wings, the resulting prediction may be very different.

P7     → The butterfly effect is a hallmark of *chaotic systems*. Simple systems are described by linear equations in which, for example, increasing a cause produces a proportional increase in an effect. In contrast, chaotic systems are described by nonlinear equations, which allow for subtler and more intricate interactions. For example, the economy is nonlinear because a rise in interest rates does not automatically produce a corresponding change in consumer spending. Weather is nonlinear because a change in the wind speed in one location does not automatically produce a corresponding change in another location.

P8  → Despite their name, chaotic systems are not necessarily random. In fact, many chaotic systems have a kind of underlying order that explains the general features of their behavior even while details at any particular moment remain unpredictable. In a sense, many chaotic systems—like the weather—are "predictably unpredictable." Our understanding of chaotic systems is increasing at a tremendous rate, but much remains to be learned about them.

14. According to the passage, why will it be difficult to predict weather?

Ⓐ We have to learn more about chaotic systems.
Ⓑ We don't communicate globally.
Ⓒ We need more powerful computers.
Ⓓ We must understand the physical laws of atoms.

15. The word particular in the passage is closest in meaning to

Ⓐ basic
Ⓑ specific
Ⓒ unusual
Ⓓ new

16. The word govern in the passage is closest in meaning to

Ⓐ change
Ⓑ control
Ⓒ show
Ⓓ explain

17. Why does the author mention "a car" in paragraph 3?

Ⓐ The car is an example of how conditions are used to make predictions.
Ⓑ The author digresses in order to tell a story about a car.
Ⓒ The car introduces the concept of computer models.
Ⓓ The mathematical equations for the car are very simple to understand.

Paragraph 3 is marked with an arrow [→].

18. Why do the predictions disagree for the computer model described in paragraph 5?

Ⓐ The conditions at the beginning were very different.
Ⓑ The model was not accurately programmed.
Ⓒ Computer models cannot predict weather.
Ⓓ Over time models are less reliable.

Paragraph 5 is marked with an arrow [→].

19. Why is weather considered a chaotic system?

Ⓐ Because it is made up of random features
Ⓑ Because it is not yet very well understood
Ⓒ Because it is described by nonlinear equations
Ⓓ Because it does not have an orderly structure

20. Based on information in paragraph 6, which of the following best explains the term "butterfly effect"?

   ⓐ Slight variations in initial conditions can cause very different results.
   ⓑ A butterfly's wings can be used to predict different conditions in various locations.
   ⓒ The weather is as difficult to predict as the rate of a butterfly's wings when it flaps them.
   ⓓ A butterfly flaps its wings in one location, which automatically produces a result in another place.

   Paragraph 6 is marked with an arrow [➜].

21. Why does the author mention "the economy" in paragraph 7?

   ⓐ To contrast a simple system with a chaotic system
   ⓑ To provide an example of another chaotic system
   ⓒ To compare nonlinear equations with linear equations
   ⓓ To prove that all nonlinear systems are not chaotic

   Paragraph 7 is marked with an arrow [➜].

22. The word random in the passage is closest in meaning to

   ⓐ practical
   ⓑ objective
   ⓒ controlled
   ⓓ unorganized

23. The word features in the passage is closest in meaning to

   ⓐ problems
   ⓑ exceptions
   ⓒ characteristics
   ⓓ benefits

24. In paragraph 8, what does the author suggest about our knowledge of chaotic systems?

   ⓐ It will never allow us to make accurate predictions.
   ⓑ It has not improved very much over the years.
   ⓒ It reveals details that can be predicted quite accurately.
   ⓓ It requires more research by the scientific community.

   Paragraph 8 is marked with an arrow [➜].

25. Look at the four squares [■] that show where the following sentence could be inserted in the passage.

   **For next week's weather, the new model may yield a slightly different prediction.**

   Where could the sentence best be added?

   Click on a square [■] to insert the sentence in the passage.

26. **Directions:** An introduction for a short summary of the passage appears below. Complete the summary by selecting the THREE answer choices that mention the most important points in the passage. Some sentences do not belong in the summary because they express ideas that are not included in the passage or are minor points from the passage. *This question is worth 2 points.*

**Because weather is a chaotic system, it is very difficult to predict.**

● 

● 

● 

### Answer Choices

Ⓐ The accuracy of weather prediction will improve as we make progress in the application of computers to equations.

Ⓑ It is very easy to make predictions about the location of a car when you know where it is and how fast it is going.

Ⓒ A slight variation in initial conditions will cause a very different prediction for weather over the long term.

Ⓓ Because weather is chaotic but not random, it may be described by nonlinear equations that provide for sensitive interactions.

Ⓔ The economic system demonstrates chaotic behavior, and it must be represented by a nonlinear equation.

Ⓕ Weather is predictable only within a time frame of a few weeks because of the nature of scientific prediction.

### *Reading 3*

The following reading passage was adapted from *Gilbert's Living with Art*, Eighth Edition by Mark Gettein, McGraw-Hill Companies, Inc., 2008.

### *"Building with Arches"*

#### Round Arch and Vault

 P1    → Although the round arch was used by the ancient peoples of Mesopotamia several centuries before our common era, it was most fully developed by the Romans, who perfected the form in the 2nd century B.C.E. The arch has many virtues. In addition to being an attractive form, it enables the architect to open up fairly large spaces in a wall without risking the building's structural soundness. These spaces admit light, reduce the weight of the walls, and decrease the amount of material needed. As utilized by the Romans, the arch is a perfect semicircle, although it may seem elongated if it rests on columns. It is constructed from wedge-shaped pieces of stone that meet at an angle always perpendicular to the curve of the arch. Because of tensions and compressions inherent in the form, the arch is stable only when it is complete, when the topmost stone, the **keystone,** has been set in place. For this reason an arch under construction must be supported from below, usually by a wooden framework.

**P2**  → Among the most elegant and enduring of Roman structures based on the arch is the Pont du Gard at Nimes, France, built about 15 C.E. when the empire was nearing its farthest expansion. At this time, Roman industry, commerce, and agriculture were at their peak. Engineering was applied to an ambitious system of public-works projects, not just in Italy but in the outlying areas as well. The Pont du Gard functioned as an aqueduct, a structure meant to transport water, and its lower level served as a footbridge across the river. That it stands today virtually intact after nearly two thousand years (and is crossed by cyclists on the route of the famous Tour de France bicycle race) testifies to the Romans' brilliant engineering skills. Visually, the Pont du Gard exemplifies the best qualities of arch construction. Solid and heavy, obviously durable, it is shot through with open spaces that make it seem light and its weight-bearing capabilities effortless.

**P3**  → When the arch is extended in depth—when it is, in reality, many arches placed flush one behind the other—the result is called a **barrel vault**. This vault construction makes it possible to create large interior spaces. The Romans made great use of the barrel vault, but for its finest expression we look many hundreds of years later, to the churches of the Middle Ages.

**P4**  → The church of Sainte-Foy, in the French city of Conques, is an example of the style prevalent throughout Western Europe from about 1050 to 1200—a style known as **Romanesque**. Earlier churches had used the Roman round arch and barrel vault so as to add height to their churches. Until this period most churches had beamed wooden roofs, which not only posed a threat of fire but also limited the height to which architects could aspire. With the stone barrel vault, they could achieve the soaring, majestic space we see in the nave of Sainte-Foy to span the spaces between the interior columns that ultimately held up the roof. With the Romanesque style, builders set a stone barrel vault as a ceiling over the nave, hiding the roof structure from view. The barrel vault unified the interior visually, providing a soaring, majestic climax to the rhythms announced by the arches below.

**Pointed Arch and Vault**

**P5**  → While the round arch and vault of the Romanesque era solved many problems and made many things possible, they nevertheless had certain drawbacks. For one thing, a round arch, to be stable, must be a semicircle; therefore, the height of the arch is limited by its width. Two other difficulties were weight and darkness. Barrel vaults are both literally and visually heavy, calling for huge masses of stone to maintain their structural stability. They exert an outward thrust all along their base, which builders countered by setting them in massive walls that they dared not weaken with light-admitting openings. The **Gothic** period in Europe, which followed the Romanesque, solved these problems with the pointed arch. Ⓐ

**P6**  The pointed arch, while seemingly not very different from the round one, offers many advantages. Ⓑ Because the sides arc up to a point, weight is channeled down to the ground at a steeper angle, and therefore the arch can be taller. The vault constructed from such an arch also can be much taller than a barrel vault. C Architects of the Gothic period found they did not need heavy masses of material throughout the curve of the vault, as long as the major points of intersection were reinforced. D

**Glossary**

nave:  the long central area in a church with aisles on each side

27. Why does the author mention the "keystone" in paragraph 1?

   A To explain the engineering of an arch
   B To provide historical background on arches
   C To point out one of the virtues of arches
   D To suggest an alternative to the arch

Paragraph 1 is marked with an arrow [→].

28. The word inherent in the passage is closest in meaning to

   A uncertain
   B unsatisfactory
   C expansive
   D essential

29. The Pont du Gard mentioned in paragraph 2 has all of the following characteristics EXCEPT

   A it was an aqueduct
   B it is still being used
   C it was built 2,000 years ago
   D it was repaired recently

Paragraph 2 is marked with an arrow [→].

30. The word virtually in the passage is closest in meaning to

   A obviously
   B accurately
   C routinely
   D practically

31. According to paragraph 3, what is the advantage of a barrel vault?

   A It was used in the Middle Ages.
   B Many arches were joined.
   C The space inside was larger.
   D It was a typical Roman look.

Paragraph 3 is marked with an arrow [→].

32. What can be inferred from paragraph 4 about Romanesque architecture?

    Ⓐ Arches and barrel vaults were used in the designs.
    Ⓑ Wood beams characterized the buildings.
    Ⓒ The structures were smaller than those of Roman style.
    Ⓓ The architecture was popular during the Roman occupation.

    Paragraph 4 is marked with an arrow [➔].

33. Which of the sentences below best expresses the information in the highlighted statement in the passage? The other choices change the meaning or leave out important information.

    Ⓐ Architects wanted to build higher ceilings in churches, but they were limited because of the fire hazard caused by wooden beams in the roofs.
    Ⓑ The majority of the churches prior to this time were constructed with wooden roofs that caused a considerable fire hazard because of their height.
    Ⓒ The wood beams in the roofs of most churches before this period were a concern because of fire and the constraints they imposed on the height of the ceiling.
    Ⓓ The limitations on the architecture of the churches were a result of the construction materials and the limited vision of the architects.

34. The word achieve in the passage is closest in meaning to

    Ⓐ retain
    Ⓑ accomplish
    Ⓒ decorate
    Ⓓ finance

35. The word ultimately in the passage is closest in meaning to

    Ⓐ partially
    Ⓑ frequently
    Ⓒ carefully
    Ⓓ finally

36. According to paragraph 5, why are Romanesque churches so dark?

    Ⓐ It was a characteristic of construction with pointed arches.
    Ⓑ It was too difficult to make windows in the heavy materials.
    Ⓒ Openings for light could have compromised the structure.
    Ⓓ Reinforcements covered the areas where light could shine in.

    Paragraph 5 is marked with an arrow [➔].

37. How did Gothic architects extend the height of their arches?

    Ⓐ By using barrel vaults
    Ⓑ By designing pointed arches
    Ⓒ By including a nave
    Ⓓ By adding windows

38. Look at the four squares [■] that show where the following sentence could be inserted in the passage.

    **These reinforcements, called ribs, are visible in the nave ceiling of Reims Cathedral.**

    Where could the sentence best be added?

    Click on a square [■] to insert the sentence in the passage.

39. **Directions:** Complete the table by matching the phrases on the left with the headings on the right. Select the appropriate answer choices and drag them to the type of architecture to which they relate. TWO of the answer choices will NOT be used. *This question is worth 4 points.*

    To delete an answer choice, click on it. To see the passage, click on **View Text**.

| Answer Choices | Round Arch |
|---|---|
| A  Allowed architects to create a taller arch | ● |
| B  Used in fortresses so that the soldiers could see out | ● |
| C  Represented the Romanesque style of architecture | ● |
| D  Similar to arches constructed in the ancient world | ● |
| E  Popular in many structures of the Gothic period | **Pointed Arch** |
| F  Required special building materials for construction | ● |
| G  Prevalent in churches during the Middle Ages | ● |
| H  Associated with structures that include barrel vaults | ● |
| I  Permitted openings in or around them for light | |

## *Reading 4*

The following reading passage was adapted from *Biology*, Eighth Edition by Neil A. Campbell, et al., Pearson Education, Inc., 2008.

### *"The Evolution of Birds"*

**The Origin of Birds**

P1    Analysis of birds and of reptilian fossils indicate that birds belong to the group called *therapods*. Several species of dinosaurs closely related to birds had feathers with vanes, and a wider range of species had filamentous feathers. Such findings imply that feathers evolved long before powered flight. Among the possible functions of these early feathers were insulation, camouflage, and courtship display.

**Derived Characteristics of Birds**

P2    → Many of the characteristics of birds are adaptations that facilitate flight, including weight-saving modifications that make flying more efficient. For example, birds lack a urinary bladder, and the females of most species have only one ovary. Living birds are also toothless, an adaptation that trims the weight of the head.

P3    A bird's most obvious adaptations for flight are its wings and feathers. Feathers are made of the protein B-keratin, which is also found in the scales of other reptiles. The shape and arrangement of the feathers form the wings into airfoils, and they illustrate some of the same principles of aerodynamics as the wings of an airplane. Power for flapping the wings comes from contractions of large pectoral (breast) muscles anchored to a keel on the sternum (breastbone). Some birds, such as eagles and hawks, have wings adapted for soaring on air currents and flap their wings only occasionally; other birds, including hummingbirds, must flap their wings continuously to stay aloft. Among the fastest birds are the appropriately named swifts, which can fly up to 170 km/hr.

P4    A Flight provides numerous benefits. B It enhances hunting and scavenging; many birds consume flying insects, an abundant, highly nutritious food resource. C Flight also provides ready escape from earthbound predators and enables some birds to migrate great distances to exploit different food resources and seasonal breeding areas. D

P5    Flying requires a great expenditure of energy from an active metabolism. Birds are endothermic; they use their own metabolic heat to maintain a high, constant body temperature. Feathers, and in some species layers of fat, provide insulation that enables birds to retain their body heat. The lungs have tiny tubes leading to and from elastic air sacs that improve airflow and oxygen uptake. This efficient respiratory system with a four-chambered heart keeps tissues well supplied with oxygen and nutrients, supporting a high rate of metabolism.

P6    Flight also requires both acute vision and fine muscle control. Birds have excellent eyesight. The visual and motor areas of the brain are well developed, and the brain is proportionately larger than those of amphibians and nonbird reptiles. Birds generally display very complex behaviors, particularly during breeding season, when they engage in elaborate courtship rituals.

P7    How did flight evolve in the therapods? In one scenario, feathers may have enabled the small, running dinosaurs chasing prey or escaping predators to gain extra lift as they jumped up into the air. Or, small dinosaurs could have gained traction as they ran up hills by flapping their feathered forelimbs—a behavior seen in birds today. In a third scenario, some dinosaurs could have climbed trees and glided, aided by feathers. Whether birds took to the air from the ground up or from the trees down, an essential question being studied by scientists ranging from paleontologists to engineers is how their efficient flight stroke evolved.

P8    → By 150 million years ago, feathered therapods had evolved into birds. *Archaeopteryx*, which was discovered in a German limestone quarry in 1861, remains the earliest known bird. It had feathered wings but retained ancestral characteristics such as teeth, clawed digits in its wings, and a long tail. *Archaeopteryx* flew well at high speeds, but unlike a present-day bird, it could not take off from a standing position. Fossils of later birds from the Cretaceous show a gradual loss of certain ancestral dinosaur features, such as teeth and clawed forelimbs, as well as the acquisition of innovations found in extant birds, including a short tail covered by a fan of feathers.

**Glossary**
Cretaceous: a time period, 144–65 million years ago

40. Which of the sentences below best expresses the information in the highlighted statement in the passage? The other choices change the meaning or leave out important information.

    Ⓐ Results of investigations indicate that birds probably flew before they had feathers.
    Ⓑ Analysis suggests that birds did not fly immediately after they had developed feathers.
    Ⓒ The time frame for the evolution of feathers is not clear from the studies cited.
    Ⓓ According to researchers, birds developed feathers in order to achieve flight.

41. The word modifications in the passage is closest in meaning to

    Ⓐ made different
    Ⓑ made better
    Ⓒ made smaller
    Ⓓ made modern

42. According to paragraph 2, how did birds adapt to achieve efficient flight?

    Ⓐ They developed new, lighter organs.
    Ⓑ Their muscles became smaller over time.
    Ⓒ Most of their weight was distributed in their heads.
    Ⓓ Heavy teeth disappeared during evolution.

    Paragraph 2 is marked with an arrow [→].

43. In paragraph 3, how does the author explain the term "keratin"?

   Ⓐ By identifying it in feathers and scales
   Ⓑ By comparing it to airfoils
   Ⓒ By providing a definition in the text
   Ⓓ By describing the way that it looks

   Paragraph 3 is marked with an arrow [➔].

44. According to paragraph 3, which of the following is true about the wings of birds?

   Ⓐ All birds flap their wings constantly by using breast muscles.
   Ⓑ Eagles and hawks have wings that propel them at 170 km/hr.
   Ⓒ The airfoils of birds function like the wings on airplanes.
   Ⓓ Wings are attached to airfoils in the bird's skeletal structure.

   Paragraph 3 is marked with an arrow [➔].

45. The word principles in the passage is closest in meaning to

   Ⓐ criticism
   Ⓑ examples
   Ⓒ topics
   Ⓓ rules

46. The word elaborate in the passage is *opposite* in meaning to

   Ⓐ simple
   Ⓑ quiet
   Ⓒ sad
   Ⓓ short

47. The word essential in the passage is closest in meaning to

   Ⓐ very clear
   Ⓑ very important
   Ⓒ very difficult
   Ⓓ very new

48. According to the passage, how did therapods develop flight?

   Ⓐ Engineers believe that they flapped their wings to gain lift.
   Ⓑ Scientists have proposed several different possibilities for flight.
   Ⓒ Paleontologists think that they glided down from high trees.
   Ⓓ Researchers confirm that flight began with running and jumping.

49. According to paragraph 8, what can be inferred about *Archaeopteryx*?

   Ⓐ A feathered fantail was prominent.
   Ⓑ Lift off was achieved by running or gliding.
   Ⓒ Teeth had been replaced by a beak.
   Ⓓ The habitat extended throughout Europe.

   Paragraph 8 is marked with an arrow [➔].

50. All of the following are mentioned as adaptations to the bird's anatomy to accommodate flight EXCEPT

    Ⓐ the arrangement of feathers
    Ⓑ a high metabolic rate
    Ⓒ very sharp eyes
    Ⓓ small legs and feet

51. Look at the four squares [■] that show where the following sentence could be inserted in the passage.

**Furthermore, migration allows birds to avoid climates that are too hot or too cold during certain seasons.**

Where could the sentence best be added?

Click on a square [■] to insert the sentence in the passage.

52. **Directions:** An introduction for a short summary of the passage appears below. Complete the summary by selecting the THREE answer choices that mention the most important points in the passage. Some sentences do not belong in the summary because they express ideas that are not included in the passage or are minor points from the passage. *This question is worth 2 points.*

**Birds evolved 150 million years ago.**

- ●
- ●
- ●

### Answer Choices

Ⓐ Birds and reptiles are most probably related.

Ⓑ Feathers are among the most unusual evolutionary changes.

Ⓒ Many structural adaptations were required for birds to fly.

Ⓓ Therapods are relatively small, meat-eating dinosaurs.

Ⓔ There are a number of advantages for creatures that fly.

Ⓕ Migration patterns are typical of many species of birds.

# LISTENING SECTION

 **Model Test 4, Listening Section, Track 75**

The Listening Section tests your ability to understand spoken English that is typical of inter-actions and academic speech on college campuses. During the test, you will listen to conver-sations, lectures, and discussions, and you will answer questions about them.

This is the short format for the Listening Section. On the short format, you will listen to two conversations, two lectures, and two discussions. After each listening passage, you will answer 5–6 questions about it.

You will hear each passage one time. You may take notes while you listen, but notes are not graded. You may use your notes to answer the questions.

Choose the best answer for multiple-choice questions. Follow the directions on the page or on the screen for computer-assisted questions. Click on **Next** and then on **OK** to go on to the next question. You cannot return to previous questions.

The Listening Section is divided into sets. Each set includes one conversation, one lecture, and one discussion. You will have 10 minutes to answer all of the questions for each set. You will have 20 minutes to answer all of the questions on the short format. A clock on the screen will show you how much time you have to complete your answers for the section. The clock does NOT count the time you are listening to the conversations, lectures, and discussions.

## *Listening 1 "Professor's Office"*

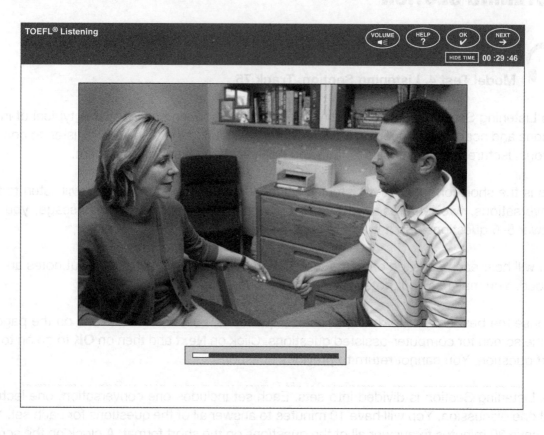

1. Why does the man go to see his professor?

   Ⓐ To take a makeup test for a class that he missed

   Ⓑ To explain why he has been absent from class

   Ⓒ To turn in an extra credit project to the professor

   Ⓓ To ask the professor how to bring up his grade

2. Why did Ernie get a low grade on the last test?

   Ⓐ He does not understand the material.

   Ⓑ He is not a very good student.

   Ⓒ He did not have time to finish it.

   Ⓓ He was in a hurry to leave the class.

3. What do we know about the test?

   Ⓐ There were 100 questions on it.

   Ⓑ It was worth 25 percent of the final grade.

   Ⓒ The test was an extra credit assignment.

   Ⓓ The questions were very difficult.

4. Why does the professor say this:

&#9398; Because she doesn't understand what the man wants her to do
&#9399; Because she has finished the discussion about the man's problem
&#9400; Because she wants the man to be more specific about his plan
&#9401; Because she does not want to do what the man suggests

5. What can be inferred about the professor?

&#9398; She tries to be fair to all of her students.
&#9399; She is not very flexible about her policies.
&#9400; She does not have very many students.
&#9401; She is not sure what she wants to do.

## Listening 2 "Anthropology Class"

6. Which of the following is the main topic of the lecture?

    Ⓐ A progressive view of agriculture
    Ⓑ The conditions for the development of agriculture
    Ⓒ A comparison of hunter-gatherers and farmers
    Ⓓ The negative effects of agriculture on early farmers

7. What are two key characteristics of hunter-gatherers mentioned in the lecture?

    Click on 2 answer choices.

    Ⓐ They were taller than farmers.

    Ⓑ They ate less well than farmers.

    Ⓒ They lived longer than farmers.

    Ⓓ They were less physically fit than farmers.

8. Why does the professor say this:

    Ⓐ To emphasize the point that he has just made
    Ⓑ To indicate that another point will be made
    Ⓒ To demonstrate that the point is his opinion
    Ⓓ To regain the students' attention for the next point

9. How does the professor organize his lecture?

    Ⓐ He contrasts older theories of agriculture with newer ones.
    Ⓑ He makes an argument for the revisionist view of agriculture.
    Ⓒ He defines revisionism by giving examples of early farmers.
    Ⓓ He provides a chronological account of early farmers.

10. Which of the following statements best summarizes the position of the revisionists?

    Ⓐ The agricultural revolution affected all human activity.
    Ⓑ The development of agriculture had a positive influence on nutrition.
    Ⓒ Agriculture contributed to the health risks for early farmers.
    Ⓓ Agricultural people had to move from place to place to plant crops.

11. In the lecture, the professor describes the relationship between health and agriculture. Indicate whether each of the following is true or false. Click in the correct box for each phrase.

|   |   | Yes | No |
|---|---|---|---|
| A | Epidemics were spread by crowded towns and trade. | | |
| B | Crop failures threatened the entire population. | | |
| C | Wars with invading hunter-gatherers devastated them. | | |
| D | Unbalanced diets contributed to malnutrition. | | |
| E | Hard labor damaged their bones. | | |

*Listening 3  "Business Class"*

12. What is the discussion mainly about?

    &Ⓐ Commercials on television
    Ⓑ Marketing brand-name products
    Ⓒ A book by Rob Frankel
    Ⓓ Selling Aunt Ruby's chicken

13. Why does the professor say this:

    Ⓐ To emphasize the importance of commercials
    Ⓑ To correct something that he said earlier
    Ⓒ To identify the time limits for most commercials
    Ⓓ To relate new information to a previous example

14. According to the professor, why do consumers develop brand loyalty?

    Ⓐ They have a relationship with the personality that the product projects.
    Ⓑ They are able to recognize the brand easily when they see it.
    Ⓒ They tend to make decisions based on recommendations by friends.
    Ⓓ They find a product that they like and continue to buy it.

15. How does the professor emphasize his point about branding?

    Ⓐ He uses Aunt Ruby's chicken as an example.
    Ⓑ He defines it by contrasting it with related concepts.
    Ⓒ He refers to a book that he has written.
    Ⓓ He shows a familiar commercial in class.

16. Why does Susan mention laundry detergent?

    Ⓐ To give an example of price wars
    Ⓑ To show that consumers buy different brands
    Ⓒ To name an industry that introduces new brands
    Ⓓ To clarify the concept of brand loyalty

17. According to the discussion, what would be a good way to sell a product?

    Ⓐ Design a good logo to present the product to the public
    Ⓑ Hire a celebrity that customers like and relate to
    Ⓒ Make it easy for consumers to recognize the packaging
    Ⓓ Increase the customer service for the product

*Listening 4 "Professor's Office"*

18. Why does the student go to see her professor?

&#9398; She needs a new course syllabus.
&#9399; She has questions about the project.
&#9400; She wants to change a requirement.
&#9401; She is trying to enroll in the class.

19. Why does the student say this:

&#9398; She thinks the requirement is important.
&#9399; She is not sure about the percentage.
&#9400; She wants the professor to change his mind.
&#9401; She is surprised that the project is worth so much.

20. How will the professor grade the project?

    Ⓐ He will grade the group based on their presentation in class.
    Ⓑ He will give each student an individual grade and a group grade.
    Ⓒ He has the group give individual grades for each member.
    Ⓓ He gives the group a grade based on their leadership.

21. What advice does the professor provide about group work?

    Click on 2 answer choices.

    Ⓐ Spend class time on the project.

    Ⓑ Find people with similar schedules.

    Ⓒ Use Google documents.

    Ⓓ Email the group regularly.

22. What is the professor's attitude toward the student?

    Ⓐ He does not mind explaining the requirements.
    Ⓑ He does not want to accept another student in class.
    Ⓒ He is not pleased about repeating the instructions.
    Ⓓ He is rushed because it is time for his class.

## Listening 5 "Biology Class"

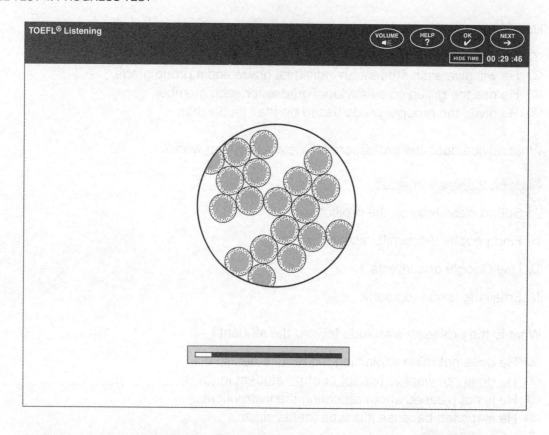

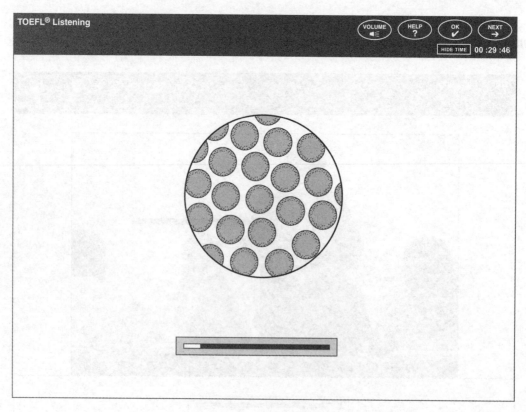

23. What aspect of blood does the professor mainly discuss?

    Ⓐ An explanation of stem cells
    Ⓑ A process for blood transfusion
    Ⓒ A method for producing artificial blood
    Ⓓ A discussion of blood typing

24. Why does the student say this:

    Ⓐ She is apologizing for disagreeing with the professor.
    Ⓑ She is interrupting politely to ask a question.
    Ⓒ She is talking to herself during the lecture.
    Ⓓ She is changing the subject of the professor's talk.

25. Why does the professor mention fingerprints?

    Ⓐ To demonstrate that blood types are different for individuals
    Ⓑ To explain how most of the blood tests are performed
    Ⓒ To explain why O blood is considered universal
    Ⓓ To help students remember the different antigens

26. In cross matching, how does a compatible match appear under the microscope?

    Ⓐ All of the cells are at an equal distance from each other.
    Ⓑ The arrangement of the cells looks like two parallel lines.
    Ⓒ The cells tend to group together in a large clump.
    Ⓓ The red cells and the plasma separate in an irregular pattern.

27. Why does the professor mention artificial blood?

    Ⓐ She is referring to the textbook.
    Ⓑ She is answering a question.
    Ⓒ She is reporting her research.
    Ⓓ She is joking with the students.

28. What does the professor imply when she says this:

    Ⓐ She is very uncertain about the risks of the research.
    Ⓑ She is somewhat interested in doing research in this area.
    Ⓒ She is withdrawing her support for future research.
    Ⓓ She agrees that research should continue in spite of problems.

## *Listening 6 "Orientation Session"*

29. What is this discussion mainly about?

   Ⓐ Success in college
   Ⓑ How to read faster
   Ⓒ Academic study skills
   Ⓓ Research on college students

30. How does the professor organize the discussion?

   Ⓐ She cites research to support her arguments.
   Ⓑ She gives a demonstration of her theory.
   Ⓒ She debates the issues with her students.
   Ⓓ She shares strategies that she developed.

31. Why does the professor mention running?

   Ⓐ To digress from the topic with a personal story
   Ⓑ To make a comparison between reading and running
   Ⓒ To show that reading requires physical effort
   Ⓓ To clarify the times two rule

32. Why does the professor say this:

   Ⓐ She doesn't think the point is very important.
   Ⓑ She is trying to finish the lecture on time.
   Ⓒ She thinks the idea will fit in better later on.
   Ⓓ She doesn't want the student to interrupt her.

33. The professor mentions several negative habits. Match these habits to the explanations. Click on the habit and drag it to the correct explanation.

| Habit | Explanation |
|---|---|
|  | Pauses that the eye makes |
|  | Reading the same words more than once |
|  | Moving your lips while reading |

   Ⓐ Fixating
   Ⓑ Auditory reading
   Ⓒ Regressing

34. What would the professor probably like the students to do?

    Ⓐ Spend more time studying outside of class
    Ⓑ Use their dictionaries when they are reading
    Ⓒ Take one of her classes at the college
    Ⓓ Get help at the Learning Center

 **Please turn off the audio. There is a 10-minute break between the Listening Section and the Speaking Section.**

# SPEAKING SECTION

 **Model Test 4, Speaking Section, Track 76**

The Speaking Section tests your ability to communicate in English in an academic setting. During the test, you will be presented with six speaking questions. The questions ask for a response to a single question, a conversation, a talk, or a lecture. The prompts and questions are presented only one time.

You may take notes as you listen, but notes are not graded. You may use your notes to answer the questions. Some of the questions ask for a response to a reading passage and a talk or a lecture. The reading passages and the questions are written, but the directions will be spoken.

Your speaking will be evaluated on both the fluency of the language and the accuracy of the content. You will have 15–20 seconds to prepare and 45–60 seconds to respond to each question. Typically, a good response will require all of the response time and the answer will be complete by the end of the response time.

You will have about 20 minutes to complete the Speaking Section. A clock on the screen will show you how much time you have to prepare each of your answers and how much time you have to record each response.

*Independent Speaking Question 1 "A City"*

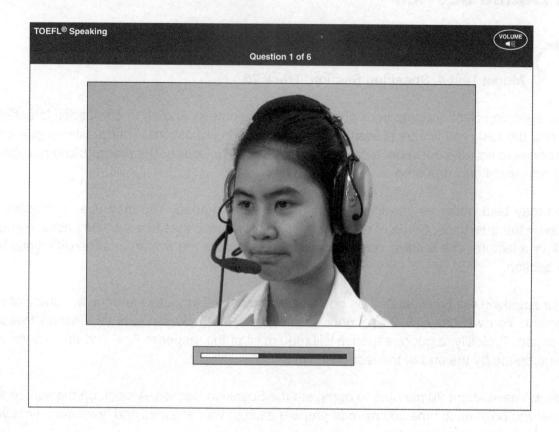

 Listen for a question about a familiar topic.

**Question**
Which city in the world would you like to visit? Use specific reasons and details to explain your choice.

Preparation Time: 15 seconds
Recording Time: 45 seconds

## *Independent Speaking Question 2 "Schools"*

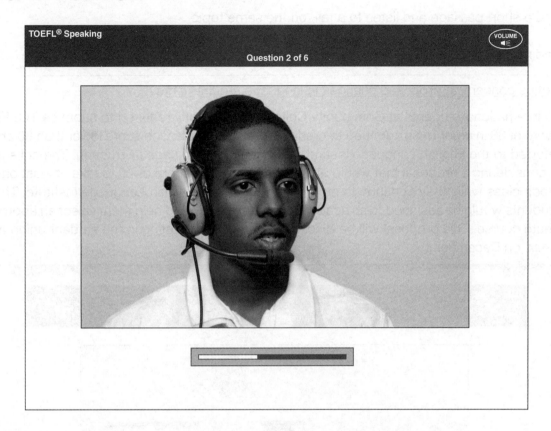

 Listen for a question that asks your opinion about a familiar topic.

**Question**
Agree or disagree with the following statement:

A coeducational school is a better environment than a school that provides education for men only or women only. Use specific reasons and examples to support your opinion.

Preparation Time: 15 seconds
Recording Time: 45 seconds

### *Integrated Speaking Question 3 "English Requirements"*

Read a short passage and listen to a talk on the same topic.

Reading Time: 45 seconds

---

Notice concerning proposed changes in language requirements

All international students at Community College are currently required to submit a TOEFL score of 80 in order to be admitted to credit classes. Students who score lower than 80 are referred to the English Language Institute for additional language instruction. The college is considering a proposal that would allow students with a score of 75 to take at least one credit class while they continue to study part time in the English Language Institute. The students would be assigned to an academic advisor who would help them select an appropriate course. This proposal will be discussed at a public meeting in the student union at 7 P.M. on December 1.

---

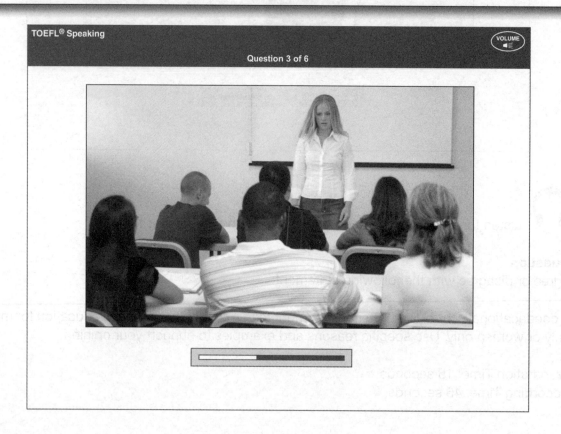

 Now listen to a student who is speaking at the meeting. She is expressing her opinion about the policy for international students.

### Question
The student expresses her opinion of the policy for international students. Report her opinion and explain the reasons that she gives for having that opinion.

Preparation Time: 30 seconds
Recording Time: 60 seconds

## Integrated Speaking Question 4 "Myths and Legends"

Read a short passage and then listen to part of a lecture on the same topic.

Reading Time: 45 seconds

---

Myths and Legends

Myths are stories that explain the origin of events from the distant past, as, for example, how the universe was created, how human beings and animals populated the Earth, the reason for death, and the nature of the afterlife. Myths are usually tied to religious beliefs and involve beings with supernatural powers. In contrast, legends are stories about more recent times, and the characters are often real people with heroic qualities that reflect the values of their culture. Because the heroes in legends become larger than life as the legend is retold and embellished, they may actually be attributed with supernatural powers like their mythological counterparts. This blurs the distinction between mythology and legends.

---

TOEFL® Speaking                                                        VOLUME

Question 4 of 6

---

 Now listen to part of a lecture in an anthropology class. The professor is talking about the legend of Paul Bunyan.

## Question

Using the main points and examples from the reading, explain the differences between myths and legends. Then refer to the lecture to explain why Paul Bunyan would be considered a legend.

Preparation Time: 30 seconds
Recording Time: 60 seconds

## *Integrated Speaking Question 5 "Roommate"*

 Now listen to a conversation between a student and her advisor.

### Question

Describe the woman's problem and the two suggestions that her advisor makes about how to handle it. What do you think the woman should do, and why?

Preparation Time: 20 seconds
Recording Time: 60 seconds

## *Integrated Speaking Question 6 "Urban Wildlife"*

 Now listen to part of a lecture in a biology class. The professor is discussing the types of habitats for wildlife found in cities.

### Question
Using the main points and examples from the lecture, describe the two general types of habitats for wildlife found in urban areas.

Preparation Time: 20 seconds
Recording Time: 60 seconds

# WRITING SECTION

The Writing Section tests your ability to write essays in English similar to those that you would write in college courses. During the test, you will write two essays.

**The Integrated Essay.** First you will read an academic passage and then you will listen to a lecture on the same topic. You may take notes as you read and listen, but notes are not graded. You may use your notes to write the essay. The reading passage will disappear while you are listening to the lecture, but the passage will return to the screen for reference when you begin to write your essay. You will have 20 minutes to plan, write, and revise your response. Typically, a good essay for the integrated topic will require that you write 150–225 words.

**The Independent Essay.** You will read a question on the screen. It usually asks for your opinion about a familiar topic. You will have 30 minutes to plan, write, and revise your response. Typically, a good essay for the independent topic will require that you write 300–350 words.

A clock on the screen will show you how much time you have left to complete each essay.

## *Integrated Essay "Sales Principles"*

You have 20 minutes to plan, write, and revise your response to a reading passage and a lecture on the same topic. First, read the passage and take notes. Then, listen to the lecture and take notes. Finally, write your response to the writing question. Typically, a good response will require that you write 150–225 words.

**Reading Passage**
Time: 3 minutes

---

Three basic principles have been shown to increase sales. The first principle is to make more calls. To get more orders, it only makes sense to make more calls. In addition to contacting more potential customers, the salesperson will also get better at making calls because of the practice. Although the exact number of calls to increase the volume of sales will vary with the product, encouraging the sales force to add even a few more calls to their goals has produced good results for all types of businesses.

The second principle, contacting people who hold higher positions in the organization, is effective for two reasons. In the first place, it is more efficient to contact someone with the authority to approve the sale. If the call is made to a lower-level employee, a salesperson may be referred higher and a second call may be necessary. In the second place, if the call is made to a person who holds a lower position, that employee will probably have to take the idea up the line to a higher-level supervisor and will probably not be able to make as strong a case for the sale as the salesperson who made the original contact.

Clearly, closing is the most important part of a sale. If a salesperson continues the conversation without closing, the sale may be lost. Rushing the customer is not a good idea, but when potential objections have been addressed, creating a sense of urgency with some kind of deadline or incentive, and doing it earlier rather than later, will improve the chances of making the sale.

---

**Model Test 4, Writing Section, Track 77**

 Now listen to a lecture on the same topic as the passage that you have just read.

**Question**

Summarize the main points in the lecture, and then explain how they cast doubt on the ideas in the reading passage.

*Independent Essay "Lifestyle"*

**Question**

**Many people believe that it is very important to make large amounts of money, while others are satisfied to earn a comfortable living.**

Analyze each viewpoint and take a stand. Give specific reasons and examples for your position.

# MODEL TEST 4

## ANSWER KEYS

Use the following Answer Keys to check your scores on the Reading and Listening Sections of Model Test 4.

### READING SECTION

| *Reading 1* | *Reading 2* | *Reading 3* | *Reading 4* |
|---|---|---|---|
| 1. C | 14. A | 27. A | 40. B |
| 2. A | 15. B | 28. D | 41. A |
| 3. A | 16. B | 29. D | 42. D |
| 4. B | 17. A | 30. D | 43. A |
| 5. B | 18. D | 31. C | 44. C |
| 6. B | 19. C | 32. A | 45. D |
| 7. B | 20. A | 33. C | 46. A |
| 8. A | 21. B | 34. B | 47. B |
| 9. C | 22. D | 35. D | 48. B |
| 10. C | 23. C | 36. C | 49. B |
| 11. D | 24. D | 37. B | 50. D |
| 12. A | 25. B | 38. D | 51. C |
| 13. B, C, E | 26. C, D, F | 39. C, D, G, H: Round | 52. A, C, E |
|  |  | A, E, I: Pointed |  |

## LISTENING SECTION

| *Listening Set 1* | *Listening Set 2* |
|---|---|
| 1.  D | 18.  B |
| 2.  C | 19.  A |
| 3.  B | 20.  B |
| 4.  D | 21.  B, C |
| 5.  A | 22.  A |
| 6.  D | 23.  D |
| 7.  A, C | 24.  B |
| 8.  B | 25.  A |
| 9.  B | 26.  A |
| 10.  C | 27.  B |
| 11.  A, B, D: Yes | 28.  D |
| 12.  B | 29.  B |
| 13.  D | 30.  A |
| 14.  A | 31.  B |
| 15.  B | 32.  C |
| 16.  D | 33.  A, C, B |
| 17.  B | 34.  D |

# EXPLANATORY AND EXAMPLE ANSWERS, MODEL TEST 4

Go to the Barron's TOEFL site to study detailed Explanatory Answers for the Reading and Listening Sections, and Outlines, Example Answers, and Checklists for the Speaking and Writing Sections of Model Test 4.

# MODEL TEST 5: PROGRESS TEST

## READING SECTION

The Reading Section tests your ability to understand reading passages like those in college textbooks. The reading passages are presented in one complete section, which allows you to move to the next passage and return to a previous passage to change answers or answer questions that you may have left blank. The passages are about 700 words in length.

This is the short format for the Reading Section. On the short format, you will read three passages. After each passage, you will answer 12–14 questions about it. You may take notes while you read, but notes are not graded. You may use your notes to answer the questions. Some passages may include a word or phrase that is underlined in blue. Click on the word or phrase to see a glossary definition or explanation.

Choose the best answer for multiple-choice questions. Follow the directions on the page or on the screen for computer-assisted questions. Most questions are worth 1 point, but the last question in each passage is worth more than 1 point.

Click on **Next** to go to the next question. Click on **Back** to return to previous questions. You may return to previous questions for all of the passages.

You can click on **Review** to see a chart of the questions you have answered and the questions you have not answered. From this screen, you can return to the question you want to answer.

Although you can spend more time on one passage and less time on another passage, you should try to pace yourself so that you are spending about 20 minutes to read each passage and answer the questions for that passage. You will have 60 minutes to complete all of the passages and answer all of the questions on the short format. A clock on the screen will show you how much time you have to complete the Reading Section.

## Reading 1

The following reading passage was adapted from *Geosystems: An Introduction to Physical Geography*, Seventh Edition by Robert W. Christopherson, Pearson Education, Inc., 2009.

### "Rising Sea Levels"

P1    Sea level must be expressed as a range of values that are under constant reassessment. During the last century, sea level rose 10–20 cm (4–8 inches), a rate 10 times higher than the average rate during the last 3,000 years. The 2007 IPCC (Intergovernmental Panel on Climate Change) forecast scenarios for global mean sea level rise this century, given regional variations, are

- Low forecast: 0.18 m (7.1 in.)
- Middle forecast: 0.39 m (15.4 in.)
- High forecast: 0.59 m (23.2 in.)

P2    Observations since 1961 show the average global ocean temperature increased to depths of 3,000 m and the ocean absorbed more than 80% of climate system heating. Such warming causes thermal expansion of seawater, contributing to sea level rise. Mountain glaciers and snow cover declined on average in both hemispheres, contributing to sea level rise. Mount Kilimanjaro in Africa, portions of the South American Andes, and the Himalayas will very likely lose most of their glacial ice within the next two decades, affecting local water resources. Glacial ice continues its retreat in Alaska.

P3    Surrounding the margins of Antarctica, and constituting about 11% of its surface area, are numerous ice shelves, especially where sheltering inlets or bays exist. Covering many thousands of square kilometers, these ice shelves extend over the sea while still attached to continental ice. The loss of these ice shelves does not significantly raise sea level, for they already displace seawater. The concern is for the possible surge of grounded continental ice that the ice shelves hold back from the sea.

P4    → Although ice shelves constantly break up to produce icebergs, some large sections have recently broken free. In 1998 an iceberg the size of Delaware broke off the Ronne Ice Shelf, southeast of the Antarctic Peninsula. In March 2000 an iceberg tagged B-15 broke off the Ross Ice Shelf (some 90° longitude west of the Antarctic Peninsula), measuring *twice* the size of Delaware, 300 km by 40 km or 190 mi by 25 mi. Since 1993, six ice shelves have disintegrated in Antarctica. About 8,000 km (3,090 mi) of ice shelf are gone, changing maps, freeing up islands to circumnavigation, and creating thousands of icebergs. [A] Larsen-A suddenly disintegrated in 1995. [B] In only 35 days in early 2002, Larsen-B collapsed into icebergs. [C] Larsen C, the next segment to the south, is losing mass on its underside. This ice loss is likely a result of the 2.5°C (4.5°F) temperature increase in the peninsula region in the last 50 years. [D] In response to the increasing warmth, the Antarctic Peninsula is sporting new vegetation growth, reduced sea ice, and disruption of penguin feeding, nesting, and fledging activities.

P5 → A loss of polar ice mass, augmented by melting of alpine and mountain glaciers (which experienced more than a 30% decrease in overall ice mass during the last century) will affect sea-level rise. The IPCC assessment states that "between one-third to one-half of the existing mountain glacier mass could disappear over the next hundred years." Also, "there is conclusive evidence for a worldwide recession of mountain glaciers. . . . This is among the clearest and best evidence for a change in energy balance at the Earth's surface since the end of the 19th century."

P6    Unfortunately, the new measurements of Greenland's ice loss acceleration did not reach the IPCC in time for its report. Scientists are considering at least a 1.2 m (3.94 ft) high case for estimates of sea-level rise this century as more realistic given Greenland's present losses coupled with mountain glacial ice losses worldwide. According to Rahmstorf and colleagues, the data now available raise concerns that the climate system, in particular sea level, may be responding more quickly than climate models indicate. . . . The rate of sea-level rise for the past 20 years is 25% faster than the rate of rise in any 20-year period in the preceding 115 years. . . . Since 1990, the observed sea level has been rising faster than the rise projected by models. These increases would continue beyond 2100 even if greenhouse gas concentrations were stabilized.

P7 → A quick survey of world coastlines shows that even a moderate rise could bring changes of unparalleled proportions. At stake are the river deltas, lowland coastal farming valleys, and low-lying mainland areas, all contending with high water, high tides, and higher storm surges. Particularly tragic social and economic consequences will affect small island states—which are unable to adjust within their present country boundaries—disruption of biological systems, loss of biodiversity, reduction in water resources, and evacuation of residents among the impacts there. There could be both internal and international migrations of affected human populations, spread over decades, as people move away from coastal flooding from the sea-level rise.

1. The word range in the passage is closest in meaning to

   Ⓐ function
   Ⓑ scale
   Ⓒ version
   Ⓓ lack

2. The word likely in the passage is closest in meaning to

   Ⓐ suddenly
   Ⓑ probably
   Ⓒ hopefully
   Ⓓ actually

3. Why does the author mention "the state of Delaware" in paragraph 4?

   Ⓐ To include the North American continent in the discussion
   Ⓑ To impress the reader with the size of the icebergs
   Ⓒ To emphasize the problems of coastal regions
   Ⓓ To solicit support from residents in the United States

   Paragraph 4 is marked with an arrow [➔].

4. According to paragraph 4, why is there more new plant life in Antarctica recently?

   Ⓐ The mountain glaciers have melted.
   Ⓑ The land masses have split into islands.
   Ⓒ The icebergs have broken into smaller pieces.
   Ⓓ The temperature has risen by a few degrees.

   Paragraph 4 is marked with an arrow [➔].

5. It may be inferred from this passage that icebergs are formed for which reason?

   Ⓐ By a drop in ocean temperatures
   Ⓑ When an ice shelf breaks free
   Ⓒ From intensely cold islands
   Ⓓ If mountain glaciers melt

6. In paragraph 5, how does the author explain the loss of polar and glacial ice?

   Ⓐ Stating an educated opinion
   Ⓑ Referring to data in a study
   Ⓒ Comparing sea levels worldwide
   Ⓓ Presenting his research

   Paragraph 5 is marked with an arrow [➔].

7. The word conclusive in the passage is closest in meaning to

   Ⓐ definite
   Ⓑ independent
   Ⓒ unique
   Ⓓ valuable

8. Which of the sentences below best expresses the information in the highlighted statement in the passage? The other choices change the meaning or leave out important information.

   Ⓐ The IPCC did not have the data about ice loss in Greenland before the report was published.
   Ⓑ This year, the report from Greenland did not measure the new ice loss for the IPCC.
   Ⓒ The new measurements by the IPCC did not include Greenland's ice loss this time.
   Ⓓ Greenland's recent ice loss had not accelerated enough to be reported to the IPCC.

9. According to paragraph 7, why will people move away from the coastlines in the future?

   Ⓐ It will be too warm for them to live there.
   Ⓑ The coastlines will have too much vegetation.
   Ⓒ Flooding will destroy the coastal areas.
   Ⓓ No agricultural crops will be grown on the coasts.

   Paragraph 7 is marked with an arrow [➔].

10. Which of the following statements most accurately reflects the author's opinion about rising sea levels?

    Ⓐ Sea levels would rise without global warming.
    Ⓑ Rising sea levels can be reversed.
    Ⓒ The results of rising sea levels will be serious.
    Ⓓ Sea levels are rising because of new glaciers.

11. The word impacts in the passage is closest in meaning to

    Ⓐ confusion
    Ⓑ disadvantages
    Ⓒ features
    Ⓓ influences

12. Look at the four squares [■] that show where the following sentence could be inserted in the passage.

    **The Larsen Ice Shelf, along the east coast of the Antarctic Peninsula, has been retreating slowly for years.**

    Where could the sentence best be added?

    Click on a square [■] to insert the sentence in the passage.

13. **Directions:** An introduction for a short summary of the passage appears below. Complete the summary by selecting the THREE answer choices that mention the most important points in the passage. Some sentences do not belong in the summary because they express ideas that are not included in the passage or are minor points from the passage. *This question is worth 2 points.*

**Global warming is causing a rise in sea levels, with accompanying changes in coastal boundaries as well as social and economic ramifications.**

- 
- 
- 

### Answer Choices

A  The ice shelf called Larsen-A suddenly disintegrated in 1995.

B  Even an average rise in sea levels will cause serious social and economic changes.

C  Continental ice shelves and grounded ice sheets from Antarctica to the Polar cap are melting into the oceans.

D  It is predicted that many human migrations inland will occur along flooded coastal regions.

E  The melting of glacial ice on high mountain ranges will affect regional water resources worldwide.

F  Scientists at NASA have concluded that the ice sheet in Greenland is melting at a rate of about 1 meter every year.

## *Reading 2*

The following reading passage was adapted from *Gardner's Art Through the Ages*, Thirteenth Edition by Fred S. Kleiner, Wadsworth, 2009.

### *"Organic Architecture"*

P1  → One of the most striking personalities in the development of early-twentieth-century architecture was Frank Lloyd Wright (1867–1959). Wright moved to Chicago, where he eventually joined the firm headed by Louis Sullivan. Wright set out to create "architecture of democracy." Always a believer in architecture as "natural" and "organic," Wright saw it as serving free individuals who have the right to move within a "free" space, envisioned as a nonsymmetrical design interacting spatially with its natural surroundings. He sought to develop an organic unity of planning, structure, materials, and site. Wright identified the principle of continuity as fundamental to understanding his view of organic unity: "Classic architecture was all fixation. . . . Now why not let walls, ceilings, floors become seen as component parts of each other? . . . This ideal, profound in its architectural implications . . . I called . . . continuity."

P2    Wright manifested his vigorous originality early, and by 1900 he had arrived at a style entirely his own. In his work during the first decade of the twentieth century, his cross-axial plan and his fabric of continuous roof planes and screens defined a new domestic architecture.

P3    → Wright fully expressed these elements and concepts in Robie House, built between 1907 and 1909. Like other buildings in the Chicago area he designed at about the same time, he called this home a "prairie house." Wright conceived the long, sweeping ground-hugging lines, unconfined by abrupt wall limits, as reaching out toward and capturing the expansiveness of the Midwest's great flatlands. Abandoning all symmetry, the architect eliminated a façade, extended the roofs far beyond the walls, and all but concealed the entrance. Wright filled the "wandering" plan of the Robie House with intricately joined spaces (some large and open, others closed), grouped freely around a great central fireplace. Ⓐ (He believed strongly in the hearth's age-old domestic significance.) Wright designed enclosed patios, overhanging roofs, and strip windows to provide unexpected light sources and glimpses of the outdoors as people move through the interior space. Ⓑ These elements, together with the open ground plan, create a sense of space-in-motion inside and out. Ⓒ The flow of interior space determined the sharp, angular placement of exterior walls. Ⓓ

P4    The Robie House is a good example of Wright's "naturalism," his adjusting of a building to its site. In this particular case, however, the confines of the city lot constrained the building-to-site relationship more than did the sites of some of Wright's more expansive suburban and country homes. The Kaufmann House, nicknamed "Fallingwater" and designed as a weekend retreat at Bear Run near Pittsburgh, is a prime example of the latter. Perched on a rocky hillside over a small waterfall, this structure extends the Robie House's blocky masses in all four directions. Since the completion of this residence, architects and the public alike have marveled at the fluid interplay between interior and exterior. In designing Fallingwater, Wright, in keeping with his commitment to an "architecture of democracy," sought to incorporate the structure more fully into the site, thereby ensuring a fluid, dynamic exchange between the interior of the house and the natural environment outside. Rather than build a house overlooking or next to the waterfall, Wright decided to build it over the waterfall, because he believed that the inhabitants would become desensitized to the waterfall's presence and power if they merely overlooked it. To take advantage of the location, Wright designed a series of terraces on three levels from a central core structure. The contrast in textures between concrete, painted metal, and natural stones in its walls enlivens its shapes, as does Wright's use of full-length strip windows to create a stunning interweaving of interior and exterior space.

P5    → The implied message of Wright's new architecture was space, not mass—a space designed to fit the patron's life and enclosed and divided as required. Wright took special pains to meet his client's requirements, often designing all the accessories of a house. In the late 1930s, he acted on a cherished dream to provide good architectural design for less prosperous people by adapting the ideas of his prairie house to plans for smaller, less expensive dwellings. The publication of Wright's plans brought him a measure of fame in Europe, especially in Holland and Germany. The issuance in Berlin in 1910 of a portfolio of his work and an exhibition of his designs the following year stimulated younger architects to adopt some of his ideas about open plans. Some forty years before his career ended, his work was already of revolutionary significance.

14. Which of the following is the main idea of this passage?

    Ⓐ The design of Robie House
    Ⓑ Twentieth-century architecture
    Ⓒ Frank Lloyd Wright's work
    Ⓓ Residences of the Midwest

15. What did Wright mean by the term "organic" in paragraph 1?

    Ⓐ Fixation
    Ⓑ Ideal
    Ⓒ Continuity
    Ⓓ Classic

Paragraph 1 is marked with an arrow [➔].

16. The phrase his own in the passage refers to

    Ⓐ style
    Ⓑ originality
    Ⓒ work
    Ⓓ plan

17. The word conceived in the passage is closest in meaning to

    Ⓐ utilized
    Ⓑ noticed
    Ⓒ created
    Ⓓ examined

18. The word Abandoning in the passage is closest in meaning to

    Ⓐ Influencing
    Ⓑ Modifying
    Ⓒ Perfecting
    Ⓓ Discontinuing

19. It can be inferred from paragraph 3 that the author gives details for the design of the Robie House for which reason?

   Ⓐ The design included both indoor and outdoor plans.
   Ⓑ Robie House included many of Wright's original ideas.
   Ⓒ All of the accessories of the house were included in the design.
   Ⓓ Wright lived in Robie House between 1907 and 1909.

   Paragraph 3 is marked with an arrow [➜].

20. The word prime in the passage is closest in meaning to

   Ⓐ most important
   Ⓑ most numerous
   Ⓒ most common
   Ⓓ most accepted

21. How was "Fallingwater" different from the "Robie House"?

   Ⓐ "Fallingwater" was an earlier example of naturalism than "Robie House."
   Ⓑ "Fallingwater" was much smaller than "Robie House" because it was a retreat.
   Ⓒ "Fallingwater" was better suited to the site with views through huge windows.
   Ⓓ "Fallingwater" was built with an open floor plan, unlike "Robie House."

22. According to paragraph 5, why did Wright begin to build smaller versions of his prairie designs?

   Ⓐ To publish his plans in Europe
   Ⓑ To give the middle class a good design
   Ⓒ To help younger architects with their work
   Ⓓ To begin a revolution in architecture

   Paragraph 5 is marked with an arrow [➜].

23. According to paragraph 5, why did Wright's work become well known in Europe?

   Ⓐ His plans were published and he held exhibitions.
   Ⓑ He visited several universities and gave lectures.
   Ⓒ His revolutionary ideas appealed to younger architects.
   Ⓓ He was already very famous in the United States.

   Paragraph 5 is marked with an arrow [➜].

24. According to the passage, a prairie house has all of the following features EXCEPT

   Ⓐ a central fireplace
   Ⓑ enclosed patios
   Ⓒ an inviting entrance
   Ⓓ strip windows

25. Look at the four squares [■] that show where the following sentence could be inserted in the passage.

**Wright matched his new and fundamental interior spatial arrangement in his exterior treatment.**

Where could the sentence best be added?

Click on a square [■] to insert the sentence in the passage.

26. **Directions:** An introduction for a short summary of the passage appears below. Complete the summary by selecting the THREE answer choices that mention the most important points in the passage. Some sentences do not belong in the summary because they express ideas that are not included in the passage or are minor points from the passage. *This question is worth 2 points.*

**By 1900, Frank Lloyd Wright had developed a unique style of architecture.**

• 

• 

• 

**Answer Choices**

A  Wright spent a few years extending his influence to Europe where he was well known.

B  Frank Lloyd Wright had attended the University of Wisconsin prior to taking a position with a Chicago firm.

C  Wright became famous for spaces that were true to their organic functions.

D  "Fallingwater," like other suburban and country homes that Wright built, joined the structure to the natural setting.

E  Wright was interested in the design of German building blocks for children created by Friedrich Froebel.

F  Robie House and other buildings in Chicago were examples of an organic structure called a "prairie house."

## Reading 3

The following reading passage was adapted from "New Women in the Ice Age" by Heather Pringle in *Applying Cultural Anthropology: An Introductory Reader*, Sixth Edition by Aaron Podolefsky and Peter J. Brown. Published by The McGraw-Hill Companies, Inc., 2003.

### "New Women of the Ice Age"

P1    The status of women in a society depends in large measure on their role in the economy. The reinterpretation of the Paleolithic past centers on new views of the role of women in the food-foraging economy. Amassing critical and previously overlooked evidence from Dolní Věstonice and the neighboring site of Pavlov, researchers Olga Soffer, James Adovasio, and David Hyland now propose that human survival there had little to do with men hurling spears at big-game animals. Instead, observes Soffer, one of the world's leading authorities on Ice Age hunters and gatherers and an archeologist at the University of Illinois in Champaign-Urbana, it depended largely on women, plants, and a technique of hunting previously invisible in the archeological evidence—net hunting. "This is not the image we've always had of Upper Paleolithic macho guys out killing animals up close and personal," Soffer explains. "Net hunting is communal, and it involves the labor of children and women. And this has lots of implications."

 → Many of these implications make her conservative colleagues cringe because they raise serious questions about the focus of previous studies. European archeologists have long concentrated on analyzing broken stone tools and butchered big-game bones, the most plentiful and best preserved relics of the Upper Paleolithic era (which stretched from 40,000 to 12,000 years ago). From these analyses, researchers have developed theories about how these societies once hunted and gathered food. Most researchers ruled out the possibility of women hunters for biological reasons. Adult females, they reasoned, had to devote themselves to breast-feeding and tending infants. "Human babies have always been immature and dependent," says Soffer. "If women are the people who are always involved with biological reproduction and the rearing of the young, then that is going to constrain their behavior. They have to provision that child. For fathers, provisioning is optional."

P3 → To test theories about Upper Paleolithic life, researchers looked to ethnography, the scientific description of modern and historical cultural groups. While the lives of modern hunters do not exactly duplicate those of ancient hunters, they supply valuable clues to universal human behavior. In many historical societies, Soffer observes, women played a key part in net hunting, since the technique did not call for brute strength nor did it place young mothers in physical peril. Among Australian Aborigines, for example, women as well as men knotted the mesh, laboring for as much as two or three years on a fine net. Among Native American groups, they helped lay out their handiwork on poles across a valley floor. Then the entire camp joined forces as beaters. Fanning out across the valley, men, women, and children alike shouted and screamed, flushing out game and driving it in the direction of the net. "Everybody and their mother could participate," says Soffer. "Some people were beating, others were screaming or holding the net. And once you got the net on these animals, they were immobilized. You didn't need brute force. You could club them, hit them any old way."

P4 → People seldom returned home empty-handed. Researchers living among the net hunting Mbuti in the forests of the Congo report that they capture game every time they lay out their woven traps, scooping up 50 percent of the animals encountered. "Nets are a far more valued item in their panoply of food-producing things than bows and arrows are," says Adovasio. So lethal are these traps that the Mbuti generally rack up more meat than they can consume, trading the surplus with neighbors. Other net hunters traditionally smoked or dried their catch and stored it for leaner times.

P5 → A Soffer doubts that the inhabitants of Dolní Věstonice and Pavlov were the only net makers in Ice Age Europe. B Camps stretching from Germany to Russia are littered with a notable abundance of small-game bones, from hares to birds like ptarmigan. And at least some of their inhabitants whittled bone tools that look much like the awls and net spacers favored by historical net makers. C

P6    Although the full range of their activities is unlikely ever to be known for certain, there is good reason to believe that Ice Age women played a host of powerful roles. D And the research that suggests those roles is rapidly changing our mental images of the past. For Soffer and others, these are exciting times.

27. The word authorities in the passage is closest in meaning to

  Ⓐ policies
  Ⓑ experts
  Ⓒ interpretations
  Ⓓ tradition

28. How do Soffer's theories compare with those of more conservative researchers?

  Ⓐ They are in agreement for the most part regarding the activities that women performed.
  Ⓑ Soffer has based her theories on archeological evidence that her colleagues had not considered.
  Ⓒ Conservative researchers are doubtful about the studies of stone tools and big-game bones.
  Ⓓ Her theories are much more difficult to prove because she relies on modern cultural evidence.

29. The word implications in the passage is closest in meaning to

  Ⓐ defects
  Ⓑ advantages
  Ⓒ suggestions
  Ⓓ controversies

30. What can be inferred about Dr. Soffer from paragraph 2?

  Ⓐ She does not agree that women should be the primary caretakers for children.
  Ⓑ She is probably not as conservative in her views as many of her colleagues.
  Ⓒ She is most likely a biologist who is doing research on European women.
  Ⓓ She has recently begun studying hunting and gathering in the Upper Paleolithic era.

  Paragraph 2 is marked with an arrow [→].

31. The word constrain in the passage is closest in meaning to

  Ⓐ limit
  Ⓑ plan
  Ⓒ notice
  Ⓓ improve

32. Which of the sentences below best expresses the information in the highlighted statement in the passage? The other choices change the meaning or leave out important information.

    Ⓐ Historically, net hunting was considered too dangerous for women because it required physical strength that they did not possess.
    Ⓑ Women throughout history have participated in societies by teaching their children how to use net hunting.
    Ⓒ In many societies, the women did not participate in net hunting because hunting was an exception to historical traditions.
    Ⓓ Because, historically, net hunting was not perilous and did not require great strength, women have been important participants in it.

33. Based on the information in paragraph 3, which of the following best explains the term "net hunting"?

    Ⓐ An approach to hunting developed by Australian fishermen
    Ⓑ A very dangerous method of hunting large animals
    Ⓒ A way for the camp to protect women and children from wild animals
    Ⓓ A hunting technique that includes the entire community

    Paragraph 3 is marked with an arrow [➔].

34. Why does the author mention "Native American and Aborigine" groups in paragraph 3?

    Ⓐ To give examples of modern groups in which women participate in net hunting
    Ⓑ To demonstrate how net hunting should be carried out in modern societies
    Ⓒ To describe net hunting techniques that protect the women in the group
    Ⓓ To contrast their net hunting techniques with those of the people in the Congo

    Paragraph 3 is marked with an arrow [➔].

35. According to paragraph 4, which of the following is true about hunting in the Congo?

    Ⓐ The Mbuti value their nets almost as much as their bows and arrows.
    Ⓑ Trade with other tribes is limited because all food must be stored.
    Ⓒ Net hunters are successful in capturing half of their prey.
    Ⓓ Vegetables are the staple part of the diet for the Mbuti people.

    Paragraph 4 is marked with an arrow [➔].

36. According to paragraph 5, why does Soffer conclude that net hunting was widespread in Europe during the Ice Age?

    Ⓐ Because there are a lot of small game still living in Europe
    Ⓑ Because tools to make nets have been found in camps throughout Europe
    Ⓒ Because the bones of small animals were found in Dolní Věstonice and Pavlov
    Ⓓ Because German and Russian researchers have verified her data

    Paragraph 5 is marked with an arrow [➔].

37. The word roles in the passage is closest in meaning to

    Ⓐ problems
    Ⓑ developments
    Ⓒ locations
    Ⓓ functions

38. Look at the four squares [■] that show where the following sentence could be inserted in the passage.

**Such findings, agree Soffer and Adovasio, reveal just how shaky the most widely accepted reconstructions of Upper Paleolithic life are.**

Where could the sentence best be added?

Click on a square [■] to insert the sentence in the passage.

39. **Directions:** An introduction for a short summary of the passage appears below. Complete the summary by selecting the THREE answer choices that mention the most important points in the passage. Some sentences do not belong in the summary because they express ideas that are not included in the passage or are minor points from the passage. *This question is worth 2 points.*

**Although previous studies denied the participation of women in hunting parties during the Paleolithic era, more recent research provides evidence that they were involved in important hunts.**

    ●

    ●

    ●

### Answer Choices

Ⓐ The Upper Paleolithic era extended from 40,000 to 12,000 years ago, a time also referred to as the Ice Age.

Ⓑ Net hunting involves the entire community, including women and children as well as men in the hunt for animals.

Ⓒ Australian Aborigines work for as many as three years weaving and knotting a net for hunting small game.

Ⓓ Modern net hunting in the Congo and Australia supports new theories that identify woman as participants in Paleolithic hunting.

Ⓔ The introduction of farming methods during the agricultural revolution changed the status of women.

Ⓕ Paleolithic sites such as Dolní Věstonice and Pavlov provide evidence of net hunting that was previously overlooked.

# LISTENING SECTION

 **Model Test 5, Listening Section, Track 78**

The Listening Section tests your ability to understand spoken English that is typical of inter-actions and academic speech on college campuses. During the test, you will listen to conver-sations, lectures, and discussions, and you will answer questions about them.

This is the long format for the Listening Section. On the long format, you will listen to three conversations, three lectures, and three discussions. After each listening passage, you will answer 5–6 questions about it. Only two conversations, two lectures, and two discussions will be graded. The other passages are part of an experimental section for future tests. Because you will not know which conversations, lectures, and discussions will be graded, you must try to do your best on all of them.

You will hear each passage one time. You may take notes while you listen, but notes are not graded. You may use your notes to answer the questions.

Choose the best answer for multiple-choice questions. Follow the directions on the page or on the screen for computer-assisted questions. Click on **Next** and then on **OK** to go on to the next question. You cannot return to previous questions.

The Listening Section is divided into sets. Each set includes one conversation, one lecture, and one discussion. You have 10 minutes to answer all of the questions for each set. You will have 30 minutes to answer all of the questions on the long format. A clock on the screen will show you how much time you have to complete your answers for the section. The clock does NOT count the time you are listening to the conversations, lectures, and discussions.

## Listening 1 "Professor's Office"

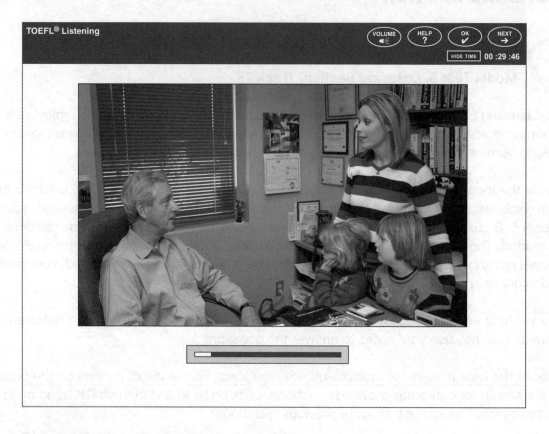

1. Why does the woman go to see her professor?

   Ⓐ To get advice about memorizing information
   Ⓑ To clarify several terms that she doesn't understand
   Ⓒ To get permission to bring her children to class
   Ⓓ To ask a question about classroom procedures

2. What do semantic memory and episodic memory have in common?

   Ⓐ They are both included in short-term memory.
   Ⓑ They do not concentrate on each step in the process.
   Ⓒ They are subcategories of declarative memory.
   Ⓓ They are the two major types of long-term memory.

3. When the professor gives the example of riding a bicycle, what kind of memory is he referring to?

   Ⓐ Declarative memory
   Ⓑ Episodic memory
   Ⓒ Procedural memory
   Ⓓ Semantic memory

4. What does the student mean when she says this: 🎧

   Ⓐ She wants confirmation that the professor understands.
   Ⓑ She is worried that the professor may not be able to remember.
   Ⓒ She remembers something else that she needs to say.
   Ⓓ She disagrees with the professor's example about vocabulary.

5. What does the professor suggest?

   Ⓐ He wants the woman to come back to his office again.
   Ⓑ He expects the woman to ask questions in writing.
   Ⓒ He offers to respond to additional questions by email.
   Ⓓ He does not think that the woman will have more questions.

## Listening 2 "History Class"

6. What is the lecture mainly about?

   Ⓐ Provisions of the Homestead Act
   Ⓑ How to construct a log cabin
   Ⓒ Frontier homes in the West
   Ⓓ Early construction materials

7. How does the professor organize his lecture?

   Ⓐ He makes a persuasive argument in favor of sod homes.
   Ⓑ He narrates stories about life on the Western frontier.
   Ⓒ He explains the process for becoming a homesteader.
   Ⓓ He contrasts several types of homes in the West.

8. What does the professor imply about construction materials for early homes?

   Ⓐ Settlers used the materials from the natural environment.
   Ⓑ Not many of the materials from that era have survived.
   Ⓒ Most of the supplies had to be shipped in by railroad.
   Ⓓ Wagons and tents were used in constructing homes.

9. What is the evidence for the inexpensive price of a sod home?

   Ⓐ Short stories and novels
   Ⓑ Letters written to relatives
   Ⓒ Newspaper advertisements
   Ⓓ Personal records and accounts

10. Why does the professor say this:

  Ⓐ To criticize the sod house
  Ⓑ To demonstrate uncertainty
  Ⓒ To draw a conclusion
  Ⓓ To uphold an opinion

11. In the lecture, the professor identifies attributes for different frontier homes. Indicate whether each attribute refers to a sod house or a log cabin. Click in the correct box for each phrase.

|  |  | Sod House | Log Cabin |
|---|---|---|---|
| A | A mud roof |  |  |
| B | A rock foundation |  |  |
| C | Chinked walls |  |  |
| D | Notching techniques |  |  |
| E | Thick brick insulation |  |  |

### Listening 3 "Geology Class"

TOEFL® Listening

VOLUME ◄≡   HELP ?   OK ✔   NEXT →

HIDE TIME   00 :29 :46

12. What is this discussion mainly about?

    Ⓐ How to exploit nonrenewable mineral resources
    Ⓑ The exploitation of minerals in protected environments
    Ⓒ Pollution as a by-product of mineral exploitation
    Ⓓ The economic and environmental costs of exploiting minerals

13. According to the professor, what are two problems that can be anticipated when roads are cut into an area for mining?

    Click on 2 answer choices.

    Ⓐ The labor is difficult to retain.

    Ⓑ The natural landscape is damaged.

    Ⓒ The roadbeds create waste piles.

    Ⓓ The ecosystem is disturbed.

14. Why does the professor say this:

    Ⓐ As encouragement for a more complete answer
    Ⓑ Because he doesn't understand the student's answer
    Ⓒ To give another student an opportunity to speak
    Ⓓ For positive reinforcement of a correct answer

15. What option is proposed as an alternative when all of the mineral resources in easily accessible locations have been depleted?

    Ⓐ Converting to nonrenewable resources
    Ⓑ Concentrating on conservation of the resources
    Ⓒ Developing synthetic resources to replace minerals
    Ⓓ Using new technology to search the area again

16. What does the professor imply about the environmental costs of mineral exploitation?

    Ⓐ He thinks that the environmental costs are less than the economic costs.
    Ⓑ He regrets that the environment is damaged during mineral exploitation.
    Ⓒ He opposes mineral exploitation when it is done close to urban areas.
    Ⓓ He believes in exploiting the resources in national parks and historic reserves.

17. What does the professor want the students to do in this class session?

    Ⓐ Listen carefully and take notes
    Ⓑ Bring in alternative ideas to present
    Ⓒ Ask questions and draw conclusions
    Ⓓ Prepare for a quiz at the end

## Listening 4 "Professor's Office"

18. Why does the student go to the professor's office?

   Ⓐ To change his schedule
   Ⓑ To apply for a job
   Ⓒ To introduce himself
   Ⓓ To help the professor

19. What does the professor mean when she says this: 🎧

   Ⓐ She does not want the man to be uncomfortable.
   Ⓑ She thinks that the responsibilities are too difficult.
   Ⓒ She is concerned that the man will be bored.
   Ⓓ She is worried that the man will not try to help her.

20. What experience does the man have that may be helpful?

   Ⓐ He knows how to operate the grading machine.
   Ⓑ He has answered the telephone in a law office.
   Ⓒ He has used computer programs for office work.
   Ⓓ He has been a work-study student in another office.

21. What is the pay for the work-study position?

   Ⓐ An hourly rate for sixteen hours per week regardless of the activity.
   Ⓑ An hourly rate for the time spent working but not for studying.
   Ⓒ A higher rate for working and a lower rate for studying.
   Ⓓ A weekly rate depending on the number of hours worked.

22. What can we assume about the meeting?

   Ⓐ The professor was impressed with the student.
   Ⓑ The student is not interested in the opportunity.
   Ⓒ The secretary will not need to interview the student.
   Ⓓ The work is very difficult to accomplish.

## Listening 5 "Music Appreciation Class"

23. What is the main purpose of the lecture?

    Ⓐ To explain chamber music
    Ⓑ To give examples of composers
    Ⓒ To congratulate the University Quartet
    Ⓓ To introduce madrigal singing

24. What is the origin of the term *chamber music*?

    Ⓐ A medieval musical instrument
    Ⓑ An old word that means "small group"
    Ⓒ A place where the music was played
    Ⓓ A name of one of the original musicians

25. Which of the following are the key characteristics of chamber music in the Classical Period?

    Click on 2 answer choices.

    Ⓐ Orderly structures

    Ⓑ Complex melodies

    Ⓒ Longer pieces

    Ⓓ Amateur musicians

26. What does the professor mean when she says this about Beethoven:

   Ⓐ She doubts that Beethoven could have written the quartets.
   Ⓑ She is in admiration of Beethoven's exceptional talent.
   Ⓒ She thinks that the later quartets could have been improved.
   Ⓓ She is inviting the students to question her information.

27. Why does the professor mention Impressionism?

   Ⓐ She is comparing the experimentation in art with that in music.
   Ⓑ She is making a transition into a discussion of art in the Modern Period.
   Ⓒ She is giving an example of the work of the Romantics.
   Ⓓ She is telling a story that includes some of the Impressionist painters.

28. How did the professor organize the lecture?

   Ⓐ She compared different types of musical compositions.
   Ⓑ She arranged the information in chronological order.
   Ⓒ She argued the advantages and disadvantages.
   Ⓓ She responded to questions that the students asked.

### Listening 6 "Botany Class"

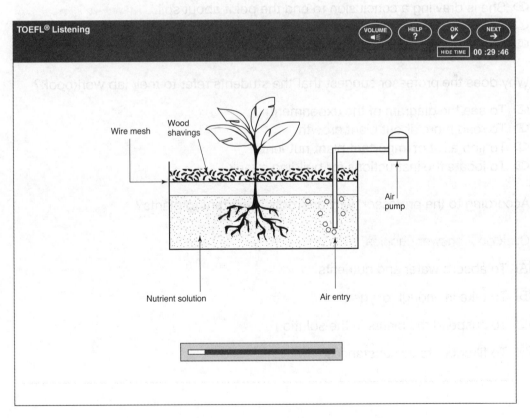

29. What is this discussion mainly about?

    Ⓐ Growing plants without soil
    Ⓑ Mixing nutrients in water
    Ⓒ Identifying chemicals in soil
    Ⓓ Solving problems in the water

30. Why does the professor talk about the history of hydroponics?

    Ⓐ She wants to put the modern method in historical context.
    Ⓑ She is trying to prove that hydroponics is a new idea.
    Ⓒ She is following the information in the textbook very closely.
    Ⓓ She digressed from the subject for a long time.

31. According to the professor, what is the greatest advantage of hydroponics?

    Ⓐ The plants are less likely to develop soil-borne diseases.
    Ⓑ The cultivation requires much less labor than traditional methods.
    Ⓒ The water can be recycled in a hydroponic environment.
    Ⓓ Less space is needed to produce a large number of plants.

32. Why does the professor say this:

    Ⓐ She is making a statement to generate further discussion.
    Ⓑ She is drawing a conclusion to end the point about soil.
    Ⓒ She is answering the question that was posed about regions.
    Ⓓ She is trying to understand what the student just said.

33. Why does the professor suggest that the students refer to their lab workbook?

    Ⓐ To see the diagram of the experiment
    Ⓑ To read more about plant growth
    Ⓒ To find a list of important plant nutrients
    Ⓓ To locate the instructions for building a tank

34. According to the professor, why are roots important to plants?

    Click on 2 answer choices.

    Ⓐ To absorb water and nutrients

    Ⓑ To take in enough oxygen

    Ⓒ To suspend the plants in the solution

    Ⓓ To filter out toxic substances

## Listening 7 "Library"

35. Why does the man approach the librarian?

    Ⓐ He needs an explanation of his assignment.
    Ⓑ He is looking for an encyclopedia.
    Ⓒ He needs help finding some data.
    Ⓓ He is trying to find the reference section.

36. What does the woman mean when she says this:

    Ⓐ She is showing comprehension.
    Ⓑ She is expressing surprise.
    Ⓒ She is talking to herself.
    Ⓓ She is dismissing the man.

37. What does the librarian imply?

    Ⓐ The man can find a chart in an encyclopedia.
    Ⓑ The professor has explained the assignment clearly.
    Ⓒ The library has a very good reference section.
    Ⓓ The man should not change the assignment.

38. What example does the librarian give for the assignment?

    Ⓐ A relative comparison of home prices
    Ⓑ Average family income in several countries
    Ⓒ International business around the world
    Ⓓ Global economic patterns in this decade

39. What will the man do with the information?

    Ⓐ Show it to the librarian
    Ⓑ Write a report for class
    Ⓒ Draw a chart or a graph
    Ⓓ Decide where to live

### Listening 8 "Engineering Class"

40. What is this lecture mainly about?

   Ⓐ Reinforced concrete in buildings
   Ⓑ The stresses caused by earthquakes
   Ⓒ Earthquake-resistant structures
   Ⓓ Understanding construction sites

41. Which technique is used to reinforce walls?

   Ⓐ Cross bracing
   Ⓑ Shear cores
   Ⓒ Bolting
   Ⓓ Base isolators

42. Which two materials are used in base isolators?

   Click on 2 answer choices.

   Ⓐ Rubber

   Ⓑ Steel

   Ⓒ Concrete

   Ⓓ Soil

43. What happens to fill dirt during an earthquake?

     Ⓐ It allows the building to sway.
     Ⓑ It reduces earthquake damage.
     Ⓒ It becomes unstable and collapses.
     Ⓓ It creates mild shock waves.

44. Why does the professor say this:

     Ⓐ He is introducing a new major point.
     Ⓑ He is trying to get the students to participate.
     Ⓒ He is drawing a conclusion about engineering.
     Ⓓ He is disagreeing with his previous comment.

45. What does the professor think about computer sensors for buildings?

     Ⓐ He thinks this is a superior method for preserving buildings.
     Ⓑ He finds the research on sensors for pistons very encouraging.
     Ⓒ He is more concerned about the potential for people to be injured.
     Ⓓ He doubts that the concept will result in design improvements.

### Listening 9 "Art History Class"

Photo of Jackson Pollock painting
Photograph by Hans Namuth
Courtesy Center for Creative Photography, University of Arizona
© 1991 Hans Namuth Estate

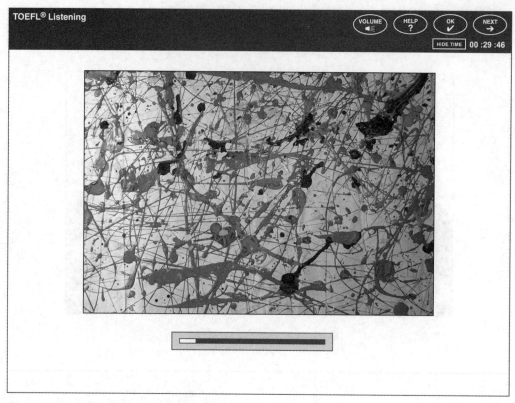

46. What is this discussion mainly about?

    Ⓐ Artists in New York
    Ⓑ Post Impressionists
    Ⓒ Abstract Expressionism
    Ⓓ The Guggenheim collection

47. To what did some critics compare Pollock's work?

    Ⓐ Nature
    Ⓑ Dancing
    Ⓒ Chaos
    Ⓓ Houses

48. According to the professor, what defines action art?

Click on 2 answer choices.

    Ⓐ Control

    Ⓑ Design

    Ⓒ Coincidence

    Ⓓ Imbalance

49. Why does the professor say this:

    Ⓐ He is helping the student to find the exact word.
    Ⓑ He is correcting something that the student said.
    Ⓒ He is changing the topic of the discussion.
    Ⓓ He is trying to regain the floor to continue.

50. What is interesting about the painting, "Lavender Mist?"

    Ⓐ The unusual color
    Ⓑ The texture of the paint
    Ⓒ The artist's handprints
    Ⓓ The number of copies

51. What is the professor's opinion of Pollock?

    Ⓐ He thinks that Pollock was an excellent illustrator.
    Ⓑ He argues that Pollock's work was influential.
    Ⓒ He expresses reservations about Pollock's work.
    Ⓓ He agrees with Pollock's critics.

 **Please turn off the audio. There is a 10-minute break between the Listening Section and the Speaking Section.**

# SPEAKING SECTION

**Model Test 5, Speaking Section, Track 79**

The Speaking Section tests your ability to communicate in English in an academic setting. During the test, you will be presented with six speaking questions. The questions ask for a response to a single question, a conversation, a talk, or a lecture. The prompts and questions are presented only one time.

You may take notes as you listen, but notes are not graded. You may use your notes to answer the questions. Some of the questions ask for a response to a reading passage and a talk or a lecture. The reading passages and the questions are written, but the directions will be spoken.

Your speaking will be evaluated on both the fluency of the language and the accuracy of the content. You will have 15–20 seconds to prepare and 45–60 seconds to respond to each question. Typically, a good response will require all of the response time and the answer will be complete by the end of the response time.

You will have about 20 minutes to complete the Speaking Section. A clock on the screen will show you how much time you have to prepare each of your answers and how much time you have to record each response.

*Independent Speaking Question 1 "A Tourist Attraction"*

 Listen for a question about a familiar topic.

## Question

Your friend's cousin is going to visit your country and you promised to show her some interesting places. Which one would be more interesting?

- A beautiful landscape
- A historical city
- Your home

Use specific reasons and details to explain your choice.

Preparation Time: 15 seconds
Recording Time: 45 seconds

## *Independent Speaking Question 2 "Success"*

 Listen for a question that asks your opinion about a familiar topic.

### Question

Some people believe that the best way to succeed is to set goals and work hard to achieve them. Other people think that hard work is not as important as good luck. Which point of view do you think is true, and why? Use specific reasons and examples to support your opinion.

Preparation Time: 15 seconds
Recording Time: 45 seconds

## *Integrated Speaking Question 3 "Auto Registration"*

Read a short passage and listen to a talk on the same topic.

Reading Time: 45 seconds

---

Policy for Vehicles on Campus

Vehicles parked on campus by students, faculty, or staff must be registered with the Campus Police Department. Parking permits are required for both part-time and full-time students. Permits may be purchased at the Campus Police Department, which is located at the south entrance to the campus or at the Business Office in the Administration Building. The fee per vehicle is $20. Please be advised that you must have a permit for every vehicle that you park in campus lots. Parking enforcement will begin one week after the first day of each semester.

---

 Now listen to a student who is speaking at the meeting. She is expressing her opinion about the policy.

**Question**

The student expresses her opinion of the policy for vehicle registration. Report her opinion and explain the reasons that she gives for having that opinion.

Preparation Time: 30 seconds
Recording Time: 60 seconds

### Integrated Speaking Question 4 "Stress"

Read a short passage and then listen to part of a lecture on the same topic.

Reading Time: 45 seconds

> #### Stress
>
> Stress is defined as a mental and physical condition that occurs when an adjustment or adaptation must be made to the environment. Unpleasant conditions or events cause stress, as, for example, financial problems, divorce, health issues, or pressure at work. However, a certain amount of stress occurs even when the adjustment is to a condition perceived as desirable. Exercise, dating, moving to a new home, or taking a trip are all stressful situations. Although short-term stress is usually harmless, the consequences of long-term stress can be dangerous to health. Factors that decrease the consequences of stress are the ability to predict stressful situations and the level of control over them that can be achieved.

 Now listen to part of a lecture in a psychology class. The professor is talking about an experiment.

### Question
Explain the causes of stress and relate them to the experiment with rats.

Preparation Time: 30 seconds
Recording Time: 60 seconds

## *Integrated Speaking Question 5 "Art Project"*

 Now listen to a conversation between a student and her friend.

## Question
Describe the woman's problem and the two suggestions that her friend makes about how to handle it. What do you think the woman should do, and why?

Preparation Time: 20 seconds
Recording Time: 60 seconds

## *Integrated Speaking Question 6 "Caverns"*

 Now listen to part of a lecture in a geology class. The professor is discussing caverns.

### Question
Using the main points and examples from the lecture, describe the two kinds of rock formations in a cavern, and explain how the professor helps his students remember the difference between the two.

Preparation Time: 20 seconds
Recording Time: 60 seconds

# WRITING SECTION

The Writing Section tests your ability to write essays in English similar to those that you would write in college courses. During the test, you will write two essays.

**The Integrated Essay.** First you will read an academic passage and then you will listen to a lecture on the same topic. You may take notes as you read and listen, but notes are not graded. You may use your notes to write the essay. The reading passage will disappear while you are listening to the lecture, but the passage will return to the screen for reference when you begin to write your essay. You will have 20 minutes to plan, write, and revise your response. Typically, a good essay for the integrated topic will require that you write 150–225 words.

**The Independent Essay.** You will read a question on the screen. It usually asks for your opinion about a familiar topic. You will have 30 minutes to plan, write, and revise your response. Typically, a good essay for the independent topic will require that you write 300–350 words.

A clock on the screen will show you how much time you have left to complete each essay.

## *Integrated Essay "Competition in the Classroom"*

You have 20 minutes to plan, write, and revise your response to a reading passage and a lecture on the same topic. First, read the passage and take notes. Then, listen to the lecture and take notes. Finally, write your response to the writing question. Typically, a good response will require that you write 150–225 words.

## Reading Passage
Time: 3 minutes

Although cooperation is currently the most popular paradigm in classrooms, competition has a number of advantages. Research on classrooms in which competition is encouraged has demonstrated that competition can increase motivation and productivity while students are having fun.

Competition has long been used in classrooms to motivate students, encouraging them to do their best work. Like athletes who improve when they train with others who are equal or superior performers, students tend to improve in a competitive learning setting. Considerable evidence suggests that motivation is especially enhanced among high achieving students in a competitive classroom.

One of the main advantages of competition is that it creates an environment in which students push each other to excel and thereby increase productivity. For example, in classrooms where students compete to read the most books, the total number of books that each student reads increases as compared with classrooms without similar competitive goals.

Perhaps because competition has long been associated with sports and games, it is fun for students. Teachers often use team-based competitions to make academic material more interesting and entertaining. Some common examples are spelling bees, science project competitions, and group quizzes in which teams answer questions and receive points for correct answers. Competition is useful when an otherwise uninteresting lesson is presented as a game. Most would agree that playing is more enjoyable than memorizing by rote for the big test. In fact, students who participate in the Science Olympiad, a national competitive event, report that the main reason for joining the team is to have fun.

**Model Test 5, Writing Section, Track 80**

 Now listen to a lecture on the same topic as the passage that you have just read.

**Question**

Summarize the main points in the lecture, and then explain how they cast doubt on the ideas in the reading passage.

*Independent Essay "Technological Innovations"*

**Question**

**Advances in transportation and communication like the airplane and the telephone have changed the way that nations interact with each other in a global society. Choose another technological innovation that you think is important.**

Give specific reasons and examples for your choice.

# MODEL TEST 5

## ANSWER KEYS

Use the following Answer Keys to check your scores on the Reading and Listening Sections of Model Test 5.

### READING SECTION

| *Reading 1* | *Reading 2* | *Reading 3* |
|---|---|---|
| 1. B | 14. C | 27. B |
| 2. B | 15. C | 28. B |
| 3. B | 16. A | 29. C |
| 4. D | 17. C | 30. B |
| 5. B | 18. D | 31. A |
| 6. B | 19. B | 32. D |
| 7. A | 20. A | 33. D |
| 8. A | 21. C | 34. A |
| 9. C | 22. B | 35. C |
| 10. C | 23. A | 36. B |
| 11. D | 24. C | 37. D |
| 12. A | 25. B | 38. C |
| 13. B, C, E | 26. C, D, F | 39. B, D, F |

## LISTENING SECTION

| *Listening Set 1* | *Listening Set 2* | *Listening Set 3* |
|---|---|---|
| 1.  B | 18.  B | 35.  C |
| 2.  C | 19.  C | 36.  B |
| 3.  C | 20.  C | 37.  D |
| 4.  A | 21.  A | 38.  B |
| 5.  C | 22.  A | 39.  C |
| 6.  C | 23.  A | 40.  C |
| 7.  D | 24.  C | 41.  A |
| 8.  A | 25.  A, D | 42.  A, B |
| 9.  D | 26.  B | 43.  C |
| 10.  B | 27.  A | 44.  A |
| 11.  A, E: Sod | 28.  B | 45.  B |
|      B, C, D: Log | 29.  A | 46.  C |
| 12.  D | 30.  A | 47.  B |
| 13.  B, D | 31.  D | 48.  A, C |
| 14.  A | 32.  A | 49.  A |
| 15.  C | 33.  C | 50.  C |
| 16.  B | 34.  A, C | 51.  B |
| 17.  C | | |

 # EXPLANATORY AND EXAMPLE ANSWERS, MODEL TEST 5

Go to the Barron's TOEFL site to study detailed Explanatory Answers for the Reading and Listening Sections, and Outlines, Example Answers, and Checklists for the Speaking and Writing Sections of Model Test 5.

# MODEL TEST 6: PROGRESS TEST

## READING SECTION

The Reading Section tests your ability to understand reading passages like those in college textbooks. The reading passages are presented in one complete section, which allows you to move to the next passage and return to a previous passage to change answers or answer questions that you may have left blank. The passages are about 700 words in length.

This is the long format for the Reading Section. On the long format, you will read four passages. After each passage, you will answer 12–14 questions about it. You may take notes while you read, but notes are not graded. You may use your notes to answer the questions. Some passages may include a word or phrase that is underlined in blue. Click on the word or phrase to see a glossary definition or explanation. Only three passages will be graded. The other passage is part of an experimental section for future tests. Because you will not know which passages will be graded, you must try to do your best on all of them.

Choose the best answer for multiple-choice questions. Follow the directions on the page or on the screen for computer-assisted questions. Most questions are worth 1 point, but the last question in each passage is worth more than 1 point.

Click on **Next** to go to the next question. Click on **Back** to return to previous questions. You may return to previous questions for all of the passages.

You can click on **Review** to see a chart of the questions you have answered and the questions you have not answered. From this screen, you can return to the question you want to answer.

Although you can spend more time on one passage and less time on another passage, you should try to pace yourself so that you are spending about 20 minutes to read each passage and answer the questions for that passage. You will have 80 minutes to complete all of the passages and answer all of the questions on the long format. A clock on the screen will show you how much time you have to complete the Reading Section.

## Reading 1

The following reading passage was adapted from *Biology: The Unity and Diversity of Life*, Tenth Edition by Cecie Starr and Ralph Taggart, Brooks-Cole, 2004.

### "Exotic and Endangered Species"

P1 → When you hear someone bubbling enthusiastically about an **exotic species**, you can safely bet the speaker isn't an ecologist. This is a name for a resident of an established community that was deliberately or accidentally moved from its home range and became established elsewhere. Unlike most imports, which can't take hold outside their home range, an exotic species permanently insinuates itself into a new community.

P2    Sometimes the additions are harmless and even have beneficial effects. More often, they make native species **endangered species**, which by definition are extremely vulnerable to extinction. Of all species on the rare or endangered lists or that recently became extinct, *close to 70 percent owe their precarious existence or demise to displacement by exotic species.* Two examples are included here to illustrate the problem.

P3    During the 1800s, British settlers in Australia just couldn't bond with the koalas and kangaroos, so they started to import familiar animals from their homeland. In 1859, in what would be the start of a wholesale disaster, a northern Australian landowner imported and then released two dozen wild European rabbits *(Oryctolagus cuniculus).* Good food and good sport hunting—that was the idea. An ideal rabbit habitat with no natural predators was the reality.

P4    Six years later, the landowner had killed 20,000 rabbits and was besieged by 20,000 more. The rabbits displaced livestock, even kangaroos. Now Australia has 200 to 300 million hippityhopping through the southern half of the country. They overgraze perennial grasses in good times and strip bark from shrubs and trees during droughts. You know where they've been; they transform grasslands and shrublands into eroded deserts. They have been shot and poisoned. Their warrens have been plowed under, fumigated, and dynamited. Even when all-out assaults reduced their population size by 70 percent, the rapidly reproducing imports made a comeback in less than a year. Did the construction of a 2,000-mile-long fence protect western Australia? No. Rabbits made it to the other side before workers finished the fence.

P5 → In 1951, government workers introduced a myxoma virus by way of mildly infected South American rabbits, its normal hosts. This virus causes *myxomatosis.* The disease has mild effects on South American rabbits that coevolved with the virus but nearly always had lethal effects on *O. cuniculus.* Biting insects, mainly mosquitoes and fleas, quickly transmit the virus from host to host. Having no coevolved defenses against the novel virus, the European rabbits died in droves. But, as you might expect, natural selection has since favored rapid growth of populations of *O. cuniculus* resistant to the virus.

P6 → In 1991, on an uninhabited island in Spencer Gulf, Australian researchers released a population of rabbits that they had injected with a calcivirus. The rabbits died quickly and relatively painlessly from blood clots in their lungs, hearts, and kidneys. In 1995, the test virus escaped from the island, possibly on insect vectors. It has been killing 80 to 95 percent of the adult rabbits in Australian regions. At this writing, researchers are now questioning whether the calcivirus should be used on a widespread scale, whether it can jump boundaries and infect animals other than rabbits (such as humans), and what the long-term consequences will be.

P7 A vine called kudzu (*Pueraria lobata*) was deliberately imported from Japan to the United States, where it faces no serious threats from herbivores, pathogens, or competitor plants. In temperate parts of Asia, it is a well-behaved legume with a well-developed root system. It *seemed* like a good idea to use it to control erosion on hills and highway embankments in the southeastern United States. A With nothing to stop it, though, kudzu's shoots grew a third of a meter per day. Vines now blanket streambanks, trees, telephone poles, houses, and almost everything else in their path. Attempts to dig up or burn kudzu are futile. Grazing goats and herbicides help, but goats eat other plants, too, and herbicides contaminate water supplies. B Kudzu could reach the Great Lakes by the year 2040.

P8 → On the bright side, a Japanese firm is constructing a kudzu farm and processing plant in Alabama. The idea is to export the starch to Asia, where the demand currently exceeds the supply. C Also, kudzu may eventually help reduce logging operations. D At the Georgia Institute of Technology, researchers report that kudzu might become an alternative source for paper.

1. Based on the information in paragraph 1, which of the following best explains the term "exotic species"?

    Ⓐ Animals or plants on the rare species list
    Ⓑ A permanent resident in an established community
    Ⓒ A species that has been moved to a different community
    Ⓓ An import that fails to thrive outside of its home range

    Paragraph 1 is marked with an arrow [→].

2. The word bond in the passage is closest in meaning to

    Ⓐ move
    Ⓑ connect
    Ⓒ live
    Ⓓ fight

3. According to the author, why did the plan to introduce rabbits in Australia fail?

   Ⓐ The rabbits were infected with a contagious virus.
   Ⓑ Most Australians did not like the rabbits.
   Ⓒ No natural predators controlled the rabbit population.
   Ⓓ Hunters killed the rabbits for sport and for food.

4. The word normal in the passage is closest in meaning to

   Ⓐ obvious
   Ⓑ prior
   Ⓒ significant
   Ⓓ usual

5. All of the following methods were used to control the rabbit population in Australia EXCEPT

   Ⓐ they were poisoned
   Ⓑ their habitats were buried
   Ⓒ they were moved to deserts
   Ⓓ they were surrounded by fences

6. Why does the author mention "mosquitoes and fleas" in paragraph 5?

   Ⓐ Because they are the origin of the myxoma virus
   Ⓑ Because they carry the myxoma virus to other animals
   Ⓒ Because they die when they are infected by myxoma
   Ⓓ Because they have an immunity to the myxoma virus

   Paragraph 5 is marked with an arrow [➡].

7. According to paragraph 6, why was the Spencer Gulf experiment dangerous?

   Ⓐ Insect populations were exposed to a virus.
   Ⓑ Rabbits on the island died from a virus.
   Ⓒ The virus may be a threat to humans.
   Ⓓ Some animals are immune to the virus.

   Paragraph 6 is marked with an arrow [➡].

8. The word consequences in the passage is closest in meaning to

   Ⓐ stages
   Ⓑ advantages
   Ⓒ results
   Ⓓ increases

9. Why does the author give details about the "kudzu farm" and "processing plant" in paragraph 8?

    Ⓐ To explain why kudzu was imported from abroad
    Ⓑ To argue that the decision to plant kudzu was a good one
    Ⓒ To give a reason for kudzu to be planted in Asia
    Ⓓ To offer partial solutions to the kudzu problem

    Paragraph 8 is marked with an arrow [➜].

10. The word exceeds in the passage is closest in meaning to

    Ⓐ surpasses
    Ⓑ destroys
    Ⓒ estimates
    Ⓓ causes

11. Which of the following statements most accurately reflects the author's opinion about exotic species?

    Ⓐ Exotic species should be protected by ecologists.
    Ⓑ Importing an exotic species can solve many problems.
    Ⓒ Ecologists should make the decision to import an exotic species.
    Ⓓ Exotic species are often disruptive to the ecology.

12. Look at the four squares [■] that show where the following sentence could be inserted in the passage.

    **Asians use a starch extract from kudzu in drinks, herbal medicines, and candy.**

    Where could the sentence best be added?

    Click on a square [■] to insert the sentence in the passage.

13. **Directions:** An introduction for a short summary of the passage appears below. Complete the summary by selecting the THREE answer choices that mention the most important points in the passage. Some sentences do not belong in the summary because they express ideas that are not included in the passage or are minor points from the passage. ***This question is worth 2 points.***

**Exotic species often require containment because they displace other species when they become established in a new environment.**

- 
- 
- 

### Answer Choices

A Rabbits were able to cross a fence 2,000 miles long that was constructed to keep them out of western Australia.

B Methods to control exotic species include fences, viruses, burning, herbicides, natural predators, and harvesting.

C Rabbits that were introduced in Australia and kudzu which was introduced in the United States are examples of species that caused problems.

D Researchers may be able to develop material from the kudzu vine that will be an alternative to wood pulp paper.

E The problem is that exotic species make native species vulnerable to extinction.

F A virus that is deadly to rabbits may have serious effects for other animals.

### *Reading 2*

The following reading passage was adapted from *Gardner's Art Through the Ages*, Thirteenth Edition by Fred S. Kleiner, Wadsworth, 2009.

### *"Paleolithic Art"*

P1    From the moment in 1879 that cave paintings were discovered at Altamira, scholars have wondered why the hunter-artists of the Old Stone Age decided to cover the walls of dark caverns with animal images. Various answers have been given, including that they were mere decoration, but this theory cannot explain the narrow range of subjects or the inaccessibility of many of the paintings. In fact, the remoteness and difficulty of access of many of the cave paintings and the fact that they appear to have been used for centuries are precisely what have led many scholars to suggest that the prehistoric hunters attributed magical properties to the images they painted. According to this argument, by confining animals to the surfaces of their cave walls, the artists believed they were bringing the beasts under their control. Some have even hypothesized that rituals or dances were performed in front of the images and that these rites served to improve the hunters' luck. Still others have stated that the painted animals may have served as teaching tools to instruct new hunters about the character of the various species they would encounter or even to serve as targets for spears.

P2     In contrast, some scholars have argued that the magical purpose of the paintings and reliefs was not to facilitate the *destruction* of bison and other species. Instead, they believe prehistoric painters created animal images to assure the *survival* of the herds Paleolithic peoples depended on for their food supply and for their clothing. A A central problem for both the hunting-magic and food-creation theories is that the animals that seem to have been diet staples of Old Stone Age peoples are not those most frequently portrayed. B

P3     Other scholars have sought to reconstruct an elaborate mythology based on the cave paintings, suggesting that Paleolithic humans believed they had animal ancestors. Still others have equated certain species with men and others with women and also found sexual symbolism in the abstract signs that sometimes accompany the images. C Almost all of these theories have been discredited over time, and art historians must admit that no one knows the intent of these paintings. D In fact, a single explanation for all Paleolithic murals, even paintings similar in subject, style, and *composition* (how the motifs are arranged on the surface), is unlikely to apply universally. The works remain an enigma—and always will—because before the invention of writing, no contemporaneous explanations could be recorded.

P4 → That the paintings did have meaning to the Paleolithic peoples who made and observed them cannot, however, be doubted. In fact, signs consisting of checks, dots, squares, or other arrangements of lines often accompany the pictures of animals.

P5 → Representations of human hands are also common. At Pech-Merle in France, painted hands accompany representations of spotted horses. These and the majority of painted hands at other sites are "negative"; that is, the painter placed one hand against the wall and then brushed or blew or spat pigment around it. Occasionally, the painter dipped a hand in the pigment and then pressed it against the wall, leaving a "positive" imprint. These handprints, too, must have had a purpose. Some researchers have considered them "signatures" of cult or community members or, less likely, an individual artist. But like everything else in Paleolithic art, their meaning is unknown.

P6 → The mural (wall) paintings at Pech-Merle also allow some insight into the reason certain subjects may have been chosen for a specific location. One of the horses may have been inspired by the rock formation in the wall surface resembling a horse's head and neck. Old Stone Age painters and sculptors frequently and skillfully used the caves' naturally irregular surfaces to help give the illusion of real presence to their forms. Altamira bison, for example, were painted over bulging rock surfaces. In fact, prehistorians have observed that bison and cattle appear almost exclusively on convex surfaces, whereas nearly all horses and hands are painted on concave surfaces. What this signifies has yet to be determined.

14. According to paragraph 1, why was the cave art difficult to find?

    &#9398; The artists were probably trying to keep their work a secret from their tribe.
    &#9399; The artists could have begun their painting while they were confined in the caves.
    &#9400; The artists may have chosen a location deep in the caves to hold ceremonies.
    &#9401; The artists had to practice before they made images that more people could see.

Paragraph 1 is marked with an arrow [➜].

15. According to paragraph 1, Paleolithic people may have used cave art for all of the following purposes EXCEPT

    &#9398; people may have danced in front of the images
    &#9399; hunters could have used the figures for target practice
    &#9400; leaders might have performed magical rituals in the caves
    &#9401; animals may have been kept in the caves near the drawings

Paragraph 1 is marked with an arrow [➜].

16. The word access in the passage is closest in meaning to

    &#9398; admission
    &#9399; meaning
    &#9400; site
    &#9401; research

17. The word facilitate in the passage is closest in meaning to

    &#9398; specify
    &#9399; permit
    &#9400; assist
    &#9401; discover

18. The word discredited in the passage is closest in meaning to

    &#9398; not attentive
    &#9399; not believed
    &#9400; not hopeful
    &#9401; not organized

19. By which means does the author explain the term "composition"?

    Ⓐ Giving an example
    Ⓑ Providing a definition
    Ⓒ Contrasting it with motifs
    Ⓓ Referring to art historians

20. Which of the sentences below best expresses the information in the highlighted statement in the passage? The other choices change the meaning or leave out important information.

    Ⓐ It is true that the paintings were meaningful to the Paleolithic peoples.
    Ⓑ Doubtless, the Paleolithic peoples were the ones who made the paintings.
    Ⓒ There is no doubt about the meaning of the Paleolithic paintings.
    Ⓓ Paintings that had meaning for the Paleolithic peoples are doubtful.

21. The phrase an individual in the passage is closest in meaning to

    Ⓐ a popular
    Ⓑ an exceptional
    Ⓒ a single
    Ⓓ an unknown

22. According to paragraph 5, why did artists leave a positive imprint of their hands on cave paintings?

    Ⓐ It represents human beings in the cave paintings.
    Ⓑ It could have been a way for them to sign their work.
    Ⓒ It was a hunter's handprint among the herd of animals.
    Ⓓ It might have been a pleasing image without much meaning.

    Paragraph 5 is marked with an arrow [➔].

23. According to paragraph 6, why do scholars believe that the artists selected certain surfaces for their work?

    Ⓐ The stone was easy to carve because it was very soft.
    Ⓑ The animals in hunting grounds nearby provided inspiration.
    Ⓒ The artists used the natural formations to create realistic shapes.
    Ⓓ The location of the caves had a magical significance to them.

    Paragraph 6 is marked with an arrow [➔].

24. Which of the following statements most accurately reflects the author's opinion about the purpose of cave paintings?

    Ⓐ The cave paintings were part of a hunting ritual.
    Ⓑ Artists were honoring their animal ancestors in cave paintings.
    Ⓒ The exact purpose of cave paintings is not known.
    Ⓓ Decoration was probably the main reason for painting in caves.

25. Look at the four squares [■] that show where the following sentence could be inserted in the passage.

**At Altamira, for example, faunal remains show that red deer, not bison, were eaten.**

Where could the sentence best be added?

Click on a square [■] to insert the sentence in the passage.

26. **Directions:** An introduction for a short summary of the passage appears below. Complete the summary by selecting the THREE answer choices that mention the most important points in the passage. Some sentences do not belong in the summary because they express ideas that are not included in the passage or are minor points from the passage. *This question is worth 2 points.*

**The purpose of the art discovered on cave walls is a topic of discussion among scholars.**

- 
- 
- 

**Answer Choices**

A The surface of the walls in the caves may have inspired some of the subjects, and handprints may have been signatures.

B It is possible that the paintings were created as part of a magical ritual either to guarantee a good hunt or an abundance of animals.

C At Altamira, excavations indicate that the protein diet of the inhabitants was probably deer rather than bison.

D Perhaps the artists were paying homage to their animal ancestors by recreating their mythology in the pictures.

E The art may be more recent than first assumed when the caves were originally discovered in the late 1800s.

F It has been documented that almost all of the horses and hands were painted on concave surfaces at Pech-Merle.

## *Reading 3*

The following reading passage was adapted from *Management*, Fourth Edition by Pamela S. Lewis, et al., South Western, 2004.

### *"Group Decision Making"*

#### Advantages of Group Decision Making

P1 → Committees, task forces, and ad hoc groups are frequently assigned to identify and recommend decision alternatives or, in some cases, to actually make important decisions. In essence, a group is a tool that can focus the experience and expertise of several people on a particular problem or situation. Thus, a group offers the advantage of greater total knowledge. Groups accumulate more information, knowledge, and facts than individuals and often consider more alternatives. Each person in the group is able to draw on his or her unique education, experience, insights, and other resources and contribute those to the group. The varied backgrounds, training levels, and expertise of group members also help overcome tunnel vision by enabling the group to view the problem in more than one way.

P2 → Participation in group decision making usually leads to higher member satisfaction. People tend to accept a decision more readily and to be better satisfied with it when they have participated in making that decision. In addition, people will better understand and be more committed to a decision in which they have had a say than to a decision made for them. As a result, such a decision is more likely to be implemented successfully.

#### Disadvantages of Group Decision Making

P3 → While groups have many potential benefits, we all know that they can also be frustrating. [A] One obvious disadvantage of group decision making is the time required to make a decision. [B] The time needed for group discussion and the associated compromising and selecting of a decision alternative can be considerable. [C] Time costs money, so a waste of time becomes a disadvantage if a decision made by a group could have been made just as effectively by an individual working alone. [D] Consequently, group decisions should be avoided when speed and efficiency are the primary considerations.

P4    A second disadvantage is that the group discussion may be dominated by an individual or subgroup. Effectiveness can be reduced if one individual, such as the group leader, dominates the discussion by talking too much or being closed to other points of view. Some group leaders try to control the group and provide the major input. Such dominance can stifle other group members' willingness to participate and could cause decision alternatives to be ignored or overlooked. All group members need to be encouraged and permitted to contribute.

P5 → Another disadvantage of group decision making is that members may be less concerned with the group's goals than with their own personal goals. They may become so sidetracked in trying to win an argument that they forget about group performance. On the other hand, a group may try too hard to compromise and consequently may not make optimal decisions. Sometimes this stems from the desire to maintain friendships and avoid disagreements. Often groups exert tremendous social pressure on individuals to conform to [P6] established or expected patterns of behavior. Especially when they are dealing with important and controversial issues, interacting groups may be prone to a phenomenon called *groupthink*.

→ Groupthink is an agreement-at-any-cost mentality that results in ineffective group decision making. It occurs when groups are highly cohesive, have highly directive leaders, are insulated so they have no clear ways to get objective information, and—because they lack outside information—have little hope that a better solution might be found than the one proposed by the leader or other influential group members. These conditions foster the illusion that the group is invulnerable, right, and more moral than outsiders. They also encourage the development of self-appointed "mind guards" who bring pressure on dissenters. In such situations, decisions—often important decisions—are made [P7] without consideration of alternative frames or alternative options. It is difficult to imagine conditions more conducive to poor decision making and wrong decisions.

Recent research indicates that groupthink may also result when group members have preconceived ideas about how a problem should be solved. Under these conditions, the team may not examine a full range of decision alternatives, or it may discount or avoid information that threatens its preconceived choice.

27. In paragraph 1, the author states that groups frequently do which of the following?

   Ⓐ Generate more options than individuals
   Ⓑ Agree on the way that the problem should be approached
   Ⓒ Make recommendations instead of decisions
   Ⓓ Are chosen to participate because of their experience

   Paragraph 1 is marked with an arrow [→].

28. According to paragraph 2, why do group decisions tend to be more successful?

   Ⓐ When more people are involved, there are more ideas from which to choose.
   Ⓑ People are more accepting of decisions when they have been involved in them.
   Ⓒ Implementing ideas is easier with a large number of people to help.
   Ⓓ People like to be participants in decisions that are successful.

   Paragraph 2 is marked with an arrow [→].

29. The word considerable in the passage is closest in meaning to

    Ⓐ valuable
    Ⓑ significant
    Ⓒ predictable
    Ⓓ unusual

30. The word Consequently in the passage is closest in meaning to

    Ⓐ About now
    Ⓑ Without doubt
    Ⓒ Before long
    Ⓓ As a result

31. According to paragraph 3, why can group discussion be problematic?

    Ⓐ Individual decisions are always more effective.
    Ⓑ It takes more time for a group to arrive at a decision.
    Ⓒ It costs more to pay all of the group members.
    Ⓓ Interaction among group members can be a problem.

Paragraph 3 is marked with an arrow [➔].

32. What can be inferred about a group leader?

    Ⓐ A good leader will provide goals for the group to consider and vote on.
    Ⓑ The purpose of the leader is to facilitate the participation of all of the members.
    Ⓒ A group leader should be the dominant member of the group.
    Ⓓ Expectations for group behavior must be presented by the group leader.

33. The word controversial in the passage is closest in meaning to

    Ⓐ accepted
    Ⓑ debatable
    Ⓒ recent
    Ⓓ complicated

34. According to paragraph 5, how does the author explain compromise in a group?

    Ⓐ The group may try to make a better decision by compromising.
    Ⓑ A compromise may be the best way to encourage groupthink.
    Ⓒ Compromising may allow the group members to remain friends.
    Ⓓ To compromise can help one member to reach a personal goal.

Paragraph 5 is marked with an arrow [➔].

35. The phrase the one in the passage refers to

     Ⓐ solution
     Ⓑ information
     Ⓒ hope
     Ⓓ leader

36. What does the term "mind guards" refer to?

     Ⓐ People who conform to the group opinion without thinking
     Ⓑ Group members who try to force others to agree with the group
     Ⓒ Members of the group who are the most ethical and influential
     Ⓓ Those people who disagree without offering an alternative view

37. According to paragraph 6, why are alternative solutions often rejected in groupthink?

     Ⓐ Dissenters exert pressure on the group.
     Ⓑ Group leaders are not very creative.
     Ⓒ Information is not made available.
     Ⓓ The group is usually right.

Paragraph 6 is marked with an arrow [→].

38. Look at the four squares [■] that show where the following sentence could be inserted in the passage.

**In fact, the traditional group is prone to a variety of difficulties.**

Where could the sentence best be added?

Click on a square [■] to insert the sentence in the passage.

39. **Directions:** An introduction for a short summary of the passage appears below. Complete the summary by selecting the THREE answer choices that mention the most important points in the passage. Some sentences do not belong in the summary because they express ideas that are not included in the passage or are minor points from the passage. ***This question is worth 2 points.***

**Group decision making has both advantages and disadvantages.**

- 
- 
- 

### Answer Choices

A Groupthink is a very ineffective type of group decision in which either influential members propose decisions and pressure the group to agree without considering alternatives or the group has already predetermined their decision.

B Group decisions are beneficial because more people contribute their ideas, more information is available, and the members are more committed to a successful outcome because they have participated.

C Many different kinds of groups are assigned the task of making decisions or recommending alternatives for important choices that will affect them and other people.

D Problems associated with group decisions are that compromise requires time for discussion, some members control participation, and social relationships can negatively affect decisions.

E Group decisions should be avoided when one member of the group is likely to dominate the other members and impose a group decision without listening to everyone's point of view.

F So called "mind guards" often appear in groups with a view to putting pressure on members of the group who do not agree with the ideas or would like to consider alternatives to the decision proposed.

## Reading 4

The following reading passage was adapted from *The Solar System*, Sixth Edition by Michael A. Seeds, Brooks-Cole, 2008.

### "Four Stages of Planetary Development"

**Planetary Development**

P1  → The planet Earth has passed through four-stages of planetary development. All terrestrial planets pass through these same stages to some degree, but some planets evolved further or were affected in different ways.

**The Four Stages**

P2  The first stage of planetary evolution is *differentiation*, the separation of material according to density. Earth now has a dense core and a lower-density crust, and that structure must have originated very early in its history. Differentiation would have occurred easily if Earth were molten when it was young. Two sources of energy could have heated Earth. First, heat of formation was released by in-falling material. A <u>meteorite</u> hitting Earth at high velocity converts most of its energy of motion into heat, and the impacts of a large number of meteorites would have released tremendous heat. If Earth formed rapidly, this heat would have accumulated much more rapidly than it could leak away, and Earth was probably molten when it formed. A second source of heat requires more time to develop. The decay of radioactive elements trapped in the Earth releases heat gradually; but, as soon as Earth formed, that heat began to accumulate and helped melt Earth. That would have helped the planet differentiate.

P3  While Earth was still in a molten state, meteorites could leave no trace, but in the second stage in planetary evolution, *cratering*, the young Earth was battered by meteorites that pulverized the newly forming crust. The largest meteorites blasted out crater basins hundreds of kilometers in diameter. As the solar nebula cleared, the amount of debris decreased, and after the late heavy bombardment, the level of cratering fell to its present low level. Although meteorites still occasionally strike Earth and dig craters, cratering is no longer the dominant influence on Earth's geology. As you compare other worlds with Earth, you will discover traces of this intense period of cratering on every old surface in the solar system.

P4  → The third stage, *flooding*, no doubt began while cratering was still intense. The fracturing of the crust and the heating produced by radioactive decay allowed molten rock just below the crust to well up through fissures and flood the deeper basins. You will find such flooded basins with solidified lava flows on other worlds, such as the Moon, but all traces of this early lava flooding have been destroyed by later geological activity in Earth's crust. On Earth, flooding continued as the atmosphere cooled and water fell as rain, filling the deepest basins to produce the first oceans. A Notice that on Earth flooding involves both lava and water, a circumstance that we will not find on most worlds. B

P5    The fourth stage, *slow surface evolution*, has continued for the last 3.5 billion years or more. C Earth's surface is constantly changing as sections of crust slide over each other, push up mountains, and shift continents. D Almost all traces of the first billion years of Earth's geology have been destroyed by the active crust and erosion.

### Earth as a Planet

P6    All terrestrial planets pass through these four stages, but some have emphasized one stage over another, and some planets have failed to progress fully through the four stages. Earth is a good standard for comparative planetology because every major process on any rocky world in our solar system is represented in some form on Earth.

P7    Nevertheless, Earth is peculiar in two ways. First, it has large amounts of liquid water on its surface. Fully 75 percent of its surface is covered by this liquid; no other planet in our solar system is known to have such extensive liquid water on its surface. Water not only fills the oceans but also evaporates into the atmosphere, forms clouds, and then falls as rain. Water falling on the continents flows downhill to form rivers that flow back to the sea, and in so doing, the water produces intense erosion. You will not see such intense erosion on most worlds. Liquid water is, in fact, a rare material on most planets. Your home planet is special in a second way. Some of the matter on the surface of this world is alive, and a small part of that living matter is aware. No one is sure how the presence of living matter has affected the evolution of Earth, but this process seems to be totally missing from other worlds in our solar system. Furthermore, the thinking part of life on Earth, humankind, is actively altering our planet.

### Glossary
meteorite:  a mass that falls to the surface of a planet from space
planetology:  the study of planets

40. Why does the author mention the "Earth" in paragraph 1?

   Ⓐ To explain the stages in planetary development for the Earth in detail
   Ⓑ To contrast the evolution of the Earth with that of other planets
   Ⓒ To demonstrate that the Earth passed through similar stages to those of most planets
   Ⓓ To give an example of exploration of the terrestrial planets

Paragraph 1 is marked with an arrow [➔].

41. Which of the sentences below best expresses the information in the highlighted statement in the passage? The other choices change the meaning or leave out important information.

    Ⓐ The Earth may have been liquid because the heat collected faster than it dissipated if the formation took place quickly.
    Ⓑ Because of the rapid formation of the Earth, the crust took a long time to cool before it became a solid.
    Ⓒ The liquid core of the Earth was created when the planet first formed because the heat was so high and there was little cooling.
    Ⓓ The cooling caused the Earth to form much more quickly as it met with the intense heat of the new planet.

42. The word pulverized in the passage is closest in meaning to

    Ⓐ melted into liquid
    Ⓑ broken into small parts
    Ⓒ frozen very hard
    Ⓓ washed very clean

43. The word dominant in the passage is closest in meaning to

    Ⓐ most limited
    Ⓑ most likely
    Ⓒ most rapid
    Ⓓ most important

44. What can be inferred about radioactive matter?

    Ⓐ It is revealed by later activity.
    Ⓑ It generates intense heat.
    Ⓒ It is an important stage.
    Ⓓ It floods the planet's crust.

45. According to paragraph 4, how were the oceans formed?

    Ⓐ Ice gouged out depressions in the Earth.
    Ⓑ Rain filled the craters made by meteorites.
    Ⓒ Earthquakes shifted the continents.
    Ⓓ Molten rock and lava flooded the basins.

    Paragraph 4 is marked with an arrow [➜].

46. According to the passage, which stage occurs after cratering?

    Ⓐ Flooding
    Ⓑ Slow surface evolution
    Ⓒ Differentiation
    Ⓓ Erosion

47. What is the author's opinion of life on other planets?

    Ⓐ She does not know whether life is present on other planets.
    Ⓑ She is certain that no life exists on any planet except Earth.
    Ⓒ She does not express an opinion about life on other planets.
    Ⓓ She thinks that there is probably life on other planets.

48. Look at the four squares [■] that show where the following sentence could be inserted in the passage.

**At the same time, moving air and water erode the surface and wear away geological features.**

Where could the sentence best be added?

Click on a square [■] to insert the sentence in the passage.

49. All of the following are reasons why the Earth is a good model of planetary development for purposes of comparison with other planets EXCEPT

    Ⓐ the Earth has gone through all four stages of planetary evolution
    Ⓑ life on Earth has affected the evolution in a number of important ways
    Ⓒ all of the fundamental processes on terrestrial planets have occurred on Earth
    Ⓓ there is evidence of extensive cratering both on Earth and on all other planets

50. The word peculiar in the passage is closest in meaning to

    Ⓐ different
    Ⓑ better
    Ⓒ interesting
    Ⓓ new

51. The word process in the passage is closest in meaning to

    Ⓐ procedure
    Ⓑ improvement
    Ⓒ regulation
    Ⓓ definition

52. **Directions:** An introduction for a short summary of the passage appears below. Complete the summary by selecting the THREE answer choices that mention the most important points in the passage. Some sentences do not belong in the summary because they express ideas that are not included in the passage or are minor points from the passage. *This question is worth 2 points.*

**There are four stages of development for the terrestrial planets.**

- 
- 
- 

## Answer Choices

A All rocky planets go through different stages in their evolution because of variations in composition.

B In spite of several unique features, the Earth is a good example of how a planet proceeds through the stages.

C Fewer meteorites fall to Earth now than in the earlier stages of the planet's evolutionary history.

D About three quarters of the surface of the Earth is submerged by the water in its oceans.

E Differentiation and cratering are early stages that are influenced by in-falling meteorites.

F Flooding includes both lava and water, while slow surface evolution causes shifting in the crust.

# LISTENING SECTION

**Model Test 6, Listening Section, Track 81**

The Listening Section tests your ability to understand spoken English that is typical of interactions and academic speech on college campuses. During the test, you will listen to conversations, lectures, and discussions, and you will answer questions about them.

This is the short format for the Listening Section. On the short format, you will listen to two conversations, two lectures, and two discussions. After each listening passage, you will answer 5–6 questions about it.

You will hear each passage one time. You may take notes while you listen, but notes are not graded. You may use your notes to answer the questions.

Choose the best answer for multiple-choice questions. Follow the directions on the page or on the screen for computer-assisted questions. Click on **Next** and then on **OK** to go on to the next question. You cannot return to previous questions.

The Listening Section is divided into sets. Each set includes one conversation, one lecture, and one discussion. You will have 10 minutes to answer all of the questions for each set. You will have 20 minutes to answer all of the questions on the short format. A clock on the screen will show you how much time you have to complete your answers for the section. The clock does NOT count the time you are listening to the conversations, lectures, and discussions.

## *Listening 1 "Professor's Office"*

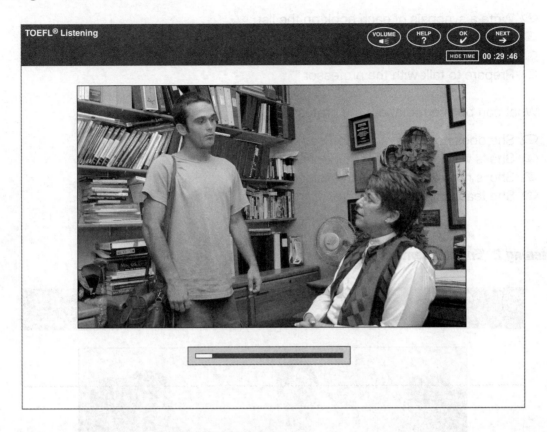

1. Why does the man go to see his professor?

   Ⓐ To borrow some books for his project
   Ⓑ To hand in the first book report
   Ⓒ To ask about the professor's requirements
   Ⓓ To talk about literary movements

2. How is the second part of the reading list different from the first part?

   Ⓐ More minority authors are represented.
   Ⓑ All of the writers are from North America.
   Ⓒ It includes books from the Post Modern Period.
   Ⓓ In addition to novels, some plays are on the list.

3. What does the man mean when he says this:

   Ⓐ He does not understand the term.
   Ⓑ He is interested in the idea.
   Ⓒ He is not sure how to pronounce it.
   Ⓓ He thinks that the word is humorous.

4. What will the man probably do before the next meeting?

    Ⓐ Write a synopsis of each book on the list
    Ⓑ Make a list of books that he wants to read
    Ⓒ Finish the art project on his computer
    Ⓓ Prepare to talk with the professor

5. What can be inferred about the professor?

    Ⓐ She does not have regular office hours.
    Ⓑ She is willing to help her students.
    Ⓒ She is not very flexible with assignments.
    Ⓓ She teaches British literature.

## Listening 2 "Environmental Science Class"

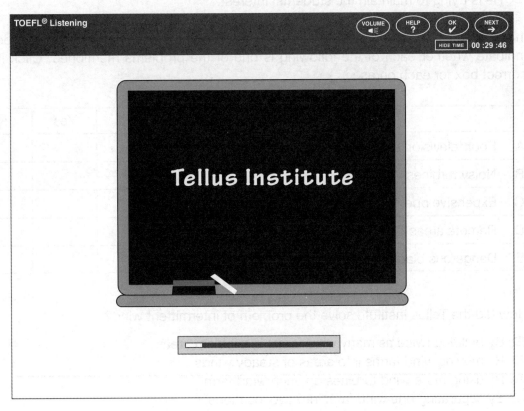

6. What aspect of wind power is the lecture mainly about?

   Ⓐ Electrical power in California
   Ⓑ Alternative energy sources
   Ⓒ Problems associated with turbines
   Ⓓ Wind as a renewable energy option

7. Which two regions of the United States have the greatest potential for supplying wind power?

   Click on 2 answer choices.

   Ⓐ The Eastern Seaboard

   Ⓑ The Midwestern Plains

   Ⓒ The Desert Southwest

   Ⓓ The Pacific Northwest

8. Why does the professor say this:

   Ⓐ He is disagreeing with the figures.
   Ⓑ He is expressing surprise at the statistics.
   Ⓒ He is correcting a previous statement.
   Ⓓ He is trying to maintain the students' interest.

9. In the lecture, the professor identifies several problems associated with wind power. Indicate whether each of the following is one of the problems mentioned. Click in the correct box for each phrase.

   |   |                           | Yes | No |
   |---|---------------------------|-----|----|
   | A | Poor television reception |     |    |
   | B | Noisy turbines            |     |    |
   | C | Expensive operating costs |     |    |
   | D | Remote areas              |     |    |
   | E | Dangerous blades for birds |    |    |

10. How did the Tellus Institute solve the problem of intermittent wind?

    Ⓐ By building twice as many wind farms in problem areas
    Ⓑ By moving wind farms into areas of steady winds
    Ⓒ By using more wind turbines on each wind farm
    Ⓓ By separating one wind farm into two locations

11. What is the professor's opinion about the future of wind power?

     Ⓐ He thinks that wind power will require more research before it becomes practical.
     Ⓑ He supports the use of wind power only as a secondary source of energy.
     Ⓒ He feels that most of the world's energy problems will be solved by wind power.
     Ⓓ He believes that there are too many problems associated with wind power.

### *Listening 3 "Philosophy Class"*

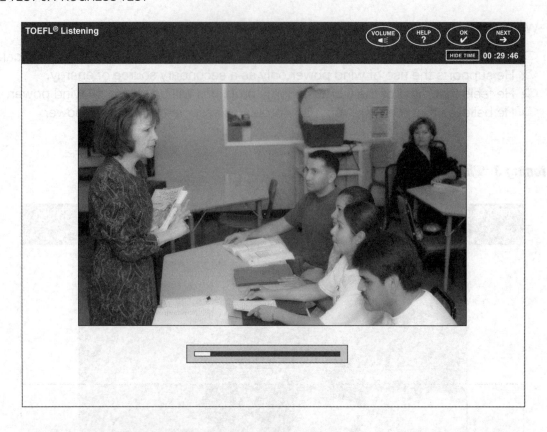

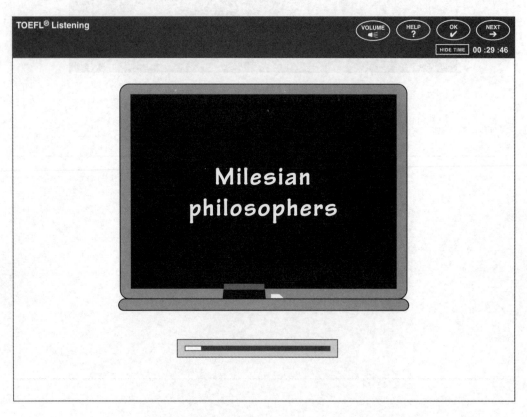

12. What is the discussion mainly about?

    Ⓐ The laws of motion
    Ⓑ The origin of water
    Ⓒ The nature of the universe
    Ⓓ The spirit of the world

13. Why does the student mention evolutionary theory?

    Ⓐ He is digressing from the main topic.
    Ⓑ He is trying to embarrass the professor.
    Ⓒ He is expressing doubt about Greek philosophy.
    Ⓓ He is comparing evolution to Anaximander's theory.

14. Why does the professor say this:

    Ⓐ She is not happy with the student's response.
    Ⓑ She is introducing an alternative view.
    Ⓒ She is going to expand on the comment.
    Ⓓ She is ending the discussion.

15. What view did the three Milesian philosophers share?

    Ⓐ They all believed that the mythology had a basis in fact.
    Ⓑ They introduced a scientific approach to explaining nature.
    Ⓒ They thought that water was the original element.
    Ⓓ They all agreed with the teachings of Socrates.

16. What can be inferred about the early Greek philosophers?

    Ⓐ They were exploring the physical sciences.
    Ⓑ They recorded many of the Greek myths.
    Ⓒ They were primarily interested in religion.
    Ⓓ They had contact with other European scholars.

17. What does the professor mean when she says this:

    Ⓐ She is expressing strong agreement.
    Ⓑ She is introducing doubt.
    Ⓒ She is maintaining a neutral position.
    Ⓓ She is asking the students to agree.

## *Listening 4 "Professor's Office"*

18. Why does the woman want to talk with her professor?

    Ⓐ She wants to make an appointment outside of office hours.
    Ⓑ She needs to get him to approve the topic for her research.
    Ⓒ She has some questions about the report she is writing.
    Ⓓ She would like a recommendation for a job in the lab.

19. What advice does the professor give the woman?

    Ⓐ Have some friends read the research
    Ⓑ Refer to the explanation in the textbook
    Ⓒ Ask a chemistry major to help her
    Ⓓ Include more references in the report

20. What does the professor offer to do?

    Ⓐ Read a draft of the report before she submits it
    Ⓑ Help her find some better references
    Ⓒ Show her how to complete the experiment
    Ⓓ Give her a job in the laboratory

21. Why does the professor say this: 🎧

    Ⓐ He realizes that she won't have time to revise the report.
    Ⓑ He is concerned that she will not complete the research.
    Ⓒ He recalls that he will not be available to help her.
    Ⓓ He wants her to get an extension to finish the project.

22. What is the professor's opinion of the woman?

    Ⓐ He assumes that she is too busy to work.
    Ⓑ He is very impressed with her attitude.
    Ⓒ He thinks that she is not a serious student.
    Ⓓ He wants her to change her major to chemistry.

## Listening 5 "Biology Class"

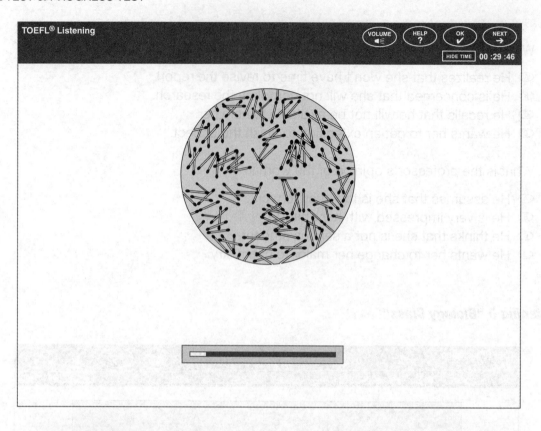

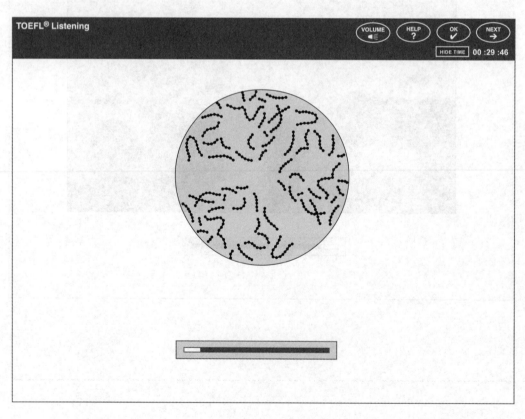

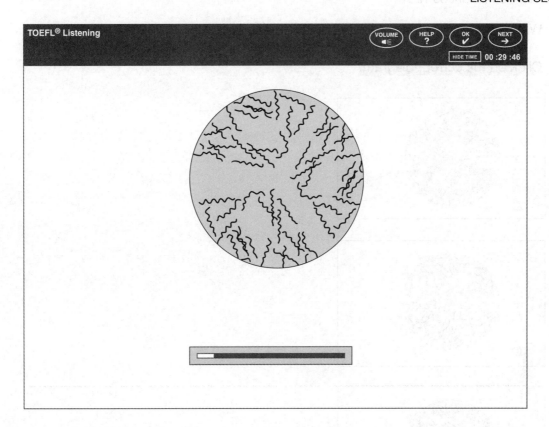

23. What aspect of bacteria is this lecture mainly about?

    Ⓐ How microscopic organisms are measured
    Ⓑ The use of bacteria for research in genetics
    Ⓒ Diseases caused by bacterial infections
    Ⓓ The three major types of bacteria

24. Which of the following slides contain cocci bacteria?

Click on the correct diagram.

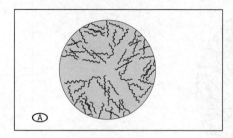

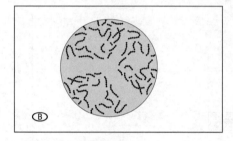

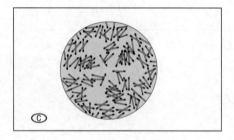

25. Which two characteristics are common in bacteria?

Click on 2 answer choices.

A  They have one cell.

B  They are harmful to humans.

C  They reproduce quickly.

D  They die when exposed to air.

26. Why are bacteria being used in the research study at the university?

     Ⓐ Bacteria have unusual cell formations.
     Ⓑ Bacteria live harmlessly on the skin.
     Ⓒ Bacteria are similar to other life forms.
     Ⓓ Bacteria cause many diseases in humans.

27. How does the professor help the students to remember the types of bacteria?

     Ⓐ He shows them many examples of slides.
     Ⓑ He tells them to look at specimens in the lab.
     Ⓒ He uses the first letter to represent the shape.
     Ⓓ He explains the various DNA structures.

28. Why does the professor say this:

     Ⓐ He is showing the students some slides.
     Ⓑ He does not want the students to ask questions.
     Ⓒ He wants the students to pay attention.
     Ⓓ He thinks that the information is very clear.

## *Listening 6 "Literature Class"*

29. What is the discussion mainly about?

    Ⓐ The life of author Jonathan Swift
    Ⓑ A narrative of the fourth voyage of Gulliver
    Ⓒ A description of the Houyhnhnms
    Ⓓ The literature of the 1700s

30. What does Gulliver learn about himself?

    Ⓐ He is like the Yahoos in many ways.
    Ⓑ He does not want to return to England.
    Ⓒ He wants to write about his experience.
    Ⓓ He is afraid of the Houyhnhnm.

31. In the discussion, the professor describes the characteristics of the Yahoos. Indicate whether each of the following is one of their characteristics. Click in the correct box for each sentence.

|   |                                      | Yes | No |
|---|--------------------------------------|-----|----|
| A | They eat flowers.                    |     |    |
| B | They have a foul odor.               |     |    |
| C | They engage in an immoral lifestyle. |     |    |
| D | They are satirical caricatures of humans. |  |    |
| E | They live in trees.                  |     |    |

32. Why does the professor say this:

    Ⓐ She is criticizing the author.
    Ⓑ She is asking the students a question.
    Ⓒ She is preparing to draw a conclusion.
    Ⓓ She is changing the subject.

33. According to the professor, what kind of book is *Gulliver's Travels*?

    Ⓐ A biography of Jonathan Swift
    Ⓑ A satire about mankind
    Ⓒ A history of politics in England
    Ⓓ A children's story about animals

34. What can we infer about the literature of the period?

    Ⓐ Satire was very popular.
    Ⓑ Most books were nonfiction.
    Ⓒ It copied the style of Swift.
    Ⓓ The tone was not very serious.

 **Please turn off the audio. There is a 10-minute break between the Listening Section and the Speaking Section.**

# SPEAKING SECTION

**Model Test 6, Speaking Section, Track 82**

The Speaking Section tests your ability to communicate in English in an academic setting. During the test, you will be presented with six speaking questions. The questions ask for a response to a single question, a conversation, a talk, or a lecture. The prompts and the questions are presented only one time.

You may take notes as you listen, but notes are not graded. You may use your notes to answer the questions. Some of the questions ask for a response to a reading passage and a talk or a lecture. The reading passages and the questions are written, but the directions will be spoken.

Your speaking will be evaluated on both the fluency of the language and the accuracy of the content. You will have 15–20 seconds to prepare and 45–60 seconds to respond to each question. Typically, a good response will require all of the response time and the answer will be complete by the end of the response time.

You will have about 20 minutes to complete the Speaking Section. A clock on the screen will show you how much time you have to prepare each of your answers and how much time you have to record each response.

## Independent Speaking Question 1  "A Good Son or Daughter"

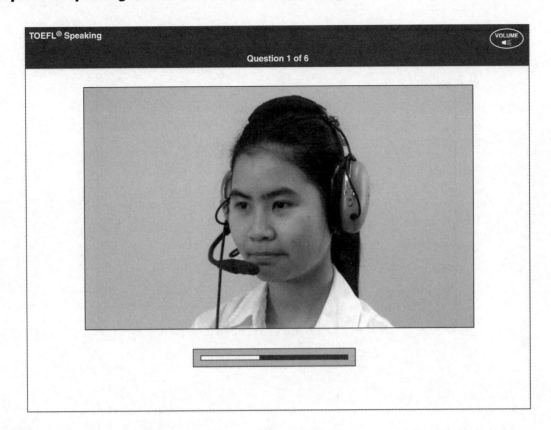

 Listen for a question about a familiar topic.

### Question
In your opinion, what are the characteristics of a good son or daughter in a family? Use specific examples and details to explain your answer.

Preparation Time: 15 seconds
Recording Time: 45 seconds

## *Independent Speaking Question 2  "Job Opportunities"*

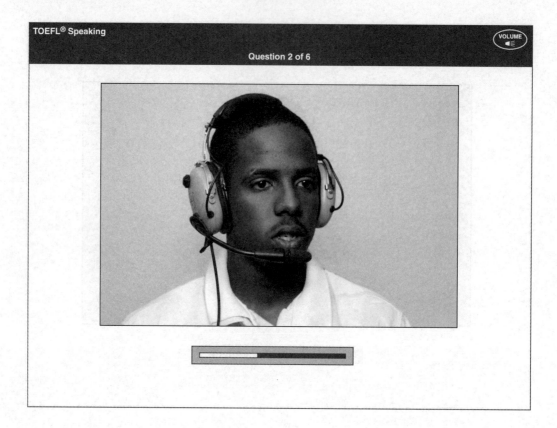

  Listen for a question that asks your opinion about a familiar topic.

**Question**

Some people are attracted to jobs that include a great deal of travel. Other people prefer jobs that allow them to return to their homes every evening. Which type of job opportunity would you prefer, and why? Use specific reasons and examples to support your opinion.

Preparation Time: 15 seconds
Recording Time: 45 seconds

## *Integrated Speaking Question 3 "Excused Absence"*

Read a short passage and listen to a talk on the same topic.

Reading Time: 45 seconds

---

<u>Policy for Excused Absence</u>

You may request an excused absence once per semester without explanation. Just email me and specify the date that you will be absent from class. If you plan to be absent on the day of a test or an exam, however, you must provide an explanation and make arrangements for a makeup test or exam. Please see me in my office for an excused absence from a test or exam. If you must be absent for more than one session, your grade may be affected. Your grade may be lowered one letter for each additional absence after the excused absence.

---

 Now listen to a student who is talking with friends about the policy.

**Question**
The student expresses his opinion of the professor's policy for excused absences. Report his opinion and explain the reasons that he gives for having that opinion.

Preparation Time: 30 seconds
Recording Time: 60 seconds

## *Integrated Speaking Question 4 "Insects"*

Read a short passage and then listen to part of a lecture on the same topic.

Reading Time: 45 seconds

---

### Insects

An insect belongs to the class of invertebrates called arthropods. Regardless of size, all adult insects have a similar body structure, which includes a head, a thorax, and an abdomen. The head contains not only the brain and mouth but also the sensory organs, usually a pair of eyes and a pair of antennae. The thorax is the central part of the insect's body where the wings and legs are attached, allowing the insect to move in the air and on feeding surfaces. Typically, insects have three pairs of legs and two pairs of wings. The third part of the insect's body structure consists of an abdomen where food is processed and the reproductive organs are found.

---

TOEFL® Speaking

Question 4 of 6

VOLUME

 Now listen to part of a lecture in a biology class. The professor is talking about insects.

**Question**

Describe the structure of an insect and explain why a spider is not strictly considered an insect.

Preparation Time: 30 seconds
Recording Time: 60 seconds

## *Integrated Speaking Question 5 "Meeting People"*

 Now listen to a conversation between a student and his friend.

**Question**
Describe the man's problem and the two suggestions that his friend makes about how to handle it. What do you think the man should do, and why?

Preparation Time: 20 seconds
Recording Time: 60 seconds

*Integrated Speaking Question 6 "Skinner Box"*

 Now listen to part of a lecture in a psychology class. The professor is discussing the Skinner Box.

**Question**
Using the main points and examples from the lecture, describe the Skinner Box and then explain how the device is used in psychology experiments.

Preparation Time: 20 seconds
Recording Time: 60 seconds

# WRITING SECTION

The Writing Section tests your ability to write essays in English similar to those that you would write in college courses. During the test, you will write two essays.

**The Integrated Essay.** First you will read an academic passage and then you will listen to a lecture on the same topic. You may take notes as you read and listen, but notes are not graded. You may use your notes to write the essay. The reading passage will disappear while you are listening to the lecture, but the passage will return to the screen for reference when you begin to write your essay. You will have 20 minutes to plan, write, and revise your response. Typically, a good essay for the integrated topic will require that you write 150–225 words.

**The Independent Essay.** You will read a question on the screen. It usually asks for your opinion about a familiar topic. You will have 30 minutes to plan, write, and revise your response. Typically, a good essay for the independent topic will require that you write 300–350 words.

A clock on the screen will show you how much time you have left to complete each essay.

## Integrated Essay "Formation of the Moon"

You have 20 minutes to plan, write, and revise your response to a reading passage and a lecture on the same topic. First, read the passage and take notes. Then, listen to the lecture and take notes. Finally, write your response to the writing question. Typically, a good response will require that you write 150–225 words.

**Reading Passage**
Time: 3 minutes

Although most scientists would agree that the Moon is critical for the formation of life on Earth, there is no consensus about the way that the Moon formed. Although there are several additional theories to explain the way that the Moon came into being, three hypotheses are commonly debated among lunar scientists.

The fission theory maintains that the Moon was once part of the Earth and became separated early in the formation of the solar system, probably while the Earth was spinning rapidly. The large piece of the Earth's surface that formed the Moon is believed to have broken off from the Pacific Ocean basin.

The co-accretion theory, also called the condensation theory, contends that the Moon was formed at the same time as the Earth from the original nebula of interstellar dust and gas that comprised the young solar system. In other words, the Moon was a sister planet that formed, like the Earth, by the aggregation of small particles into a single, much larger body. This event probably took place shortly after the Big Bang, about 13 billion years ago.

The giant impact theory states that the Moon was formed from the debris of an indirect collision between the Earth and a planetary body about the size of Mars. It is estimated that the collision occurred about 4.5 billion years ago. Initially, there would have been a number of pieces from both Earth and the collision planet that would have orbited Earth, but eventually, they would have coalesced to form a ball of molten rock about the size of today's Moon.

**Model Test 6, Writing Section, Track 83**

 Now listen to a lecture on the same topic as the passage that you have just read.

**Question**

Summarize the main points in the lecture and then explain how they cast doubt on the ideas in the reading passage.

### Independent Essay "Learning a Foreign Language"

**Question**

**Many people have learned a foreign language in their own country; others have learned a foreign language in the country in which it is spoken. Which is better?**

Give the advantages of each and support your viewpoint.

# MODEL TEST 6

## ANSWER KEYS

Use the following Answer Keys to check your scores on the Reading and Listening Sections of Model Test 6.

### READING SECTION

| *Reading 1* | *Reading 2* | *Reading 3* | *Reading 4* |
|---|---|---|---|
| 1.  C | 14.  C | 27.  A | 40.  C |
| 2.  B | 15.  D | 28.  B | 41.  A |
| 3.  C | 16.  A | 29.  B | 42.  B |
| 4.  D | 17.  C | 30.  D | 43.  D |
| 5.  C | 18.  B | 31.  B | 44.  B |
| 6.  B | 19.  B | 32.  B | 45.  B |
| 7.  C | 20.  A | 33.  B | 46.  A |
| 8.  C | 21.  C | 34.  C | 47.  B |
| 9.  D | 22.  B | 35.  A | 48.  D |
| 10.  A | 23.  C | 36.  B | 49.  B |
| 11.  D | 24.  C | 37.  C | 50.  A |
| 12.  C | 25.  B | 38.  A | 51.  A |
| 13.  B, C, E | 26.  A, B, D | 39.  A, B, D | 52.  B, E, F |

## LISTENING SECTION

| *Listening Set 1* | *Listening Set 2* |
|---|---|
| 1. C | 18. C |
| 2. A | 19. A |
| 3. B | 20. A |
| 4. D | 21. A |
| 5. B | 22. B |
| 6. D | 23. D |
| 7. B, D | 24. B |
| 8. C | 25. A, C |
| 9. A, B, E: Yes | 26. C |
| 10. D | 27. C |
| 11. A | 28. D |
| 12. C | 29. B |
| 13. D | 30. A |
| 14. C | 31. B, C, D: Yes |
| 15. B | 32. B |
| 16. A | 33. B |
| 17. B | 34. D |

# EXPLANATORY AND EXAMPLE ANSWERS, MODEL TEST 6

Go to the Barron's TOEFL site to study detailed Explanatory Answers for the Reading and Listening Sections, and Outlines, Example Answers, and Checklists for the Speaking and Writing Sections of Model Test 6.

# MODEL TEST 7: PROGRESS TEST

## READING SECTION

The Reading Section tests your ability to understand reading passages like those in college textbooks. The reading passages are presented in one complete section, which allows you to move to the next passage and return to a previous passage to change answers or answer questions that you may have left blank. The passages are about 700 words in length.

This is the short format for the Reading Section. On the short format, you will read three passages. After each passage, you will answer 12–14 questions about it. You may take notes while you read, but notes are not graded. You may use your notes to answer the questions. Some passages may include a word or phrase that is underlined in blue. Click on the word or phrase to see a glossary definition or explanation.

Choose the best answer for multiple-choice questions. Follow the directions on the page or on the screen for computer-assisted questions. Most questions are worth 1 point, but the last question in each passage is worth more than 1 point.

Click on **Next** to go to the next question. Click on **Back** to return to previous questions. You may return to previous questions for all of the passages.

You can click on **Review** to see a chart of the questions you have answered and the questions you have not answered. From this screen, you can return to the question you want to answer.

Although you can spend more time on one passage and less time on another passage, you should try to pace yourself so that you are spending about 20 minutes to read each passage and answer the questions for that passage. You will have 60 minutes to complete all of the passages and answer all of the questions on the short format. A clock on the screen will show you how much time you have to complete the Reading Section.

### *Reading 1*

The following reading passage was adapted from *Environmental Science: Earth as a Living Planet*, Sixth Edition by Daniel B. Botkin and Edward A. Keller, John Wiley and Sons, Inc., 2007.

### *"The Hydrologic Cycle"*

P1 → The hydrologic cycle is the transfer of water from the oceans to the atmosphere to the land and back to the oceans. The processes involved include evaporation of water from the oceans; precipitation on land; evaporation from land; and runoff from streams, rivers, and subsurface groundwater. The hydrologic cycle is driven by solar energy, which evaporates water from oceans, freshwater bodies, soils, and vegetation. Of the total 1.3 billion cubic km water on Earth, about 97% is in ocean, and about 2% is in glaciers and ice caps. The rest is in freshwater on land and in the atmosphere. Although it represents only a small fraction of the water on Earth, the water on land is important in moving chemicals, sculpturing landscape, weathering rocks, transporting sediments, and providing our water resources. The water in the atmosphere—only 0.001% of the total on Earth—cycles quickly to produce rain and runoff for our water resources.

P2 → Especially important from an environmental perspective is that rates of transfer on land are small relative to what's happening in the ocean. For example, most of the water that evaporates from the ocean falls again as precipitation into the ocean. On land, most of the water that falls as precipitation comes from evaporation of water from land. This means that regional land-use changes, such as the building of large dams and reservoirs, can change the amount of water evaporated into the atmosphere and change the location and amount of precipitation on land—water we depend on to raise our crops and supply water for our urban environments. Furthermore, as we pave over large areas of land in cities, storm water runs off quicker and in greater volume, thereby increasing flood hazards. Bringing water into semi-arid cities by pumping groundwater or transporting water from distant mountains through aqueducts may increase evaporation, thereby increasing humidity and precipitation in a region.

P3    Approximately 60% of water that falls by precipitation on land each year evaporates to the atmosphere. A smaller component (about 40%) returns to the ocean surface and subsurface runoff. A This small annual transfer of water supplies resources for rivers and urban and agricultural lands. B Unfortunately, distribution of water on land is far from uniform. C As human population increases, water shortages will become more frequent in arid and semi-arid regions, where water is naturally nonabundant. D

P4 → At the regional and local level, the fundamental hydrological unit of the landscape is the drainage basin (also called a watershed or catchment). A drainage basin is the area that contributes surface runoff to a particular stream or river. The term *drainage basin* is usually used in evaluating the hydrology of an area, such as the stream flow or runoff from hill slopes. Drainage basins vary greatly in size, from less than a hectare (2.5 acres) to millions of square kilometers. A drainage basin is usually named for its main stream or river, such as the Mississippi River drainage basin.

P5  → The main process in the cycle is the global transfer of water from the atmosphere to the land and oceans and back to the atmosphere. Notice that more than 97% of Earth's water is in the oceans; the next largest storage compartment, the ice caps and glaciers, accounts for another 2%. Together, these account for more than 99% of the total water, and both are generally unsuitable for human use because of salinity (seawater) and location (ice caps and glaciers). Only about 0.001% of the total water on Earth is in the atmosphere at any one time. However, this relatively small amount of water in the global water cycle, with an average atmospheric residence time of only about 9 days, produces all our freshwater resources through the process of precipitation.

P6  → Water can be found in either liquid, solid, or gaseous form at a number of locations at or near Earth's surface. Depending on the specific location, the residence time may vary from a few days to many thousands of years. However, as mentioned, more than 99% of Earth's water in its natural state is unavailable or unsuitable for beneficial human use. Thus, the amount of water for which all the people, plants, and animals on Earth compete is much less than 1% of the total.

P7   As the world's population and industrial production of goods increase, the use of water will also accelerate. The world per capita use of water in 1975 was about 185,000 gal/year. And the total human use of water was about 700 m$^3$/year or 2000 gal/day. Today, world use of water is about 6,000 km$^3$/year or about $1.58 \times 10^{15}$ gal/year, which is a significant fraction of the naturally available freshwater.

P8   Compared with other resources, water is used in very large quantities. In recent years, the total mass (or weight) of water used on Earth per year has been approximately 1000 times the world's total production of minerals, including petroleum, coal, metal ores, and nonmetals.

1. Which of the sentences below best expresses the information in the highlighted statement in the passage? The other choices change the meaning or leave out important information.

   Ⓐ It is the hydrologic cycle that causes water to evaporate from plants, soil, and bodies of water inland as well as from the oceans.
   Ⓑ Solar energy is the source of power for the hydrologic cycle, which begins by evaporating water from plants, soil, oceans, and freshwater sources.
   Ⓒ The evaporation of water from the oceans, freshwater sources, plants, and soils is a natural process, which we call the hydrologic cycle.
   Ⓓ Energy from the sun and the hydrologic cycle are power sources for plants that require water from the oceans and freshwater sources.

2. Based on information in paragraph 1, which of the following best explains the term "hydrologic cycle"?

   Ⓐ The movement of water from freshwater bodies into the oceans
   Ⓑ Solar energy in the atmosphere that produces rain over land and oceans
   Ⓒ Water resources from oceans and freshwater sources inland
   Ⓓ Transportation of water from oceans into the atmosphere and onto the land

   Paragraph 1 is marked with an arrow [→].

3. The phrase The rest in the passage refers to

   Ⓐ oceans
   Ⓑ ice caps
   Ⓒ glaciers
   Ⓓ water

4. According to paragraph 1, why is freshwater considered important?

   Ⓐ It evaporates more quickly than water in the ocean.
   Ⓑ It is the largest source of water on Earth.
   Ⓒ It determines the landscape of rocks and sediment.
   Ⓓ It is the runoff that empties into the oceans.

   Paragraph 1 is marked with an arrow [→].

5. Based on information in paragraph 2, how do man-made water resources such as reservoirs and lakes affect the water cycle?

   Ⓐ They increase the danger of flooding in the areas surrounding them.
   Ⓑ They cause changes in the patterns of rainfall in the immediate area.
   Ⓒ They provide water sources for agricultural purposes in dry areas.
   Ⓓ They improve the natural flow of water into the oceans.

   Paragraph 2 is marked with an arrow [→].

6. The word component in the passage is closest in meaning to

   Ⓐ error
   Ⓑ part
   Ⓒ estimate
   Ⓓ source

7. The word fundamental in the passage is closest in meaning to

   Ⓐ diverse
   Ⓑ common
   Ⓒ basic
   Ⓓ attractive

8. Why does the author mention the "Mississippi River" in paragraph 4?

   Ⓐ The Mississippi River is an example of a drainage basin.
   Ⓑ The Mississippi River is one of the largest rivers in the region.
   Ⓒ The Mississippi River is used in evaluating the runoff from hills.
   Ⓓ The Mississippi River is named for the area surrounding it.

   Paragraph 4 is marked with an arrow [→].

9. According to paragraph 5, which of the following is true about the global transfer of water?

   Ⓐ Most rainwater stays in the atmosphere for less than a week.
   Ⓑ Glaciers are a better source of water than the oceans.
   Ⓒ Most of the water in the world is currently in the water cycle.
   Ⓓ Less than 1 percent of the water can be used for human consumption.

   Paragraph 5 is marked with an arrow [→].

10. According to paragraph 6, why is water a problem?

    Ⓐ There is not enough water available in liquid form in the world.
    Ⓑ Bringing water to the surface of the Earth can be difficult.
    Ⓒ A comparatively small amount of Earth's water is suitable for human use.
    Ⓓ Most of the naturally accessible water is too old to be used safely.

    Paragraph 6 is marked with an arrow [→].

11. The word significant in the passage is closest in meaning to

    Ⓐ rare
    Ⓑ small
    Ⓒ important
    Ⓓ regular

12. Look at the four squares [■] that show where the following sentence could be inserted in the passage.

    **As a result, water shortages occur in some areas.**

    Where could the sentence best be added?

    Click on a square [■] to insert the sentence in the passage.

13. **Directions:** An introduction for a short summary of the passage appears below. Complete the summary by selecting the THREE answer choices that mention the most important points in the passage. Some sentences do not belong in the summary because they express ideas that are not included in the passage or are minor points from the passage. *This question is worth 2 points.*

**The hydrologic cycle transfers water from the oceans to the atmosphere, from the atmosphere to the land, and back to the oceans.**

- 
- 
- 

### Answer Choices

A The global problem is the availability of water that is suitable for human use where and when it is needed.

B Only about 0.001% of the total water on Earth is in the atmosphere at a particular point in time.

C Solar energy causes the evaporation of oceans and freshwater lakes and rivers into the atmosphere.

D Water shortages will probably become more common as more people begin to live in desert regions.

E Precipitation in the form of rainfall replenishes the water in the ocean and in drainage basins on land.

F Desalination is a key solution to the problem of adequate water supplies for human use.

## Reading 2

The following reading passage was adapted from *Life Span Development*, Twelfth Edition by John W. Santrock, McGraw-Hill Companies, Inc., 2009.

### "Piaget's Cognitive Development Theory"

P1    Jean Piaget, the famous Swiss developmental psychologist, changed the way we think about the development of children's minds. **Piaget's theory** *states that children go through four stages as they actively construct their understanding of the world.* Two processes underlie this cognitive construction of the world: organization and adaptation. To make sense of our world, we organize our experiences. For example, we separate important ideas from less important ideas and we connect one idea to another. In addition to organizing our observations and experiences, we adapt, adjusting to new environmental demands.

P2    As the infant or child seeks to construct an understanding of the world, said Piaget, the developing brain creates **schemes**. These are actions or mental representations that organize knowledge.

P3    → **Assimilation and Accommodation.** To explain how children use and adapt their schemes, Piaget offered two concepts: assimilation and accommodation. Assimilation occurs when children use their existing schemes to deal with new information or experiences. Accommodation occurs when children adjust their schemes to take new information and experiences into account. Think about a toddler who has learned the word *car* to identify the family's car. The toddler may call all moving vehicles on roads "cars," including motorcycles and trucks; the child has assimilated these objects to his or her existing scheme. But the child soon learns that motorcycles and trucks are not cars and fine-tunes the category to exclude motorcycles and trucks, accommodating the scheme.

P4    Assimilation and accommodation operate even in the very young infant's life. Newborns reflexively suck everything that touches their lips; they assimilate all sorts of objects into their sucking scheme. By sucking different objects, they learn about their taste, texture, shape, and so on. After several months of experience though, they construct their understanding of the world differently. Some objects, such as fingers and the mother's breast, can be sucked, but others, such as fuzzy blankets, should not be sucked. In other words, they accommodate their sucking scheme.

P5    Piaget also held that we go through four stages in understanding the world. Each of the stages is age-related and consists of distinct ways of thinking. Remember, it is the *different* way of understanding the world that makes one stage more advanced than another; knowing *more* information does not make the child's thinking more advanced, in the Piagetian view. This is what Piaget meant when he said the child's cognition is *qualitatively* different in one stage compared to another. Ⓐ What are Piaget's four stages of cognitive development?

P6    Ⓑ The *sensorimotor stage,* which lasts from birth to about 2 years of age, is the first Piagetian stage. In this stage, infants construct an understanding of the world by coordinating sensory experiences (such as seeing and hearing) with physical, motoric actions—hence the term *sensorimotor*. Ⓒ At the end of the stage, 2-year-olds have sophisticated sensorimotor patterns and are beginning to operate with primitive symbols. Ⓓ

P7    → The *preoperational stage,* which lasts from approximately 2 to 7 years of age, is Piaget's second stage. In this stage, children begin to go beyond simply connecting sensory information with physical action. However, according to Piaget, preschool children still lack the ability to perform what he calls *operations*, which are internalized mental actions that allow children to do mentally what they previously did physically. For example, if you imagine putting two sticks together to see whether they would be as long as another stick without actually moving the sticks, you are performing a concrete action.

P8  → The *concrete operational stage,* which lasts from approximately 7 to 11 years of age, is the third Piagetian stage. In this stage, children can perform operations, and logical reasoning replaces intuitive thought as long as reasoning can be applied to specific or concrete examples. For instance, concrete operational thinkers cannot imagine the steps necessary to complete an algebraic equation, which is too abstract for thinking at this stage of development.

P9  → The *formal operational stage,* which appears between the ages of 11 and 15, is the fourth and final Piagetian stage. In this stage, individuals move beyond concrete experiences and think in abstract and more logical terms. As part of thinking more abstractly, adolescents develop images of ideal circumstances. They might think about what an ideal parent is like and compare their parents to this ideal standard. They begin to entertain possibilities for the future and are fascinated with what they can be. In solving problems, formal operational thinkers are more systematic, developing hypotheses about why something is happening the way it is, then testing these hypotheses in a deductive manner.

14. The word underlie in the passage is closest in meaning to

   Ⓐ establish
   Ⓑ support
   Ⓒ combine
   Ⓓ complicate

15. Which of the sentences below best expresses the information in the highlighted statement in the passage? The other choices change the meaning or leave out important information.

   Ⓐ Our new experiences require that we adjust in order to understand information that we have never seen.
   Ⓑ Understanding new ideas is easier if we include observations and personal experiences.
   Ⓒ We engage in both organization of what we see and experience and adaptation of novel ideas.
   Ⓓ Thinking must include direct observation and experiences in order to organize the information.

16. Why does the author mention a "car" in paragraph 3?

    Ⓐ To explain the concepts of assimilation and accommodation
    Ⓑ To demonstrate how a toddler responds to a new experience
    Ⓒ To prove that a young child cannot engage in problem solving
    Ⓓ To provide an example of the first stage of cognitive development

    Paragraph 3 is marked with an arrow [➔].

17. The word adjust in the passage is closest in meaning to

    Ⓐ change
    Ⓑ improve
    Ⓒ hide
    Ⓓ find

18. The word distinct in the passage is closest in meaning to

    Ⓐ new
    Ⓑ simple
    Ⓒ different
    Ⓓ exact

19. The word sophisticated in the passage is closest in meaning to

    Ⓐ limited
    Ⓑ complex
    Ⓒ useful
    Ⓓ necessary

20. Based on the information in paragraph 7, which of the following best explains the term "operations"?

    Ⓐ Symbolic thought
    Ⓑ Mental actions
    Ⓒ Physical activity
    Ⓓ Abstract reasoning

    Paragraph 7 is marked with an arrow [➔].

21. According to paragraph 8, why would a 10-year-old be unable to solve algebra problems?

    Ⓐ Algebra requires concrete operational thinking.
    Ⓑ A 10-year-old has not reached the formal operational stage.
    Ⓒ A child of 10 does not have logical reasoning abilities.
    Ⓓ An algebra problem has too many steps in order to solve it.

    Paragraph 8 is marked with an arrow [➔].

22. In paragraph 9, why does the author mention "parents"?

    (A) Teenagers are already thinking about their roles in the future.
    (B) Parents are very important teachers during the final stage of development.
    (C) The comparison of real and ideal parents is an example of abstract thinking.
    (D) Adolescents tend to be critical of their parents as part of their development.

    Paragraph 9 is marked with an arrow [→].

23. What can be inferred from the passage about people who are older than 15 years of age?

    (A) They must have completed all of Piaget's stages of cognitive development.
    (B) They are probably in the formal operational stage of development.
    (C) They have mastered deductive reasoning and are beginning to learn intuitively.
    (D) They may still not be able to solve problems systematically.

24. All of the following refer to Piaget's theory EXCEPT

    (A) even very young infants may engage in constructing the way that they understand the world
    (B) both assimilation and accommodation are processes that we can use to help us adapt to new information
    (C) when children learn more information, then their thinking is at a higher stage of development
    (D) operations require a more advanced stage of development than symbolic representation

25. Look at the four squares [■] that show where the following sentence could be inserted in the passage.

    **At the beginning of this stage, newborns have little more than reflexive patterns with which to work.**

    Where could the sentence best be added?

    Click on a square [■] to insert the sentence in the passage.

26. **Directions:** An introduction for a short summary of the passage appears below. Complete the summary by selecting the THREE answer choices that mention the most important points in the passage. Some sentences do not belong in the summary because they express ideas that are not included in the passage or are minor points from the passage. *This question is worth 2 points.*

**Jean Piaget proposed a theory of cognitive development in children.**

- 
- 
- 

### Answer Choices

A Assimilation and accommodation are two processes that allow children to organize schemes.

B Four age-related stages build upon each other to encourage different ways of thinking and developing.

C Logical reasoning is applied to specific or concrete examples, replacing intuition as a mental process.

D A toddler learns that there are different categories for vehicles, including cars, motorcycles, and trucks.

E Children are active participants in cognitively constructing their understanding of the world around them.

F Imagination plays a central role in children during the early stages of their development.

## Reading 3

The following reading passage was adapted from *Language Files 10*, Tenth Edition by the Department of Linguistics, the Ohio State University, 2007.

### *"Speech and Writing"*

P1 → One of the basic assumptions of modern linguistics is that speech is primary and writing is secondary. The most immediate manifestation of language is speech and not writing. Writing is simply the representation of speech in another physical medium. Spoken language encodes thought into a physically transmittable form, while writing, in turn, encodes spoken language into a physically preservable form. Writing is a three-stage process: thinking of an idea, expressing it in mental grammar, and then transferring it to written form. All units of writing, whether letters or characters, are based on units of speech, i.e., words, sounds, or syllables. When linguists study language, therefore, they take the spoken language as their best source of data and their object of description except in instances of languages like Latin for which there are no longer any speakers.

P2    You may think that with the advent of so many "instant messaging" programs, writing can now be as immediate as speech. But it is important to remember that even though the written form can be nearly immediate these days, there is still an extra step between conceptualizing the message you want to communicate and the reception of that idea, if you have to write it— regardless of whether you do so longhand or type it into a computer.

P3    There are several reasons for maintaining that speech is primary and writing is secondary. Ⓐ Writing is a later historical development than spoken language. Ⓑ **Archeological evidence** indicates that writing was first utilized in Sumer, that is, modern-day Iraq, about 6,000 years ago. Ⓒ As far as physical and cultural anthropologists can tell, spoken language has probably been used by humans for hundreds of thousands of years. Ⓓ

P4  → **Writing does not exist everywhere** that spoken language does. This seems hard to imagine in our highly literate society, but the fact is that there are still many communities in the world where a written form of language is not used. Even in those cultures using a writing system, there are individuals who fail to learn the written form of their language. In fact, the majority of the Earth's inhabitants are illiterate, though quite capable of spoken communication. However, no society uses only a written language with no spoken form.

P5    **Writing must be taught**, whereas spoken language is acquired automatically. All children, except children with serious learning disabilities, naturally learn to speak the language of the community in which they are brought up. They acquire the basics of their native language before they enter school, and even if they never attend school, they become fully competent speakers. Writing systems vary in complexity, but regardless of their level of sophistication, they must all be taught.

P6    **Neurolinguistic evidence** (studies of the brain in action during language use) demonstrates that the processing and production of written language is overlaid on the spoken language centers in the brain. Spoken language involves several distinct areas of the brain; writing uses these areas and others as well.

P7    Despite all this evidence, it is a widely held misconception that writing is more perfect than speech. To many people, writing somehow seems more correct and more stable, whereas speech can be careless, corrupted, and susceptible to change. Some people even go so far as to identify "language" with writing and to regard speech as a secondary form of language used imperfectly to approximate the ideals of the written language.

P8  → What gives rise to the misconception that writing is more perfect than speech? There are several reasons. Writing can be edited, and so the product of writing is usually more aptly worded and better organized, containing fewer errors, hesitations, and incomplete sentences than are found in speech. This "perfection of writing" can be explained by the fact that writing is the result of deliberation, correction, and revision, while speech is the spontaneous and simultaneous formulation of ideas; writing is therefore less subject to the constraint of time than speech is. Writing must be taught and is therefore ultimately associated with education and educated speech. Since the speech of the educated is more often than not set up as the "standard language," writing is associated indirectly with the varieties of language that people tend to view as "correct." However, the association of writing with the standard variety is not a necessary one, as evidenced by the attempts of writers to transcribe faithfully the speech of their characters. Mark Twain's *Huckleberry Finn* and John Steinbeck's *Of Mice and Men* contain examples of this. Writing is more physically stable than spoken language, which consists of nothing more than sound waves traveling through the air, and is therefore ephemeral and transient. Writing tends to last, because of its physical medium (characters on some surface), and can be preserved for a very long time. Spelling does not seem to vary from individual to individual or from place to place as easily as pronunciation does. Thus, writing has the appearance of being more stable especially in the modern era. Of course, spelling does vary, as exemplified by the differences between the American ways of spelling *gray* and words with the suffixes *-ize* and *-ization* as compared with the British spelling of *grey* and *-ise* and *-isation*. Writing could also change if it were made to follow the changes of speech. The fact that people at various times try to carry out spelling reforms amply illustrates this possibility.

27. According to paragraph 1, what can be inferred about linguistic research?

    Ⓐ Linguists do not usually study Latin.
    Ⓑ Research on writing is much easier.
    Ⓒ Studies always require several sources.
    Ⓓ Researchers prefer speech samples.

    Paragraph 1 is marked with an arrow [→].

28. According to paragraph 4, what is true about literacy?

    Ⓐ Only a minority of the world's population can read and write.
    Ⓑ Literate populations are more capable than other groups.
    Ⓒ The modern world has a very highly literate population.
    Ⓓ Many people fail to become literate because it is difficult.

    Paragraph 4 is marked with an arrow [→].

29. Which of the sentences below best expresses the information in the highlighted statement in the passage? The other choices change the meaning or leave out important information.

    Ⓐ Writing that has a very complex system must be learned.
    Ⓑ All writing has to be taught because the systems are variable.
    Ⓒ In spite of complex features in writing systems, people can learn them.
    Ⓓ Both simple and complex writing systems require direct instruction.

30. The word approximate in the passage is closest in meaning to

   Ⓐ make better than
   Ⓑ come close to
   Ⓒ take out of
   Ⓓ get on with

31. The word deliberation in the passage is closest in meaning to

   Ⓐ work
   Ⓑ thought
   Ⓒ time
   Ⓓ intelligence

32. Why does the author mention "Mark Twain" and "John Steinbeck" in paragraph 8?

   Ⓐ To demonstrate that speech cannot be transcribed
   Ⓑ To provide examples of two good writing styles
   Ⓒ To prove that a nonstandard variety can be written
   Ⓓ To contrast varieties of speech for their characters

   Paragraph 8 is marked with an arrow [➔].

33. The word transient in the passage is closest in meaning to

   Ⓐ unimportant
   Ⓑ temporary
   Ⓒ interesting
   Ⓓ clear

34. According to paragraph 8, what is true about spelling?

   Ⓐ Spelling does not change from one geographical region to another.
   Ⓑ British and American spellings are more similar than pronunciation.
   Ⓒ Pronunciation in English is not related to spelling changes.
   Ⓓ Changes in spelling are occasionally initiated because of speech.

   Paragraph 8 is marked with an arrow [➔].

35. The phrase this possibility in the passage refers to

   Ⓐ writing could also change
   Ⓑ the changes of speech
   Ⓒ people try to carry out
   Ⓓ spelling reforms illustrate

36. Which of the following statements most closely represents the author's opinion?

   Ⓐ Speech and writing have historical similarities.
   Ⓑ Standard speech is the best model for writing.
   Ⓒ Writing is not more perfect than speech.
   Ⓓ Writing should not change like speech does.

37. How does the author organize the passage?

    Ⓐ Cause and effect
    Ⓑ Chronological narrative
    Ⓒ Persuasive argument
    Ⓓ Contrastive analysis

38. Look at the four squares [■] that show where the following sentence could be inserted in the passage.

    **The Sumerians probably devised written characters for the purpose of maintaining inventories of livestock and merchandise.**

    Where could the sentence best be added?

    Click on a square [■] to insert the sentence in the passage.

39. **Directions:** Complete the table by matching the phrases on the left with the headings on the right. Select the appropriate answer choices and drag them to the type of language to which they relate. TWO of the answer choices will NOT be used. *This question is worth 4 points.*

    To delete an answer choice, click on it. To see the passage, click on **View Text**.

**Answer Choices**

Ⓐ Not observable in brain activity

Ⓑ A primary form of language

Ⓒ Direct representation of thought

Ⓓ A three-stage process

Ⓔ An earlier development

Ⓕ Associated with education

Ⓖ Contains fewer errors

Ⓗ No regional variations

Ⓘ Acquired naturally

**Speech**

• 
• 
• 
• 

**Writing**

• 
• 
•

# LISTENING SECTION

 **Model Test 7, Listening Section, Track 84**

The Listening Section tests your ability to understand spoken English that is typical of inter-actions and academic speech on college campuses. During the test, you will listen to conver-sations, lectures, and discussions, and you will answer questions about them.

This is the long format for the Listening Section. On the long format, you will listen to three conversations, three lectures, and three discussions. After each listening passage, you will answer 5–6 questions about it. Only two conversations, two lectures, and two discussions will be graded. The other passages are part of an experimental section for future tests. Because you will not know which conversations, lectures, and discussions will be graded, you must try to do your best on all of them.

You will hear each passage one time. You may take notes while you listen, but notes are not graded. You may use your notes to answer the questions.

Choose the best answer for multiple-choice questions. Follow the directions on the page or on the screen for computer-assisted questions. Click on **Next** and then on **OK** to go on to the next question. You cannot return to previous questions.

The Listening Section is divided into sets. Each set includes one conversation, one lecture, and one discussion. You have 10 minutes to answer all of the questions for each set. You will have 30 minutes to answer all of the questions on the long format. A clock on the screen will show you how much time you have to complete your answers for the section. The clock does NOT count the time you are listening to the conversations, lectures, and discussions.

## *Listening 1 "Professor's Office"*

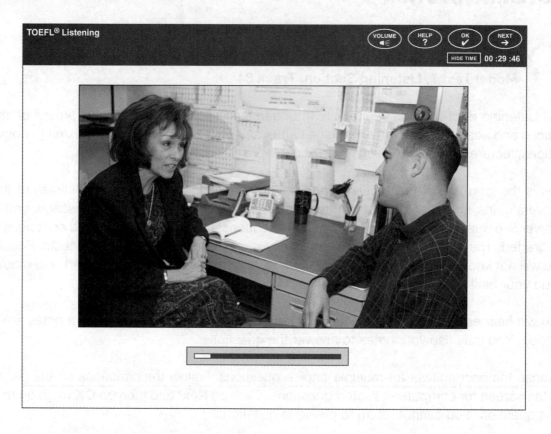

1. Why does the man go to see his professor?

   Ⓐ He wants to withdraw from the class.
   Ⓑ He needs to ask the professor a question.
   Ⓒ His professor promised to give him a tape.
   Ⓓ His professor asked him to come to the office.

2. Why does the student say this:

   Ⓐ He is disrespectful.
   Ⓑ He is surprised.
   Ⓒ He is sorry.
   Ⓓ He is happy.

3. What does the professor mean when she says this:

   Ⓐ She is warning the student that she could take more serious action.
   Ⓑ She is indicating that she is not sure what she wants to do.
   Ⓒ She is asking the man to come up with a solution for the situation.
   Ⓓ She is forgiving the man for causing a problem in her class.

4. How does the professor feel about questions in class?

    Ⓐ She would rather answer questions during her office hours.
    Ⓑ She thinks that students who ask questions are showing interest.
    Ⓒ She does not like students to be disrespectful by asking questions.
    Ⓓ She wants her students to help each other instead of asking questions.

5. What will the man probably do during the next class?

    Ⓐ He will ask fewer questions.
    Ⓑ He will tape record the lecture.
    Ⓒ He will refer to the outline in the book.
    Ⓓ He will participate more in the discussion.

### Listening 2 "Art Class"

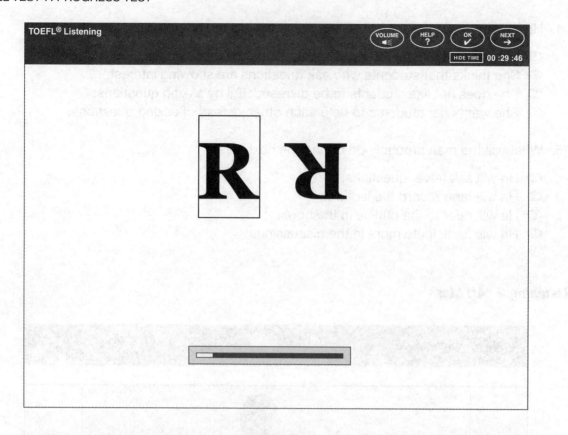

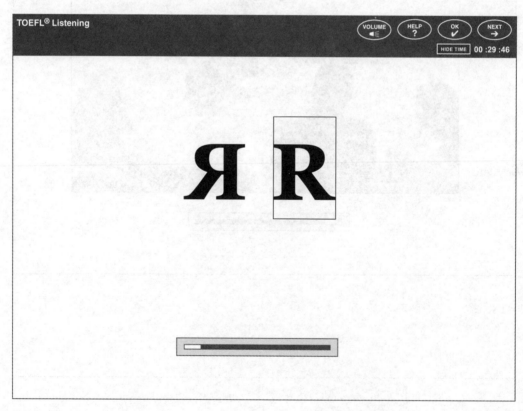

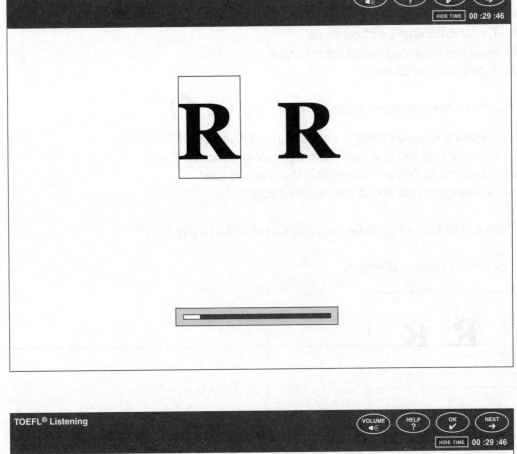

6. What is this lecture mainly about?

    Ⓐ Symmetry in the visual arts
    Ⓑ The characteristics of patterns
    Ⓒ How the brain organizes information
    Ⓓ A definition of beauty

7. What does the professor mean when he says this:

    Ⓐ He plans to give others an opportunity to speak.
    Ⓑ He is talking too fast and intends to slow down.
    Ⓒ He needs to correct something that he has said.
    Ⓓ He wants to talk about that subject later.

8. Which of the following slides represents reflection symmetry?

    Click on the correct diagram.

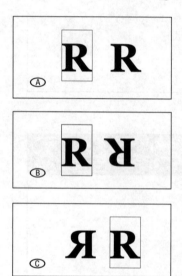

9. How is it possible to recognize an object when only part of it is visible?

    Ⓐ The brain recognizes symmetry and visualizes the whole.
    Ⓑ The object is often familiar enough to be recognized.
    Ⓒ The pieces are large even though some are missing.
    Ⓓ The principles for identification can be learned.

10. In addition to a system for organization, what characteristics define a pattern?

   Click on 2 answer choices.

   Ⓐ  A basic unit

   Ⓑ  An image

   Ⓒ  Repetition

   Ⓓ  Rotation

11. What assignment does the professor give his students?

   Ⓐ  They are supposed to identify patterns in the classroom.
   Ⓑ  They should be prepared for a quiz on this lecture.
   Ⓒ  They need to go to the lab to complete an experiment.
   Ⓓ  They have to design a pattern that includes symmetry.

### Listening 3 "Sociology Class"

12. How does the professor organize the discussion?

   Ⓐ  By defining gang activity, using information from articles
   Ⓑ  By contrasting gang activity with noncriminal organizations
   Ⓒ  By reading part of an article on gang activity to the class
   Ⓓ  By reporting her research on gang activity in the local area

13. What was surprising about Thrasher's study?

    Ⓐ The size of the study, which included 1300 gangs
    Ⓑ The excellent summary by the student who located the research
    Ⓒ The changes that were reported in the history of gangs
    Ⓓ The fact that gang activity has been prevalent for so long

14. According to the study by Moore, what causes gang activity?

    Ⓐ Cliques that form in high school
    Ⓑ Normal feelings of insecurity in teens
    Ⓒ Abusive family members in the home
    Ⓓ Loyalty to family already in the gang

15. Why does the professor say this:

    Ⓐ To show that she does not agree with the response
    Ⓑ To encourage the student to give an example
    Ⓒ To indicate that she does not understand
    Ⓓ To praise the student for his answer

16. What is the role of women in gangs?

    Ⓐ They are full members of the gangs.
    Ⓑ They are protected by the gangs.
    Ⓒ They are a support system for the gangs.
    Ⓓ They have little contact with gangs.

17. In the discussion, the students identify aspects of gang activity. Indicate whether each of the following is one of the aspects. Click in the correct box for each phrase.

|   |   | Yes | No |
|---|---|---|---|
| A | A replacement for high school cliques | | |
| B | A group socialized on the streets | | |
| C | A peer group that is 14–20 years old | | |
| D | Young people who have dropped out of school | | |
| E | A group that makes careful plans | | |

## Listening 4 "Professor's Office"

18. Why did the student go to see his professor?

    Ⓐ To transfer from on campus to an online class
    Ⓑ To drop the course because it is an overload
    Ⓒ To get some advice about improving his grade
    Ⓓ To enroll in another class with the professor

19. Why did the man take an online course?

    Ⓐ He wanted to study over the weekend.
    Ⓑ He takes most of his courses online.
    Ⓒ He did not want to have an overload.
    Ⓓ He preferred the online professor.

20. What is the student's problem?

    Ⓐ He is not succeeding in the discussions.
    Ⓑ He got a low grade on his papers.
    Ⓒ He does not do well on tests.
    Ⓓ He does not manage time well.

21. How can the man improve his discussion posts?

Click on 2 answer choices.

A  Use journal references.

B  Make the posts shorter.

C  Enter the discussion earlier.

D  Provide his opinion.

22. What will the student probably do?

Ⓐ He will write an extra paper.
Ⓑ He will work online before the weekend.
Ⓒ He will join the professor's on-campus class.
Ⓓ He will agree with some of the posts.

### Listening 5 "Biology Class"

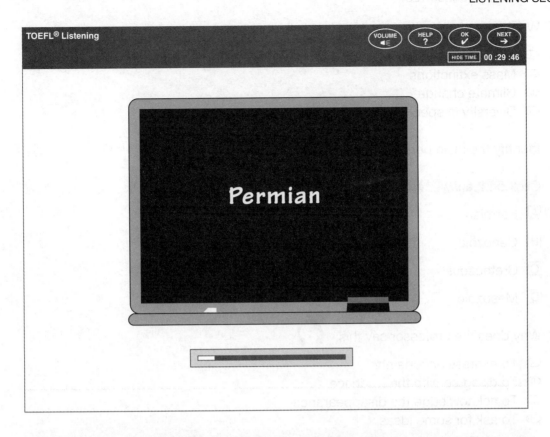

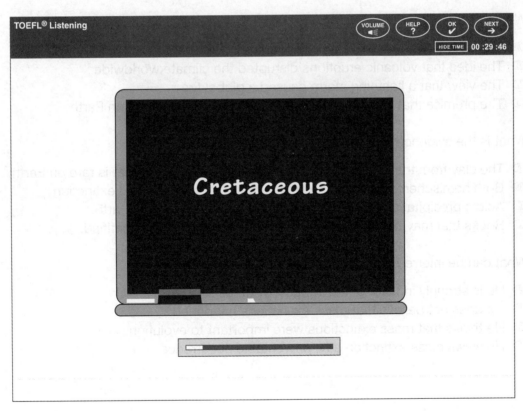

23. What aspect of the fossil record is this lecture mainly about?

    Ⓐ The impact hypothesis
    Ⓑ Mass extinctions
    Ⓒ Climate change
    Ⓓ Diversity in species

24. Identify the main periods of mass extinction.

    Click on 2 answer choices.

    A Permian

    B Cenozoic

    C Cretaceous

    D Mesozoic

25. Why does the professor say this:

    Ⓐ To express uncertainty
    Ⓑ To disagree with the evidence
    Ⓒ To acknowledge the disappearance
    Ⓓ To ask for some ideas

26. What is the impact hypothesis?

    Ⓐ The theory that the continents drifted and collided with each other
    Ⓑ The idea that volcanic eruptions disrupted the climate worldwide
    Ⓒ The view that a lightning storm caused a global fire
    Ⓓ The premise that an asteroid crashed, blocking the sunlight on Earth

27. What is the evidence for the impact hypothesis?

    Ⓐ The clay from the Cretaceous period contains an element that is rare on Earth.
    Ⓑ Both hemispheres suffered the same amount of damage and extinction.
    Ⓒ Acidic precipitation is still not evenly distributed across the Earth.
    Ⓓ Rocks that may have been part of an asteroid have been identified.

28. What can be inferred about the professor's opinion?

    Ⓐ He is strongly in favor of the impact hypothesis.
    Ⓑ He does not believe that mass extinctions happened.
    Ⓒ He thinks that mass extinctions were important to evolution.
    Ⓓ He views mass extinction as a preventable occurrence.

*Listening 6 "Anthropology Class"*

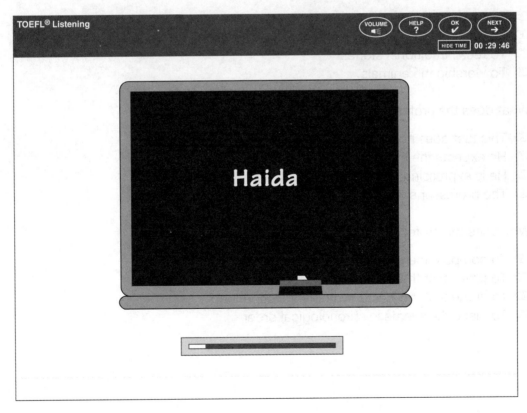

29. Which of the following is an important reason the Haida people carve totem poles?

    Ⓐ To frighten away spirits
    Ⓑ To decorate the village
    Ⓒ To recall traditional stories
    Ⓓ To worship the animals

30. What does the professor mean when he says this:

    Ⓐ This fact does not directly relate to the topic.
    Ⓑ He expects the students to write down the definition.
    Ⓒ He is expressing uncertainty about the information.
    Ⓓ The professor should not be talking about this tradition.

31. Why does the professor mention the coat of arms of Canada?

    Ⓐ To compare the symbolism to that of a totem pole
    Ⓑ To prove that the Haida live in Canada
    Ⓒ To argue that the Haida symbols are superior
    Ⓓ To place the events in chronological order

32. What does the saying *low man on the totem pole* mean?

    Ⓐ A very good representative member of the group
    Ⓑ A person who begins to tell an important story
    Ⓒ A person who has the least status among the members
    Ⓓ A member of the community who is not accepted

33. Why do the master carvers work on the bottom figures?

    Ⓐ Master carvers are usually too old to work at the top of the pole.
    Ⓑ The figures near the bottom are more visible to the public.
    Ⓒ The totem pole is too large for just one carver to complete.
    Ⓓ The last carving is an honor reserved for the masters.

34. What does the professor mean when he says this:

    Ⓐ He is indicating that the information to follow is very reliable.
    Ⓑ He is showing the class that he knows a great deal about the information.
    Ⓒ He is signaling that the students should learn this information.
    Ⓓ He is informing the students that there may be more information.

## Listening 7 "Professor's Office"

35. Why does the man go to see his professor?

    Ⓐ He is worried about the professor's class.
    Ⓑ He wants to bring up the grade in her class.
    Ⓒ He would like some advice about his classes.
    Ⓓ He needs to get the woman's signature.

36. Why does the man say this:

    Ⓐ He is apologizing for the problem.
    Ⓑ He is asking the woman to explain.
    Ⓒ He is thinking of what to say next.
    Ⓓ He is correcting the professor politely.

37. What is the man's problem?

    Ⓐ He is taking too many classes this semester.
    Ⓑ He is failing one of his required courses.
    Ⓒ He has a problem with his academic advisor.
    Ⓓ He took classes with heavy reading assignments.

38. What does the professor suggest?

    Ⓐ Registration for a course in how to read faster
    Ⓑ Extra help sessions to bring up the grade in her class
    Ⓒ Immediate withdrawal from one of the courses
    Ⓓ Intensive study until the end of the semester

39. What can we infer about the situation?

    Ⓐ The student will probably talk with his advisor before registration next term.
    Ⓑ The professor believes that the student will probably not take her advice.
    Ⓒ The date for changing the student's schedule has probably passed already.
    Ⓓ The professor is probably the student's academic program advisor.

## Listening 8 "Psychology Class"

40. What is the lecture mainly about?

    Ⓐ Neurotransmitters
    Ⓑ Seasonal affective disorder
    Ⓒ Genetic research
    Ⓓ The National Institute of Mental Health

41. What are neurotransmitters?

    Ⓐ Chemical imbalances
    Ⓑ Chemicals in the brain
    Ⓒ Images of the brain
    Ⓓ Genetic triggers

42. What happens when there is a reduction of light during the winter months?

    Ⓐ An increase in melatonin may cause a chemical imbalance.
    Ⓑ The pineal gland begins functioning to compensate.
    Ⓒ The retina of the eye opens to receive more light.
    Ⓓ The mental processes in the brain are slower.

43. Why does the professor think that the acronym S.A.D. is unsuitable?

    Ⓐ She did not participate in creating the acronym.
    Ⓑ It does not reflect the seriousness of the problem.
    Ⓒ Some of her patients object to the acronym.
    Ⓓ The acronym is not an abbreviation for the words.

44. What does the professor mean when she says this:

    Ⓐ She is reminding the students of previous facts.
    Ⓑ She is disagreeing with the statistics.
    Ⓒ She is indicating that the example is unimportant.
    Ⓓ She is expressing uncertainty about the information.

45. In the lecture, the professor reports the preliminary results of her research. Indicate whether each of the following is one of the findings. Click in the correct box for each sentence.

|   |   | Yes | No |
|---|---|---|---|
| A | Morning exposure for the treatment is superior. | | |
| B | A regular sleep schedule supports therapy. | | |
| C | Eye damage occurs in only a few subjects. | | |
| D | Sessions of less than two hours are preferable. | | |
| E | Fluorescent lighting cannot be used for therapy. | | |

### Listening 9 "Physics Class"

46. What is the discussion mainly about?

    Ⓐ The theory of everything
    Ⓑ Einstein's unified field theory
    Ⓒ Advances in brain theory
    Ⓓ Theoretical mathematics

47. How does the professor explain the closed string?

    Ⓐ He refers the students to a website.
    Ⓑ He rewords the definition in the book.
    Ⓒ He compares it with a thin rubber band.
    Ⓓ He contrasts it with an open string.

48. Why does the professor say this:

    Ⓐ He does not expect the student to answer the question.
    Ⓑ He does not know the answer to the question.
    Ⓒ He does not want to continue the debate in class.
    Ⓓ He does not want to influence the woman's thinking.

49. According to the discussion, what reason does the man give for rejecting string theory?

    Ⓐ There may have been errors in the mathematical calculations.
    Ⓑ Strings have not been observed in a laboratory.
    Ⓒ String theory does not prove the theory of everything.
    Ⓓ The experiments were not performed correctly.

50. What can be inferred about the students?

&#9398; They have not formed opinions about the theory.
&#9399; They do not agree with the professor's point of view.
&#9400; They have reached different conclusions about the theory.
&#9401; They have changed their minds during the discussion.

51. Why does the professor suggest that the students visit a website?

&#9398; The textbook does not have the latest information about the topic that they will debate.
&#9399; The website should provide objective data, which they can use for the next discussion.
&#9400; The professor wants the students to understand the history of the theory they are studying.
&#9401; The site will prepare the students to complete mathematical calculations before the next class.

 **Please turn off the audio. There is a 10-minute break between the Listening Section and the Speaking Section.**

# SPEAKING SECTION

 **Model Test 7, Speaking Section, Track 85**

The Speaking Section tests your ability to communicate in English in an academic setting. During the test, you will be presented with six speaking questions. The questions ask for a response to a single question, a conversation, a talk, or a lecture. The prompts and questions are presented only one time.

You may take notes as you listen, but notes are not graded. You may use your notes to answer the questions. Some of the questions ask for a response to a reading passage and a talk or a lecture. The reading passages and the questions are written, but the directions will be spoken.

Your speaking will be evaluated on both the fluency of the language and the accuracy of the content. You will have 15–20 seconds to prepare and 45–60 seconds to respond to each question. Typically, a good response will require all of the response time and the answer will be complete by the end of the response time.

You will have about 20 minutes to complete the Speaking Section. A clock on the screen will show you how much time you have to prepare each of your answers and how much time you have to record each response.

*Independent Speaking Question 1 "A Book"*

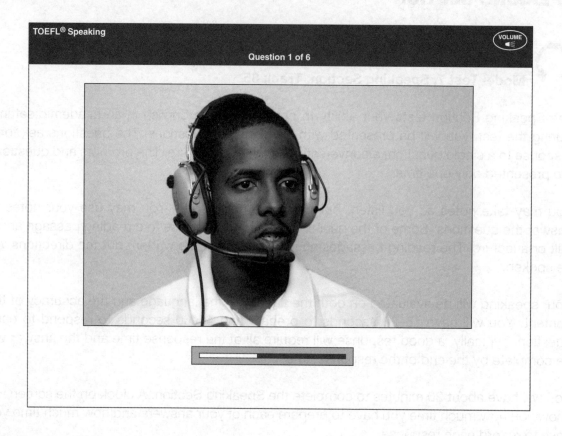

  Listen for a question about a familiar topic.

**Question**

Think about a book that you have enjoyed reading. Why did you like it? What was especially interesting about the book? Use specific details and examples to support your response.

Preparation Time: 15 seconds
Recording Time: 45 seconds

## *Independent Speaking Question 2 "Foreign Travel"*

 Listen for a question that asks your opinion about a familiar topic.

### Question
Agree or disagree with the following statement:

Traveling independently is better than traveling as part of a tour group.

Use specific reasons and examples to support your opinion.

Preparation Time: 15 seconds
Recording Time: 45 seconds

## *Integrated Speaking Question 3 "Old Main"*

Read a short passage and listen to a talk on the same topic.

Reading Time: 45 seconds

---

Notice Concerning Old Main

The college will be celebrating the one-hundredth anniversary of the founding of the school by renovating Old Main, the original building. Two alternative plans are being considered. One plan would leave the outer structure intact and concentrate on electrical and plumbing upgrades as well as minor structural support. The other plan would demolish all of the building except the clock tower, which would form the centerpiece of a new structure. An open meeting is scheduled for Friday afternoon at three o'clock in the Old Main auditorium.

---

 Now listen to a professor who is speaking at the meeting. She is expressing her opinion about the proposals.

### Question

The professor expresses her opinion of the plan for the renovation of Old Main. Report her opinion and explain the reasons that she gives for having that opinion.

Preparation Time: 30 seconds
Recording Time: 60 seconds

## *Integrated Speaking Question 4  "Pangea"*

Read a short passage and then listen to part of a lecture on the same topic.

Reading Time: 45 seconds

---

Pangea

Plate tectonics assumes that the Earth's outer layer is comprised of slabs called plates, which are constantly in motion, changing the position of land masses and seascapes relative to each other throughout history. The plates move slowly but continuously at a rate of 2 inches every year. The movement may be caused by the unequal distribution of heat and pressure below them. Very hot material within the mantle, the layer of rock inside the Earth, moves upward while a cooler layer descends, putting the outer crust of the continents in motion. Several large plates include an entire continent with its seafloor; however, the plate boundaries do not correspond precisely with the continents recognized today.

---

TOEFL® Speaking

Question 4 of 6

VOLUME

---

 Now listen to part of a lecture in a geography class. The professor is talking about Pangea.

**Question**
Explain how plate tectonics relates to the theory of *continental drift.*

Preparation Time: 30 seconds
Recording Time: 60 seconds

## *Integrated Speaking Question 5 "Headaches"*

 Now listen to a short conversation between a student and her friend.

### Question

Describe the woman's problem and the two suggestions that her friend makes about how to handle it. What do you think the woman should do, and why?

Preparation Time: 20 seconds
Recording Time: 60 seconds

## *Integrated Speaking Question 6 "Fax Machines"*

 Now listen to part of a lecture in a business class. The professor is discussing the way that a fax machine transmits and receives data.

**Question**

Using the main points and examples from the lecture, describe the three parts of a fax machine and then explain how the fax process works.

Preparation Time: 20 seconds
Recording Time: 60 seconds

# WRITING SECTION

The Writing Section tests your ability to write essays in English similar to those that you would write in college courses. During the test, you will write two essays.

**The Integrated Essay.** First you will read an academic passage and then you will listen to a lecture on the same topic. You may take notes as you read and listen, but notes are not graded. You may use your notes to write the essay. The reading passage will disappear while you are listening to the lecture, but the passage will return to the screen for reference when you begin to write your essay. You will have 20 minutes to plan, write, and revise your response. Typically, a good essay for the integrated topic will require that you write 150–225 words.

**The Independent Essay.** You will read a question on the screen. It usually asks for your opinion about a familiar topic. You will have 30 minutes to plan, write, and revise your response. Typically, a good essay for the independent topic will require that you write 300–350 words.

A clock on the screen will show you how much time you have left to complete each essay.

## Integrated Essay "Urban Forest Plan"

You have 20 minutes to plan, write, and revise your response to a reading passage and a lecture on the same topic. First, read the passage and take notes. Then, listen to the lecture and take notes. Finally, write your response to the writing question. Typically, a good response will require that you write 150–225 words.

### Reading Passage
Time: 3 minutes

The city enjoys urban forests not only in the city square, the municipal parks, and golf courses, but also along many streets in the city. The forest, boasting almost 700,000 trees, was planted during the late 17th century, but since the 1920s, planting has not kept pace with the losses from age, disease, storms, and development. An urban forest plan is needed that incorporates the following points: legislation to protect the existing forest, support to maintain and conserve the trees, and a public information campaign.

Legislation would have to include a temporary moratorium on development in areas where mature trees would be harmed and ordinances that would protect and nurture mature trees currently growing on industrial, institutional, and residential land.

Support to maintain and conserve the trees should be twofold. First, public funds should be allocated for this purpose. An adequate budget for maintenance of trees in parks and along city streets must be included in several city departments and funded by a small increase in city taxes. Equally important, however, private funds should be solicited through initiatives such as memorial tree plantings, adopt-a-tree programs, and a tree endowment fund.

As the final portion of the plan, a public information campaign would be essential to educate local residents and businesses. Otherwise, the advantages of the urban forests would not be understood and, therefore, not encouraged. Besides enhancing the landscape and improving the lifestyle of residents and visitors, trees mitigate air pollution, provide natural shade, cool the surrounding area, and reduce ultraviolet radiation. They also provide habitats for wildlife in the city.

**Model Test 7, Writing Section, Track 86**

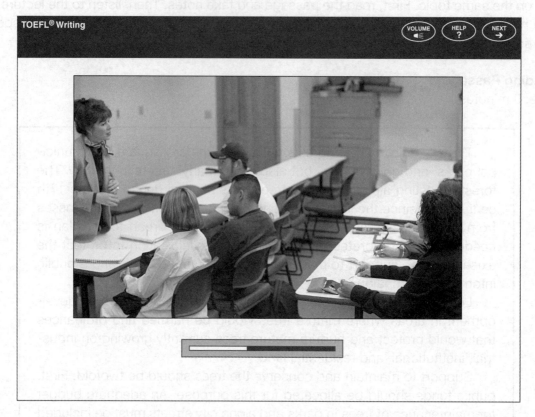

TOEFL® Writing                    VOLUME ◄    HELP ?    NEXT →

 Now listen to a lecture on the same topic as the passage that you have just read.

**Question**

Summarize the main points in the lecture, and then explain how they cast doubt on the ideas in the reading passage.

## Independent Essay "Study Abroad"

**Question**

**You are planning to study abroad. What do you think you will like and dislike about this experience? Why?**

Use specific reasons and details to support your answer.

# MODEL TEST 7

## ANSWER KEYS

Use the following Answer Keys to check your scores on the Reading and Listening Sections of Model Test 7.

### READING SECTION

| *Reading 1* | *Reading 2* | *Reading 3* |
|---|---|---|
| 1.  B | 14.  B | 27.  D |
| 2.  D | 15.  C | 28.  A |
| 3.  D | 16.  A | 29.  D |
| 4.  C | 17.  A | 30.  B |
| 5.  B | 18.  C | 31.  B |
| 6.  B | 19.  B | 32.  C |
| 7.  C | 20.  B | 33.  B |
| 8.  A | 21.  B | 34.  D |
| 9.  D | 22.  C | 35.  A |
| 10.  C | 23.  A | 36.  C |
| 11.  C | 24.  C | 37.  C |
| 12.  C | 25.  C | 38.  C |
| 13.  A, C, E | 26.  A, B, E | 39.  B, C, E, I: Speech |
| | | D, F, G: Writing |

## LISTENING SECTION

| *Listening Set 1* | *Listening Set 2* | *Listening Set 3* |
|---|---|---|
| 1. D | 18. C | 35. C |
| 2. B | 19. A | 36. B |
| 3. A | 20. A | 37. D |
| 4. B | 21. A, C | 38. C |
| 5. B | 22. B | 39. A |
| 6. A | 23. B | 40. B |
| 7. D | 24. A, C | 41. B |
| 8. C | 25. A | 42. A |
| 9. A | 26. D | 43. B |
| 10. A, C | 27. A | 44. D |
| 11. D | 28. C | 45. A, B: Yes |
| 12. A | 29. C | 46. A |
| 13. D | 30. A | 47. C |
| 14. B | 31. A | 48. D |
| 15. B | 32. C | 49. B |
| 16. C | 33. B | 50. C |
| 17. A, B: Yes | 34. D | 51. B |

 # EXPLANATORY AND EXAMPLE ANSWERS, MODEL TEST 7

Go to the Barron's TOEFL site to study detailed Explanatory Answers for the Reading and Listening Sections, and Outlines, Example Answers, and Checklists for the Speaking and Writing Sections of Model Test 7.

# MODEL TEST 8: PROGRESS TEST

## READING SECTION

The Reading Section tests your ability to understand reading passages like those in college textbooks. The reading passages are presented in one complete section, which allows you to move to the next passage and return to a previous passage to change answers or answer questions that you may have left blank. The passages are about 700 words in length.

This is the long format for the Reading Section. On the long format, you will read four passages. After each passage, you will answer 12–14 questions about it. You may take notes while you read, but notes are not graded. You may use your notes to answer the questions. Some passages may include a word or phrase that is underlined in blue. Click on the word or phrase to see a glossary definition or explanation. Only three passages will be graded. The other passage is part of an experimental section for future tests. Because you will not know which passages will be graded, you must try to do your best on all of them.

Choose the best answer for multiple-choice questions. Follow the directions on the page or on the screen for computer-assisted questions. Most questions are worth 1 point, but the last question in each passage is worth more than 1 point.

Click on **Next** to go to the next question. Click on **Back** to return to previous questions. You may return to previous questions for all of the passages.

You can click on **Review** to see a chart of the questions you have answered and the questions you have not answered. From this screen, you can return to the question you want to answer.

Although you can spend more time on one passage and less time on another passage, you should try to pace yourself so that you are spending about 20 minutes to read each passage and answer the questions for that passage. You will have 80 minutes to complete all of the passages and answer all of the questions on the long format. A clock on the screen will show you how much time you have to complete the Reading Section.

## *Reading 1*

The following reading passage was adapted from *Western Civilization*, Seventh Edition by Jackson J. Spielvogel, Wadsworth, 2009.

### *"Prosperity in the Early Empire"*

P1    The Early Roman Empire was a period of considerable prosperity. Internal peace resulted in unprecedented levels of trade. Merchants from all over the empire came to the chief Italian ports of Puteoli on the Bay of Naples and Ostia at the mouth of the Tiber. The importation of large quantities of grain to feed the populace of Rome and an incredible quantity of luxury items for the wealthy upper classes in the west led to a steady drain of gold and silver coins from Italy and the west to the eastern part of the empire.

P2    → Long-distance trade beyond the Roman frontiers also developed during the Early Empire. Developments in both the Roman and Chinese Empires helped foster the growth of this trade. Although both empires built roads chiefly for military purposes, the roads also came to be used to facilitate trade. Moreover, by creating large empires, the Romans and Chinese not only established internal stability but also pacified bordering territories, thus reducing the threat that bandits posed to traders. As a result, merchants developed a network of trade routes that brought these two great empires into commercial contact.

P3    → Most important was the overland Silk Road, a regular caravan route between West and East. The Silk Road received its name from the Chinese import of silk cloth, which became a popular craze among Roman elites, leading to a vast outpouring of silver from Rome to China, provoking the Roman emperor to grumble that the ladies and their baubles were transferring too much money to foreign lands. The silk trade also stimulated a degree of mutual curiosity between the two great civilizations, but, unfortunately, not much mutual knowledge or understanding. So far as it is known, no personal or diplomatic contacts between the two civilizations ever took place. But two great empires at the extremes of the Eurasian supercontinent had for the first time been linked together in a commercial relationship.

P4    → Although Roman roads were excellent, most goods traveled by boat through the Mediterranean and beyond. Vast numbers of amphoras, large two-handled pottery jars, were used to transport olive oil and wine, as well as such luxury items as pepper, cloves, and incense. Amphoras could be stacked to transport large quantities of goods. Roman merchant ships could stack between 5,000 and 10,000 amphoras in their holds. Rome became the warehouse of the world, where whatever was raised or manufactured everywhere was always in Rome in abundance. In addition to the imported grain that fed the populace, numerous luxury goods were available in the shops. Since many Romans despised trade, most shops were run by slaves or freedmen. A famous stone relief from Ostia in the second century A.D. shows a shopkeeper selling groceries and livestock. In addition to the local produce, two monkeys from overseas are available as pets.

P5    Increased trade helped stimulate manufacturing. The cities of the east still produced items made in Hellenistic times. Ⓐ The first two centuries of the empire also witnessed the high point of industrial development in Italy. Ⓑ Some industries became concentrated in certain areas, such as bronze work in Capua and pottery in Arretium in Etruria. Ⓒ Much industrial production remained small-scale and was done by individual artisans, usually freedmen or slaves. In the course of the first century, Italian centers of industry experienced increasing competition from the provinces. Ⓓ Pottery produced in Gaul, for example, began to outsell Italian pottery from Arretium.

P6    Despite the prosperity from trade and commerce, agriculture remained the chief occupation of most people and the underlying basis of Roman prosperity. While the large landed estates, the *latifundia*, still dominated agriculture, especially in southern and central Italy, small peasant farms persisted, particularly in Etruria and the Po valley. Although large estates concentrating on sheep and cattle raising used slave labor, the lands of some *latifundia* were worked by free tenant farmers called *coloni*. The *colonus* was essentially a sharecropper who paid rent in labor, produce, or sometimes cash.

P7    In considering the prosperity of the Roman world, it is important to remember the enormous gulf between rich and poor underlying it. The development of towns and cities, so important to the creation of any civilization, is based to a large degree on the agricultural surpluses of the countryside. In ancient times, the margin of surplus produced by each farmer was relatively small. Therefore, the upper classes and urban populations had to be supported by the labor of a large number of agricultural producers who never found it easy to produce much more than enough for themselves. Although still primarily an agrarian economy, the Roman Empire provided the single currency and stable conditions necessary for an expansion of trade in various commodities and products. An extensive system of roads and shipping routes facilitated trade.

1.  The word steady in the passage is closest in meaning to

    Ⓐ constant
    Ⓑ expected
    Ⓒ rapid
    Ⓓ large

2. According to paragraph 2, why did the Chinese and the Romans build a system of roads?

    Ⓐ The promotion of commercial interests
    Ⓑ Rapid transportation of supplies and soldiers
    Ⓒ Establishment of intercultural relationships
    Ⓓ Demonstration of advances in engineering

    Paragraph 2 is marked with an arrow [→].

3. The word transferring in the passage is closest in meaning to

   Ⓐ using
   Ⓑ moving
   Ⓒ hiding
   Ⓓ planning

4. According to paragraph 3, how was the Silk Road named?

   Ⓐ The road was compared to silk because it was very smooth.
   Ⓑ Goods imported by land from China were wrapped in silk.
   Ⓒ Silk from China was transported along this trade route.
   Ⓓ The word *silk* sounded like the old Roman name for the route.

   Paragraph 3 is marked with an arrow [➔].

5. Which of the sentences below best expresses the information in the highlighted statement in the passage? The other choices change the meaning or leave out important information.

   Ⓐ Roman roads and boats were better than those of any other Mediterranean power.
   Ⓑ Sea routes were preferred for Mediterranean trade in spite of the superior roads by the Romans.
   Ⓒ The Romans were very successful at building roads and navigating the Mediterranean for trade.
   Ⓓ Roman goods traded throughout the Mediterranean were very high quality.

6. According to paragraph 4, what advantage did amphoras have in shipping?

   Ⓐ Liquids could be transported in amphoras.
   Ⓑ Amphoras could be stored efficiently.
   Ⓒ Warehouses contained goods in amphoras.
   Ⓓ Amphoras were manufactured in Gaul.

   Paragraph 4 is marked with an arrow [➔].

7. Why does the author mention "a stone relief" from Ostia in paragraph 4?

   Ⓐ Ostia is an ancient trading center on the caravan route.
   Ⓑ The scene in the carving shows the class structure.
   Ⓒ The carving provides evidence of international trade.
   Ⓓ The carving is an example of luxury goods in Roman cities.

   Paragraph 4 is marked with an arrow [➔].

8. According to the passage, what can be inferred about the economy in the Early Roman Empire?

    Ⓐ Manufacturing and industrial production were centralized in Rome.
    Ⓑ Slave labor had been replaced by freedmen who worked for wages.
    Ⓒ Agriculture was still the most important part of the economic system.
    Ⓓ Large estates were being divided into smaller farms and ranches.

9. The word persisted in the passage is closest in meaning to

    Ⓐ became smaller
    Ⓑ worked very hard
    Ⓒ fought with each other
    Ⓓ continued to exist

10. The word extensive in the passage is closest in meaning to

    Ⓐ very strong
    Ⓑ very new
    Ⓒ very large
    Ⓓ very costly

11. All of the following are mentioned as reasons why trade flourished in the Early Roman Empire EXCEPT

    Ⓐ control of borders
    Ⓑ standard currency
    Ⓒ caravan routes
    Ⓓ improved vehicles

12. Look at the four squares [■] that show where the following sentence could be inserted in the passage.

**Other industries, such as brickmaking, were pursued in rural areas on large landed estates.**

Where could the sentence best be added?

Click on a square [■] to insert the sentence in the passage.

13. **Directions:** An introduction for a short summary of the passage appears below. Complete the summary by selecting the THREE answer choices that mention the most important points in the passage. Some sentences do not belong in the summary because they express ideas that are not included in the passage or are minor points from the passage. *This question is worth 2 points.*

**The Early Roman Empire was prosperous because of trade, commerce, and agriculture.**

- 
- 
- 

### Answer Choices

A Wealthy Romans purchased a large variety of imported grain and luxury items from abroad.

B Trade throughout the Early Roman Empire and beyond was carried out using a large system of roads and sea routes.

C Trade encouraged the increase and spread of industry and manufacturing into the provinces.

D The Silk Road was an important caravan route that linked the Roman Empire with the Chinese Empire.

E The owners of large estates as well as small farmers, provided the agricultural base for the Roman Empire.

F Towns and cities in the provinces began to grow during the Early Roman Empire.

## Reading 2

The following reading passage was adapted from *Biology*, Eighth Edition by Neil A. Campbell et al., Pearson Education, Inc., 2008.

### "Altruism"

P1  → Many social behaviors are selfish; that is, they benefit the individual at the expense of others, especially competitors. Even in species in which individuals do not engage in antagonistic behavior, most adaptations that benefit one individual will indirectly harm others. Ⓐ It is easy to understand the pervasive nature of selfishness if natural selection shapes behavior. Ⓑ Behavior that maximizes an individual's survival and reproductive success is favored by selection, regardless of how much damage such behavior does to another individual, a local population, or even an entire species. How, then, can we explain observed examples of what appears to be "unselfish" behavior? Ⓒ

P2  On occasion, some animals behave in ways that reduce their individual fitness but increase the fitness of other individuals in the population; this is our functional definition of *altruism* or selflessness. Ⓓ Consider the Belding's ground squirrel, which lives in some mountainous regions of the western United States and is vulnerable to predators such as coyotes and hawks. A squirrel that sees a predator approach often gives a high-pitched alarm call that alerts unaware individuals to retreat to their burrows. Note that, for the squirrel that warns others, the conspicuous alarm behavior increases the risk of being killed because it brings attention to the caller's location.

P3  Another example of altruistic behavior occurs in honeybee societies, in which the workers are sterile. The workers themselves never reproduce, but they labor on behalf of a single fertile queen. Furthermore, the workers sting intruders, a behavior that helps defend the hive but results in the death of those workers.

P4  Altruism is also observed in naked mole rats, highly social rodents that live in underground chambers and tunnels in southern and northeastern Africa. The naked mole rat, which is almost hairless and nearly blind, lives in colonies of 75 to 250 or more individuals. Each colony has only one reproducing female, the queen, who mates with one to three males, called kings. The rest of the colony consists of nonreproductive females and males who forage for underground roots and tubers and care for the queen, the kings, and new offspring. The nonreproductive individuals may sacrifice their own lives in trying to protect the queen or kings from snakes or other predators that invade the colony.

P5    How can a Belding's ground squirrel, a worker honeybee, or a naked mole rat enhance its fitness by aiding members of the population that may be its closest competitors? How can altruistic behavior be maintained by evolution if it does not enhance the survival and reproductive success of the self-sacrificing individuals?

P6    The selection for altruistic behavior is most readily apparent in the act of parents sacrificing for their offspring. When parents sacrifice their own well being to produce and aid offspring, this actually increases the fitness of the parents because it maximizes their genetic representation in the population. However, individuals sometimes help others who are not their offspring.

P7    → Biologist William Hamilton proposed that an animal could increase its genetic representation in the next generation by "altruistically" helping close relatives other than its own offspring. Like parents and offspring, full siblings have half their genes in common. Therefore, selection might also favor helping siblings or helping one's parents produce more siblings. This possibility led to Hamilton's idea of *inclusive fitness*, the total effect an individual has on proliferating its genes by producing its own offspring and by providing aid that enables other close relatives, who share many of those genes, to produce offspring.

P8    → If kin selection explains altruism, then the examples of unselfish behavior we observe among diverse animal species should involve close relatives. This is in fact the case, but often in complex ways. Like most mammals, female Belding's ground squirrels settle close to their site of birth, whereas males settle at distant sites. Since nearly all alarm calls are given by females, they are most likely aiding close relatives. In the case of worker bees, who are all sterile, anything they do to help the entire hive benefits the only permanent member who is reproductively active—the queen, who is their mother.

P9    In the case of naked mole rats, DNA analyses have shown that all the individuals in a colony are closely related. Genetically, the queen appears to be a sibling, daughter, or mother of the kings, and the nonreproductive mole rats are the queen's direct descendants or her siblings. Therefore, when a nonreproductive individual enhances a queen's or king's chances of reproducing, the altruist increases the chance that some genes identical to its own will be passed to the next generation.

14. According to paragraph 1, why is selfish behavior logical in nature?

Ⓐ Most species are programmed to engage in antagonistic behavior with other species.
Ⓑ Natural selection favors individuals in a species that conform to the behavior of the group.
Ⓒ Adaptations that encourage survival for individuals also tend to be selfish behaviors.
Ⓓ Competition among individuals in a social species is not an example of selfish behavior.

Paragraph 1 is marked with an arrow [→].

15. The word benefit in the passage is closest in meaning to

    Ⓐ control
    Ⓑ limit
    Ⓒ change
    Ⓓ help

16. According to the author, which of the following is a definition of *altruism*?

    Ⓐ Living within a social structure that rewards interaction
    Ⓑ Risking harm to protect another member of the population
    Ⓒ Becoming fit in order to escape from dangerous predators
    Ⓓ Behaving in ways that benefit the individual instead of the group

17. The word conspicuous in the passage is closest in meaning to

    Ⓐ noticeable
    Ⓑ important
    Ⓒ dangerous
    Ⓓ loud

18. The word nearly in the passage is closest in meaning to

    Ⓐ a short time ago
    Ⓑ sometimes
    Ⓒ less
    Ⓓ almost

19. The word maintained in the passage is closest in meaning to

    Ⓐ changed
    Ⓑ supported
    Ⓒ understood
    Ⓓ organized

20. According to paragraph 7, why do animals help close relatives?

    Ⓐ The animal's genes are passed to the next generation.
    Ⓑ Animals have close emotional bonds with kinship groups.
    Ⓒ The aid is mutual in a population of close relatives.
    Ⓓ Siblings and parents are important to animals with offspring.

    Paragraph 7 is marked with an arrow [➔].

21. Which of the sentences below best expresses the information in the highlighted statement in the passage? The other choices change the meaning or leave out important information.

    Ⓐ Altruism is not explained by kin selection because unselfish behavior does not always occur among close relatives in a variety of animal species.

    Ⓑ A variety of animal species are observed to practice unselfish behavior within groups of close relatives if kinship is known.

    Ⓒ Close relationships should account for altruism among a variety of species, unless kin selection explains unselfish behavior.

    Ⓓ If altruism is explained by kinship, close relatives should be the ones participating in unselfish behavior among different animal species.

22. According to paragraph 8, why would male Belding's ground squirrels be less likely to make alarm calls?

    Ⓐ Males do not live close to their kinship group.

    Ⓑ Most of the males do not reproduce.

    Ⓒ Unlike males, females sacrifice for their offspring.

    Ⓓ The queen is the only permanent member of the colony.

    Paragraph 8 is marked with an arrow [➜].

23. Why does the author mention "DNA analyses" in paragraph 9?

    Ⓐ The results suggest that kinship may influence altruism among naked mole rats.

    Ⓑ Genetic research increased reproduction among queens and kings in naked mole rat colonies.

    Ⓒ Establishing relationships among naked mole rats is the first step in observing several generations.

    Ⓓ Naked mole rats are not reproducing enough offspring for the colonies to survive.

    Paragraph 9 is marked with an arrow [➜].

24. All of the following are mentioned as examples of altruistic behavior EXCEPT

    Ⓐ making alarm calls to the group

    Ⓑ stinging predators to defend others

    Ⓒ feeding disabled members

    Ⓓ caring for reproductive individuals

25. Look at the four squares [■] that show where the following sentence could be inserted in the passage.

**For example, superior foraging ability by one individual may leave less food for others.**

Where could the sentence best be added?

Click on a square [■] to insert the sentence in the passage.

26. **Directions:** An introduction for a short summary of the passage appears below. Complete the summary by selecting the THREE answer choices that mention the most important points in the passage. Some sentences do not belong in the summary because they express ideas that are not included in the passage or are minor points from the passage. *This question is worth 2 points.*

**Altruism is behavior among animals that reduces their individual fitness and increases the fitness of others in the population.**

● 

● 

● 

### Answer Choices

Ⓐ Workers that sting intruders in the honey-bee hive will die.

Ⓑ Examples of altruism in animals are found among close relatives.

Ⓒ Hamilton's theory of inclusive fitness claims that kinship explains altruism.

Ⓓ Alarm calls are very common among mammals, while insects leave trails.

Ⓔ Ground squirrels, honeybees, and mole rats risk their lives to protect others.

Ⓕ There is evidence that some animals have a gene that encourages altruism.

## *Reading 3*

The following reading passage was adapted from *Geosystems: An Introduction to Physical Geography*, Seventh Edition by Robert W. Christopherson, Pearson Education, Inc., 2009.

### *"Solar Energy"*

P1    Any surface that receives light from the Sun is a *solar collector*. But the diffuse nature of solar energy received at the surface requires that it be collected, concentrated, transformed, and stored to be useful. Space heating is the simplest application. Windows that are carefully designed and placed allow sunlight to shine into a building, where it is absorbed and converted into sensible heat—an everyday application of the greenhouse effect. An average building in the United States receives 6 to 10 times more energy from the Sun hitting its exterior than is required to heat the inside.

P2    A *passive solar system* captures heat energy and stores it in a "thermal mass," such as water-filled tanks, adobe, tile, or concrete. An *active solar system* involves heating water or air in a collector and then pumping it through a plumbing system to a tank where it can provide hot water for direct use or for space heating.

P3    Solar energy systems can generate heat energy of an appropriate scale for approximately half the present domestic applications in the United States, which include heating and water heating. In marginal climates, solar-assisted water and space heating is feasible as a backup; even in New England and the Northern Plains states, solar collection systems prove effective.

P4    Focusing (concentrating) mirrors, such as Fresnel lenses or parabolic (curved surface) troughs and dishes can be used to attain very high temperatures to heat water or other heat-storing fluids. Kramer Junction, California, northeast of Los Angeles, in the Mojave Desert near Barstow, has the world's largest operating solar electric-generating facility, with a capacity of 150 megawatts, that is, 150 million watts. Long troughs of computer-guided curved mirrors concentrate sunlight to create temperatures of 390°C (735°F) in vacuum-sealed tubes filled with synthetic oil. The heated oil heats water; the heated water produces steam that rotates turbines to generate cost-effective electricity. The facility converts 23% of the sunlight it receives into electricity during peak hours, and operation and maintenance costs continue to decrease.

P5    → Producing electricity by photovoltaic cells (PVs) is a technology used in spacecraft since 1958. Familiar to us all are the solar cells in pocket calculators (hundreds of million now in use). When light shines upon a semiconductor material in these cells, it stimulates a flow of electrons (an electrical current) in the cell. PV cells are arranged in modules that can be assembled in large arrays.

P6     The efficiency of these cells has improved to the level that they are generally cost-competitive, especially if government policies and subsidies were to be balanced evenly among all energy sources. A typical residential array features 36 panels, generating 205 W each, 7380 W total, at a 21.5% conversion efficiency. People who live in a home with this type of installation would be able to run their electric meters in reverse and supply electricity to the power grid.

P7     → Rooftop photovoltaic electrical generation is now cheaper than power line construction to rural sites. For example, hundreds of thousands of homes in Mexico, Indonesia, the Philippines, South Africa, India, Norway, and elsewhere have PV roof systems. Rural villages in developing countries could benefit greatly from the simplest, most cost-effective solar application—the solar panel cooker. A For example, people in Kenya walk many kilometers collecting fuel for wood cooking fires. B Using solar cookers, villagers are able to cook meals and sanitize their drinking water without scavenging for wood. C These solar devices are simple, yet efficient, reaching temperatures between 107°C–127°C (225°F–260°F). D

P8     In less-developed countries, the money for electrification, a centralized technology, is not available despite the push from more developed countries and energy corporations for large capital-intensive power projects in those countries. In reality, the pressing need is for decentralized energy sources, appropriate in scale to everyday needs, such as cooking, heating water, and pasteurization. Net per capita cost for solar cookers is far less than for centralized electrical production, regardless of fuel source.

P9     Solar energy is a wise choice for the future. It is directly available to the consumer; it is based on a renewable energy source of an appropriate scale for end-use needs; and most solar strategies are labor-intensive, rather than capital-intensive as in centralized, nonrenewable power production. Whether or not we follow the alternative path of solar energy is a matter of political control and not technological innovation. Much of the technology is ready for installation and is cost-effective when all direct and indirect costs are considered.

**Glossary**
Photovoltaic cells (PVs): cells that are capable of producing voltage when exposed to light

27. According to the passage, which of the following would be a good example of a passive solar system?

    Ⓐ Pumps that supply hot air to heat a building
    Ⓑ A system of pipes that feed into a hot-water heater
    Ⓒ Space heaters with hot water as the source
    Ⓓ Storage tanks that hold solar-heated water

28. The word feasible in the passage is closest in meaning to

    Ⓐ certain
    Ⓑ possible
    Ⓒ simple
    Ⓓ perfect

29. The word generate in the passage is closest in meaning to

    Ⓐ replace
    Ⓑ save
    Ⓒ cause
    Ⓓ find

30. Why does the author mention "pocket calculators" in paragraph 5?

    Ⓐ To compare them with more modern technologies
    Ⓑ To provide an example that readers will recognize
    Ⓒ To explain why the Sun is being underutilized
    Ⓓ To summarize the history of solar power

Paragraph 5 is marked with an arrow [→].

31. According to the passage, what can be assumed about PVs?

    Ⓐ PV technology does not have widespread applications.
    Ⓑ Government policies do not support the use of PVs.
    Ⓒ PVs are less efficient than electricity for residential use.
    Ⓓ The power grid is not compatible with PV systems.

32. The word typical in the passage is closest in meaning to

    Ⓐ similar
    Ⓑ changed
    Ⓒ valuable
    Ⓓ usual

33. According to paragraph 7, what is the advantage of the solar cooker?

     Ⓐ Solar cookers would allow people to have clean water and hot food without burning wood.
     Ⓑ The solar cookers are easy to use even though they are still not very efficient.
     Ⓒ Small PV cookers could be installed on the roofs to provide solar cooking for rural homes.
     Ⓓ With training, many people would be able to learn how to use a solar cooker.

     Paragraph 7 is marked with an arrow [→].

34. The phrase this type of installation in the passage refers to

     Ⓐ energy sources
     Ⓑ residential array
     Ⓒ electric meters
     Ⓓ power grid

35. According to the passage, how does the author feel about centralized power in less-developed countries?

     Ⓐ He would like more developed countries to stop supporting expensive centralized projects.
     Ⓑ He believes that large corporations should invest capital in centralized power projects.
     Ⓒ He thinks that centralized electrical production should be generated from solar power.
     Ⓓ He argues against decentralized electrification because it is not as effective as centralization.

36. Which of the sentences below best expresses the information in the highlighted statement in the passage? The other choices change the meaning or leave out important information.

     Ⓐ When technology for alternative solar power advances, then the politicians will exercise better control.
     Ⓑ Politics is more influential than new technologies in determining the use of solar power as an alternative energy source.
     Ⓒ Solar power is the best alternative for energy because the technology is acceptable to the politicians.
     Ⓓ Controlling the politicians matters more than investigating alternative sources of energy such as solar power.

37. All of the following are mentioned as advantages of solar power EXCEPT

     Ⓐ relatively inexpensive investment
     Ⓑ renewable resource
     Ⓒ direct availability to user
     Ⓓ newest technology

38. Look at the four squares [■] that show where the following sentence could be inserted in the passage.

   **Consequently, each village and refugee camp is surrounded by impoverished land, stripped of wood.**

   Where could the sentence best be added?

   Click on a square [■] to insert the sentence in the passage.

39. **Directions:** An introduction for a short summary of the passage appears below. Complete the summary by selecting the THREE answer choices that mention the most important points in the passage. Some sentences do not belong in the summary because they express ideas that are not included in the passage or are minor points from the passage. *This question is worth 2 points.*

   **Solar power is a comparatively cheap, renewable source of energy.**

   - 
   - 
   - 

### Answer Choices

A  Both passive and active solar systems are capable of generating heat energy effectively.

B  Wood for fuel and cooking is still a common source of energy in many parts of the world.

C  PV cells are an efficient way to power heating and cooking devices, especially in rural areas.

D  Special construction material is designed to provide roof-top solar power in new homes.

E  Decentralized solar energy is better than centralized systems for developing nations.

F  Renewable solar power will replace all other sources of energy in the future.

## Reading 4

The following reading passage was adapted from *Gardner's Art Through the Ages*, Thirteenth Edition by Fred S. Kleiner, Wadsworth, 2009.

### *"Tattoo in Polynesia"*

P1    Even though the Polynesians were skillful navigators, various island groups remained isolated from one another for centuries by the vast distances they would have to cover in open outriggers. This geographical separation allowed distinct regional styles to develop within a recognizable general Polynesian style.

P2    Throughout Oceanic cultures, body decoration was an important means of representing cultural and personal identity. In addition to clothing and ornaments, body adornment most often took the form of tattoo. Tattooing was common among Micronesian cultures, but it was even more extensively practiced in Polynesia. Indeed, the English term *tattoo* is Polynesian in origin, related to the Tahitian, Samoan, and Tongan word *tatau* or *tatu*. In New Zealand, the markings are called *moko*. Within Polynesian cultures, tattooing reached its zenith in the highly stratified societies—New Zealand, the Marquesas Islands, Tahiti, Tonga, Samoa, and Hawaii. Both sexes displayed tattoos. In general, men had more tattoos than did women, and the location of tattoos on the body differed. For instance, in New Zealand, the face and buttocks were the primary areas of male tattooing, whereas tattoos appeared on the lips and chin of women.

P3    Historically, tattooing served a variety of functions in Polynesia beyond personal beautification. It indicated status, because the quantity and quality of tattoos often reflected rank. In the Marquesas Islands, for example, tattoos completely covered the bodies of men of high status. Certain patterns could be applied only to ranking individuals, but commoners also had tattoos, generally on a less extensive scale than elite individuals. A For identification purposes, slaves had tattoos on their foreheads in Hawaii and on their backs in New Zealand. B There were also accounts of defeated warriors being tattooed. In some Polynesian societies, tattoos identified clan or familial connections. The markings could also serve a protective function by in essence wrapping the body in a spiritual armor. C On occasion, tattoos marked significant events. In Hawaii, for example, a tattooed tongue was a sign of grief. D

P4    → Priests who were specially trained in the art form usually applied the tattoos. Rituals, chants, or ceremonies often accompanied the procedure, which took place in a special structure. Tattooing involves the introduction of black, carbon-based pigment under the skin with the use of a bird-bone tattooing comb or chisel and a mallet. In New Zealand, a distinctive technique emerged for tattooing the face. In a manner similar to Maori woodcarving, a serrated chisel created a groove in the skin to receive pigment, thereby producing a colored line.

P5    → Polynesian tattoo designs were predominantly geometric, and affinities with other forms of Polynesian art are evident. For example, the curvilinear patterns in Maori facial *moko* recall the patterns found on *poupou*, decorated wall panels in Maori meeting houses. Depending on their specific purpose, many tattoos could be "read" or deciphered. For facial tattoos, the Maori generally divided the face into four major symmetrical zones: the left and right forehead down to the eyes, the left lower face, and the right lower face. The right-hand side conveyed information on the father's rank, tribal affiliations, and social position, while the left-hand side provided matrilineal information. Smaller secondary facial zones imparted information about the tattooed individual's profession and position in society.

P6    → Te Pehi Kupe was the chief of the Ngato Toa in the early nineteenth century. The upward and downward koru (unrolled spirals) in the middle of his forehead connote his descent from two paramount tribes. The small design in the center of his forehead documents the extent of his domain—north, south, east, and west. The five double koru in front of his left ear indicate that the supreme chief (the highest rank in Maori society) was part of his matrilineal line. The designs on his lower jaw and the anchor-shaped koru nearby reveal that Te Pehi Kupe was not only a master carver but descended from master carvers as well.

P7    → An engraving depicts a Marquesan warrior from Nukahiva Island covered with elaborate tattoo patterns. The various tattoo patterns marking his entire body seem to subdivide his body parts into zones on both sides of a line down the center. Some tattoos accentuate the joint area, whereas others separate muscle masses into horizontal and vertical shapes. The warrior also covered his face, hands, and feet with tattoos. In Polynesia, nobles and warriors accumulated tattoo patterns to enhance their status and beauty. Tattoos also wrapped a warrior's body in spiritual armor.

P8    Largely as a result of missionary pressure in the nineteenth century, tattooing virtually disappeared in many Oceanic societies, but some Pacific peoples have revived tattooing as an expression of cultural pride.

40. The word extensively in the passage is closest in meaning to

     Ⓐ secretly
     Ⓑ completely
     Ⓒ probably
     Ⓓ naturally

41. Which of the sentences below best expresses the information in the highlighted statement in the passage? The other choices change the meaning or leave out important information.

     Ⓐ Women usually had fewer tattoos than men, and they were not applied on the same parts of the body.
     Ⓑ Generally, men and women had about the same number of tattoos, but they were applied in a different way.
     Ⓒ As a rule, women and men from the same general location had different tattoos on their bodies.
     Ⓓ Tattoos do not look the same on men and women because their bodies are different.

42. The word function in the passage is closest in meaning to

     Ⓐ purpose
     Ⓑ example
     Ⓒ method
     Ⓓ part

43. According to paragraph 4, how is tattoo applied to the face in New Zealand?

     Ⓐ Priests use a bird-bone to introduce pigment under the skin.
     Ⓑ A woodcarver uses a chisel and a mallet to create scars.
     Ⓒ Black carbon-based pigment is injected in facial designs.
     Ⓓ Colored lines are cut into the face with a special chisel.

     Paragraph 4 is marked with an arrow [➡].

44. The word predominantly in the passage is closest in meaning to

     Ⓐ by chance
     Ⓑ after all
     Ⓒ for the most part
     Ⓓ now and then

45. Why does the author mention *poupou* in paragraph 5?

     Ⓐ To compare the patterns with those in facial tattoos
     Ⓑ To confirm that Maori decorate their meeting houses
     Ⓒ To demonstrate how the designs are deciphered
     Ⓓ To identify the purpose of decorations in Maori culture

     Paragraph 5 is marked with an arrow [➡].

46. The word specific in the passage is closest in meaning to

     Ⓐ possible
     Ⓑ best
     Ⓒ usual
     Ⓓ exact

47. According to paragraph 6, which of the following does NOT describe Te Pehi Kupe?

    Ⓐ A respected master carver
    Ⓑ A descendent of the supreme chief
    Ⓒ A member of the Ngato Toa
    Ⓓ A female chief of the highest rank

Paragraph 6 is marked with an arrow [➜].

48. Which of the following can be inferred about the Marquesan warrior mentioned in paragraph 7?

    Ⓐ One of the tattoos indicates that he was captured in battle.
    Ⓑ His high rank among Marquesans was easily recognized.
    Ⓒ The pattern of tattoos could indicate that he was a young man.
    Ⓓ He was probably a Polynesian priest as well as a warrior.

Paragraph 7 is marked with an arrow [➜].

49. All of the following are mentioned as symbolic reasons for tattoos EXCEPT

    Ⓐ social position
    Ⓑ tribal membership
    Ⓒ marital status
    Ⓓ profession

50. According to paragraph 8, what is the current situation in Oceania?

    Ⓐ The teaching of missionaries encouraged people to continue tattooing their bodies.
    Ⓑ The Oceanic peoples no longer continue the practice of tattooing in modern societies.
    Ⓒ Many older members of the societies hold traditional tattooing ceremonies in secret.
    Ⓓ Tattooing is now being practiced by some people in Oceania as part of a cultural revival.

Paragraph 8 is marked with an arrow [➜].

51. Look at the four squares [■] that show where the following sentence could be inserted in the passage.

**The pain the tattooed person endured was a sign of respect for the deceased.**

Where could the sentence best be added?

Click on a square [■] to insert the sentence in the passage.

52. **Directions:** An introduction for a short summary of the passage appears below. Complete the summary by selecting the THREE answer choices that mention the most important points in the passage. Some sentences do not belong in the summary because they express ideas that are not included in the passage or are minor points from the passage. ***This question is worth 2 points.***

**Polynesians practiced tattooing as an important means of representing individual and group identity.**

- ●

- ●

- ●

## Answer Choices

A  Tattooing served many purposes, including social status, membership in families and professions, and spiritual protection.

B  The patterns in Maori tattoos are similar to designs used in the decoration of their houses.

C  Polynesian tattoos have recently become popular in many other parts of the world.

D  Designs are usually tattooed in four zones on the body and their meaning can be interpreted.

E  Techniques for tattooing involve the introduction of pigment under the skin, using a sharp instrument.

F  Ancient engravings and carvings depict leaders with intricate tattoos on their faces.

# LISTENING SECTION

 **Model Test 8, Listening Section, Track 87**

The Listening Section tests your ability to understand spoken English that is typical of interactions and academic speech on college campuses. During the test, you will listen to conversations, lectures, and discussions, and you will answer questions about them.

This is the short format for the Listening Section. On the short format, you will listen to two conversations, two lectures, and two discussions. After each listening passage, you will answer 5–6 questions about it.

You will hear each passage one time. You may take notes while you listen, but notes are not graded. You may use your notes to answer the questions.

Choose the best answer for multiple-choice questions. Follow the directions on the page or on the screen for computer-assisted questions. Click on **Next** and then on **OK** to go on to the next question. You cannot return to previous questions.

The Listening Section is divided into sets. Each set includes one conversation, one lecture, and one discussion. You have 10 minutes to answer all of the questions for each set. You will have 20 minutes to answer all of the questions on the short format. A clock on the screen will show you how much time you have to complete your answers for the section. The clock does NOT count the time you are listening to the conversations, lectures, and discussions.

## *Listening 1 "Professor's Office"*

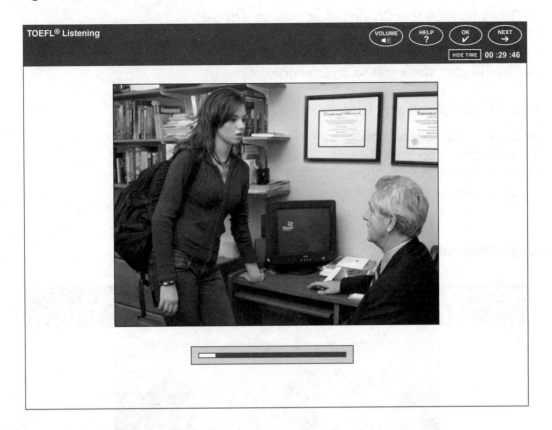

1. Why does the student visit the professor?

   Ⓐ She would like a letter of recommendation.
   Ⓑ She needs advice about two opportunities.
   Ⓒ She is applying for a teaching position.
   Ⓓ She wants to discuss his research project.

2. What does the man mean when he says this:

   Ⓐ He is clarifying his position to Jane.
   Ⓑ He is congratulating Jane.
   Ⓒ He is offering to help Jane.
   Ⓓ He is giving another option to Jane.

3. How could Professor Chang help Jane?

   Ⓐ He could offer Jane a teaching assistantship.
   Ⓑ He could give Jane advice about her future.
   Ⓒ He could promote Jane's business in Asia.
   Ⓓ He could help Jane secure a job at Harvard.

4. What does the professor think that Jane should do?

    Ⓐ Talk with Professor Chang before making a decision.
    Ⓑ Send in the contract for the teaching position.
    Ⓒ Find out more about the job responsibilities.
    Ⓓ Decide what she wants to do after graduation.

5. What can be inferred about Jane from this conversation?

    Ⓐ Jane is in graduate school.
    Ⓑ Jane graduated from Harvard.
    Ⓒ Jane's family lives in China.
    Ⓓ Jane is an excellent teacher.

## Listening 2 "Environmental Science Class"

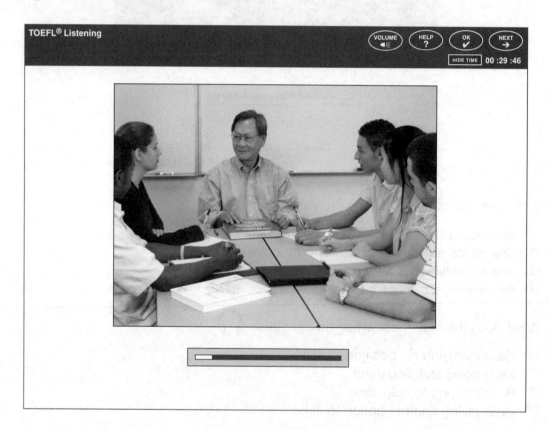

6. What is the main topic of the lecture?

&#9398; Recycling
&#9399; Global recession
&#9400; Waste management
&#9400; World markets

7. Which example does the professor provide to explain "repurposing"?

&#9398; Refilling a water bottle when it is empty
&#9399; Using a water bottle as a sprinkler
&#9400; Making new bottles from old water bottles
&#9401; Repairing a broken lid on a water bottle

8. How do global recessions affect recycling?

&#9398; The recycling business slows down because of lower prices.
&#9399; Global recessions increase business for used items.
&#9400; More people recycle during an economic downturn.
&#9401; Warehouses are a good business during recessions.

9. Why does the professor say this: 🎧

    Ⓐ To invite questions
    Ⓑ To express disapproval
    Ⓒ To prove his views
    Ⓓ To move on to the next point

10. How is aluminum different from other recycled materials?

Click on 2 answer choices.

    Ⓐ It costs more to produce new products.

    Ⓑ It can be sold in the same place that it is collected.

    Ⓒ It is not used as much as other recyclables.

    Ⓓ It is easier to recycle aluminum cans.

11. What is the professor's point of view about recycling?

    Ⓐ Political activism is more important than economics.
    Ⓑ It is still a good idea to recycle while the markets adjust.
    Ⓒ Recycling is not as important as reducing and reusing.
    Ⓓ Economic factors are a major influence on recycling.

### Listening 3 "Sociology Class"

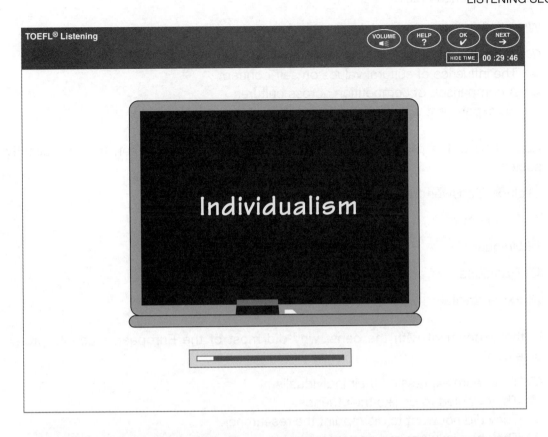

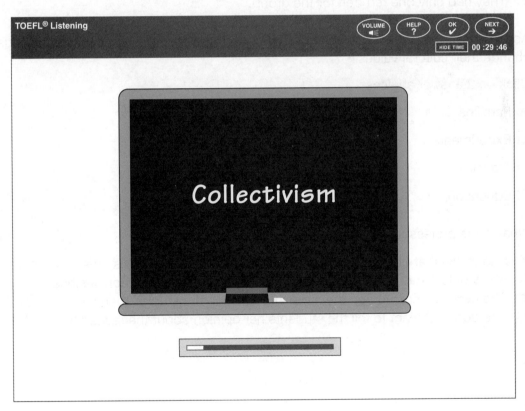

12. What is the discussion mainly about?

    Ⓐ The problem of individual achievement in groups
    Ⓑ The influence of cultural values on self-concept
    Ⓒ A comparison of competition across cultures
    Ⓓ An experiment with students from different countries

13. According to the professor, what are two attributes of a person from a collectivistic society?

    Click on 2 answer choices.

    Ⓐ Cooperative

    Ⓑ Unique

    Ⓒ Traditional

    Ⓓ Experimental

14. In the experiment with the pens, why did most of the European students prefer the blue pen?

    Ⓐ They were expressing their individualism.
    Ⓑ They wanted to be like their friends.
    Ⓒ They did not want to disappoint the researcher.
    Ⓓ They had only one red pen for the group.

15. According to the professor, which of the following factors might influence individuals to change their cultural values?

    Click on 2 answer choices.

    Ⓐ Families

    Ⓑ Experiments

    Ⓒ Travel

    Ⓓ Education

16. What is the professor's opinion about the research on women?

    Ⓐ She thinks that only broad generalizations can be made at this time.
    Ⓑ She would like to see more research results before drawing conclusions.
    Ⓒ She believes that women are more interested in the studies than men.
    Ⓓ She does not want to tell the students her opinion about the research.

17. In the discussion, the professor identifies general characteristics of individualism and collectivism that define a person's identity. Indicate whether each characteristic refers to an individualistic or a collectivistic characteristic. Click in the correct box for each phrase.

|   | | Collectivistic | Individualistic |
|---|---|---|---|
| A | Tradition | | |
| B | Extended family | | |
| C | Competition | | |
| D | Ambition | | |

## Listening 4 "Dormitory"

18. What problem does the woman have?

&#9398; She is not getting along with her roommate.
&#9399; Her room requires some maintenance.
&#9400; The R.A. is not available to help her.
&#9401; She is locked out of her dorm room.

19. Why does the man say this:

&#9398; He is a very expressive person.
&#9399; He is joking with the woman.
&#9400; He is not sure about the information.
&#9401; He does not want to insult the woman.

20. What does the woman consider an emergency?

   Ⓐ A cracked window
   Ⓑ A broken bookshelf
   Ⓒ A dirty room
   Ⓓ A broken lock

21. Why does the woman prefer to stay in the room she was assigned?

   Ⓐ She doesn't want to change roommates.
   Ⓑ She likes living on the seventh floor.
   Ⓒ She prefers to live by herself.
   Ⓓ She would have to go to another dorm.

22. What will the woman probably do?

   Ⓐ Make the repairs herself
   Ⓑ Meet with the R.A. to solve the problem
   Ⓒ Call maintenance to meet her at the room
   Ⓓ Get the man to help her move

## Listening 5 "Anthropology Class"

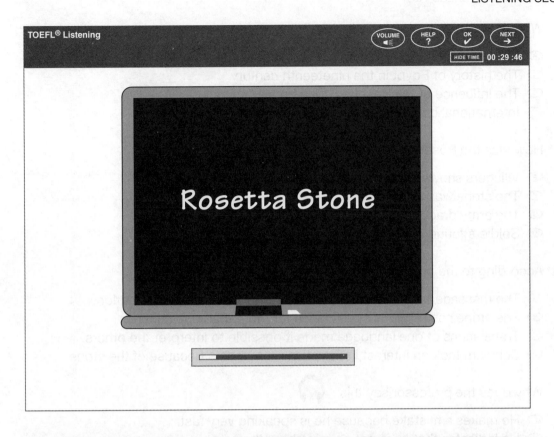

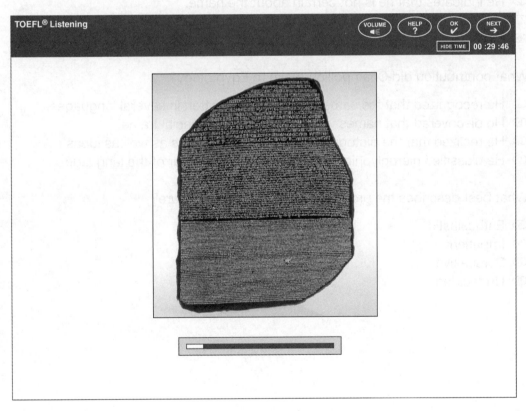

23. What is the main topic of this lecture?

    Ⓐ Military contributions to science and scholarship
    Ⓑ The history of Egypt in the nineteenth century
    Ⓒ The influence of the Rosetta Stone on hieroglyphics
    Ⓓ International cooperation in early Egyptology

24. How was the Rosetta Stone discovered?

    Ⓐ Villagers showed it to some soldiers.
    Ⓑ The stone was uncovered in an old fort.
    Ⓒ The army dragged it out of the Nile River.
    Ⓓ Soldiers found it in a construction site.

25. According to the professor, why is the Rosetta Stone important?

    Ⓐ The message on the stone records important historical information.
    Ⓑ The stone has religious significance for more than one culture.
    Ⓒ Translations of one language made it possible to interpret the others.
    Ⓓ Scholars took an interest in Egyptian monuments because of the stone.

26. Why does the professor say this:

    Ⓐ He makes a mistake because he is speaking very fast.
    Ⓑ He indicates that he is not certain about the name.
    Ⓒ He demonstrates his knowledge of the topic.
    Ⓓ He lets students know that they should take notes.

27. What contribution did Champollion make to Egyptology?

    Ⓐ He recognized that the same message was written in several languages.
    Ⓑ He discovered that names were identified by a special frame.
    Ⓒ He realized that the pictographs represented sounds as well as ideas.
    Ⓓ He classified hieroglyphics and described a grammar of the language.

28. What best describes the professor's attitude in this lecture?

    Ⓐ Enthusiastic
    Ⓑ Impatient
    Ⓒ Persuasive
    Ⓓ Undecided

## *Listening 6 "Geology Class"*

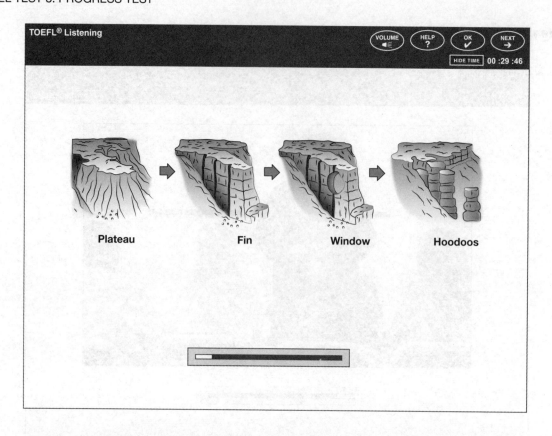

29. What is the discussion mainly about?

  Ⓐ A comparison of mineral deposits in hoodoos
  Ⓑ A new definition of hoodoo formations
  Ⓒ An explanation of the processes that create hoodoos
  Ⓓ A theory of the way that wind affects hoodoos

30. According to the professor, what contributes to the colors in the rock formations?

  Click on 2 answer choices.

  Ⓐ Dolomite

  Ⓑ Minerals

  Ⓒ Light

  Ⓓ Acid

31. According to the book, what is *frost wedging*?

  Ⓐ Freezing temperatures that cause ice to support cracks in the hoodoos
  Ⓑ Water that expands when it freezes and breaks rocks into pieces
  Ⓒ A unique microclimate that exposes canyons to extreme temperatures
  Ⓓ A kind of chemical weathering that occurs when rain soaks into limestone

32. What causes the uneven shapes of hoodoos?

  Ⓐ Unequal rates of erosion for different rocks in the hoodoo
  Ⓑ Variations in wind speed and direction around the hoodoo
  Ⓒ Acid rain that attacks the limestone and dissolves the hoodoo
  Ⓓ Gravity that causes cracked hoodoos to fall into the canyons

33. In the lecture, the professor identifies the steps in which the hoodoos are formed. Click on the step and drag it to the correct box to put the steps in order.

| Step | Order |
| --- | --- |
|  | 1 |
|  | 2 |
|  | 3 |
|  | 4 |

  Ⓐ Fin
  Ⓑ Plateau
  Ⓒ Hoodoo
  Ⓓ Window

34. What does the professor mean when she says this:

- Ⓐ She wants the students to offer their opinions.
- Ⓑ She is confirming an obvious statement.
- Ⓒ She signals that she is not sure of the information.
- Ⓓ She will introduce an opposing point of view.

 **Please turn off the audio. There is a 10-minute break between the Listening Section and the Speaking Section.**

# SPEAKING SECTION

 **Model Test 8, Speaking Section, Track 88**

The Speaking Section tests your ability to communicate in English in an academic setting. During the test, you will be presented with six speaking questions. The questions ask for a response to a single question, a conversation, a talk, or a lecture. The prompts and questions are presented only one time.

You may take notes as you listen, but notes are not graded. You may use your notes to answer the questions. Some of the questions ask for a response to a reading passage and a talk or a lecture. The reading passages and the questions are written, but the directions will be spoken.

Your speaking will be evaluated on both the fluency of the language and the accuracy of the content. You will have 15–20 seconds to prepare and 45–60 seconds to respond to each question. Typically, a good response will require all of the response time and the answer will be complete by the end of the response time.

You will have about 20 minutes to complete the Speaking Section. A clock on the screen will show you how much time you have to prepare each of your answers and how much time you have to record each response.

## Independent Speaking Question 1 "A Goal"

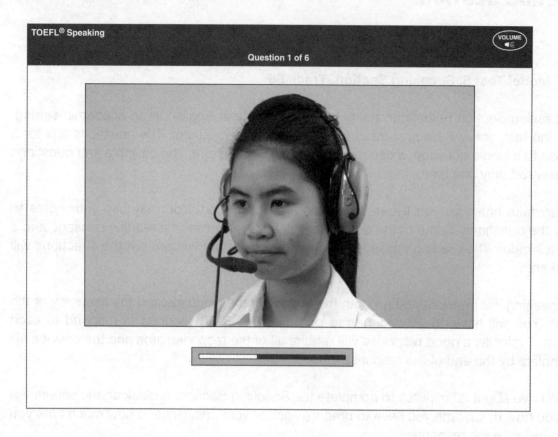

 Listen for a question about a familiar topic.

**Question**

Talk about a goal that you have set and achieved. What was the goal? How did you accomplish it? Include specific reasons and details to explain your choice.

Preparation Time: 15 seconds
Recording Time: 45 seconds

## *Independent Speaking Question 2 "Gifts"*

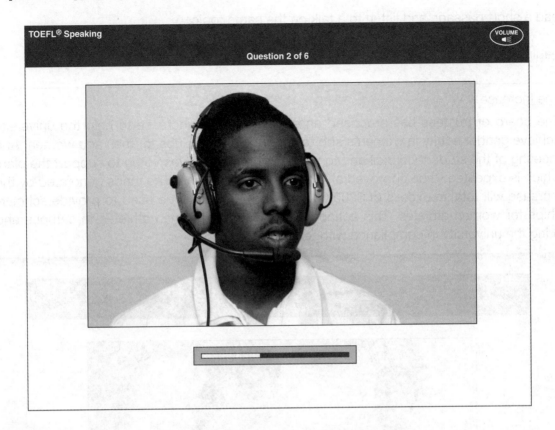

 Listen for a question that asks your opinion about a familiar topic.

**Question**

Some people give gift cards for special occasions so that recipients can choose something they like. Other people select a gift for recipients to open at the celebration. Which type of gifts do you prefer to give, and why? Use specific reasons and examples to support your opinion.

Preparation Time: 15 seconds
Recording Time: 45 seconds

## Integrated Speaking Question 3 "Women's Sports"

Read a short passage and listen to a talk on the same topic.

Reading Time: 45 seconds

---

### Fee Increase

The board of trustees has proposed an eighty-dollar fee increase to help the university achieve gender equity in women's sports and fund sports clubs for men and women. At a meeting of the student council on Monday, the representatives voted to support the plan, which is expected to be approved at the next board meeting. The funds generated by the increase will total in excess of $800,000, most of which will be used to provide scholarships for women athletes. This action will attract more women athletes to campus and bring the university in compliance with federal legislation.

---

 Now listen to a student who is talking with friends about the decision.

### Question

The student expresses her opinion of the university's decision to increase fees. Report her opinion and explain the reasons that she gives for having that opinion.

Preparation Time: 30 seconds
Recording Time: 60 seconds

### *Integrated Speaking Question 4 "Dramatic License"*

Read a short passage and then listen to part of a lecture on the same topic.

Reading Time: 45 seconds

---

Dramatic License

*Dramatic license*, or artistic license, is a term to explain the distortion of facts by an artist or writer to make his or her work more interesting or exciting. As such, dramatic license is at the discretion of the artist, intended to be accepted by the public. It is useful when historical information is unavailable or when not enough information is available for a longer work. However, the use of dramatic license often causes disagreement. When some are offended by the reinterpretation of facts, the artist or writer points out that the works are not intended to be a documentary, but art or literature that should be appreciated for its artistic value.

---

 Now listen to part of a lecture in a literature class. The professor is talking about dramatic license.

**Question**
Summarize the reading and then explain how the lecture relates to it.

Preparation Time: 30 seconds
Recording Time: 60 seconds

*Integrated Speaking Question 5 "Lost Data"*

 Now listen to a conversation between a student and his friend.

**Question**
Describe the man's problem and the two suggestions that his friend makes about how to handle it. What do you think the man should do and why?

Preparation Time: 20 seconds
Recording Time: 60 seconds

*Integrated Speaking Question 6 "Definition of a Planet"*

 Now listen to part of a lecture in an astronomy class. The professor is discussing the definition of a planet.

**Question**
Using the main points and examples from the lecture, define a planet and explain why Pluto is no longer considered a planet.

Preparation Time: 20 seconds
Recording Time: 60 seconds

# WRITING SECTION

The Writing Section tests your ability to write essays in English similar to those that you would write in college courses. During the test, you will write two essays.

**The Integrated Essay.** First you will read an academic passage and then you will listen to a lecture on the same topic. You may take notes as you read and listen, but notes are not graded. You may use your notes to write the essay. The reading passage will disappear while you are listening to the lecture, but the passage will return to the screen for reference when you begin to write your essay. You will have 20 minutes to plan, write, and revise your response. Typically, a good essay for the integrated topic will require that you write 150–225 words.

**The Independent Essay.** You will read a question on the screen. It usually asks for your opinion about a familiar topic. You will have 30 minutes to plan, write, and revise your response. Typically, a good essay for the independent topic will require that you write 300–350 words.

A clock on the screen will show you how much time you have left to complete each essay.

### Integrated Essay "The Vinland Map"

You have 20 minutes to plan, write, and revise your response to a reading passage and a lecture on the same topic. First, read the passage and take notes. Then, listen to the lecture and take notes. Finally, write your response to the writing question. Typically, a good response will require that you write 150–225 words.

### Reading Passage

Time: 3 minutes

The Vinland map is important not only because it is a fifteenth-century map of the world, but also because it contains unique information about the Norse exploration of the Americas. In fact, the map shows a landmass southwest of Greenland in the Atlantic that is labeled *Vinland*. The map describes this region as having been visited by Europeans in the eleventh century. Presented to the world in 1965 with an accompanying text published by the British Museum and Yale University, the map was authenticated because of its strong resemblance to a world map made in the 1420s by Italian mariner Andrea Bianco with the addition of the Vinland feature.

Another aspect of the map that persuaded experts of its authenticity was the parchment. Using radiocarbon dating, the University of Arizona in cooperation with the Smithsonian Institution concluded that the age of the parchment was between 1423 and 1445, which fits the time period for a genuine artifact that would predate the arrival of Columbus in the New World. As such, the Vinland map would be the first known cartographic representation of North America and would offer persuasive evidence that there was contact by Norsemen long before the voyages documented in the thirteenth century.

Further evidence to verify the age of the map was collected and analyzed in several studies of ink samples; however, the absence of similar studies for maps of the same age that contain titanium, along with the potential for chemical reactions over time, have made it unwise to publish conclusive explanations. Also problematic is the fact that carbon-14 dating cannot be used on lines as thin as the ink lines on the map, so data on the ink is rather inconclusive.

### Model Test 8, Writing Section, Track 89

 Now listen to a lecture on the same topic as the passage that you have just read.

### Question
Summarize the main points in the lecture and explain how they cast doubt on the ideas in the reading passage.

### *Independent Essay "Standardized Tests"*

### Question
Agree or disagree with the following statement:

**Standardized tests like the TOEFL provide sufficient information to determine whether students should be admitted to a college or university.**

Give reasons and examples to support your opinion.

# MODEL TEST 8

## ANSWER KEYS

Use the following Answer Keys to check your scores on the Reading and Listening Sections of Model Test 8.

### READING SECTION

| Reading 1 | Reading 2 | Reading 3 | Reading 4 |
|---|---|---|---|
| 1.  A | 14.  C | 27.  D | 40.  B |
| 2.  B | 15.  D | 28.  B | 41.  A |
| 3.  B | 16.  B | 29.  C | 42.  A |
| 4.  C | 17.  A | 30.  B | 43.  D |
| 5.  B | 18.  D | 31.  B | 44.  C |
| 6.  B | 19.  B | 32.  D | 45.  A |
| 7.  C | 20.  A | 33.  A | 46.  D |
| 8.  C | 21.  D | 34.  B | 47.  A |
| 9.  D | 22.  A | 35.  A | 48.  B |
| 10.  C | 23.  A | 36.  B | 49.  C |
| 11.  D | 24.  C | 37.  D | 50.  D |
| 12.  C | 25.  B | 38.  B | 51.  D |
| 13.  B, C, E | 26.  B, C, E | 39.  A, C, E | 52.  A, D, E |

## LISTENING SECTION

| *Listening Set 1* | *Listening Set 2* |
|---|---|
| 1. B | 18. B |
| 2. B | 19. D |
| 3. C | 20. D |
| 4. D | 21. C |
| 5. D | 22. B |
| 6. A | 23. C |
| 7. B | 24. D |
| 8. A | 25. C |
| 9. D | 26. B |
| 10. A, B | 27. D |
| 11. D | 28. A |
| 12. B | 29. C |
| 13. A, C | 30. B, C |
| 14. A | 31. B |
| 15. C, D | 32. A |
| 16. B | 33. 1 B, 2 A, 3 D, 4 C |
| 17. A, B: Collectivistic | 34. B |
| C, D: Individualistic | |

# EXPLANATORY AND EXAMPLE ANSWERS, MODEL TEST 8

Go to the Barron's TOEFL site at *http://bit.ly/Barrons-TOEFL* to study detailed Explanatory Answers for the Reading and Listening Sections, and Outlines, Example Answers, and Checklists for the Speaking and Writing Sections of Model Test 8.

# 9
# SCORE ESTIMATES

## ✔ *Estimate your score*

## IMPORTANT BACKGROUND INFORMATION

It is not possible for you to determine the exact score that you will receive on the TOEFL iBT®. There are three reasons why this is true. First, the testing conditions on the day of your official TOEFL will affect your score. If you are in an uncomfortable room, if there are noisy distractions, if you are upset because you arrived in a rush, or if you are very nervous, then these factors can affect your score.

The administration of a model test is more controlled. First, you will probably not be as stressed when you take one of the tests in this book. Second, the model tests in the book are designed to help you practice the most frequently tested item types on the official TOEFL iBT®. Because they are constructed to teach as well as to test, there is more repetition in TOEFL model tests than there is on official TOEFL iBT® tests. Tests that are not constructed for exactly the same purposes are not exactly comparable. Third, the TOEFL scores received by the same student will vary from one official TOEFL examination to another official TOEFL examination by as many as 20 points, even when the examinations are taken on the same day. In testing and assessment, this is called a standard error of measurement. Therefore, a TOEFL score cannot be predicted precisely, even when two official tests are used. Nevertheless, you would like to know how close you are to your goal. To do that, take the model tests online, and your score will be calculated automatically. If you prefer to take the model tests in the book instead of online, you can use the following procedure to estimate your TOEFL iBT® score. Remember, an estimate is an approximation.

## PROCEDURE FOR SCORING

The official TOEFL iBT® tests have either a longer Reading Section or a longer Listening Section. The extra part on each test contains experimental questions that will not be graded as part of your score. You will need to do your best on all of the questions because you will not know which questions are experimental. The model tests in this book have either a longer Reading Section or a longer Listening Section. Use the procedure below with the charts on the following pages to determine your score estimate for each TOEFL iBT® model test.

## Test with a short Reading Section and a long Listening Section

1. Count the total number of correct answers for the Reading Section. This is your raw score. Now find the scaled score that corresponds to the raw score on the reference chart. This is your section score for the Reading Section.

2. Count the total number of correct answers for the Listening Section. Multiply the number by .66 and round to the nearest whole number. This is your raw score. Now find the scaled score that corresponds to the raw score on the reference chart. This is your section score for the Listening Section.

3. Rate each of the six questions for the Speaking Section on a holistic scale 0–4, add the six scores, and divide by 6. This is your raw score. Now find the scaled score that corresponds to the raw score on the reference chart. This is your section score for the Speaking Section.

4. Rate each essay for the Writing Section on a holistic scale 0–5, add the two scores, and divide by 2. This is your raw score. Now find the scaled score that corresponds to the raw score on the reference chart.

5. Add the scaled scores for all four sections. This is your TOEFL estimate.

## Test with a long Reading Section and a short Listening Section

1. Count the total number of correct answers for the Reading Section. Multiply the number by .75 and round to the nearest whole number. This is your raw score. Now find the scaled score that corresponds to the raw score on the reference chart. This is your section score for the Reading Section.

2. Count the total number of correct answers for the Listening Section. This is your raw score. Now find the scaled score that corresponds to the raw score on the reference chart. This is your section score for the Listening Section.

3. Rate each of the six questions for the Speaking Section on a holistic scale 0–4, add the six scores and divide by 6. This is your raw score. Now find the scaled score that corresponds to the raw score on the reference chart. This is your section score for the Speaking Section.

4. Rate each essay for the Writing Section on a holistic scale 0–5, add the two scores, and divide by 2. This is your raw score. Now find the scaled score that corresponds to the raw score on the reference chart.

5. Add the scaled scores for all four sections. This is your TOEFL estimate.

**Note:** The automatic scoring of the tests online is more exact because the algorithm accounts for questions that are worth more than 1 point. Nevertheless, your estimates using this procedure will give you a good idea of your progress.

# REFERENCE CHARTS

## Reading

| Raw Score | Scaled Score |
|---|---|
| 39 | 30 |
| 38 | 29 |
| 37 | 29 |
| 36 | 28 |
| 35 | 27 |
| 34 | 26 |
| 33 | 25 |
| 32 | 24 |
| 31 | 23 |
| 30 | 22 |
| 29 | 21 |
| 28 | 20 |
| 27 | 19 |
| 26 | 18 |
| 25 | 17 |
| 24 | 16 |
| 23 | 15 |
| 22 | 14 |
| 21 | 13 |
| 20 | 12 |
| 19 | 11 |
| 18 | 9 |
| 17 | 8 |
| 16 | 7 |
| 15 | 6 |
| 14 | 5 |
| 13 | 4 |
| 12 | 3 |
| 11 | 2 |
| 10 | 1 |
| 9 | 0 |
| 8 | 0 |
| 7 | 0 |
| 6 | 0 |
| 5 | 0 |
| 4 | 0 |
| 3 | 0 |
| 2 | 0 |
| 1 | 0 |
| 0 | 0 |

## Listening

| Raw Score | Scaled Score |
|---|---|
| 34 | 30 |
| 33 | 29 |
| 32 | 29 |
| 31 | 28 |
| 30 | 27 |
| 29 | 26 |
| 28 | 25 |
| 27 | 23 |
| 26 | 22 |
| 25 | 21 |
| 24 | 19 |
| 23 | 18 |
| 22 | 17 |
| 21 | 15 |
| 20 | 14 |
| 19 | 13 |
| 18 | 11 |
| 17 | 10 |
| 16 | 9 |
| 15 | 8 |
| 14 | 7 |
| 13 | 6 |
| 12 | 5 |
| 11 | 5 |
| 10 | 4 |
| 9 | 3 |
| 8 | 3 |
| 7 | 2 |
| 6 | 2 |
| 5 | 1 |
| 4 | 0 |
| 3 | 0 |
| 2 | 0 |
| 1 | 0 |
| 0 | 0 |

## Speaking

| Raw Score | Scaled Score |
|-----------|--------------|
| 4.0 | 30 |
| 3.5 | 27 |
| 3.0 | 23 |
| 2.5 | 19 |
| 2.0 | 15 |
| 1.5 | 11 |
| 1.0 | 8 |
| 0 | 0 |

## Writing

| Raw Score | Scaled Score |
|-----------|--------------|
| 5.0 | 30 |
| 4.5 | 28 |
| 4.0 | 25 |
| 3.5 | 22 |
| 3.0 | 20 |
| 2.5 | 17 |
| 2.0 | 14 |
| 1.5 | 11 |
| 1.0 | 8 |
| 0 | 0 |

# EXAMPLES FOR SCORING MODEL TESTS

## Example of TOEFL iBT® Model Test with Long Reading Section

| Reading Section | Correct Answers | Raw Score | Scaled Score |
|-----------------|-----------------|-----------|--------------|
| 4 passages 52 questions | 46 × .75  = | 34.5 = 35 | 27 |

| Listening Section | Correct Answers | Raw Score | Scaled Score |
|-------------------|-----------------|-----------|--------------|
| 6 passages 34 questions | 30 | 30 | 27 |

| Speaking Section | Holistic Rating | Scaled Score |
|------------------|-----------------|--------------|
| Speaking Question 1 | 4 | |
| Speaking Question 2 | 4 | |
| Speaking Question 3 | 3 | |
| Speaking Question 4 | 3 | |
| Speaking Question 5 | 4 | |
| Speaking Question 6 | 3 | |
| Average number of ratings | 3.5 | 27 |

| Writing Section | Holistic Rating | Scaled Score |
|-----------------|-----------------|--------------|
| Integrated essay | 4 | |
| Independent essay | 5 | |
| Average number of ratings | 4.5 | 28 |

**TOTAL**

**Add scaled scores for all sections**                          109

## Example of TOEFL iBT® Model Test with Long Listening Section

| Reading Section | Correct Answers | Raw Score | Scaled Score |
|---|---|---|---|
| 3 passages 39 questions | 36 | 36 | 28 |

| Listening Section | Correct Answers | Raw Score | Scaled Score |
|---|---|---|---|
| 9 passages 51 questions | 44 × .66 = | 29.0 = 29 | 26 |

| Speaking Section | Holistic Rating | Scaled Score |
|---|---|---|
| Speaking Question 1 | 4 | |
| Speaking Question 2 | 4 | |
| Speaking Question 3 | 3 | |
| Speaking Question 4 | 3 | |
| Speaking Question 5 | 4 | |
| Speaking Question 6 | 3 | |
| Average number of ratings | 3.5 | 27 |

| Writing Section | Holistic Rating | Scaled Score |
|---|---|---|
| Integrated essay | 4 | |
| Independent essay | 5 | |
| Average number of ratings | 4.5 | 28 |

**TOTAL**
**Add scaled scores for all sections**                                          109

## SCORE COMPARISONS

| Common European Framework (CEFR) | Internet TOEFL (iBT) | Institutional TOEFL (ITP) |
|---|---|---|
| C1 | 110–120 | 627–677 |
| B2 | 87–109 | 543–626 |
| B1 | 57–86 | 460–542 |

**Note:** TOEFL scores are also reported as they relate to the Common European Framework of Reference (CEFR), which is an internationally recognized measure of language proficiency. The equivalency chart above cites equivalencies determined by major research studies; however, they are only estimates of individual scores.

# FEEDBACK

A feature of the official TOEFL score report is feedback. A general analysis of your strengths and weaknesses will be included with the numerical score. The Barron's online site that supplements this book provides an automatic score report at the end of each model test.

# OPTIONS FOR PERSONAL EVALUATION

## SPEAKING

### ➤ SpeechRater™

Your Speaking Section score on the TOEFL iBT® is determined by human raters. SpeechRater™ is an automated prediction of the score that a human rater would probably assign to your responses. This computer rating includes some, but not all, of the features that a human rater considers in evaluations—pronunciation, vocabulary, grammar, and fluency. Although the scoring will provide experience, the actual score may not be the same as your TOEFL score.

## WRITING

### ➤ Criterion e-rater®

Your Writing Section score on the TOEFL iBT® is a combination of evaluations that include both human and computer raters. E-rater® is an automated prediction of the combined score that a human rater and a computer rater would probably assign to your responses. This computer rating includes some, but not all of the features that a human rater considers in evaluations—organization, style, grammar, vocabulary, complexity, and mechanics. The scoring will provide experience and is more advanced than the SpeechRater™; however, the actual score may not be exactly the same as your TOEFL score.

For more information about these personal evaluation options, including the current fees, visit *www.ets.org/toefl*. Click on **TOEFL Practice Online**.

# 10
# RESOURCES

## ✔ *Use resources to support your preparation*

## WEBSITES FOR TOEFL

*These websites may include short commercials as well as fee-based media and services, but many free options are also included on the sites. Click on the free material to practice English and help you prepare for the TOEFL.*

### SHORT AUDIO OR VIDEO CLIPS

*www.bbc.co.uk*
Video and written scripts. Click on **Earth** or **Nature**.

*www.history.com*
Short video clips and articles under a variety of academic topics. Click on **History** or **Science and Technology**. TV programs on the site are not as helpful.

*www.openculture.com*
Online courses that include lectures in various academic subjects. The lectures are presented by professors from some of the leading colleges and universities. They are delivered as free YouTube audio or video files.

*www.smithsonianmag.com*
Short videos with excellent narration. Click on **Video**. Subscriptions for a fee, but downloads are free.

*www.ted.com/talks*
Thought-provoking talks by experts in various fields of study. Subtitles are available in a limited number of languages.

*www.video.nationalgeographic.com*
Part of the National Geographic Society. Use the following short video categories: *Animals and Nature* (also listed as *Wildlife*), *Environment, Science and Space, and Travel and Culture*. Full feature films are also found on this site, but they are not as useful for TOEFL preparation as the short clips.

## READING PASSAGES

*www.encyclopedia.com*
Offers unlimited possibilities for short reading passages on academic topics from reliable research sources. To solve the problem of what to choose, click on **Featured Topics**. After a trial period, you may be asked to pay a small fee to continue using the site, but you are not obligated to continue.

*en.wikipedia.org*
A free encyclopedia that is written in English and edited by the general public. Click on **Featured Articles** to search for interesting topics by academic category. There is no charge to read the articles in Wikipedia.

## SPEAKING AND PRONUNCIATION

*www.dictionary.com*
A free talking dictionary. First click on the search icon and then type in a word or phrase and click on the speaker icon. Although it may seem slow at times, the words or phrases are pronounced very well.

## WRITING

*www.owl.english.purdue.edu*
The Purdue University Online Writing Lab. Click on **English as a Second Language** for ESL resources.

# TUTORS AND ONLINE TEACHERS

*Tutoring websites may charge a fee or you may be able to exchange tutoring in your language for free tutoring in English.*

Check out all the sites before you make a commitment to tutoring. They are listed here in alphabetical order. If a free trial is offered, use that opportunity to meet a potential tutor. Be sure to emphasize that you are preparing for the TOEFL. Some tutors are not familiar with the test and will not be as helpful to you. One excellent way to use tutoring to your benefit, even if the tutor does not have much experience with the TOEFL, is to ask your tutor to respond to TOEFL Speaking questions so that you can listen to good models for that section of the test. When you listen to good models, you learn how to speak!

*www.conversationexchange.com*

*www.italki.com*

*www.language-exchanges.org*

*www.nativemonks.com*

*www.verbalplanet.com*

*www.verbling.com*

# DR. SHARPE'S WEBSITE

Dedicated to the students and teachers worldwide who are preparing themselves or others for the Test of English as a Foreign Language (TOEFL iBT®), Dr. Sharpe's website is the place to ask questions about this book or her other books, or to learn more about TOEFL test preparation. Contact Dr. Sharpe at *sharpe@teflprep.com* or use the contact space on her website.

*www.teflprep.com*

# TOEFL iBT® RESOURCE CENTERS

*Contact a local TOEFL iBT® Resource Center for general information about the TOEFL. These centers cannot help you register for the test or provide you with your scores.*

**France**
**ETS Global B.V.**
Email: *lberkowitz@etsglobal.org*
Phone: **+33153631430**
Website: *www.etsglobal.org*

**Germany**
**ETS Global B.V.**
Email: *tkryaninko@etsglobal.org*

**India**
**Learning Links Foundation**
1209 Padma Tower 1, 5 Rajendra Place, New Delhi, 110008 INDIA
Email: *toeflinfo@learninglinksindia.org*
Phone: **+91 9 7112 37111**
Website: *http://www.learninglinksindia.org*

**Japan**
**CIEE**
Cosmos Aoyama, 5-53-67 Jingumae, Shibuya-ku, Tokyo 150-8355, Japan
Email: *toefl@cieej.or.jp*
Phone: **(81 3) 5467 5477**
Website: *http://www.cieej.or.jp*

**Mexico**
**IIE Mexico**
Berlin 18 60 Piso Col. Juarez, Mexico City C.P. 06600
Email: *toeflibtinfo@iie.org*
Phone: **55925260**

**Poland**
**ETS Global in Poland**
ul. Barska 28/30, Block B, 2nd Floor, 02-315 Warszawa
Email: *jwrzesinska@etsglobal.org*
Phone: **+48 22 890 00 17 ext. 13**
Website: *www.etsglobal.org*

**Saudi Arabia**
**AMIDEAST**
Al Kindi Plaza  #59 Diplomatic Quarters P.O. Box 352,
Riyadh 11411  Kingdom of Saudi Arabia
Email: *saudiarabia@amideast.org*
Phone: **01-483-8800**

**Taiwan**
**Chun Shin**
2F, No.45, Sec2, Fu Xing S Rd, Taipei 106 Taiwan, ROC
Email: *service@toefl.com.tw*
Phone: **(88 6) 2 2701 7389**
Website: *www.toefl.com.tw*

**Turkey**
**ETS Global B.V.**
Email: *yarsin@etsglobal.org*

**United Arab Emirates**
**AMIDEAST**
CERT Technology Park Higher Colleges of Technology Muroor Road (4th Street)
PO Box 5464 Abu Dhabi, Abu Dhabi
Email: *uae.testing@amideast.org*
Phone: **(971-2) 445-6720**
Fax: **(971-2) 443-1489**

# TEACHING TIPS

These ideas work for me. I invite you to try some of them in your classes.

## ➤ 1. Begin with a positive message.

It can be very simple. For instance, "The highest tower is built one brick at a time."
If we put a new message in the same place every time—on a slide or on the board—students
will learn to look for it when they come into the room. Music serves the same purpose. It sets
a positive mood for the session.

## ➤ 2. Write three important goals for the class so that students can see them.

Three goals are manageable for one class session. When they are visible, they keep us all on track. At the end of the class, referring to the goals gives everyone a sense of progress and closure for the day.

## ➤ 3. Arrange for model tests to be taken in a lab or at home on the honor system.

Our time with students is too valuable for us to spend four hours proctoring each model test. That would add up to twenty-eight hours of class time for all of the model tests in this book.

## ➤ 4. Allow students to grade the Reading and Listening Sections of their model tests.

When students take responsibility for grading the objective sections of their model tests and for referring to the Explanatory Answers, we save hours that we would have had to use doing routine clerical tasks. If the students take the model tests on the computer, the scoring for these sections will be done automatically; if they are using the book, the Answer Key is printed after each test. This will afford us the time we need to concentrate on answering questions.

## ➤ 5. Ask students to send their questions on email before class.

When students refer to the Explanatory Answers, many questions are resolved for them without asking the teacher. If students write down their questions, sometimes the answer becomes apparent to them at this stage. The questions that they bring to class are really worth discussion. If we have them on email, we can prepare our answers for the question-and-answer session at the beginning of the next class. We always have the answer!

## ➤ 6. When several students have the same question, prepare a short presentation.

When the question is repeated, it gives us an indication of what our students need to know. By using their questions for class preparation, we show that we are teaching people, not subjects.

## ➤ 7. Present the PowerPoint slides in Review Chapter 4 and show the students how to choose an answer.

Let the students "listen in" on our thought processes as we decide why answers are incorrect and which answer choice is correct. For example, we might say, "I know that A is not correct because the professor did not include this research in his lecture. Choice B looks possible, but it is not complete. The choice leaves out the second part of the answer. That means it must be either Choice C or D. I know that D is not correct because the professor said that there were three types, not two. It must be Choice C." Modeling *how* to think helps students *learn* to think when they see similar test items.

## ➤ 8. Use class time to present frequently tested item types and practice academic skills.

Present the slides from Chapter 4 in class. Take the quizzes in class, using "Think, Answer, Compare, Discuss." Give students time to think and respond to each answer independently, compare their answers to the correct answers, and discuss why that choice is a good one. Then focus on the academic skills in Chapter 5.

## ➤ 9. Focus on speaking and writing in class.

Provide many good models of responses to speaking and writing questions in class. Show students how to use the checklists to evaluate speaking and writing.

## ➤ 10. Assign speaking tasks and writing tasks as homework.

Have students turn in speaking assignments and essays. Students can send sound files with one-minute responses to speaking tasks. Spend grading time on these important sections. Bring samples of good work to class—good organization, good openings, good support statements, good closings. Let's catch our students doing something good to use as an example.

## ➤ 11. Don't worry about covering all the material in the book.

This book has more material than most teachers need for a course, but all of it was written for self-study as well as for classroom instruction. That means that students can work on their own for "extra credit," and all of the pages don't have to be referred to in class. In my experience, when we teachers try to cover too much, we are the only ones who can keep up. The material gets covered, but the students don't understand it. I trust that teachers know which pages to select for the students in our classes.

## ➤ 12. Provide counseling and encouragement as part of the class routine.

Ideally, one minute at the end of class can be used for a pep talk, a cheer, or a success story about a former student. This is one of my favorite cheers: T-O-E-F-L! We're making progress! We're doing well! T-O-E-F-L! I also like to stand by a poster at the door when students are leaving my class. The last thing they see is the affirmation on the poster: "I know more today than I did yesterday. I am preparing. I will succeed." Some students want a handshake, a high five, or a hug. Others just smile and say good-bye. Some hang by the door, and I know that they need to talk. Every excellent TOEFL prep teacher I know is also a very good counselor. You probably are, too.

# PERSPECTIVES FOR TEACHERS

In the Middle Ages, a man approached two stonemasons and asked them what they were doing. The first stonemason replied, "I am laying stones." The other answered, "I am building a cathedral."

I have been teaching TOEFL preparation classes since 1970 and writing TOEFL materials since 1975. As I go into my classes, I ask myself: Am I teaching TOEFL prep or am I helping students achieve their career goals? As I prepare each new edition of my books, I ask myself: Am I writing TOEFL preparation books or am I making tools that will help students succeed on the TOEFL and *after* the TOEFL? It is a very different perspective and inspires in a different way.

Certainly, we have seen many changes in the TOEFL across the decades. Often Educational Testing Service has revised the TOEFL in an effort to keep pace with changes in our ESL/EFL teaching paradigms, and occasionally the revisions in the TOEFL have produced changes in our teaching paradigms in something referred to as a *washback effect*.

This is probably the most challenging time in TOEFL preparation that I have experienced because the Internet-Based TOEFL (iBT) is more than a revision. It is a completely different kind of test, which requires a new approach to learning. Our students will have to demonstrate their ability to integrate the language skills by completing tasks similar to those that they will be expected to accomplish in academic settings. They will have to speak and write at high levels of proficiency.

Eventually, I believe that the changes on the TOEFL iBT® will be beneficial for our students and for us, their teachers.

# ACKNOWLEDGMENTS

With affection and appreciation, I acknowledge my continued indebtedness to the friends, family, and colleagues who have been part of the TOEFL team for so many years.

**Dr. Jayne Harder, former Director of the English Language Institute at the University of Florida** for initiating me into the science of linguistics and the art of teaching English as a second language;

**Robert and Lillie Sharpe, my parents** for their assistance in typing and proofreading previous editions and for their enthusiastic encouragement throughout my career;

**The late Dr. Tom Clapp, former Dean of Continuing Education at the University of Toledo** for the maturity and confidence that I gained during our marriage because he believed in me;

**Carole Berglie, former Editor at Barron's Educational Series, Inc.** for her guidance in seeing the first edition of the manuscript through to publication;

**Kristen Girardi, Editor at Kaplan Test Prep, Inc.** for assembling an expert team, providing leadership, and creating an environment that encouraged our best work, as well as for her invaluable insights and wise counsel during every stage of development and production;

**Alison Maresca, Production Editor at Kaplan Test Prep, Inc.** for the creative suggestions and designs, large and small, that have improved every chapter;

**John Rockwell, Editor and President of Rockwell Audio Media** for casting and directing the talented voices and bringing the script to life;

**Kathy Telford, Proofreader at Proofreaders Plus** for her attention to the important details, her positive approach to errors, and her friendship;

**Dennis Oliver, Professor at Estrella Mountain Community College** for collaborating on the original version of *Glossary of Campus Vocabulary*;

**John T. Osterman, my husband—a special thank you** for the unconditional love and the daily interest in and support for my writing career, as well as for checking my math in the evaluation tables. Each revision of this book is better than the last, and every new and revised year with John is the best year of my life.